ss Cataloging-in-Publication Data

rea data networking with switched multi-megabit data
V. Klessig, Kaj Tesink

raphical references and index.
807-4
ti-megabit data service.   I. Tesink, Kaj.

K58   1995   94-18960
                                      CIP

pt
Mona Pompili
DeLuca Design
Murray
inator: Linda Behrens
t: Shirley McGuire

4807-4

national (UK) Limited, *London*
ustralia Pty. Limited, *Sydney*
da, Inc., *Toronto*
anoamericana, S.A., *Mexico*
dia Private Limited, *New Dehli*
pan, Inc., *Tokoyo*
Asia Pte. Ltd, *Singapore*
all do Brasil, Ltda., *Rio de Janeiro*

Library of Cong

Klessig, Robert
 SMDS : wid
service / Rober
 p.   cm. —
 Includes bibl
 ISBN 0-13-8
 1. Switched
II. Title
TK5105.875.

SMDS

Wide-Area Data Networ
Switched Multi-megabit D

Robert W. Klessig, Ph.D.
Manager, Business Developr
3Com Corporation

Kaj Tesink
Distinguished Member of Technic
Bell Communications Research, Inco

Publisher: Al
Project Mana
Cover Desigr
Copy Editor:
Production C
Editorial Ass

©
A
E

The authors
efforts incl
their effecti
consequenti
these progra

Printed in

10 9 8 7

ISBN 0

==*An Alan R. Apt Book*==

Prentice Hall, Englewood Cliffs, New Jers

Prentice-F
Prentice-F
Prentice-F
Prentice-F
Prentice-F
Prentice-F
Simon &
Editoria

To our Parents

Trademark Information

Foreword

It is a pleasure to introduce this book on Switched Multi-megabit Data Service.

We are witnessing an industry in formation. It is like watching a volcano being born. It is brought about by the tremendous drop in the price of computers and communications in the past decade. That price drop shows no sign of abating. The result has been the eruption of a new market for computer networking that has caught the attention of the telephone companies. SMDS is the telecommunications industry's first real attempt to understand what people actually do with computing and communications and then offer them products and services that help them achieve their goals.

If you want to offer fast, cheap, and reliable wide-area data networking services to your customers, then everything you need to know is contained in this book. Fortunately, that is not a prison sentence. Also, fortunately, you probably don't have to read every paragraph to get at what you need for your job. The excellent table of contents can guide your travels through the pages. The authors have taken great pains to be clear as opposed to being condescendingly authoritative. They obviously know not only the topics but also the pain of understanding large technical documents that describe protocols in their entirety.

Hidden in the text you will find many insights on to how to save money on your WAN data service purchases. For example, when selecting a service class for your site, you would probably look at the 10-megabit offering and buy it if you used Ethernet on your site. The authors point out that you might consider buying the 4-megabit offering if it is priced much below the 10-megabit offering because you probably can't drive the interface at that higher rate unless you have an unusual application. Now why is that? It is because the people who bring you

SMDS are telephone people who like to deliver what they promise, and the engineering of the SMDS cloud has been done so you can hit the interface at the rate you paid for on a continuous basis. So, maybe you can get away with buying a lower class of service than you might first reach for. Another example is the cost analysis of SMDS, which nicely demonstrates the increasing cost benefits of a public switched service as your network becomes more complicated.

Why is this book even necessary? The regulatory environment in the United States has dismantled the "one-system" approach to provisioning telephony. You cannot buy end-to-end service from one carrier anymore. Thus many internal interfaces have to be exposed so anyone can "carry the ball" part way down the field. This has the side effect of making it possible to build some pretty elaborate systems that were not envisioned in the past. It has forced the telephone industry to understand what its customers are doing because customers have so many alternatives available to them.

The authors have done an excellent job of describing the SMDS "service" offering. They point out quite emphatically the difference between a "service" offering and a "technology" offering. Thus they explain what is different about SMDS and ISDN, Frame Relay, ATM, and SONET: SMDS is what the customer "sees"; the others are technologies that the carriers use to deliver the service to the customer. In addition, they provide a rigorous description of the service as well as insights into the reasoning (and occasionally lack of reasoning) behind the various features. Many of these insights are the kind that can be furnished only by those who did the actual work on SMDS. A sort of "those who wrote the book on SMDS" have actually written a book.

Equally important, the authors have pulled together an impressive amount of material describing how SMDS fits into your network. Are you running TCP/IP, Netware, and AppleTalk? You'll find how to run these protocols (and more) over SMDS in this book. You say you have nonroutable protocols in your network? You are covered again with a chapter on bridging over SMDS that contains new material that has not been published before. And, for once, here is a book that gives the attention to network management that it deserves. Almost a quarter of the book is devoted to describing how you can manage SMDS as a component of your network.

This book is a fundamental contribution to the art of wide area data networking. Its completeness, the guidance to the reader at the beginning of every chapter, the many examples, and the pointers to additional sources of information help make this book accessible to a wide audience, and a must for all those interested in data networking.

We have all been waiting patiently through many false starts in the quest of "dialtone for data." With SMDS, perhaps the time has finally come.

Dan Lynch
Chairman and Founder
Interop
Foster City, CA

Preface

Data Communications in the 1980s and 1990s saw the proliferation of the Local Area Network. This has led to the need to connect these LANs across widely separated sites to create Wide Area Networks (WANs). Dedicated lines have been the telephone carrier service offering most commonly used with bridges and routers to build a WAN. Although effective solutions to WAN connectivity, these configurations tended to be expensive and inflexible. This provided an opportunity for the telephone carriers to offer new services tailored to LAN interconnection. Switched Multi-megabit Data Service (SMDS) is such a service. It was designed from the ground up, for ease of interconnection of LANs, to support the dominant protocols in the market (e.g., IP and IPX). SMDS provides the flexibility and cost effectiveness for LAN/WAN connectivity that has thus far been unavailable.

This book is all about SMDS and it has four goals:

- To provide an in-depth description of SMDS features, access protocols, and performance objectives.

- To provide one tutorial/reference book that shows how SMDS can be used for bridging and routing with commonly deployed data-networking protocols and how SMDS relates to technologies like Asynchronous Transfer Mode ATM and Frame Relay.

- To convey a historical perspective to help explain many of the key decisions that shaped SMDS.

- To provide a comprehensive user's guide for SMDS.

Who Should Read This Book

This book focuses on SMDS service features, their background, and their potential applications by SMDS customers. It also focuses on the equipment to access SMDS. As such, this book can serve as a concise reference to planners, designers, and suppliers of SMDS, and as a practical and detailed guide for SMDS customers and suppliers of data communications equipment for SMDS access. Consultants and network planners will find useful material that compares SMDS with other current and future data-networking solutions, and the data-network manager will appreciate the details on management aspects of SMDS. The teacher, scholar, researcher and student will find valuable background on why the service is the way it is. Where possible, we discuss relevant issues for both North American and other SMDS environments.

Organization of This Book

The material in this book falls into six categories: Introduction and Overview, Service Description, Access Protocols, Routing and Bridging with SMDS, Network Management, and Sources for Additional Information.

Introduction and Overview

Chapter 1 gives a *historical perspective* to SMDS and provides rationales for its development. It also describes the roles of different industry organizations in the development of SMDS. Chapter 2 is an overview of SMDS. It describes the role of SMDS in some of the more popular data-networking architectures. Then SMDS features are briefly discussed along with the reasoning behind them. Finally, the *economics* of SMDS are examined as well as how SMDS relates to current and future technologies, such as *Frame Relay* and *Asynchronous Transfer Mode* (ATM). Readers who already are familiar with the basics of SMDS can skip this chapter.

Service Description

SMDS is a service rather than a technology. Chapter 3 contains a detailed service description of SMDS and includes all service features. This material is essential if one is to derive the most benefit from the use of SMDS. Chapter 7 details the SMDS performance objectives and presents the reasoning behind each of the objectives.

Access Protocols

SMDS can be accessed through four different methods; through the *SMDS Interface Protocol* (SIP), through the *Data Exchange Interface* (DXI), through Frame Relay, and through ATM. Chapter 4 is a detailed description of the SMDS Interface Protocol. It includes recommendations for the "minimal" CPE implementation. And, it also details the use of DS1, E1, DS3, and E3 physical transmission facilities for SMDS. Chapter 5 describes a common method of interfacing to SMDS by the use of a special Channel Service Unit/Data Service Unit (CSU/DSU). The DXI, the interface between the CSU/DSU and a data-networking device such as a router, is described. The use of this protocol as a direct means of accessing SMDS is also covered. Chapter 6 presents the details of using the Frame Relay protocol for accessing SMDS. This approach is referred to as *SIP Relay*. Chapter 13 describes the details for accessing and supporting SMDS with ATM. Appendix A provides background material on the Distributed Queue Dual Bus (DQDB) as an aid in understanding the details of SIP. Appendix C contains background information on the *Cyclic Redundancy Check* (CRC).

Routing and Bridging with SMDS

Chapters 8 and 9 describe how SMDS can be used with routers and bridges. Chapter 8 details the use of SMDS to carry many of the popular network-layer protocols. Industry specifications are described, as well as some new material. The protocols covered include TCP/IP, OSI, AppleTalk, XNS, Netware, 3+, 3+Open, VINES, and DECnet Phase IV and Phase V. Chapter 9 contains new material on the use of SMDS for bridging.

Network Management

Chapters 10 through 12 present a detailed description of the network-management aspects of SMDS. Chapter 10 provides background on network management and SMDS. The basics of the Simple Network Management Protocol (SNMP) and the Management Information Base (MIB) are presented. Chapter 11 describes the management of SMDS CPE. Chapter 12 deals with managing SMDS by use of the SMDS Customer Network Management Service, which is based on SNMP. Appendix B contains Management Information Base (MIB) information that supplements Chapter 12.

Sources for Additional Information

Appendix D provides practical guidance on contact information for industry groups relevant for SMDS, how to obtain SMDS specifications, and how to join electronic discussion groups on SMDS.

Acknowledgments

This book was made possible by the many people who played a role in bringing SMDS to reality. Any attempt to name them all is doomed to failure. Thus, we will only attempt to acknowledge those who were there at the very beginning.

Chris Hemrick deserves first mention for having the vision and audacity to suggest that a telephone company should offer a connectionless data service. She backed up her heresy with long hours of hard work and debate to fill in the details of SMDS and to convince the RBOCs to at least let the rebellion continue if not enthusiastically accept the concept.

Warren Gifford, Howard Sherry, and Stagg Newman played early key roles by being managers who didn't believe in just paying lip service to the concept of employee empowerment. Their advice, support, and risk-taking were critical in the survival of SMDS as a project in its early days.

A group of brilliant and creative people contributed to the initial design of SMDS in Winter of 1987. These included Ed Isganitis, Fran Knapp, Joe Lawrence, Jon Shantz, and Kiho Yum. It was brainstorming at its best. Another milestone of SMDS was the pioneering work on *Customer Network Management Service*. The early contributors in this design were Tracy Brown, Dave Piscitello, Patrick Sher, and Grace Wrigley.

The following people also made important contributions to the development of SMDS and also reviewed the parts of this book that deal with their areas of expertise: Tony Clark, Cedric Druce, Max Figueroa, Jay Gill, Mary Kelly, Deirdre Kostick, Paul Sanchirico, Marco Sosa, and Wayne Tsou. We also thank Chris Camley, Scott Ginsburg, Rolf Hahn, Johann Hölzle, Jay Israel, Alan Oppenheimer, Radia Perlman, Mike Skrzypczak, and Eric Vanuska for their reviews of selected parts of this book. Special thanks go to Dave Piscitello for having the perseverance to review the entire manuscript.

Bell Communications Research and 3Com Corporation provided us logistical support and day jobs to support our writing habit. Shirley McGuire and Mona Pompili provided valuable editorial and production assistance.

Finally, we must acknowledge our editor, Alan Apt. We wish we had his patience.

Bob Klessig
Kaj Tesink

Contents

1

Introduction

This book is about *Switched Multi-megabit Data Service* (SMDS). The name says it all:

- *Switched*: SMDS provides the capability for communications between any subscribers just like the telephone network. In fact, SMDS even uses telephone numbers to identify subscribers (or at least their data communications equipment).

- *Multi-megabit*: SMDS is intended for the interconnection of LANs and therefore provides bandwidth similar to LANs. The multi-megabit nature of SMDS makes it the first Broadband (greater than 2.048 Mbps) public carrier service to be deployed.

- *Data*: SMDS is intended for carrying traffic found on today's LANs. This is generally called data but in fact includes other types of traffic, e.g., images. The industry is rife with hyperbole about multimedia and video-on-demand. Yet, compared to the nearly 40 million PCs currently connected to LANs, the market for these non-data services is a mere grease spot on the information highway. SMDS is meant to meet the substantial and growing need for high-speed LAN interconnection.

- *Service*: When it comes to public carrier data services, there is much confusion between technology and service.[1] SMDS is a service. It is not a technology or a protocol. It will follow the time-honored tradition

---

[1]This must be related to the data aspect since no such confusion exists for voice services. No one chooses their interexchange telephone service provider based on the protocols used to control the carrier's telephone switches.

of public carrier services; the service features will stay constant while the technology used in the carrier network is repeatedly improved. For example, SMDS is the first switched service based on ATM technology.

This book is a comprehensive treatment of SMDS, bringing together in one source all material, including some not previously published, required by both SMDS customers and data networking equipment suppliers. The book contains historical insights and rationales for the features of SMDS that are not available in any other publicly available publications.

This chapter describes some of the history behind SMDS, including the fundamental concepts and philosophy underlying the development of the service. It also enumerates sources of SMDS specifications.

1.1   The Problem: Market Perception of Telephone Companies

The history of SMDS can be viewed as beginning in July of 1982 when IEEE Project 802 initiated a new Working Group, IEEE P802.6, to develop standards for Metropolitan Area Networks (MANs). The key significance of the formation of IEEE P802.6 was that it reflected the realization among LAN vendors that there was a market for the connection of LANs across wide areas. Furthermore, it was perceived that existing standards activities were not adequately addressing this potential market. When considering wide-area connectivity, it was natural to think of telephone carriers. The 1982 statement of direction for the telephone industry was the Integrated Services Digital Network (ISDN). Unfortunately, there was significant concern among LAN vendors about the adequacy of ISDN for meeting the LAN interconnection market. The greatest concern was the lack of bandwidth.[2]

Unfortunately for the telephone carriers, the lack of credibility for LAN interconnection was not limited to the dim view of ISDN. In 1982, telephone networks were considered to be slow and error-prone. To a large extent this view was accurate, given the analog technology of the telephone networks and the modem technology of the day, which was the typical approach for both switched and private-line wide-area data connectivity. The only plausible carrier alternatives to the telephone companies in the early 1980s were the Community

---

[2]At the time, the emphasis was on the 16 Kbps D Channel for providing the data part of ISDN. Another possibility was to use the 64-Kbps B Channel. Either approach would introduce a speed bottleneck. The time to transmit a 1000-byte packet on a CSMA/CD [802.3] (10-Mbps) LAN is 0.8 ms. To do the same on a B Channel takes 125 ms. It was hard to argue that using ISDN would provide transparent LAN interconnection.

Antenna Television (CATV) providers. As a result, more out of desperation than enthusiasm, the initial MAN protocol proposals were based on the use of CATV technology.

The formation of Working Group IEEE P802.6 stimulated work to begin within Bell Laboratories to develop high-speed data services that would be suitable for LAN interconnection. After the breakup of the Bell System, this work was continued by Bell Communications Research (Bellcore).[3] In 1985 and 1986, Bellcore in cooperation with NYNEX and US WEST carried out successful concept trials of MAN token-ring technology to interconnect LANs across a metropolitan area.

As the MAN trials concluded in 1986, Bellcore work on defining a new, high-speed, data service began. There were a number of goals:

- *The service should be aimed at LAN interconnection.* The LAN market had moved into a dynamic growth phase, with ever-increasing numbers being installed, and market projections were highly optimistic. It did not take a great leap of faith to believe that a service that allowed the transparent interconnection of LANs across a wide area would find a significant market.

- *The service should offer more value than fast private lines.* By the time the MAN trials were completed, the position of the North American telephone carriers with respect to high-speed data communications had improved somewhat. The conversion of the telephone networks to digital transmission technology had made 1.544-Mbps DS1 (Digital Signal 1) private-line service viable. This service in conjunction with the advent of remote bridges made possible the interconnection of LANs with a bandwidth starting to approach that of the LANs. However, being simply a provider of private line services for data was not considered a desirable business strategy. The inevitable arrival of local competition was expected to lead to private lines becoming a commodity.[4] Thus, features and capabilities that provide customers with value beyond that available from private lines were considered vital.

- *The service should help RBOCs shed the image of being incapable of providing data communications services.* The demand for POTS (plain

---

[3]Bellcore is a research and development company owned and principally funded by the Regional Bell Operating Companies (RBOCs). Among its activities is the definition of services that can be supported by the regulated networks of the RBOCs in order to foster nationwide service consistency. SMDS is the result of such service-definition work.

[4]Being in the private line business is derisively referred to as being a WACCO (wire and cable company).

old telephone service) was expected to experience low, single-digit growth rates, whereas data communications (such as LAN interconnection) were expected to grow much faster. Therefore, it was vital that a useful data service be deployed quickly to build market presence and credibility for the RBOCs.

In addition to the above goals, there was a significant constraint. Because of the funding and ownership arrangements, Bellcore work on defining new services was constrained to focus on services that can be offered by the regulated network entities within the RBOCs. In this case, a key implication of this constraint was that the equipment that the regulated network provider owns, and that is on the customer's premises, is highly constrained in functionality. Another constraint was that the service cannot provide connectivity between Local Access and Transport Areas (LATAs) without the use of an Interexchange Carrier.

1.2   A Solution: SMDS

The fundamental concept underlying SMDS is the exploitation of existing solutions for LAN interconnection. Figure 1.1 illustrates a typical approach to LAN interconnection in the local area. By using high-performance bridges or routers, LANs can be interconnected by means of backbone LANs. The approach for SMDS is to make the service look like a backbone LAN, as shown in Figure 1.2. This simple but elegant approach was conceived by Christine Hemrick while she was employed by Bellcore.

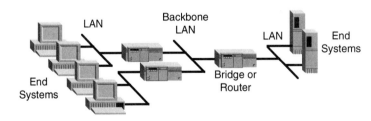

Figure 1.1 Local area interconnection of LANs

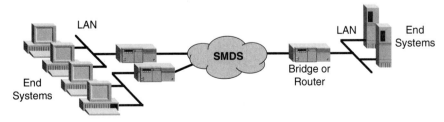

Figure 1.2 Interconnection of LANs using SMDS

This basic approach to SMDS was established in late 1986. In early 1987, work began in earnest to flesh out the details of the service. In pursuing this work, several principles were followed:

1. *Be market-driven:* The intended market for SMDS, high-speed interconnection of LANs, was well defined right from the beginning, and this was invaluable in keeping the work focused. It was believed that this market would soon blossom. This was of great concern because of the difficulty and long lead times involved in deploying new telephone-carrier-based services. Hence, the work was approached with a great sense of urgency. Furthermore, it was felt that the market opportunity, by the time the service could be deployed, would be for speeds above DS1 (1.544 Mbps). The assumption was that, once a DS1 private-line data network was installed (along with the organization to maintain it), it would be difficult to induce a customer to migrate to the public network unless she needed a step up in performance.[5] By all indications, by the time SMDS could be deployed, DS1 private-line data networks would be widely deployed. Consequently, the initial work was limited to defining DS3 (44.736 Mbps) interface rates [772.1]. The addition of DS1 interface rates was relatively easy and was done in 1989 [772.2]. Low-speed (e.g., 56 Kbps), low-cost access to SMDS was defined in 1993 [1239] [1240]. The specification of DS1 and slower interface rates was intended to make SMDS economically attractive to a larger share of the LAN interconnection market. The addition of European interface rates was straightforward and was done in 1993 [ESIG002].

2. *Respect customers' existing data network investment:* No matter how wonderful the service that is offered by a carrier, if making use of it requires substantial changes to the customer's installed data network, the service will be unattractive. The basic concept of making SMDS look like a LAN addresses this principle. SMDS is synergistic with many existing data-networking architectures (see Chapters 8 and 9), and thus it has very little impact on the installed base of end systems, LANs, bridges, and routers. Group Addressing (a form of multicast; see Chapters 3, 8, and 9) is an example of an element of SMDS that addresses this principle.

3. *Emphasize service attributes:* A criticism that can be leveled at ISDN is that it was derived by looking at what was possible to implement in a

---

[5]In retrospect, this assumption was not necessarily valid. The aggressive tariffs for DS1 SMDS and the benefits of not having to manage a "rats nest" of DS1 private lines have proved to be strong inducements to customers to buy DS1-based access to SMDS. (See Chapter 2.)

telephone network without much consideration for the usefulness of the resulting services (or even what the services might be). In defining SMDS, a conscious effort was made to ignore network implementation issues and instead focus on what is useful to the customer. For example, Group Addressing is very useful to the customer, but its implementation details were not addressed by Bellcore until 1990, [1059] three years after it was first specified as a service feature for SMDS.

4. *Minimize innovation:* Given the urgency of getting a useful LAN interconnection service deployed, it was imperative that unnecessary innovation be avoided. In particular, this meant avoiding the temptation to design the "glorious ultimate service" that would support all applications using Intelligent Network concepts. By the time such a service could be deployed, one could expect completely different communications technologies to have taken over the market, perhaps of the type envisioned in *The President's Analyst.*[6]

5. *Hit the dates:* In early 1987, it was believed that 1991 was a realistic goal for the first deployment of SMDS. Earlier deployment was viewed as desirable from a market timing point of view. The realities of deploying a new service suggested that 1991 was optimistic but realistic. In the end, Bell Atlantic derived revenue from a "pre-SMDS" service in December of 1991. At the time of this writing, most of the RBOCs, GTE, and MCI are deploying SMDS, several Interexchange Carriers in addition to MCI have announced SMDS plans, telephone carriers in other parts of the world (e.g., Europe) have announced SMDS plans, SMDS Customer Network Management has been deployed, and SMDS Interest Groups are operating in North America, Europe, and the Pacific Rim.

1.3   Sources of Specifications for SMDS

A number of different organizations have been or are involved in activities related to SMDS. Each is described below including descriptions of the material in this book that each organization developed. Contact information for each organization is provided in Appendix D.

---

[6]*The President's Analyst* is a movie from the late 1960s (predivestiture), in which TPC (The Phone Company) proposes injecting small wireless communications devices into the brains of all newborns as a way to save money on telephone-plant investment.

1.3.1   Bell Communications Research (Bellcore)

Bellcore is a research and development company owned and principally funded by the Regional Bell Operating Companies (RBOCs). One of the objectives of Bellcore is to provide specifications of services that can be offered by the RBOCs and thus promote consistency in telecommunications service throughout the United States. SMDS is one such service. The majority of the material in this book is drawn from Bellcore Technical Requirements and Technical Advisories; see the references at the end of the text: [772], [772.1], [772.2], [772.3], [772.3S], [773], [1059], [1060], [1062], [1062R], [1239], and [1240].

1.3.2   SMDS Interest Group (SIG)

The SIG is an industry consortium that was formed in early 1991 to promote SMDS. By mid-1992, over 50 companies had joined. An example of one important activity of the SIG is the specification of interfaces to allow the use of a special SMDS Channel Service Unit/Data Service Unit (CSU/DSU) to allow access to the service [SIG001] [SIG002]. Chapter 5 is based primarily on these documents. The SIG also drew up specifications for access to SMDS through Frame Relay and ATM [SIG006] [SIG008]. Another important focus of the SIG is the specification of ways to carry various network-layer protocols over SMDS [SIG003] [SIG019]. These specifications are the basis for parts of Chapter 8.

1.3.3   European SMDS Interest Group (ESIG)

The ESIG is the European counterpart to the SIG. It is promoting SMDS in Europe and to that end has developed specifications such as physical-layer protocols for access to SMDS that are compatible with the European digital transmission hierarchy [ESIG002]. This specification is covered in Chapter 4.

1.3.4   European Telecommunications Standards Institute (ETSI)

ETSI is developing standards for Metropolitan Area Networks and thus has developed Physical Layer Convergence Procedures for the European digital transmission hierarchy [ETSI213] [ETSI214]. These have been adopted for SMDS by the ESIG, as described in Chapter 4.

1.3.5   Pacific Rim Frame Relay/ATM/SMDS Interest Group (PR FASIG)

The PR FASIG was formed in late 1992 to promote data services in the Pacific Rim. One PR FASIG activity may be the development of specifications for providing SMDS in Pacific Rim countries.

1.3.6   Internet Engineering Task Force (IETF)

The IETF looks at issues concerning the Internet and considers the use of SMDS in that context. For example, it has developed a specification for carrying Internet Protocol (IP) over SMDS [RFC1209]. This specification is described in Chapter 8. The IETF is also responsible for the development of specifications based on the Simple Network Management Protocol (SNMP), [Rose] [RFC1157] including some that are used for SMDS [RFC1304] [RFC1406] [RFC1407] as discussed in Chapters 10, 11, and 12.

1.3.7   IEEE Project 802

The work of two working groups, IEEE P802.1 and IEEE P802.6 are described in this book. IEEE P802.1 is developing standard methods for remote bridging [802.1g]. This specification is the basis of Chapter 9.

As described in Chapter 4, the SMDS Interface Protocol has certain compatibility with the standard developed by IEEE P802.6 [802.6]. Much of Chapter 4 and all of Appendix A are based on this standard.

1.4   Focus of This Book

This book looks at SMDS from a customer and applications perspective. This is in contrast to the Bellcore requirements documents that are related to SMDS. Because of the Modified Final Judgment,[7] the RBOCs are not allowed to manufacture the equipment that they use in their networks, and they are not allowed to carry long-distance traffic. Consequently, Bellcore requirements are targeted at (potential) suppliers of equipment for RBOC networks and other network providers who must be involved if SMDS is to be widely offered in the United States.

In the United States, telecommunications regulation has evolved in such a way that many network providers coexist and compete in offering service. In

---

[7]*Modified Final Judgment* (MFJ) is the umbrella term used to refer to the consent decree that resulted in the breakup of AT&T in 1984. Does anyone believe that this is the *final* judgment? (And how do you modify something that was final anyway?)

particular, there are Local Exchange Carriers (LECs) and Interexchange Carriers (IECs). LECs provide service within a single Local Access and Transport Area (LATA), while IECs are free to offer service between LATAs. Figure 1.3 shows some possible configurations involving LECs and IECs in providing SMDS. (The connection between IEC 1 and IEC 2 is shown in gray to emphasize the fact that the vigorous competition among Interexchange Carriers has inhibited the deployment of connections between IEC networks.) The complexity of these arrangements has resulted in a significant portion of Bellcore work being devoted to provision of SMDS by interconnected carrier networks.

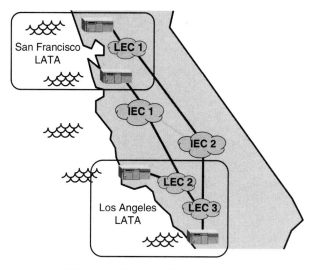

LEC: Local Exchange Carrier
IEC: Interexchange Carrier
LATA: Local Access and Transport Area

Figure 1.3 Examples of interconnected networks providing SMDS

The details of intercarrier provision of SMDS and the details of the equipment in the public network are of secondary importance to SMDS customers and their data communications equipment suppliers. Thus, this book focuses on the material contained in the SMDS service description requirements documents [772] [773] [1060] [1062] [1062R]. When discussing the material in the Bellcore requirements, we provide expanded descriptions of complex requirements, and we provide historical perspective and the rationale behind the requirements. In addition, material is presented that is not covered by the Bellcore requirements. For example, the SIG and the IETF have established specifications on how SMDS can be used in various important networking architectures, and this material is included here. Another example is customer premises equipment (CPE) implementation of the SMDS Interface Protocol

(SIP). In several places, the SMDS requirements, such as [772] and [773], leave options open for the CPE, and we make recommendations on how to close them.

2

Overview of SMDS

This chapter provides a high-level description of SMDS. It can be viewed as an "executive overview" of the service. Readers who have had no experience with SMDS will find this chapter helpful in understanding the essentials of SMDS without having to wade through all of the details in the rest of the book. Readers familiar with SMDS may want to skip this chapter.

The first section describes the general use of SMDS by explaining how SMDS can be used in different networking architectures. The next section highlights the key features of the service by making extensive use of examples. The rationale behind the features is also explained. The third section illustrates the economics of SMDS with a simple example. The fourth section describes the various access protocols for SMDS. The chapter concludes with a discussion of some technologies for providing SMDS and comparisons of SMDS with some other services targeted at LAN interconnection.

2.1   Role of SMDS in a Data Communications Environment

SMDS was designed with the expectation that it would be used as a physical network in an internet. However, SMDS can play other roles as well. The various roles are described further in this section.

To better understand the potential roles of SMDS, it is helpful to take a brief look at the SMDS Interface Protocol (SIP). The Level 3 Protocol Data Unit (L3_PDU) is the component of SIP that supports the SMDS features. All service features and performance objectives for SMDS are defined in terms of the transfer and treatment of L3_PDUs. Figure 2.1 shows a simplified format of the

L3_PDU. Chapter 4 gives a complete description of SIP. When sending information, Customer Premises Equipment (CPE) that accesses SMDS constructs the L3_PDU by filling in the DESTINATION ADDRESS field, the SOURCE ADDRESS field, and the INFORMATION field. Each L3_PDU contains complete addressing information, and thus can be delivered independently of other L3_PDUs. This type of service is called a *datagram* service. Unless there is an error, these fields are *unchanged* when the L3_PDU is delivered to the destination CPE.

Destination Address	Source Address	Information
8 bytes	8 bytes	≤9188 bytes

Figure 2.1 Simplified L3_PDU format

2.1.1 Routing with SMDS

The environment of a potential SMDS customer will probably contain a number of Local Area Networks (LANs) and Wide Area Network (WAN) services. Examples of LANs include CSMA/CD [802.3] (commonly called Ethernet), Token Bus, [802.4] Token Ring, [802.5] and Fiber Distributed Data Interface (FDDI) [FDDI]. Examples of WAN services include DS1 private lines and X.25 packet switching. The LANs and WAN services are integrated into a single network by an internetworking protocol implemented in routers and end systems. This configuration is generally referred to as an *internet,* and each LAN and WAN service is called a *physical network.* (Several LANs are often bridged together to form a larger physical network.)

SMDS was explicitly designed to play the role of a physical network in an internet. An example of this role is portrayed in Figure 2.2, which shows the use of SMDS by TCP/IP [RFC791] [RFC793]. In this configuration, a router that is using SMDS to send an IP packet to another router (or an end system) must determine the proper SMDS DESTINATION ADDRESS from the IP address of the recipient system. The details of this use of SMDS are described in Chapter 8 and in [RFC1209].

The TCP/IP architecture is very similar to many other internet architectures and the use of SMDS in these architectures is much like that shown in Figure 2.2. Chapter 8 also describes the use of SMDS with OSI, AppleTalk, XNS, Netware (IPX), 3Com's 3+ and 3+Open, VINES, DECnet Phase IV, and DECnet Phase V.

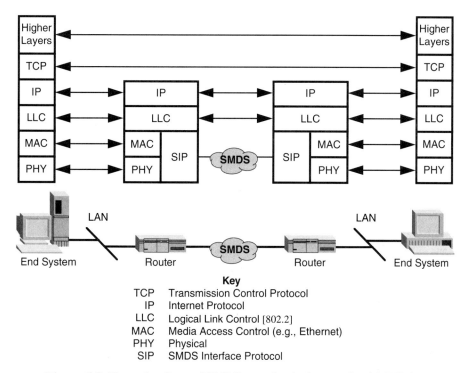

Key

TCP	Transmission Control Protocol
IP	Internet Protocol
LLC	Logical Link Control [802.2]
MAC	Media Access Control (e.g., Ethernet)
PHY	Physical
SIP	SMDS Interface Protocol

Figure 2.2 Example of use of SMDS as a physical network with TCP/IP

2.1.2   Bridging with SMDS

As explained in Chapter 1, SMDS is designed to look like a backbone LAN. Thus, another possible way to use SMDS is with bridges. Figure 2.3 shows the use of SMDS with bridges and TCP/IP [RFC791] [RFC793]. Virtually all IEEE 802 LANs and FDDI use 48-bit MAC addresses, while SMDS uses telephone numbers based on [E.164]. As described in Chapter 9, the different address spaces will make Translation Bridging difficult, and thus we expect that any use of SMDS with bridges will make use of Encapsulation Bridging. In other words, the MAC frame is copied into the SMDS INFORMATION field by the bridge that is using SMDS to send to another bridge. Chapter 9 describes these bridging approaches based on [802.1g].

2.1.3   Multiplexing with SMDS

Although switching is a major capability of SMDS, SMDS can be used to emulate private lines. As an example of this, Figure 2.4 illustrates the use of SMDS for multiplexing. In Figure 2.4, each service interface has two SMDS addresses associated with it. Each multiplexer has two ports, which we assume

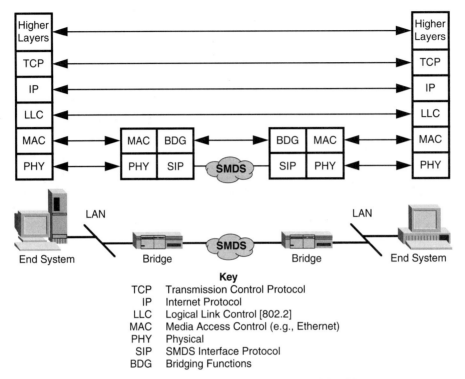

Key

TCP	Transmission Control Protocol
IP	Internet Protocol
LLC	Logical Link Control [802.2]
MAC	Media Access Control (e.g., Ethernet)
PHY	Physical
SIP	SMDS Interface Protocol
BDG	Bridging Functions

Figure 2.3 Example of the use of SMDS with bridges

have a frame-based, link-level protocol such as HDLC or SDLC. When a frame is received on port 1, it is encapsulated in the L3_PDU INFORMATION field and the DESTINATION ADDRESS field is set to the Transmit Address (C). This L3_PDU is delivered to the multiplexer with ports 3 and 4, and this multiplexer determines that port 3 should receive the frame by matching C with the Receive Address of port 3. Thus, in this example, ports 1 and 3, 2 and 6, and 4 and 5 appear to be directly connected.

Many other variations of multiplexing are clearly possible, as well as various combinations of bridging, routing, and multiplexing. Like the paths worn in the grass of a new college campus, new ways of using SMDS will probably emerge as the service becomes widely deployed and used.

2.2   Overview of Key SMDS Features

The key features of SMDS are described in the following subsections. The intent is to provide simple descriptions along with commentary on the rationale for their inclusion in the service. Full descriptions of these features are provided in Chapter 3.

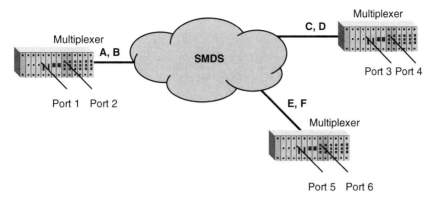

Port	Transmit address	Receive address	Connects to port
1	C	A	3
2	F	B	6
3	A	C	1
4	E	D	5
5	D	E	4
6	B	F	2

Figure 2.4 Example of the use of SMDS for multiplexing

2.2.1   SMDS Addressing

SMDS addresses use numbers structured according to [E.164]. This is just a fancy way of saying telephone numbers. The choice of the E.164 number structure is based on several considerations. First, the most prevalent network-layer protocols, IP and IPX, [Novell2] are independent of the structure of physical network addresses and, as shown in Chapter 8, all of the internetworking protocols can work with E.164 numbers used as physical network addresses. Second, use of telephone numbers greatly facilitates deployment in the telephone networks. Modern telephone networks have extensive computerized operations-support systems for such functions as service-record inventory and billing. As might be expected, these operations-support systems are typically keyed to telephone numbers. Therefore, the use of a different addressing scheme makes integrating SMDS into the current telephone network operations-support systems difficult and is in conflict with the goal of expeditious deployment of the service. Finally, a comprehensive administrative structure exists for telephone numbers — another plus for *quick* deployment of the service.

The format of an SMDS address is a 4-bit address type followed by up to 15 Binary Coded Decimal (BCD) digits structured according to [E.164]. This coding is chosen to facilitate routing within a service-provider network as described in [1059]. More details on E.164 numbering can be found in Section 3.4.1.

The interface between a customer's CPE and the service provider's network is called the *Subscriber Network Interface* (SNI). Up to 16 SMDS addresses can be assigned to a given SNI.[1] One motivation for the ability to have more than one address per SNI is the support of multiplexing, as described in Section 2.1.3. Another is the ability for a customer to have both public (well known) and private addresses; this is described in Section 2.2.5.

2.2.2   Unicasting

When an L3_PDU is transmitted across the SNI with an Individual Destination Address (as indicated by the address-type field), the L3_PDU is delivered to the SNI associated with the Destination Address. An exception to this occurs when the Destination Address is assigned to the source SNI. In this case, the L3_PDU is not delivered back to the source SNI. This exception accounts for the possibility of multiple CPE attached to the SNI, as described in 2.4.1.

Since the full Destination Address is contained in every L3_PDU, there is no need for the CPE to be burdened with setting up and maintaining a connection before transmitting to any destination.

2.2.3   Group Addressing (Multicasting)

When an L3_PDU is transmitted across the SNI with a Group Destination Address (as indicated by the type field), the L3_PDU is delivered to the SNIs associated with Individual Addresses that compose the group identified by the destination Group Address. Figure 2.5 shows an example of Group Addressing.

Only one copy of the L3_PDU is delivered to an SNI, even if the SNI is identified by more than one Individual Address in the Group Address components. For example, the SNI with assigned addresses B and H in Figure 2.5 receives only one copy of the L3_PDU even though both B and H are part of the Group Address G. A copy of the L3_PDU is never delivered to the SNI from which it originated.

As shown in Figure 2.5, the Source Address need not be a component of the Group Address. An example of the value of this is the ESHello message of OSI CLNP, which is described in Chapter 8. Any OSI end system can send to a Group Address identifying all OSI intermediate systems even though the end system is not a member of the group. This distinguishes SMDS Group Addressing from the X.25 concept of a Closed User Group.

---

[1]At low-speed access to SMDS, this number is 2. See Chapter 3.

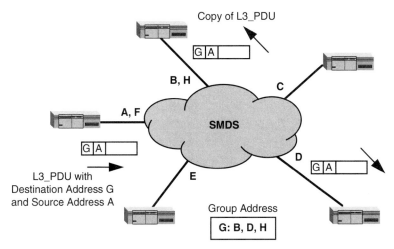

Figure 2.5 Example of Group Addressing

2.2.4 Source Address Validation

When an L3_PDU is sent to SMDS, the Source Address is checked to see if it is assigned to the originating SNI. If the Source Address is not assigned to the originating SNI, the L3_PDU is not delivered. An example of Source Address Validation is shown in Figure 2.6.

Source Address Validation is motivated by two considerations. First, in the case of charging on a per-L3_PDU basis, the Source Address *must* be validated to ensure that the proper customer is charged. Second, Source Address Validation helps to prevent "spoofing" at the SIP level, where the sender of an L3_PDU attempts to fool the receiver into believing that the L3_PDU was sent by a different source.

2.2.5 Address Screening

Address Screening is a feature that lets a customer restrict communications based on SMDS addresses. The restrictions are defined by tables associated with each SNI called Address Screens. An Individual Address Screen is a table consisting of Individual Addresses. A Group Address Screen is a table consisting of Group Addresses. An L3_PDU is the subject of two types of Address Screening. With Destination Address Screening, the Destination Address of the L3_PDU is compared against an Address Screen.[2] With Source Address

---

[2]It is natural to think of Destination Address Screening as being implemented at the ingress point of the service-provider network. However, it can be implemented anywhere in the network without any change to the service feature.

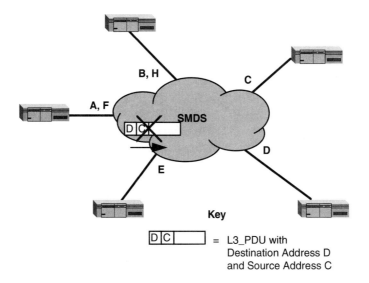

Figure 2.6 Example of Source Address Validation

Screening, the Source Address is compared against an Address Screen.[3] An Address Screen can contain either alowed addresses or disalowed addresses. An L3_PDU whose compared address (source or destination) matches an entry in a screen with disalowed addresses is discarded, while an L3_PDU whose compared address fails to match any entries in a screen with alowed addresses is discarded.

Figure 2.7 illustrates an example of the use of Address Screens to limit communications across an SNI. The Individual Address Screen and the Group Address Screen are shown for the SNI with assigned addresses B and H. Both of these screens contain alowed addresses. L3_PDUs sent from this SNI into the service-provider network are subject to Destination Address Screening. Examples in Figure 2.7 are the L3_PDUs sent from B to G and from H to C. For the L3_PDU from B to G, the Group Address Screen is used because the Destination Address is a Group Address. In this case, a match is found, and the L3_PDU is not discarded. For the L3_PDU from H to C, the Individual Address Screen is used because the Destination Address is an Individual Address. In this case, a match is not found and the L3_PDU is discarded.

L3_PDUs addressed to be delivered to this SNI, (i.e., with Destination Address B, H, or G) are subject to Source Address Screening. Since a Source Address is always an Individual Address, the Individual Address Screen for this SNI is used for Source Address Screening. In Figure 2.7, the L3_PDUs from C to

---

[3]It is natural to think of Source Address Screening as being implemented at the egress point of the service-provider network. However, it can be implemented anywhere in the network without any change to the service feature.

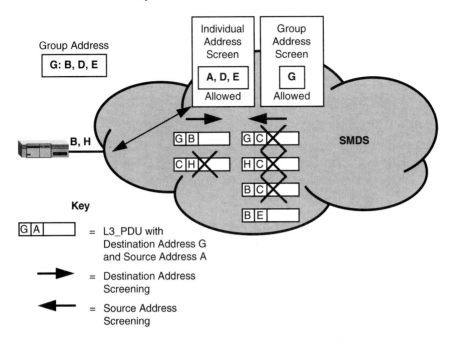

Figure 2.7 Simple example of Address Screening

G (discarded), from C to H (discarded), from C to B (discarded), and from E to B (not discarded) are all subjected to the Source Address Screening for this SNI. The screens shown for this example SNI are those that would make this SNI part of a virtual private network consisting of A, B, D, E, and H. To complete the virtual private network, complementary screens are needed for the SNIs serving A, D, and E.

A more complex configuration of Address Screens can be used to effect the simultaneous use of "public" and "private" addresses on the same SNI.[4] This could be useful to a company by allowing the company customers and prospective customers to communicate via the public address, while intracompany communications could be limited to the private address. In this arrangement, multiple Individual and Group Address Screens are used. Each screen is pointed to by addresses associated with the SNI. Individual Address Screens can be pointed to by either Individual Addresses assigned to the SNI or by Group Addresses that have at least one component that is an Individual Address assigned to the SNI. Group Address Screens can only be pointed to by Individual Addresses assigned to the SNI.

---

[4]This more complex form of Address Screening is called out as an *Objective* in [772] as opposed to a *Requirement*. Consequently it may not be supported in early offerings of SMDS. Check with your service provider before planning to use this feature.

Figure 2.8 shows an example of how this works. In this example, B is the private address, and H is the public address. H points to empty Address Screens that are disallowed. Thus, the L3_PDU from C to H is checked (Source Address Screened) against the empty Individual Address Screen. Since there is not a match (the screen is empty) and the screen "contains" disalowed addresses, the L3_PDU is delivered. The L3_PDU from C to B is checked (Source Address Screened) against the {B, G: A, D, E} Individual Address Screen and is discarded because there is no match and the screen contains alowed addresses. The L3_PDU from B to C is Destination Address Screened using the {B, G: A, D, E} screen and discarded, while the L3_PDU from H to C is not discarded. The net result of the screening configuration in this example is that B can only exchange L3_PDUs with A, D, and E (and G), while H is unrestricted.

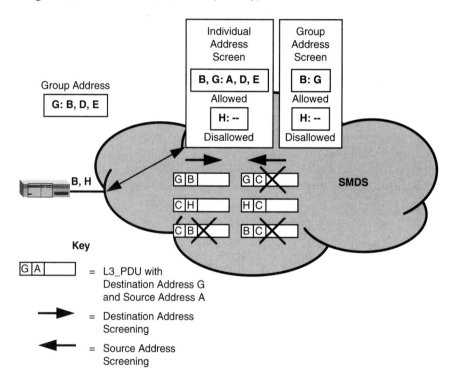

Figure 2.8 Example of Address Screening with public and private addresses

Notice that it is possible to have configuration conflicts between Address Screening and Group Addressing. For example, it is possible that Group Address Screens could be such that all L3_PDUs sent to a given Group Address are always discarded. Another potential problem is a mistake in setting up the screens, thus preventing communications that are intended to be allowed. The use of the Customer Network Management features, as described in Chapter 12, aids in the timely detection and correction of such errors.

2.2.6   Access Classes

The bit rate of DS3 (44.736 Mbps) is approximately 28 times faster than the bit rate of DS1 (1.544 Mbps) and 672 times faster than SMDS based on DS0 access (see Section 2.4). This is a large difference when considering average throughput of potential SMDS customers. On the other hand, the higher rate of DS3 can be very advantageous for bursts of data such as a large FDDI frame. The time to send a maximum-size FDDI frame (4500 bytes) on a DS1-based SNI is approximately 31 ms. On a DS3-based SNI the same transmission takes only approximately 1.1 ms.[5]

It is clear that, if a service-provider network is designed assuming full usage of all DS3-based SNIs, then many more resources will be deployed in the service-provider network than will be used. The Access Class concept is intended to allow a simple characterization of usage that will allow more efficient network implementation. The resulting economies can then be shared with the SMDS customers via low tariffs. Access Classes are only defined for DS3-based and E3-based SNIs.

Access Classes allow for bursts of traffic but still limit the long-term sustained traffic rate. A burst is one or more L3_PDUs sent back-to-back at the *full DS3 bit rate*. (Thus, the Access Class approach is *not* "fractionalizing" the DS3.) An Access Class is described by a Credit Manager Algorithm which is rigorously defined in Chapter 4. An L3_PDU delivered to SMDS will be forwarded to its destination(s) if the available credit equals or exceeds the length of the L3_PDU INFORMATION field. If the credit is not sufficient, the L3_PDU is discarded. The credit builds up continuously until it reaches a maximum. Whenever an L3_PDU is forwarded, the credit is reduced by the number of bytes in the L3_PDU INFORMATION field. Figure 2.9 illustrates the credit calculation. Because the full DS3 bit rate can be used if credit is available, the 4500-byte L3_PDU shown in Figure 2.9 can traverse the SNI in approximately 1.1 ms.

The long-term maximum data transfer rate, called the Sustained Information Rate (SIR), is just the rate of credit buildup. Five different Access Classes are defined for DS3-based SNIs. Figure 2.10 shows the SIRs for these Access Classes. Four different Access Classes are defined for E3-based SNIs. Figure 2.11 shows the SIRs for these Access Classes. In both cases, the first three classes correspond to the common LAN data rates of 4, 10, and 16 Mbps. The other classes represent higher data rates. Chapter 4 shows how these SIRs are calculated.

---

[5]These timing calculations are based on the fact that SIP on DS3 carries 96,000 L2_PDUs per second, and each L2_PDU contains up to 44 bytes of an L3_PDU as payload. Chapter 4 contains the details.

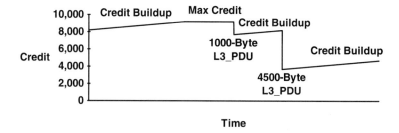

Figure 2.9 Credit Manager Algorithm example

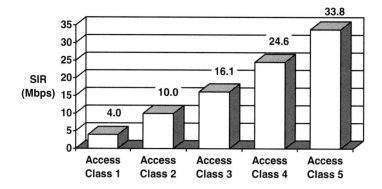

Figure 2.10 Sustained Information Rates for DS3-based SNIs

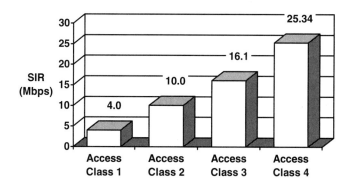

Figure 2.11 Sustained Information Rates for E3-based SNIs

From Figure 2.9, it is clear that bursts of L3_PDUs can be transmitted when sufficient credit is available. The maximum burst is the number of INFORMATION field bytes that can be transmitted in back-to-back L3_PDUs at the full DS3 or E3 bit rate without any of the L3_PDUs exceeding the available credit, when at the start of the burst the credit is at the maximum value. Chapter 4 shows how to calculate the maximum burst, and the results are presented in

Figures 2.12 and 2.13. The time to send such a burst is independent of the SIR because bursts are sent at the full DS3 or E3 bit rate. For example, the maximum burst of over 10 Kbytes takes approximately 2.5 ms to send across the DS3-based SNI.

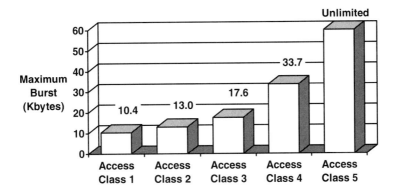

Figure 2.12 Maximum Burst Sizes for DS3-based SNIs

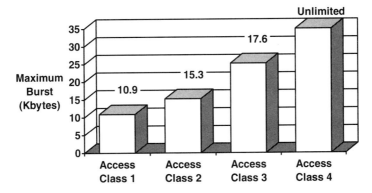

Figure 2.13 Maximum Burst Sizes for E3-based SNIs

There is some similarity[6] between the concept of Access Class and the concept of Committed Information Rate (CIR) of Frame Relay [FRF-1]. However, a key difference is that when a Frame Relay frame exceeds the CIR, it can be marked for priority discard and then discarded if congestion is experienced in the network. With Access Classes, if an L3_PDU exceeds the available credit, it is always discarded. The motivation for this is to avoid unpredictable service performance for customers and simpler network implementation. By always discarding, SMDS keeps a customer from experiencing random, degraded performance as a result of having a poorly

---

[6]Access Classes appear to predate CIR, having been first published in 1988 [772.1].

selected Access Class. Poor Access Class selection will cause high data loss, which will immediately manifest itself as high delay and low throughput or even broken transport-layer connections. This should stimulate immediate corrective action, for example, through the use of Customer Network Management (see the next subsection), and lead to more predictable future performance.

2.2.7   Customer Network Management

As discussed in Chapter 1, the underlying concept of SMDS is to provide a service that looks like a backbone LAN. One important property of today's LANs is that they can be monitored and configured from a remote Network Management Station (NMS). As internets have grown larger with more physical networks, this network management capability has become critical to the effective operation of the internets. Consequently, it is viewed as imperative that SMDS offer the customer the ability to remotely manage and configure the service. This service feature is called Customer Network Management (CNM).

Because the vast majority of existing NMSs use the Simple Network Management Protocol (SNMP) [Rose] [RFC1157], the SMDS network management feature uses this protocol to communicate with an agent within the service-provider network. The concept is shown in Figure 2.14. The customer's NMS sends requests to the agent, which in turn carries out the commands from the NMS. As explained in Chapter 12, two kinds of information are available: that dealing with SNIs and that dealing with subscription parameters. For example, the agent can retrieve performance measurements from various elements in the service-provider network and forward the result to the NMS. Similarly, the agent can effect changes in the customer's service features, such as modifying an Address Screen.

In combination with the management of SMDS CPE, SMDS CNM Service provides NMSs with a valuable tool to manage an internet that uses SMDS. The management of SMDS CPE and SMDS CNM service are thoroughly described in Chapters 10, 11, and 12.

2.3   SMDS Economics

General statements about the environment in which a particular carrier service is economically attractive are very difficult to make. Tariffs, number of customer locations, and traffic patterns are but a few of the important factors. However, some of the dynamics can be illustrated by example, and that is what is done in this section.

In our example, we compare the cost of SMDS with that of dedicated DS1 connections. The comparison is done in terms of equivalent monthly charges.

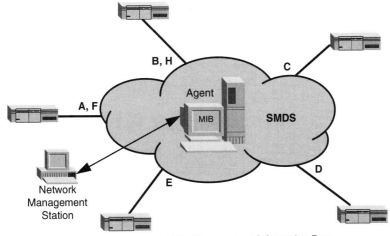

MIB: Management Information Base

Figure 2.14 Customer network management concept

The tariff and equipment-cost assumptions are presented in Table 2.1.[7] Tariffs for SMDS are still evolving. Most of the early RBOC intra-LATA offerings include a flat-rate tariff for each SNI. Tariffs based on traffic and/or distance may be offered in the future. For our comparisons, we assume a flat-rate tariff. We also assume the use of a special SMDS CSU/DSU[8] which is a common configuration (see Section 2.4.1).

Item	First cost ($)	Monthly charge ($)	Equivalent monthly charge ($)
Per-mile charge for DS1		20.00	20.00
Access charge per end for DS1		340.00	340.00
CSU/DSU	2500.00		83.33
Router port	3000.00		100.00
SMDS tariff per SNI		700.00	700.00
CSU/DSU for SMDS	5000.00		166.67

Note: The equivalent monthly charge is computed from first cost by dividing by 30, which is based on a 3-year amortization and approximately a 13% interest rate.

Table 2.1 Assumptions for economic comparison (North America, 1993)

---

[7]We believe that these numbers are representative for North America in 1993. They are not meant to be definitive statements of any tariffs or equipment costs. In fact, in general both equipment cost and tariffs are expected to fall over time. Your mileage may vary.

[8]When a frame-based access protocol is used to access SMDS (see Section 2.4.2), a special CSU/DSU is not needed, and the CSU/DSU cost is the same for both the dedicated DS1 connection and SMDS.

For each dedicated DS1 connection, we assume that the length is 10 miles. Because the DS1 tariff is assumed to be related to distance, the results of our comparison are highly dependent on this assumption. We also assume that the traffic is such that a single location will not overload a single DS1 SNI. Finally, we have assumed that service installation charges are the same and, therefore, we have not included them in the comparison.

Because the DS1 connections are assumed to be 10 miles, the monthly tariff is 10 times the per-mile charge plus twice the access charge (one access charge for each end of the connection). The monthly equipment charge for each dedicated DS1 connection (two ends) is two times the router-port charge plus two times the CSU/DSU charge. Thus, the total monthly charge for each dedicated DS1 connection is 200.00 + 680.00 + 166.66 + 200.00 = $1246.66. For each SMDS SNI (one end), the monthly charge is the tariff plus the monthly charge for a router port plus the monthly charge for a CSU/DSU for SMDS, which equals 700.00 + 100.00 + 166.67 = $966.67.

The above calculations show that if just two locations, 10 miles apart, are to be communicating, the monthly charge for a single dedicated DS1 connection ($1246.66) is less than the cost for the two-SMDS SNI arrangement ($1933.34). However, the comparison becomes more interesting as the number of locations increases.

If a full mesh of DS1s is used, which maintains one hop between all locations, the monthly charges are as shown in Figure 2.15. Beginning with the addition of a third location, SMDS becomes significantly less expensive than dedicated DS1 connections. As the number of locations increases, the SMDS advantage increases dramatically because the monthly charges for SMDS grow linearly, while the monthly charges for the full mesh of dedicated DS1 connections grow quadratically.

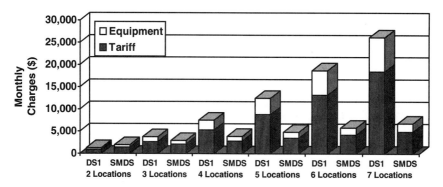

Figure 2.15 Economics of private-line, full-mesh topology and SMDS

Of course it is unlikely that a full mesh of dedicated DS1 connections will be used for a large number of locations. The least expensive topology for dedicated DS1 connections is to connect all locations to a single hub location. Thus, *n − 1* connections are used for *n* locations. The results of this comparison are shown in Figure 2.16. In this case, SMDS and dedicated DS1 connections are just about equal in monthly charges for four locations with the SMDS having the advantage for larger numbers of locations, and dedicated DS1 connections having the advantage for two and three locations.

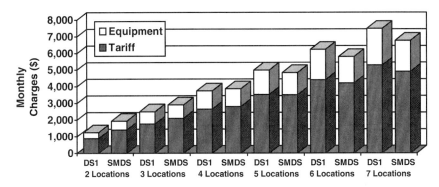

Figure 2.16 Economics of private-line hub topology and SMDS

Actual dedicated DS1 configurations are likely to fall somewhere in between the previous two described above. In order to estimate the intermediate case, we use a partial mesh topology. In this topology, each location has two dedicated DS1 connections, one to each of two of the other locations. The results are shown in Figure 2.17. Even for this moderate level of connectivity for the dedicated DS1 connections, SMDS has lower monthly charges beginning with three locations.

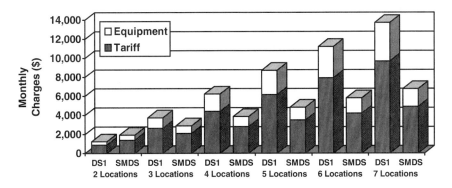

Figure 2.17 Economics of private-line, partial-mesh topology and SMDS

The above examples illustrate that SMDS looks more and more attractive as the number of communicating locations increases. This is exactly the behavior that is needed for a successful public switched service.

2.4   Access Protocols for SMDS

In order to access SMDS, an access protocol that can carry the L3_PDU is required. Bellcore, in [772], specifies a protocol based on the Distributed Queue Dual Bus (DQDB) [802.6]. Subsequent to the publication of [772], access protocols based on the SMDS Data Exchange Interface (DXI) [SIG001] and on Frame Relay have been specified for access to SMDS [SIG005] [1239] [SIG006] [1240]. These three access protocols are briefly described in the following subsections. Then we discuss access to SMDS via Asynchronous Transfer Mode (ATM).

2.4.1   Distributed Queue Dual Bus Access (DQDB) to SMDS

DQDB is a protocol designed for a shared-medium network. It can be used for the equipment in a service-provider network and it is also the basis of SIP. Section 2.5 describes the former use, while in this section we focus on the latter use.

One of the motivations for basing SIP on DQDB is that it allows multiple CPE to access SMDS over a single physical access arrangement, as shown in Figure 2.18. (A thorough discussion of the pros and cons of basing SIP on DQDB is provided in Chapter 4.) However, typical configurations involve single CPE, as shown in Figure 2.19. As shown in this figure, SIP can be terminated in a single CPE device, such as a router, or it can be implemented in two devices using a special Channel Service Unit/Data Service Unit (CSU/DSU). The interface between the CSU/DSU and the router is the SMDS Data Exchange Interface (DXI) [SIG001]. This arrangement is fully described in Chapter 5.

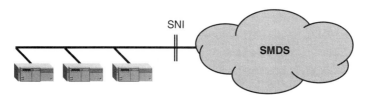

Figure 2.18 Multiple CPE access to SMDS

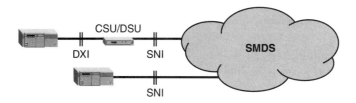

Figure 2.19 Single CPE access to SMDS

SIP is said to be based on DQDB because a device that it conforms with [802.6] can successfully access SMDS. However, as described in Chapter 4, for single-CPE access, a subset of [802.6] is all that is required. SIP supports data rates of 1.544 Mbps (DS1), 2.048 Mbps (E1), 34.368 Mbps (E3), and 44.736 Mbps (DS3).

2.4.2   SMDS Data Exchange Interface (DXI) Access to SMDS

The SMDS Interest Group first developed the DXI [SIG001] as an interface between a router or end system and a special CSU/DSU that would allow existing routers and end systems to access SMDS without the need for hardware upgrades. This was useful because hardware for SIP was not yet widely available. However, it requires that this new hardware be incorporated in the CSU/DSU (i.e., existing CSU/DSUs cannot be used). As a consequence, the SMDS Interest Group went on to specify the use of the DXI for direct-service access [SIG005]. MCI, in its HyperStream[SM] SMDS [MCI], has eliminated the need for a special CSU/DSU by making the DXI the service access protocol for speeds between 56 Kbps and 1.536 Mbps.

The DXI is based on HDLC procedures [ISO3309]. The encapsulation of L3_PDUs in the HDLC frame is shown in Figure 2.20. Details are presented in Chapter 5.

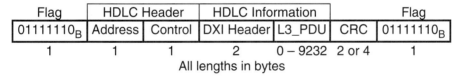

Figure 2.20 Encapsulation of the L3_PDU in the DXI

Bellcore has published a technical service description, [1239], for SMDS for the case where the SNI is based on the DXI, which is referred to as Low-Speed SMDS. The SNI uses a DS0 transmission path with bit rates of either 56 Kbps or 64 Kbps, although there is a suggestion[9] that a bit rate of 1.536 Mbps might be offered. Bellcore requirements [1239] call out some differences from [772] with regard to the service features of Low-Speed SMDS. Most of the differences involve reduced addressing capabilities (e.g., the number of Individual Addresses that can be assigned to an SNI). The motivation for the reduced feature set is ease of implementation by the service provider. Chapter 3 details the differences in features for Low-Speed SMDS. The SIG, in [SIG005], allows for use of the DXI at speeds of 56, 64, n×56, and n×64 Kbps, only

---

[9]The suggestion is in the form of a "Conditional Requirement" that begins, "If a LEC chooses to offer a DS1 access rate . . ." and specifies a physical layer for DS1.

observing that service feature implications for speeds above E1 (2.048 Mbps) are under study.

2.4.3   Frame Relay Access to SMDS

Frame Relay can be discussed as either a technology or a service. In this section we discuss Frame Relay as a technology for supporting access to SMDS. (In subsection 2.6.1 we discuss Frame Relay as a service.) The use of the Frame Relay protocol to access SMDS is called *SIP Relay,* and the service access interface is called the *SIP Relay Interface* (SRI) [SIG006] [1240].

The Frame Relay protocol is based on HDLC procedures, [ISO3309] and thus it can be used to access SMDS much as described in the previous subsection. Figure 2.21 shows the encapsulation of the L3_PDU in the Frame Relay frame. The details of this encapsulation can be found in Chapter 5, [SIG006], and [1240]. The DATA LINK CONNECTION IDENTIFIER (DLCI) in the frame header is set to a special value to identify the SIP Relay Interface Permanent Virtual Circuit (SRI PVC). This value is not universally defined and thus will be defined by each service provider.

Flag	Frame Relay Header	Frame Relay Information		Flag
01111110_B	DLCI = SRI PVC	L3_PDU	CRC	01111110_B
1	2	0 – 9232	2	1

all lengths in bytes

Figure 2.21 Encapsulation of the L3_PDU in the Frame Relay frame

Given the similarity of Frame Relay encapsulation to DXI encapsulation, one might wonder why both protocols are needed. The answer lies in the intended uses. The previous subsection discussed the motivation for the DXI. From the customer's point of view, an advantage of Frame Relay access to SMDS is that both Frame Relay service (see Section 2.6.1) and SMDS can be accessed over a single interface. Since the tariff for a service includes a large component for the access line, using a single access line can yield significant savings compared to paying for two access lines, one for each service. The single access line can also yield savings by avoiding the use of a bridge or router port.

A service-provider motivation for the use of Frame Relay access to SMDS can be explained with the use of Figure 2.22. Consider a carrier that has an existing network of Frame Relay switches. For simplicity, this network is represented by a single Frame Relay switch in Figure 2.22. By using the encapsulation of the L3_PDU of Figure 2.21, the existing Frame Relay network can transparently carry the L3_PDU to a location where the SMDS service features and switching can be performed, shown as the combination of an interworking unit and an SMDS Switching System in Figure 2.22. Use of a

Frame Relay Permanent Virtual Circuit (FRPVC) allows the identification of the source service interface to allow support of Source Address Validation and Address Screening. Thus, the use of Frame Relay Access to SMDS allows the carrier to leverage the existing investment in Frame Relay technology in offering SMDS.

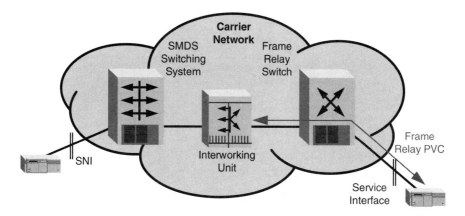

Figure 2.22 Frame Relay access to SMDS

Bellcore has published a technical service description for SIP Relay [1240]. The SMDS features supported by SIP Relay differ from those in [772]. Most of the differences involve reduced addressing capabilities. For example, only two Individual Addresses can be assigned to an SRI PVC. The details of these differences are noted in Chapter 3.

2.4.4   Asynchronous Transfer Mode (ATM) Access to SMDS

ATM is a technology for switching and multiplexing based on 53-byte packets called *cells*. Multiplexing is accomplished by breaking each traffic stream into cells and labeling the cells with a unique 24-bit code in the header of the cell. Each label corresponds to what is called a *Virtual Channel Connection* (VCC). Thus, on a single physical interface to a network, multiple services can be accessed by using a different VCC for each service. This is illustrated in Figure 2.23.

The protocols that are used for accessing SMDS over ATM are very similar to SIP.[10] This follows from the cell orientation of SIP, where L2_PDUs are also 53 bytes. One very important identical aspect of the protocol with SIP is that the service-feature-related fields of the L3_PDU are the same. The protocol layering

---

[10]Of course, close doesn't count in protocols as it does in horseshoes, dancing, and hand grenades.

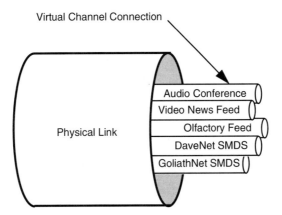

Figure 2.23 Accessing SMDS using ATM

for accessing SMDS over ATM is shown in Figure 2.24. Chapter 13 presents the details of the protocols shown in this figure.

SIP Level 3
AAL3/4 SAR
ATM
PHY

Note: AAL3/4 SAR refers to an ATM protocol for carrying large, variable-length packets in multiple cells (see Chapter 13).

Figure 2.24 Protocol layering for accessing SMDS using ATM

2.5   Technologies for Providing SMDS

SMDS is a service, not a technology. In a properly designed service-provider network, the customer should be unaware of and unconcerned with the technology being used by the service provider. The customer will only be concerned with the tariff, the features supported, and the performance. In principle, even supersonic carrier pigeons could be used to provide SMDS.[11] As the technology in the service provider network improves, the SMDS customer will not need to make any changes except to enjoy improved performance and lower tariffs.

---

[11]In 1983, a short discussion actually occurred at an IEEE P802.6 meeting regarding the suitability of using supersonic carrier pigeons for Metropolitan Area Networks. After about two minutes with a calculator, it was concluded that the latency would be too great. Who says standards making is all serious business?

Early implementations in service provider networks have used what can be described as Metropolitan Area Network technology, which is typically dedicated only to SMDS. In the longer term, technology intended for supporting multiple services, such as Asynchronous Transfer Mode, may be used. The next subsections describe these approaches.

2.5.1   Metropolitan Area Network Technology

One approach to implementing SMDS in a service-provider network is to use Metropolitan Area Network (MAN) technology. In the example illustrated in Figure 2.25, a Distributed Queue Dual Bus (DQDB) running on high-speed transmission systems is used to connect four central offices. In each central office is one or more Customer Access Nodes. CANs terminate SNIs and implement the various SMDS features such as Address Screening. (Note that because the CANs terminate the SNIs, aberrant behavior on the part of CPE cannot disrupt the operation of the DQDB that connects the telephone central offices.) The CANs also make use of the Connectionless MAC capability of DQDB to send L3_PDUs to the CAN(s) that terminate the destination SNI(s).

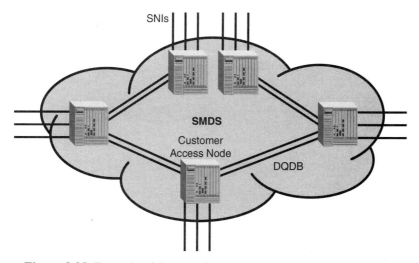

Figure 2.25 Example of the use of MAN technology to provide SMDS

One of the reasons that MAN technology was considered attractive in the early work on SMDS was that this approach could be implemented quickly [Hemrick]. Indeed, the first trials and service implementations of SMDS by Bell Atlantic used this approach.

2.5.2 Broadband Integrated Services Digital Network

The Broadband Integrated Services Digital Network (BISDN) is the follow-on concept to the Integrated Services Digital Network (ISDN). BISDN differs from ISDN in that it is intended to provide much higher bandwidth, and that it will be based on ATM. Because ATM offers the promise of being able to support all forms of communications traffic, it is expected to provide the foundation on which telephone carriers will eventually implement all services.[12]

For SMDS, the multiplexing capability of ATM can be used in an arrangement like the one shown in Figure 2.26. An ATM permanent virtual channel exists between the CPE and a device that provides the SMDS features, the SMDS Feature Processor. In effect, the ATM infrastructure is used to transfer L3_PDUs between points that can process them. The SMDS Feature Processor can use another permanent virtual channel to deliver the L3_PDU to the appropriate destination.

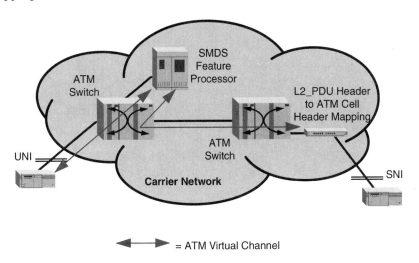

Figure 2.26 Example of providing SMDS using Asynchronous Transfer Mode

Figure 2.26 illustrates support of SMDS by both the SNI and the ATM User Network Interface (UNI). For the UNI access, the ATM permanent virtual channel connects the CPE with the SMDS Feature Processor. With the SNI access, the permanent virtual channel can connect a simple mapping function to the SMDS Feature Processor. The mapping function need only map between the SIP L2_PDU NETWORK CONTROL INFORMATION field (see Section 4.6.2) and the ATM Cell Header. (Chapter 13 provides more detail on providing SMDS with

---

[12]Clearly this is a *very* long-term vision. The non-ATM installed investment in telephone networks that is not written off is huge and will take a very long time to replace.

ATM.) Thus, the deployment of ATM will not obviate the support of the SNI. Also, when the ATM UNI is used for SMDS access, perhaps to accrue the benefits of a multiservices interface, the L3_PDU will continue to be used on top of ATM protocols.[13]

2.6   Comparison with Other LAN Interconnection Services

SMDS is not the only new carrier service that is targeted at LAN interconnection. In the past few years, there has been substantial interest in the industry in how these new services relate to each other.[14] In particular, the relationship of Frame Relay Service and SMDS has been of high interest, and this is discussed in the next section. Then, we compare SMDS with what we call *native* LAN service. Finally we compare SMDS with Cell Relay Service (CRS), which we expect to be one of the first public-carrier, ATM-based services.

2.6.1   Frame Relay Service

In Section 2.4.3, we discussed Frame Relay as a technology. In this section, we are concerned with Frame Relay in the context of a service. Frame Relay Service can be viewed as consisting of two different services; Frame Relay Permanent Virtual Circuit Service (FRPVC) and Frame Relay Switched Virtual Circuit Service (FRSVC). Both are compared with SMDS in the next two subsections.

2.6.1.1   Frame Relay Permanent Virtual Circuit Service (FRPVC)

With FRPVC a customer can use a single service interface to exchange data with equipment connected to several other service interfaces. The bit rate of the service interface can range from 56 Kbps up to 2.048 Mbps. Connectivity between two service interfaces is established via a request to the service provider to configure a virtual connection between the service interfaces. Forms that the request can take include a telephone call, a paper mail message, or facsimile transmission. The time from when the request is made to the time that the virtual connection is available can range from a few minutes to several weeks. Given this interval and the fact that there is usually a significant installation fee for each virtual connection, a customer will tend to leave the virtual connections in

---

[13]We are quite amused by claims that ATM will replace SMDS. That is like saying in 1955 that jet aircraft were going to replace airline passengers. Luckily, the airline industry realized that jet aircraft were going to replace DC-6s.

[14]In the recent past, some players in the industry have attempted to position these services as if they were in a competitive "fight-to-the-death." These activities reminded us of professional wrestling promoters manufacturing nonexistent grudges in an attempt to sell more tickets, in this case to industry seminars and debates on the services.

place once they are established. Hence these connections are called *permanent virtual connections* (PVCs).

For each connection established at a service interface, there is (typically) a 10-bit identifier, called a DATA LINK CONNECTION IDENTIFIER (DLCI), assigned. To send data to a particular destination, the attached CPE forms a frame whose header contains the DLCI value assigned to the PVC to the intended destination and transmits it across the service interface. The maximum frame size is usually 1600 bytes.

Because of the duration of the PVCs, FRPVC is much like a private-line service and is ideal for private networks. Although SMDS can easily be used as a private-line replacement, with Address Screening providing similar levels of privacy, the ability to reach any SMDS subscriber's interface by simply using the proper E.164 address makes SMDS much better suited for public networking.

SMDS Group Addressing is another key difference. Such a multicasting capability is not available with FRPVC. The impact is that the methods of implementing routing and bridging are different with FRPVC. Chapters 8 and 9 show how SMDS Group Addressing is extensively exploited for routing and bridging respectively. This is not to say that doing routing and bridging over FRPVC is not well understood. Bridging and routing implementations over private lines are very mature, and thus the private-line nature of FRPVC makes migration straightforward. However, as the number of permanent virtual connections becomes large, the exchange of routing information on each connection becomes burdensome compared to the simplicity when Group Addressing is used to exchange routing information. For example, if a router is connected to FRPVC with 100 PVCs across the interface, the router has to send 100 hello messages, one for each PVC, across the interface in order to maintain adjacency with the routers on the other end of each PVC. When a topology change occurs, swarms of update messages are exchanged on each PVC, which can look like an update message storm compared to the total bandwidth of the FRPVC interface.

Other key differences between SMDS and FRPVC include the following:

- Maximum interface bit rate: up to 44.736 Mbps versus 2.048 Mbps

- Maximum user information in each data unit: 9188 bytes versus 1600 bytes (typical).

2.6.1.2   Frame Relay Switched Virtual Circuit Service (FRSVC)

FRSVC is like FRPVC with the additional capability for dynamic (e.g., sub second) virtual connection setup and clearing. The setup and clearing are accomplished through a signaling protocol[15] that operates between the CPE and the network providing FRSVC. This protocol is a variation on the connection-signaling protocol of ISDN. We expect[16] that the addressing used to identify end points for these connections will be based on E.164; and thus FRSVC will have public-service capability similar to that of SMDS.

However, the signaling protocol makes the CPE implementation and operation more complex than for SMDS. First, there is the signaling protocol itself, which is nontrivial. Second, since FRSVC tariffs will probably include a connection holding-time charge, the CPE will need to decide when to establish and when to clear a connection. Poor connection management can mean poor performance caused by excessive connection setups and clearings or excessive carrier charges for long-lived idle connections.

In other aspects, FRSVC and SMDS compare much the same as FRPVC and SMDS, as described in the previous section.

2.6.2   Native LAN Service

In a native LAN service the subscriber network interface is a standard LAN such as Ethernet or FDDI. Several such interfaces are tied together as if the carrier network was a multiport store-and-forward repeater. Figure 2.27 shows how such a service might work with for Ethernet. Any frame originated by A or B will be seen by C, D, E, and F. Thus all end systems appear to be on a single Ethernet, except that end systems attached to different service interfaces will never collide with each other, since the store-and-forward repeaters do the Ethernet MAC protocol. This is the simplest implementation of a native LAN service. More sophisticated implementations could include filtering to reduce extraneous traffic and could also participate in the management of a bridging spanning tree. In all cases, the result is that all service interfaces are part of a MAC layer network.

A native LAN service has the advantage that it is accessed with the LAN MAC protocol. Thus no special interface hardware is necessary to access the service. This is simpler than SMDS, but it also has some disadvantages. First, it is strictly intended for private network applications. Second, the number of devices attached to the service should be limited to prevent the management difficulties that can emerge with large, flat networks, such as broadcast storms.

---

[15]It is hard to imagine a useful communications protocol that is not used to "signal" information between the communicating entities. However, the term "signaling" is deeply rooted in telecommunications culture predating "protocols" and even telegraph. "Signaling protocol" usually refers to procedures to setup, maintain, and release connections.

[16]As of this writing, FRSVC has not yet been announced by any carrier.

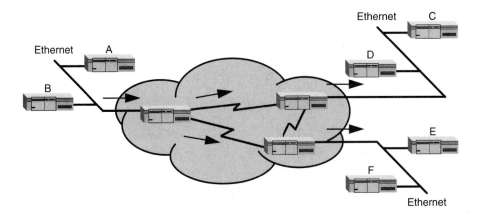

Figure 2.27 Example of Ethernet native LAN service

2.6.3   Cell Relay Service

In recent years, the communications industry has developed a huge interest in ATM. In all of the hoopla, ATM has come to stand for many things including the following:

- A high-speed, scalable communications technology

- A galactic-scale communications architecture for the ultimate, ubiquitous, all-singing, all-dancing communications infrastructure

- A basis for the next generation of high-end public carrier services.

ATM as the basis for new public carrier services is our focus here. Because of the ATM promise for very high-speed and performance, it is natural to think of ATM as the basis for a LAN interconnection service. We expect that SMDS will be one of these ATM-based services (see Chapter 13). However, in order to expedite ATM-based service availability, other, less feature-rich, ATM-based services will also probably be offered that will be suitable for LAN interconnection.

As of this writing, the details of these first ATM-based services are just emerging, although several public carriers have announced plans for such services [1408]. Therefore, we must make some educated guesses as to what the initial ATM-based services will entail. We refer to our conjecture about a generic ATM-based service as Cell Relay Service (CRS).

CRS provides permanent virtual connections between service interfaces. It is very much like today's FRPVC but with some important differences:

1. The bit rate of the service interface will be much higher, with 44.736 Mbps (DS3) being first offered, and 155.52 Mbps Synchronous Optical Network (SONET) STS-3c being offered later.

2. The unit of data transfer will be the ATM Cell with a fixed size payload of 48 bytes instead of a variable-length HDLC frame.

3. Twenty-four bits will be available for virtual connection identification instead of the 10 bits for FRPVC.

4. Instead of the CIR, CRS will use the Generic Cell Rate Algorithm (GCRA) as defined in [UNI3] and [1408].

5. Because of the need for hardware to convert between ATM cells and large variable length LAN frames, a special ATM CSU/DSU will be needed to access CRS during its early years of availability. The interface between the CSU/DSU and a router or end system is called the *ATM Data Exchange Interface* (ATM DXI) [ATM1].

The net effect is that CRS will be very much like FRPVC[17] except that it will have higher performance. Thus, the comparison of CRS with SMDS is identical to the comparison of FRPVC with SMDS, with the exception that CRS and SMDS will have similar bit rates for their service interfaces.

CRS SVCs have been the subject of much speculation, but as of this writing, no firm plans have been announced by public carriers. If provided, CRS SVCs will be much like FRSVC, except that they will have higher performance. Thus, the comparison of FRSVC and SMDS will also apply to this case.

---

[17]This is an explicit goal of Mode 1A of the ATM DXI [ATM1].

3

Service Description

SMDS provides for the transport of data packets at multi-megabit speeds. In [772], these packets are called *SMDS data units* when discussed in the context of the *service* that SMDS provides, and *SIP L3 Protocol Data Units*, *SIP L3_PDUs* or *L3_PDUs* when the protocol is discussed that transports these packets. For simplicity, in this book we always refer to L3_PDUs.

The features that accompany this transport give SMDS its unique character. Chapter 2 has introduced an overview of key SMDS features. This chapter describes the service and its features in detail. We will describe CPE arrangements for access to networks that provide SMDS. Subsequently, we present a detailed description of the SMDS features. We conclude the chapter with a summary of SMDS subscription parameters. To illustrate the use of the respective features, we will first introduce the networking configuration of a hypothetical company, the Bodacious Data Corporation, and illustrate the SMDS features with examples in that configuration.[1] The network configuration of this company is also used for examples in subsequent chapters in this book.

Most of this material is based on Bellcore specifications [772] and [1060]. The European specifications, [ESIG001] and [ESIG006], are virtually identical. Thus, we will refer mostly to [772] and [1060], but explain the few situations where particular North American or European specifications apply. Contrary to [772] and [1060], the presented material takes the perspective of SMDS customers and CPE designers.

---

[1]Only Dave Piscitello could come up with a name like Bodacious Data. It was sported on buttons handed out at SMDS demonstrations during the Interop '91 trade show.

SMDS customers should find this chapter useful in contemplating and configuring their use of SMDS. CPE designers will be interested in the exact details and rationale of the respective SMDS features.

3.1   The Bodacious Data Corporation

The Bodacious Data Corporation specializes in nautical charts. They further participate in government projects and special contracts to study and track oceanic wildlife and produce charts of seasonal migration patterns. Bodacious Data started their operations from Edgar Town on the island of Martha's Vineyard, where they occupy two separate buildings, focusing on the North American coast and the North Atlantic. They expanded by opening a branch office in nearby Cutty Hunk. Recently, they opened another branch office in San Juan, Puerto Rico, extending their operations to the Caribbean Sea.

At all locations, the Bodacious Data Corporation produces nautical charts on common workstations, usually with small teams sharing the work on a particular chart. Marine-life migration reports are produced on personal computers, tapping information in several file servers distributed over the various sites, with a number of people working on a particular report. Personnel administration is run on minicomputers in Edgar Town, with regular communications with all branch offices. A key to the success of the corporation is a corporate data network that allows for low cost and distributed operations. The network consists of LANs at all locations. The locations were initially interconnected by leased lines. Recently, these leased lines have been replaced by SMDS, which fits into the corporate network as shown in Figure 3.1. The Bodacious Data Corporation regularly works with Competing Products, Inc., which is a small supplier that does the actual printing of the charts. Subsequent sections will illustrate how the Bodacious Data Corporation makes use of SMDS.

3.2   SMDS Access Arrangements

Figures 3.2 and 3.3. show the basic concepts relevant for accessing SMDS. SMDS customer equipment that exchanges L3_PDUs through one or more service-provider networks is called SMDS *Customer Premises Equipment* (CPE).

The demarcation between SMDS CPE and SMDS is called the *Subscriber Network Interface* (SNI). The SNI marks the physical and administrative boundary between the service provider and service customers.

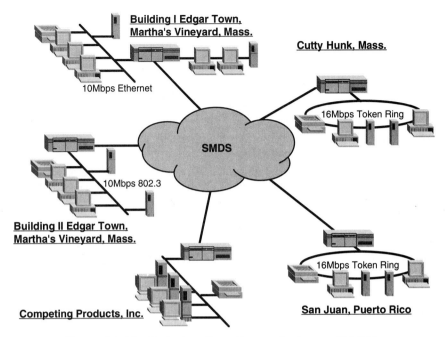

Figure 3.1 The Bodacious Data Corporation's use of SMDS

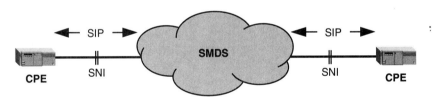

Figure 3.2 SMDS access through SIP

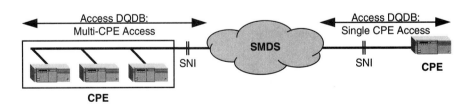

Figure 3.3 Access DQDB configurations

SMDS Interface Protocol (SIP) is a protocol used to access the service and is discussed in the next section.

3.2.1   SMDS Access Protocols

SMDS CPE accesses SMDS by means of a protocol. SMDS is a service, and does not refer to a particular technology. Thus, SMDS could potentially be supported by many different access protocols, although today just a few exist. The importance of this observation is that, as more technologies become available to provide SMDS, the service can be kept unchanged, which minimizes the impact on equipment that uses the service.[2]

- SIP is the predominant SMDS access protocol in use in 1993. We discuss SIP [772] in detail in Chapter 4. SIP operates over a variety of physical transmission facilities (i.e., DS1 and DS3 in North America, and E1 and E3 in Europe).

- The DXI (Data Exchange Interface) is an HDLC-based [ISO3309] SIP variant, and is already being used for access to SMDS at speeds up to DS1 [MCI] [SIG005] [1239]. Chapter 5 discusses this access method.

- SIP Relay refers to a Frame Relay-based access method to SMDS [SIG006] [1240]. Chapter 6 discusses this access method.

- A SIP variant based on Asynchronous Transfer Mode (ATM) [UNI3] is specified in [SIG008], and i· explained in Chapter 13. This access variant could, for example, be provided over Synchronous Optical Network (SONET) transmission facilities [253].

3.2.2   CPE and SNI

SMDS CPE is typically owned by customers of the service, and is located on their premises. Typical SMDS CPE includes intermediate systems such as bridges and routers that are capable of executing SIP and that employ SMDS to communicate between geographically dispersed locations. However, SMDS may also serve end systems directly when they are properly equipped with SIP interfaces. Examples of such end systems may range from mainframes to PCs.

Typically, customers will connect a single station to an SNI for access to SMDS. This type of access is known as *single-CPE Access*. However, SIP [772] allows multiple stations to connect to a single SNI. This arrangement is referred to as *multi-CPE Access*. Similar to LAN technologies such as Ethernet and Token Ring, SIP can use a shared physical medium with potentially many stations. The technology that is used for SIP is called *Distributed Queue Dual Bus* (*DQDB*) and has been standardized as IEEE Std 802.6-1990 [802.6] by

---

[2]All current access protocols share a common protocol format (SIP Level 3—see Chapter 4). This format is expected to be preserved in future access protocols.

IEEE. DQDB relies on the use of two unidirectional buses. The SMDS access arrangement based on SIP is referred to as an *Access DQDB*. Figure 3.3 shows Access DQDBs for single-CPE and multi-CPE Access. The expectation expressed in [772] is that the number of stations that may use an Access DQDB will not exceed 16. Chapter 4 discusses the technical details of these arrangements.

SMDS access protocols other than SIP, (SMDS DXI [SIG005], Frame Relay [SIG006], and ATM-based [SIG008] access) do not make use of DQDB. The single-CPE Access arrangement applies in these cases.

The SNI marks the administrative and physical boundary between customer and service provider. From the provider's point of view, SMDS can only be "provided" from SNI to SNI (see Figures 3.1–3.3). This situation applies especially to the United States for regulated carriers. On the other hand, some European carriers may also control CPE, in which case the service may be guaranteed from application to application. From a customer perspective, the relevant service to consider is the one as seen by the applications that make use of SMDS, and that are run by the CPE stations. In the design of SMDS, certain assumptions had to be made about CPE behavior and configurations. These assumptions follow.

- CPE executes the access protocol correctly with no significant degradation of performance within the CPE. For example, the performance objectives discussed in Chapter 7 apply (necessarily) between SNIs. These objectives are to a large extent based on the needs of expected applications that are run in the CPE stations.

- CPE is configured according to one of two possible configurations (i.e., single-CPE or multi-CPE). The assumption for multi-CPE is that local traffic on the Access DQDB may take place (even though SMDS will ignore it) but that this traffic will not disrupt or degrade SMDS traffic.

While different stations on an Access DQDB could, from a technical perspective, belong to different subscribers, SMDS makes the constraint that all stations belong to the same subscriber. A dedicated Access DQDB must be used for each subscriber.[3] DQDB, like a LAN, is a promiscuous medium, and subscribers should not be able to degrade each other's traffic performance, nor should subscribers be able to capture traffic meant for other subscribers. In an analogy with telephones, extensions are allowed, but not party lines.

---

[3]A subscriber in this context is, for example, a corporation purchasing an SNI, and not the department LAN managers who may share the Access DQDB and who (presumably) have a trusted relationship regarding their use of the Access DQDB.

3.2.3   Networks Providing SMDS

SMDS may consist of one or more interconnected SMDS Switching Systems (SSs) that are capable of communicating with SMDS CPE through the access protocol. A network will transport customer traffic to the appropriate destination and apply the SMDS features. A network also performs customer billing and maintains administration of customer information, such as subscription parameters. Networks providing SMDS may be mutually interconnected [1060]. Several networks may be traversed for communication between CPE. For example, intercontinental traffic typically uses more than one carrier.

The network ingress is the point where SMDS traffic enters a network. The network egress is the point where SMDS traffic exits the network. Ingress and egress play important and different roles with regard to several SMDS features. Figure 3.4 illustrates these network concepts.

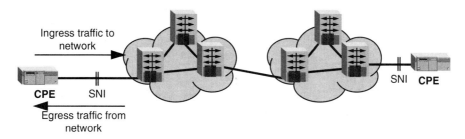

Figure 3.4 Interconnected networks providing SMDS

3.2.4   Service Access Integration

A carrier providing SMDS may offer SMDS through the same network-access facilities that are used for the provision of other network services. For example, a subscriber DS1 access circuit may be configured so that a portion of the DS1 bandwidth is dedicated to access to SMDS, while another portion is used for voice applications. This arrangement is called *multiservice access*. The advantage to subscribers is a potential cost saving on their carrier-access facilities.

Figure 3.5 illustrates an example scenario, where voice and SMDS traffic are multiplexed over the same access circuit. Digital cross-connect systems in the carrier network route the respective DS1 fractions to their destinations. A CSU/DSU (Channel Service Unit/Data Service Unit, described in Chapter 5) performs a similar function at customer premises. Further examples of this arrangement are described in Chapter 5 and in [MCI].

Multiservice access is expected to be exploited more often with ATM-based access to SMDS (see Chapter 13). An implication of multiservice access

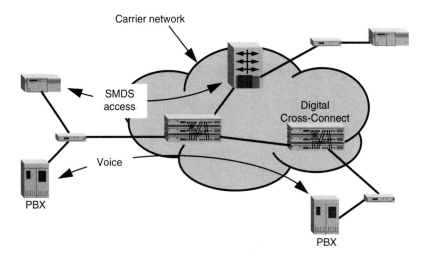

Figure 3.5 Example of multiservice access using fractional DS1

configurations is that bandwidth allocation on the access circuit must be such that different traffic streams for the respective applications will not disrupt each other, or otherwise compromise each other's service objectives.

3.2.5   Use of SMDS by Applications

SMDS provides high-speed packet transport. L3_PDUs are the packets sent over an SNI. They carry the customer's information that is transparent to SMDS access protocols and all the networks that it traverses. Conversely, the customer's applications that use SMDS, for example, protocols such as IP, are merely concerned with the end-to-end behavior of SMDS, and not with the individual pieces of equipment that participate in providing the service. In order to divorce the actual service from mundane (but complex) things such as interface cards, networks, cabling, and so on, an abstraction technique is used. This rather old service decomposition technique [Vissers] is also extensively used to describe the Open Systems Interconnection architecture and related services [ISO7498]. Figure 3.6 shows this abstraction.

The abstract service that is relevant for SMDS applications (the applications and higher level protocols in Figure 3.6) is provided through SMDS Service Access Points or SMDS SAPs. The inherent complexities of the abstract service provider (everything between the SMDS SAPs, such as SIP interface cards, cabling, networks, etc.) are not relevant for these applications. SMDS Addresses (discussed later in this chapter) actually identify SMDS SAPs, and are used by SMDS applications to identify the source and destination of L3_PDUs. The abstract service may in turn be used by other protocols, such as TCP/IP. Chapters 8 and 9 describe several routing and bridging applications.

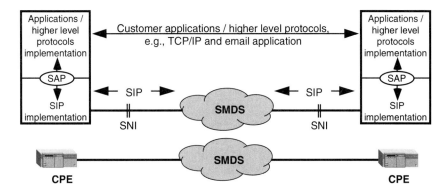

Figure 3.6 Service at SNIs and service at SMDS Service Access Points

Information from SMDS applications is passed across SAPs, and is transported between SAPs by L3_PDUs. The basic structure of an L3_PDU is shown in Figure 3.7.

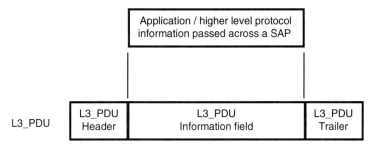

Figure 3.7 SAPs and L3_PDUs

The implementation of the SIP in CPE may be distributed over multiple pieces of equipment (e.g., a CSU/DSU and a router; see Chapter 5), just as the implementation of the higher level protocols and applications may be distributed over multiple pieces of equipment, for example, a router (IP functions of Figure 3.6), connected through a LAN to a mail server (TCP/IP and electronic mail functions of Figure 3.6).

It is important to appreciate the distinction between SMDS SAPs and SNIs with respect to SMDS service provision. The primary concern from the perspective of applications that use SMDS is the service observed at SMDS SAPs. Provision of that service requires good behavior of both CPE and participating networks. Regulated service providers in the United States can only control the service between SNIs. Thus, engineering assumptions (discussed in Section 3.2.2) for these networks have to be made about CPE performance and the use of the service observed at SNIs.[4] SMDS customers should configure their SMDS access equipment so that these assumptions are not compromised, in order to allow proper operation of the service provided at SMDS SAPs.

3.3   Service Features for the Transport of L3_PDUs

Because one of the major applications contemplated for SMDS is LAN interconnection, a design criterion was that SMDS should fit easily into leading data communications architectures. Thus, SMDS is designed to look like a LAN to the SMDS user. To this end, the major characteristic of SMDS is connectionless packet (or datagram) transport. Together with other control information, each L3_PDU contains the addresses of its source and destination, and is routed to its destination independently of other L3_PDUs. Figure 3.8 shows an example of this approach.

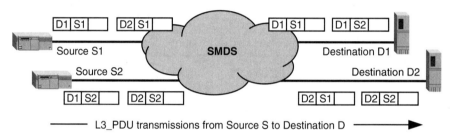

Figure 3.8 L3_PDU transport

The connectionless approach has been widely adopted in leading communications architectures (see Chapters 8 and 9). Examples of other connectionless services are those provided by Ethernet and FDDI. In contrast, services such as those provided by X.25 rely on an initial establishment of a virtual circuit between source and destination, and subsequent labeling of data units with their virtual circuit identifier. No management of virtual circuits is necessary for SMDS, which decreases the complexity and cost of accessing the service. This approach, in combination with features such as Group Addressing, gives SMDS its LAN-like appearance and allows it to fit easily into leading communications architectures (see Chapters 8 and 9).

Connectionless communication does not require each "hop" in a network that a datagram traverses to confirm correct receipt of the datagram to the source.

---

[4]This distinction also finds its way into other terminology. In literature on SMDS one will often find phrases like "submitting SDUs to an SNI," "addressing SNIs," "receiving SDUs from an SNI," etc. This terminology is tailored to the responsibilities of the service provider, and disregards the equipment at customer premises.

Rather, for those applications that require it, error detection and receipt confirmation are performed by end-to-end protocols across the interconnected networks. Examples of such protocols are TCP and the OSI Transport Protocol. The wide deployment of this approach allows for a simple design of SMDS, and suggests rather simple use of the service by CPE, and high performance by both CPE and networks that provide SMDS.

A rigorous set of performance objectives is used in SMDS to achieve LAN-like performance, including LAN-like ratios for parameters such as misdelivered L3_PDUs, errored L3_PDUs, or missequenced L3_PDUs (see Chapter 7).[5]

SMDS provides for two basic L3_PDU transport services:

1. Transport of Individually Addressed L3_PDUs (unicasting), which allows for transport of L3_PDUs between a source and a single destination.

2. Transport of Group Addressed L3_PDUs (multicasting), which allows for transport of L3_PDUs between a source and multiple destinations. The SMDS Group Addressing capability is similar to that found in most LAN products.

Transport and delivery of L3_PDUs are complemented by a number of SMDS features. Section 3.4 explains these features in detail.

3.3.1   Unicasting—Individually Addressed L3_PDUs

The basic operation of Individually Addressed L3_PDUs is shown in Figure 3.9. This figure shows the view of SMDS applications at the SMDS SAPs discussed in Section 3.2.5. For each L3_PDU, the source needs to specify its own address (the Source Address) and a Destination Address for which the L3_PDU is intended. The Destination Address is said to be an Individual Destination Address when there is exactly one intended recipient of the L3_PDU.

It is expected that all public SMDS carriers will use SMDS addresses that are structured according to [E.164], the addressing plan for the ISDN era, which is discussed in Section 3.4.1.

A source may include a Carrier Selection indication (see below) in an L3_PDU, and up to 9188 bytes of SMDS Information.[6] Figure 3.9 shows that the DESTINATION ADDRESS, the SOURCE ADDRESS, the CARRIER SELECTION, and the INFORMATION fields of L3_PDUs are delivered to the destination unchanged.

SMDS allows for transport of 0-9188 bytes of Information; thus, it supports most networking technologies that may be connected to SMDS, without the need

---

[5]In addition, associated with SMDS, CNM service may be provided to aid in speedy troubleshooting and problem isolation (see Chapters 10 and 12).

[6]Access through Frame Relay may support a smaller information field. See Chapter 6.

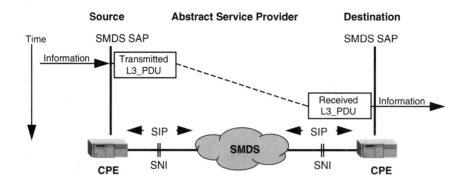

Parameter	Transmitted L3_PDU	Received L3_PDU
SMDS Individual Source Address	Mandatory	Mandatory (=)
SMDS Individual Destination Address	Mandatory	Mandatory (=)
Carrier Selection	Optional	Optional (=)
SMDS Information (≤ 9188 bytes)	Optional	Optional (=)

(=): Required when present in the Transmitted L3_PDU, and unchanged in the Received L3_PDU.

Figure 3.9 Individually Addressed L3_PDUs

of further segmentation and reassembly. The maximum L3_PDU size also guides implementors on issues such as buffer-size requirements and bit-error detection. Table 3.1 shows maximum-information field sizes of PDUs for common networking technologies.

L3_PDUs addressed to the same SNI over which they were received at the network ingress are not delivered. In the case of a multi-CPE configuration, returning them to that SNI could result in the destination station receiving two copies of the same L3_PDU, which burdens applications unnecessarily.

SMDS accommodates the United States system of Local Exchange Carriers (LECs) and Interexchange Carriers (IECs) by allowing customers to select their preferred IEC. This affords IEC interexchange service offerings equal access to customers directly connected to a LEC network. There are two ways for customers to choose their preferred IEC. In the first way, known as *preselection*, customers choose their preferred carrier as part of the service subscription process. In the second way, known as *overriding*, customers can explicitly choose their preferred carrier on a per-L3_PDU basis. An explicit per-L3_PDU selection of a preferred carrier (the Carrier Selection indication) overrides a preselected carrier. Section 3.4.7 discusses Carrier Selection.

Networking technology	Maximum PDU size	Maximum information field size
Ethernet / IEEE 802.3 [802.3]	1526 bytes	1500 bytes
Token Bus / IEEE 802.4 [Martin]	9210 bytes[a]	8191 bytes
Token Ring / IEEE 802.5 [802.5][b] 4 Mbps 16 Mbps	4500 bytes ≈16000 bytes	4479 bytes ≈16000 bytes
FDDI - Basic Mode [FDDI]	4500 bytes	4478 bytes
FDDI - Hybrid Mode [Kessler]	8600 bytes	8578 bytes

[a] Excluding the Preamble. The size of the Preamble depends on the modulation method [Martin].

[b] The maximum size depends on the maximum token-holding time. Taking the 10-ms holding time, and assuming a 1-ms ring latency yields for 4 Mbps a maximum frame size of 4500 bytes. Similarly, a 16-Mbps Token Ring can support a maximum frame size of about 16,000 bytes.

Table 3.1 Maximum PDU sizes

3.3.2   Multicasting—Group Addressed L3_PDUs

Figure 3.10 shows the basic operation of Group Addressed L3_PDUs, and illustrates the view of SMDS applications at the SMDS SAPs discussed in Section 3.2.5. For each L3_PDU, the source needs to specify its own Source Address and a Destination Address that identifies a group of destinations for which the L3_PDU is intended. This Destination Address is called a Group Address. Group Addresses (values) are allocated by the SMDS provider. The list of members is established by separate procedures between customers and SMDS service administrators (see Section 3.4.2 and Chapter 12).

As with Individual Addresses, it is expected that all public SMDS carriers will use SMDS Group Addresses structured according to [E.164] (see Section 3.4.1).

Group Addressed L3_PDUs, like Individually Addressed L3_PDUs, can carry up to 9188 bytes of SMDS Information.[7]

Figure 3.10 shows that the DESTINATION ADDRESS, the SOURCE ADDRESS, the CARRIER SELECTION, and the INFORMATION fields of L3_PDUs are delivered to the destination unchanged. The reason for delivering the Group Address instead of the Individual Address that is the member of the group (see Section 3.4.2) is that the Group Address conveys information about which group is the intended destination. For example, addresses on an SNI may be members of multiple Group Addresses to support different data-networking architectures, as

---

[7]Access through Frame Relay may support a smaller information field. See Chapter 6.

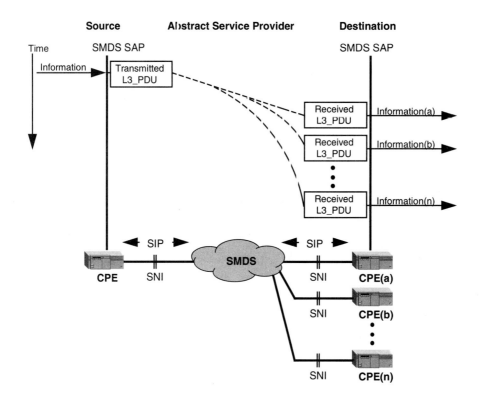

Parameter	Transmitted L3_PDU	Received L3_PDU
SMDS Individual Source Address	Mandatory	Mandatory (=)
SMDS Group Destination Address	Mandatory	Mandatory (=)
Carrier Selection	Optional	Optional (=)
SMDS Information (≤ 9188 bytes)	Optional	Optional (=)

(=): Required when present in the Transmitted L3_PDU, and unchanged in the Received L3_PDU.

Figure 3.10 Group Addressed L3_PDUs

discussed in Chapters 8 and 9. It also allows different levels of trust to be applied to the processing of L3_PDUs, depending on which Group Address is used.

The Source Address of a station does not need to belong to a Group Address in order for the station to send to it. This is an important difference from the Closed User Group facility for X.21 and X.25 networks, with which Group Addressing is sometimes erroneously compared.[8]

---

[8]This confusion is quite puzzling to the authors; Group Addressing is a multicasting capability, while Closed User Group is an access-control feature.

The service definition specifies that each member of the Group Address should receive precisely one L3_PDU. This seems quite unremarkable at first glance, but observe that several members of a Group Address may share the same SNI. To accommodate this correctly, SMDS delivers only one copy of a Group Addressed L3_PDU to an SNI that is shared by multiple members of that Group Address.[9] It also ensures that when the source of the L3_PDU shares an SNI with one or more members of the Group Address, SMDS will not copy the L3_PDU back to that SNI.

Carrier Selection also applies to Group Addressed L3_PDUs (see Section 3.4.7).

We use the configuration of the Bodacious Data Corporation to illustrate an example. In Figure 3.11, when station A sends an L3_PDU addressed to G2, copies of the L3_PDU are delivered to the SNIs of B and C. When station D sends an L3_PDU addressed to G2, copies of the L3_PDU are delivered to the SNIs of A, B and C.

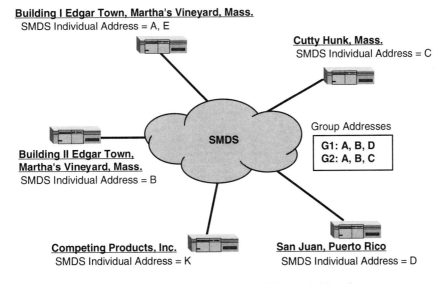

Building I Edgar Town, Martha's Vineyard, Mass.
SMDS Individual Address = A, E

Cutty Hunk, Mass.
SMDS Individual Address = C

SMDS

**Building II Edgar Town,
Martha's Vineyard, Mass.**
SMDS Individual Address = B

Group Addresses

G1: A, B, D
G2: A, B, C

Competing Products, Inc.
SMDS Individual Address = K

San Juan, Puerto Rico
SMDS Individual Address = D

Figure 3.11 Example of the use of Group Addressing

SMDS Group Addressing differs from the broadcast mechanism commonly used on LANs in that a broadcast is used to reach all possible destinations on a network, and a multicast is meant to reach a specific set of destinations. For SMDS this set must be preconfigured.

SMDS does not support a broadcast capability. The reason for this choice is well illustrated in [Comer1], when raising the question whether a network that is

---

[9]There is one catch to this rule, which is related to which network is resolving the Group Address. This is described in Section 3.4.2.

connected to another network through a gateway should broadcast messages generated on the local network be passed along by the gateway to the next network. The answer to this question for SMDS is no. The gateway in question is generalized to mean SMDS, and to pass along a broadcast implies that all networks of all subscribers connected by SMDS receive this broadcast. Not only would this action generate large amounts of traffic and consume resources on all connected equipment, it is improbable that this would be the true intention of the sender. Rather, it is likely that the sender wants to reach a small set of known stations (e.g., within a corporate internet), for example, in order to transport routing information, as is common in several networking architectures. A multicast capability addresses these needs more efficiently.

3.4   Address- and Transport-Related Features

In this section we take a look at each of the features associated with SMDS.

3.4.1   SMDS Addresses

SMDS applications use SMDS addresses to identify the source and destination of L3_PDUs. Networks providing SMDS use SMDS addresses to route L3_PDUs from their source SNI to their destination SNI, subject to various SMDS features. SMDS addresses have a variable length, and are composed as shown in Figure 3.12.

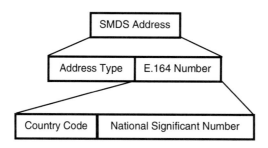

Figure 3.12 SMDS address structure

The components are as follows:

- *Address Type:* This part distinguishes between Individual Addresses and Group Addresses.

- *E.164 Number:* This part contains a number that conforms to the CCITT E.164 numbering plan.

- *Country Code:* This part of the E.164 Number identifies the country that has allocated the *National Significant Number*. It can contain 1 to 3 decimal digits.

- *National Significant Number:* A variable number of decimal digits allocated by the numbering authority of the country identified by the *Country Code*.

The parts are described in the following subsections.

3.4.1.1   Address Type

Both Individual and Group Addresses for SMDS conform to the CCITT E.164 numbering format. However, the same number may be used for both a particular Individual Address and for a particular Group Address. The semantics of a particular address are determined "by the context of its use" [772]. This context is determined by the Address Type. Thus, each half of the SMDS address space precisely matches E.164, and the two halves are distinguished by the value of the Address Type.

The Address Type is a hexadecimal digit that assumes the value C_H (1100_B) for Individual Addresses and E_H (1110_B) for Group Addresses. The notational convention is

$< C | E > <$ some decimal E.164 value $>$.

For example

C18097585254$_H$ represents an SMDS Individual Address, and
E18097585254$_H$ represents an SMDS Group Address.

Chapters 4 and 8 show that many protocols that use SMDS addresses use a fixed-length format of 16 hexadecimal digits. The fixed length is obtained by padding the address with binary 1's (F_H):

$< C | E > <$ some decimal E.164 value $>$ <padding F's>

Thus the same two SMDS addresses given above can also be represented by the following hexadecimal strings:

C18097585254FFFF$_H$
E18097585254FFFF$_H$

3.4.1.2   E.164 Number

CCITT Recommendation E.164 defines the numbering plan for the ISDN era [E.164]. This numbering format is also used for the broadband flavor of

ISDN (BISDN). SMDS is considered to be an early BISDN service. The E.164 numbering plan closely follows the international numbering for telephony [E.163]. While E.163 specifies a maximum number length of 12 decimal digits, E.164 allows for an addressing space of 15 decimal digits, giving a larger address space to the national significant portion of the address. The current telephony numbering is therefore subsumed by the ISDN numbering plan.

The E.163/164 numbering plan allows for "abbreviated" dialing patterns for the convenience of telephone service users. For example, in the United States, a local call requires dialing only 7 digits, while a long-distance call requires 10 digits preceded by a prefix of 1 to indicate long-distance calling. SMDS, used by computerized equipment, does not benefit from abbreviated dialing patterns. SMDS addresses are specified in their entirety[10] which guarantees global uniqueness and avoids the need to implement and recognize local prefixes.

3.4.1.3   Country Code

The Country Code is used to designate a country or geographical area,[11] and consists of 1–3 decimal digits. Country Codes are allocated by the ITU and defined in CCITT Recommendation E.163 [E.163]. Most telephone directories will also list commonly used Country Codes. Some Country Code examples follow:

North America	1
The Netherlands	31
Nigeria	234

3.4.1.4   National Significant Number

The National Significant Number, sometimes also called the *National Number*, is allocated by a designated national numbering authority. For North America, currently 10 decimal digits are used for the National Significant Number, structured in accordance with the North American Numbering Plan (NANP) [2775]. We will discuss some basic properties and usage of these SMDS addresses as defined in [772].

SMDS addresses allocated according to [772] have a hierarchical structure, mainly based on geography, to facilitate efficient routing. Figure 3.13 shows the

---

[10]At first glance, this seems to be contradicted by [772], which requires that SMDS addresses consist of 10-digit numbers preceded by a *prefix* of 1. The prefix actually represents the Country Code of 1, and results in the specification of full international numbers. This requirement reflects the fact that [772] was primarily written for the use of the RBOCs.

[11]Country Codes do not always correspond exactly to a country. For example, the Country Code of 1 (World Numbering Zone 1) corresponds to all of North America, and also includes some island groups such as Bermuda, the Bahamas, and island groups in the Antilles such as the Virgin Islands.

structure of these SMDS addresses. Additional structures exist under NANP, such as the N11 codes for Directory Assistance, and Ancillary SACs where 10 digits are used to determine the carrier. These structures are not supported for SMDS.

Country Code = 1	Numbering Plan Area Code, or Service Access Code	Local Number

Figure 3.13 SMDS address structure in North America [772]

The Numbering Plan Area (NPA) Code and Service Access Code (SAC) consist of three decimal digits. NPA Codes and SACs are distinguished by their values [2775].

3.4.1.4.1   NPA Code

The NPA Code identifies geographical areas within the scope of the NANP (Area Codes in telephone directories). L3_PDUs with NPA codes in their individual Destination Address are routed according to the location of the address.[12]

3.4.1.4.2   SAC

SMDS supports two types of SACs: Embodied SACs and External SACs.[13] Embodied SACs indicate that the three digits immediately following the Embodied SAC identify the carrier serving the address. Hence, an originating LEC network will attempt to route L3_PDUs with Embodied SAC destination addresses directly to the carrier identified in the address.[14] In contrast, L3_PDUs with External SACs in the destination address are routed by an originating LEC network directly to the sender's preferred carrier, as determined by Carrier Selection (see Section 3.4.7).

3.4.1.4.3   Mobility

It would be convenient if SMDS addresses had a certain amount of mobility. For example, when a router has to be moved from one SNI to another one, the retention of the same value for its SMDS address might avoid the need for updating the customer's routing tables. Address mobility is an objective for SMDS. The degree of mobility may differ across SMDS providers and, if provided, may be limited to mobility within the serving area of the same

---

[12]Routing by the originating carrier of L3_PDUs with an NPA Code in the Destination Address is also a function of Carrier Selection. See Section 3.4.7.

[13]In telephony, 900 numbers are an example of an Embodied SAC, and 700 numbers are an example of an External SAC.

[14]If the carrier identified by the Embodied SAC address is not directly connected by the origination carrier, that carrier will drop the L3_PDU (see Section 3.4.7).

switching system. The Local Number has a typical structure that is relevant for address mobility. The first three digits after the NPA most often determine a particular serving switching system, and the last four digits in those cases are used by that switching system to determine the SNI. In fact, [772] requires that all addresses beginning with the same NPA and three following digits should be assigned to the same switching system. This is for administrative reasons, and also simplifies the design of switching and routing. The implication is that address mobility is restricted to the geographical serving area of the switching system.[15]

3.4.1.5   Subscription Parameters for Address Allocation

The subscription parameters for Individual and Group Addresses are subject to a number of engineering constraints on switching system implementations. These constraints are meant to preserve switching system simplicity, but at the same time to avoid limitations on common applications expected for SMDS.

3.4.1.5.1   *Maximum Number of SMDS Individual Addresses Identifying an SNI*

There are three motivations for the need to have multiple addresses per SNI:

- It is possible to allocate multiple addresses to a single SMDS station, that is, to distinguish between different applications. For example, the station may be a multiprotocol router, with XNS and TCP/IP communicating over SMDS.[16]

- These addresses can be associated with different Address Screens to allow the simultaneous use of private and public access on the same SNI.

- Multi-CPE configurations may be used on Access DQDBs.

Table 3.2 shows the maximum number of addresses per SNI. These numbers are chosen to allow both a reasonable number of applications per station, and multi-CPE arrangements. The limitations for low-speed access methods are specified in [1239] and [1240], and are related to how early networks for this low-speed service are expected to be implemented. Users should check with their service provider for any restrictions for this feature.

---

[15]For telephone service, this limitation can be overcome using a special arrangement called a *foreign exchange line*. A similar arrangement could theoretically be used for SMDS if there is a market for it.

[16]Chapters 8 and 9 explain that this distinction is more typically made via the LLC or LLC/SNAP multiplexing technique. However, these techniques are not universally applied.

Access method	Individual Addresses per SNI	Remarks
High-speed access (≥ DS1)	≤ 16	A higher value may be supported in the future [772].
Low-speed access (Chapters 5 and 6)	≤ 2 [1239] [1240]	[1239] and [1240] list 2 as a requirement and 16 as an objective.

Table 3.2 Maximum number of Individual Addresses per SNI

3.4.1.5.2   *Maximum Membership of an SMDS Group Address*

A Group Address can represent up to 128 Individual Addresses. To prevent looping problems, and for network simplicity, Group Addresses are not allowed to be members of another Group Address. The figure of 128 is thought to be adequate for Group Addressing needs (see, for example, Chapters 8 and 9) during early SMDS deployment,[17] and may be raised to 2048 in the future [772].

3.4.1.5.3   *Maximum Number of SMDS Group Addresses Identifying an Individual Address*

Table 3.3 gives the maximum number of Group Addresses of which a particular Individual Address can be a member. The figure of 32 is in line with the current common capacity for multicast addresses on Ethernet and FDDI adapters. The limitations for low-speed access methods are specified in [1239] and [1240] and are related to how early networks for this low-speed service are expected to be implemented.

Access method	Group Addresses per Individual Address	Remarks
High-speed access (≥ DS1)	≤ 32	A higher value may be supported in the future [772].
Low-speed access (Chapters 5 and 6)	≤ 3 [1239] [1240]	[1239] and [1240] list 3 as a requirement and 32 as an objective.

Table 3.3 Maximum number of Group Addresses per Individual Address

---

[17]Another concern is the processing time that might be needed to replicate Group Addressed L3_PDUs to a long list of recipients.

3.4.1.5.4   Maximum Number of SMDS Group Addresses Identifying an SNI

An SNI is identified by a Group Address if one or more Individual Addresses assigned to the SNI is a member of that Group Address. The maximum number of Group Addresses per SNI is shown in Table 3.4. The limitations for low-speed access methods are specified in [1239] and [1240], and are related to how early networks for this low-speed service are expected to be implemented.

Access method	Group Addresses per SNI	Remarks
High speed access (≥ DS1)	≤ 48	A higher value may be supported in the future [772].
Low speed access (see Chapters 5 and 6)	≤ 3 [1239] [1240]	[1239] and [1240] list 3 as a requirement and 48 as an objective.

Table 3.4 Maximum number of Group Addresses per SNI

3.4.2   Use and Administration of Group Addresses

A Group Address identifies a configured list of Individual Addresses. The service provider maintaining that list uses it to replicate and route L3_PDUs with that Group Address as their destination. Thus, SMDS customers must interact with the provider of SMDS in order to configure Group Addresses in accordance to their needs. We will explain the administration aspects of Group Addresses using the earlier Bodacious Data Corporation example. Figure 3.14 shows an extended example, where SMDS is provided to Bodacious Data by three interconnected carrier networks. (Section 3.4.7 explains the rules for Carrier Selection.) Figure 3.14 shows two key concepts, Group Address Sponsor, and Group Address Agent, which we explain in the next sections.

3.4.2.1   Group Address Sponsor

A Group Address Sponsor is a person or organization that requests the creation of and subsequent changes to a Group Address with a Group Address Agent. In our example, the Group Address Sponsor is located in the Edgar Town Building II location. FasterTel is the Group Address Agent. Technically, each of the Group Addresses used by Bodacious Data may have its own sponsor. It may be more practical for all Group Addresses for Bodacious Data to be handled by the same sponsor. A given Group Address can have only one sponsor.

The Group Address Sponsor, on behalf of the maintenance personnel of all prospective members of the Group Address, interacts with the Group Address

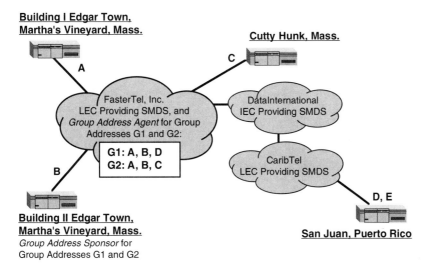

Figure 3.14 Group Address Sponsor and Group Address Agent

Agent to create, modify, or delete the Group Addresses that it sponsors. For this purpose, the sponsor must maintain a list of the Group Addresses it creates and lists of the members of each group. This interaction may be done by telephone, fax, or electronic mail. Direct management of Group Addresses by the Group Address Sponsor through Customer Network Management (see Chapter 12) can simplify this interaction. In performing this function, the objectives of the Group Address Sponsor include the following:

1. Proper configuration of the Group Address for applications (see Chapter 8 and 9), including staying within the constraints on the number of Group Addresses that are supported on the SNIs.

2. Proper configuration of any SMDS Address Screens (see Section 3.4.3).

3. Avoidance of the potential for "remotely generated duplicate L3_PDUs." We will describe the background of this issue in the next section. The implication for a Group Address Sponsor is that *membership in a particular Group Address of multiple Individual Addresses associated with the same SNI should be avoided*, and only one of these Individual Addresses should be identified for membership in a given Group Address. In some practical scenarios failure to meet this constraint may cause multiple copies of the same L3_PDU to be delivered to that SNI.

3.4.2.2   Group Address Agent

The Group Address Agent serves as the centralized administrator for a Group Address. In our example, FasterTel serves as the Group Address Agent. However, either of the other carriers could serve that function. Technically, each of the Group Addresses used by Bodacious Data may have its own Group Address Agent. It may be more practical for all Group Addresses for Bodacious Data Corporation to be handled by the same Group Address Agent.[18] A given Group Address can have only one Group Address Agent. The duties of the Group Address Agent include the following:

- The Group Address Agent interacts with a Group Address Sponsor to handle requests for the creation, modification, or deletion of Group Addresses, or provides Group Address membership information. The Group Address Agent also notifies the sponsor when changes become effective, or are denied due to Group Address limitations (see Section 3.4.1.5). For these purposes, the Group Address Agent maintains lists of the Group Addresses it creates and of the members of each group. The modification of Group Addresses and the process of obtaining membership information can be simplified through Customer Network Management (see Chapter 12).

- The Group Address Agent interacts with carrier maintenance personnel to put Group Address requests into effect and to verify that requests can be honored. (This may include personnel from other carriers.)

Group Addressed L3_PDUs must be replicated according to the membership list of the Group Address. Often, this function is completely performed by the carrier network of the Group Address Agent. However, arrangements may exist between carrier networks that allow partial replication of the Group Address by the network of the Group Address Agent, while parts that pertain to addresses in other carrier networks are replicated by those networks. This technique, known as *Nested Group Addressing* [1060], is meant to avoid unnecessary traffic between carrier networks and does normally not concern customers. However, it has one *implication* for SMDS customers: it avoids the potential of what we call remotely generated duplicate L3_PDUs.

Consider again Figure 3.14, but assume that G1 = {A, B, D, E}. If the FasterTel network performs complete Group Address replication, an L3_PDU from A and addressed to G1 will probably result in separate copies being sent to B, D, and E.[19] The network of CaribTel will then deliver two copies to the SNI

---

[18]It should be appreciated that the Group Address Agent is an administrative concept, and that the extent of this service may differ per carrier.

[19]Unless the network of FasterTel knows that D and E reside on the same SNI. It can be appreciated that, in general, this may not be the case.

of D and E. Nested Group Addressing causes FasterTel to send a single copy to the network of CaribTel with a Nested Group Address N, agreed to between the carriers. CaribTel administers N = {D, E}; its network knows that D and E reside on the same SNI and that only one copy has to be delivered.

3.4.3   Address Screening

SMDS Address Screening is designed to facilitate the use of the public service for virtual private networking. These screens can be configured to allow communication only between a specified set of addresses, or, alternatively, to exclude communication with certain addresses.

The operation of Address Screening is defined by lists of addresses called *Address Screens* associated with each SNI. There are two kinds of Address Screening: Source Address Screening and Destination Address Screening. Source Address Screening is the process of deciding to deliver or discard an L3_PDU based on its Source Address. Destination Address Screening is the process of deciding to deliver or discard an L3_PDU based on its Destination Address.

There are two screen types associated with an SNI. An Individual Address Screen consists of a list of Individual Addresses. It is used for Destination Address Screening for Individually Addressed L3_PDUs and for Source Address Screening for both Individually Address and Group Addressed L3_PDUs. A Group Address Screen consists of a list of Group Addresses. It is used for Destination Address Screening for Group Addressed L3_PDUs. Thus, the Group Address is screened, and not the set of Individual Addresses it represents.[20]

A screen always consists of either a set of *allowed addresses*, signifying a list of addresses with which communication can take place, or a set of *disallowed addresses*, signifying a list of addresses with which communication is prohibited. If an SMDS address is screened against a list of allowed addresses, and a match is found in the list, the L3_PDU will pass the screen. If no match is found the L3_PDU is discarded. The opposite happens when an SMDS address is screened against a list of disallowed addresses. If a match is found, the L3_PDU is discarded. If no match is found, the L3_PDU passes the screen.

Figure 3.15 shows an example of an Address Screen configuration for the Bodacious Data Corporation. The example uses inclusive (allowed) screens. Traffic to and from non-Bodacious Data sources is locked out. The traffic to and from the SNI of Competing Products is not screened in Figure 3.15. We could

---

[20]The implementation of the Address Screening processing can take place anywhere in the service-provider network. However, it is conceptually intuitive that Destination Address Screening takes place close to the ingress and that Source Address Screening takes place near the egress.

configure the screens of the SNI of Competing Products, so as to exclude (disallow) any traffic to or from Bodacious Data with the following:

Individual Address Screen = Disallowed {A, B, C, D, E}
Group Address Screen = Disallowed {G1, G2}

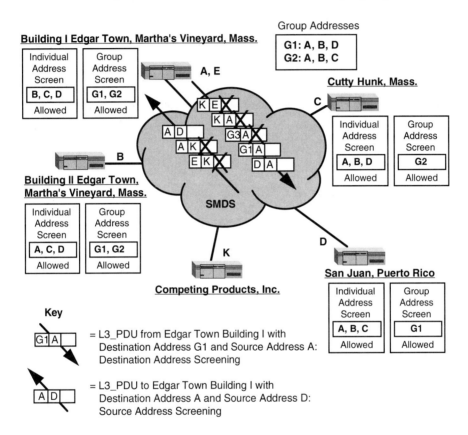

Figure 3.15 Example Address Screen configuration

From this simple example, we may conclude that Address Screens must be carefully configured, and that misconfiguration is possible. For example, omission of G1 in the Group Address Screen of the San Juan SNI results in L3_PDUs addressed to G1 not being delivered when sent from the San Juan SNI. As we will see in Chapters 8 and 9, Group Addressed L3_PDUs are commonly used for the exchange of routing and neighbor discovery information. If the configuration prevents these L3_PDUs from being delivered, other communication with this address may become impossible. Customer Network Management (see Chapter 12) is designed to help ensure correct configuration.

3.4.3.1   Single Address Screen Pair per SNI

The support of one Individual Address Screen and one Group Address Screen per SNI means that traffic to and from all addresses on an SNI is screened by these two screens, as in the example of Figure 3.15. The Individual and Group Address Screens are currently subject to an engineering constraint. Together they can consist of up to 128 SMDS addresses per SNI. This is considered a reasonable initial bound on the number of addresses in a private virtual network using SMDS. At the same time, it avoids the delay that would be caused by searching long address lists, and limits the memory that needs to be allocated for Address Screening. In the future, 2048 addresses in the combined screens may be supported [772]. The Customer Network Management Service can be used conveniently to track the number of addresses that have been used in the combined screens (see Chapter 12).

3.4.3.2   Multiple Address Screens per SNI

Since an SNI may support up to 16 addresses, it is desirable to allow for traffic to and from different addresses on an SNI to be screened differently. This would make it possible to refine the configuration of individual station addresses on an SNI to particular applications.

Each address assigned to an SNI is associated with exactly one Individual Address Screen and is also associated with exactly one Group Address Screen. Each Group Address that contains an Individual Address assigned to the SNI is associated with exactly one Individual Address Screen. Table 3.5 contains the rules for selecting the Address Screen to use for each L3_PDU.

Type of screening	Destination Address type	Type of screen	Address association
Destination	Individual	Individual	Source Address
Destination	Group	Group	Source Address
Source	Individual	Individual	Destination Address
Source	Group	Individual	Destination Address

Table 3.5 Address Screen selection

Section 2.2.5 describes the possibility of configuring public and private addresses by associating the public address to an empty disallowed screen (i.e., L3_PDUs to and from that address are not screened). Figure 3.16 shows this possibility in the Bodacious Data configuration. Configured in this manner, all interenterprise traffic to and from Bodacious Data can be cleared through a single device, that is, the device with SMDS Address E.

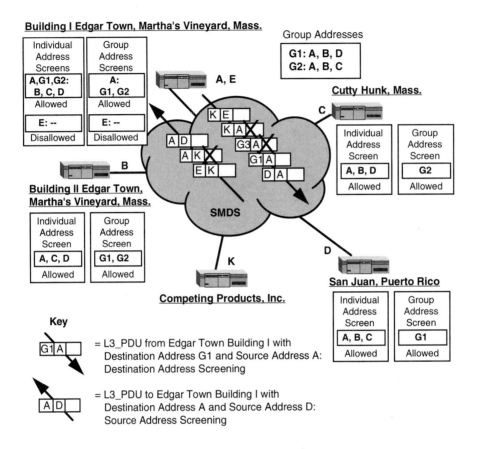

Figure 3.16 Example of a configuration with multiple Address Screens per SNI

Another example is a configuration where the nodes with addresses E and K are configured to communicate only with each other; for example,

Individual Address Screen associated with E	=	Allowed {K},
Group Address Screen associated with E	=	Allowed {-},
Individual Address Screen associated with K	=	Allowed {E},
Group Address Screen associated with K	=	Allowed {-}.

The support of four Individual Address Screens and four Group Address Screens per SNI is an *objective* in [772], and may not be universally supported in initial service offerings. Users should check with their service provider to determine the number of Address Screens supported per SNI.

The single-screen and multiscreen scenarios have the same limit on the number of addresses that can be supported in the combined Address Screens, that is, 128. In the future, 2048 addresses in the combined screens may be supported [772].

3.4.4   **Source Address Validation**

Source Address Validation is a service access-control feature. The Source Address of each L3_PDU is verified at the ingress SNI[21] to determine whether it belongs to the list of SMDS addresses assigned to that SNI. The L3_PDUs with improper Source Addresses are discarded.

The example in Figure 3.17 shows that two SMDS addresses, A and E, are allocated to the SNI for Edgar Town Building I. SMDS will discard all L3_PDUs from this SNI with a Source Address that is not A or E.

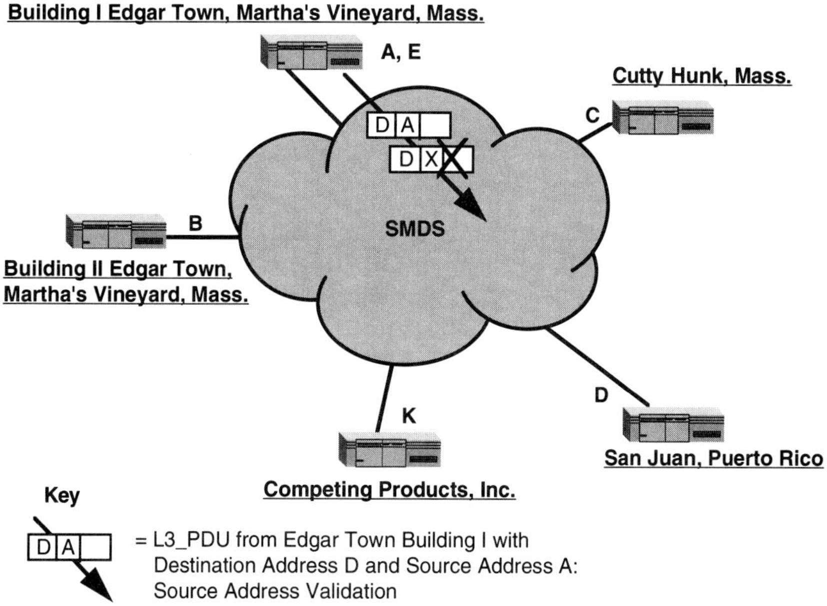

Figure 3.17   Example of Source Address Validation

The motivation for Source Address Validation is twofold:

- It allows accurate billing and traffic data to be collected in the case of charging on a per-L3_PDU basis.

---

[21]The implementation of Source Address Validation can take place anywhere in the service provider network. However, it is conceptually intuitive that Source Address Validation takes place close to the ingress SNI.

- It helps to prevent spoofing, where the sender of an L3_PDU attempts to fool the receiver that the L3_PDU was sent by a different source, and allows Address Screening to work properly.[22]

3.4.5   Multiple Data Units in Transit Concurrently

The concurrent transport of multiple data units is an artifact of the protocol that is used for communication over an Access DQDB [802.6]. The protocol employs a procedure for segmenting L3_PDUs into small slots of a fixed length, and allows slots from different L3_PDUs to be intermingled. It is therefore possible for multiple L3_PDUs to be in transit concurrently. Figure 3.18 shows an example of two L3_PDUs in transit concurrently from CPE to a network providing SMDS. This characteristic requires that buffer space must be allocated for several L3_PDUs that are to be sent simultaneously, and for received portions of L3_PDUs that are waiting for reassembly. Logic is required to keep track of the state of L3_PDUs in transit.

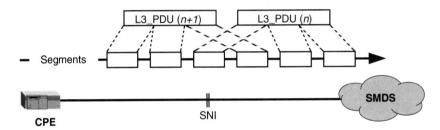

Figure 3.18 Example of Multiple Data Units in Transit Concurrently

Both SMDS and the CPE need a good understanding of the maximum number of L3_PDUs that can be in transit concurrently. This allows them to allocate resources effectively, and to keep costs down.

Two subscription parameters address this issue. Table 3.6 shows their values:

- The maximum number of concurrent L3_PDUs in transit from CPE to SMDS (MCDUs In).

- The maximum number of concurrent L3_PDUs in transit from SMDS to CPE (MCDUs Out). In this case, the service-provider network buffers L3_PDUs, in order to avoid discard.

---

[22]This is also an argument against sharing an Access DQDB among multiple subscribers. A network providing SMDS can validate Source Addresses only for an Access DQDB as a whole; it cannot discover improper generation of those addresses by individual stations on the bus.

SMDS access protocol	MCDUs In	MCDUs Out
SIP based on DQDB or ATM (Chapters 4 and 13)	1 or 16	1 or 16
SIP based on DXI or Frame Relay (Chapters 5 and 6)	1	1

Table 3.6 Subscription values for MCDUs In and MCDUs Out

For SMDS access protocols that do not support segmentation and reassembly, the value of these parameters is set to 1. For other access protocols, the values can be 1 (no L3_PDU interleaving) or 16. The value of 16 is deemed to be reasonable in terms of costs and required implementation complexity. For an Access DQDB, these parameters apply to the combined stations, not to individual stations. Single-CPE arrangements will typically use the value of 1. Multi-CPE arrangements will typically use the value of 16.

3.4.6 Access Classes

As a result of the different physical transmission facilities and access protocols for access to SMDS, the maximum effective bandwidth for L3_PDUs varies. Table 3.7 summarizes these variations.

While high speeds may be necessary to meet low delay requirements, subscribers do not always need the sustained throughput that would be obtainable over high-speed access paths. For example, a subscriber who wants to connect a 10 Mbps Ethernet to a DS3-based SMDS access path does not need the full DS3 bandwidth. For this reason, Access Classes have been defined. Access Classes also benefit the engineering of service-provider networks, in that resource requirements become more predictable. In turn, this results in cost savings on implementation, which can be reflected in the rate structure for the service.

Access Classes have only been defined for DS3- and E3-based access; it was determined that customers with lower-speed access paths would not benefit from access below the maximum effective bandwidth. Furthermore, only *ingress* Access Classes have been defined. The service-provider network strategy at the *egress* is to avoid unnecessary buffering of information, and to forward L3_PDUs to the CPE whenever possible.[23] Access Classes are established at subscription time.

---

[23]In early versions of the requirements for SMDS, egress Access Classes were specified [772.1] [772.2] [772.3]. However, internetworking suppliers indicated that their equipment would not benefit from such traffic smoothing.

Physical access facilities	Access protocol	Approximate maximum effective bandwidth
DS3	SIP (Chapter 4)	34 Mbps (subject to the Access Class feature)
DS3-based ATM[a]	SIP/ATM (Chapter 13)	34 Mbps (subject to the Access Class feature)
E3	SIP (Chapter 4)	25 Mbps (subject to the Access Class feature)
E3-based ATM[a]	SIP/ATM (Chapter 13)	25 Mbps (subject to the Access Class feature)
E1	SIP/DXI (Chapter 5)	1.9 Mbps
E1	SIP (Chapter 4)	1.5 Mbps
DS1	SIP/DXI (Chapter 5)	1.5 Mbps
DS1	SIP (Chapter 4)	1.1 Mbps
$n \times 56$, or $n \times 64$ Kbps	SIP/DXI (Chapter 5)	$n \times 56$, or $n \times 64$ Kbps
Frame Relay access facilities ($n \times 56$, or $n \times 64$ Kbps, up to E1 [SIG006])	SIP Relay (Chapter 6)	$n \times 56$, or $n \times 64$ Kbps

[a]ATM access based on DS3 and E3 facilities is specified in [SIG008], and supports Virtual Connections with bandwidths corresponding to DS1, E1, E3, and DS3. Higher speed access facilities, e.g., STS-3c may be specified in the future. Other Virtual Connection bandwidths, such as those corresponding to Access Classes in Table 3.8 are anticipated in the future. See Chapter 13.

Table 3.7 Maximum effective bandwidth

The design of Access Classes has a number of objectives:

- From the subscriber's perspective, the Access Class mechanism should put limits on the Sustained Information Rate (SIR, the rate of information transfer that can be sustained over long periods), but should have only a small impact on "bursts" of data that are typical for applications expected to run over SMDS. Access Classes may therefore put limits on the *duration* of bursts.

- The Access Classes should match common classes of CPE in terms of SIR but, in the interest of simplicity, they should avoid unnecessary further tweaking. The first three Access Classes match the potential traffic on 4- and 16-Mbps Token Ring LANs (IEEE Std. 802.5-1985 [802.5]), and 10-Mbps Ethernets (or IEEE Std. 802.3-1985 [802.3]) respectively.

- From the service provider's perspective, the mechanism should be simple to implement, so that savings in network resources are not offset by the complexity of the Access Class mechanism. Furthermore, the mechanism should have a negligible impact on switch performance.

To meet these requirements, a Credit Manager Algorithm is used. *Credit*, in terms of bytes, increments periodically with time until it reaches a maximum. It is decremented by the number of bytes in the INFORMATION field of each L3_PDU that enters the network. L3_PDUs for which not enough credit is available are discarded. The maximum number of L3_PDU bytes that can be sent in contiguous (uninterrupted) L3_PDUs is called the *Maximum Burst Size*. The parameters of the algorithm are tailored to common traffic patterns on LANs. Section 4.9 describes details of the Credit Manager Algorithm. Table 3.8 shows the Access Classes with the respective service parameter values for SIR and burst duration. Additional Access Classes may be added in the future, for example, when SMDS becomes available at even higher speeds (see Chapter 13).

Service access path	Access Class	SIR (Mbps)	Maximum Burst Size (Kbytes)
E1, DS1, or lower	Not Applicable	See Table 3.7	∞
DS3	1	4	10.4
	2	10	13.0
	3	16	17.5
	4	25	33.6
	5	34	∞
E3	1	4	10.9
	2	10	15.2
	3	16	25.2
	4	25	∞

Table 3.8 Access Classes

Access Class 4 for E3, and Access Class 5 for DS3 correspond to the situation where the full effective bandwidth can be used continuously.

Table 3.7 can be used as an aid in appropriate Access Class selection. To illustrate some of the concepts, we will use the simple example shown in Figure 3.19, in which a router is attached to a 10-Mbps Ethernet and to a DS3 SNI.

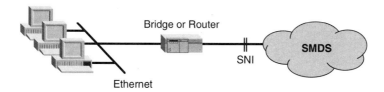

Figure 3.19 Access Class selection example

For this example, a choice of Access Class 2 is guaranteed to not impact performance due to discarded L3_PDUs, because the Ethernet cannot deliver data to the router faster than the Sustained Information Rate of 9.96 Mbps. However, if the tariff for Access Class 2 is significantly more than the tariff for Access Class 1, it is probably wise to use Access Class 1. It is very likely that the average utilization on the Ethernet is not greater than the SIR of 3.99 Mbps, or if the utilization is higher, it is unlikely that the average traffic destined for SMDS exceeds the SIR. Furthermore, the Access Class Maximum Burst Size is almost seven maximum-size Ethernet frames (see Table 3.8), which is also very unlikely to be exceeded.

A similar analysis can be done for other simple configurations like that of Figure 3.19. More complex configurations, such as having multiple LANs attached to the router, will require more sophisticated analysis and more knowledge of the underlying traffic patterns. The Customer Network Management features described in Chapter 12 can be used to track both discards due to Access Class enforcement and SNI utilization. Thus, Access Class decisions can be validated and revised if necessary.

Access Classes should not be confused with common techniques to fractionalize, sub-rate or channelize bandwidth, which limit the information rate and imply increased delays, as opposed to the SIR. The Access Class concept is also sometimes erroneously compared with plain throughput. The distinction is that where *throughput* refers to the average information rate, Access Classes also define burst duration, which allow for predictable traffic patterns. For example, it is possible to use the Credit Manager Algorithm to define two Access Classes with the same SIR, but with different Maximum Burst Sizes.

3.4.7 Carrier Selection

Carrier Selection is a capability that is relevant for cases where L3_PDUs need to traverse multiple, interconnected networks. The idea is to offer senders of L3_PDUs the ability to select their preferred carrier(s). Our discussion explains the feature as defined in [772] and [1060], which is expected to be offered by the U.S. Local Exchange Carriers (LECs).[24]

Figure 3.20 shows a typical U.S. example. The Bodacious Data Corporation obtains access to SMDS through two different hypothetical LECs. Two different hypothetical Interexchange Carriers (IECs) provide interexchange services. Carrier Selection is used to select the preferred IEC.

There are two means of Carrier Selection:

1. Carrier Pre-selection represents the simplest way to select a long-distance carrier. At subscription time, or later through a service order

---

[24]The operation of the Carrier Selection feature is highly influenced by the U.S. regulatory environment. Since such externalities do not uniformly apply in other parts of the world, other countries may choose to use the Carrier Selection feature in a different way.

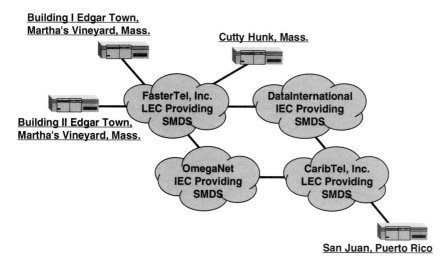

Figure 3.20 Example of intercarrier traffic

or Customer Network Management (see Chapter 12), a subscriber indicates the preferred carrier for each SNI. Interexchange L3_PDUs from these SNIs that do not have an explicit Carrier Selection (overriding), are routed by the LEC network to that preferred carrier. This feature applies per SNI, and does not distinguish among traffic from individual Source Addresses on an SNI.

2. In the second means of Carrier Selection, overriding, a carrier is *explicitly indicated* in the L3_PDU. This indication overrides the preselected carrier. Thus, senders can select their preferred carrier on a per-L3_PDU basis.[25]

In the example of Figure 3.20, DataInternational may be the preselected carrier at all SNIs. OmegaNet may be selected on a per-L3_PDU basis by including the Carrier Selection option.

U.S. carriers are governed by legal and regulatory guidelines; hence, often rather complicated routing conditions apply. The following provides a simplified view of these conditions in North America from the perspective of SMDS customers trying to configure their Carrier Selection options (or trying to figure out why L3_PDUs got lost due to improper Carrier Selection usage). Readers interested in more background on carrier rights and duties are referred to [2775].

---

[25]While the service as well as the protocol allow for the specification of more than one carrier, the specifications [772] and [1060] state that the local service provider will act only on the first carrier in the list.

3.4.7.1   Carrier Identification Code

IECs in North America are identified by a three digit decimal code, called the *Carrier Identification Code* (CIC) [93]. Some examples of CIC values follow:

MCI Telecomm Corporation—SouthEast	898
Metromedia Long Distance	011
US Sprint (Telenet, ISACOMM, LT/USA)	777
St. Thomas & San Juan Tel. Co.	097
AT&T Communications	288

3.4.7.2   Individually Addressed L3_PDUs Without Overriding

When an Individually Addressed L3_PDU uses no overriding, the originating LEC will route it on the basis of the following criteria for Carrier Selection:

- If the Destination Address is served by the originating LEC or by another local service provider within the LATA, the L3_PDU is routed for delivery to that address.

- If the Destination Address is outside the LATA, the L3_PDU is routed to the preselected carrier.

The *exception* is when the Destination Address starts with a 1 (North America), has an Embodied SAC (see Section 3.4.1.4), and the originating LEC is not the embodied carrier. In that case the L3_PDU is routed to the embodied carrier for further delivery. If the originating LEC is the embodied carrier, the originating LEC will deliver the L3_PDU. The originating LEC will make its best effort to reach the embodied or preselected carrier. No alternative carriers will be attempted.

3.4.7.3   Individually Addressed L3_PDUs with Overriding

When an Individually Addressed L3_PDU uses overriding, the originating LEC will route it on the basis of the following criteria for Carrier Selection:

- The L3_PDU is routed to the explicitly selected carrier. This can include any traffic local to the LEC network; explicit Carrier Selection overrides the determination by the local provider as to whether it can deliver to the Destination Address itself. If the selected carrier is unavailable, the L3_PDU is discarded.

The *exception* is when the Destination Address starts with a 1 (North America), and has an Embodied SAC (see Section 3.4.1.4). The use of an Embodied SAC-based Destination Address in combination with the use of explicit Carrier Selection is considered an error, and the L3_PDU will be discarded.

One further *potential exception* exists. Under certain conditions, and in some jurisdictions, some carriers may not be authorized to provide service. This situation would result in an L3_PDU discard. It is beyond the scope of this book to describe the legalities of this case.

Yes, reader, this is confusing, and awkward to implement in CPE. The simplest implementation is to presubscribe to your favorite carrier, and leave it to your local service provider to distinguish between local and long-distance traffic, and between NPAs and embodied SACs.

3.4.7.4   Carrier Selection and Group Addressing

Carrier Selection is the same for Individually Addressed and Group Addressed L3_PDUs. If the network to which the L3_PDU is submitted is the Group Address Agent, that network replicates the Group Address and produces the appropriate number of copies of the L3_PDU. The Carrier Selection procedures, including overriding, if any, in the original L3_PDU, are applied to each copy (based on the respective Individual Addresses that are used within and among the networks to route these copies). If the Group Address Agent is outside the LATA, the Carrier Selection procedures are applied to the submitted Group Addressed L3_PDU. After reaching the network of the Group Address Agent, this L3_PDU is replicated., if the Group Address Agent is a LEC, any copies with destinations outside the LATA of the Group Address Agent are returned to the IEC from which the original L3_PDU was received.

For example, in Figure 3.21 FasterTel is the Group Address Agent for Group Address G. Thus, a Group Addressed L3_PDU sent by A is replicated by the FasterTel network. One copy is delivered to B. Carrier Selection procedures are applied to select the IEC for the copy for D. A Group Addressed L3_PDU sent by D must first be routed to the network of the Group Address Agent (FasterTel). Thus, Carrier Selection procedures are applied to this L3_PDU. After arrival at the FasterTel network, the L3_PDU is replicated, and copies are delivered to A and B.

A consequence of the treatment of Carrier Selection for Group Addressed L3_PDUs is that a single IEC will be used for all copies of the L3_PDU. In other words, Group Addressed L3_PDUs that require interexchange transport can only be copied to destinations and serving carriers that can be reached by the same IEC. In practice, this is unlikely to be a problem. However, a large SMDS customer with locations that cannot be reached through the same IEC needs to take special measures to overcome this limitation (e.g., a separate SMDS Group Address for each IEC that it wants to use).

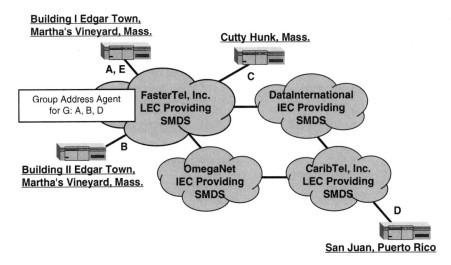

Figure 3.21 Example of Group Addressed intercarrier traffic

3.4.7.5   CPE Configuration

Several strategies can be implemented to make use of the Carrier Selection feature. The simplest implementation could rely on the preselected carrier for all destinations, and not use the overriding capability. This approach is straightforward and has few drawbacks. The drawbacks, however, include the possibility that the preselected carrier does not serve all destinations that a user needs to communicate with, in which case overriding must be used for some destinations. Another drawback might be that different carriers may charge different rates for certain destinations. Routers that use SMDS may have to implement a routing table that binds particular destination addresses to the use of appropriate carriers.

3.4.8   End-User Blocking

End-user blocking actually refers to a feature that can be offered in North America by LECs to IECs. An IEC may request the local carrier to discard all traffic that originates from a certain SNI and that would use that IEC. Likely targets for such requests might be customers of the IEC who are not meeting their subscription obligations (e.g., have not paid their bills). Figure 3.22 illustrates an example.

Users will experience this feature as L3_PDU loss for all destinations for which a carrier is used that requested blocking. No on-line notification is provided. However, Customer Network Management (see Chapter 12) provides users with the ability to trace the L3_PDU loss to end-user blocking, including the carrier that requested the blocking.

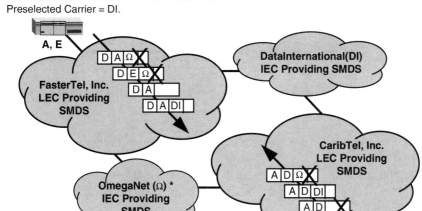

Building I Edgar Town, Martha's Vineyard, Mass.
Preselected Carrier = DI.

A, E

DataInternational(DI)
IEC Providing SMDS

FasterTel, Inc.
LEC Providing
SMDS

CaribTel, Inc.
LEC Providing
SMDS

OmegaNet (Ω) *
IEC Providing
SMDS

D

Key

DAΩ = L3_PDU with Destination Address D, Source   **San Juan, Puerto Rico**
Address A, and a Carrier Selection field set to Ω: Preselected Carrier = Ω
end-user blocking

* OmegaNet has requested FasterTel to block traffic from Edgar Town Building I, and
CaribTel to block traffic from San Juan.

Figure 3.22 Example of end-user blocking

3.5   Summary of Subscription Parameters

As shown in previous sections, prospective SMDS users need to consider a number of subscription parameters. Table 3.9 summarizes these parameters and the ranges of their values.

Subscription features and parameters	Range
Individual Addresses per SNI	$1 \leq n \leq 16$ [a]
Members (Individual Addresses) of a Group Address	$1 \leq n \leq 128$ per Group Address (may go up to 2048 in the future)
Number of Group Addresses of which any Individual Address can be a member	$0 \leq n \leq 32$ (may go up in the future)[a]
Number of Group Addresses identifying an SNI	$0 \leq n \leq 48$ per SNI (may go up in the future)[a]
Number of addresses in the combined number of Individual and Group Address Screens per SNI	$0 \leq n \leq 128$ (may go up to 2048 in the future)
Number of Individual Address Screens per SNI	$1 \leq n \leq 4$ [b]
Number of Group Address Screens per SNI	$1 \leq n \leq 4$ [b]
Access Classes (Sustained Information Rate for network ingress)	4, 10, 16, 25, 34 Mbps for DS3-based SNIs 4, 10, 16, 25 Mbps for E3-based SNIs
MCDUs In	1 or 16 (may go up in the future) 1 for low-speed access
MCDUs Out	1 or 16 (may go up in the future) 1 for low-speed access

[a] For low-speed access, some providers may offer a smaller range, as described in Section 3.4.1.

[b] Users should check with their service provider to determine if values greater than 1 are supported.

Table 3.9 Subscription parameters and features

4

SMDS Interface Protocol

To realize the benefits of SMDS, it is necessary to use equipment that can access the service. Such equipment must necessarily implement the protocol that the SMDS provider supports for access to the service. Such a protocol was specified by Bellcore and is called the *SMDS Interface Protocol* (SIP) [772]. This is the interface protocol that the RBOCs and GTE have stated that they will use for their offerings of SMDS. MCI has announced plans to offer HyperStream[SM] SMDS, which makes use of SIP and also includes an access protocol based on the *SMDS Data Exchange Interface Protocol* (DXI) [SIG005] [SIG001]. Several RBOCs also plan to use DXI based access to SMDS. As of this writing, other carriers, for example in Europe, are also planning service offerings similar to SMDS. In this chapter, we limit our focus to SIP, as specified in [772], [ESIG002], and [ESIG003] while the DXI is described in Chapter 5. In addition, an access protocol based on Frame Relay is described in Chapter 6, and an access protocol based on Asynchronous Transfer Mode (ATM) is described in Chapter 13. Also, because they are very dependent on the details of SIP, the details of the Access Class algorithm are presented in this chapter.

CPE designers should find the chapter useful in designing SMDS equipment. SMDS customers will be most interested in the overview material (Sections 4.1, 4.2, and 4.3) and the description of the Access Class algorithm (Section 4.9).

4.1   Role of SIP

As described in Chapter 3, (see Figure 3.2) SIP allows CPE to access SMDS. It is the mechanism by which CPE and SMDS exchange L3_PDUs. Unfortunately, some confusion has developed surrounding the role of SIP. Therefore, it is worth noting some things that SIP is not.

SIP is not the service. SIP is only a means to access SMDS. Indeed, SIP has undergone very significant changes since first specified [772.1] [772.2] [772.3] [772.3S] [772]. For all of these changes, the essential features of the service, such as addressing, address screening, and so on, are fundamentally unchanged. Furthermore, we will probably see other protocols for accessing SMDS. This is further underscored by the access protocols described in Chapters 5, 6, and 13, which support essentially the same service features.

SIP is not the way service-provider networks are implemented. SIP is an access protocol and not a network protocol. It falls far short of the functionality needed to "glue" together switches and transmission systems into a viable network. In [1059], Bellcore provides an example of a protocol, the *Inter-Switching System Interface Protocol* (ISSIP), that does have sufficient functionality for implementing a network to provide SMDS.

SIP is not the protocol for connecting between carrier networks. When multiple carrier networks are interconnected to provide SMDS, the interface between networks requires substantially more functionality than that provided by SIP. Bellcore, in [1060], specifies a protocol for connecting carrier networks, the *Inter-Carrier Interface Protocol* (ICIP).

SIP is not IEEE Std. 802.6-1990. As explained in the next section, there is a strong relationship between SIP and IEEE Std. 802.6-1990; however, the two protocols have some dramatic differences. SIP is defined across a single interface, the SNI. IEEE Std. 802.6-1990 is a shared-medium protocol defined for multiple interfaces that uses the *Distributed Queue Dual Bus* (DQDB) algorithm. (Appendix A provides background on DQDB.)

4.2   Relationship to IEEE Std. 802.6-1990

SIP is designed so that a CPE device conforming to IEEE Std. 802.6-1990 can access SMDS when used on the customer side of the SNI. Conformance to IEEE Std. 802.6-1990 is sufficient; it is not necessary. As described later in this chapter, it is possible to implement a nonconforming subset of IEEE Std. 802.6-1990 in CPE that is compatible with SIP.

4.2.1   Why SIP Is Aligned with IEEE Std. 802.6-1990

The key features of SMDS do not require many of the SIP functions. For example, Chapters 5 and 6 illustrate how HDLC procedures can be the basis for an access protocol for SMDS. The first requirements document issued by Bellcore for SMDS, [772.1], specified a protocol to run on top of the payload of DS3, whose format is shown in Figure 4.1. Like HDLC, this protocol is much simpler than SIP. So why is SIP so complex?

Field	Length in bytes
Starting Delimiter	2
Length	2
Length Check	2
Control Indicator	1
Destination Address	8
Source Address	8
Reserved	2
Carrier Indicator	1
Carrier Select	2
Information	≤ 8191
Frame Check Sequence	4

Figure 4.1 First SMDS interface protocol

SIP is complex because of its alignment with IEEE Std. 802.6-1990. This alignment is the result of a decision made by the *SMDS Early Availability Task Force* (SEATF) in the Fall of 1988. SEATF was a committee of representatives from each of the Bellcore Client Companies and Bellcore.[1] This was well after the issuance of [772.1]. The decision was not taken without significant debate. The arguments for aligning with the then yet-to-be-completed IEEE Std. 802.6-1990 included the following:

- *Industry acceptance:* There was a belief that the computer networking industry would more readily accept a protocol that was a formal public standard rather than one that was a Bellcore "standard." *Belief* is used above because, at the time, there was little evidence either way on this point.

- *Positioning for BISDN:* Since the proposal for the IEEE standard was to use short, fixed-length cells and it was expected that BISDN protocols would also use fixed-length cells, the use of such a protocol

---

[1]The Bellcore Client Companies consisted of the seven RBOCs, Southern New England Telephone, and Cincinnati Bell, Inc.

for SIP would migrate customers toward BISDN, and it would speed the deployment of BISDN in the telephone networks.

- *Support of multiple CPE:* There was a belief that a customer would want to attach multiple stations to an SNI. The protocol in [772.1] was designed for only a single device on the customer side of the SNI. The yet-to-be-completed IEEE Std. 802.6-1990 offered the potential (the standard was not very close to completion at the time of the decision) of being able to support multi-CPE configurations, where a single customer could attach multiple devices to the single SNI and even have those devices communicate with each other as well as access SMDS.

- *Availability of network equipment:* A major U.S.-based telephone network equipment supplier was refusing to commit to develop network equipment for SMDS unless SIP conformed to a formal public standard.

Arguments against aligning with IEEE Std. 802.6-1990 included the following:

- *Unnecessary complexity:* The market for multi-CPE configurations was highly uncertain[2] and thus the use of a complex protocol such as was being developed by IEEE P802.6 would increase the cost of accessing the service without any likely corresponding benefit.

- *Uncertain time to market:* By aligning with the emerging IEEE standard, the completion of the standard would be put in the critical path to availability of the service. Progress in creating standards is difficult to predict, except that it always takes longer than expected.

It is not now and may never be possible to judge the appropriateness of the SEATF decision. As Chapter 5 shows, the bridge and router vendors have been reluctant to implement the full SIP. The added complexity has been developed by the CSU/DSU vendors, with an attendant increase in the cost of the CSU/DSU device. This suggests that the industry acceptance argument was unfounded, while the unnecessary complexity argument was valid. Furthermore, having been intimately involved in the standards process and the writing of the

---

[2]Multiple CPE means that a shared-medium network is shared by two administrative entities: the SMDS customer and the SMDS provider. Furthermore, one organization is charging the other for the use of the medium. Under these conditions, administration, trouble sectionalization, and maintenance will be critical to customer acceptance. For example, in a multi-CPE configuration, heavy traffic between two CPE stations can make it appear that SMDS is not meeting the performance objectives. Robust administration, trouble sectionalization, and maintenance were (and continue to be) difficult and unsolved problems. Hence, the market for the multi-CPE configuration was (and continues to be) highly speculative.

Bellcore requirements, we can authoritatively say that the alignment delayed the issuance of final Bellcore SIP requirements by at least 18 months. On the other hand, had the network-equipment suppliers continued to refuse to build SMDS equipment based on Bellcore requirements, SMDS would have never reached the market.

Thus, the design requirements for SIP include more than the support of a high-speed, connectionless packet transport. In addition, SIP must align with IEEE Std. 802.6-1990 and allow the multi-CPE configuration. These requirements are discussed further in the following subsections.

4.2.2   Multi-CPE Configurations

Figure 4.2 depicts the Access DQDB drawn to show multiple stations and an SMDS Switching System (SS) in the service provider network. (Background on DQDB is given in Appendix A.)

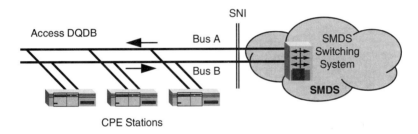

Figure 4.2 Access DQDB with a multi-CPE configuration

The IEEE standard, [802.6], specifies a topology with two buses, Bus A and Bus B, that have slightly different functions. In addition, each bus requires a function at the originating end, called *Head-of-Bus,* to do such things as generate empty slots. For the purposes of specifying SIP, [772] defines the SS as the collection of functions that terminate the dual bus in the service-provider network, and the direction of transmission toward the CPE is defined as Bus A. SIP (and thus the functionality of the SS) are defined so that the CPE stations "believe" that they are attached to an open bus topology DQDB as defined by [802.6], with the Head-of-Bus A role being played by the SS. This is how the alignment with IEEE Std. 802.6-1990 and the multi-CPE configuration support design requirements are met. There are a number of implications:

1. The SS must generate the appropriate DQDB Layer-Management Information as defined in [802.6]. This is necessary for both the data transfer on the Access DQDB and the reconfiguration of the CPE Stations in the event of a failure.

2. CPE stations that conform to IEEE Std. 802.6-1990 can exchange information among themselves (local traffic) using the Access DQDB. Such local traffic on Bus B will reach the SS which must recognize it as local traffic and ignore it.[3]

3. The SS must honor requests (according to the DQDB protocol) for free bandwidth on Bus A to allow local communications among the CPE stations on Bus A.

In designing SIP in the face of these demanding requirements, the primary principle was to place complexity in the SS when that could allow a less complex CPE implementation.

4.2.3 Single CPE

Figure 4.3 shows the Access DQDB with a single CPE station attached.

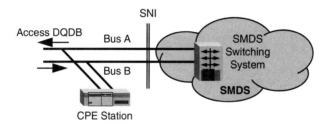

Figure 4.3 Access DQDB with a single CPE configuration

For this configuration, the complexity of both the SS and the CPE can be less than for the multi-CPE configuration. For example, in this configuration there is no contention for bandwidth, and thus there is no need to implement the DQDB algorithm for obtaining access to the medium. Indeed, the single CPE needs only implement a small subset of IEEE Std. 802.6-1990, and this is further elucidated in Section 4.8.

Simplifying the SS is another matter. Given the SEATF directive to support the multi-CPE configuration, the SS cannot be simplified. What can be done is to add a second, simpler interface especially for the single-CPE case. This has two serious drawbacks:

---

[3]The fact that local traffic is seen by the SMDS provider could be a cause of concern over privacy and is yet another reason mitigating against the market acceptance of the multi-CPE configuration. This concern may be addressable by the *eraser node* function, which is a subject of future standardization by IEEE P802.6.

1. Multiple SS interfaces have to be maintained in inventory and the provisioning for a new SMDS customer would have to make sure the proper interface was installed.

2. If a customer wants to change CPE configurations, the change must be coordinated with the SS configuration, which raises the potential for delays and service disruptions.

Luckily, it was possible to design SIP so that the SS need not be aware of the configuration of the CPE.[4] Therefore, a single SIP suffices for both of the CPE configurations.

4.3   SIP Architecture and Overview

The IEEE standard, [802.6], makes use of a complex, multiple-layer architecture to specify the DQDB protocol. This is appropriate because [802.6] is dealing with a complex, multiple-access protocol that has the potential to carry both packet data and isochronous traffic (e.g., real-time voice and video). Since SIP does not specify multiple services access and needs to carry only packet data, a much simpler layering is employed in its specification. (SMDS is expected to be made available via a multiple-services network interface with the availability of the UNI for BISDN, as described in Chapter 13.)

As depicted in Figure 4.4, SIP is specified by the use of three layers named *SIP Level 1*, *SIP Level 2*, and *SIP Level 3*. SIP Level 1 is further divided into two sublayers, the Physical Medium Dependent (PMD) Layer and the Physical Layer Convergence Procedure (PLCP) Layer.

SIP Level 3
SIP Level 2
SIP Level 1: PLCP Sublayer
SIP Level 1: PMD Sublayer

Figure 4.4 SIP layers

The protocol data units associated with each layer are denoted by L1_PDU, L2_PDU, and L3_PDU respectively. The use of the word level is an attempt to emphasize that the SIP layers are not meant to bear any relationship to the layers in the OSI Reference Model.[5] [ISO7498]

---

[4]It should be noted that the authors are not yet aware of any tests of a multi-CPE configuration with any SMDS Switching System. The lack of market interest in the multi-CPE configuration has made such testing a low priority.

[5]The OSI Reference Model mandates three layers for internetworking: physical, link, and network layers. This corresponds to the view on internetworking in the 1970s when the OSI

4.3.1   SIP Level 3 Overview

The primary role of SIP Level 3 is to provide the information necessary to support the service features of SMDS. In particular, this level carries the SMDS User Information and the associated Source Address and Destination Address. It also carries the information for Carrier Selection if present. Finally, it provides error checking for transmission errors and the loss of L2_PDUs.

Because of the close relationship with the service features, the L3_PDU remains unchanged when SMDS is offered via the ATM UNI (see Chapter 13) just as it has remained unchanged for all access protocols defined subsequently to SIP (see Chapters 5 and 6).

4.3.2   SIP Level 2 Overview

SIP Level 2 provides a means to delimit the L3_PDUs, and it provides various error-detection capabilities. The L3_PDU delimitation is accomplished by means of segmentation and reassembly. Figure 4.5 provides an overview of this process. At the transmitter, SIP Level-3 protocol information is appended to the SMDS User Information using both a header and a trailer. The resulting L3_PDU is then segmented into fixed-length units. Each segment has SIP Level-2 protocol information appended using both a header and a trailer. This header identifies each resulting L2_PDU as either a beginning, continuation, or end of message. At the receiver, the process is reversed to reconstruct the original SMDS User Information.

4.3.3   SIP Level 1 Overview

The role of SIP Level 1 is four-fold. First, it provides the transmission of bits across the physical transmission medium. Second, it delimits the L2_PDUs within the bit stream. Third, it carries the DQDB Layer Management Information that is generated by the SS. Finally, it has provisions for monitoring the underlying transmission system to allow detection of failures or marginal error performance.

Reference Model was designed, and in particular to X.25. Other network technologies, like LANs, did not meet this layering model. Sometimes many more than three layers were used to provide internetworking services. Caught in a three-layer straight jacket, OSI sublayering was invented, in particular in the network layer [ISO8648]. The result is that comparison of a protocol like IEEE Std. 802.6-1990 with OSI is often a fruitless exercise. A more fruitful OSI architecture would have been an internetworking protocol like [ISO8473] riding over physical networks (e.g., X.25, SMDS) or network interfaces, where the physical networks may use an arbitrary number of layers. This is the Internet model.

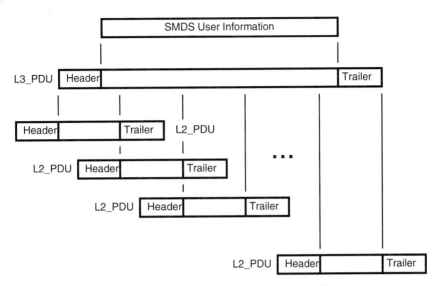

Figure 4.5 SIP segmentation and reassembly

4.3.4   Pipelining and Reassembly

SSs can operate in two modes: pipelining or reassembly. *Pipelining* is defined as the forwarding of part of the L3_PDU before the information required to construct the L3_PDU from all of the associated L2_PDUs is available. As an example, consider two SNIs on a single SS. Suppose that an L2_PDU with the first portion of an L3_PDU is received by the SS on one SNI, and further suppose that the Destination Address is associated with the other SNI. This L2_PDU contains all of the SMDS addressing information, and thus the SS could analyze the addresses and send an L2_PDU on the outgoing SNI before having received all of the L3_PDU on the incoming SNI. This would be a case of pipelining. *Reassembly* occurs when the SS waits for the entire L3_PDU to arrive on the incoming SNI before starting to send on the outgoing SNI. The two concepts are depicted in Figures 4.6 and Figure 4.7, respectively.

One motivation for pipelining is the reduction in store-and-forward delay. In the example above, suppose that the SNIs are both DS1, that the L3_PDU requires 210 L2_PDUs (the maximum-length L3_PDU), and that the SS has 5 ms of processing delay. As will be discussed, 10 L2_PDUs are transmitted every 3 ms on a DS1 SNI. Thus if the SS is operating in reassembly mode, the delay would be two L3_PDU store-and-forward delays (one for each Access DQDB) plus 5 ms. This is $2 \times (210 \times 3/10) + 5 = 131$ ms. If the SS is pipelining, the delay is one L3_PDU store-and-forward delay plus the 5 ms plus the store-and-forward delay of one L2_PDU, or $(210 \times 3/10) + 5 + 3/10 = 68.3$ ms. This is a significant delay reduction. Note however, that the advantage becomes less as

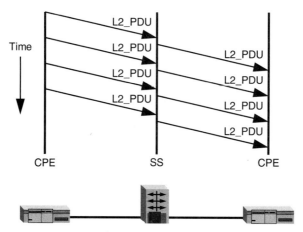

Figure 4.6 Example of pipelining with an L3_PDU of four L2_PDUs

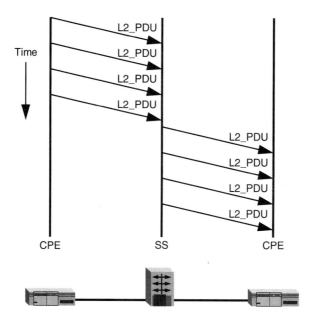

Figure 4.7 Example of reassembly with an L3_PDU of four L2_PDUs

the length of the L3_PDU becomes less. Also, if one or both of the SNIs are DS3, then the delay advantage all but vanishes.

Another motivation for pipelining that has been expressed by SS suppliers is complexity reduction. It would appear that less buffer memory is required when pipelining. However, the limit on the number of Multiple Data Units in Transit Concurrently (see Section 3.4.5) suggests that the SS will have to do substantial buffering, even when pipelining. Nevertheless, during the development of the SMDS requirements, some SS suppliers strongly advocated that the requirements not preclude pipelining by the SS. Consequently, [772] allows pipelining by the SS.

For our purposes here, the primary impact is on what it means for SMDS to *discard* an L3_PDU. If an SS is operating in a pipelining mode, it is possible for an error to be detected (e.g., a transmission error in an L2_PDU) after a portion of the L3_PDU has been delivered across the destination SNI. Therefore, in order to allow pipelining in the SS, the definition of the L3_PDU discard includes the case where SMDS deliberately delivers only a fragment of the L3_PDU. For CPE, discard means that the content of the information field of the L3_PDU is not made available to the higher-layer protocol, which is a more conventional definition of discard.

4.4   Bit-Transmission Order

In the descriptions that follow, protocol fields are transmitted left to right and top to bottom when there is more than one row. The bits comprising a field are transmitted most significant (leftmost bit) first. If the field value is decimal digits, the leftmost digit is transmitted first, and the most significant bit of the binary representation is transmitted first. This convention is illustrated in Figure 4.8.

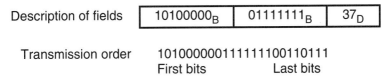

Description of fields | 10100000_B | 01111111_B | 37_D |

Transmission order   10100000011111111100110111
                         First bits   Last bits

Figure 4.8 Example of bit-transmission order

Figure 4.8 also makes use of the notation that we use for specifying protocol field values. Subscript B indicates binary, subscript D indicates Binary Coded Decimal, and subscript H indicates hexadecimal. For example,

$$37_D = 00110111_B = 37_H.$$

4.5   SIP Level 3 Description

Figure 4.9 shows the format of the L3_PDU.

All of the fields except the BETAG (see Section 4.5.2) are delivered unchanged by SMDS. Those fields that are underlined in Figure 4.9 are not processed by SMDS. Thus, they can be populated in any way by the sending

Field	Length
Header	
Reserved	1 byte
BEtag (Beginning-End Tag)	1 byte
BAsize (Buffer Allocation Size)	2 bytes
DA (Destination Address)	8 bytes
SA (Source Address)	8 bytes
HLPI (Higher Layer Protocol Identifier)	6 bits
PL (Pad Length)	2 bits
QOS (Quality of Service)	4 bits
CIB (CRC32 Indicator Bit)	1 bit
HEL (Header Extension Length)	3 bits
Brdg (Bridging)	2 bytes
HE (Header Extension)	12 bytes
Info (Information)	≤ 9188 bytes
Trailer	
PAD	0 - 3 bytes
CRC32 (32-bit Cyclic Redundancy Check)	4 bytes
Reserved	1 byte
BEtag (Beginning-End Tag)	1 byte
Length	2 bytes

Figure 4.9 SIP Level 3 Protocol Data Unit format

CPE. However, as is discussed below, improper values in these fields could cause the receiving CPE to discard the L3_PDU.

Each of the fields of the L3_PDU is discussed in the following subsections. In many cases, [772] specifies action that the SS shall take and leaves open the question of what the CPE should do.[6] In these situations, we discuss the alternative actions and in some cases make recommendations on what the CPE actions should be.

4.5.1 Reserved Fields

RESERVED fields currently have no defined function and should always contain 0. IEEE P802.6 defined them to allow the possibility of changing the interpretation of other existing fields. For example, if a device is pipelining, it may not know the ultimate length of the information to be sent. In this case, BUFFER ALLOCATION SIZE may only be an estimate of the length. A code in the first RESERVED field could indicate this to the receiving station. It is very unlikely

---

[6]The reason for this is that Bellcore requirements are primarily aimed at the suppliers of telephone network equipment. Furthermore, the legal constraints on the RBOCs with respect to CPE motivate Bellcore to write requirements that make as few specifications on CPE as possible.

that SIP would ever be modified to make use of either RESERVED field. The SS
sets them to 0. CPE should also set them to 0.

4.5.2   Beginning-End Tag Fields

BETAG fields are present to detect the loss of both the last L2_PDU of an
L3_PDU and the first L2_PDU of the next L3_PDU. When transmitting
L3_PDUs, both the CPE and the SS should increment (modulo 256) the value in
the BETAG fields for each L3_PDU. Thus, if an L3_PDU is received with
different values in the BETAG fields, it must be concluded that an error occurred,
namely that fragments of different L3_PDUs were combined into a single
L3_PDU. Thus, when the values in the two BETAG fields of an L3_PDU are not
equal, the L3_PDU is to be discarded by both SMDS and the CPE. Figure 4.10
illustrates an example of the use of the BETAG fields.

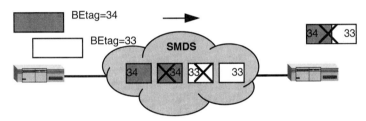

Figure 4.10 Example of the use of the BETAG field

4.5.3   Buffer Allocation Size Field and Length Field

Both the BUFFER ALLOCATION SIZE and the LENGTH should contain the number
of bytes contained in the L3_PDU, beginning with the DESTINATION ADDRESS
up to and including the CRC32, if present.[7] Thus, if an L3_PDU is received with
different values in these two fields, or if the amount of bytes received does not
agree with the common value, then it is concluded that an error has occurred. In
such a case, SMDS discards the L3_PDU.

Bellcore [772] does not specify an action for CPE in the face of this error.
Such an error is indicative of one or more lost L2_PDUs and hence corrupted
SMDS User Information. We recommend that CPE discard L3_PDUs with this
error condition.

---

[7]As noted in Section 4.5.1, IEEE P802.6 might sometime in the future define a protocol
where the value of the BUFFER ALLOCATION SIZE could be different from the value of the LENGTH
field. It is very unlikely that SIP would ever be modified in this way.

4.5.4 Destination Address Field

As implied by the name, the DESTINATION ADDRESS field contains the address of the intended recipient of the SMDS User Information. It is subdivided into two subfields, as illustrated in Figure 4.11.

Address_Type	Address
4 bits	60 bits

Figure 4.11 Address subfields

The ADDRESS_TYPE subfield indicates whether the DESTINATION ADDRESS is an Individual or Group Address. A value of 1100_B indicates an Individual Address, while a value of 1110_B indicates a Group Address. This is consistent with [802.6], where 1100_B means publicly administered, 60-bit Individual Address, and 1110_B means publicly administered, 60-bit Group Address. Any other value is invalid for SMDS, and the L3_PDU is discarded.

The ADDRESS subfield contains the Destination Address. Proper formatting of this field will depend on the number-administration authority for the destination. In North America, SSs conforming to [772] and [1060] only attempt to analyze ADDRESS subfields that conform to the North American Numbering Plan (see Section 3.4.1). Such addresses begin with 0001_B in the 4 most significant bits. If the 4 most significant bits are not equal to 0001_B, the SS forwards the L3_PDU to an IEC, on the assumption that the destination is outside of the LATA. Figure 4.12 shows the acceptable formats for the ADDRESS subfield in North America as specified by [772] and [1060]. If the 4 most significant bits contain 0001_B, the next 40 bits must contain BCD encoded decimal digits, followed by 16 bits set to 1_B. These last 16 bits are not padding, as defined in [802.6] since the ADDRESS_TYPE subfield indicates 60 bits of address. If the most significant 4 bits contain any value other than 0001_B, then the next 56 bits can contain any value. If the ADDRESS subfield does not have the proper format, SMDS discards the L3_PDU.

For service providers adhering to [ESIG001], for example in Europe, the L3_PDU is discarded if the ADDRESS subfield does not conform to [E.164] (see Section 3.4.1).

How should CPE process the ADDRESS_TYPE and ADDRESS subfields? If the station is only going to be used in the single-CPE configuration, then no processing of these fields is required if one is willing to trust SMDS to only deliver L3_PDUs to the proper SNI. (Section 7.4.3 describes the performance objective for such misdelivered L3_PDUs.) If such trust is not held, then there may be a market for a capability to discard L3_PDUs whose DESTINATION ADDRESS does not contain a value assigned to the SNI.

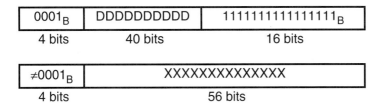

0001$_B$	DDDDDDDDD	1111111111111111$_B$
4 bits	40 bits	16 bits

≠0001$_B$	XXXXXXXXXXXXX
4 bits	56 bits

D   Binary Coded Decimal Digit (4 bits)
X   Don't Care Nibble (4 bits)

Figure 4.12 Valid ADDRESS subfield formats for the DESTINATION ADDRESS

The multi-CPE configuration mandates processing of these fields. In order to receive an L3_PDU, a station in a multi-CPE configuration must examine the content of the DESTINATION ADDRESS field to see if it contains an address assigned to the station. If it does, then the station copies the L3_PDU from the Access DQDB. If local traffic is to be supported, the station might also need to recognize values in the ADDRESS_TYPE subfield in addition to 1100$_B$ and 1110$_B$. For example, [802.6] defines values for 48-bit addresses, 16-bit addresses, and privately administered 60-bit addresses.

4.5.5 Source Address Field

The SOURCE ADDRESS field contains the address of the sender of the L3_PDU. Like the DESTINATION ADDRESS field, it is composed of two subfields, as shown in Figure 4.11. If the ADDRESS_TYPE subfield contains any other value than 1100$_B$, SMDS discards the L3_PDU. (It makes no sense to have a Group Address as the Source Address.)

If the service provider uses addresses structured according to the North American Numbering Plan, then the acceptable format for the ADDRESS subfield for ingress L3_PDUs is as shown in Figure 4.13. If the ADDRESS subfield does not have an acceptable format, the ingress L3_PDU is discarded [772].

0001$_B$	DDDDDDDDD	1111111111111111$_B$
4 bits	40 bits	16 bits

Figure 4.13 Valid ADDRESS subfield format for the ingress SOURCE ADDRESS field

Bellcore [1060] is ambiguous about allowed formats for the ADDRESS subfield upon egress. The Bellcore document, [1060], clearly implies the relaxation on the requirements in [772] on the DESTINATION ADDRESS field to allow the second format shown in Figure 4.12. We believe that the intent is to apply a similar relaxation for the SOURCE ADDRESS field on egress.[8] This interpretation allows communication between an SNI offered by a service provider adhering to the North American Numbering Plan (e.g., an RBOC) and an SNI offered by a service provider using a different addressing structure (e.g., an IEC).[9]

For service providers adhering to [ESIG001], for example in Europe, the L3_PDU is discarded if the ADDRESS subfield does not conform to [E.164] (see Section 3.4.1) for both ingress and egress.

Processing of the SOURCE ADDRESS field by receiving CPE is not required. CPE features such as additional security or department charge-back might motivate such processing, but these are beyond the scope of SMDS.

4.5.6 Higher Layer Protocol Identifier Field

SMDS does not process the HIGHER LAYER PROTOCOL IDENTIFIER field. The field is present to align SIP with IEEE Std. 802.6-1990 and corresponds to the IMPDU PROTOCOL IDENTIFICATION field of the standard. We recommend that the use of this field be consistent with [802.6], which specifies the values shown in Table 4.1. An example of the use of this field for identifying LLC is the specification for carrying IP [RFC791] over SMDS in [RFC1209],[10] which is discussed in Chapter 8.

Decimal value	Protocol
1	LLC
48 - 63	Available for local administration
0, 2 - 47	Reserved for future standardization by IEEE P802.6

Table 4.1 Recommended use of the HIGHER LAYER PROTOCOL IDENTIFIER field

---

[8]This relaxation cannot be done on ingress, because the service provider would only assign addresses based on the North American Numbering Plan; thus any Source Address not abiding by the first format in Figure 4.12 must fail the Source Address Validation check.

[9]This is a hypothetical arrangement. As of this writing, we are not aware of any IEC plans to use a numbering structure that is not consistent with the North American Numbering Plan.

[10]The title of [RFC1209], *The Transmission of IP Datagrams over the SMDS Service,* appears to have used the word *service* redundantly. This title arose from an effort on the part of the RBOCs and Bellcore to make SMDS into a service mark. This would have meant that SMDS would become just four letters and not an acronym, and thus the word *service* would need to be added. Thus Bellcore proposed the title of [RFC1209] with the extra word. When it was finally realized that making SMDS a Bellcore service mark would lead to a proliferation of names (Interexchange Carriers are unlikely to use a Bellcore service mark to name a service), the effort was abandoned. The title of [RFC1209] remains as an artifact of this activity.

4.5.7 PAD and PAD Length Fields

In order to facilitate processing, the PAD field is sized to make the L3_PDU 32-bit aligned. Since the only two fields of the L3_PDU that are not necessarily 32-bit aligned are the INFORMATION and PAD fields, the length of the PAD field can be calculated from the following formula:

PAD LENGTH = 3 − ((number of INFORMATION bytes + 3) mod 4).

The PAD LENGTH field allows the receiving device (SS or CPE) to find the end of the INFORMATION field. The PAD field, when present, contains all 0s.

4.5.8 Quality of Service Field

SMDS does not process the QUALITY OF SERVICE field. The field is present to align SIP with IEEE Std. 802.6-1990 and corresponds to the concatenation of the IMPDU QOS_DELAY and QOS_LOSS fields of the standard. For consistency with the standard, we recommend that this field be set to 0000_B.

4.5.9 32-bit Cyclic Redundancy Check and CRC32 Indication Bit Fields

In early drafts of [802.6], a 32-bit CRC was included to detect bit errors. In the winter of 1989, this was replaced by a 10-bit CRC on each segment. The motivation for the change was to align with the emerging BISDN Standards. Nevertheless, debate continued about the adequacy of 10-bit CRCs for detecting errors.[11] Eventually, an optional 32-bit CRC was added in order to reach a consensus.

The CRC32 field is not processed by SMDS. However, it is necessary for SMDS to know when it is present. This is accomplished by the CRC32 INDICATION BIT. If the CRC32 field is present, the CIB is set to 1. Otherwise it is set to 0. This is all that is required for transporting the L3_PDU. However,

---

[11]Proponents of the CRC32 were concerned with small bursts of bit errors occurring within the payload of the Derived MAC Protocol Data Unit (the equivalent of the payload of the L2_PDU). For such an event, the probability that the 10-bit CRC (see Section 4.6) would fail to detect the errors is $2^{-10} = .977 \times 10^{-3}$ which was considered too large. If the bit errors are randomly distributed, then the vast majority of errors are single-bit errors which the 10-bit CRC always detects. Finally, if the error bursts are large and impact other fields of the Derived MAC Protocol Data Unit, the errors in these fields will very likely be detected (see Section 4.6). We believe that typical telephone transmission equipment (e.g., T1 systems) will generate errors that are either random single-bit errors or bursts of bit errors that are longer than several L2_PDUs, and thus the 10-bit CRC is sufficient. Use of the protocol in other transmission environments might require the use of the CRC32.

to ensure interoperability between CPE, it is necessary that the transmitting CPE calculate the CRC32 field as specified in Section 6.5.1.6 of [802.6], and it is necessary that the receiving CPE at least be able to detect its presence.

4.5.10 Header Extension Length Field

The IEEE [802.6] defines a variable-length IMPDU HEADER EXTENSION field, whose length is indicated in an IMPDU HEADER EXTENSION LENGTH field. To facilitate processing, SIP makes use of a fixed-length HEADER EXTENSION field. Thus, the HEADER EXTENSION LENGTH field always contains the value 011_B to indicate a length of three 32-bit words (i.e., 12 bytes). If the HEADER EXTENSION LENGTH field contains any value other than 011_B, SMDS discards the L3_PDU.

Bellcore [772] does not put requirements on CPE with respect to processing this field. If CPE is designed for the single-CPE configuration, then all data received will be from SMDS, and a value of other than 011_B is indicative of an error. Thus, for this case, we recommend that CPE drop L3_PDUs whose HEADER EXTENSION LENGTH fields do not contain 011_B. For the multi-CPE configuration case, the situation is less clear. Local communications on the Access DQDB may involve protocol data units with varying sizes of the HEADER EXTENSION FIELD. For CPE designed for this environment, it is probably reasonable to accept any value in the range 000_B to 101_B, which are the valid values specified in [802.6].

4.5.11 Bridging Field

SMDS does not process the BRIDGING field. The field is present to align SIP with IEEE Std. 802.6-1990 and corresponds to the IMPDU BRIDGING field of [802.6]. This field is currently reserved for future use,[12] and stations are required to set it to 0. Therefore, we recommend that CPE set this field to 0. (The use of SMDS by bridges is described in Chapter 9.)

4.5.12 Header Extension Field

The HEADER EXTENSION field is currently used to identify the SIP version number and to allow per-L3_PDU carrier selection. However, the coding of this field is flexible enough to allow additional uses in the future. The HEADER EXTENSION field is composed of subfields, as illustrated in Figure 4.14.

---

[12]The envisioned use is for DQDB bridges. Such bridges could make use of this field to communicate with each other (e.g., to indicate the number of bridges an IMPDU has traversed). Such uses are expected to be transparent to the stations.

Element Length	Element Type	Element Value	...	Element Length	Element Type	Element Value	HE PAD
1	1	Variable		1	1	Variable	Variable

Lengths are in bytes.

Figure 4.14 Header Extension Field format

The HEADER EXTENSION field is always 12 bytes in length. The subfields follow:

ELEMENT LENGTH: This field contains the length in bytes of itself plus the lengths of the ELEMENT TYPE field and ELEMENT VALUE field that immediately follow it.

ELEMENT TYPE: This field contains a code that identifies the type of information in the immediately following ELEMENT VALUE field. The various types of elements are described below.

ELEMENT VALUE: The content of this field depends on its type. The values and formats for this field are described below.

HE PAD: This field is meant to fill whatever bytes of the HEADER EXTENSION field that are not used by the fields listed above. It begins with at least 1 byte of zeros. This means that when the HEADER EXTENSION field is processed, it will appear to be an ELEMENT LENGTH of 0, thus indicating the end of the HEADER EXTENSION FIELD elements. As can be seen below, the HE PAD can vary from 0 to 9 bytes in length.

Table 4.2 shows the possible values and meanings for the ELEMENT TYPE field.

Element type	Meaning
0	Version
1	Carrier Selection
2 – 127	Reserved
128 – 255	For use by other entities

Table 4.2 Element Types

The values 2 – 127 are reserved for future use by Bellcore. Such a new element could be used in implementing a new feature for SMDS. The values 128 – 255 could be defined by anyone. An example is an Interexchange Carrier defining an ELEMENT TYPE for a service feature offered by the carrier.[13] The authors are only aware of the two defined element types in Table 4.2. Each type is described below.

4.5.12.1　Version Element Field

The VERSION ELEMENT field is insurance against the possibility of changes in SIP. Should this occur, the new protocol could be identified by this element. This would allow "bilingual" equipment (probably the SS) to work with all generations of equipment. As of this writing, 1 is the only valid value for this element. Furthermore, this element must always be present as the first element in the HEADER EXTENSION field. Consequently, the first three bytes of the HEADER EXTENSION field contain the value $00000011\ 00000000\ 00000001_B$.

A strict reading of [772] could lead one to conclude that several instances of the VERSION ELEMENT field are allowed in the HEADER EXTENSION field. Since there is no useful function for multiple instances, this is clearly not the intent of [772].

4.5.12.2　Carrier Selection Field

The CARRIER SELECTION field can be used to specify up to three carriers. In North America, a carrier is specified by means of its Carrier Identification Code (CIC),[14] which is encoded by four BCD digits (see Chapter 3). For CICs with three digits, the leading (most significant) digit is 0_D. The number of carriers in an element can be deduced from the value in the ELEMENT LENGTH, as shown in Table 4.3.

Number of carriers	Element length
1	4
2	6
3	8

Table 4.3 Number of carriers and ELEMENT LENGTH

CARRIER SELECTION elements can appear anywhere in the HEADER EXTENSION field other than the first element. However, SMDS only processes

---

[13]During the development of [772], one IEC suggested that the unused portion of the HEADER EXTENSION field might be used for this purpose. This is why only the first byte of the HE PAD is required to be zero, which allows the remaining bytes to be used to carry information. However, use of the HE PAD is fraught with danger because the definition of new HEADER EXTENSION elements will "squeeze" the HE PAD. (Idle bits are the devil's playground.)

[14]Both [772] and [1060] use the term *SMDS Carrier Identification Codes*. This reflects the possibility that the codes used to identify carriers for SMDS might be different from the codes used for voice services. For simplicity, we use CIC.

this kind of element when it immediately follows the version element (i.e., it is the second element in the HEADER EXTENSION field). Furthermore, if the CARRIER SELECTION element that is processed contains more than one CIC, only the first (most significant) CIC is processed by the network providing the source SNI.[15] Figure 4.15 shows examples of valid HEADER EXTENSION fields.

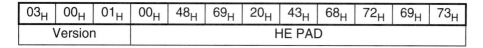

03_H	00_H	01_H	00_H	48_H	69_H	20_H	43_H	68_H	72_H	69_H	73_H
Version			HE PAD								

No carrier selection. (This HE PAD contains a message to the Mother of SMDS.)

03_H	00_H	01_H	06_H	01_H	02_H	88_H	00_H	97_H	00_H	00_H	00_H
Version			Carrier Selection						HE PAD		

AT&T (0288_H) and St. Thomas & San Juan Telephone Company (0097_H) selected.

Figure 4.15 Examples of valid HEADER EXTENSION fields

The following HEADER EXTENSION field errors cause SMDS to discard the L3_PDU:

- The VERSION element does not appear first in the HEADER EXTENSION field.

- The value for the VERSION element is not 1.

- The second element is a CARRIER SELECTION element and the value of the ELEMENT LENGTH is not 4, 6, or 8.

- The second element is a CARRIER SELECTION element and the first CIC is not four BCD digits.

Bellcore [772] does not specify actions for the CPE regarding the HEADER EXTENSION field. Since no CPE use is currently defined for this field, we recommend that the CPE ignore this field.

---

[15]The CICs that are not processed may be of significance to a network that is not providing the SNI. For example, the second CIC in a CARRIER SELECTION element could specify an international carrier. In North America, the Interexchange Carrier (specified by the first CIC) could use the second CIC to route an L3_PDU toward an international destination.

4.5.13 Information Field

The INFORMATION field varies in length between 0 and 9188 bytes.[16] It is meant to carry the SMDS User Information.

4.6 SIP Level 2 Description

SIP Level 2 provides a means to delimit the L3_PDUs, and it provides various error-detection capabilities. Figure 4.16 shows the format of the L2_PDU.

	Field	Length
Header	Access Control	8 bits
	Network Control Information	32 bits
	Segment Type	2 bits
	Sequence Number	4 bits
	Message Identifier	10 bits
	Segmentation Unit	44 bytes
Trailer	Payload Length	6 bits
	Payload CRC	10 bits

Figure 4.16 SIP Level 2 Protocol Data Unit format

Each of the fields of the L2_PDU is discussed in the following subsections. As with the L3_PDU, [772] leaves open the question of how the CPE should handle some of the fields. In these situations, we discuss the alternative actions and in some cases make recommendations on what the CPE actions should be.

4.6.1 Access Control Field

The ACCESS CONTROL field is used to identify L2_PDUs that contain information (i.e., that are not empty), and it can be used by CPE to request the SS to free bandwidth on Bus A for local communications. It can be viewed as composed of subfields. The subfields are different depending on the direction of transmission. Figure 4.17 shows the subfields for the CPE-to-SS direction.

The BUSY subfield indicates when the L2_PDU contains information. As will be seen from the description of the SIP Level 1 protocols, L2_PDUs must be continuously transmitted. We refer to each time an L2_PDU must be sent as an *L2_PDU transmit opportunity*. When an L2_PDU transmit opportunity occurs

---

[16]At one time during the development of IEEE Std. 802.6-1990, the IMPDU overhead was proposed to be 28 bytes. The information field length was then set to 9188, so that a full-size IMPDU would be exactly 9K bytes. Later the overhead changed, but no one bothered to change the information field length.

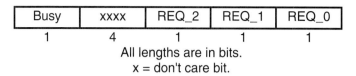

Busy	xxxx	REQ_2	REQ_1	REQ_0
1	4	1	1	1

All lengths are in bits.
x = don't care bit.

Figure 4.17 ACCESS CONTROL field for the CPE to SS direction

and a device has nothing to send, an empty L2_PDU must be transmitted. BUSY = 0 means that the L2_PDU is empty, and all fields other than the ACCESS CONTROL field should be ignored by the SS. Busy = 1 means that the L2_PDU contains information, and the SS should process the other fields of the L2_PDU.

The four "don't care" bits correspond to bits reserved for isochronous transmission and the eraser node function described in [802.6]. *Isochronous* refers to a capability to reserve bandwidth that is available for transmitting in a periodic fashion. The eraser node is a function that allows bandwidth to be reused; it erases the BUSY subfield. Since the SS ignores these bits, it is conceivable that, in the multi-CPE configuration, local isochronous traffic and eraser nodes could be accommodated. However, [802.6] does not standardize these aspects, and therefore we recommend that these bits be set to zero.

The REQ_0, REQ_1, and REQ_2 subfields, when set to 1, are interpreted by the SS as requests for bandwidth on Bus A for local communications (see Figure 4.2). For each instance of one of these fields set, an empty L2_PDU will be generated on Bus A by the SS. This SS behavior is necessary to allow local communications in the multi-CPE configuration. When the CPE sets these bits, the net effect is to reduce the bandwidth that is available to the SS for delivering L3_PDUs. Indeed, if either the REQ_1 or REQ_2 subfield is always set to 1, no SMDS traffic can be delivered by the SS. Consequently, for CPE designed for the single-CPE configuration, we recommend that these three fields always be set to 0. For the multi-CPE configuration, the REQ_1 and REQ_2 subfields should always be set to 0, and the REQ_0 subfield should be set according to [802.6].

Figure 4.18 shows the subfields for the ACCESS CONTROL field for the SS-to-CPE direction. The BUSY subfield has the same meaning and is set the same as for the CPE-to-SS direction. The remaining bits are always set to 0 by the SS. This means that the SS never requests empty L2_PDUs on Bus B, which is appropriate because the SS never transmits on Bus B.

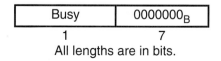

Busy	0000000_B
1	7

All lengths are in bits.

Figure 4.18 Access Control field for the SS to CPE direction.

Bellcore [772] requires the SS to set all bits of empty L2_PDUs to 0. This is consistent with [802.6] and is necessary to support CPE transmitting local traffic on Bus A, since [802.6] specifies that such transmission can be done by "or writing" into all fields after the ACCESS CONTROL field. In [772], Bellcore does not place any requirements on how CPE populate these fields for empty L2_PDUs. For consistency with [802.6], we recommend that CPE populate all fields after the ACCESS CONTROL field with 0s for empty L2_PDUs.

4.6.2   Network Control Information Field

The NETWORK CONTROL INFORMATION field corresponds to several fields defined in [802.6]. It has no use in SMDS and is therefore always set to the same value: 11111111 11111111 11110000 00100010_B = $FFFFF022_H$, for nonempty L2_PDUs. The first 20 bits correspond to the Virtual Circuit Identifier (VCI) defined in [802.6]. In the context of IEEE Std. 802.6-1990, the VCI can identify connectionless data (VCI is all 1s) or connection-oriented data.[17] SMDS uses the connectionless-data VCI.[18] The next 4 bits are set to 0, as specified in [802.6]. The last 8 bits are the result of a CRC calculation that is specified in [802.6].

Any L2_PDU with a NETWORK CONTROL INFORMATION field that does not contain $FFFFF022_H$ is discarded by the SS. This is because such an L2_PDU can contain an error, can be local traffic in a multi-CPE configuration, or can be empty. Once again, [772] does not specify the action to be taken by the CPE. CPE designed for the multi-CPE configuration should process this field according to the specifications for the corresponding fields in [802.6]. For CPE designed for the single-CPE configuration, we recommend discarding any L2_PDU whose NETWORK CONTROL INFORMATION field does not contain $FFFFF022_H$.

4.6.3   Segment Type Field

The SEGMENT TYPE field is used for the reassembly of an L3_PDU from its associated L2_PDUs. It indicates the relative position of the SEGMENTATION UNIT field with respect to the segmentation of the L3_PDU. Table 4.4 shows the meaning of the values for this field. For the case where the L3_PDU does not fit within the SEGMENTATION UNIT field, the L2_PDU with the most significant bytes of the L3_PDU has a SEGMENT TYPE field = BOM, the L2_PDU with the

---

[17]Connection-oriented data is a subject for possible future standardization by IEEE P802.6.

[18]In principle, the presence of the VCI in IEEE Std. 802.6-1990 could be used to extend SIP to support a multiple-services interface. Each service provider will have to make a business decision regarding this extension. We expect that the RBOCs will not extend SIP but will use protocols based on the emerging ITU BISDN standards for a multiple-services interface. The single-service SNI will continue to be supported, of course.

least significant bytes of the L3_PDU has a SEGMENT TYPE field = EOM, and the remaining L2_PDUs carrying the L3_PDU have a SEGMENT TYPE field = COM. Should an L3_PDU fit within a single SEGMENTATION UNIT field, the SEGMENT TYPE field is set to SSM.[19]

Value	Meaning
00_B	Continuation of Message (COM)
01_B	End of Message (EOM)
10_B	Beginning of Message (BOM)
11_B	Single Segment Message (SSM)

Table 4.4 SEGMENT TYPE values

4.6.4   Sequence Number Field

The SEQUENCE NUMBER field is for detecting lost L2_PDUs. When multiple L2_PDUs are needed to transmit an L3_PDU, this field for the BOM can have an arbitrary value and is incremented modulo 16 for each subsequent L2_PDU carrying SEGMENTATION UNIT fields for the same L3_PDU. When only an SSM is needed to carry the L3_PDU, this field can have an arbitrary value.[20]

4.6.5   Message Identifier Field

The MESSAGE IDENTIFIER (MID) field is used to allow association of L2_PDUs with an L3_PDU. It allows multiple L3_PDUs to be interleaved on the SNI. MCDUs Out and MCDUs In (see Section 3.4.5) specify the maximum number of L3_PDUs that can be interleaved. The MID is set to the same value for all L2_PDUs carrying a given L3_PDU. The SS sets the MID to 0 for SSMs. The SS uses MID values in the range 1 through $(2^9 - 1)$ for L2_PDUs that are not SSMs. In fact, the SS uses a single MID value when the MCDUs Out is 1, and it uses 16 MID values when MCDUs Out is 16. The reason for this is as follows. Consider a reassembly process active in the CPE, and suppose the EOM associated (via the MID value) with this process is lost, for example, due to a transmission error on the SNI. If the MID value is not used again for a long time, the resources

---

[19]The small size of the SEGMENTATION UNIT field compared to the overheads of protocols such as IP suggest that the SSM may be quite rare. Cedric Druce has predicted that the SSM will be like the Quark: theoretically possible, but never observed [Druce].

[20]This setting of the SEQUENCE NUMBER field is less complex than that specified in [802.6] where the sequence must be maintained across L2_PDUs with the same value in the MESSAGE IDENTIFIER field. The procedure in [802.6] is consistent with the SIP procedure.

allocated for the reassembly process are either lost for this time, or a timer (as specified in [802.6]) must be used to recover the resources. When the SS uses 1 or 16 MID values, the CPE does not need a timer. When the maximum number of concurrent data units need to be sent to the CPE, the MID associated with the lost reassembly process will be used by the SS. When the CPE receives a BOM with an MID value associated with an existing reassembly process, that process is abandoned and reinitialized for the new L3_PDU. Thus, even without a timer, the CPE will never have more than MCDUs Out active reassembly processes than the number of MCDUs Out.

Bellcore [772] does not specify what values the CPE should use, except to use 0 for SSMs. For CPE designed for the single-CPE configuration, any nonzero value can be used for BOMs, COMs, and EOMs. The simplest thing to do would be to use a single value (say 1) for MCDUs In equal to 1, and 16 values (say 1,2,...,16) for MCDUs In equal to 16. CPE designed for the multi-CPE configuration need to be more complex. The key to selecting an MID value in the case of the multi-CPE configuration is that it must be unique among all stations transmitting on the same bus. The MID Page Allocation Protocol[21] specified in [802.6] provides a method for distributing MID values that meets this requirement. The DQDB Layer Management Information that is generated by the SS is such that, if all stations are using this protocol, then the SS reserves all MID values in the range 1 to $(2^9 - 1)$ for its own use. This leaves the range 2^9 to $(2^{10} - 1)$ for use by the CPE. Consequently, we recommend that CPE designed for the multi-CPE configuration implement the MID Page Allocation Protocol as specified in Section 10.3 of [802.6]. (Appendix A describes the MID Page Allocation Protocol.)

L2_PDUs are discarded by both the CPE and the SS if:

- MID = 0, and SEGMENT TYPE field = BOM, COM, EOM.

- MID ≠ 0, and SEGMENT TYPE field = SSM.

In contrast to the CPE, the SS cannot assume that the CPE will continually reuse MID values. Therefore, [772] and [ESIG003] specify that the SS must maintain a timer for each active reassembly process. The timer is started upon receipt of a BOM and is terminated upon receipt of the next EOM with an MID value matching that of the BOM. If the timer reaches a certain value, the

---

[21]One might conclude from the name of this protocol that it allocates MID values in groups (pages). However, this is not the case. The values are allocated one at a time. At one time in the development of IEEE Std. 802.6-1990, the MESSAGE IDENTIFIER field was proposed to be 14 bits, and MID values were allocated in pages of 4. In an attempt to maintain alignment with the emerging BISDN standards, four bits were taken away from the MESSAGE IDENTIFIER field when the draft document was nearly complete, and it was deemed easier to leave the name of the protocol unchanged and simply define a page to equal 1.

Message Receive Interval (MRI), the reassembly process is terminated, and the corresponding L3_PDU is discarded. Table 4.5 shows the values for MRI for each Digital Transmission Level (see Section 4.7).

Digital transmission level	MRI (ms)
DS1	200 [772]
DS3	100 [772]
E1	200 [ESIG003]
E3	100 [ESIG003]

Table 4.5 Message Receive Interval values

In the cases of SNIs based on DS1 and E1 with MCDUs In = 16, it is possible for large L3_PDUs to be discarded due to the MRI being exceeded, even though no L2_PDUs are lost. To understand the mechanism, suppose that M concurrent L3_PDUs are being sent without any gaps in the L2_PDUs. In other words, for a given L3_PDU, the L2_PDUs derived from it are separated by $(M - 1)$ L2_PDUs from the other L3_PDUs. Now consider what happens to an L3_PDU that requires L L2_PDUs to be transmitted across the SNI. After the BOM is received by the SS, the timer is started. A total of $M \times (L - 1)$ L2_PDUs will need to be received by the SS to complete the L3_PDU. Thus, to avoid the discard of the L3_PDU by the SS, L must satisfy

$$\frac{M \times (L - 1)}{R} < 200 \text{ ms},$$

where R is the rate at which L2_PDUs are carried on the SNI. R = 3333.3 L2_PDUs/sec for DS1 (see Section 4.7.1), and R = 4210.5 L2_PDUs/sec for E1 (see Section 4.7.3). Solving for L and multiplying by 44 yields the largest L3_PDU that will not be discarded given M concurrent L3_PDUs:

$$\text{Maximum Length L3\_PDU} = 44 \times \text{floor}\left[\frac{0.2 \times R}{M} + 1\right] \text{bytes},$$

where floor[x] is the largest integer $\leq x$. Figure 4.19 shows the results of this calculation. This figure accounts for the fact that the largest valid L3_PDU (including header and trailer) is 9232 bytes. Even in the case where there are 16 concurrent L3_PDUs, a full size CSMA/CD frame can be accommodated.

In order to receive local traffic in the multi-CPE configuration, CPE must maintain a timer to measure an interval analogous to the MRI. Consequently, the MRI was included in the SMDS Management Information Base for both CPE and the SS (see Chapters 11 and 12).   ·

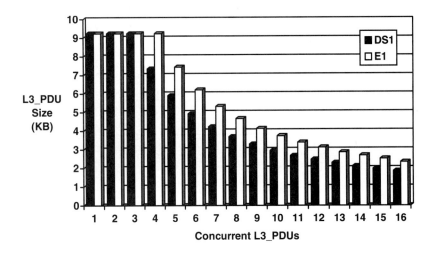

Figure 4.19 Largest L3_PDU versus concurrent L3_PDUs

4.6.6 Segmentation Unit Field

The SEGMENTATION UNIT field contains the partial L3_PDU. Its 44 bytes are sufficient to contain the 36 bytes of the L3_PDU header (see Figure 4.9), and thus it facilitates pipelining (see Section 4.3.4).

4.6.7 Payload Length Field

The PAYLOAD LENGTH field indicates how much of the SEGMENTATION UNIT field contains data. Given the structure of the L3_PDU, only certain values are valid, as shown in Table 4.6. However, the SS will accept as valid the values indicated in the last column of Table 4.6. Use of these acceptable values facilitates the use of hardware that conforms to [802.6] for implementing the SNI on the SS. This follows from two facts. First, [802.6] does not require a check for 4-byte integral values in the PAYLOAD LENGTH field. Second, [802.6] allows HEADER EXTENSION field lengths of 0, 4, 8, 12, 16, and 20 bytes, which means that in [802.6], the SSM can have PAYLOAD LENGTH field values of 28, 32, 36, 40, and 44. The SS discards any L2_PDUs with PAYLOAD LENGTH field values other than those shown in the last column of Table 4.6. Here again, [772] does not put requirements on CPE for checking this field. Given the length-checking mechanisms in the L3_PDU, we recommend that CPE not implement such a check.

Segment Type field	Valid values	Accepted by the SS
BOM	44	44
COM	44	44
EOM	4,8,12,16,20,24,28,32,36,40,44	4,5,6, . . .,44
SSM	40,44	28,29,30, . . .,44

Table 4.6 Valid and acceptable values for the PAYLOAD LENGTH field

4.6.8 Payload CRC Field

The PAYLOAD CRC field is used to detect transmission errors. It is populated with the value that results from the following procedure. Set all of the bits of the PAYLOAD CRC field to 0. Divide the contents of the SEGMENT TYPE, SEQUENCE NUMBER, MESSAGE IDENTIFIER, SEGMENTATION UNIT, PAYLOAD LENGTH, and PAYLOAD CRC fields, treated as a polynomial, by the generator polynomial of degree 10, $G(x) = x^{10} + x^9 + x^5 + x^4 + x^1 + 1$ (see Appendix C). The resulting remainder, with the most significant bit the highest coefficient, is the value of the PAYLOAD CRC field.

At the receiver, the equivalent of the following procedure is followed. Divide the received contents of the SEGMENT TYPE, SEQUENCE NUMBER, MESSAGE IDENTIFIER, SEGMENTATION UNIT, PAYLOAD LENGTH, and PAYLOAD CRC fields, by $G(x)$. If the remainder is not all 0s, discard the L2_PDU.

4.7   SIP Level 1 Description

There are several different Level-1 protocols for SIP. The North American protocols are based on data rates and formats that are part of the North American Digital Transmission Hierarchy [T1.107]. The European protocols are based on the European Digital Transmission Hierarchy [G.703] [G.704] [G.751]. The CCITT has specified the relationship between these hierarchies in [G.702]. The levels that are defined for use by SMDS are shown in Table 4.7. Higher rates based on SONET [253] are not shown but are contemplated for SMDS in the future.

The first North American Level-1 protocol is DS1, which has a raw bit rate of 1.544 Mbps. The second North American Level-1 protocol is DS3 which has a raw bit rate of 44.736 Mbps. Although it might be more convenient for the SMDS customer if the Physical Medium Dependent part of SIP was based on common LAN standards, using the North American Digital Transmission Hierarchy has compelling advantages for early deployment of SMDS. The

North America		Europe	
Level	**Bit rate (Mbps)**	**Level**	**Bit rate (Mbps)**
DS1	1.544	E1	2.048
DS3	44.736	E3	34.368

Table 4.7 Digital Hierarchy Levels Used by SMDS

advantage is that using DS1 and DS3 allows great flexibility in the placing of the SMDS Switching System. For example, as illustrated in Figure 4.20, within a LATA, a single SS can be initially deployed. For SMDS customers served by a central office not containing the SS, it is relatively easy to take the DS1 or DS3 path for the customer and connect it via digital cross-connects (DSX) and existing digital transmission systems from the serving central office to the central office with the SS. In other words, SMDS can be made available over a wide area, such as a LATA, by placing only a single SS within the area. Clearly this will facilitate early availability for SMDS deployment.

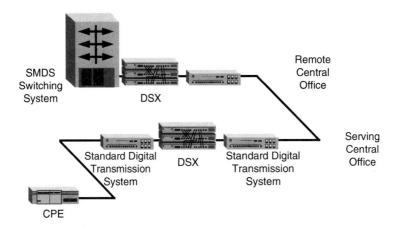

Figure 4.20 Remote access to an SMDS Switching System via DS1

The European peers of DS1 and DS3 are E1 and E3, with the nominal bit rates of 2.048 Mbps and 34.368 Mbps respectively. Selection of these digital transmission techniques for SMDS in Europe has advantages similar to those for DS1 and DS3 in North America.

Level 1 of SIP consists of two parts. The first part is the Physical Medium Dependent (PMD) part. It provides the transmission of bits between peers as well as extensive maintenance, monitoring, and operations support. The second is the additional protocol needed specifically for SMDS, called the Physical

Layer Convergence Procedure (PLCP).[22] The PLCP provides delimitation of L2_PDUs within the PMD bit stream as well as maintenance, monitoring, and operations support. Because standard digital transmission rates and formats are used for the Physical Medium Dependent part of Level-1 SIP, we do not include details of this aspect of the protocols. Rather, we focus on the PLCP. Details on DS1, DS3, E1, and E3 can be found in [773], [G.703], [G.704], [G.751], [ESIG002], and additional references cited there. These references contain extensive requirements on the SS for supporting Level-1 management, such as Loopback, Send Code, Alarm State, Errored Seconds, Severely Errored Seconds, Severely Errored Framing Seconds, Unavailable Seconds, Bipolar Violations, and Coding Violations. Because these requirements are in support of management, their details are included in Chapters 11 and 12.

4.7.1   SIP Level 1 Based on DS1

SIP Level 1 based on DS1 is meant for customers with moderate bandwidth needs, either because their aggregate traffic does not justify DS3, or their applications do not require the high-speed performance that DS3 can deliver. The initial SMDS offerings in North America were based on DS1. There were a number of reasons for this. DS1 SIP was the first protocol implemented in both CPE and SSs. The complexity of SIP, because of its alignment with IEEE Std. 802.6-1990, means that full performance for DS3 requires highly customized hardware, which makes implementations more time-consuming than for DS1. Another factor was that attractive tariffs for the DS1 interface were possible, which in turn meant that a significant early market could be developed.

4.7.1.1   DS1 Physical Medium Dependent Protocol

The DS1 PMD is based on the Extended Superframe (ESF) and is illustrated in Figure 4.21. This is a frame of 3-ms duration that is composed of 24 rows of 193 bits. The first bit of each row, called the *framing bit* (F-bit), is used for framing and various maintenance and operations functions. The philosophy of the use of ESF is to have CPE provide substantial information to the SS regarding the performance of the DS1 transmission path. The SS provides similar information to CPE. This facilitates SNI management and reliability. The details can be found in [773].

The 24 framing bits of an Extended Superframe follow the pattern shown in Figure 4.22. The D-bits form a 4-Kbps channel that is used to convey performance information to the other end. Details on their use are provided in Chapter 11. The C-bits are used for a CRC. The CRC that is used is the CRC-6.

---

[22]This term was originally used in IEEE Std. 802.6-1990. The claim was that this is not a protocol but a procedure. The distinction escapes us, but we will use the same term to avoid compounding any confusion.

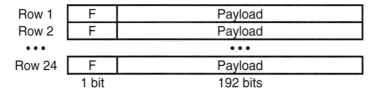

Figure 4.21 Extended Superframe

The C-bits are populated as follows. Set the F-bits temporarily to 1s. Then the contents of the frame (4632 bits, treated as a polynomial) are multiplied by x^6. Divide (modulo 2) the result by the generator polynomial of degree 6, $G(x) = x^6 + x + 1$. The resulting remainder is placed in the C-bits of the *subsequent* frame, such that the most significant bit is the highest coefficient, placed in the first C-bit (bit 194 of the frame). The remaining F-bits are used for frame alignment. The alignment signal is 001011_B. Further details on the F-bits can be found in [773].

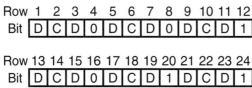

Figure 4.22 Extended Superframe framing bits

Older transmission facilities for DS1 require that long strings of 0s not occur within the signal. This is accomplished by setting up to every eighth bit to 1.[23] Newer systems use a different line coding to avoid this lack of data transparency. Unfortunately, different carriers have implemented different coding. One code is called *Bipolar with 8-Zero Substitution* (B8ZS). The other is called *Zero Byte Time Slot Interchange* (ZBTSI). Either method meets the SIP Level-1 specification in [773]. However, equipment implementing different coding techniques will not interoperate. Therefore, it is important for SMDS customers to determine which technique is used by their carrier and insure that the proper CPE configuration is used. If there is a choice, we recommend the use of B8ZS due to its superior robustness.

4.7.1.2   DS1 Physical Layer Convergence Procedure

Figure 4.23 shows the format of the DS1 PLCP Frame. As already described, this frame is meant to delimit L2_PDUs and provide maintenance, monitoring, and operations support.

This DS1 PLCP Frame is carried within the payload bits of the ESF, and each bit following an F-bit is the beginning of a PLCP byte. The DS1 PLCP

---

[23]Hence, in North America, 56 Kbps (7/8 of 64 Kbps) and not 64 Kbps digital lines are widely available.

1111011000101000$_B$	00100101$_B$	00000000$_B$	L2_PDU	
1111011000101000$_B$	00100000$_B$	00000000$_B$	L2_PDU	
1111011000101000$_B$	00011100$_B$	00000000$_B$	L2_PDU	
1111011000101000$_B$	00011001$_B$	00000000$_B$	L2_PDU	
1111011000101000$_B$	00010101$_B$	00000000$_B$	L2_PDU	
1111011000101000$_B$	00010000$_B$	B1	L2_PDU	
1111011000101000$_B$	00001101$_B$	G1	L2_PDU	
1111011000101000$_B$	00001000$_B$	M2	L2_PDU	
1111011000101000$_B$	00000100$_B$	M1	L2_PDU	
1111011000101000$_B$	00000001$_B$	C1	L2_PDU	Trailer
2 bytes	1 byte	1 byte	53 bytes	6 bytes

Key

B1	Bit Interleaved Parity
G1	PLCP Path Status
M1, M2	SIP Level 1 Control Information
C1	Cycle/Stuff Counter

Figure 4.23 DS1 PLCP Frame format

Frame can begin on any byte within the ESF payload. The DS1 PLCP Frame contains 4608 bits, which is exactly the size of the payload of the ESF (192×24 = 4608). Therefore, the DS1 PLCP Frame period is 3 ms. Given that each L2_PDU can carry 44 bytes of L3_PDU, the DS1 L3_PDU Bandwidth is

$$\text{DS1 L3\_PDU Bandwidth} = \left[\frac{10 \text{ L2\_PDUs}}{3 \times 10^{-3} \text{ sec}}\right] \times \left[44 \frac{\text{bytes}}{\text{L2\_PDU}}\right] \times \left[8 \frac{\text{bits}}{\text{byte}}\right]$$

$$= 1.1733 \text{ Mbps.}$$

The first column of the DS1 PLCP Frame is a 16-bit framing pattern. The second column is used to identify the row number of the DS1 PLCP Frame. When a receiver finds a framing pattern and row number followed by another framing pattern and proper row number 54 bytes (or 60 bytes if the first row number is 00000001$_B$) later, it declares itself as In-Frame. If a receiver detects a framing word with errors in both bytes of the word, then it declares itself Out-Of-Frame (OOF). Also, if two consecutive row-number bytes are invalid or not sequential, then the receiver declares itself OOF. If the OOF condition persists for 24 ms $\pm$ 1 ms, the receiver declares a Loss-Of-Frame (LOF) condition.[24]

---

[24]The OOF and LOF conditions are used to set the LINK STATUS SIGNAL field in the G1 byte, as described below.

The B1 byte is a BIT INTERLEAVED PARITY-8 (BIP-8) code. The first bit of the BIP-8 is set to 1 if the parity of the first bits of the bytes of the previous DS1 PLCP Frame, excluding the trailer, is odd. The second bit of the BIP-8 is computed in a like manner based on the second bits of the bytes of the previous DS1 PLCP Frame, excluding the trailer, and so on for the other bits of the BIP-8.

The G1 byte is the PLCP STATUS byte. The PLCP STATUS is used to convey PLCP performance information from the receiver to the transmitter. It is composed of three subfields, as depicted in Figure 4.24.

Far-End Block Error	Yellow Signal	Link Status Signal
4 bits	1 bit	3 bits

Figure 4.24 PLCP STATUS subfields

The FAR-END BLOCK ERROR (FEBE) contains the number of errors detected by the last received BIP-8. In other words, the last BIP-8 is compared against the receiver's calculation for the PLCP Frame covered by the BIP-8. The number of parity errors (0 to 8) is inserted in the FEBE.

The YELLOW SIGNAL is set to 1 when a PLCP LOF is detected on the incoming PLCP Frame for $2.5 \pm .5$ seconds. Once set, the YELLOW SIGNAL continues to be set until the PLCP LOF ceases for 15 ± 5 seconds. At that time, the YELLOW SIGNAL is set to 0 until the next failure condition.

The LINK STATUS SIGNAL arises from the reconfiguration capability defined in [802.6], which allows a dual bus to reconfigure itself in the face of a link failure. The value is dependent on the framing state of the incoming PLCP Frame and the incoming value of the LINK STATUS SIGNAL. The logic for setting the LINK STATUS SIGNAL is presented in Table 4.8.

Framing state	Incoming Link Status Signal	Outgoing Link Status Signal
Out-Of-Frame	XXX	110_B
Loss-Of-Frame	XXX	011_B
In-Frame	000_B	000_B
In-Frame	110_B	000_B
In-Frame	011_B	110_B

Table 4.8 LINK STATUS SIGNAL logic

The M1 and M2 bytes carry the SIP Level 1 Control Information. This is described in Section 4.7.5.

The C1 byte is called the CYCLE/STUFF COUNTER. For the DS1 PLCP, it has no function. It is included to maintain similarity with the format of the DS3 PLCP Frame. It is always set to 00000000_B.

The TRAILER is used to pad out the DS1 PLCP Frame so that it is equal in length to the ESF payload. Each of the 6 bytes is set to 11001100_B.

4.7.2   SIP Level 1 Based on DS3

SIP Level 1 based on DS3 is meant for customers with high bandwidth needs. Although higher-speed SNIs based on SONET [253] will be offered in the future, the lack of widespread deployment of SONET makes DS3 the preferred approach for early SMDS deployment.

4.7.2.1   DS3 Physical Medium Dependent Protocol

Figure 4.25 shows the DS3 M-Frame. A DS-3 M-frame consists of 7 subframes that are each divided into 8 blocks of 85 bits. A block consists of one overhead (O) bit and 84 bits of payload. The DS3 M-Frame duration is 106.4 µsec which gives a payload bandwidth of slightly more than 44.21 Mbps. The overhead bits are used for various framing, maintenance, and operations functions. Among such functions is the C-Bit Parity Application [T1.107a]. Because much telephone network equipment does not implement the C-Bit Parity Application, [773] does not specify its use. However, new CPE DS3 hardware is likely to include this capability. As described in [SIG.cbit], there is a remote chance that CPE executing the C-Bit Parity Application could experience problems when connected to an SS that does not support the application. Therefore, as recommended in [SIG.cbit], we recommend that CPE with the C-Bit Parity Application have the option to disable the application.

4.7.2.2   DS3 Physical Layer Convergence Procedure

Figure 4.26 shows the format of the DS3 PLCP Frame. As already described, this frame is meant to delimit L2_PDUs and provide maintenance, monitoring, and operations support. It has a very similar structure to that of the DS1 PLCP Frame.

The DS3 PLCP Frame can appear anywhere within the DS3 payload, provided that the first bit after each DS3 M-Frame overhead bit is the first bit of a DS3 PLCP Frame nibble. Since the duration of the DS3 PLCP Frame averages 125 µsec, its start is forever changing relative to the start of the DS3 M-Frame, which has a duration of 106.4 µsec. Given that each L2_PDU can carry 44 bytes of L3_PDU, the DS3 L3_PDU Bandwidth is

Subframe 1	O	Payload	O	Payload	O	Payload	O	Payload
	O	Payload	O	Payload	O	Payload	O	Payload
Subframe 2	O	Payload	O	Payload	O	Payload	O	Payload
	O	Payload	O	Payload	O	Payload	O	Payload
Subframe 3	O	Payload	O	Payload	O	Payload	O	Payload
	O	Payload	O	Payload	O	Payload	O	Payload
Subframe 4	O	Payload	O	Payload	O	Payload	O	Payload
	O	Payload	O	Payload	O	Payload	O	Payload
Subframe 5	O	Payload	O	Payload	O	Payload	O	Payload
	O	Payload	O	Payload	O	Payload	O	Payload
Subframe 6	O	Payload	O	Payload	O	Payload	O	Payload
	O	Payload	O	Payload	O	Payload	O	Payload
Subframe 7	O	Payload	O	Payload	O	Payload	O	Payload
	O	Payload	O	Payload	O	Payload	O	Payload

```
1    84    1    84    1    84    1    84
```
Lengths are in bits

Figure 4.25 DS3 M-Frame format

1111011000101000_B	00101101_B	00000000_B	L2_PDU	
1111011000101000_B	00101001_B	00000000_B	L2_PDU	
1111011000101000_B	00100101_B	00000000_B	L2_PDU	
1111011000101000_B	00100000_B	00000000_B	L2_PDU	
1111011000101000_B	00011100_B	00000000_B	L2_PDU	
1111011000101000_B	00011001_B	00000000_B	L2_PDU	
1111011000101000_B	00010101_B	00000000_B	L2_PDU	
1111011000101000_B	00010000_B	B1	L2_PDU	
1111011000101000_B	00001101_B	G1	L2_PDU	
1111011000101000_B	00001000_B	M2	L2_PDU	
1111011000101000_B	00000100_B	M1	L2_PDU	
1111011000101000_B	00000001_B	C1	L2_PDU	Trailer

```
2 bytes        1 byte      1 byte      53 bytes   52 or 56 bits
```

Key

B1	Bit Interleaved Parity
G1	PLCP Path Status
M1, M2	SIP Level 1 Control Information
C1	Cycle/Stuff Counter

Figure 4.26 DS3 PLCP Frame format

$$\text{DS3 L3\_PDU Bandwidth} = \left[\frac{12 \text{ L2\_PDUs}}{125 \times 10^{-6} \text{ sec}}\right] \times \left[44 \frac{\text{bytes}}{\text{L2\_PDU}}\right] \times \left[8 \frac{\text{bits}}{\text{byte}}\right]$$

$$= 33.792 \text{ Mbps.}$$

The first column of the DS3 PLCP Frame is a 16-bit framing pattern. The second column is used to identify the row number of the DS3 PLCP Frame. When a receiver finds a framing pattern and row number followed by another framing pattern and the next row number at the proper place in the serial bit stream, it declares itself as In-Frame. If a receiver detects a framing word with errors in both bytes of the word, then it declares itself Out-Of-Frame (OOF). Also, if two consecutive row-number bytes are invalid or not sequential, then the receiver declares itself OOF. If the OOF condition persists for 1 ms, the receiver declares a Loss-Of-Frame (LOF) condition.[25]

The B1 byte is a BIT INTERLEAVED PARITY-8 (BIP-8) code. The first bit of the BIP-8 is set to 1 if the parity of first bits of the bytes of the previous DS3 PLCP Frame, excluding the trailer, is odd. The second bit of the BIP-8 is computed in a like manner based on the second bits of the bytes of the previous DS3 PLCP Frame, excluding the trailer, and so on for the other bits of the BIP-8.

The G1 byte is the PLCP STATUS byte. The PLCP STATUS is used to convey PLCP performance information from the receiver to the transmitter. It is composed of three subfields as depicted in Figure 4.24. These subfields, FAR-END BLOCK ERROR (FEBE), YELLOW SIGNAL , and LINK STATUS SIGNAL have the same functions and interpretations as the fields of the same name in the DS1 PLCP (see Section 4.7.1.2).

The M1 and M2 bytes carry the SIP LEVEL 1 CONTROL INFORMATION. This is described in Section 4.7.5.

The value of the CYCLE/STUFF COUNTER is correlated with the length of the TRAILER. Table 4.9 shows the encoding of the CYCLE/STUFF COUNTER and the related TRAILER lengths.

Bellcore [773] requires the SS to cycle through the CYCLE/STUFF COUNTER codes and to stuff (using 14 trailer nibbles) in the third frame in such a manner that the DS3 PLCP Frame has an average period of 125 μsec. We recommend that CPE operate in the same way.

---

[25]The OOF and LOF conditions are used to set the LINK STATUS SIGNAL field in the G1 byte, as described below.

Cycle/Stuff code	Frame in cycle	Trailer length (nibbles)
11111111_B	1	13
00000000_B	2	14
01100110_B	3 (not stuff)	13
10011001_B	3 (stuff)	14

Table 4.9 CYCLE/STUFF COUNTER codes and TRAILER length

4.7.3   SIP Level 1 Based on E1

E1 is the European peer of the North American DS1. The nominal bit rate is 2.048 Mbps. The physical and electrical characteristics of the E1 signal are standardized in [G.703] and [ESIG002]. The E1 transmission frame is standardized in [G.704].

4.7.3.1   E1 Physical Medium Dependent Protocol

The E1 transmission frame as used for SMDS is depicted in Figure 4.27 [ESIG002]. The frame is 32 bytes long, of which the first byte is used as frame overhead, and the 17th byte is filled with the HDLC flag. The transmission-frame rate is 8 KHz, which makes the frame duration 125 μsec. This corresponds to a payload bandwidth of 1.920 Mbps.

(See Figure 4.28)	E1 Payload	01111110_B	E1 Payload
1 byte	15 bytes	1 byte	15 bytes

Figure 4.27 E1 Frame format

The 17th byte, the Signaling Slot, is not used in this case, and is always filled with the HDLC flag 01111110_B. The first byte, Slot 0, is used for alignment and to convey management information. This is defined in [G.704] and shown in Figure 4.28. The alignment signal is 0011011_B.

Alignment Frame	Si	0	0	1	1	0	1	1
Non-alignment Frame	Si	1	A	Sa4	Sa5	Sa6	Sa7	Sa8
Bit	1	2	3	4	5	6	7	8

Figure 4.28 Slot 0 of the E1 frame

For SMDS, the first bit in Slot 0 is used for the CRC-4 multiframe structure, which is explained below. The A-bit in the non-alignment frame indicates the remote alarm status: 1 signifies an alarm, and 0 indicates normal operation. Bits Sa4, Sa7, and Sa8 are not used for SMDS and should be set to 1 by the CPE. Bits Sa5 and Sa6 are used in loopback situations, as described in Chapters 11 and 12.

The purpose of the CRC-4 procedure in the first bit of the E1 frame is to provide additional protection against simulation of the frame-alignment signal. The recommendation, [G.704], defines the procedure to use it. The CRC-4 multiframe structure is recreated in Figure 4.29.

Sub-multiframe	Frame									
	0	C1	0	0	1	1	0	1	1
	1	0	1	A	Sa4	Sa5	Sa6	Sa7	Sa8
	2	C2	0	0	1	1	0	1	1
1	3	0	1	A	Sa4	Sa5	Sa6	Sa7	Sa8
	4	C3	0	0	1	1	0	1	1
	5	1	1	A	Sa4	Sa5	Sa6	Sa7	Sa8
	6	C4	0	0	1	1	0	1	1
	7	0	1	A	Sa4	Sa5	Sa6	Sa7	Sa8
	8	C1	0	0	1	1	0	1	1
	9	1	1	A	Sa4	Sa5	Sa6	Sa7	Sa8
	10	C2	0	0	1	1	0	1	1
2	11	1	1	A	Sa4	Sa5	Sa6	Sa7	Sa8
	12	C3	0	0	1	1	0	1	1
	13	E	1	A	Sa4	Sa5	Sa6	Sa7	Sa8
	14	C4	0	0	1	1	0	1	1
	15	E	1	A	Sa4	Sa5	Sa6	Sa7	Sa8
		1	2	3	4	5	6	7	8	bit

Figure 4.29 CRC-4 Multiframe structure

Figure 4.29 shows that each CRC-4 multiframe is composed of two sub-multiframes, each consisting of eight E1 frames, which corresponds to the CRC-4 block size (2,048 bits). A set of C1-C4 bits contains the CRC calculated over the *previous* sub-multiframe, with C1 being the most significant bit of the CRC. The CRC value is encoded by first setting the C-bits of a sub-multiframe to 0. Then the contents of the sub-multiframe (treated as a polynomial) are multiplied by x^4 and the result is divided (modulo 2) by the generator polynomial of degree 4, $G(x) = x^4 + x + 1$. The resulting remainder is placed in the C-bits of the next sub-multiframe.[26] The E-bits are used to flag received errored sub-multiframes. One E-bit should be set from 1 to 0 for each received errored sub-multiframe within 1 second after receipt.

---

[26]As an interesting exercise, the reader is challenged to determine the number of CRCs that "protect" a SIP protocol stack.

4.7.3.2   E1 Physical Layer Convergence Procedure

Figure 4.30 shows the format of the E1 PLCP Frame as standardized in [ETSI213]. The format is very similar to that of the DS1 PLCP, but in this case the frame consists of 10 rows of 57 bytes.

1111011000101000_B	00100101_B	00000000_B	L2_PDU
1111011000101000_B	00100000_B	00000000_B	L2_PDU
1111011000101000_B	00011100_B	00000000_B	L2_PDU
1111011000101000_B	00011001_B	00000000_B	L2_PDU
1111011000101000_B	00010101_B	F1	L2_PDU
1111011000101000_B	00010000_B	B1	L2_PDU
1111011000101000_B	00001101_B	G1	L2_PDU
1111011000101000_B	00001000_B	M2	L2_PDU
1111011000101000_B	00000100_B	M1	L2_PDU
1111011000101000_B	00000001_B	C1	L2_PDU
2 bytes	1 byte	1 byte	53 bytes

Key

B1	Bit Interleaved Parity
G1	PLCP Status
M1, M2	SIP Level 1 Control Information
C1	Cycle/Stuff Counter

Figure 4.30 E1 PLCP Frame format

The first two columns, the 16-bit framing pattern and the row identification, are identical with that of the DS1 PLCP (compare with Figure 4.23, starting from the last row). The next column is also largely the same, and has only two deviations. ETSI has reserved the F1 byte for future standardization of PLCP peer-to-peer communication. However, for the time being, the F1 byte is set to 00000000_B, which makes it identical to the DS1 PLCP case. No Trailer is needed.

The CYCLE/STUFF COUNTER C1 therefore has no function in this case and is set to 00000000_B. The L3_PDU Bandwidth is calculated in the same way as shown for the DS1 and DS3 cases. The E1 PLCP Frame contains 4560 bits, which corresponds to the payload of 19 E1 frames. Thus, the E1 PLCP Frame period is 19×125 μsec = 2.375 ms, and the E1 L3_PDU Bandwidth is

$$\text{E1 L3\_PDU Bandwidth} = \left[\frac{10 \text{ L2\_PDUs}}{2.375 \times 10^{-3} \text{ sec}}\right] \times \left[44 \frac{\text{bytes}}{\text{L2\_PDU}}\right] \times \left[8 \frac{\text{bits}}{\text{byte}}\right]$$

$$= 1.4821 \text{ Mbps.}$$

4.7.4   SIP Level 1 Based on E3

E3 is the European peer of DS3. The nominal bit rate is 34.368 Mbps. The physical and electrical characteristics of the E3 signal are standardized in [G.703]. The E3 transmission frame is standardized in [G.751].

4.7.4.1   E3 Physical Medium Dependent Protocol

The frame as used for SMDS is depicted in Figure 4.31 [ESIG002]. The E3 transmission frame is 1536 bits long, of which the first 16 bits are the frame overhead. The transmission frame rate is 22.375 KHz which corresponds to a payload bandwidth of 34.01 Mbps. The REMOTE ALARM INDICATION is set to 1 for an alarm condition. The bit for NATIONAL USE is set to 1 if not used.

1111010000_B	Remote Alarm Indication	National Use	1100_B	E3 Payload
10 bits	1 bit	1 bit	4 bits	1520 bits

Figure 4.31 E3 Frame format

4.7.4.2   E3 Physical Layer Convergence Procedure

Figure 4.32 shows the format of the E3 PLCP Frame as standardized in [ETSI214]. The format is very similar to that of the DS3 PLCP, but in this case the frame consists of 9 rows of 57 bytes.

The first two columns, the 16-bit framing pattern and the row identification, are identical with those of the DS3 PLCP (compare with Figure 4.26, starting from the last row). The next column is also largely the same, and has only two deviations. ETSI has reserved the F1 byte for future standardization of PLCP peer-to-peer communication. However, for the time being, the byte is set to 00000000_B, which makes it identical to the DS3 PLCP case. The other difference is the encoding of the CYCLE/STUFF COUNTER C1 and the related TRAILER length. Table 4.10 shows the C1 values and the corresponding TRAILER lengths [ESIG002].

The calculation of the E3 L3_PDU Bandwidth is the same as for the DS3 L3_PDU Bandwidth (see Section 4.7.2.2). Like the DS3 PLCP Frame, the E3 PLCP Frame is 125 μsec, but the E3 PLCP Frame contains 9 L2_PDUs instead of 12. Thus, the E3 L3_PDU Bandwidth is 3/4 of the DS3 L3_PDU bandwidth:

1111011000101000$_B$	00100000$_B$	00000000$_B$	L2_PDU	
1111011000101000$_B$	00011100$_B$	00000000$_B$	L2_PDU	
1111011000101000$_B$	00011001$_B$	00000000$_B$	L2_PDU	
1111011000101000$_B$	00010101$_B$	F1	L2_PDU	
1111011000101000$_B$	00010000$_B$	B1	L2_PDU	
1111011000101000$_B$	00001101$_B$	G1	L2_PDU	
1111011000101000$_B$	00001000$_B$	M2	L2_PDU	
1111011000101000$_B$	00000100$_B$	M1	L2_PDU	
1111011000101000$_B$	00000001$_B$	C1	L2_PDU	Trailer
2 bytes	1 byte	1 byte	53 bytes	17 to 21 bytes

Key

B1	Bit Interleaved Parity
G1	PLCP Status
M1, M2	SIP Level 1 Control Information
C1	Cycle/Stuff Counter

Figure 4.32 E3 PLCP Frame format

Cycle/Stuff code	Trailer length (bytes)
00111011$_B$	17
01001111$_B$	18
01110101$_B$	19
10011101$_B$	20
10100111$_B$	21

Table 4.10 E3 PLCP CYCLE/STUFF COUNTER codes and TRAILER length

$$\text{E3 L3\_PDU Bandwidth} = \left[\frac{9 \text{ L2\_PDUs}}{125 \times 10^{-6} \text{ sec}} \right] \times \left[44 \frac{\text{bytes}}{\text{L2\_PDU}} \right] \times \left[8 \frac{\text{bits}}{\text{byte}} \right]$$

$$= 25.344 \text{ Mbps.}$$

4.7.5   SIP Level 1 Control Information

The SIP LEVEL 1 CONTROL INFORMATION, carried in the PLCP M1 and M2 bytes, corresponds to the DQDB Layer Management Information of [802.6]. In the context of [802.6], it is used to effect reconfiguration of the dual bus topology in the face of failures, and it is used to distribute MIDs. However, since the SS never participates in a DQDB reconfiguration, it does not process the SIP

Level 1 Control Information that is received from CPE. In addition, the codes that the SS generates are restricted when compared to what can be generated according to [802.6].

There are two types of SIP Level 1 Control Information bytes. In the context of [802.6], Type 0 is used for reconfiguration, and Type 1 is used for MID distribution. One of each type is contained in each PLCP Frame. If the M1 byte contains the first type, then M2 contains the second type and vice versa. Figures 4.33 and 4.34 show the fields for the two types of SIP Level 1 Control Information bytes. The first bit in each byte indicates the type.

0_B	Bus Identification	SubNetwork Configuration
1 bit	2 bits	5 bits

Figure 4.33 Type 0 SIP Level 1 Control Information format

1_B	0_B	Page Reservation	Page Counter Modulus	Page Counter Control
1 bit	1 bit	2 bits	2 bits	2 bits

Figure 4.34 Type 1 SIP Level 1 Control Information format

The SS populates these fields as follows. The Bus Identification field is set to 01_B. In the context of [802.6], this is identifying the transmission path from the SS as Bus A. The SubNetwork Configuration field is set to 11011_B. In the context of [802.6], this is specifying that a Default Slot Generator is present, namely the SS; that the Head-of-Bus, the SS, is stable; and that an External Timing Source, the SS, is present.

The Page Reservation field, the Page Counter Modulus field, and the Page Counter Control field are set according to a cycle of period 1023. Table 4.11 defines how these fields are set. In the context of [802.6], these values reserve the MID values 1 through 511 for use by the SS. Thus, CPE using the MID allocation algorithm (see Appendix A) can use MID values 512 through 1023.[27]

Since the SS does not process the incoming SIP Level 1 Control Information, CPE is free to set it to any arbitrary value. For multi-CPE configurations, we recommend following the specifications in Section 10 of [802.6]. For the single-CPE configuration, constant values can be used, as described in Section 4.8.3.

---

[27]Recall that the SS does not check that CPE stations are using MID values within this range. The generation of Type 1 SIP Level 1 Control Information is to facilitate the Multi-CPE configuration.

Cycle number	Page Reservation	Page Counter Modulus	Page Counter Control
1 through 511	11_B	(Cycle Number) mod 4	10_B
512 through 1022	00_B	(Cycle Number) mod 4	10_B
1023	00_B	(Cycle Number) mod 4	01_B

Table 4.11 Codes for Type 1 SIP LEVEL 1 CONTROL INFORMATION

4.8   Recommended Minimum CPE Implementation

Although SIP was designed so that CPE conforming to [802.6] could access the service, such conformance is not necessary. In this section we make recommendations for CPE implementations that are less complex than full conformance to [802.6] requires. Our recommendations are organized according to the SIP layers.

4.8.1   Minimum SIP Level 3 Implementation

We expect that Level 3 will be where CPE vendors will try to differentiate their products. For example, the ability of CPE to check the Destination Address of a received L3_PDU to confirm that it is correct could be a security feature that double-checks SMDS. Another example is the ability to generate and validate the optional 32-bit CRC. Hence, we have just one recommendation for Level 3.

We recommend against the use of the HEADER EXTENSION field for Carrier Selection (Explicit Carrier Selection). Instead, we recommend that Carrier Pre-selection be used and that the Customer Network Management features described in Chapter 12 be used to attain flexible Carrier Selection. The reason for this recommendation is that the Carrier Selection features specified in [1060] require complex configuration within CPE to attain desirable service behavior when using Explicit Carrier Selection.[28] For example, if Explicit Carrier Selection is used and the Destination Address for the L3_PDU is an Embodied SAC (see Section 3.4.1), then the L3_PDU will be discarded by SMDS. Another possible example arises when (some) LECs use the Carrier Selection specified in Section 3.5.3 of [1060]. For these LECs, as described in Section 3.4.7, it is likely that the use of Explicit Carrier Selection with an L3_PDU that has a Destination

---

[28]These carrier-selection procedures defined in [1060] are a straight adaptation of the rules that apply to telephone calls, with each L3_PDU treated like a telephone call for the purposes of carrier selection. There is no technical reason for this alignment. Rather than speculate on the business reasons for this approach, we prefer to view it as another "Great Moment in Divestiture."

Address within the same LATA will result in the L3_PDU being discarded. For other LECs, the same situation will result in delivery of the L3_PDU. Clearly, to avoid this inconsistent and confusing behavior will require that complex data bases be maintained in the CPE.[29] By far the most straightforward solution is to use Carrier Pre-selection and to ensure that the HEADER EXTENSION field is always populated as in the first example in Figure 4.15.

4.8.2   Minimum SIP Level 2 Implementation

The assumptions underlying the minimum Level-2 implementation are:

1. Single-CPE configuration

2. MCDUs In = MCDUs Out = 1.

Because there is no interleaving of L3_PDUs, only two MID values are needed; 0 for SSMs and an arbitrary value for BOMs, COMs, and EOM. A reasonable value is 1000000001_B. Therefore, the L2_PDUs generated reduce to the cases shown in Figure 4.35.

In receiving, the CPE discards all empty L2_PDUs (which have the first bit set to 0). Nonempty L2_PDUs with invalid PAYLOAD CRC fields or invalid NETWORK CONTROL INFORMATION fields are also discarded. Nonempty L2_PDUs with valid PAYLOAD CRC fields and valid NETWORK CONTROL INFORMATION fields whose SEGMENT TYPE fields contain SSM are processed by extracting the data from the SEGMENTATION UNIT field and initiating the L3_PDU processing. All other L2_PDUs are passed to a single reassembly process, whose behavior is described by the state machine shown in Figure 4.36. In Figure 4.36, the conditions that cause a state transition are listed above the arrow representing the transition. The actions taken in association with each state transition are listed below the corresponding arrow. Each state transition is discussed below.

- **(IA1)** This is the normal initiation of a reassembly. In addition to storing the fragment of the L3_PDU, the system calculates the expected value of the next SEQUENCE NUMBER field.

- **(AA1)** This is the normal continuation of a reassembly when a COM is received. The fragment of the L3_PDU is appended to the fragments already received, and the expected value of the next SEQUENCE NUMBER field is updated.

---

[29]One possible way to deal with this problem is to have SMDS customers include a lawyer in their network management staff. This might not make the customer's network perform better, but it does provide someone to blame for the problems.

00000 . . . 0$_B$
53 bytes

Empty L2_PDU

80FFFFF022$_H$	40 bits
11$_B$	2 bits
Sequence Number	4 bits
0000000000$_B$	10 bits
Segmentation Unit	44 bytes
Payload Length	6 bits
Payload CRC	10 bits

SSM L2_PDU

80FFFFF022$_H$	40 bits
10$_B$, 00$_B$, or 01$_B$	2 bits
Sequence Number	4 bits
1000000001$_B$	10 bits
Segmentation Unit	44 bytes
Payload Length	6 bits
Payload CRC	10 bits

BOM, COM, and EOM L2_PDU

Figure 4.35 Minimum implementation L2_PDUs

- **(AI1)** This is the normal completion of a reassembly process. The last fragment of the L3_PDU is appended to the fragments already received to complete the reconstruction of the L3_PDU.

- **(AA2)** This represents an error condition, typically that an EOM was lost. The received BOM causes a new reassembly to be initiated. This transition is dependent on the SS using a single MID value as specified in [772].

- **(II1)** This represents an error that is the loss of a BOM. The COMs and EOM associated with the lost BOM are discarded.

- **(AI2)** This transition is the result of a lost COM or EOM, as detected by the SEQUENCE NUMBER field. The partially constructed L3_PDU is discarded.

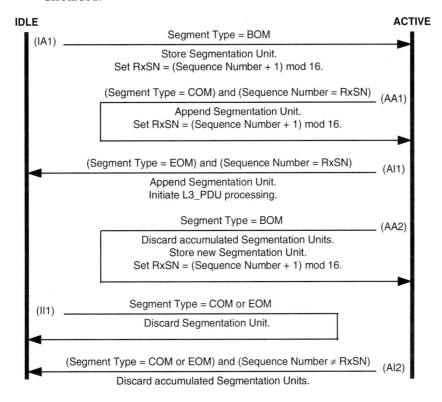

Figure 4.36 Minimum implementation reassembly process

4.8.3   Minimum SIP Level 1 Implementation

Once again we assume the single-CPE configuration. Since the SS ignores the SIP LEVEL 1 CONTROL INFORMATION and both reconfiguration and MID allocation are meaningless in the single-CPE configuration case, the SIP LEVEL 1 CONTROL INFORMATION can be set to arbitrary, constant values. For Type 0, we recommend the value 01000010_B, which, in the context of [802.6], corresponds to Bus B, Default Slot Generator is not present, Head-of-Bus is stable, and External Timing Source is not present.[30] For Type 1, we recommend the value 00000001_B, which, in the context of [802.6] means that MID Page 1 is not reserved (see Appendix A).

---

[30]These are values consistent with [802.6] for the Type 0 values generated by the SS.

4.9 Access Class Implementation

This section contains a detailed description of how Access Classes are defined. Section 3.4.6 discusses the use of Access Classes. The design goals for the Access Class definition include simplicity, limited constraint on bursts of data, and the potential for implementation of a parallel algorithm in CPE. The latter goal deserves some discussion.

If SMDS tariffs are very sensitive to the Access Class, then there may be motivation for buffering in the CPE to allow the use of a lower Access Class. In other words, it might be desirable for a traffic smoothing function to be implemented in the CPE. The algorithm is designed to allow this option.

Access Classes are implemented with a Credit Manager Algorithm. The algorithm is a leaky bucket procedure. Consider a bucket with a leak in the bottom. Pouring a single glass of water (a burst) into the bucket will not overflow the bucket. Indeed, depending on the relative sizes of the glass and bucket, several glasses could be dumped into the bucket, but there is a limit (the maximum credit) on how many glasses can be quickly poured into the bucket before it starts to overflow. If there is a time interval when no glasses are poured, the leak creates additional capacity (credit) in the bucket for future glasses. Note that the long-term average rate of water pouring is just the leak rate of the bucket.[31]

In the Credit Manager Algorithm, the rate at which credit is incremented is expressed by a number of L2_PDUs received as opposed to a time interval. This is done to give both the SS and the CPE a common timing reference, namely counts of L2_PDUs. Since the PLCPs for DS3 and E3 carry an integral number of L2_PDUs every 125 µsec, the 8-MHz clock can also be used as the reference for the Credit Manager Algorithm.

4.9.1 Access Class Parameters

Three parameters define an instance of an Access Class:

1. C_{max} is the maximum amount of credit that can accrue. The credit is set to this value when the Credit Manager Algorithm is started.

2. I_{inc} is the interval between increments in the available credit, measured in received L2_PDUs (both empty and nonempty). I_{inc} is always integer-valued.

3. N_{inc} is the amount the credit is incremented every I_{inc} L2_PDU times.

---

[31]This ignores the fact that, in real leaky buckets, the flow rate will vary with the water level in the bucket. Such an approximation is reasonable, since things like gravity and mass do not exist above OSI Layer 1.

4.9.2   Credit Manager Algorithm Description

The Credit Manager Algorithm is described below as a series of steps and branches. This series of steps is carried out each time an L2_PDU (either empty or nonempty) is received by the SS. Three variables are used in the algorithm:

1. *Debit* is the amount of credit that an L3_PDU will consume if enough credit is available.

2. *Balance* is the credit available at any given instance of the reception of an L2_PDU. The initial value of *Balance* is C_{max}.

3. *Count* is the number of L2_PDUs that must be received before the next credit increment. The initial value of *Count* is I_{inc}.

In addition, the algorithm must check for valid BOMs and SSMs. BOMs and SSMs are valid if the following are true:

1. The NETWORK CONTROL INFORMATION field is valid (see Section 4.6.2).

2. The MID value is 0 for SSMs and $\neq 0$ for BOMs.

3. The PAYLOAD LENGTH field is valid (see Section 4.6.7).

4. The PAYLOAD CRC field is valid (see Section 4.6.8).

5. The format of the DESTINATION ADDRESS field[32] is valid (see Section 4.5.4).

6. The DESTINATION ADDRESS is not an Individual Address associated with the ingress SNI.

The steps in the Credit Manager Algorithm follows:

Step 1:   If the L2_PDU is a valid BOM or SSM, go to Step 2; else, go to Step 3.

Step 2:   Set *Debit* = max(0, BASIZE − 36).[33] If *Balance* < *Debit*, discard the L3_PDU; else, set *Balance* = *Balance* − *Debit*.

---

[32]Recall that the L3_PDU address fields are contained in BOMs and SSMs.

[33]Ideally, the *Debit* should equal the number of bytes in the INFORMATION field. The precise length of the INFORMATION field is BASIZE − PAD LENGTH − 32 if the CRC32 is not present. It is BASIZE − PAD LENGTH − 36 if the CRC32 is present. The extra accuracy of these calculations is not deemed to justify the added implementation complexity, and thus the BASIZE − 36 approximation is used. Note that this approximation can be a negative number, and thus the max function is used in the algorithm.

Step 3:   Set *Count* = *Count* − 1. If *Count* = 0, set *Count* = I_{inc} and set *Balance*
            = min(C_{max}, *Balance* + N_{inc}).

4.9.3   CPE Version of the Credit Manager Algorithm

It is probably impossible to implement the Credit Manager Algorithm in the
multi-CPE configuration. Therefore, we assume the single-CPE configuration.
Furthermore, we assume that MCDUs In = 1.

The Credit Manager Algorithm in the CPE makes use of the same
parameters and variables as for the SS version (see Sections 4.9.1 and 4.9.2).
The algorithm follows:

Step 1:   If the L2_PDU to be sent is nonempty and is either a BOM or a
            SSM, go to Step 2; else, go to Step 3.

Step 2:   Set *Debit* = max(0, BASIZE − 36). If *Balance* ≥ *Debit*, transmit the
            L2_PDU, and set *Balance* = *Balance* − *Debit*; else, send an empty
            L2_PDU and try to send the current L2_PDU at the next transmit
            opportunity.

Step 3:   Set *Count* = *Count* − 1. If *Count* = 0, set *Count* = I_{inc}, and set
            Balance = min(C_{max}, *Balance* + N_{inc}).

If the SS finds all BOMs and SSMs to be valid, then the CPE and the SS
will have synchronized views of the available credit. In the case that not all
BOMs and SSMs are found to be valid by the SS (e.g., there is a transmission
error on the SNI), the SS view of the remaining credit will be higher than the
CPE view. Thus, CPE running this algorithm can successfully avoid discard of
L3_PDUs by the SS due to Access Class Violation. Furthermore, both sides will
become resynchronized during idle periods when both values of *Balance* will
increase to C_{max}.

4.9.4   Access Class Parameter Values

In choosing an Access Class, it is important to understand how the Credit
Manager Algorithm parameters relate to the maximum information transfer rate
that can be sustained, the Sustained Information Rate (SIR), and the amount of
allowed "burstiness." The SIR for DS3-based SNIs is just the rate at which credit
is incremented. It is given by the following equation:

$$\text{SIR}_{\text{DS3}} = \left[8\,\frac{\text{bits}}{\text{byte}}\right] \times \left[\frac{12\ \text{L2\_PDUs}}{125\ \mu\text{sec}}\right] \times \left[\frac{N_{\text{inc}}\ \text{bytes}}{I_{\text{inc}}\ \text{L2\_PDUs}}\right]\ \text{Mbps}.$$

For E3-based SNIs, the SIR is given by the following equation:

$$\text{SIR}_{\text{E3}} = \left[8\,\frac{\text{bits}}{\text{byte}}\right] \times \left[\frac{9\ \text{L2\_PDUs}}{125\ \mu\text{sec}}\right] \times \left[\frac{N_{\text{inc}}\ \text{bytes}}{I_{\text{inc}}\ \text{L2\_PDUs}}\right]\ \text{Mbps}.$$

The burstiness is a bit more complex. As the L2_PDUs of an L3_PDU are transmitted, the Credit Manager Algorithm replenishes the credit. Thus, if an L3_PDU is sized to just exhaust the available credit (*Balance* = 0 after Step 2), by the time the L3_PDU is completed, there will usually be credit available, and another smaller L3_PDU can be sent. If we define a burst as the amount of L3_PDU bytes that can be sent in contiguous L3_PDUs, then an estimate of the Maximum Burst Size can be made as follows. If we assume that each L2_PDU contains 44 bytes of payload, then it represents 44 bytes of spent credit. However, it also results in credit being incremented by about $N_{\text{inc}}/I_{\text{inc}}$. Thus, there is a net rate of credit loss for each nonempty L2_PDU. Dividing this rate into C_{max} yields an estimate of the number of L2_PDUs in a Maximum Burst. Multiplying by 44 for the payload in each L2_PDU yields the following result:

$$\text{Maximum Burst Size} = \left[\frac{C_{\text{max}}}{44 - \dfrac{N_{\text{inc}}}{I_{\text{inc}}}}\right] \times 44\ = \left[\frac{I_{\text{inc}} \times C_{\text{max}}}{44 \times I_{\text{inc}} - N_{\text{inc}}}\right] \times 44\ \text{bytes}.$$

Since this equation is independent of the L2_PDU rate, it applies to both DS3-based and E3-based access to SMDS.

As described in Section 3.4.6, the parameters for the Credit Manager Algorithm are chosen such that SIRs exist to match common LAN transmission rates. The C_{max} parameter is chosen to guarantee that at least one maximum-size L3_PDU can be transmitted. Table 4.12 shows the SIR and Maximum Burst Size for the five Access Classes currently defined for SMDS with DS3-based access. Table 4.13 shows the SIR and Maximum Burst Size for the four Access Classes currently defined for SMDS with E3-based access.

Tables 4.12 and 4.13 can be used as aids in determining the appropriate Access Class. Approaches to choosing a proper Access Class are discussed in Chapter 3.

Class number	Parameters			Sustained Information Rate (Mbps)	Maximum Burst Size (bytes)
	N_{inc}	I_{inc}	C_{max}		
1	26	5	9188	3.99	10419
2	13	1	9188	9.98	13041
3	21	1	9188	16.12	17577
4	32	1	9188	24.57	33689
5	—	—	—	33.79	∞

Note: The Credit Manager Algorithm is not applied for Access Class 5, and thus no parameters are defined

Table 4.12 Details of the Access Classes for DS3-based access to SMDS

Class number	Parameters			Sustained Information Rate (Mbps)	Maximum Burst Size (bytes)
	N_{inc}	I_{inc}	C_{max}		
1	7	1	9188	4.03	10926
2	35	2	9188	10.08	15256
3	28	1	9188	16.13	25267
4	—	—	—	25.34	∞

Note: The Credit Manager Algorithm is not applied for Access Class 4, and thus no parameters are defined

Table 4.13 Details of the Access Classes for E3-based access to SMDS

5

Data Exchange Interface

As the CPE for SMDS has evolved, a very common method of implementing SIP is to implement the higher levels in a router or end system, and the lower levels in a separate device, the Channel Service Unit/Data Service Unit (CSU/DSU). The interface between the CSU/DSU and the router or end system is the SMDS Data Exchange Interface Protocol (DXI) [SIG001]. This arrangement is illustrated in Figure 5.1. The primary reason for this configuration is that it allows the router or end system to access SMDS with only a software upgrade for the support of SIP Level 3. (For simplicity in the remainder of the chapter, we call the device connected to the CSU/DSU via the DXI a *router*, with the understanding that it could also be an end system.) The lower levels of the DXI use commonly implemented physical and link layer protocols.

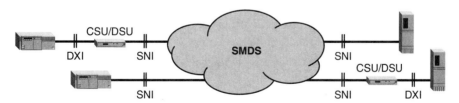

Figure 5.1 CPE with integrated and separate CSU/DSU configuration

Interestingly, the use of the DXI has since its inception been taken beyond its original purpose. MCI [MCI] announced its use of the DXI as the basis for direct access to SMDS (albeit, based on different physical transmission facilities), and has proposed a specification for this purpose. This simple approach has been adopted by the SIG and by Bellcore [SIG005] [1239].

This chapter describes the DXI in Sections 5.1 and 5.2. Direct access to SMDS via the DXI is discussed in Section 5.3. There is also a management protocol associated with the DXI, the DXI *Local Management Interface* (LMI) [SIG002], which is described in Chapter 11.

CPE designers should find this chapter helpful in evaluating the various CPE alternatives for accessing SMDS. SMDS users should find this chapter useful for understanding the DXI and the needs of their SMDS access configuration.

5.1   CSU/DSU Function

In North America, special equipment is traditionally used at customer premises to isolate and protect network facilities from harmful signals and voltages over the access line. This was required by the U.S. Federal Communications Commission, and is usually implemented by devices called *Channel Service Units*, or *CSUs*. In the last decade, a competitive industry developed that resulted in CSUs with additional functions beyond their original purpose. For example, the CSU/DSU vendors developed expertise for obtaining certification from carriers around the world, a significant undertaking, given the many carriers and the variations in the requirements for their interfaces. An informative overview of this development is described in [Brown] and [RuxLiles].

Originally, the CSU would perform functions such as checking bipolar violations (see Chapter 11) and performing loopbacks. The need to transport data besides voice traffic introduced additional functionality. These devices are usually referred to as *Data Service Units* or *DSUs*. The Extended Superframe Format (ESF, see Section 4.7) introduced additional capabilities for the monitoring and management of the circuit. The result was that CSU/DSUs became much more than simple line terminators. They could now also provide flexible and useful management functions. Today, many CSU/DSUs can be configured to connect to DS1 and DS3, as well as to E1 and E3.

For SMDS, the existence of the CSU/DSU market meant that there were technical alternatives to connect CPE to SMDS. On the one hand, routers, bridges or host computers can implement the CSU/DSU functions directly. We call this the *Integrated DSU Configuration*. On the other hand, separate CSU/DSUs can be used, which avoids the need for integrating these functions in devices such as routers. However, this means that two separate devices are required to connect to SMDS, and that these devices must communicate with each other. We call this approach the *Separate CSU/DSU Configuration*. Both configurations have been implemented and are illustrated in Figure 5.1. Note that there are no restrictions on communication between different configurations.

The Separate CSU/DSU Configuration approach has been defined by router and CSU/DSU vendors in the SMDS Interest Group (SIG). A major motivation for this development was to allow support of SMDS by the installed base of routers without the need for hardware upgrades.[1] The DXI is the specification of the protocol that is needed between the CSU/DSU and the other CPE, and is based on common, well-understood technology. The DXI specification requires the CSU/DSU to terminate all protocol levels of SIP except the SIP Level 3. Thus, the CSU/DSU will take care of SIP Level 2, including the segmentation and reassembly functions. L3_PDUs are carried between CSU/DSU and CPE, such as hosts, bridges, and routers, via the simpler HDLC-based DXI protocol.[2] The DXI does not require segmentation and reassembly of L3_PDUs. The DXI uses physical interfaces that are also commonly used for bridges and routers, such as V.35 and EIA 422A.

5.2   Data Exchange Interface Protocol

The DXI is based on the use of HDLC frames via an appropriate physical interface. Figure 5.2 shows the protocol stacks that are used.

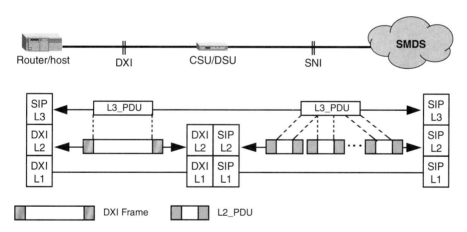

Figure 5.2 Protocols used for the DXI

Figure 5.2 shows that all functions and error checks of SIP Level 2 are performed in the CSU/DSU. The CSU/DSU does not perform the functions and error checks of SIP Level 3.

---

[1]In addition, the router community was interested in supporting SMDS, but wary of investing in hardware development for DS1, DS3, and SIP Level 2. On the other hand, the CSU/DSU vendors saw an opportunity in expanding their product line with SMDS CSU/DSUs.

[2]This bears witness to the reluctance of some CPE vendors to implement all complexities of the SIP protocol stack.

5.2.1 DXI Physical Interface

The DXI physical interface depends on the physical interface used for accessing SMDS. A number of alternative physical interfaces can be used. Table 5.1 shows the relationship between the physical interfaces for DXI and SIP.

SMDS access	Alternative DXI physical interfaces	
	Physical aspects	Electrical aspects
DS1 (1.544 Mbps)	EIA 530A [EIA530A]	EIA 422A [EIA422A]
E1 (2.048 Mbps)	EIA 449 [EIA449]	EIA 422A [EIA422A]
	CCITT V.35 [V.35]	CCITT V.35 [V.35]
	CCITT X.21 [X.21]	CCITT X.27/V.11 [X.27, V.11]
DS3 (44.736 Mbps) E3 (34.368 Mbps)	HSSI [EIA613]	HSSI [EIA612]

Table 5.1 DXI physical interface requirements

Most of these specifications are all well established and widely implemented. The HSSI (High Speed Serial Interface) was originally specified by Cisco Systems, Inc., and T3plus Networking, Inc. The specification, which now is supported by a multitude of vendors [Hindin] and is standardized by ANSI, [EIA612] [EIA613] was designed to accommodate serial transmission speeds up to 52 Mbps.

The DXI allows for the support of non-HSSI, lower-speed interfaces such as V.35 or EIA449 for SNIs that use Access Classes (Section 3.4.6) with sustained information rates lower than the full available bandwidths. This may seem useful with regard to traffic going towards the network that is providing SMDS, but recall that SMDS does not enforce Access Classes for traffic sent from the network to the CPE, in order to avoid unnecessary buffering and delays and to leave any SMDS data unit discard or buffer strategy to the destination CPE. The implication is that the CSU/DSU must implement a mechanism to appropriately buffer or discard any traffic surplus that it cannot immediately relay across the DXI.

The DXI specification requires a clock signal from the CSU/DSU to the router or host. For HSSI, a nominal rate of 44.736 MHz (DS3 access) or 34.368 MHz (E3 access) must be used. A non-HSSI interface should use the clock rate supported by that interface. Note that due to the difference in protocol overhead between the DXI and SIP, the router or host can potentially overflow the CSU/DSU input buffer. For example, a DS1 CSU/DSU clocks in L3_PDUs from the DXI interface at 1.544 Mbps, while the effective SNI bandwidth is 1.17 Mbps. The implication is that the CSU/DSU must implement a mechanism to appropriately buffer or discard any traffic surplus that it cannot immediately relay across the SNI.

5.2.2   DXI Link Level

L3_PDUs are transported over the DXI via traditional HDLC frames [ISO3309]. Each HDLC frame transports one complete L3_PDU. This means that the CSU/DSU is responsible for the segmentation and reassembly of L3_PDUs into and from L2_PDUs. Note that this means that MCDUs In could be set to 1 (see Section 3.4.5). If MCDUs Out is set greater than 1, then the CSU/DSU must be able to buffer multiple incomplete L3_PDUs as they are received across the SNI.

HDLC has been widely implemented for a variety of purposes, and represents well-understood technology. Figure 5.3 shows the basic frame structure for DXI.

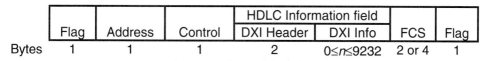

Figure 5.3 HDLC frame structure for DXI

5.2.2.1   Frame Delimiting

A FLAG marks the beginning or end of a frame and consists of the binary pattern 01111110_B. Stations continuously hunt for this sequence and use it for frame synchronization. A FLAG may double as the end of one frame and the beginning of the subsequent frame. In order to avoid a bit pattern within the frame being misconstrued as a FLAG, HDLC uses a bit-stuffing technique. When preparing a frame for transmission, a 0-bit is inserted after each occurrence of five contiguous 1s. Thus the receiving station will only recognize real FLAGS. The receiving station will remove the stuffed 0s again, restoring the original frame contents. The DXI requires that the time between frames will be filled by contiguous FLAGS. When a pattern of seven 1s is encountered within a frame, it is considered an abort sequence, and the frame is discarded.

5.2.2.2   Control Field

The CONTROL field in HDLC typically distinguishes frame types and performs a number of functions for each type of frame, such as maintaining sequence numbers for numbered information frames. The DXI uses HDLC Unnumbered Information (UI) frames for the transfer of L3_PDUs. In addition, a special Test frame for diagnostic purposes is used. The interpretation of the CONTROL field, shown in Table 5.2, is quite simple. UI frames use a CONTROL field with the value 00000011_B. The Test frame uses the value $111P0011_B$. The

P represents the POLL/FINAL bit that is commonly used in protocols such as LAPB, (the link protocol for X.25) and CCITT LAPD [Q.921], used for ISDN and Frame Relay. A Command frame (see Section 5.2.2.3) with the POLL/FINAL bit set to 1 by a sending station is used to solicit (poll) a response from the station to which the frame is addressed. The receiving station uses a Response (see Section 5.2.2.3) frame with the POLL/FINAL bit set to 1 to indicate a result of a previously received poll command.

Frame type	Control bits 8-1							
UI Frame, carrying an L3_PDU or LMI_PDU	0	0	0	0	0	0	1	1
Test Frame	1	1	1	P/F	0	0	1	1

Table 5.2 Use of the CONTROL field

5.2.2.3   Address Field

The 1-byte ADDRESS field is structured as shown in Table 5.3.

Frame type	Direction	Address bits 8-1						C/R	AE
		Logical Link Identifier					Station Address		
Command	To DSU	L	L	L	L	L	1	0	1
Response	To DSU	L	L	L	L	L	1	1	1
Command	From DSU	L	L	L	L	L	0	1	1
Response	From DSU	L	L	L	L	L	0	0	1

Table 5.3 Use of the ADDRESS field

The UI frames are not tagged with sequence numbers, and can only be Command frames. The Test frame may be either a Command frame or a Response frame.

Figure 5.4 shows the use of the DXI logical links. The LOGICAL LINK IDENTIFIER, which consists of the five L bits in Table 5.3, separates data flows for different applications. L3_PDUs use link number 00000_B. LMI PDUs, which are used for management purposes (see Chapter 11), use link number 00001_B. Links $10000_B - 11111_B$ are available for any proprietary use. The remaining link numbers are reserved in [SIG001] for possible future allocation.

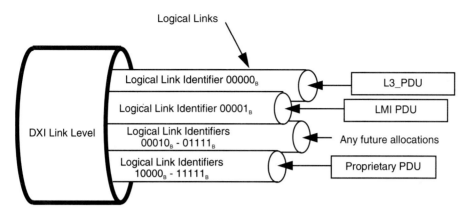

Figure 5.4 Use of the DXI logical links

The STATION ADDRESS bit in the ADDRESS field determines the receiving station. The CSU/DSU is defined as having address 1. The host, router or bridge processing L3_PDUs has address 0.

The C/R-bit in the ADDRESS field distinguishes Command and Response frames. Its use is the same as the C/R-bit defined in, for example, LAPD. As shown in Table 5.3, the CSU/DSU does this by using 0 for Commands and 1 for Responses. The router uses 1 for Commands and 0 for Responses.

The ADDRESS EXTENSION bit (AE-bit) indicates whether more bytes in the ADDRESS field will follow. Since the ADDRESS field in this case is only one byte, the bit is set to 1, indicating the end of the field.

5.2.2.4   Information Field

The HDLC INFORMATION field in Figure 5.3 shows two subfields. The first two bytes contain the DXI Header field. The remainder of the INFORMATION field contains the DXI INFORMATION field. This field will contain either an L3_PDU, or LMI information (see Chapter 11). The choice for a two-byte length for the DXI HEADER was caused by a desire for 32-bit alignment of the frame.[3] Given the maximum length of a L3_PDU of 9232 bytes, the overall length of the DXI INFORMATION field is $2 \leq n \leq 9234$.[4]

Frames with only the Header present in the INFORMATION field are referred to as *Null frames* or *Null PDUs* in the DXI. The DXI specification stipulates that only one Null frame may be sent by the CSU/DSU, after which no Null frames may be sent before the next L3_PDU is transmitted. The rationale for this decision is an attempt to avoid overloading of the router with Null frames. The DXI HEADER subfield is shown in Table 5.4.

---

[3]The ADDRESS, CONTROL, and HEADER fields together are 32 bits long. The L3_PDU is also 32-bit aligned (see Section 4.5.7).

[4]HDLC permits the transmission of empty frames. These should be ignored by the receiver.

Purpose	DXI Header bits 16–1															
No congestion	0	0	0	0	0	0	0	0	0	0	0	0	0	0	0	0
Congestion	0	0	0	0	0	0	0	0	0	0	0	0	0	0	1	0

Table 5.4 Use of the DXI HEADER subfield

Bit 2 of the DXI HEADER field represents a CONGESTION bit. The use of the other bits has not been defined. They are set to zero and should be ignored. The intent of the CONGESTION bit is to signal from the CSU/DSU to its DXI peer (for example, a host or a router) whether a congestion condition exists at the CSU/DSU. Setting the bit to 1 indicates a congestion condition. The use of this bit in the direction towards the CSU/DSU is not specified, and the value of the bit is set to 0. A similar bit has been specified elsewhere, for example for Frame Relay [FRF-1]. Its exact use will depend on the capabilities of the receiver. However, there is substantial disagreement in the industry about the value and use of this mechanism. As is observed by [Comer1] and others, the central issue is not how to send control messages but when. There is also no common understanding of the required actions that need to be taken upon receipt of a CONGESTION bit set to 1.[5] In the absence of a common procedure, most vendors have refrained from implementing any procedure to use this bit; thus, we recommend that the CONGESTION bit not be used (set to 0) and be ignored upon receipt.

5.2.2.5   Frame Check Sequence Field

The FRAME CHECK SEQUENCE (FCS) field is 16 or 32 bits long. The FCS is used to check whether transmission errors have occurred in a received frame. The 16-bit version is the default, and is calculated according to [ISO3309] (see Appendix C). The generator polynomial of degree 16 is

$$G(x) = x^{16} + x^{12} + x^5 + 1.$$

The generator polynomial of degree 32 is

---

[5]Potential alternative procedures in a congestion situation at a CSU/DSU could include (a) PDU discard (CONGESTION bit not used); (b) piggyback CONGESTION bit set to 1 on an L3_PDU; (c) send DXI Null frames with CONGESTION bit set to 1 (d) set the CONGESTION bit to 1 when the queue length in the CSU/DSU reaches a certain threshold, and so on. Given this variety of alternatives, a router is unlikely to know the CSU/DSU strategy in this regard. Neither does it know how transient the condition is. Thus, the router would have no other options than trying to buffer packets on each receipt of a CONGESTION bit set to 1, trying to inform the source(s) of a congestion condition with whatever appropriate mechanism was available, or relying on end-to-end protocols such as TCP for recovery from the congestion condition.

$$G(x) = x^{32} + x^{26} + x^{23} + x^{22} + x^{16} + x^{12} + x^{11} + x^8 + x^7 + x^5 +$$
$$x^4 + x^2 + x^1 + 1.$$

The 32-bit version provides for improved error detection for large frames. Since the DXI does not provide for any negotiating capabilities on this level, the use of the 16- or 32-bit FCS must be preconfigured.

5.2.2.6   Test Frames

The Test frame can be used on any logical link. However, its only specified use is described as the Heart Beat Poll procedure on logical link number 1. This procedure is designed for a DXI station to periodically check the status of the link with the other station. To this end, each station is required to maintain a timer, called the *Heart Beat Poll Timer*, that determines the length of the period between sending Heart Beat Poll Test Command frames. The length of the interval measured by this timer is implementation-specific. After sending such a frame (with the POLL/FINAL bit set to 1), another timer, the No Acknowledgment Timer, is started. If 5 seconds elapse before a Heart Beat Poll Test Response frame is received, a downstream problem is assumed.[6] No further Test Command frames are allowed to be sent before receipt of the Response or expiration of the No Acknowledgment Timer. Upon receipt of a Test Command frame, the receiving station is required to return any data in the INFORMATION field in a Test Response frame with the POLL/FINAL bit set to 1. Parsing of that data is not required.

A very high frequency of Heart Beat Poll messages will unnecessarily consume bandwidth, while a very low frequency jeopardizes the objectives of the Heart Beat Poll procedure. Therefore we recommend that the interval between Heart Beat Poll messages ranges from 1 to 5 seconds.

5.2.2.7   Bit Transmission Order

Bytes of the HDLC header and the HDLC INFORMATION field will be transmitted starting with their lower order bit (the Least Significant Bit, or LSB) first. As per HDLC, the FCS is transmitted starting with the bit representing the highest coefficient of the polynomial value of the field (see Appendix C and [ISO3309]).

The bit-order of transmission of the INFORMATION field, which contains an L3_PDU (see Chapter 4) or an SNMP-like LMI packet (see Chapter 11), is different from the order of bit transmission of L3_PDUs when carried in L2_PDUs, and from the order of bit transmission for SNMP, both of which are transmitted starting with the Most Significant Bit (MSB) first. However, this

---

[6]The precise semantics of this condition are not described and are left to the implementor.

difference does not require the CSU/DSU to reassemble the whole packet. The bit reordering can be performed on a byte basis.

5.2.2.8   Pipelining

For the CPE-to-SMDS direction, the BUFFER ALLOCATION SIZE (see Section 4.5.3) allows the CSU/DSU to pipeline (see Section 4.3.4) since the BUFFER ALLOCATION SIZE is carried in the header of the L3_PDU. Thus, the CSU/DSU does not have to wait for the HDLC closing FLAG to determine the length of the L3_PDU. For the SMDS to CPE direction, pipelining is theoretically possible, but not done in today's CSU/DSUs.

5.3   DXI-Based Direct Access to SMDS

In recognition of the simplicity of the DXI, MCI has included a DXI-based SMDS access protocol in its service offering. Based on this approach, the SIG has standardized DXI-based access in [SIG005], and Bellcore has specified detailed requirements in [1239].

5.3.1   DXI Use for Direct Access

The basic approach is shown in Figure 5.5. Comparing this figure with Figure 5.2, one can intuitively understand that in the direct DXI-based access configuration, the CSU/DSU is simplified and therefore less costly. Since the CSU/DSU in this configuration does not perform any SMDS-specific functions, existing CSU/DSUs can be used.

This access method has initially been introduced for SMDS access speeds below DS1. The physical level for the SNI (the L1* in Figure 5.5) consists of appropriate transmission facilities for these speeds. Speeds of DS1 and higher may be supported in the future. The SIG specifies this access method for access speeds of 56, 64, n x 56 and n x 64 Kbps.[7] Actual service provision may differ per service provider.[8]

The following restrictions to the DXI apply, when used for direct access to SMDS [SIG005].

---

[7]Service provision at speeds as low as 64 Kbps is driven by a desire for broad market coverage, and goes significantly beyond the original SMDS design objectives, which position SMDS as a backbone LAN (see Chapter 1). For example, many LAN applications require performance objectives in the range of the figures shown in Chapter 7. Since delays caused by low-speed lines are significantly longer than what is often needed for a LAN backbone, delay-sensitive applications, such as client-server applications, should be used with caution via this type of access.

[8]For example, MCI supports access speeds of 64, 128, 256, 512, 768, and 1024 Kbps via this method [MCI].

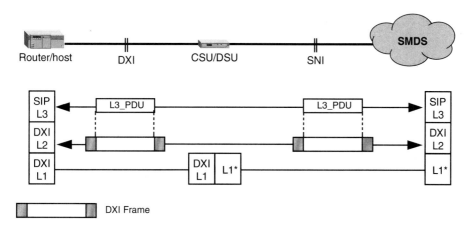

DXI Frame

Figure 5.5 Protocols used for the DXI

- The Heart Beat Poll procedure must be supported, but it must be possible to disable it.

- The LMI (see Chapter 11) is not supported.

5.3.2   Service Aspects of DXI-Based Access

The SMDS features MCDUs In, MCDUs Out, and Access Classes do not apply to this type of access. Since there is no need for segmentation and reassembly of L3_PDUs, there is no potential to send multiple data units in transit concurrently. Access Classes only apply for DS3- or E3-based access.

For access at speeds below DS1, Bellcore [1239] also makes some restrictions in the service. The underlying assumption is that CPE for these access rates has fewer networking needs. Therefore, some adjustments in the ranges of some address features have been defined. These adjustments allow simplification of the implementation of the service and are noted in Chapter 3.

5.3.3   Multiservice Access

SMDS access by n × 56 and n × 64 Kbps can be realized by provisioning a DS1 circuit between CPE and the carrier network that is providing SMDS, and allocating an appropriate fraction of the available bandwidth to SMDS. Thus, it is possible to allocate other fractions of the access circuit to other applications such as voice, provided that this multiservice access arrangement is supported by the carrier (see, for example, [MCI]). Digital cross-connect systems in the carrier network connect the respective DS1 fractions to their appropriate destinations. Figure 5.6 shows an example where voice and SMDS traffic are multiplexed over the same access circuit.

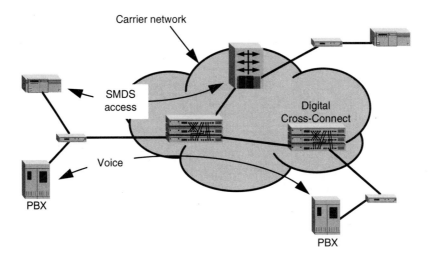

Figure 5.6   Example of multiservice access using fractionalized DS1

6

SIP Relay Access to SMDS

The key features of SMDS, described in Chapter 3, are based on the DESTINATION ADDRESS, SOURCE ADDRESS, and INFORMATION fields of the L3_PDU. Thus, any protocol that can transfer these three pieces of information across a physical link with adequate error detection can serve as the access protocol for SMDS. HDLC procedures can easily serve as the basis of such a protocol [ISO3309]. The DXI (see Chapter 5) is an example of this use of HDLC procedures. Another example of the use of HDLC procedures is the Frame Relay Protocol known as Link Access Procedures Frame-mode (LAPF) [FRF-1]. This method of access is referred to as the SIP Relay Interface (SRI) [SIG006] [1240].

This chapter describes SIP Relay access to SMDS by first presenting some background on Frame Relay and then the motivation for the use of SIP Relay access to SMDS. Finally, the details of the SRI protocols are described. The chapter concludes with a discussion of some of the service aspects of SIP Relay access to SMDS.

The two primary sources of material for this chapter are [SIG006] and [1240]. There are some differences between these two specifications. These are identified and we recommend which specification to follow.

CPE designers should find the chapter useful in designing SMDS equipment for the SRI. SMDS customers should find the chapter useful in choosing among the access options for SMDS, if multiple options are available from the customer's service providers.

6.1   Brief Tutorial on Frame Relay

This section presents a very brief tutorial on Frame Relay. For a thorough description of this technology, we recommend [T1.617] and [FRF-1].

Frame Relay is a technology that allows a device with a single physical interface to exchange data units with multiple destinations. This is accomplished with virtual connections, as illustrated in Figure 6.1. When a router (or similar CPE) sends a data unit into the Frame Relay network, it attaches a label to it called the DATA LINK CONNECTION IDENTIFIER (DLCI). This allows the Frame Relay network to forward the data unit to the proper service interface. Similarly, when the Frame Relay network delivers a data unit to the router, the appropriate DLCI is attached, so that the router can identify the source of the data unit. The establishment of the virtual connections can be accomplished administratively (e.g., via a paper service order), in which case the connection is called a Permanent Virtual Connection (PVC). SRI is based on the use of a PVC.

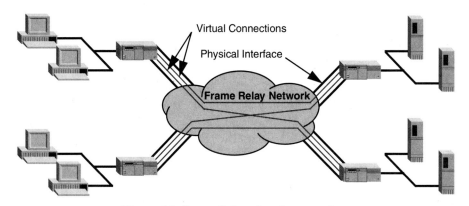

Figure 6.1 Frame Relay virtual connections

Figure 6.2 shows the LAPF format. The FLAGS and FRAME CHECK SEQUENCE are the same as described in Chapter 5. The bit stuffing of HDLC procedures is used, and thus the opening and closing FLAGS are used to delimit the frame [ISO3309]. The FRAME CHECK SEQUENCE is used to detect bit errors in the HEADER and INFORMATION fields. The default maximum INFORMATION field size is 262 bytes, although typical implementations use a much larger and more practical maximum size. Bellcore [1369] calls for a maximum length of 4096 bytes.

Figure 6.3 shows the details of the LAPF HEADER. The fields of the LAPF Header are described below.

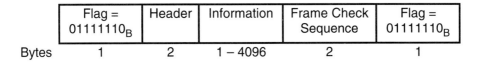

Figure 6.2 LAPF format

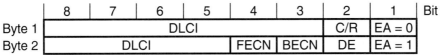

Note: The order of bit transmission is right-to-left, top-to-bottom.

Key

DLCI	Data Link Connection Identifier
C/R	Command/Response
FECN	Forward Explicit Congestion Notification
BECN	Backward Explicit Congestion Notification
DE	Discard Eligibility
EA	Extended Address

Figure 6.3 LAPF header

- DATA LINK CONNECTION IDENTIFIER: This field identifies the virtual connection that is associated with the frame. Bit 8 of byte 1 is the most significant bit of the DLCI, while bit 5 of byte 2 is the least significant bit. The values of 0 and 1023_D are reserved for special functions.

- COMMAND/RESPONSE: This field is ignored and carried transparently by the Frame Relay network.

- EXTENDED ADDRESS: By setting the second instance of this field to 0, the DLCI can be extended up to 23 bits. EA = 1 indicates that no more address bytes follow. Such an extension is not needed for the SRI.

- FORWARD EXPLICIT CONGESTION NOTIFICATION: The Frame Relay network sets this bit to 1 to indicate that the frame encountered congestion. This is an indication that the CPE should consider reducing the rate of data being sent into the Frame Relay network in the direction of the frame carrying the FECN = 1 on the virtual connection identified by the DLCI in the frame.[1]

- BACKWARD EXPLICIT CONGESTION NOTIFICATION: The Frame Relay network sets this bit to 1 to indicate that new frames sent into the

---

[1]We are not aware of any mechanism to enforce this behavior of the CPE. Perhaps the Protocol Police will pay a nighttime visit to the owner of the misbehaving CPE. Notice also the similarity to the dilemmas described for the DXI Congestion bit (see Section 5.2.2.4).

network in the opposite direction of the frame carrying the BECN = 1 may encounter congestion. This is an indication that the CPE should consider reducing the rate of data being sent into the Frame Relay network on the virtual connection identified by the DLCI in the frame.

- DISCARD ELIGIBILITY: This bit is set by the Frame Relay network for frames that violate the Committed Burst Size. (Committed Burst Size is part of the characterization of traffic for a given virtual connection and is described below.) When it becomes necessary to discard frames, the Frame Relay network attempts to discard frames with this bit set before discarding frames with the bit not set.

For each virtual connection, a Committed Information Rate (CIR) is defined. The CIR concept is similar to Access Classes, as described in Chapters 3 and 4. The CIR is expressed in bits per second and is the average bit rate that the Frame Relay network commits to transport for the virtual connection under normal conditions. The Committed Burst Size is the maximum number of bits that the network will transport over a given Measurement Interval, T. The CIR equals the Committed Burst Size divided by T.

6.2   Motivation for SIP Relay Access to SMDS

The primary motivation for SIP Relay access to SMDS is to allow carriers to leverage their Frame Relay network equipment in providing SMDS. Figure 6.4 is adapted from [1240] and illustrates this concept. A carrier that has deployed a Frame Relay network can provide SMDS via an SRI by establishing a PVC, called the *SIP Relay Interface Permanent Virtual Circuit* [1240] (SRI PVC), from the Frame Relay Service Interface through the Frame Relay network to SMDS. Thus, all customers that the carrier can reach with the Frame Relay network can be offered SMDS.

Figure 6.5 shows additional detail of this carrier arrangement. An interworking unit can be used to interconnect an SMDS Switching System (SS) and a Frame Relay switch. The interworking unit terminates several SRI PVCs. Frames for each of these SRI PVCs are converted to and from SIP Levels 1, 2, and 3 on an interface on the SS. From the SS point of view, the SMDS customers using SIP Relay appear as multiple CPE attached to the SNI. Because of this, the interworking unit also performs appropriate Address Screening and Group Addressing functions in order to provide all SMDS features to these customers.

Another potential advantage of SIP Relay is that a CPE can access both Frame Relay service and SMDS over one physical interface. This may reduce total tariff charges by reducing the number of physical interfaces to the carrier network. It may also reduce the cost of CPE for the same reason.

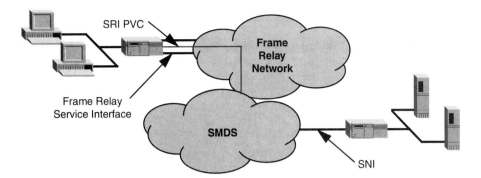

Figure 6.4 Frame Relay network access to SMDS

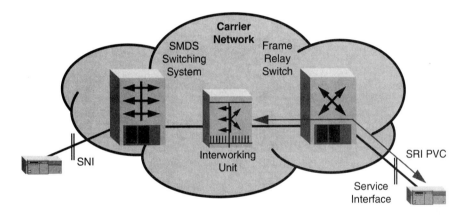

Figure 6.5 Interworking SRIs and SNIs

6.3   SRI Protocol

The SRI Protocol consists of three levels as shown in Figure 6.6. Each level is described in the following subsections.

Level 3	SIP Level 3
Level 2	LAPF
Level 1	$N \times 56$ Kbps or $N \times 64$ Kbps

Figure 6.6 SRI protocol levels

6.3.1   SRI Protocol Level 3

Level 3 of the SRI Protocol is identical to the Level 3 of SIP, as described in Section 4.5.

6.3.2   SRI Protocol Level 2

Level 2 of the SRI Protocol is based on LAPF, as illustrated in Figure 6.7 [SIG006]. Comparing Figure 6.7 with Figure 6.2 reveals two differences. First, the INFORMATION field can contain up to 9232 bytes for SRI, which is larger than for Frame Relay. Second, the FRAME CHECK SEQUENCE can contain four bytes. The SMDS Interest Group [SIG006] makes the use of four bytes optional and recommends the use of four bytes for frames larger than 4096 bytes. Since the size of the FRAME CHECK SEQUENCE is a matter of equipment configuration, this does not mean changing the size frame-by-frame. Instead, it means that four bytes should always be used if frames larger than 4096 bytes will be frequently carried over the interface.

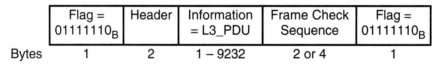

Figure 6.7 LAPF for SRI Protocol Level 2

Bellcore [1240] differs from [SIG006] with respect to the maximum size of the INFORMATION field and the use of the four-byte FRAME CHECK SEQUENCE. Instead of mandating 9232 bytes, [1240] calls for a maximum of 4096 bytes and support of only the two-byte FRAME CHECK SEQUENCE. Support of 9232 bytes of information and the four-byte FRAME CHECK SEQUENCE by the service provider is a Conditional Requirement.[2]

When the maximum INFORMATION field size specified by [1240] is used, there is a potential interworking problem between a CPE attached to an SNI and one attached to an SRI. The CPE attached to the SNI can send L3_PDUs to the CPE attached to the SRI that are larger than 4096 bytes, and such L3_PDUs will not be delivered. Two solutions to this problem come to mind:

1. Always limit the size of the L3_PDU to 4096 for *all* interfaces accessing SMDS.

---

[2]In Bellcore requirements documents, Conditional Requirements are requirements that only apply if some condition is met. In this case, the condition can be paraphrased as follows: "If the carrier decides to support 9232 bytes . . . ."

2.   Maintain information on the maximum size L3_PDU that can be sent to each E.164 address that is to be used as a destination, which effectively means multiple packet sizes for a physical network in an internet.

The first solution is simple but reduces the utility of SMDS. The second solution will be either an administrative nightmare or will require new negotiation procedures between CPE attached to SMDS interfaces. Neither of these appear attractive to us, and thus we recommend that all service providers support 9232 bytes.[3]

The SRI LAPF Header is identical to that of Figure 6.3. For a given SRI, a single DLCI value is used for the transport of all L3_PDUs. This value, the SRI PVC, is configurable on a per-SRI basis. Thus, when configuring CPE to access the service, the customer and the service provider must agree on a single value as part of the service-provisioning process.

6.3.3   SRI Protocol Level 1

SRI Protocol Level 1 can be any of the physical layers of [FRF-1]. The SMDS Interest Group [SIG006] states the intent that level 1 should support speeds of 56, 64, N × 56, and N × 64 Kbps up to and including E1 (2.048 Mbps).

Bellcore [1240] differs from [SIG006] in that it calls for access rates of 56, 64, 768, and 1536 Kbps. This set of speeds seems adequate to us, and thus we recommend that [1240] be followed.

6.3.4   Status Signaling

ANSI [T1.617] (Annex D) and [FRF-1] define protocols for determining the status of PVCs on a Frame Relay service interface. The SMDS Interest Group [SIG006] specifies the use of the protocols in [FRF-1] for the SRI, while [1240] requires support of both of the status-signaling protocols for tracking the status of the SRI PVC. We recommend that the status signaling of [1240] be implemented.

6.3.5   Committed Information Rate

The SMDS Interest Group [SIG006] is silent about the use of CIR on the SRI. In contrast, [1240] requires the use of the CIR mechanism on the SRI PVC. Use of

---

[3]The immense wit and charm of the authors may not be sufficient to convince all service providers to follow this recommendation. Therefore, we also recommend that customers check with their service providers to determine the maximum L3_PDU size that is supported. *Caveat emptor.*

the CIR on the SRI PVC certainly seems to be indicated when the service interface is supporting the SRI PVC as well as other Frame Relay PVCs.[4]

6.4   Service Aspects of SRI

The use of the SRI Protocol affects two SMDS features. First, because of the slow data rate, the Access Class feature does not apply. Second, Multiple Data Units in Transit Concurrently (see Section 3.4.5) is equal to one because the use of a frame oriented protocol means that only one data unit can be sent at a time. This fact is noted in both [SIG006] and [1240].

Although it is not required by the protocol, [1240] also changes some of the other features, such as the number of addresses that can be assigned to a PVC SRI. The motivation for these changes is simplification of implementation of the service and is related to the use of the interworking unit shown in Figure 6.5. Bellcore [1240] uses the term *Access Server* for this function.

Figure 6.8 shows an example of the impact on addressing support when the interworking unit is used. In this example, the interworking unit is supporting eight SRI PVCs. If we suppose that these SRI PVCs are serving 64-Kbps SRIs, then the interworking unit can exploit a single DS1-based SNI on the SS by multiplexing as indicated in Figure 6.8.[5] This provides a cost-effective implementation, because the relatively expensive SS interface can be shared across eight customers. However, only 16 Individual Addresses can be assigned to an SNI, and this limits the number of addresses per SRI PVC to two — the number called out in [1240]. Thus the somewhat reduced feature set specified in [1240] reflects the trade-off between feature support and network implementation cost. These service-feature restrictions are listed in Chapter 3.

---

[4]In what may be an oversight, [1240] states performance objectives for SIP Relay that seem to be independent of the CIR mechanism. It is reasonable to expect that L3_PDUs in frames that have their DISCARD ELIGIBILITY bit set, because of exceeding the Committed Burst Size, will have an elevated not-delivered ratio. Therefore, we believe that the performance objectives of [1240] only apply to frames within the CIR.

[5]Proper implementation of SMDS features requires the interworking unit to perform functions in addition to multiplexing. For example, it will have to implement Group Addressing across the multiple SRIs.

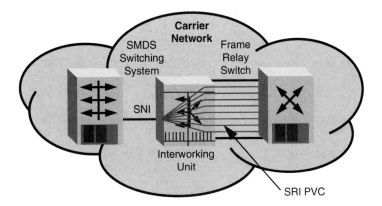

Figure 6.8 Address-support limitation in the SRI

7

Performance and Quality-of-Service Objectives

This chapter describes and discusses the performance and quality-of-service objectives for SMDS. Understanding the performance of SMDS is important to both SMDS customers and CPE designers. For SMDS customers, this information will aid in network design and facilitate making the most effective use of SMDS. CPE vendors can use this information in designing equipment to work effectively with the service.

The framework for the definition of SMDS performance and quality-of-service objectives is influenced by the fact that SMDS is a public carrier service, and this framework is the first point of discussion. Next the scope of the objectives is described. The chapter then concludes with descriptions and discussions of the three categories of objectives: Availability, Accuracy, and Delay.

7.1 Framework for SMDS Objectives

As discussed in Chapter 1, the fundamental approach to the definition of SMDS is to provide a LAN-like service that extends over a wide area. However, in terms of performance and quality-of-service, SMDS differs from a LAN in a number of important ways.

First, a LAN is typically operated and used by a single organization or company, while SMDS is intended to involve many different organizations. When SMDS is used, some of the organizations involved (the SMDS customers) pay other organizations (the public carriers). This customer-supplier relationship was the primary reason that performance and quality-of-service objectives were formulated for SMDS. By providing performance and quality-of-service objectives, the SMDS provider gives the SMDS customer an indication of what her money is buying. The word "indication" in the previous sentence is significant. The specification of performance and quality-of-service objectives for public, high-speed data services is an evolving art. Consequently, as can be seen in the descriptions in this chapter, some of the performance and quality-of-service objectives (primarily Availability objectives), are not yet completely defined. Furthermore, there are no common methods defined yet for measuring performance and quality-of-service.[1] Without such measurement methods, it is impossible to determine if the provider of SMDS is meeting the objectives. Thus, the SMDS performance and quality-of-service objectives contained in [772] are not yet sufficient to be the basis of a contract, but they can be considered a statement of intent on the part of the service provider.

A second significant difference between SMDS and a LAN is its geographical extent. The fact that SMDS will cover wide areas means that certain performance and quality-of-service aspects will differ from those typically found on a single LAN. For example, the longer distances covered by SMDS necessarily mean that SMDS will have larger delays than those typically found on a LAN. SMDS performance and quality-of-service objectives help the customer understand how SMDS differs from a LAN.

A third difference between SMDS and a LAN is that regulatory constraints apply to some of the potential SMDS providers: the seven U.S. Regional Bell Operating Companies (RBOCs). The particular constraint that is of interest to this discussion is that the RBOCs cannot include the CPE in a service offered by the regulated network. For example, a router that an SMDS customer uses to achieve wide-area connectivity cannot be part of SMDS.

The implications of this constraint are significant. As discussed in Chapter 3, the performance and quality-of-service that an SMDS customer experiences when using SMDS will depend on the performance of the CPE used to access SMDS. However, this is under the control of the SMDS customer, and therefore it would be an academic exercise to include the CPE in the SMDS performance and quality-of-service objectives. Instead, the approach that is taken is illustrated in Figure 7.1.

SMDS performance and quality-of-service objectives are specified from SNI to SNI. The SNI is the physical point of demarcation between the equipment supplied by the SMDS customer and the network equipment supplied by the public carrier that is offering SMDS. Thus, the performance and quality-of-

---

[1]Standardized definitions and associated values of performance and quality-of-service do not exist for LANs. However, some provocative studies in this area can be found in [Gusella].

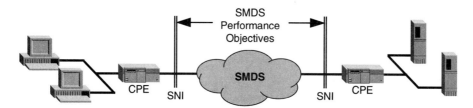

Figure 7.1 Framework for SMDS performance and quality-of-service objectives

service objectives can be viewed as an indication of the performance and quality-of-service that "perfect protocol analyzers" should observe when attached to SNIs.

7.2   Scope of the Performance and Quality-of-Service Objectives

Figure 7.1 is an oversimplification in that it implies a single service-provider network. In reality, several networks operated by different public carriers can stand between SNIs. For example, in the United States, two LECs and one or more IECs can be involved in carrying data between two SNIs. Figure 7.2 illustrates this possible arrangement.

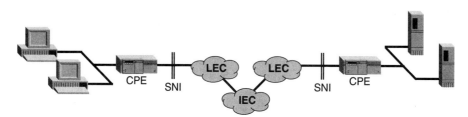

Figure 7.2 Example of multiple networks providing SMDS

In the example of Figure 7.2, the level of performance and quality-of-service between the SNIs will depend on the performance and quality-of-service of each of the three intervening networks. The performance and quality-of-service objectives described below *do not apply to this type of arrangement.* The requirements in [772] were prepared for the use of the U.S. RBOCs, and thus, by the terms of the divestiture agreement, it applies only to RBOC LEC intra-LATA networks. The performance and quality-of-service objectives described here *only apply to communications among SNIs served by a single LEC network.* Performance and quality-of-service objectives for the case of Figure 7.2 will require detailed agreements among the network providers involved, and such agreements have yet to be concluded.[2]

The setting of the SMDS performance and quality-of-service objectives requires striking a balance between two sometimes conflicting considerations. The first consideration is the SMDS customer needs. If customer needs are not met, there is no point in offering the service. On the other hand, it is also pointless to set objectives that are obviously unattainable and thus not credible (e.g., setting delay objectives which require that the speed of light be exceeded). Of course neither factor is completely understood at this time and thus the performance and quality-of-service objectives may change as experience is gained with SMDS.

7.3   Availability Objectives

Availability is the ratio (expressed as a percentage) of actual service time to scheduled service time.[3] It is an SNI-to-SNI concept. At any particular time, the service can be available for some SNI pairs and not available for other SNI pairs. Thus, availability can be viewed as the probability that communications can be accomplished between a given pair of SNIs at a given time.

The determination of availability is based on availability decision parameters for the particular SNI pair. An example of such a parameter could be the ratio of L3_PDUs not delivered. Each parameter has an associated outage threshold. For example, the threshold might be stated as more than 5 in 1000 L3_PDUs not delivered in a given second. Actual service time is the sum of time intervals during which all availability decision parameter values are equal to or better than the associated outage threshold. Definition of the availability decision parameters and the associated outage thresholds is still un er study. However, it is expected that the parameters will be based on the performance and quality-of-service objectives in the next two sections. The example used above, the L3_PDU not-delivered ratio, is actually covered by a separate accuracy objective (see Section 7.4). Using these parameters for availability definitions is convenient since the parameters are clearly defined. However, the outage threshold for a given parameter will typically be less stringent than the accuracy objective for that parameter.

It is expected that the definition of the availability decision parameters and associated outage thresholds will need to wait until more experience is obtained

---

[2][1060] contains performance and quality-of-service objectives for Exchange Access SMDS, which is the service that the LEC networks provide to the IEC network in the context shown in Figure 7.2.

[3]The definitions of performance and quality-of-service parameters in this section are based on [X.137].

in the use of SMDS by customers and in the implementation of large service-provider networks.

7.3.1   Scheduled Service Time

The Scheduled Service Time is the time that the service is planned to be offered and is clearly a key element in the service availability objectives. SMDS is a public service, which means that communication needs will span many SMDS customers across diverse geographical areas and time zones. Furthermore, SMDS allows machines to communicate, and most machines involved in data processing and communications do not "sleep" according to predictable schedules.

> The **SMDS Scheduled Service Time Objective** is 24 hours a day, 7 days a week.

The important implication of this objective for the SMDS customer is that there is no need to coordinate the operation of his data network (and thus the operation of his enterprise) with scheduled downtime for SMDS.

7.3.2   Mean Time Between Service Outages

Service availability can viewed as depending on two things: the length of time between service outages and the length of such outages. Numerous outages, even of short duration, can be very disruptive to the applications dependent on the service. Thus, the objective for uninterrupted service intervals is set aggressively.

> The **SMDS Mean Time Between Service Outages Objective** is no less than 3500 hours.

Until some experience is gained with the implementation of SMDS, the statistical nature of the time between service outages will be a matter of conjecture. However, as a perspective on this objective, we can divide the hours in a year (8,760) by 3500 to estimate about 2.5 service outages per year.

7.3.3   Mean Time to Restore

If a service outage occurs, it should be remedied quickly. Requirements [301] for RBOC X.25 networks specify a time to restore of 3.5 to 4 hours. Given the premium nature of SMDS, the lower value is used.

The **SMDS Mean Time to Restore Objective** is no more than 3.5 hours.

7.3.4 Availability

The two previous objectives can be used to estimate the availability. A cycle consists of an interval of service availability followed by an interval of service outage. The fraction of time that the service is available for a cycle can be estimated as 3500/(3500 + 3.5) = .999000999. Rounding this result yields the value for the availability objective.

The **SMDS Availability Objective** is 99.9%.

Another way of expressing this objective is that the service should be unavailable no more than 8.76 hours per year.

Table 7.1 summarizes the SMDS availability objectives.

Objective	Value
Scheduled Service Time	24 hours a day, 7 days a week
Mean Time Between Service Outages	No less than 3500 hours
Mean Time To Restore	No more than 3.5 hours
Availability	99.9%

Table 7.1 Summary of Availability Objectives

The implication of these availability objectives is that SMDS should provide sufficient availability for all but the most demanding SMDS customer applications. SMDS availability should be better than private lines because of the internal network capability to route around failures [1059]. The weak link will probably be the transmission facility from the customer premises to the serving central office. Therefore, for applications that need higher availability, redundancy for this weak link will be required. We suggest either special arrangements with the SMDS provider to obtain diverse, redundant access links or integration of additional data networking services from alternative network providers.

7.4   Accuracy Objectives

Accuracy refers to the level of errors that occur during the transfer of SMDS customer data. Since the service is the transfer of variable-length SMDS User Information, all of the accuracy objectives are stated in terms of L3_PDUs. (See

Chapter 4 for the complete definition of L3_PDU.) Five types of errors are addressed by these objectives: L3_PDUs Not Delivered, Errored L3_PDUs, Misdelivered L3_PDUs, Duplicated L3_PDUs, and Missequenced L3_PDUs. The definitions of all but the last error are based on [X.140].

Each objective is stated as a ratio of L3_PDUs delivered and/or not delivered across an SNI by SMDS. Thus, each SNI has five objectives for error ratios associated with it.

Missequenced L3_PDUs are only defined for Individually Addressed L3_PDUs. The other errors apply to both Individually and Group Addressed L3_PDUs. For the ratios associated with these other errors, Group Addressed L3_PDUs will contribute to the ratios associated with several SNIs. For example, suppose a Group Addressed L3_PDU is destined for both SNI A and SNI B but is only delivered to SNI A. For the ratio associated with SNI A, this counts as a delivered L3_PDU. For the ratio associated with SNI B, this counts as a lost L3_PDU.

7.4.1 L3_PDU Not-Delivered Ratio

The L3_PDU Not-Delivered Ratio is the ratio of the number of *lost L3_PDUs* to the total number L3_PDUs presented to SMDS across an SNI. Lost L3_PDUs include those L3_PDUs that contain errors that SIP detects when properly processed. For example, if an L2_PDU contains errored bits in its payload so that the payload CRC will detect the error, then the L3_PDU associated with this L2_PDU is a lost L3_PDU.

Lost L3_PDUs do not include L3_PDUs discarded by the proper operation of SMDS features. For example, L3_PDUs discarded due to Address Screening and Access Class enforcement are not considered as lost L3_PDUs, since their discard is not due to improper service provider operation.

The L3_PDU Not-Delivered Ratio is probably the least aggressive of all of the performance objectives. The reason is the embedded digital transmission facilities in RBOC telephone network access links (the transmission facility from the customer premises to the serving central office). It is anticipated that transmission errors on copper-based T1 facilities will be the dominant cause of lost L3_PDUs. Under normal operation, bit-error rates on this type of facility can be as high as 10^{-8}. If each bit error is uncorrelated with the other bit errors, the probability of a 1200-byte L3_PDU containing a bit error can be calculated[4] to

---

[4]If we assume a full 44 bytes of L3_PDU overhead, $\lceil 1244/44 \rceil = 29$ L2_PDUs are needed. Thus, the total number of bits transmitted is $29 \times 53 \times 8 = 12296$. If $p = 10^{-8}$, then the probability of an error is $1 - (1 - p)^{12296} = 1.23 \times 10^{-4}$. The assumption that the bit errors are uncorrelated is conservative, since correlation between the bit errors will result in fewer L3_PDUs having errors,

be approximately 10^{-4}. The use of a 1200-byte average data field is reasonable for the case of a DS1 interface since it yields a reasonable packet transmission delay for the slow speed SNI and is consistent with maximum packet sizes typically found on today's data networks.

> The **SMDS L3_PDU Not-Delivered Ratio Objective** is 1×10^{-4} for collections of L3_PDUs whose user data fields average 1200 bytes.

The loss of an L3_PDU should not mean the loss of data, since transport-layer protocols (or the equivalent) running above SMDS will detect the loss and automatically recover. Therefore, the impact of lost L3_PDUs will manifest itself as delay as the recovery protocol retransmits the information, possibly after waiting for a timer to expire. The size of this delay is dependent on the L3_PDU size, the transmission window, the delay between the devices running the recovery protocol, and transmission rate. Our advice is to keep the L3_PDU size at less than 1200 bytes when accessing SMDS on a DS1-based SNI.

7.4.2   Errored L3_PDU Ratio

An errored L3_PDU is an L3_PDU that contains bits in error, extra bits, or missing bits[5] such that the plethora of error checking-facilities[6] will fail to detect the error(s). Since the optional 32-bit CRC is not checked by SMDS, this error-checking facility is not included in this definition of errored L3_PDU. The Errored L3_PDU Ratio is the number of errored L3_PDUs delivered divided by the sum of the number of successfully delivered L3_PDUs and the number of errored L3_PDUs delivered.

In establishing an objective for this ratio, the example of existing standard LAN protocols is used. These protocols typically use a 32-bit CRC. A conservative estimate of the probability of an error being undetected by this CRC is $2^{-32} = 2.33 \times 10^{-10}$. When this is multiplied by the probability of a maximum length L3_PDU containing a bit error, approximately $1 - (1 - 10^{-8})^{9000 \times 8} =$

---

and those that have errors will tend to have multiple bit errors. Such bunching of bit errors is typical on copper-based transmission facilities.

[5]From the definition of SIP, all bits of an L3_PDU, except possibly the bits in the BETAG fields, should be delivered unchanged.

[6]During the development of IEEE Standard 802.6-1990, the error-checking mechanisms in the protocol proliferated like weeds. The fertilizer was provided by the usual committee consensus-building and a desire by some participants to design the ultimate error-checking protocol for use with cell-based protocols. SMDS is not the ultimate service, but the commitment to align SMDS with IEEE 802.6 meant that SIP must bear the resulting burden.

7.2×10^{-4}, we obtain about 1.7×10^{-13}. Adding some margin for error[7] yields the objective.

The **SMDS Errored L3_PDU Ratio Objective** is 5×10^{-13}.

It should be noted that a draft of the IEEE Project 802 functional requirements [802Req] suggested that undetected errors should not occur with a probability greater than 5×10^{-14} per octet of data transferred. Since $5 \times 10^{-14} \times 9188 = 4.59 \times 10^{-10}$, the SMDS objective implies better performance than that proposed in the IEEE draft for maximum-length L3_PDUs.

The implication for SMDS customers is that networking configurations that depend successfully on LANs to not deliver errored data can be equally successfully used with SMDS.[8]

7.4.3 Misdelivered L3_PDU Ratio

A misdelivered L3_PDU is an L3_PDU received across an SNI not associated with the Destination Address of the L3_PDU. In other words, the L3_PDU was intended for a different SNI. The Misdelivered L3_PDU Ratio is the number of misdelivered L3_PDUs received across the SNI divided by the sum of the number of successful L3_PDUs, the number of errored L3_PDUs, and the number of misdelivered L3_PDUs received across the SNI. Such misdelivery is likely to result from failure of the routing function in one or more SMDS Switching Systems. It is assumed that the nature of the routing function will be similar to existing packet switches, and thus the objective is based on existing requirements [301].

The **SMDS Misdelivered L3_PDU Ratio Objective** is 5×10^{-8}.

Misdelivered L3_PDUs should not have serious impact on the SMDS customer beyond the consumption of bandwidth on the SNI. Either the receiving CPE will filter out the L3_PDU because of the improper Destination Address, or a similar filtering will occur based on a higher-layer address (e.g., IP). For the above objective, the bandwidth impact is negligible.

---

[7]Pun intended.

[8]If you are really concerned about undetected errors, the optional CRC32 of the L3_PDU (see Section 4.5.9) can also be used to detect errors. The effect is to multiply 5×10^{-13} by 2^{-32} to obtain 1.16×10^{-24}. This number is so small that we believe it to approximate the probability that buttered bread will fall buttered side up.

7.4.4   Duplicated L3_PDU Ratio

When CPE transmits an L3_PDU to SMDS, only one copy of that L3_PDU should be delivered across a given destination SNI. This is true even when the L3_PDU is Group Addressed and several addresses associated with the SNI are members of the group (see Section 3.3.2). When more than one copy of the L3_PDU is delivered, each additional copy is defined as a *duplicated L3_PDU*. A duplicated L3_PDU could cause serious problems for protocols running on top of SIP that use unnumbered data units. An example of such a protocol is IEEE Std 802.2-1989 [802.2], Logical Link Control when using Type 2 (connection-oriented) Operation which uses unnumbered acknowledgments. The Duplicated L3_PDU Ratio is the number of duplicated L3_PDUs divided by the total number of L3_PDUs delivered across an SNI.

In determining the objective, it is assumed that duplicated L3_PDUs will arise from routing function failures in SMDS Switching Systems. Therefore, the same reasoning that was applied to the L3_PDU Misdelivered Ratio Objective is applied to this objective.

The **SMDS Duplicated L3_PDU Ratio Objective** is 5×10^{-8}.

7.4.5   Missequenced L3_PDU Ratio

The missequenced performance objective is undoubtedly the most complex of all of the objectives. It is motivated by the observation that certain uses of SMDS will employ protocols on top of SIP that were designed under the assumption that they would be used on top of a sequential, bit-oriented physical medium. In other words, the design assumption was that protocol data units would never get out of order. An example of such a protocol is IEEE Std 802.2-1989 [802.2] Logical Link Control when using Type 2 (connection-oriented) Operation. This is the protocol typically used when bridging token ring LANs [802.5]. It can be shown (see Chapter 8) that missequenced protocol data units can lead to undesirable behavior (e.g., RESETs) by devices that conform to [802.2].

The situation is further complicated by the slotted nature of SIP.[9] It is possible that L3_PDUs can be interleaved, as shown in Figure 7.3. In this example, two L3_PDUs are interleaved. Which one is first? According to [802.6], L3_PDU number 2 is first. This makes sense because at the receiving system, L3_PDU number 2 will be the first PDU to be complete and ready for processing by the protocol running on top of SIP.

---

[9]The use of small cells in ATM is very similar to the use of slots in SIP. Consequently, the definition of sequentiality described here must also apply when SMDS is accessed via ATM. See Chapter 13.

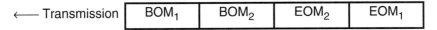

Figure 7.3 Example of the interleaving of L3_PDUs, using L2_PDUs

Now consider the case where the sequence of L2_PDUs in the example of Figure 7.3 is transmitted across an SNI to SMDS, and both L3_PDUs are destined for the same egress SNI. One approach would be to deliver the L2_PDUs across the egress SNI exactly as they arrived across the ingress SNI. However, this is generally not possible. If the egress SNI has 1 as the maximum number of concurrent data units (see Section 3.4.5), then the sequence of Figure 7.3 violates the service feature.[10] So, a sequentiality objective must be more than a simple-minded relay of L2_PDUs.

To define a meaningful objective, it is necessary to consider where L3_PDU sequentiality is important. In fact, it is only important for service data units being exchanged between two SAPs for the protocol running on top of SIP. It is reasonable to assume that these SAPs will be identified by a unique SMDS address. Therefore, sequentiality need only be maintained for L3_PDUs being sent between a specific pair of SMDS addresses. Furthermore, according to IEEE Std 802.6-1990, when a device conforming to [802.6] uses the connectionless MAC procedures, it must finish transmitting a connectionless PDU before starting another PDU (i.e., it must send one connectionless PDU at a time). Thus, the sequence of L2_PDUs of Figure 7.3 should not occur for L3_PDUs with the same Source Address. This simplifies the implementation of the service-provider network.

Unfortunately, there is another factor that must be considered. Figure 7.4 shows a case where L2_PDU order is changed, but protocols depending on L3_PDU sequentiality would operate properly. This sequence is acceptable because the relative order of the EOMs is maintained. But now suppose the CPE behind the receiving SNI is designed so that the one-at-a-time property of [802.6] is assumed. An example might be a bridge based on [802.6]. In such a case the output sequence of Figure 7.4 could well cause this receiving CPE to behave improperly. Another consideration is the case of SMDS provided by multiple interconnected carriers. Maintaining sequentiality is much easier for a service provider if the input sequences are like those of Figure 7.4. Consequently, if the L2_PDU order is changed by one of the networks as in Figure 7.4, implementation of the receiving interconnected network is more difficult. Thus the definition of sequentiality must preclude this case.

The above discussion leads to the following rather complicated definition of missequencing. An individually addressed L3_PDU is defined to be missequenced if the following two conditions both hold:

---

[10]This illustrates that SMDS is more than just cell-relay. It is quite common to see SMDS erroneously labeled as cell-relay.

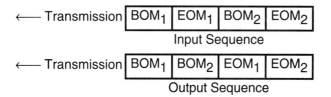

Figure 7.4 Example of changed L2_PDU order

1. It is sent across the ingress SNI without any interleaved L2_PDUs from other L3_PDUs with the same Source and Destination Address.

2. The EOM (or SSM) segment of the L3_PDU is delivered to the destination SNI after a BOM (or SSM) segment of another L3_PDU that was sent later with the same Source and Destination Address.

In other words, L3_PDUs for a given source and destination that enter the network noninterleaved should exit the network noninterleaved and in the same order as they entered the network. The Missequenced L3_PDU Ratio is the number of missequenced Individually Addressed L3_PDUs divided by the total number of Individually Addressed L3_PDUs delivered across the SNI.

Based on requirements [1059] on the internals of a service-provider network, the only time an L3_PDU may be missequenced is when there is a topology change such as a transmission system failure. Thus, the objective is set aggressively.

The **SMDS Missequenced L3_PDU Ratio Objective** is 1×10^{-9}.

Table 7.2 summarizes the SMDS accuracy objectives.

Objective	Value
L3_PDU Not-Delivered Ratio	1×10^{-4}
Errored L3_PDU Ratio	5×10^{-13}
Misdelivered L3_PDU Ratio	5×10^{-8}
Duplicated L3_PDU Ratio	5×10^{-8}
Missequenced L3_PDU Ratio	1×10^{-9}

Table 7.2 Summary of Accuracy Objectives

7.5   Delay Objectives

The performance objective of most interest in data networks is probably delay. In the case of SMDS, it is the delay of L3_PDUs that is meaningful. Unfortunately, in defining the delay objectives, there are a number of complications that must be ignored. Most of these complications arise from the slotted nature of SIP and the possibility that there may be multiple CPE devices attached to an SNI using SIP.

The delay of interest is the time interval from the transmission of the first bit of an L3_PDU by the sending CPE to the reception at the destination CPE of the last bit of the L3_PDU. But what if there are several CPE devices attached to the ingress SNI? They could create contention for bandwidth on the access DQDB both for local traffic and for access to SMDS. Thus the delay seen could be greatly impacted; yet all of this impact is beyond the control of SMDS. Now consider the egress SNI. Local traffic could contend for bandwidth on the access DQDB, thus delaying the L3_PDU delivery by the network. Again, this is beyond the control of SMDS. Another factor impacting the delay is having more L3_PDUs ready for delivery than the limit on the maximum number of concurrent data units in transit (MCDUs Out; see Section 3.4.5).

Since it is not at all clear how to factor these DQDB issues into a definition of delay objectives, they are explicitly ignored. For SIP-based access, the delay objectives apply only to L3_PDUs for which (1) the transmission across both SNIs is in contiguous SIP L2_PDUs, (2) there is no contention for bandwidth between the network and CPE on the access DQDB, and (3) the MCDUs Out limit is not exceeded on the egress SNI. Similarly, for ATM- and SRI- based access, a "guaranteed" information rate is assumed for virtual connections to transport SMDS information. These simplifying assumptions are not needed for DXI-based access, since bandwidth contention is not applicable to this access type.

With the aid of Figure 7.5, the calculations underlying the delay objectives can be described. Three delay components are included in the calculation: two access path delays (d_1 and d_3) plus the delay across the service provider network (d_2). The values of d_1 and d_3 will depend on the type of access path. For example, for DS3-based SIP access, d_1 and d_3 are computed by dividing the number of L2_PDUs in the L3_PDU by 96,000 L2_PDUs per second, as provided by the DS3 PLCP (see Section 4.7.2). There are 210 L2_PDUs in a maximum-size L3_PDU, and thus $d_1 = d_3 = 210/96,000 = 2.19$ ms.[11] The same calculation applies to ATM-based access where SMDS is supported over an

---

[11]Recall that these objectives are intended for the service of a single U. S. LEC network, as defined in Section 7.1 and Figure 7.1, and thus the propagation time can be ignored in these calculations.

ATM virtual connection with a cell rate of 96,000 cells per second. SIP-based access over a DS1 (or ATM-based access over a virtual connection providing the same bandwidth) yields 10 L2_PDUs (or ATM cells) every 3 ms (see Section 4.7.1). Thus $d_1 = d_3 = 210 \times (3/10) = 63$ ms. Similar calculations can be done for SIP-based E1 or E3 access or ATM-based access providing equivalent bandwidth.

For DXI-based access and SRI-based access, the HDLC frame overhead can be ignored, and d_1 and d_3 can be derived by dividing the size of the L3_PDU by the available bandwidth. Recall that for Frame Relay-based access, the maximum size L3_PDU may not always be supported. For example, a 1600-byte L3_PDU on an SRI 64 Kbps virtual connection implies $d_1 = d_3 = (1600 \times 8/64,000) = 200$ ms. For the maximum size L3_PDU on a DXI DS1 access path, $d_1 = d_3 = 48$ ms.

To complete the calculation, engineering judgment is applied to estimate that 15 ms should be allotted for d_2. Note that [1240] uses the same number for d_2 for SRI access, where d_2 represents the delay of the combined Frame Relay network and SMDS. The total delay is just the sum of the three components.

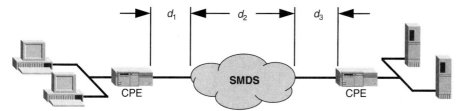

Figure 7.5 Delay components

These calculations ignore certain factors. For example, as discussed in Section 4.3.4, it may be possible to implement switching systems that do pipelining or cut-through. This can reduce the delay significantly when both access paths are DS1.[12] Another factor is the speed-matching necessary, for example, when L3_PDUs are sent from a DS3 SNI to a DS1 SNI. It is possible that buffering will occur in the network and thus impact the delay. The practical realities will not be understood until some experience is gained with network implementation and use.

---

[12]There are a number of implementation issues regarding the desirability of pipelining. Therefore, the Bellcore requirements are written to allow implementations either with or without pipelining. Network equipment vendors will choose an approach based on their product implementation.

7.5.1   Delay for Individually Addressed L3_PDUs

Using the above calculations, the delay objectives for individually addressed L3_PDUs are finally derived. They are stated as 95th percentiles, which means 95 percent of L3_PDUs should have delay less than or equal to the objective.

The **SMDS Delay for Individually Addressed L3_PDUs Objective** is given in Tables 7.3 through 7.6.

Key to SNI types	
56	56 Kbps DXI or SRI
64	64 Kbps DXI or SRI
384	384 Kbps DXI or SRI
768	768 Kbps DXI or SRI
1536	1536 Kbps DXI or SRI
DS1	DS1 SNI or ATM UNI
DS3	DS3 SNI or ATM UNI
E1	E1 SNI or ATM UNI
E3	E3 SNI or ATM UNI
N/A	Not Applicable

Note: Full bandwidth on the Frame Relay permanent virtual circuit is assumed for delays when an SRI SNI is present.

Table 7.3 Key to SNI types for delay tables

SNI A								
56	2653							
64	2488	2323						
384	1526	1361	400					
768	1430	1265	304	207				
1536	1382	1217	255	159	111			
DS1	1397	1232	270	174	126	140		
DS3	1336	1171	210	113	65	80	20	
E1	N/A	N/A	N/A	N/A	N/A	N/A	N/A	140	
E3	N/A	N/A	N/A	N/A	N/A	N/A	N/A	80	20
	56	64	384	768	1536	DS1	DS3	E1	E3
SNI B								

Table 7.4 95th percentile delay for Individually Addressed L3_PDUs (9232 bytes)

SNI A	56	64	384	768	1536	DS1	DS3	E1	E3
56	472								
64	444	415							
384	277	248	82						
768	260	232	65	48					
1536	252	223	57	40	32				
DS1	255	226	59	43	34	140			
DS3	244	215	49	32	24	80	20		
E1	N/A	N/A	N/A	N/A	N/A	N/A	N/A	140	
E3	N/A	N/A	N/A	N/A	N/A	N/A	N/A	80	20
	56	64	384	768	1536	DS1	DS3	E1	E3
				SNI B					

Table 7.5 95th percentile delay for Individually Addressed L3_PDUs (1600 bytes)

SNI A	56	64	384	768	1536	DS1	DS3	E1	E3
56	161								
64	152	143							
384	99	90	36						
768	93	84	31	26					
1536	91	82	28	23	20				
DS1	92	83	29	24	21	140			
DS3	88	79	26	20	18	80	20		
E1	N/A	N/A	N/A	N/A	N/A	N/A	N/A	140	
E3	N/A	N/A	N/A	N/A	N/A	N/A	N/A	80	20
	56	64	384	768	1536	DS1	DS3	E1	E3
				SNI B					

Table 7.6 95th percentile delay for Individually Addressed L3_PDUs (512 bytes)

The values in Tables 7.4 through 7.6 come from a number of sources. The numbers for communication among DS1 and DS3 SNIs can be found in [772]. The numbers for communication among E1 and E3 SNIs are from [ESIG003].[13] The numbers for DXI- and SRI- based access for 512- and 1600- byte L3_PDUs are from [1239] and [1240] respectively. All other numbers are the result of our calculations as described above, with calculations for ATM UNIs based on the assumption that the bandwidth allocated to the virtual connection is equivalent to either DS1 or DS3, as described in Chapter 13. Notice that the delays for 1536-Kbps DXI and SRI SNIs are lower than the delays for DS1 SNIs and ATM UNIs,

---

[13]Since these numbers are identical to the DS1 and DS3 numbers, the methodology behind them must differ from the approach described earlier.

even though the physical bit rates are the same. These differences result from the lower protocol overhead of the frame-based access protocols compared to the overhead of the cell-based access protocols. The same effect occurs for Group Addressed L3_PDUs (see Section 7.5.2).

It is interesting to note that if the L3_PDU is 38 L2_PDUs on DS1-based SNIs (which is consistent with a 1600-byte INFORMATION field), then the calculation for the DS1-to-DS1 delay is $38 \times (3/10) + 38 \times (3/10) + 15 = 37.8$ ms. Thus, the objectives in Table 7.5 may well be conservative compared to what will be achieved in practice. A similar calculation leads to the same conclusion for Table 7.6.

From the SMDS customer viewpoint, the important delay is that experienced between end systems, of which the SMDS delay is just one component. The significance of the SMDS delay is highly dependent on the configuration of a customer's network. For DS3-to-DS3, the SMDS delay will probably be comparable to other delays, such as the delay through routers and across 10-Mbps LANs.

7.5.2 Delay for Group Addressed L3_PDUs

The definition of delay for Group Addressed L3_PDUs is the same as for Individually Addressed L3_PDUs, except that it is applied to each copy. In other words, if a group has five members, an L3_PDU sent to the group from an address that is not a member results in five measurements of delay. In setting the objectives, allowance must be made for the fact that supporting Group Addressing will require more processing in the network. Once again, engineering judgment is applied, and 80 ms is added to d_2 to account for the extra network processing. Thus, the numbers in Tables 7.7 through 7.9 are derived from Tables 7.4 through 7.6 by simply adding 80 ms.

> The **SMDS Delay for Group Addressed L3_PDUs Objective** is given in Table 7.3 and Tables 7.7 through 7.9.

The larger delays for Group Addressed L3_PDUs compared to Individually Addressed L3_PDU delays are not significant so long as the use of this feature is low-volume, which should be the case when it is used for functions such as address discovery as described in Chapter 8. In actual practice, the delays of Group Addressed L3_PDUs could be comparable to the delays of Individually Addressed L3_PDUs if the internal network routing and forwarding protocols specified in [1059] are used. This is because the forwarding procedures in [1059] for Group Addressed L3_PDUs are very similar to those for Individually

SNI A	56	64	384	768	1536	DS1	DS3	E1	E3
56	2733								
64	2568	2403							
384	1606	1441	480						
768	1510	1345	384	287					
1536	1462	1297	335	239	191				
DS1	1477	1312	350	254	206	220			
DS3	1416	1251	290	193	145	160	100		
E1	N/A	N/A	N/A	N/A	N/A	N/A	N/A	220	
E3	N/A	N/A	N/A	N/A	N/A	N/A	N/A	160	100
	56	64	384	768	1536	DS1	DS3	E1	E3
					SNI B				

Table 7.7 95th percentile delay for Group Addressed L3_PDUs (9232 bytes)

Addressed L3_PDUs. However, service provider network equipment using proprietary procedures may not be as efficient as those in [1059].

SNI A	56	64	384	768	1536	DS1	DS3	E1	E3
56	552								
64	524	495							
384	357	328	162						
768	340	312	145	128					
1536	332	303	137	120	112				
DS1	335	306	139	123	114	220			
DS3	324	295	129	112	104	160	100		
E1	N/A	N/A	N/A	N/A	N/A	N/A	N/A	220	
E3	N/A	N/A	N/A	N/A	N/A	N/A	N/A	160	100
	56	64	384	768	1536	DS1	DS3	E1	E3
					SNI B				

Table 7.8 95th percentile delay for Group Addressed L3_PDUs (1600 bytes)

7.6   Summary

The performance objectives for SMDS provide an indication to the SMDS customer of the level of performance to expect from the service. These objectives are limited in two important ways. First, they only apply to RBOC intra-LATA networks. Second, measurement procedures are not defined, and

SNI A	56	64	384	768	1536	DS1	DS3	E1	E3
56	241								
64	232	223							
384	179	170	116						
768	173	164	111	106					
1536	171	162	108	103	100				
DS1	172	163	109	104	101	220			
DS3	168	159	106	100	98	160	100		
E1	N/A	N/A	N/A	N/A	N/A	N/A	N/A	220	
E3	N/A	N/A	N/A	N/A	N/A	N/A	N/A	160	100
	56	64	384	768	1536	DS1	DS3	E1	E3
					SNI B				

Table 7.9 95th percentile delay for Group Addressed L3_PDUs (512 bytes)

thus there is no conclusive way to determine if the objectives have been met. Nevertheless, the objectives establish the parameters on which the quality-of-service for SMDS is based.

Finally, we close this chapter with Table 7.10, which summarizes all of the objectives.

Objective	Value
Scheduled Service Time	24 hours a day, 7 days a week
Mean Time Between Service Outages	No less than 3500 hours
Mean Time To Restore	No more than 3.5 hours
Availability	99.9%
L3_PDU Not-Delivered Ratio	1×10^{-4}
Errored L3_PDU Ratio	5×10^{-13}
Misdelivered L3_PDU Ratio	5×10^{-8}
Duplicated L3_PDU Ratio	5×10^{-8}
Missequenced L3_PDU Ratio	1×10^{-9}
Delay DS3 and DS3, Individually Addressed	20 ms
Delay DS3 and DS1, Individually Addressed	80 ms
Delay DS1 and DS1, Individually Addressed	140 ms
Delay DS3 and DS3, Group Addressed	100 ms
Delay DS3 and DS1, Group Addressed	160 ms
Delay DS1 and DS1, Group Addressed	220 ms

Note: Only the delay objectives for DS1- and DS3- based SNIs are summarized here for the sake of brevity.

Table 7.10 Summary of objectives

8

Internetworking and SMDS

This chapter discusses how SMDS can be used with routers in internets. Chapter 9 describes how bridges can use SMDS. This chapter reviews how SMDS can be used in the following internetworking architectures: TCP/IP, OSI, AppleTalk, XNS, NetWare, VINES, 3+ and 3+Open, DECnet Phase IV, and DECnet Phase V. It is beyond the scope of this book to review all details of these architectures. We describe the main features, followed by a presentation of how SMDS fits into each architecture and a description of any particular issues relevant for the use of SMDS. Much of this chapter draws from material developed in the Internet community and in the SMDS Interest Group (SIG). Due to the varying level of detail of the SIG specifications, we describe the role of SMDS in some architectures in more depth than others. Section 8.1 describes some issues that have general relevance when using SMDS in an internet, such as protocol-multiplexing techniques, address resolution, and the support of connection-oriented reliable data streams.

CPE designers should find this chapter useful in designing SMDS equipment. SMDS customers who want to use SMDS to connect routers will find this chapter useful in configuring both their routers and the associated SMDS subscription parameters.

8.1   General Issues

Before we describe how SMDS fits into some specific architectures, we first present some issues that are common for many internetworking architectures.

8.1.1   Support of Broadcast and Multicast Datagrams

SMDS is designed to look like a LAN, even over a geographically wide area. Nevertheless, there are some differences:

- SMDS does not support a global broadcast capability.

- Multicast addresses and recipients have to be preconfigured. There are no special SMDS Group Address values set aside for specific applications; customers have to configure their own environments. There is also a limit to the maximum number of recipients. When the number of intended recipients for a particular multicast application exceeds this maximum, participating stations must be configured with multiple SMDS Group Addresses for that application.

- LANs represent a nonrecurring expense (not counting maintenance), while SMDS usually involves monthly recurring charges. The implication is that there tends to be a premium on efficient bandwidth use (e.g., avoiding unnecessary structural broadcasts).

Protocols and applications that use SMDS and that require a broadcast capability can be served by the use of the SMDS Group Addressing capability. Examples include address resolution protocols and certain routing protocols. For this to work, an SMDS user needs to identify all SMDS stations and associated SMDS addresses that are to be reached by the broadcast. Then the user must set up an SMDS Group Address, BROADCAST_GA, that includes this list of addresses. Subsequent broadcasts must be carried in L3_PDUs addressed to BROADCAST_GA. If Address Screens are used, they should at least allow communication between all addresses identified by BROADCAST_GA.

Multicast internetworking datagrams are carried by either the SMDS Individual Addressing or Group Addressing capability. Under the assumption that multiple stations of a particular multicast application connect to SMDS, an internetworking level, multicast-addressed packet can be mapped to an L3_PDU directed at a configured SMDS Group Address, MULTICAST_GA(n). If very few stations with the multicast application are connected through SMDS, the stations could use their SMDS Individual Addresses to communicate. An example of this scenario is the interconnection of two LANs with all multicast stations connected to the LANs.

All packets carried over SMDS are subject to the 9188-byte limit of the INFORMATION field of the L3_PDU. Observe that some protocol-multiplexing techniques cause the actual limit to be a few bytes less than 9188 (see Sections 8.1.3 and 8.1.4). For example, TCP/IP uses LLC1/SNAP encapsulation that consumes 8 bytes, so that 9180 bytes are left for IP packets. This is not a limitation for any of the applications discussed in this book.

8.1.2   Support of Connection-Oriented Reliable Data Streams

SMDS provides a connectionless service. Each L3_PDU is labeled with Source and Destination Addresses, and the L3_PDUs are routed independently. Inherent to this service is that packet loss and out-of-order delivery may occur, although the service objectives are such that the probability of these events happening is small (see Chapter 7). For applications that require preservation of the order of data units, the CPE must employ special procedures. Typically, this function is performed by the application itself (e.g., NFS) or by end-to-end transport protocols such as TCP [RFC793] and ISO8073 (Class 4 [ISO8073]). These protocols are well equipped to correct these events, and they can provide an application with a connection-oriented reliable data stream. Figure 8.1 shows this method. For an in-depth description of TCP and the OSI transport protocols, see, for example, [Comer1], [Rose2], and [Piscitello].

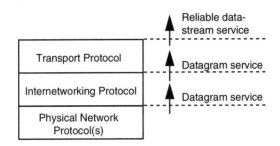

Figure 8.1 Reliable data-stream service, using an appropriate transport protocol

Another method that is employed for some LAN applications is the use of the IEEE Logical Link Control Type 2 (see also 8.1.3). LLC2 is often used for IEEE 802.5 Token Ring LANs [802.5] to support SNA (Systems Network Architecture) applications; it is a single-hop (or single MAC-bridged-LAN/WAN) protocol. If SMDS were to connect these Token Ring networks through bridges, LLC2 could be used over SMDS, as shown in Figure 8.2.

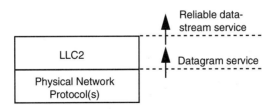

Figure 8.2 Reliable data-stream service, using LLC2

LLC Type 2 can provide a connection-oriented data link service comparable to certain HDLC procedures, [ISO4335] and [ISO7809], maintaining separate connection-establishment, data transfer, and connection-release states. LLC2 was originally designed for operation over LANs, which typically make use of shared media. In other words, packets necessarily arrive in the same order as they are sent. Since sequentiality cannot be guaranteed to be perfect with SMDS,[1] it is interesting to question the impact of L3_PDU misordering on LLC2 and the protocols and applications that use it. It is beyond the scope of this book to provide an in-depth analysis of this issue. Instead, we present a summary of an analysis performed at Bellcore [Gill] and the relevant conclusions.

Figure 8.3 shows a simplified illustration of LLC2 events. IEEE802.2/ISO8802-2 [802.2] describes the precise details. In simple terms, the events are summarized as follows. After connection establishment, data are sent, received and acknowledged using a sliding-window mechanism. The window represents the number of frames that can be sent before an acknowledgment is received. The receipt of a data frame out of order causes the recipient to signal to the sender that the frame was rejected and that it is still waiting for an earlier frame. The earlier frame may then arrive and be acknowledged, but the rejected frame has caused a gap in the sequence, so subsequent frames will be ignored. Meanwhile, the sender, having seen the frame-reject signal, will resend the frame that was out of order. Upon receipt, this frame will also be rejected; since it has been received already, the copy will be recognized as a frame outside the receive window, which will cause the recipient to initiate a link reset (or even disconnect) to resynchronize the link. The same effect will occur after the receipt of misordered acknowledgments.

For applications, the important question is how link reset and disconnect impacts the end-to-end throughput of the link. It can intuitively be understood that this will be influenced by the following:

- The actual misordering probability (P) provided by SMDS. The objective for the SMDS missequenced L3_PDU Ratio is 1×10^{-9} (see Chapter 7).

- The delay (D) experienced over SMDS (see Chapter 7).

- The time (R) that applications in the CPE require to reset or reconnect. The value of this parameter is implementation-dependent.

Another parameter that influences the equation is the time (S) that is needed by a station to emit a data packet.

---

[1]No network with switching can guarantee perfect sequentiality. Rerouting around failures and switch malfunctions that can lead to missequencing always have a nonzero probability.

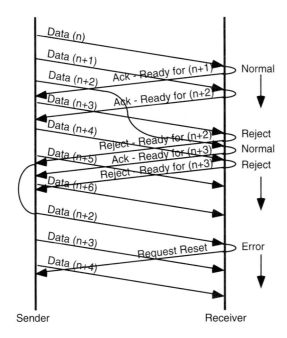

Figure 8.3 Example of LLC2 reception of out-of-sequence PDUs

Figure 8.4 shows some results of the initial analysis.[2] The first diagram assumes a reset time of 0 (immediate reset) and a packet-emission time of $S = 2$ ms which approximates the time needed to emit a maximum-size L3_PDU on a DS3-based SNI.[3] The second diagram assumes $S = 2$ ms, and a cross-network delay $D = 20$ ms, which is the objective for SMDS intra-LATA DS3-to-DS3 delay.

The diagrams show that the effect of missequenced LLC frames only causes noticeable loss of throughput when P is high, on the order of $P = 1 \times 10^{-4}$, the network delay is high, and the reset time is on the order of R = 1000 ms. Calculations show that even with an exaggerated $D = 500$ ms and $P = 1 \times 10^{-4}$, throughput is reduced by only 10–15%, and that throughput can be kept to almost 100% with $P = 1 \times 10^{-6}$. The throughput figures are quite encouraging, considering that typical network delays can be expected to remain within the stated service objectives,[4] and that the service objectives for P are substantially

---

[2]Conversation with Jay Gill, Bellcore.

[3]For slower speed access lines the effect of out-of-order delivery is smaller. This can be understood by considering S as the time difference between the emission of the first bit of two PDUs (see Figure 8.3). An increased S implies a lower loss of PDUs during the reject and reset recovery phases.

[4]A trade show demonstration in San Jose of a network with a DS1 subscriber link showed a round-trip delay of 150 ms to Geneva, Switzerland.

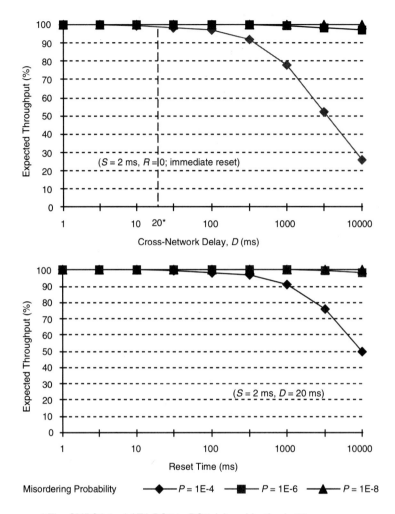

* The SMDS intra-LATA DS3-to-DS3 delay objective is 20 ms.

Figure 8.4 Some expected effects of L3_PDU misordering

better than 10^{-4}. No good statistics for values of R in common implementations are available at this time. Other possible effects of resets on higher layer protocols in implementations also need further analysis for a more precise understanding of the effects of out-of-order PDU delivery.

8.1.3 Protocol Multiplexing

Packets that are received through SMDS must carry some information that allows the receiving station to determine the type of higher layer protocol that is carried in order to process it properly. Several approaches are possible.

8.1.3.1   Ethertypes

The frame header of Ethernet includes a field called PROTOCOL TYPE (see Figure 8.5) that specifies the carried protocol. The 2-byte identifiers for this field are allocated by Xerox (see, for example, [RFC1340]).

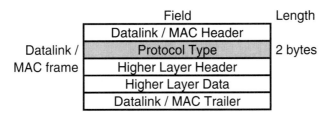

Figure 8.5 Use of the Ethernet Protocol Type

8.1.3.2   LLC/SNAP

IEEE 802 uses a method that is similar to the Ethertypes concept, but distinguishes source and destination. These fields are called SAPs (SERVICE ACCESS POINTS). These fields are part of the *Logical Link Control (LLC)* header. LLC is standardized as IEEE Std. 802.2-1985 [802.2]; it is a protocol layer designed on top of an IEEE 802 MAC layer service, as shown in Figure 8.6.

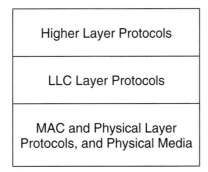

Figure 8.6 IEEE MAC and LLC protocol layers

The LLC service provides a logical link for use by higher layer protocols to transfer data. The specific functions include protocol multiplexing and an indication of the type of link service that is provided over the MAC layer service. This can be either a datagram service, LLC1, or a confirmed (connection-oriented) service, LLC2 [802.2].[5]

---

[5]Still another mode of operation, LLC3, has been standardized as a compromise between the complexity of LLC2 and the simplicity of LLC1. We are not aware of any application for this "half pregnant" protocol.

LLC1 can easily be used on top of SMDS, since both provide a datagram service. SMDS provides the MAC functions, and LLC1 adds the IEEE protocol-multiplexing capability. For a discussion of the use of LLC2, see Section 8.1.2. Unfortunately, the SAP fields that indicate the type of protocol that rides over LLC are only 1 byte long, causing the available code space to run out quickly, since only 64 SAP values can be allocated by the IEEE.[6] Therefore, IEEE defined an extension called *Sub-Network Access Protocol*, or SNAP, to allow for additional code space [802].

Figure 8.7 shows the use of LLC. In practice, the LLC Source and Destination SAP are always given the same identifier, so that this method is slightly less efficient than the original Ethernet PROTOCOL TYPE field. The SAPs are allocated by the IEEE. Table 8.1 shows some examples (see also, for example, [RFC1340]).

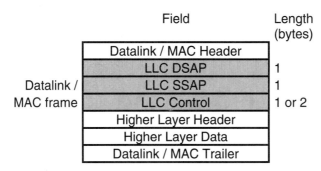

Figure 8.7 Use of IEEE LLC1

802.2 SAP	Meaning
04_H	SNA Path Control
42_H	BPDUs (Chapter 9)
AA_H	SNAP
FE_H	ISO 8473 (Section 8.3)

Table 8.1 Examples of 802.2 SAP values

When used in combination with SNAP, each SAP will indicate the value reserved for SNAP (170_D or AA_H). The CONTROL field indicates the type of operation that the LLC service provides (datagrams, etc.), and is 1 byte for LLC1, and 1 or 2 bytes for LLC2. The CONTROL field indicates the use of LLC1 by the value of 03_H (Unnumbered Information frames).

---

[6]The last 2 bits of the SAPs are reserved to distinguish global from local assignment, and to indicate use by an individual or multiple protocols.

The SNAP consists of two fields. The ORGANIZATIONALLY UNIQUE IDENTIFIER (OUI) code defines the organization that assigns the following PROTOCOL IDENTIFIER (PID). An important OUI value is 000000_H, indicating that the PID equals the Ethertypes as allocated in Ethernets (administered by Xerox). Table 8.2 shows OUI/PID values used in this book. Figure 8.8 depicts the resulting frame with LLC1/SNAP encapsulation. The LLC1/SNAP header is a simple 8-byte constant. A list is published regularly by a central Internet group, the Internet Assigned Numbers Authority (IANA) [RFC1340].

OUI		PID	
OUI Value	**Organization**	**PID value**	**Protocol**
000000_H	Ethertype	0800_H	IP
000000_H	Ethertype	0806_H	ARP / RARP
080007_H	AppleTalk	$809B_H$	AppleTalk DDP
000000_H	Ethertype	$80F3_H$	AppleTalk ARP
000000_H	Ethertype	0600_H	XNS IDP
000000_H	Ethertype	$8137_H - 8138_H$	Novell, Inc.
000000_H	Ethertype	$3C07_H - 3C0D_H$	3Com; see Section 8.7.2
$08004A_H$	Banyan	$80C4_H$	VINES IP
$08004A_H$	Banyan	$80C5_H$	VINES Echo
000000_H	Ethertype	6003_H	DECnet Phase IV
$0080C2_H$	IEEE 802.1 WG	$0001_H - 000C_H$	See Chapter 9

Table 8.2 Examples of 802.2 SNAP values

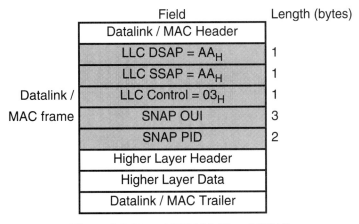

Figure 8.8 Use of IEEE LLC1 and SNAP

Given its flexibility and the large SAP/OUI/PID code space, the LLC1/SNAP technique is the most commonly used open method for protocol multiplexing. Therefore we recommend using this technique when using SMDS.

8.1.3.3   Network Layer Protocol Identifier

The CCITT and ISO have mostly relied on the use of self-identifying Network Layer (NL) protocols. This approach uses an identifier, the NETWORK LAYER PROTOCOL IDENTIFIER, or NLPID, in the first byte of a PDU. The identifier values are centrally administered by ISO/CCITT [ISO9577].[7] Most CCITT and ISO network layer protocols use this mechanism. The drawback of this method is that it is not compatible with non-CCITT/ISO protocols. Figure 8.9 shows this approach.

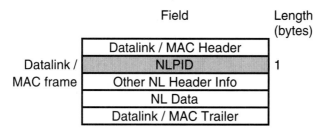

Figure 8.9 Use of the NLPID

8.1.3.4   SMDS Higher Layer Protocol Identifier

Yet another method of protocol multiplexing on top of SMDS is the use of the L3_PDU HIGHER LAYER PROTOCOL IDENTIFIER field in the L3_PDU header. This field indicates the protocol that rides directly on top of SIP Level 3. It corresponds to the IEEE Std. 802.6-1990 PROTOCOL IDENTIFICATION field [802.6] and is administered by IEEE, as discussed in Section 4.5.6. Only a code for LLC has been defined, and we recommend not using this field for protocol multiplexing, since it may not operate well between equipment of different vendors.

In practice, a combination of these protocol-multiplexing techniques is often used to overcome the problem of running protocols that have not been assigned by IEEE or ISO/CCITT.

8.1.4   Fragmentation and Reassembly

If the maximum size of a packet that needs to be transported over SMDS exceeds 9188 bytes, a fragmentation and reassembly procedure must be employed (if

---

[7]The mechanisms defined in [ISO9577] are more detailed than explained here. See, for example, [RFC1483] and [RFC1490]. We explain here only those aspects relevant for SMDS.

supported by the protocol that uses SMDS). This must also take into account any required bytes for protocol multiplexing and encapsulation. For example, LLC1 and SNAP together take up 8 bytes, so that 9180 bytes remain available for packet transport.

8.1.5   Neighbor Discovery and Address Resolution

SMDS will often be used to link LANs. In such internets, a higher (network) layer protocol is necessary to link the physical networks (the LANs and SMDS) together into a single internet. These protocols are generally referred to as *internet protocols*. Examples include Novell's IPX (Internetwork Packet Exchange), Apple's DDP (Datagram Delivery Protocol), TCP/IP's IP (Internet Protocol), and OSI's ISO 8473 (CLNP, or Connectionless Network Protocol). Because these protocols are designed to span a variety of networks, they use their own addressing discipline, which tends to be distinct from the addressing used in the underlying physical networks. Figure 8.10 shows the general picture.

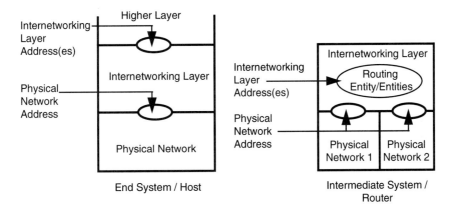

Figure 8.10 Internetworking layer and physical network addressing

For a packet to be transported over a particular physical network, it is necessary to (a) be aware of the existence of the peer system (neighbor discovery), and (b) find the binding of the address on the internet layer with the address of the physical network (address resolution). There are a number of ways to solve these problems (see also [Comer1], [Perlman], and [Piscitello]):

- *A static table in each connected router/host*
  This table contains a list of all stations that this station wishes to communicate with, and includes for each internet layer address the corresponding physical address. The advantage of this method is that it does not require the exchange of neighbor discovery and routing

messages. The drawback of this method is that changes in the network, such as the addition of a router, must be manually configured.

- *Algorithmic address binding*
  It is convenient when the address used by the physical network can be extracted from the address used on the internet layer. For example, the internet address would consist of <prefix><physical network address>. This is not often possible, since the two address spaces are usually designed and administered at different times by different organizations with different goals. However, OSI uses this method in some scenarios [ISO8348.2] [Hemrick] [SIG004].

- *A dynamic address-binding table in each router/host — address bindings on request*
  This case relies on the use of both a table in each host or router and a protocol to request a particular binding from other hosts or routers if the local table does not contain this binding. Older entries in the table are declared outdated, so that current network reconfigurations will eventually be reflected throughout the network. Address bindings are usually requested using a broadcast or multicast. Examples of this method are ARP in the TCP/IP protocol suite [RFC826] [Comer1] and AppleTalk's AARP [Apple] [Sidhu].

- *A directory or address resolution server*
  A special case of the "address bindings on request" method, this method concerns the configuration of one or more special servers in the internet, to which requests for address bindings can be directed. This method can work well, and avoids address resolution broadcast storms in large networks. Often more than one server is used for a network, in order to avoid a single point of failure for the network. An example is a dedicated ARP server.

- *A dynamic address-binding table in each router/host — advertise your presence and address binding.*
  This method is similar to the "address bindings on request" method. Instead of requesting a binding when needed, this method relies on periodic advertisement of bindings. An example of this method is OSI's ES-IS [ISO9542] [Perlman] [Piscitello].

The dynamic methods usually rely on a broadcast or multicast of the requested or advertised address binding, which can be accommodated by SMDS by setting up Group Addresses for particular communities (logical networks) of SMDS stations that need to communicate. The implication is that routing and address-binding information is only known within a logical network, and that communication between stations belonging to different logical networks is only possible via a router, that is, by traversing the same physical network (SMDS in this case) more than once. This seems somewhat wasteful, and efforts are underway to define ways to shortcut this type of routing (see, for example, [RFC1433]).[8]

8.1.6 Performance

The performance of a network affects many aspects of the protocols that make use of it.

- The settings of timers related to some protocol action at the remote end (e.g., retransmission timers) depend on the delay across the network.

- The setting of a window size (e.g., in some transport protocols) may depend on the delay across the network.

- The throughput of the network as compared with other routes to a destination.

As has been illustrated in Chapter 7, delays in networks that provide SMDS and span a very wide area are necessarily longer as compared with a single LAN, and may require special attention in cases of timer settings and nonadaptive window settings.

8.1.7 Routing

Generally speaking, routing protocols will treat SMDS as just another physical network. An appropriate routing cost or metric (in terms of delay, throughput, etc.) can be assigned to a hop over SMDS. There is one interesting difference between SMDS and LANs that may influence routing decisions. Since LANs represent a nonrecurring expense (not counting maintenance), and SMDS usually involves monthly recurring charges, there tends to be a premium on efficient bandwidth use. For example, there is more incentive to avoid situations such as unnecessary broadcasts and the routing of traffic across a public network to a router that just sends it back over the same public network to the original location.[9]

---

[8]Note also that a LAN protocol-design premise is that the set of nodes reachable by datalink broadcast is exactly the set reachable by unicast, while with SMDS there is a limit to the number of nodes that can be reached through a Group Address.

[9]This applies to situations where usage-sensitive billing is applied by the service provider. The philosophy of usage measurement for billing contained in [775] is that all L3_PDUs leaving SMDS are counted. This means that a Group Addressed L3_PDU that is delivered to n destination SNIs will cause n L3_PDUs to be counted.

8.1.8   Virtual Private Networking

Virtual private networking is a loosely used term that usually refers to the provision of public network services offered in such way that the customer appears to be the network's only user, and the network services appear to be tailored to the particular needs of that user.

SMDS has been designed to exhibit LAN-like features, even though its geographic extent may span a wide area. A distinguishing feature is the fact that SMDS is a public service that is shared among subscribers. The significance of this observation is that, without special measures, the routers of different subscribers may start talking to each other, which may not always be desired by these subscribers.

8.1.8.1   CPE-Based Access Control

One approach for SMDS CPE is to screen at protocol layers above SMDS. An example of this approach is used in the specification for running OSI over SMDS [SIG004] where passwords can be used to authenticate messages. However, in some cases it is more efficient to find a way to create a virtual private network, that is, to make SMDS appear to subscribers as a resource dedicated to their exclusive use, just like their own LANs. In other words, the stations of a subscriber should be configured as a "logical network," providing a self-contained MAC layer service, as other LANs of that subscriber do. The SMDS Address Screening and Group Addressing features can be used to accomplish this.

8.1.8.2   Address Screens

Address Screens can be set up for each participating station's SNI to allow communication only among the stations in that group and to disallow communication outside the group. Figure 8.11 shows how the example of Section 3.4.3 produces a virtual private network; the Bodacious Data routers can mutually exchange data, but data exchange with other SNIs is not allowed. This approach has the added value of preventing unwanted traffic from reaching the CPE.

8.1.8.3   Group Addresses

Another approach makes use of the fact that many of today's leading communication architectures use broadcasting or multicasting for the propagation of routing and address resolution information. Thus, for these architectures, the use of appropriate Group Addressed L3_PDUs for the transfer of routing and address resolution information would effectively contain communication within that group. This claim is based on two assumptions:

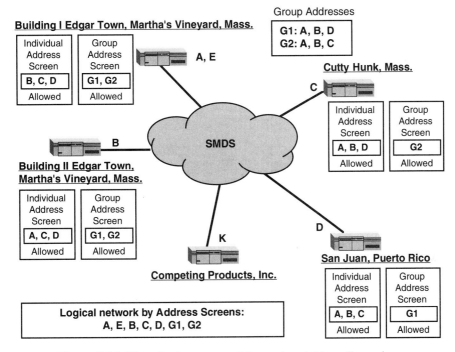

Figure 8.11 Virtual private networking, using Address Screening

- The routers have been configured to listen only to the configured Group Addresses for exchange of their routing information; they are not allowed to listen to other traffic. Recall that stations can send data to a Group Address without being members of that Group Address.

- Routing and address resolution information is distributed through the use of Group Addressed L3_PDUs only. The specifications for OSI and DEC Phase IV-over-SMDS are examples where Individually Addressed L3_PDUs may also be used.

Thus, the Group Addressing approach to virtual private networking may need to be used in combination with Address Screens or CPE-based access-control mechanisms such as passwords. Of course, when Address Screens are used, they should at least allow communication between all addresses identified by the Group Address.

The specification of IP-over-SMDS [RFC1209] introduces the term *logical subnetwork* for the Group Addressing approach. This approach is used to support most of the architectures described in this chapter.

Figure 8.12 illustrates a case where a logical AppleTalk subnetwork is created over SMDS by using an SMDS Group Address, G1. It shows that this technique can also be applied so that different routing architectures can coexist.

The Group Address G2 is used to form a logical IP subnetwork. The virtual network that the SMDS customer in Figure 8.12 has created consists of the union of all members of the two Group Addresses.

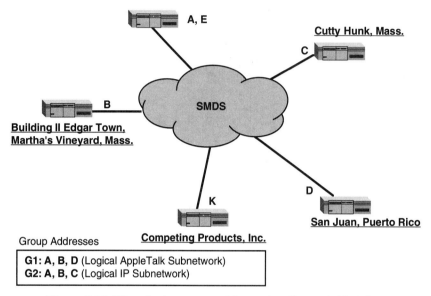

Figure 8.12 Virtual private networking, using Group Addressing

A station can be a member of both Group Addresses, to signify that it can accept both kinds of traffic. Similarly, a station can participate in multiple logical networks of the same kind (e.g., multiple IP networks). Since routing information would be exchanged within a particular logical subnetwork, traffic would be contained within that subnetwork and would not interact with traffic from another subnetwork. In this scenario, routing between logical subnetworks requires a router that is a member of both subnetworks. A particular Group Address can also be used to support different types of logical subnetworks simultaneously, using the protocol-multiplexing techniques described in section 8.1.3.

It is possible, of course, to forego the Group Address based logical subnetwork and configure a router to send individual copies of a broadcast or multicast packet to a configured set of recipients. One could argue that it is simpler to configure a router with a few SMDS Individual Addresses for broadcast purposes than to go through the trouble of registering an SMDS Group Address with the SMDS provider. The SMDS Address Screens can be used to contain traffic within a specified set of SMDS stations. This observation should be compared with the potential need for reconfiguration. The reconfiguration of a Group Address–based logical subnetwork can be performed by a single update of the SMDS Group Address.[10] If the SMDS provider supports SMDS Customer Network Management, as described in Chapter 12, this update can even be performed by a simple on-line operation by the subscriber's network manager. This is much simpler than to update the broadcast-recipients list and Address Screens of all routers if the Group Addressing scenario were not used. Furthermore, the use of Group Addresses also reduces the routing traffic on the SNI. For example, neighbor discovery messages can just be sent to a Group Address instead of to each of the members of that Group Address individually.

8.1.9   Use of SMDS Addresses

SMDS uses addresses that have to be manually configured. In some cases it is necessary to carry SMDS addressing information in protocols "above" the SMDS level. An unambiguous method with regard to bit ordering must be defined to carry these addresses. An example is the Redirect message in the OSI ES-IS protocol (see Section 8.3.3). SMDS addresses are carried in L3_PDUs as strings of 16 BCD encoded digits, and structured as follows:

$$<\text{Address Type}><\text{E.164 Address}><\text{any trailing } F_H\text{'s}>$$

As is also recommended in [RFC1209], we recommend that, unless explicitly defined otherwise, this format should also be used in any internetworking layer protocols that need to convey the SMDS physical network address, with the same bit ordering as is used in SIP: the high-order bit of the SMDS Address Type occupies the high-order bit of the first byte of the address field in which the SMDS address needs to be carried.

8.2   TCP/IP over SMDS

TCP and IP are protocols. The phrase *TCP/IP*, however, is often used loosely to refer to a suite of protocols and an architecture for internetworking. TCP/IP emerged from ARPANET during the 1970s. DARPA, faced with growing hardware diversity in their networks of leased lines, packet communications via radio, and satellite channels, needed technology to provide flexible interconnection of heterogeneous networks. By the end of the 1970s, in answer to this challenge, TCP/IP had taken firm root in research organizations and universities. Further refinement and development continues to this day. The Internet, a collection of thousands of networks and millions of users connected

---

[10]This makes the implicit assumption that changes can also be quickly provisioned by the service provider. We recommend that subscribers check with their service provider on this point.

together via the TCP/IP protocol suite, is used today as *the* backbone for continuous research and experimentation on the Internet itself, facilitating electronic mail, bulletin boards, file transfer, and a large base for gathering statistics and piloting new features. Today, TCP/IP-compatible equipment has become a *de facto* industry standard, and is sold by virtually all data communications suppliers. It is therefore important that this protocol suite be able to use SMDS as a viable service, allowing TCP/IP users to communicate over wide area distances.

The basic structure of TCP/IP internet consists of an arbitrary set of physical networks tied together by routers or gateways. The design philosophy makes only minimal assumptions about the properties of the physical networks, which may be LANs as well as WANs, packet- as well as circuit-switched, connection-oriented as well as connectionless, and may use technologies ranging from telephone lines to radio waves. The physical networks are used to span geographical distance, and the routers function to direct traffic over its next hop (physical network) on its way to the destination station. Of course, the physical networks may do some network-specific routing on their own, but TCP/IP is not really concerned about that. It acts as an overlay network spanning the collection of physical networks. See Figure 8.13.

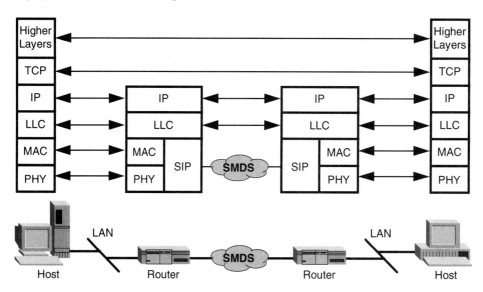

Figure 8.13 Basic TCP/IP architecture with SMDS

Figure 8.13 shows that SMDS is used as just another physical network, such as Ethernets and FDDI networks. SMDS is connected to other physical networks by means of routers that route the IP datagrams. This is quite in line with the philosophy of building TCP/IP internets. The TCP/IP protocol suite treats all networks equally [Comer1].

IP uses SMDS in the same way that it uses IEEE 802.x LAN Media Access Control (MAC) services. This is an SMDS design objective: SMDS should be able to carry any traffic that can be sent over a LAN. Of course, it is also possible to connect IP hosts directly to SMDS.

The functions performed by the IP layer can be split into two classes: generic IP, and medium-specific. Generic IP functionality is generally performed independently of the specific physical network by which the IP packet is transported. These functions include IP addressing and the exchange of control information which allow IP routers to coordinate in internetworking (routing, error recovery, network management). Medium-specific functions are concerned with direct delivery of packets between IP stations. This includes IP broadcast and multicast support, the method of how the packets are carried by the specific medium, and the coexistence of IP with other protocols that use that particular physical network. This section describes the IP medium-specific functions for the case of SMDS.

It is important to realize that there are no special protocol modifications needed in equipment to accommodate the use of the TCP/IP protocol suite over SMDS.

8.2.1   Some Properties of the TCP/IP Protocol Suite

The Internet Protocol (IP) is a connectionless, or datagram, protocol. Each PDU or packet is tagged with its source and destination IP addresses, and can be routed independently from other packets. The service supported by IP includes unicast, multicast, and broadcast.

The basic format of an IP packet is defined in [RFC791] and reproduced in Figure 8.14. Douglas Comer provides detailed discussions of IP in [Comer1] and [Comer2]. Some basic properties relevant for SMDS are discussed below.

Of particular interest for carrying IP packets over SMDS are the length of the IP packets and the way they are addressed. Figure 8.14 shows two length fields. The TOTAL LENGTH field is the relevant one for SMDS. It indicates the length of the packet measured in bytes. The HEADER LENGTH field indicates the length of the IP packet header, measured in 32-bit words. The format shows that the maximum length of the packet is 2^{16}, or 65,535 bytes. This is larger than the maximum L3_PDU size (9188 bytes). However, since IP was designed to run over a variety of networks and to hide their physical properties and constraints from IP users, a mechanism was built in to fragment IP packets that are too large to be carried in their entirety over a network that these packets need to transit. The fragments are eventually reassembled at the IP destination host. Hosts that connect to a network providing SMDS need to perform this fragmentation of large IP packets in order to transport them using SMDS. However, since the maximum L3_PDU size has been chosen so that it can accept packets received

Length in bytes	Field	
1	Version	Header Length
1	Service Type	
2	Total Length	
2	Identification	
1	Flags	Fragment Offset
1	Fragment Offset	
1	Time To Live	
1	Protocol	
2	Header Checksum	
4	Source IP Address	
4	Destination IP Address	
3	IP Options (if any)	
1	Padding	
variable	Data	

Figure 8.14 IP Packet format

from virtually all current LANs without fragmentation, IP packet fragmentation will rarely be necessary for transportation over SMDS.

The SOURCE IP ADDRESS and DESTINATION IP ADDRESS are 32-bit identifiers that are used to reach IP stations. Their notation is of the form w.x.y.z, where each portion corresponds to the decimal value of the corresponding byte in the address. IP addresses, also called *internet addresses*, are assigned by Internet Assigned Numbers Authority (IANA). Conceptually, an IP address consists of the tuple {NETID, HOSTID}. The NETID identifies a network, and the HOSTID a host on that network. The IP address space is divided into different classes, in order to make an efficient distinction between larger and smaller networks. For example, in a Class B address, the HOSTID portion is 16 bits, allowing a network size of 65,536 hosts. In a Class C address, the HOSTID portion is 8 bits, allowing for 256 hosts per network. Internet addresses are different from SMDS addresses, both in format, in use, and in administration. Internet addresses apply at the IP layer for the routing of IP packets, hop by hop, to their final destination. SMDS addresses are used to route L3_PDUs. No mathematical or administrative relationship exists between the two address spaces, and a suitable address resolution procedure is therefore necessary.

The remaining fields in the IP header are of no direct importance to SMDS. However, for example the SERVICE TYPE field, which specifies the type of transport the packet requests (low delay, high throughput, high reliability) can be used in conjunction with matching routing metrics to determine the route of a packet (e.g., SMDS or an alternative route). Refer to [RFC1340] for the use of these parameters for some applications.

Both broadcast and multicast applications of IP are in use. Common broadcast applications include the address resolution protocols and routing protocols. The use of IP multicast is defined in [RFC1112] for applications like the internet Network Time Protocol. An interesting discussion on the trade-offs in IP layer multicasting and the relationship with physical network addressing is provided in [Perlman]. A set of IP addresses has been set aside for multicast purposes. These multicast addresses, called *well-known* addresses, are assigned by IANA and are dedicated to particular applications. The broadcast applications can be supported by employing the SMDS Group Address feature. The multicast applications can also use the SMDS Group Address feature, or they can use SMDS Individual Addresses if very few stations with that application are connected via SMDS. The concept of well-known IP multicast addresses does not map to a corresponding well-known SMDS address. No well-known SMDS addresses have been reserved for this purpose. Thus, within each virtual private network a different SMDS Group Address must be defined to support a particular well-known IP address and its associated application. Table 8.3 shows some reserved IP multicast addresses registered by IANA [RFC1340].

IP address	Multicast application
224.0.0.0	Reserved
224.0.0.1	All Hosts on this Subnet
224.0.0.5	OSPFIGP* [RFC1583] — All Routers
224.0.0.6	OSPFIGP* [RFC1583] — All Designated Routers
224.0.1.1	NTP — Network Time Protocol

*OSPFIGP: Open Shortest Path First Interior Gateway Protocol

Table 8.3 Examples of well-known IP multicast addresses

8.2.2   Logical IP Networks over SMDS

The concept of IP stations that are connected to SMDS and that are configured as a Logical IP Subnetwork (LIS) is introduced in [RFC1209]. A LIS provides a self-contained MAC layer service, as other LANs of that subscriber do. To that end, an SMDS Group Address (LIS_GA) must be configured to identify all IP stations connected by SMDS that span the desired LIS. The LIS_GA is then used as broadcast or multicast address within the LIS for a broadcast or multicast IP and for address resolution (see Section 8.2.3)

The following requirements for LIS configuration are listed in [RFC1209]:

- All members of a LIS have the same IP network/subnet number (NETID). This requirement stems from the fact that IP broadcasts (HOSTID equals all one's) are restricted to a particular NETID.

- For each LIS, a single SMDS Group Address, the LIS_GA, must be configured that identifies all IP stations that form the LIS.

- All IP stations within a LIS are accessed directly over SMDS. This is a logical consequence of the definition of a LIS. All LIS members must be reachable by LIS_GA-addressed L3_PDUs. This requirement implies that LIS stations cannot be connected to SMDS by a MAC layer bridge.

- SMDS-attached IP stations that do not belong to a common LIS must use an IP router to communicate. Since only IP stations within a LIS can communicate directly, communication with other IP stations requires an extra hop, for example, via a router that is a member of more than one LIS. The latter case has one unfortunate consequence. Consider the case of three routers, where routers 1 and 2 belong to one LIS, and routers 2 and 3 to another. In this configuration, routers 1 and 3 can only communicate through router 2, even though they are connected by SMDS. Proposals to address this inefficiency are being discussed by the Internet community [RFC1433]. It should be noted that a station can belong to multiple LISs but only use one SNI with a single Individual Address.

8.2.3 Neighbor Discovery and Address Resolution

The addressing in the IP layer differs from the addressing used for SMDS. For an IP packet to be sent over SMDS, it is necessary to map the IP address in the packet to the corresponding SMDS destination address. Static address resolution tables can be used, but the most common method applied is the use of a dynamic table for address binding, called the *cache*. First, a masking technique is applied to determine whether the IP address is on the same network. If it is, then the IP/physical network address bindings are obtained via a broadcast or multicast request to other hosts or routers. The protocol used for this purpose is called *Address Resolution Protocol* (ARP) [RFC826] [Comer1]. ARP is used to obtain a binding when the cache does not already contain it, or when the entry is outdated, and thus keeps the table of reachable systems and the associated address bindings up to date. An example using SMDS is shown in Figure 8.15.

Step 1:   The ARP Request is broadcast to all members of the LIS and is carried by a Group Addressed L3_PDU directed at LIS_GA.

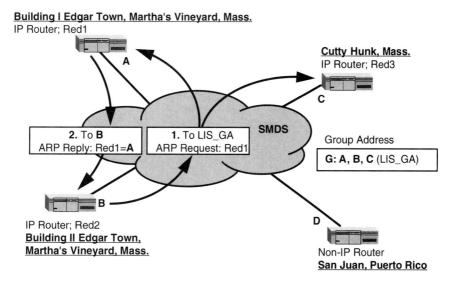

Figure 8.15 Example of the use of ARP

Step 2:   The station with the IP address to be resolved responds with the requested address binding.

Protocols like Reverse ARP (RARP) and the Bootstrap protocol take care of the initialization of the station, so that, given its physical network address, it can obtain its own IP address. The implication is that SMDS stations must know their own SMDS addresses.

ARP and RARP, like IP, are datagram protocols carried in the PDUs of the physical network in question. Figure 8.16 shows the ARP PDU format, as shown in [RFC826] and [Comer1].

Length in bytes	Field	
1	Hardware Type	
1	Protocol Type	
1	HLEN	PLEN
1	Operation	
8	Sender Hardware Address	
4	Sender IP Address	
8	Target Hardware Address	
4	Target IP Address	

Figure 8.16 ARP/RARP PDU format for SMDS

The contents of the ARP/RARP message are straightforward. The HARDWARE TYPE field determines the type of physical network that is used

(Ethernet, SMDS, etc.). The PROTOCOL TYPE field determines the type of internet protocol (IP, IPX, CLNP, etc.). HLEN and PLEN specify the lengths in bytes of the hardware address and the length of the address of the protocol specified in the protocol field respectively. The OPERATION field determines whether the message is an ARP request, ARP reply, RARP request, or RARP reply. The remaining fields specify the address bindings of the sender and the target host for which the binding is requested.

For IP-over-SMDS, the fields are used as follows [RFC1209]:

HARDWARE TYPE The code assigned for SMDS is $0E_H$ (14_D) [RFC1340].

PROTOCOL TYPE The value for IP is 0800_H (2048_D) [RFC1340].

HLEN   The length of SMDS addresses is 8 bytes.

PLEN   The length of IP addresses is 4 bytes.

8.2.4 IP Routing

The TCP/IP protocol suite accommodates quite a number of protocols to propagate routing information through an internet. These include the interior gateway protocols — *Routing Information Protocol* (RIP), derived from the RIP defined for XNS, the Hello protocol, and *Open Shortest Path First* (OSPF) for routing within a routing domain — as well as the exterior gateway protocols, *Exterior Gateway Protocol* (EGP) and the *Border Gateway Protocol* (BGP) for routing between routing domains.[11] OSPF is a link state routing protocol, while the other protocols use the distance-vector (Bellman-Ford) technique for the propagation of routing information. It is beyond the scope of this book to describe the details of all these protocols. The interested reader is referred to [Comer1] and [Perlman], and a series of RFCs including [RFC1583], [RFC1058], [RFC904], and [RFC891]. We focus here on issues that are relevant for running these protocols over SMDS.

The aspects that are of potential interest for SMDS are any particular use of broadcasts or multicasts to request or advertise routing information, and the metric that is used to describe the cost of transporting packets between two routers. Table 8.4 summarizes these properties for each of the more popular routing protocols in the TCP/IP suite.

---

[11]The IP community terms *interior gateway protocol* and *exterior gateway protocol* correspond with the OSI community terms *intradomain routing protocol* and *interdomain routing protocol*. An example of a routing domain is presented in Section 8.3.4.

Routing protocol	Route propagation	Broadcast/multicast needs	Routing metric
EGP [RFC904]	Distance vector	None	No metric
Hello [RFC891]	Distance vector	LIS_GA*	Delay (dynamic computation)
RIP [RFC1058]	Distance vector	LIS_GA*	Hops
OSPF [RFC1583]	Link state	ALL_SPF_ROUTERS_GA (used to reach all OSPF routers); ALL_DROUTERS_GA (used to reach all Designated Routers).	Throughput, Delay, Expense, Error
BGP [RFC1267]	Distance vector	None	Route comparison

*A slightly more efficient use would be to use an ALL_IP_ROUTERS_GA directed at all IP routers within the LIS. This gain in traffic efficiency must be compared with the need to request and maintain an additional Group Address. This gain may only be significant in a large LIS.

Table 8.4 Use of SMDS Group Addressing by routing protocols in the TCP/IP protocol suite

8.2.4.1   RIP and Hello

RIP is derived from the RIP developed for XNS, which is described in more detail in Section 8.5.4. It utilizes broadcasts to distribute routing information. L3_PDUs addressed to LIS_GA can be used for these broadcasts. Hello is similar to RIP in many ways, but it uses a different routing metric (i.e., link delays instead of hops). It does so by continuously estimating hop delays based on the exchange of time-stamped packets and a procedure for clock synchronization among the routers. Thus, SMDS does not pose any further special requirements for the use of these routing protocols. (Compare also with NetWare's RIP, described in Section 8.6.4.)

8.2.4.2   OSPF

A more complex situation exists for the case of OSPF, which uses the concept of Designated Router (DR) in order to keep routing traffic down. Through a dynamic procedure where OSPF routers broadcast or multicast OSPF Hello messages to each other, a router on a LAN is selected to be the DR. Routers on this LAN exchange their routing information with the DR. The DR, representing the LAN, combines the received routing information and propagates it on the internet to all other OSPF routers. Emulating this over SMDS is achieved by using the SMDS Group Address ALL_SPF_ROUTERS_GA. OSPF also recognizes a Backup DR that can take over in case the DR goes down or becomes unreachable. Thus, the Backup DR needs to listen to all routing information directed to the DR. For this purpose, yet another SMDS Group Address must be used to reach all DRs (ALL_DROUTERS_GA). As discussed under IP multicasting, some special IP addresses are reserved for OSPF multicasts. Thus, OSPF routers must be configured with the address bindings shown in Table 8.5.

IP multicast address	SMDS Group Address	Multicast application
224.0.0.5	ALL_SPF_ROUTERS_GA	All OSPF Routers
224.0.0.6	ALL_DROUTERS_GA	All OSPF DRs

Table 8.5 IP/SMDS multicast OSPF address bindings

8.2.4.3   BGP

BGP does not pose any particular requirements for SMDS. It runs on top of a reliable point-to-point transport service provided by TCP. No broadcasts or multicasts are used.

8.2.5   Carrying IP and ARP/RARP Datagrams over SMDS

Since both IP and ARP/RARP constitute datagram protocols, and SMDS provides for datagram transport, the IP and ARP/RARP packets can be carried directly by SMDS. IP uses SMDS in the same way that it uses IEEE 802.x MAC layer services. Protocol multiplexing is achieved by encapsulating IP, ARP, or RARP messages in the LLC1/SNAP format. Figure 8.17 illustrates the resulting formats as defined in [RFC1209].

	Field	Value
	L3_PDU Header	HLPI = 000001_B (LLC)
LLC	LLC DSAP	= AA_H (SNAP)
	LLC SSAP	= AA_H (SNAP)
	LLC Control	= 03_H (UI frames)
SNAP	SNAP OUI	= 000000_H (Ethertype)
	SNAP PID	= 0800_H (IP)
		= 0806_H (ARP/RARP)
	IP/ARP/RARP Packet	
	L3_PDU Trailer	

Figure 8.17 Encapsulation of IP and ARP/RARP in L3_PDUs

The PDU fields are used as follows:

- In the L3_PDU header, the HLPI is set to 1. This indicates the use of IEEE 802.2 LLC.

- The LLC DSAP and SSAP values are set to 170_D (AA_H), indicating the use of IEEE 802.1 SNAP. The LLC CONTROL field is set to the value 3_D, mandating the use of UI frames, the IEEE 802.2 LLC Type 1 mode of operation.

- The SNAP OUI is set to 0, meaning that Ethertype style of identification is applicable. The PID values are 2048_D for IP (0800_H), and 2054_D for ARP/RARP (0806_H).

The result is that a simple 8-byte constant, $AAAA030000000800_H$, is used when carrying IP packets, and that $AAAA030000000806_H$ is used for the transport of ARP/RARP packets. It follows that these packets can have a maximum size of $(9188 - 8) = 9180$ bytes. IP stations connected to SMDS should therefore set their Maximum Transfer Unit (MTU) parameter, which is used to determine the need for IP packet fragmentation to 9180.

8.2.6   IP Station Configuration for SMDS

IP stations must be configured with a number of special parameters and values in order to use SMDS, as described in RFC1209.

- The hardware address or SMDS Individual Address of the IP station using SMDS.

- The SMDS Group Address LIS_GA that identifies the members of a LIS. The list of SMDS addresses that are identified by a LIS_GA are maintained by the SMDS Group Address Agent (see Chapter 3). It is the responsibility of the Group Address Sponsor to request an update of that list if stations are added to or removed from the LIS. This may be performed via the SMDS Customer Network Management service. See Chapter 12.

- The ARP Request Address represents the SMDS address to which ARP Requests are sent. In the LIS scenario, this address could the same as LIS_GA. However, it is possible to use addresses other than LIS_GA, for example, the configuration of one or more stations as special "ARP-servers" whose function would be dedicated to provide IP/SMDS address bindings. In this case the ARP Request Address would be an SMDS Group Address identifying these servers, or it could even be an SMDS Individual Address identifying one particular server.

In addition, an IP address is needed to identify the station at the IP layer. All IP addresses in a LIS must have the same NETID.

IP-stations that are members of more than one LIS must implement multiple sets of these parameters. Multiple LISs can be supported via a single SNI, by a station with a single or with multiple SMDS addresses.

When the LIS scenario is used, and the station is configured to only listen to LIS-GA for neighbor discovery, the use of SMDS Address Screening feature is not required. If used, however, the screens should be configured to at least allow communication within the LIS (Individual Addresses and the LIS_GA).

The configuration of Group Addresses to support various routing protocols is discussed in Section 8.2.4.

8.3   OSI over SMDS

Open Systems Interconnection (OSI) refers to a communications architecture, and associated with that, a set of protocols and services. Started in the late 70s, the objective was to specify a nonproprietary way of communicating over a growing diversity of networks, using a variety of applications. OSI has been specified by formal standardization organizations, in particular the International Standardization Organization (ISO) and the International Telegraph and Telephone Consultative Committee (CCITT). These organizations follow a complex, open-review process for the formulation of their standards, involving both national and international committees. While fostering international and widespread agreements, this process is often slow in reacting to new technical developments such as the LAN explosion of the 1980s. Another consequence of the broad participation is the appearance of a greater number of options than would be practical and cost-effective in typical implementations.[12] Despite these hurdles, an impressive set of specifications has been produced. Developments on OSI continue to this day. For an informative overview of the OSI architecture and specifications, see [Piscitello] and [Rose2].

The basic architecture of OSI borrows several ideas from architectures such as XNS and TCP/IP. The architecture is much more elaborate in several ways though. Some examples follow:

- Several methods are defined to achieve internetworking. OSI recognizes two different services that the internetworking layer can

---

[12]This is understandable when considering situations where vendors promote different technical solutions. The result is sometimes that both solutions appear as options. Another result may be a deliberate vagueness in the standard, leaving it up to the marketplace to decide. A statement sometimes heard at the end of a committee meeting is, "The meeting booked progress since everybody left equally unhappy."

provide: connection-oriented, using virtual circuits, and connectionless, providing a datagram service.

- As compared with TCP/IP, OSI has defined a more detailed layering for the application-oriented, end-to-end protocols, distinguishing three different layers to support applications, and applying further sublayering in the actual application.

- The addressing scheme at the internetworking layer, the NSAP addresses, consists of an amalgamation of address spaces, including the numbering plans for telephony and telex.

SMDS can function in much the same way in the OSI architecture as it does in TCP/IP, that is, to function as one wide area link in an internet consisting of many physical networks. An architecture picture is shown in Figure 8.18.

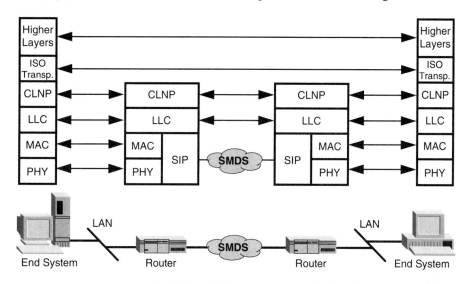

Figure 8.18 Basic OSI architecture with SMDS

This section draws most of its material from a specification by the SIG [SIG004] on the implementation of OSI over SMDS. OSI specifies two alternative network layer approaches: a connection-oriented mode, and a connectionless mode [ISO8348]. The SIG specification uses an internetworking protocol called *Connectionless-mode Network Layer Protocol* (CLNP) [ISO8473], as shown in Figure 8.18. CLNP functions in much the same way as IP (see Section 8.2). The rationale for using CLNP as opposed to a connection-oriented approach is that CLNP is a natural match for SMDS, suggesting a straightforward and simple implementation. There seems also to be no reason to forego the availability of the routing protocols associated with CLNP. Therefore we recommend this method as the preferred method to run OSI over SMDS.

However, for those scenarios where the use of the connection-oriented network service is deemed necessary, the reader is referred to the discussion on the use of LLC2 in Section 8.1.2.

8.3.1 Some Properties of CLNP

CLNP is a connectionless or datagram protocol, similar to IP. The basic format of an CLNP packet is reproduced in Figure 8.19. Each PDU, or packet, is tagged with its SOURCE ADDRESS and DESTINATION ADDRESS, and can be routed independently. The service supported by CLNP includes unicast and broadcast.[13] For a detailed discussion, see [Piscitello]. Some basic properties relevant for SMDS are discussed here.

Length in bytes	Field
1	NLPID
1	Length Indicator
1	Version/Pld Extension
1	Lifetime
1	Flags / Type
2	Segment Length
2	Checksum
1	Destination Address Length
≤ 20	Destination Address
1	Source Address Length
≤ 20	Source Address
0 or 6	Segmentation Part
Variable	Options Part
Variable	Data

Figure 8.19 CLNP packet format

Functionally, CLNP is virtually identical with IP, discussed in Section 8.2. The major difference is the use of variable length addresses in CLNP, as compared with fixed 4-byte addresses in IP.

The NLPID is the NETWORK LAYER PROTOCOL IDENTIFIER that is used for the multiplexing of ISO/CCITT protocols. The SEGMENT LENGTH specifies the entire length of the PDU in bytes. CLNP supports segmentation and reassembly. The SEGMENTATION PART in the packet header indicates to which unfragmented packet a fragment belongs; it also indicates the fragment offset and the total length of the unfragmented packet.

---

[13]The use of multicast is only partly defined at the time of publication.

The addresses used by CLNP are called Network Service Access Point (NSAP) addresses [ISO8348.2]. In hosts (called End Systems, or ESs, in OSI), they specify the Service Access Point of the OSI Network Layer as seen by the OSI Transport Layer. When used in routers (Intermediate Systems or ISs in OSI), the NSAP addresses are referred to as Network Entity Titles. For simplicity, we will just use the term *NSAP address*.

The OSI NSAP address structure was designed according to the something-for-everybody principle. The result was a very large address space that combined all the CCITT numbering plans (telephony, public data networks, ISDN, and even telex) with a number of other schemes, such as national schemes administered under ISO and its national counterparts, schemes for international organizations, and a possibility for local use. With plenty of prefixes and postfixes to spare, the structure accommodates addresses up to 160 bits long. The general outline of an NSAP address is shown in Figure 8.20.

Authority and Format Identifier (AFI)	Initial Domain Identifier (IDI)	Domain Specific Part (DSP)

Figure 8.20 NSAP address structure

Briefly, the AFI indicates what address plan is being used, and provides guidelines for the structure of the rest of the address. The IDI specifies the particular addressing authority within the address plan indicated by the AFI, and in some cases a further portion of the address. The DSP can be used to construct further subdomains in the address and is allocated by the authority indicated by the AFI/IDI. Details can be found in [ISO8348.2], [Hemrick], and [Piscitello].

Stations connected to SMDS can follow either an NSAP structure that embeds SMDS addresses directly (algorithmic address binding), or another structure. The former is quite attractive, since the address binding of NSAP address to SMDS address follows directly from the NSAP address. For example, a router that needs to send packets to one of these stations does not need to run a dynamic address-binding procedure to relate an NSAP address to an SMDS address. Thus, this approach saves both complexity and some bandwidth. Use of the format that embeds the SMDS address in the NSAP address deserves some further explanation. The AFI indicates E.164 and the IDI contains the E.164 number. We use the example in Figure 8.21 of an NSAP address with an embedded SMDS Individual Address.

The example uses an SMDS address allocated according to the North American Numbering Plan (see Chapter 3). It is an Individual Address C18097585254FFFF$_H$, which is padded with trailing F$_H$ digits to make up its fixed length of the 16 hexadecimal digits used in L3_PDUs. The NSAP address

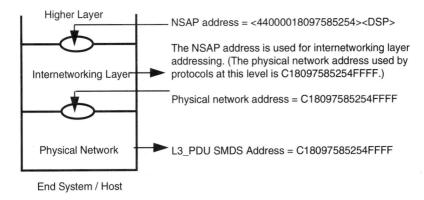

Figure 8.21 Example of an NSAP address with embedded SMDS address

structure has reserved a number of `AFI` values for E.164 addresses.[14] All values shown in Table 8.6 signify that an E.164 number follows (15 digits). An E.164 number (`IDI`) consists of a variable number of digits. Thus, in order to correctly identify the `DSP` portion of the NSAP address, the `IDI` must be padded to its maximum length of 16 digits. The `AFI` value provides the padding rules (Table 8.6).

AFI value	Meaning
44_D	Leading zero (0) digits are used for padding the IDI if the first significant E.164 digit is nonzero. The DSP consists of decimal digits.
45_D	Leading zero (0) digits are used for padding the IDI if the first significant E.164 digit is nonzero. The DSP consists of binary octets.
58_D	Leading one (1) digits are used for padding the IDI if the first significant E.164 digit is zero. The DSP consists of decimal digits.
59_D	Leading one (1) digits are used for padding the IDI if the first significant E.164 digit is zero. The DSP consists of binary octets.

Table 8.6 NSAP address `AFI` values for E.164

[14]The NSAP scheme is designed to distinguish address-allocation authorities, and not necessarily types of physical networks. For example, E.164 could imply a number of different services, such as SMDS, a telephone line, and so forth. It is also possible that a device that uses an E.164 embedded NSAP address is not even connected to a physical network that uses E.164. A consequence is that SMDS nodes that are configured to know other nodes must accompany any configured E.164 embedded NSAP addresses of those configured nodes with a flag that indicates whether or not the SMDS address can be extracted from the NSAP address.

Since SMDS E.164 addresses always start with a Country Code, and because no Country Codes starting with a zero have been allocated, leading zeros are always used for padding (i.e., the AFI values 58_H and 59_H are not used). The recipe to construct the NSAP address from an SMDS Address follows:

1. Strip the ADDRESS TYPE digit (C_H or E_H) and the trailing padding ones. This step reconstructs the decimal E.164 number needed for the target NSAP format.

2. Pad the result with leading zero digits to 15 digits. Prefix the result with the AFI value 44_D. (45_D could also be used in the example.)

3. Add the DSP portion.

To extract the SMDS address from the NSAP address, the opposite procedure is used.

The use of this type of NSAP address is recommended in [SIG004] because of its implied routing-traffic efficiency gain, but it is not required.

8.3.2   Logical OSI Networks over SMDS

OSI stations of an SMDS subscriber can be configured as a Logical OSI Subnetwork (LOS), providing a self-contained MAC layer service, like other LANs of that subscriber. In concept, a LOS is similar to the LIS discussed in Section 8.2.2. However, where a LIS is formed simply by grouping all IP stations in an SMDS Group Address, the SIG specification [SIG004] provides a variety of ways to form a LOS. In order to minimize the use of precious WAN bandwidth through unnecessary broadcasts to all members of the LOS, none of the approaches necessarily rely on the configuration of a single SMDS Group Address to address all OSI stations.

- As we will see in the next sections, neighbor discovery and routing information may be exchanged via SMDS Group Addressed L3_PDUs, Individually Addressed L3_PDUs, or a mixture of these. Thus, a LOS is maintained by configuring the OSI stations to listen to a fixed set of SMDS addresses. When a LOS is formed by configuration of one or more SMDS Group Addresses, adding a station to the LOS requires two actions:

   1. Configure the new station to listen to that SMDS Group Address.

   2. Extend the SMDS Group Address to include the SMDS address of the new station. The SMDS CNM Service can be used for this purpose (see Chapter 12).

If the OSI stations within a LOS are configured to listen to Individual Addresses, addition of a station to the LOS requires reconfiguration of multiple stations.

- Traffic can be contained within a LOS by proper configuration of the SMDS Address Screens of the OSI stations connected to SMDS. In this case, adding a station to a LOS requires updates of the Address Screens of all stations within the LOS. The SMDS CNM Service can be used for this purpose (see Chapter 12).

- An additional approach specified in [SIG004] is the use of passwords in the neighbor-greeting messages (described in the next sections). As we will see in the next sections, a new station within the LOS is only required to know some other stations within the LOS. Other stations are only in some cases required to be configured with the address information of the new station. The new station must be configured with the password(s) that maintain the integrity of the LOS.

8.3.3 Neighbor Discovery and Address Resolution

OSI's general solution to the problems of neighbor discovery and address resolution is the use of the ES-IS protocol [ISO9542]. ESs represent End Systems, or *hosts* in TCP/IP parlance. ISs are Intermediate Systems, or routers. ES-IS, a datagram protocol, is based on the method of periodically advertising your presence and address bindings to the peer systems on the same physical network. Listening stations use these announcements to keep their lists of reachable systems and the associated address bindings up-to-date. A system of timers is used to (a) determine the frequency of the advertisements (the Configuration Timer), and (b) to determine the maximum time the recorded information must be kept and is considered valid (the Holding Timer).[15] For ES-IS details, see [ISO9542], [Perlman] and [Piscitello]. ES-IS has been designed for operation over Point-to-Point links and over 802.x LANs. Since bandwidth is probably more precious for SMDS than for LANs, some refinements are made. Our description here is based on the corresponding SIG specification [SIG004].

8.3.3.1   System Types Attached to SMDS

In an SMDS environment, an efficiency gain in the ES-IS protocol exchanges can be achieved by using E.164 embedded NSAP addresses. ESs that have NSAP addresses from which their SMDS address can be extracted are called *Simple-ES*s. An IS that connects nodes to SMDS that are configured with

---

[15]While most dictionaries associate a timer with the measurement of an interval of time, these specifications associate a timer with *both* a time interval and the measurement thereof.

the same value of the E.164 portion of their NSAP address is called a *Passive IS* [SIG004]. Since the address binding automatically follows from their NSAP address, no continuous protocol exchange is necessary to keep the network informed of their existence; their existence can be verified as needed.

This approach assumes that physical networks in an internet are configured around a public network, with NSAP address allocation driven by the numbers allocated to the stations that connect to the public network. NSAP address allocation schemes that use a different approach include [X3.216], which provides guidelines for OSI NSAP address allocation in the ANSI portion of the NSAP address space, and [RFC1237], which defines the NSAP address structure for use in the Internet. For NSAP address-allocation schemes such as these two, there are two alternatives for address binding:

- *A static address-binding table.* ESs that rely on their address binding being statically configured in ISs are called *Configured-ESs*. ISs that rely on their address binding and the nodes that can be reached through them being statically configured in ISs are called *Configured-Passive-ISs*. These two types of SMDS stations only contact ISs as needed.

- *A dynamic address binding table is maintained in an IS.* The table is kept up to date by continuous protocol exchange with other systems. ESs that rely on these ISs are called *Dynamically-Learned-ESs*, and must be in continuous contact with these ISs. This procedure between Dynamically-Learned-ESs and Non-Passive-ISs uses more bandwidth than the static-binding approach. For this reason, [SIG004] recommends avoiding the use of Dynamically-Learned-ESs. Consequently, we will not detail the use of these ESs. Interested readers are referred to [SIG004]. The ISs that maintain a dynamic table of IP address bindings are called *Nonpassive-ISs*. Nonpassive-ISs run the IS-IS protocol [ISO10589] to exchange routing information with each other.

Simple-ESs, Configured-ESs, Passive-ISs, and Configured-Passive-ISs are not required to exchange messages continuously with Nonpassive-ISs. The address binding needed to reach Simple-ESs and Passive-ISs follows from their NSAP address, and, by definition, the address information of the Configured-ESs and Configured-Passive-ISs is configured in the Nonpassive-ISs.

All systems are set up with one or more SMDS Individual or Group Addresses to reach the Nonpassive-ISs they need to talk to. When they must communicate with a Nonpassive-IS, they can verify its existence by sending it a message that requires a response. Borrowing the TCP/IP name for such a procedure, this exchange is referred to as *pinging*.

Figure 8.22 summarizes the different types of SMDS stations.

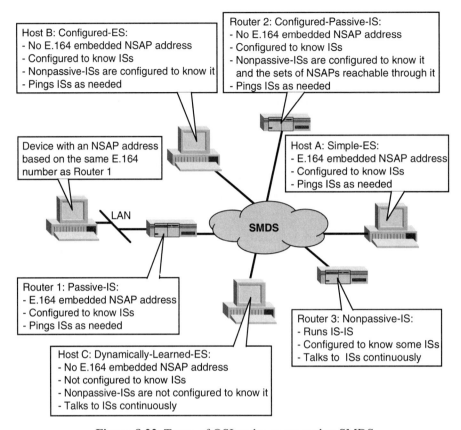

Figure 8.22 Types of OSI nodes connected to SMDS

8.3.3.2 Designated Router

A physical network that connects *n* routers results in $n(n-1)/2$ router relationships. Since it would be inefficient to model the physical network as $n(n-1)/2$ point-to-point links for the purpose of the exchange of routing information, one of the routers is used to represent the physical network itself. This router is called the *Designated Router* (DR). The idea is that the DR collects routing information from the non-DRs attached to the physical network, and, on behalf of the physical network, advertises routing information listing all ESs and ISs attached to the physical network. The neighbor-greeting procedures exploit the DR concept, as shown in the following section.

8.3.3.3 Neighbor Greeting

The message used by an ES for pinging an IS is an SMDS ES Hello, with the Holding Timer set to 0. For each ES, this is sent to each address in the configuration list, until a response is received. A non-DR that receives an SMDS ES Hello with Holding Timer set to 0 responds with an SMDS Hello Redirect.

The DR responds with an SMDS DR-ES Hello. Figure 8.23 illustrates this exchange.

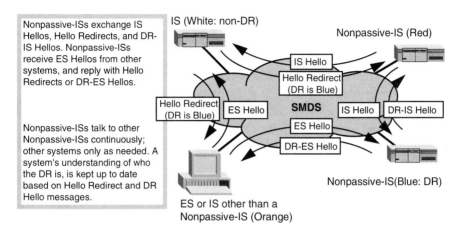

Figure 8.23 OSI neighbor greeting, using SMDS

Figure 8.23 also illustrates the basic neighbor-greeting protocol exchange between Nonpassive-ISs. The procedure for these ISs to find each other is similar, but not the same as that defined on 802.x LANs [ISO10589]. ISs that run IS-IS over 802.x LANs exchange IS Hellos to find each other, to verify each other's existence, and to exchange routing information. A standard multicast address is used for IS Hello advertisements. For running IS-IS over SMDS, the neighbor-greeting packets are modified (SMDS IS Hellos), in order to make more efficient use of the bandwidth. SMDS Redirect messages are used to prevent unnecessary multiple hops over SMDS. SMDS customers need to request an SMDS Group Address for SMDS IS Hello advertisements, or they can use Individual Addresses or a mix of both. The reason is to allow for flexibility and to circumvent the potential problem of the limits on Group Address membership.

An efficiency gain is achieved by the use of the DR. Instead of broadcasting SMDS IS Hellos to all ISs, the idea is to send only to the DR, and the DR periodically sends DR-IS Hellos to ISs. A Nonpassive-IS attached to SMDS finds the DR by initially sending SMDS IS Hellos to a preconfigured set of ISs. Non-DRs will reply with an SMDS Hello Redirect message that contains the address information of the DR. The IS will then send an SMDS IS Hello to the DR, which in turn will reply with an SMDS DR-IS Hello, establishing itself as the DR to the IS. Only Nonpassive-ISs run IS-IS. Election of the DR and the exchange of routing information are further discussed in Section 8.3.4. The message formats are specified in Section 8.3.5.

The DR establishes a minimal list of all SMDS addresses of ISs that it needs to talk to. This list is computed from its own list of configured IS SMDS addresses, the preconfigured IS SMDS addresses reported in SMDS IS Hellos (Option type 1; see Table 8.10), and the IS addresses it learns through the SMDS Source Address of SMDS IS Hellos. A "weeding" procedure is necessary to remove Individual Addresses of ISs that are also represented by a Group Address that they listen to, and that is reported in their SMDS IS Hello (see also the SMDS IS Hello format). This list is called IS-SMDS-BROADCAST-ADDRESSES.[16]

Neighbor-greeting messages can be carried in Group Addressed L3_PDUs, although this is not required. All systems must have a configured set of SMDS addresses for reaching ISs. These may be SMDS Group Addresses or Individual Addresses. For example, an SMDS customer can set up a Group Address, IS_GA, that identifies all ISs in her internet that are attached to SMDS. However, a mix of Group Addresses and Individual Addresses may also be configured, for example, when more ISs need to be identified than can be contained in a single Group Address (currently 128; see Chapter 3). Nonpassive-ISs must be configured with SMDS address information to reach Configured-ESs and Configured-Passive-ISs.

The SMDS Redirect Hello messages require that all systems maintain the address-binding list of the Nonpassive-IS they need to communicate with. As a backup, additional addresses may be kept.

More complex configurations than shown in Figure 8.23 may exist. In particular, a configuration can exist where the ES on the LAN can be reached via multiple routers that attach to SMDS. In order to take advantage of the approach with embedded E.164 NSAP addresses (i.e., the SMDS address of the router attached to SMDS can be extracted from its NSAP address), the ES must be able to be identified by a set of NSAP addresses (i.e., where the DSP is the same, but the AFI/IDI may differ).

8.3.3.4   DR Election

The identity of the DR is determined through election. The qualification of an IS to be DR consists of its configured priority, an 8-bit unsigned integer reported in the SMDS IS Hello.[17] The numerically highest priority wins. In case of a tie between two claims, the IS with the numerically highest ID wins. The ID is a portion of the NSAP address and will be discussed in Section 8.3.4.1.

---

[16]A station does not need to be a member of an SMDS Group Address in order to use it. This is a feature that distinguishes Group Addressing from X.25 Closed User Groups, with which it is sometimes erroneously compared.

[17]IS-IS reserves the most significant bit for future use, and sets it to zero.

A DR is elected by all ISs starting with the belief that they are DR and transmitting SMDS DR-IS Hellos. By exchanging Hello and Redirect messages, each will learn of other ISs, including ISs that are more qualified to be DR. An IS that has received an SMDS DR-IS Hello from a more qualified router stops seeing itself as DR: It starts transmitting SMDS IS Hellos instead of SMDS DR-IS Hellos, and only transmits them to what it now believes is the DR. Nevertheless, this may still not be the real DR. This situation is resolved by mandating that non-DRs that receive SMDS IS Hellos respond with an SMDS Redirect. The recipient of this message will test this claim by sending a single SMDS IS Hello to the address in the SMDS Redirect. Only after a positive confirmation is received in the form of a DR-IS Hello does this IS change its belief about the DR situation. Each IS maintains a Holding Timer (3 × Hello Timer) to keep track of whether the DR situation changes. When its timer expires, an IS starts claiming to be DR again, until convinced otherwise. The DR election procedure is very similar to the one for running DECnet Phase IV over SMDS, which is described in more detail in Section 8.9.3. Figure 8.24 shows an example of the DR election process.

Each IS is configured with address information to reach other ISs. This information may consist of a single SMDS Group Address, or any mixture of Individual and Group Addresses. Section 8.3.4 explains that IS-IS uses a two-level routing hierarchy. Thus, for example, a simple configuration may use an SMDS Group Address, L1IS_GA, to identify all Level 1 routers, and another one, L2IS_GA, to identify all Level 2 routers. After an IS is aware of who the DR is, it will send SMDS IS Hellos only to the DR. The DR sends SMDS DR-IS Hellos to all ISs, specifying the ISs that it has recently received messages from. This not only reduces IS Hello traffic, but it also allows for very simple configuration of a new IS. By configuring an IS with even just a single SMDS address of another IS, the procedure will guarantee that the new IS will be eventually known by all other ISs, and that it will be a full participant in the DR election process.

8.3.4 OSI Routing

Making good use of the extensive experience with routing protocols in architectures such as XNS and TCP/IP, a small set of protocols has been defined for the propagation of routing information in networks running CLNP. An in-depth description of OSI routing is provided in [Perlman]. The description in this section provides just those details relevant for running the OSI routing protocols over SMDS, and is based on [SIG004].

Figure 8.25 shows a routing topology example for The Bodacious Data Corp. (see Chapter 3), which illustrates OSI router types and their relationships according to the OSI routing framework [ISO9575]. A routing topology

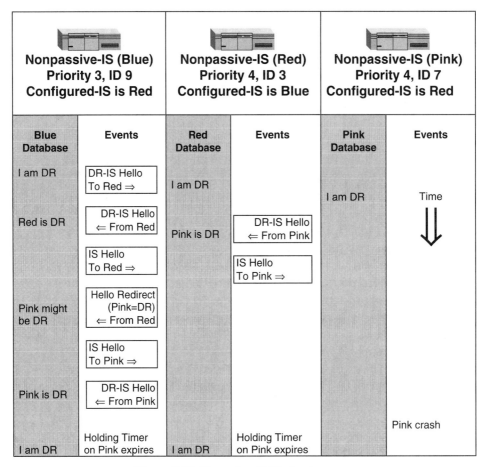

Figure 8.24 Example of DR election process

represents logical connectivity. In principle, several or even all physical connections may be provided by the same physical network. OSI distinguishes routing domains, which are administered separately. In order to reduce routing traffic, an administrative routing domain may organize routing in a hierarchy of two levels. The top level, called Level 2, routes packets between routing Areas. The bottom level, called Level 1, routes packets within an Area. The protocol that distributes routing information within an administrative routing domain is called *IS-IS* [ISO10589] and is a close cousin of OSPF [RFC1583]. Like OSPF, it is a link state routing protocol. ISs that route at Level 1 are called *Level 1 ISs*, and use Level 1 IS-IS routing rules. ISs that route at Level 2 are called *Level 2 ISs*. They perform intradomain routing between Areas, and use Level 2 routing rules. In addition, a Level 2 IS can also act as a Level 1 IS.

    Routing information between administrative routing domains is exchanged utilizing the Inter-Domain Routing Protocol (IDRP) [ISO10747]. IDRP is a

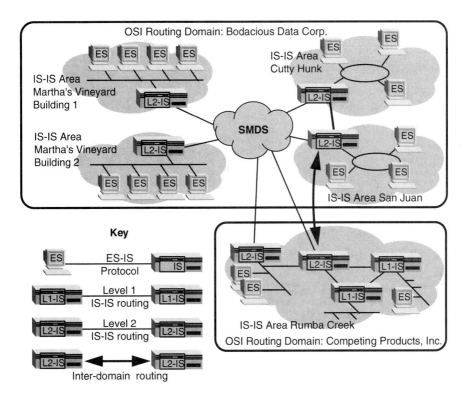

Figure 8.25 Example of OSI Routing Relationships

distance-vector routing protocol and is similar to BGP [RFC1267]. Table 8.7 summarizes some properties of IS-IS and IDRP.

Routing protocol	Main function	TCP/IP cousin	Route info propagation	Routing metric
IS-IS [ISO10589]	Intradomain routing	OSPF [RFC1583]	Link state	Default (usually throughput), Delay, Expense, Error
IDRP [ISO10747]	Interdomain routing	BGP [RFC1267]	Distance-vector	Throughput, Delay, Expense, Error, or Domain hop count

Table 8.7 Some properties of the OSI Routing Protocols

8.3.4.1 NSAP Address

Routing Areas are distinguished by their allocated NSAP addresses. Figure 8.26 depicts how NSAP addresses are partitioned for this purpose.

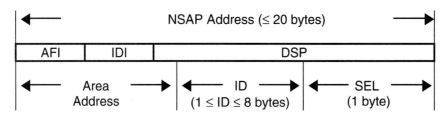

Figure 8.26 NSAP address structure used for IS-IS routing

Level 1 routers route on the ID field (System IDentifier). For example, the ID may be a 48-bit MAC address. IDs within a routing domain are of equal length. The SEL (NSAP SELector) field is used within an ES to distinguish different higher layer protocols, and is set to 0 for ISs. The ARE ADDRESS field spans at least the AFI/IDI, and distinguishes Areas. Level 2 routers advertise and route on address prefixes. An address prefix consists of an arbitrary most significant portion of an NSAP address. For example, a Level 2 router may advertise that it can route traffic to all destinations that have an NSAP address starting with the address prefix 44000018097585254_H. This is an example that uses a specific E.164 embedded NSAP address. Similarly, a router may advertise that it can reach any E.164 address, by distributing the prefix 44_H. Thus, an address prefix may be an Area Address of a destination area, or a prefix for a reachable address. Routers that are attached to SMDS and have E.164 embedded NSAP addresses are necessarily Level 2 routers, since they will have different SMDS addresses and thus different Area Addresses.

The situation where an ES can be reached via multiple ISs attached to SMDS means that it must be possible to configure multiple SMDS addresses for reaching an NSAP address prefix. We can see an example of this situation in Figure 8.25, if the Cutty Hunk LAN were connected to SMDS by two routers instead of one. The SIG specification [SIG004] suggests that the destination is initially reached by trying a round robin through the set of SMDS addresses. Once traffic is received from that destination, the received SMDS address is used for any further communication, until the NSAP/SMDS address binding is outdated due to expiration of the Holding Timer.

8.3.4.2   Routing Metric

Costs of a (logical) link are based on the routing metric that is applied. IS-IS and OSPF support the same routing metrics (see Table 8.7). For each link (e.g., via SMDS), at least the default metric must be supported. The others are optional. However, as demonstrated in [Perlman], the use of the other metrics at this point may still produce arbitrary and nonoptimal routes. Therefore, we see no compelling reason to insist on their use when routing over SMDS at this time. In order to be as accurate as possible, the cost of an SMDS link to a particular

SMDS address is the cost configured for the longest SMDS address prefix that matches that address. Table 8.8 shows an example.

	SMDS address prefix	**SMDS link cost**
C1516	(all SMDS addresses in North American area code 516)	1
C1809	(all SMDS addresses in North American area code 809)	3
C1	(all other SMDS addresses in the North American Numbering Plan)	2
C31	(all SMDS addresses in The Netherlands)	4

Table 8.8 Example of the configuration of SMDS link costs

8.3.4.3   IS-IS over SMDS

Nonpassive-ISs maintain a database that specifies the shortest paths to other systems. This database is refreshed by the exchange of routing information between Nonpassive-ISs. The packets that are used for this purpose are the IS-IS Link State PDU (LSP), the Complete Sequence Number PDU (CSNP), and the Partial Sequence Number PDU (PSNP). All of these PDUs are carried across SMDS in Individually Addressed L3_PDUs and have the same format as when used over other physical networks. These packets and the procedure for using them are specified in IS-IS [ISO10589]. However, recall that a DR is actually distributing routing information on behalf of other systems. Since the LSP, CSNP, and PSNP packets only contain NSAP address information and not the corresponding SMDS address information, it is still necessary to convey this address binding, so that systems can communicate directly. The DR will report the IS address bindings of its IS neighbors in its SMDS DR-IS Hello messages. Since this information can be sizable, the SMDS DR-IS Hello message (Option 2) can send fragments by allowing address ranges to be sent. Upon receipt of an SMDS DR-IS Hello, an IS will refresh its adjacency database for SMDS neighbors.

8.3.4.4   IDRP over SMDS

IDRP, like BGP, uses a reliable point-to-point transport service to deliver PDUs. IDRP specifies its own transport protocol for this purpose. As a consequence, as with BGP, IDRP does not put any special constraints on the use of SMDS. No multicast addresses are needed.

8.3.5 PDU Formats

Since ES-IS [ISO9542] and IS-IS [ISO10589] have been designed for operation over point-to-point links and over 802.x LANs, and given the refinements made for their use over SMDS, some of the ES-IS and IS-IS PDU formats are slightly modified as well. Figures 8.27–8.31 and Tables 8.9 and 8.10 show the message formats. These formats only apply for operation over SMDS, and do not affect information that is propagated beyond SMDS. All PDUs are shown starting with the first byte on top and the most significant bit (bit 1) on the left.

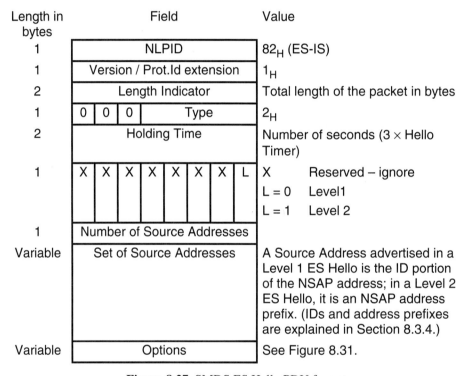

Figure 8.27 SMDS ES Hello PDU format

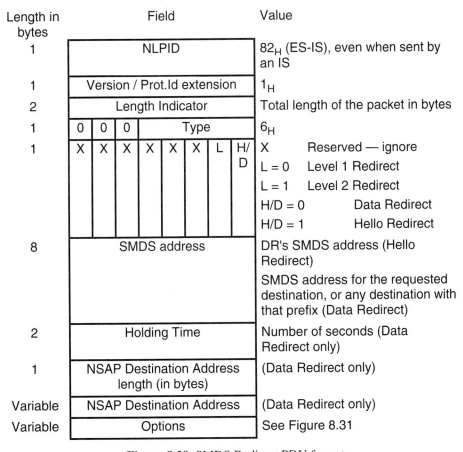

Figure 8.28 SMDS DR-to-ES Hello PDU format

Figure 8.29 SMDS Redirect PDU format

Length in bytes	Field	Value
1	NLPID	83_H (IS-IS)
1	Version / Prot.Id extension	1_H
2	Length Indicator	Total length of the packet in bytes
1	0 | 0 | 0 | Type	$0F_H$ SMDS Level 1 IS Hello 10_H SMDS Level 2 IS Hello
2	Holding Time	Number of seconds ($3 \times$ Hello Timer)
1	X | X | X | X | X | X | X | DR	X Reserved — ignore DR=0 Sender considers itself non-DR DR=1 Sender considers itself DR
1	ID length	The number of bytes this IS thinks is in the ID portion of the NSAP address
1	Maximum Area addresses	The maximum number of Area addresses this IS is prepared to keep
1	Priority	The configured priority of this IS for becoming DR
1	Link type	1_H Level 1 2_H Level 2 3_H Level 1 and Level 2
1	ID	ID length octets
8	SMDS Group Address	The Group Address that this IS receives messages on. Set to zero if none. Only present when the IS Hello is sent by a non-DR.
Variable	Option	See Figure 8.31.

Figure 8.30 SMDS DR-IS Hello and SMDS IS Hello PDU format

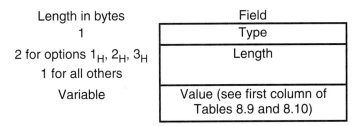

Figure 8.31 Use of the OPTIONS field

SMDS options [SIG004]	Message type applicability	Semantics
5_H	All	Password
Generic options [ISO9542]		
$C5_H$	All but the SMDS IS Hello	Security
$C3_H$	SMDS Redirect	Quality of service Maintenance
CD_H	All but the SMDS IS Hello	Priority
$E1_H$	SMDS Redirect	Address Mask
$E2_H$	SMDS Redirect	SNPA (Subnetwork Point of Attachment) Mask
$C6_H$	SMDS DR-ES Hello	Suggested ES Configuration Timer

Table 8.9 Option types

SMDS options [SIG004]	Semantics	Length in bytes
1_H	Preconfigured SMDS addresses for reaching ISs (sent by non-DR only)	$n \times 8$
2_H	IS adjacencies (sent by DR only) - Numerically lowest ID in this Hello - Numerically highest ID in this Hello - Set of ID, SMDS address bindings learned from Hellos from Nonpassive-ISs	$2 \times \text{ID\_length} + n \times (8 + \text{ID\_length})$
3_H	Preconfigured SMDS addresses for reaching ESs (sent by non-DR only)	$n \times 8$
4_H	Area addresses	$n \times 8$
5_H	Password	Variable

Table 8.10 SMDS IS Hello and SMDS DR-IS Hello options

8.3.6 Carrying CLNP, ES-IS, and IS-IS over SMDS

SMDS carries CLNP, ES-IS, and IS-IS via LLC1 encapsulation. SNAP encapsulation is not necessary. All of these ISO protocols use the self-identifying NLPID.

Figure 8.32 illustrates the resulting formats as defined in [SIG004].

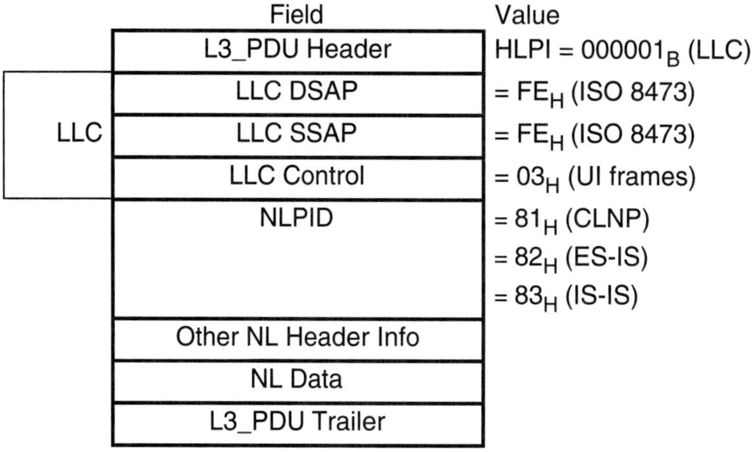

Field	Value
L3_PDU Header	HLPI = 000001_B (LLC)
LLC DSAP	= FE_H (ISO 8473)
LLC SSAP	= FE_H (ISO 8473)
LLC Control	= 03_H (UI frames)
NLPID	= 81_H (CLNP)
	= 82_H (ES-IS)
	= 83_H (IS-IS)
Other NL Header Info	
NL Data	
L3_PDU Trailer	

(LLC brackets LLC DSAP, LLC SSAP, and LLC Control fields)

Figure 8.32 Encapsulation of CLNP, ES-IS, and IS-IS in L3_PDUs

The PDU fields are used as follows:

- In the L3_PDU header, the HLPI is set to 1. This indicates the use of IEEE 802.2 LLC.

- The LLC DSAP and SSAP values are set to FE_H, indicating the use of CLNP. This includes the use of the associated ES-IS and IS-IS protocols. The LLC CONTROL field is set to the value 3_H (UI frames).

- The NLPID determines the network layer protocol that is used; it is coded as 81_H for CLNP, 82_H for ES-IS, and 83_H for IS-IS. (See also the PDU formats in the previous sections.)

The resulting protocol identifier is a 4-byte constant: $FEFE0381_H$, $FEFE0382_H$, or $FEFE0383_H$ identifying CLNP, ES-IS, or IS-IS packets.

8.3.7 OSI Station Configuration and Database Information for SMDS

The SIG specifies a detailed configuration list for OSI systems attached to SMDS [SIG004]. We present this list in Tables 8.11 and 8.12.[18] In addition, each OSI system will maintain a database with information that it learns from interactions with other systems. The SIG lists for this information are presented in Tables 8.13, 8.14, and 8.15.

Item	Configuration information
1	Configured set of IS SMDS Group and/or Individual Addresses
2	Set of NSAP/SMDS address bindings of systems reachable on SMDS:* - NSAP address prefix only if the SMDS address can be extracted, or NSAP address prefix plus one or more matching SMDS addresses - SMDS Carrier Selection (if needed)
3	The minimum time (in seconds) between pings of any one configured SMDS address for reaching ISs.
4	The ping expiration time (in seconds): When expired while pinging a particular IS SMDS address, the next address on the list will be tried.

* If not configured in a node, Nonpassive-ISs must be configured with the addresses of that node.

Table 8.11 Configuration information for OSI Systems attached to SMDS (other than Nonpassive-ISs)

Based on the configuration and database information, a number of decisions have to be made for the forwarding of a CLNP packet. The procedure specified in [SIG004] is illustrated in Figure 8.33. One additional procedure relative to the figure applies to the case where the packet is received from the transport layer, and the transport layer has the capability to notify that it cannot communicate with the destination in this packet. In case of this notification, the cache entry for the destination is deleted, or, if no entry exists, a Simple ES will delete its knowledge of the active IS and start pinging for a new one.

As explained in Section 8.3.2, the LOS can be maintained by a variety of methods, including proper use of passwords in the neighbor-greeting messages. Table 8.16 shows the configuration requirements. For example, a simple configuration could be to use a single password within a LOS for all systems.

If receive passwords are not used, their presence in received messages must be ignored.

---

[18]This shows empirical evidence of what we think must be the routing-protocol variant of Heisenberg's principle: Every increase of routing protocol and traffic efficiency is proportional to the increase in routing protocol and configuration complexity.

Item	Configuration information	Level
1	Link type: The link over SMDS can be configured as "Level 2 only" (L2 ISs), or "Not Level 2 only" (L1 and L2 for L2 ISs, L1 for L1 ISs).	L1 and L2
2	Level 1 Configured-ES addresses. For each ES: - ID, ID length (a constant for the routing domain) - SMDS address	L1 only
3	Preconfigured CLNP address prefixes: - CLNP address prefix - Flag on whether an E.164 embedded NSAP address is used. If the flag is false, one or more SMDS Addresses that must be used when forwarding packets to that CLNP address prefix. - Preferred carrier (optional)	L1 and L2
4	Link costs. Each entry contains: - SMDS address-prefix length specified in the number of bits - SMDS address prefix (padded with trailing 0's to 8 bytes) - Cost from this node to this prefix	L1 and L2
5	SMDS Group Address L1IS_GA (if any) that this node receives packets on	L1 only
6	SMDS Group Address L2IS_GA (if any) that this node receives packets on	L2 only
7	Priority for becoming Level 1 DR	L1 only
8	Priority for becoming Level 2 DR	L2 only
9	Configured set of SMDS Group and/or Individual Addresses for reaching ESs	L1 and L2
10	Configured set of SMDS Group and/or Individual Addresses for reaching Level 1 ISs	L1 only
11	Configured set of SMDS Group and/or Individual Addresses for reaching Level 2 ISs	L2 only
12	Level 1 IS-IS Hello Timer; the time (in seconds) between transmission of SMDS IS Hellos	L1 only
13	Level 2 IS-IS Hello Timer; the time (in seconds) between transmission of SMDS IS Hellos.	L2 only
14	IS-ES Hello Timer; the time (in seconds) between transmission of SMDS IS Hellos (only used if system is DR)	L1 and L2
15	Redirect cache Holding Timer; the value to put in the Redirect message Holding Timer	L1 and L2
16	Time for remembering a manually configured ES or IS SMDS address reported in an SMDS IS Hello in option types 1 or 3 (only used when system is DR)	L1 and L2

Table 8.12 Configuration information for OSI Nonpassive-ISs attached to SMDS

Item	Configuration information
1	Active IS Information: - SMDS address - Holding Timer - Time since cache entry was verified by receipt of DR-ES Hello or receipt of a Data Redirect from that SMDS address
2	Backup Active IS information (optional)
3	IS SMDS addresses pinged, plus a timestamp for each SMDS address of the last ping
4	Destination cache - NSAP address prefix (or complete address for simplicity) - Set of SMDS addresses for each prefix, with a pointer indicating which one was chosen most recently in the round-robin use of the preconfigured set of SMDS addresses. Once traffic is received from an SMDS address, the set of addresses is replaced by the single SMDS address - Time since the address binding was verified by an incoming message (a CLNP packet from that address, or a Redirect with that binding specified)

Table 8.13 Database information kept by OSI Simple-ESs, Configured-ESs, Passive-ISs, and Configured-Passive-ISs Attached to SMDS

Item	Configuration information
1	DR Information on Level 1 and /or Level 2:* - SMDS address - Holding Timer - Time since cache entry was verified by receipt of DR-ES Hello or receipt of a Data Redirect from that SMDS address
2	SMDS neighbor information (address bindings) from the DR-IS Hello (kept by non-DRs only)
3	Flags for which LSPs need to be transmitted over SMDS on Level 1 and/or Level 2
4	Redirect database (to shortcut redundant hops) for Level 1 and /or Level 2: - NSAP address prefix - SMDS address - Holding Timer - Time since cache entry was last verified

* ISs other than the DR also keep information from the DR's Hello.

Table 8.14 Database information kept by OSI Nonpassive-ISs attached to SMDS

Item	Configuration information
1	IS neighbors: - SMDS address (from the Source Address of the SMDS packet carrying an IS Hello) - CLNP ID - Holding Timer - Time since SMDS IS Hello was received - SMDS Group Address this IS receives messages on (if any) - Cost of the link across SMDS to this IS
2	The minimal set of SMDS addresses that will reach all ISs of the appropriate level (both manually configured and received in SMDS IS Hellos):* L1-IS-SMDS-BROADCAST-ADDRESSES for Level 1 and L2-IS-SMDS-BROADCAST-ADDRESSES for Level 2
3	The manually configured SMDS addresses for ISs discovered via received IS Hellos (Option 1): - SMDS address - Most recent time since that address was reported in any received SMDS ES Hello
4	The manually configured SMDS addresses for ESs discovered via received IS Hellos (Option 3): - SMDS address - Most recent time since that address was reported in any received SMDS ES Hello

*SMDS Individual Addresses that are known to be part of a Group Address in the list must be weeded out.

Table 8.15 Additional database information kept by DRs attached to SMDS

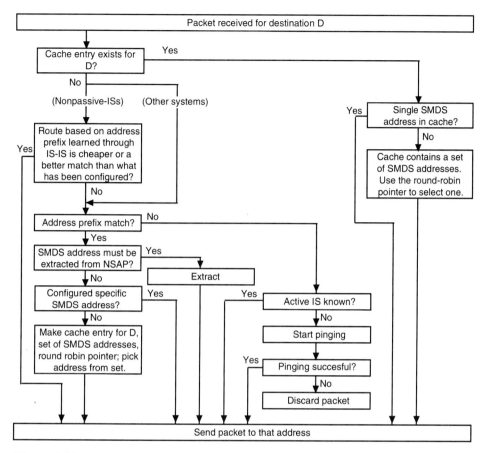

Figure 8.33 Procedure to forward CLNP packets and to maintain the destination cache

Device	Configured passwords	Transmit/ Receive	Applicability
ES	1	Transmit	SMDS ES Hello
	1 or more	Receive	SMDS DR-ES Hello SMDS Hello Redirect
Level 1 IS	1	Transmit	SMDS DR-ES Hello SMDS Hello Redirect (to ES)
	1	Transmit	SMDS L1IS Hello SMDS Hello Redirect (to IS)
	1 or more	Receive	SMDS ES Hello
	1 or more	Receive	SMDS L1IS Hello SMDS Hello Redirect (to IS)
Level 2 IS*	1	Transmit	SMDS DR-ES Hello SMDS Hello Redirect (to ES)
	1	Transmit	SMDS L2IS Hello SMDS Hello Redirect
	1 or more	Receive	SMDS ES Hello
	1 or more	Receive	SMDS L2IS Hello SMDS Hello Redirect

* A Level 2 IS that also acts as Level 1 IS also requires the Level 1 configuration

Table 8.16 Password configuration

8.4   AppleTalk over SMDS

AppleTalk is a network architecture designed by Apple Computer, Inc., to connect Apple products such as the Macintosh personal computer and LaserWriter printer, as well as non-Apple devices. While Apple products can also be connected using other architectures, such as TCP/IP, AppleTalk represents Apple's own suite of rules and protocols for internetworking.

The basic internetworking structure of the AppleTalk architecture is similar to the structure of the TCP/IP and OSI architectures. An internetworking protocol is used to tie potentially heterogeneous physical networks together via routers and gateways, and shields applications from the peculiarities of these networks. An authoritative overview of the AppleTalk architecture is described in [Apple] and [Sidhu]. Figure 8.34 shows how SMDS fits into the basic AppleTalk protocol architecture.

The internetworking function in the AppleTalk architecture is performed by the Datagram Delivery Protocol (DDP). DDP is designed to run over a variety of physical networks. The properties of these networks are adapted to the needs of AppleTalk by means of special protocols. Token Ring networks use the

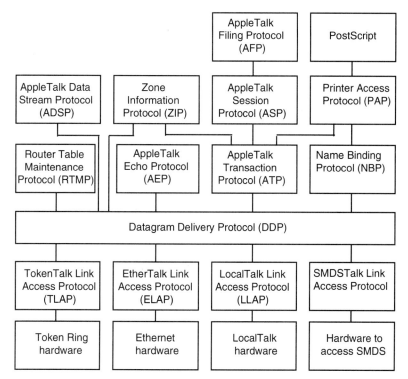

Figure 8.34 Role of SMDS in the Basic AppleTalk protocol architecture

TokenTalk Link Access Protocol (TLAP), Ethernets use the EtherTalk Link Access Protocol (ELAP), and LocalTalk networks (an Apple specific LAN) use the LocalTalk Link Access Protocol (LLAP). EtherTalk and TokenTalk use the LLC encapsulation method. By extension, SMDS can fulfill a role similar to Token Ring networks and Ethernets in this architecture, allowing AppleTalk to operate over wide areas using SMDS. Aptly named SMDSTalk, an informational specification was produced for this purpose in the SIG [SIG019]. SMDSTalk follows EtherTalk and TokenTalk by employing the LLC1/SNAP encapsulation. Figure 8.35 shows an example of an AppleTalk network configuration employing SMDS.

There are no special protocol modifications needed in equipment to accommodate the use of the AppleTalk protocol suite over SMDS.

8.4.1 Some Properties of the AppleTalk Protocol Suite

The internetworking protocol in the AppleTalk protocol suite is DDP, a datagram protocol. The service supported by DDP includes unicast, multicast, and broadcast. The format of a DDP packet is discussed in [Sidhu], and is

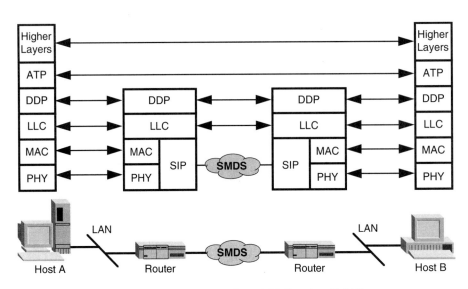

Figure 8.35 Example of AppleTalk using SMDS

reproduced in Figure 8.36. Some basic properties relevant for SMDS are discussed below.

Length in bytes	Field		
1	0	0	Hop count	Datagram Length
1	Datagram Length		
2	DDP Checksum		
2	Destination Network Number		
2	Source Network Number		
1	Destination Node ID		
1	Source Node ID		
1	Destination Socket Number		
1	Source Socket Number		
1	DDP Type		
0 – 586	Data		

Figure 8.36 DDP Packet format (extended header)

Relevant for SMDS is the maximum length of DDP packets, and the way they are addressed. The DATAGRAM LENGTH field indicates the length of the total packet, including the header, and is 10 bits long, allowing potentially 1024-byte packets. However, as shown in Figure 8.36, the actual maximum length of DDP packets is 599 bytes [Sidhu]. This is easily accommodated by SMDS, and no fragmentation and reassembly mechanism is necessary.

The DDP source and destination addresses are 32-bit identifiers consisting of the triplet {NETWORK NUMBER, NODE ID, SOCKET NUMBER}. They address both the source and destination nodes, and the processes (sockets) within these nodes that are communicating. Each AppleTalk network in an internet is assigned a range of network numbers. A node is identified by a NETWORK NUMBER from within the range of the network it connects to, and a NODE ID. The addresses are typically dynamically assigned. Therefore, to route a DDP packet over SMDS, address resolution is necessary to find the appropriate SMDS address.

8.4.2   Logical AppleTalk Networks over SMDS

Similar to the use of Logical IP Subnetworks (LIS; see Section 8.2.2) for TCP/IP networking over SMDS, AppleTalk networks that use SMDS should configure logical subnetworks over SMDS. These subnetworks are called Logical SMDSTalk AppleTalk networks (LSA) in [SIG019]. The rationale and the way to achieve this are the same as for the LIS. An SMDS Group Address (LSA_GA) is configured to identify the AppleTalk stations that form an LSA. The LSA_GA is then used as the AppleTalk broadcast address within the LSA.

An LSA configuration requires the following:

- All members of an LSA must be within the same *network number range*. This requirement has the same rationale as its IP-peer for a LIS. AppleTalk broadcast packets (NODE ID equals all one's, and NETWORK NUMBER equals zero) are directed at all stations within the network number range.

- For each LSA, a single SMDS Group Address, the LSA_GA, is configured to identify all AppleTalk stations that form the LSA.

- Similar to IP nodes within a LIS, all AppleTalk stations within an LSA are accessed directly over SMDS. This is a logical consequence of the definition of an LSA. All LSA members must be reachable by LSA_GA-addressed L3_PDUs.

- All AppleTalk stations outside an LSA are accessed via a DDP router. Since only AppleTalk stations within an LSA can communicate directly, communication with other AppleTalk stations requires an extra hop, for example via a router that is member of more than one LSA.

8.4.3   Address Resolution and Neighbor Discovery

Since AppleTalk addresses are dynamically assigned when the station is initialized, a dynamic address resolution mechanism is employed within the

AppleTalk architecture to bind the AppleTalk address with a hardware address. The method used is analogous to ARP for the TCP/IP protocol suite (see Section 8.2.3). The protocol used for AppleTalk is called the AppleTalk Address Resolution Protocol (AARP). The cache maintaining AppleTalk address/hardware address bindings is called the *Address Mapping Table* (AMT). A variation relative to ARP is that AARP uses one additional packet type called the *AARP Probe packet*. This is necessary because of the dynamic address-allocation mechanism in AppleTalk. Upon initialization, a station picks a tentative AppleTalk address (one that is not in its AMT). It uses that address in an AARP Probe packet broadcast. If the address is already in use, the target station returns a response signifying that the probing station must pick another tentative address. Details on AARP and AMT are described in [Apple] and [Sidhu]. Figure 8.37 shows the AARP packet format as shown in [Sidhu].

Length in bytes	Field
2	Hardware Type
2	Protocol Type
1	Hardware Address Length
1	Protocol Address Length
2	Function
8	Source Hardware Address
4	Source AppleTalk Address
8	Destination Hardware Address
4	Destination AppleTalk Address

Figure 8.37 AARP Request, Response, and Probe Packet format for SMDS

The contents of the AARP message are similar to those of ARP packets:

HARDWARE TYPE — The code that determines the network type. The value assigned to SMDS is $0E_H$ (14_D) [RFC1340].

PROTOCOL TYPE — The code that identifies the protocol stack for which address resolution is sought. The value for AppleTalk is $809B_H$.

FUNCTION — The packet type (Request, Response or Probe. See [Sidhu]).

HARDWARE ADDRESS LENGTH — The length of SMDS addresses is 8 bytes.

PROTOCOL ADDRESS LENGTH   The length of AppleTalk addresses is 4
                                 bytes.

DESTINATION HARDWARE ADDRESS Set to 0 in the AARP Request and
                                 Probe packets.

8.4.4 AppleTalk Routing

AppleTalk internets consist of networks connected by routers, routing DDP
packets. A number of protocols are employed to exchange the necessary
information to achieve proper routing and associated address and name mapping.
A descriptive figure [Sidhu] that is relevant for SMDS is depicted in Figure 8.38.

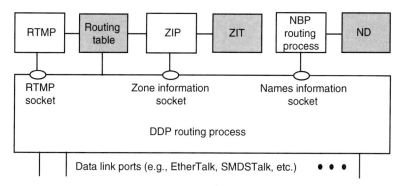

Figure 8.38 The AppleTalk routing model and SMDS

The Routing Table is maintained using the Routing Table Maintenance
Protocol (RTMP). RTMP associates the AppleTalk node address of a sending
port of a router with the duple {NETWORK NUMBER, DISTANCE}. The network
number may also be a range of network numbers. The distance is the minimum
number of hops known to the router that separate the router from that particular
network. The Routing Tables are kept up-to-date by mandating that every router
broadcast its Routing Table entries to other routers. Combined with a system of
deleting outdated entries, the inspection of received RTMP packets keeps the
Routing Table up-to-date. For details, see [Apple] and [Sidhu]. RTMP is a
datagram protocol, carried by DDP, which in turn is carried by a physical
network, such as SMDS. The required RTMP broadcasts must be mapped to
SMDS Group Addressed packets, and must be sent to the entire LSA using
SMDS. In other words, the Group Address used should be LSA_GA.

AppleTalk allows human-friendly names to be used for communicating
entities. Besides being human-friendly, this overcomes the problem of the
frequent changes in address information (dynamic address allocation). For this to
work, a dynamic binding between name and address is necessary in combination

with maintaining a Names Table in each node that contains the name/address bindings. The protocol defined for this purpose is the Name Binding Protocol (NBP). Entity names are of the form {*object*:*type*@*zone*}, where the *object* specifies a name of an entity, and the *type* specifies some attribute or description of the entity. The *zone* is a grouping of nodes within an AppleTalk internet. Zones can be used within an internet to demarcate equipment of organizations and departments, and to build a useful organization of an AppleTalk internet. Each of the three parts of the entity name can be up to 32 characters long.

The dynamic binding between zones and the range of network numbers that contain nodes on a zone is achieved by the Zone Information Protocol (ZIP). ZIP is used in combination with a Zone Information Table (ZIT) that contains the zone/network range mappings known to that router. The ZIP services are used by the NBP process to direct NBP name-lookup requests to the appropriate networks in an AppleTalk zone. The bindings between names and internet addresses are maintained in a Name Table in each node. The Names Directory (ND) refers to the collection of Name Tables in the nodes of an internet. NBP is used to find name bindings of particular entities. For details, see [Apple] and [Sidhu].

Both NBP and ZIP are datagram protocols using DDP. NBP and ZIP work internet wide. To avoid interrupting nodes outside a zone, multicasting is used wherever possible to support name-lookup requests. Zone multicast addresses on an SMDSTalk network can be supported by SMDS Group Addresses (ZONE_GA*n*). The number of zone multicast addresses is usually bound to a maximum value (253 on Ethernet and FDDI, and 19 on Token Ring). This does not limit the number of zones valid on one network, since zone names are hashed to zone multicast addresses, as described in [Sidhu]. The maximum number of zone multicast addresses for SMDSTalk has been set to 19 (ZONE_GA1 through ZONE_GA19) [SIG019]. In cases where only one zone multicast address is needed, this may be set to ZONE_GA1 = LSA_GA.

8.4.5 Carrying DDP and AARP Datagrams over SMDS

DDP and AARP, both datagram protocols, can be carried directly by SMDS. DDP and AARP both utilize IEEE LLC1/SNAP encapsulation in order to be carried over SMDS, in much the same way as discussed for IP and ARP (see Section 8.2.5). Figure 8.39 illustrates the resulting formats, as defined in [SIG019].

The PDU fields are used as follows:

- In the L3_PDU header, the HLPI is set to 1. This indicates the use of IEEE 802.2 LLC.

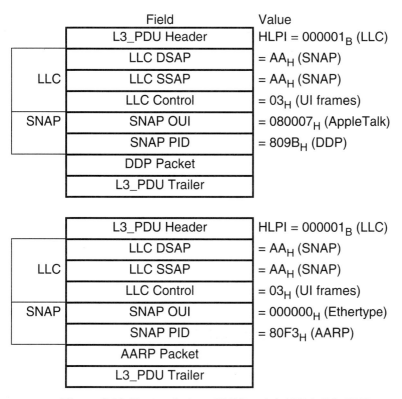

	Field	Value
	L3_PDU Header	HLPI = 000001_B (LLC)
LLC	LLC DSAP	= AA_H (SNAP)
	LLC SSAP	= AA_H (SNAP)
	LLC Control	= 03_H (UI frames)
SNAP	SNAP OUI	= 080007_H (AppleTalk)
	SNAP PID	= $809B_H$ (DDP)
	DDP Packet	
	L3_PDU Trailer	

	Field	Value
	L3_PDU Header	HLPI = 000001_B (LLC)
LLC	LLC DSAP	= AA_H (SNAP)
	LLC SSAP	= AA_H (SNAP)
	LLC Control	= 03_H (UI frames)
SNAP	SNAP OUI	= 000000_H (Ethertype)
	SNAP PID	= $80F3_H$ (AARP)
	AARP Packet	
	L3_PDU Trailer	

Figure 8.39 Encapsulation of DDP and AARP in L3_PDUs

- The LLC DSAP and SSAP values are set to 170_D (AA_H), indicating the use of IEEE 802.1 SNAP. The LLC CONTROL field is set to the value 3_D (UI frames).

- The SNAP header OUI is set to 000000_H for AARP, meaning that the Ethertype style of identification is applicable. The PID value for AARP assigned to AppleTalk is $80F3_H$. For DDP the OUI is 080007_H. The PID for DDP is $809B_H$.

The resulting 8-byte constant for LLC1/SNAP is $AAAA03080007809B_H$ when carrying DDP packets, and $AAAA0300000080F3_H$ for the transport of AARP packets.

8.4.6   AppleTalk Node Configuration for SMDS

AppleTalk nodes (routers or end stations) must be configured with a number of special parameters and values in order to use SMDS, as described in [SIG019].

- The hardware address (i.e., the SMDS Individual Address) of the AppleTalk node using SMDS.

- The SMDS Group Address LSA_GA that identifies the members of an LSA. This Group Address represents the SMDS address to which AppleTalk broadcasts should be directed (for example, AARP Requests and RTMP Data packets).

- The SMDS Group Addresses ZONE_GA1 through ZONE_GAn that identify recipients of a zone multicast to support the NBP and ZIP. Multiple instances of this address may be supported on one SMDSTalk network. The maximum is set to 19. If only one zone is supported over SMDSTalk, this address may be set to LSA_GA. Although a given node will only use one such address at any one time (it can only be in one zone), it should be configured with all the multicast addresses valid for its LSA.

It is the responsibility of the Group Address Sponsor (see Chapter 3) to request an update of that list if new stations are added to the LSA. This may be performed via the SMDS Customer Network Management service. See Chapter 12.

An AppleTalk router may be a member of more than one LSA. In that case, multiple sets of these parameters are needed.

The duration of the time-out interval while the router waits for an AARP Response should take into account the delays that are typical for wide area SMDS. SMDS delay objectives are discussed in Chapter 7.

The AARP Probe interval for SMDSTalk to determine the time-out value before a retry may be attempted is set to 1 second. The Probe retry count for SMDSTalk (the maximum number of retries [Sidhu]) is set by the SIG to 5 [SIG019].

When the LSA scenario is used, the use of the SMDS Address Screening feature is not required. If used, however, the screens should be configured to at least allow communication within the LSA (Individual Addresses, the LSA_GA, and the ZONE_GAs).

8.5   Xerox's XNS over SMDS

Xerox Network Systems (XNS) refers to a communications architecture created at the Xerox Palo Alto Research Center that arose from the PARC Universal Packet (PUP) university research project in the late 1970s. XNS has had a profound impact on architectures of leading LAN vendors as well as on OSI. It is described in [Neibaur] as a cousin of TCP/IP, and indeed, many of the design principles are very much alike. Like TCP/IP, the key of XNS is a datagram internetworking protocol, that ties an arbitrary set of physical networks together by routers and gateways. The set of XNS protocols is shown in Figure 8.40.

XNS distinguishes five communication layers. The lowest layer, layer 0, represents the physical networks, such as SMDS. While these networks, as we have seen in previous chapters, usually have a layered architecture themselves, this layering is of no particular significance from the XNS perspective. The Internetwork Datagram Protocol (IDP) fulfills the same role as IP, OSI CLNP, and AppleTalk's DDP. IDP in turn, is used by the transport protocols Sequenced Packet Protocol (SPP), which can provide a reliable, connection-oriented data stream), and Packet Exchange Protocol (PEP), which can be used for connectionless applications, and is comparable to UDP and ISO 8602. Other users of IDP are the Routing Information Protocol (RIP), the Error Protocol used for diagnostic purposes, and the Echo Protocol, which is used to verify the existence and correct operation of host systems. Details are specified in [Xerox].

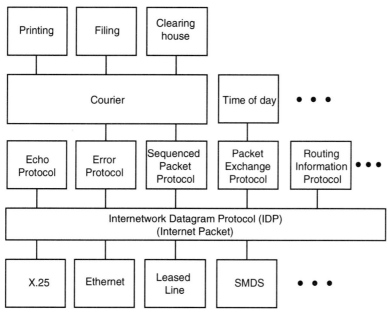

Figure 8.40 SMDS and the XNS protocol suite

Given its similarity with TCP/IP and OSI, SMDS can accommodate XNS in much the same way as those architectures. Methods to operate XNS over SMDS had not been formally specified by the SIG or by Xerox at the publication of this book. The approach we present in this section parallels the approach of [RFC1209], and requires no special protocol modifications in equipment to accommodate the use of the XNS protocol suite over SMDS.

8.5.1 Some Properties of the XNS Protocol Suite

IDP is a datagram protocol. The service supported by IDP includes unicast, multicast, and broadcast. The basic format is defined in [Xerox] and reproduced in Figure 8.41. The same packet format has been adopted for Netware's Internetwork Packet Exchange (IPX) protocol, which we discuss in Section 8.6.

Length in bytes	Field
2	Checksum
2	Length
1	Transport Control
1	Packet Type
4	Destination Network
6	Destination Host
2	Destination Socket
4	Source Network
6	Source Host
2	Source Socket
0 – 546*	Data

* IPX packets can have the size permitted by the underlying medium. See Section 8.6.1.

Figure 8.41 IDP and IPX packet format

XNS specifies a maximum IDP packet size of 576 bytes, which includes 30 bytes of header. No fragmentation and reassembly mechanism is needed to run it over SMDS.

IDP uses an address triplet {NETWORK NUMBER, NODE NUMBER, SOCKET NUMBER}. The NODE NUMBER is 6 bytes long, typically a 48-bit MAC hardware address. SMDS addresses do not fit into this field, and another type of address has to be assigned. Address resolution is necessary to find the appropriate SMDS/IDP address binding. Broadcast packets use {NODE NUMBER} = "all ones"; broadcasts are NETWORK-wide.

8.5.2 Logical Xerox Networks over SMDS

XNS stations can employ logical subnetworks, Logical XNS Subnetworks (LXSs), over SMDS using the SMDS Group Addressing feature in the same way as has been described for other protocol architectures. An SMDS Group Address (LXS_GA) must be set up for broadcast purposes that spans all participating XNS stations in a particular LXS. The requirements for stations in an LXS are similar to those for the LIS described in Section 8.2.2:

- All members of an LXS have the same NETWORK NUMBER.

- All LXS stations are accessed directly over SMDS.

- All LXS stations are configured to receive L3_PDUs addressed to LXS_GA.

- An XNS node can be a member of multiple LXSs.

- Communications between LXSs must pass through an IDP router that is a member of multiple LXSs.

8.5.3   Address Resolution and Neighbor Discovery

In the absence of a dynamic protocol for address resolution, the address binding of the a station's address triplet {NETWORK NUMBER, NODE NUMBER, SOCKET NUMBER} and the corresponding SMDS address is obtained by a static table in each XNS node that uses SMDS.

8.5.4   XNS RIP

RIP is the protocol that allows dynamic updates of the routing table in routers, and allows routers to locate other XNS routers. Routing information can be requested or may also be advertised gratuitously. A timer process allows for removal of aged entries in the routing table. The routing metric is expressed in the number of hops that separate two stations, and is independent of the use of SMDS. Routing information is usually propagated using broadcast. For SMDS, RIP broadcast packets can be mapped to LXS_GA.

8.5.5   Carrying IDP Datagrams over SMDS

IDP-over-SMDS can employ the LLC1/SNAP encapsulation method, using the identification codes allocated to Xerox XNS IDP. The resulting format is shown in Figure 8.42.

8.6   Novell's NetWare over SMDS

NetWare is the network operating system developed by Novell, Inc. NetWare is another offspring of the XNS architecture of Xerox. In particular the Internetwork Packet Exchange (IPX), Sequenced Packet Exchange (SPX), and RIP protocols are virtually the same as their peers in XNS. The basic NetWare protocol suite is shown in Figure 8.43. IPX runs some other applications than its counterpart IDP in XNS. NetBIOS is an industry standard and was written in

Field	Value
L3_PDU Header	HLPI = 000001_B (LLC)
LLC DSAP	= AA_H (SNAP)
LLC SSAP	= AA_H (SNAP)
LLC Control	= 03_H (UI frames)
SNAP OUI	= 000000_H (Ethertype)
SNAP PID	= 0600_H (XNS IDP)
IDP Packet	
L3_PDU Trailer	

Figure 8.42 Encapsulation of IDP in L3_PDUs

1984 for IBM. It handles certain input/output functions comparable with transport/session functions in the OSI model. The Service Advertising Protocol (SAP) is used by devices such as print servers and file servers to advertise their address information and supported services. The NetWare Core Protocol (NCP) is used for client/server interactions.

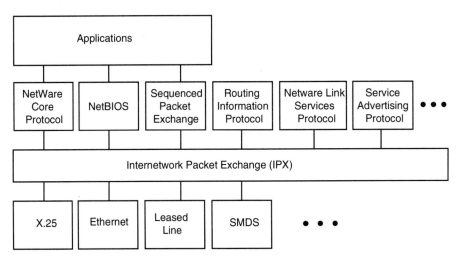

Figure 8.43 SMDS and the NetWare protocol suite

SMDS fits into the NetWare protocol suite in the same way that it fits into XNS. NetWare is discussed in more detail in [Novell1], [Novell2], [Novell3], and [Miller]. An informational specification has been prepared for the SIG on how to run IPX over SMDS [SIG042]. There are no special protocol modifications needed in equipment to accommodate the use of the NetWare protocol suite over SMDS.

8.6.1   Some Properties of the NetWare Protocol Suite

The internetworking protocol in the NetWare protocol suite is IPX, which is derived from IDP of the XNS protocol suite. The PDU format is shown in Figure 8.41. IPX packets can have the size permitted by the underlying medium. Hence, IPX packets of up to 9180 bytes can be supported over SMDS [Novell1]. All IPX stations in a logical NetWare subnetwork (see Section 8.6.2) must support and configure the same maximum.

Like IDP, IPX uses an address structure of {NETWORK NUMBER, NODE NUMBER, SOCKET NUMBER}. The NODE NUMBER is 6 bytes long, and is typically a 48-bit MAC hardware address. The Socket number identifies a process within the destination node, such as RIP or SAP. SMDS addresses do not fit into this field, and another type of address has to be assigned. Manufacturers of the interface must assign an IEEE 48-bit address (ADDRESS_IEEE) to the port accessing SMDS, which is then used as NODE NUMBER. IEEE addresses are obtained from IEEE. Address resolution is necessary to find the appropriate address binding between an IPX address and an SMDS address.

Broadcast packets use {NODE NUMBER} = "all ones". Broadcasts are NETWORK-wide. One exception is a special packet type defined in IPX, called the *IPX Type 20 Propagation Packet*. This packet is necessary to support certain protocols, such as NetBIOS, and is propagated network-wide. This has no special consequence for the use of SMDS. Upon receipt of this packet from a non-SMDS source or another VPN (see Section 8.6.2), the packet, after proper processing, is broadcast to all VPNs it has not yet traversed. A list of traversed networks is included in the packet.

8.6.2   Logical NetWare Networks over SMDS

NetWare stations can employ logical NetWare subnetworks over SMDS in a manner similar to what has been described for XNS (see Section 8.5.2). These subnetworks are called *Virtual Private Networks* (VPNs) in [SIG042]. All stations within a VPN share the same NETWORK NUMBER.

An SMDS Group Address, GLOBAL_GA, is used for broadcast purposes to reach all participating NetWare stations in a particular VPN. Communication between VPNs is achieved by two hops over SMDS via a router that is a member of both VPNs. Interestingly, GLOBAL_GA is defined as "all nodes belonging to the VPN, whether they use IPX, a different protocol, or multiple protocols." The purpose of this definition is to allow multiprotocol coexistence within the same VPN. As we will see in the next section, ARP (see Section 8.2.3) is supported for address resolution, which will allow for multiprotocol address resolution.

Another SMDS Group Address, IPX_GA, is defined in [SIG042], to allow IPX broadcasts within a VPN to all stations that use IPX. Implementations are allowed to configure IPX_GA = GLOBAL_GA. For example, this configuration applies to an IPX-only VPN. IPX Type 20 packets are transmitted within a VPN to IPX_GA.

8.6.3   Address Resolution and Neighbor Discovery

The Address Resolution Protocol (ARP) [RFC826] [Comer1] is used for IPX address resolution over SMDS. ARP is used in the same way for NetWare as for TCP/IP networks (see Section 8.2.3). The required packet format when used for operating IPX over SMDS is shown in Figure 8.44.

Length in bytes	Function
1	Hardware Type
1	Protocol Type
1	HLEN	PLEN
1	Operation
8	Sender Hardware Address
10	Sender IPX Address
8	Target Hardware Address
10	Target IPX Address

Figure 8.44 ARP PDU format for IPX-over-SMDS

For IPX-over-SMDS, the fields are used as follows [SIG042]:

HARDWARE TYPE   The code assigned for SMDS is $0E_H$ or 14_D [RFC1340]

PROTOCOL TYPE   The value for IPX is 8137_H [RFC1340]

HLEN   The length of SMDS addresses is 8 bytes

PLEN   The length of IPX addresses is 10 bytes. (The SOCKET NUMBER is not needed for ARP.)

ARP requests are sent to an SMDS Group Address, IPX_ARP_GA. A typical configuration in a multiprotocol environment is IPX_ARP_GA = GLOBAL_GA. For example, a VPN, where IP and IPX coexist, may be configured as IPX_ARP_GA = GLOBAL_GA = LIS_GA (see Section 8.2.3). However, a separate IPX_ARP_GA also allows for configuration of one or more ARP servers, separate from the node for which address resolution is requested.

8.6.4   NetWare RIP, SAP, and NLSP

With some small amendments NetWare has adopted the indomitable RIP of XNS. But where the XNS RIP carries routing information duples {NETWORK

NUMBER, INTERNETWORK DELAY}, with the delay measured in hops, NetWare carries {NETWORK NUMBER, INTERNETWORK DELAY, NUMBER OF TICKS}. There are 18.21 ticks in a second. This allows for an improved decision to select the fastest route to a destination. For high-bandwidth physical networks like Token Rings and Ethernets, [Novell1] specifies a one-tick delay, while a T1 or X.25 delay may range from 6 to 7 ticks. Delays for SMDS may therefore be set in the 1 – 6 ticks range.

The NetWare RIP model is shown in Figure 8.45. Routing information is disseminated by broadcasts. End nodes determine the best route to a network number by broadcasting a route request. Routers broadcast route requests to update their routing tables, and respond to incoming route requests. Routers also broadcast their routing information periodically and also whenever a change in the network is detected. A timer process allows for removal of aged entries in the routing table (maximum age is 3 minutes). For SMDS, RIP broadcast packets can be mapped to the SMDS Group Address IPX_GA.

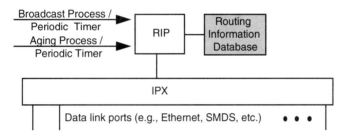

Figure 8.45 The NetWare RIP routing model

The Service Advertising Protocol, SAP, is used by nodes to advertise their services and addresses. These include print servers, file servers, archive servers, remote bridge servers, and so on. The advertisements consist of the service type, the server name, the address tuple, and the number of hops to the node. This information can be solicited via a SAP-request broadcast, and is also broadcasted at events such as start-up. SAP agents also periodically broadcast all service information known to the node. A timer process determines outdated entries in the server table and removes these (maximum age is 3 minutes). For SMDS, all of these SAP broadcast packets can be mapped to the SMDS Group Address IPX_SAP_GA, which spans all routers in a VPN. It is allowable to configure IPX_SAP_GA = IPX_GA. The NetWare SAP model is shown in Figure 8.46.

NetWare also supports a link-state routing protocol, the NetWare Link State Protocol (NLSP) [Novell2]. NLSP replaces RIP and SAP between servers and routers, but RIP and SAP are still used between an end node and its nearest router(s). NLSP has a compatibility feature supporting interoperation with RIP routers. NLSP operates for LANs somewhat differently from WANs. However, SMDS is treated as a LAN. Like RIP, NLSP makes use of the IPX service to

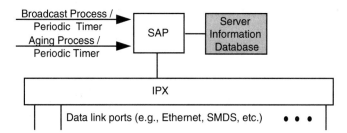

Figure 8.46 The NetWare SAP model

communicate between NLSP stations. To support broadcasts of NLSP packets within a VPN, the SMDS Group Address IPX_NLSP_GA is used. All NLSP stations are required to listen to this address. It is allowable to configure IPX_NLSP_GA = IPX_GA (which may cause slightly more traffic overhead in some topologies).

8.6.5   Carrying IPX Datagrams over SMDS

Novell has obtained both LLC SAP values and SNAP values to identify its protocols. For SMDS, the IPX encapsulation employs the LLC1/SNAP method [RFC1340]. The resulting format is shown in Figure 8.47.

	Field	Value
	L3_PDU Header	HLPI = 000001_B (LLC)
LLC	LLC DSAP	= AA_H (SNAP)
LLC	LLC SSAP	= AA_H (SNAP)
LLC	LLC Control	= 03_H (UI frames)
SNAP	SNAP OUI	= 000000_H (Ethertype)
SNAP	SNAP PID	= 8137_H (IPX)
	IPX Packet	
	L3_PDU Trailer	

Figure 8.47 Encapsulation of IPX in L3_PDUs

8.6.6   IPX Node Configuration for SMDS

NetWare nodes connected to SMDS must be configured with the following parameters and values:

- The SMDS Individual Address of the router using SMDS.

- Each router or a server within a VPN is configured with the same NETWORK NUMBER. An end node learns the NETWORK NUMBER by protocol exchange with the nearest router. If there is no router available, it uses NETWORK NUMBER zero, meaning "the directly attached network." (This makes things plug-and-play for end nodes for typical LAN media). The NODE NUMBER is the 48-bit MAC address ADDRESS_IEEE.

- For each VPN, a maximum transmission unit size, TU_MAX, is used by all stations ($584 \leq$ TU_MAX ≤ 9188).

- For each VPN, SMDS Group Addresses are used, as shown in Table 8.17.

SMDS Group Address	Purpose	Remarks
GLOBAL_GA	Allows ARP broadcasts within a multiprotocol VPN	In a IPX-only VPN: GLOBAL_GA = IPX_GA
IPX_GA	Allows IPX broadcasts within a VPN	
IPX_ARP_GA	Allows dedicated ARP servers within a VPN	When no dedicated ARP servers are used, IPX_ARP_GA = GLOBAL_GA
IPX_NLSP_GA	Allows NLSP broadcasts within a VPN	Typically, IPX_NLSP_GA = IPX_GA

Table 8.17 SMDS Group Address configuration for NetWare stations

Address Screens, if used, should at least allow communication within the VPN.

8.7   3Com's 3+ and 3+Open over SMDS

3Com Corp. has developed two major networking architectures, 3+ and 3+Open [Miller]. 3+ refers to an architecture that successfully blends the Xerox architecture for internetworking (XNS, see Section 8.5) with applications running under DOS, the Server/Redirector File-Sharing protocol of MicroSoft Corp., and, like Novell's NetWare and Banyan VINES, it also supports NetBIOS, which is running directly over IDP/SPP. A simplified protocol architecture is illustrated in Figure 8.48.

3+Open uses a more extensive architecture called the *Demand Protocol Architecture*. This refers to the use of a protocol manager that dynamically runs the binding between the hardware driver and the protocol that uses it. This feature is especially useful for personal computers running Microsoft DOS.

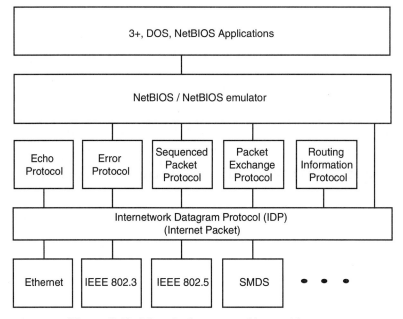

Figure 8.48 3Com 3+ internetworking architecture

Without rebooting, up to four protocols can be multiplexed at a hardware port. Supported protocol architectures include XNS, TCP/IP, AppleTalk, and *NetBIOS Protocol* (NBP), a version of NetBIOS that runs directly over the data link provided by the hardware; see Figure 8.49.

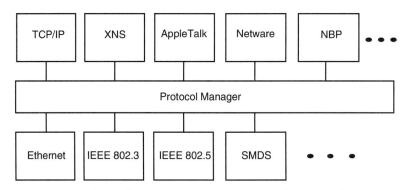

Figure 8.49 Dynamic binding between hardware port and protocol driver in 3+Open

Methods to operate 3+ and 3+Open over SMDS were not formally specified by the SIG or by 3Com at the publication of this book. We present in this section an approach that parallels [RFC1209], and that requires no special protocol modifications in equipment to accommodate the use of the 3+ and 3+Open protocol suite over SMDS.

8.7.1   Logical 3Com Networks over SMDS

Logical 3Com subnetworks to support 3+ can be achieved in the same way as is described for XNS. An SMDS Group Address, L3S_GA, is used to determine the span of the broadcasts within the *Logical 3+ Subnetwork* (L3S).

The support of logical networks for 3+Open presents an interesting case. Given the multiprotocol environment within 3+Open, two alternatives can be configured:

- Construct a single *Logical 3+Open Subnetwork* (L3S) with an SMDS Group Address (L3S_GA) that identifies all 3+Open stations that are to be reached via SMDS. This address is used for all broadcast and multicast purposes within the L3S. This alternative is simple, but may be wasteful in traffic and causes unnecessary interrupts at stations that are not configured to run all protocol architectures within 3+Open.

- Configure separate logical networks for each of the protocol architectures supported within an L3S, for example, a LIS, an LSA, a VPN, and an LXS with associated SMDS Group Addresses, as described in previous sections. No separate L3S_GA is necessary in this scenario. L3S consists of the union of the LIS, LAS, VPN, and LXS.

8.7.2   Carrying 3Com-Supported Protocols over SMDS

Fitting SMDS into the 3+ and 3+Open architecture should be straightforward, using the LLC1/SNAP encapsulation and the respective Ethertype values described earlier in this chapter for XNS and the other supported protocols. An interesting case is NBP. NBP provides a virtual circuit service, and some of its messages are sensitive to ordered delivery. On Ethernets and Token Ring networks, these messages are carried directly in the data link frame, using the Ethertype or LLC1/SNAP multiplexing technique. For this purpose, 3Com obtained a block of Ethertype codes starting with $3C_H$ [Miller], as shown in Table 8.18.[19]

As discussed earlier, ordered delivery of L3_PDUs is not guaranteed. The NBP protocol is such that this is important in some situations. While the probability of missequencing is small, it may have unforeseen effects on higher layers in the protocol stack.[20] Fortunately, 3Com offers an alternative to run

---

[19]We are unaware of the conditions that led to this fortunate code assignment to 3Com Corp.

[20]Measurements on this subject had not yet been carried out at our publication date.

Ethertype	NBP packet	Ethertype	NBP packet
$3C00_H$	Virtual Circuit Data	$3C07_H$	Datagram Data
$3C01_H$	System	$3C08_H$	Broadcast Datagram Data
$3C02_H$	Connect Request	$3C09_H$	Claim Name
$3C03_H$	Connect Response	$3C0A_H$	Delete Name
$3C04_H$	Connect Complete	$3C0B_H$	Remote Adapter Status Request
$3C05_H$	Close Request	$3C0C_H$	Remote Adapter Status Response
$3C06_H$	Close Response	$3C0D_H$	Reset

Table 8.18 Ethertypes and NBP packets

NetBIOS, that is, as an application in the XNS architecture. Also, since SMDS is expected to act mainly as a LAN interconnection service for which XNS is more suitable than the plain execution of NBP, we recommend that NetBIOS be run as an XNS application over SMDS, instead of via NBP over SMDS. In cases where NBP needs to be used directly, an SMDS Group Address is needed to accommodate NBP broadcast datagrams.

8.8   Banyan VINES over SMDS

Banyan Systems Inc.'s *Virtual Networking Systems* (VINES) supports a proprietary protocol suite derived from the XNS architecture (see Figure 8.50). The VINES architecture is designed so that it can be integrated with TCP/IP, IPX/SPX, AppleTalk, and SNA. In this section, we focus on how the native VINES protocols can make use of SMDS. The proprietary protocols are used to support applications such as NetRPC (a remote procedure call facility, formerly called MatchMaker, and comparable to XNS's Courier), a NetBIOS emulation, file-transfer services, StreetTalk (a distributed naming service), email, and printing services. Unix, DOS, OS/2, Windows, and Macintosh environments are supported. Details of the architecture and its protocols can be found in [Banyan1], [Banyan2], and [Miller].

Methods to operate VINES over SMDS had not been formally specified by the SIG or by Banyan at the publication of this book. We present in this section an approach that parallels [RFC1209], and that requires no special protocol modifications in equipment to accommodate the use of the 3+ and 3+Open protocol suite over SMDS.

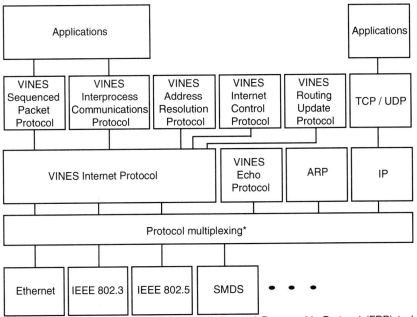

* Includes the use of the VINES Fragmentation and Reassembly Protocol (FRP) to handle large packets

Figure 8.50 Banyan VINES internetworking architecture (server side)

8.8.1   Some Properties of the VINES Protocol Suite

The internetworking protocol in the VINES proprietary protocol suite is VINES IP. VINES IP is another derivative of XNS's IDP. It can be carried over SMDS in the same way as IDP (albeit with a different protocol-multiplexing indication). For its format, see Figure 8.51. A VINES IP packet has a maximum length of 1468 bytes. Thus, the VINES Fragmentation and Reassembly Protocol (FRP) is not needed to support VINES IP over SMDS.

VINES IP uses an address structure of {NETWORK, SUBNETWORK} 6 bytes long. The NETWORK number of 4 bytes identifies a logical network of VINES nodes. The logical network has a two-level hierarchy of one server and a set of client nodes. The NETWORK number is the serial number of the server, and the SUBNETWORK number identifies a client of that server. Servers use SUBNETWORK = 1. VINES IP addresses are independent of the addresses used for the physical networks. Address resolution is necessary to find the appropriate address binding. A subnetwork-wide broadcast uses SUBNETWORK = $FFFF_H$. A network-wide broadcast sets the destination address to "all ones".

Length in bytes	Function
2	Checksum
2	Length
1	Transport Control
1	Packet Type
4	Destination Network
2	Destination Subnetwork
4	Source Network
2	Source Subnetwork
≤1450	Data

Figure 8.51 VINES IP packet format

8.8.2 Logical VINES Networks over SMDS

For the support of broadcasts among VINES stations over SMDS, the logical subnetwork concept described for other architectures can be used. We call this subnetwork a *Logical VINES Subnetwork* (LVS). As in the 3Com case, a single SMDS Group Address, LVS_GA, can be set up that spans all VINES stations attached to SMDS (including the nonnative VINES stations such as TCP/IP nodes), or separate SMDS Group Addresses can be configured to support native VINES (LVS_GA) and other protocol environments such as TCP/IP (LIS_GA) separately.

An application that requires broadcasts is StreetTalk, which supports propagation of updates for the StreetTalk naming database among its servers. Another application is the Time Service that runs on every server, and propagates time information in order to synchronize network time. Both applications make use of unreliable IPC (datagram), which is carried in VINES broadcast IP packets. When transmitted over SMDS, these packets should be addressed to LVS_GA.

8.8.3 Address Resolution, Neighbor Discovery, and Routing

The VINES Address Resolution Protocol (ARP, not to be confused with the ARP defined for TCP/IP) is used to allocate addresses to nodes that need one. VINES supports two versions of ARP. Sequenced ARP is a version of ARP introduced under VINES 5.5. Nonsequenced ARP is also supported under VINES 5.5, but also in older versions of VINES. SMDS can support both versions of ARP in the same way.

VINES makes use of a dynamic address-assignment procedure. When a client boots up, it finds an appropriate server by broadcasting a message to all servers. The client selects the first server from the server responses. This server becomes the client's routing server. The client sends a message directly to that server, asking for an address. The server will allocate an address {NETWORK, SUBNETWORK}, where NETWORK is the server's serial number, and SUBNETWORK is a unique number for that server.

VINES servers configure their own addresses as {serial number, 1}. When a VINES server boots up, it broadcasts its routing information to other servers. The VINES Routing Update Protocol (RTP) is used to broadcast routing information among servers. VINES supports two versions of RTP. Sequenced RTP is a version of RTP introduced under VINES 5.5. Nonsequenced RTP is also supported under VINES 5.5, but also in older versions of VINES. SMDS can support both versions of RTP in the same way.

When SMDS is used, the SMDS Group Address LVS_GA can be used for ARP and RTP broadcasts.

8.8.4   Carrying VINES Datagrams over SMDS

According to [Banyan2], VINES will support the LLC1/SNAP encapsulation method, using the identification codes allocated to Banyan VINES [Novell1]. The resulting format for SMDS is shown in Figure 8.52.

	Field	Value
	L3_PDU Header	HLPI = 000001_B (LLC)
LLC	LLC DSAP	= AA_H (SNAP)
	LLC SSAP	= AA_H (SNAP)
	LLC Control	= 03_H (UI frames)
SNAP	SNAP OUI	= $08004A_H$ (Banyan)
	SNAP PID	= $80C4A_H$ (VINES IP)
		= $80C5_H$ (VINES Echo)
	VINES IP/VINES Echo Packet	
	L3_PDU Trailer	

Figure 8.52 Encapsulation of VINES IP in L3_PDUs

VINES also uses the VINES Fragmentation and Reassembly Protocol (VFRP) to handle large packets. Since the maximum size of VINES IP packets is 1468 bytes, SMDS can carry these packets directly.

8.9   DECnet Phase IV over SMDS

DECnet Phase IV forms the current core of DEC's internetworking architecture. The architecture is described in [DEC1] and [DEC2]. SMDS fulfills the same role in DECnet as it does in most other internetworking architectures, that is, SMDS provides physical network connectivity to the internetworking layer (see Figure 8.53).[21]

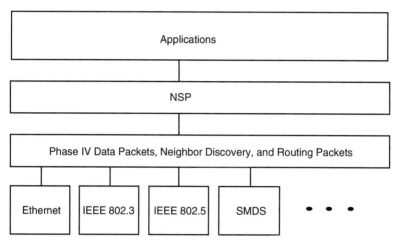

Figure 8.53 Simplified DEC Phase IV architecture

A specification on how to run DECnet Phase IV over SMDS has been published by the SMDS Interest Group [SIG003]. This section recaps the essence of that specification. There are no special protocol modifications needed in equipment to accommodate the use of the DECnet Phase IV protocol suite over SMDS.

8.9.1   Some Properties of the DECnet Phase IV Protocol Suite

DECnet Phase IV represents another architecture that relies on a datagram-based internetworking protocol. The basic format of the DEC Phase IV Data packet is defined in [DEC2] and reproduced in Figure 8.54.

---

[21]Interestingly, the Phase IV internetworking protocol was initially called *Transport Protocol*, and the end-to-end protocol on top of that was called *Network Services Protocol*. This seemed quite logical since, after all, the real transport of packets is at the internetworking layer. Unfortunately, OSI discussions in ISO and CCITT included many telephone-service providers who had a different idea about network services and reversed the two labels. This made Phase IV descriptions pretty confusing, so that the labels were quietly dropped and only the acronym NSP was retained.

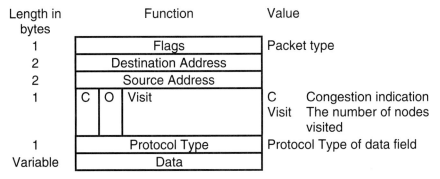

Figure 8.54 DEC Phase IV Data packet format

Phase IV addresses consist of the tuple {AREA, HOST}. The {AREA} is 6 bits long, and the {HOST} is 10 bits. Address resolution is necessary to run Phase IV datagrams over SMDS. The following description uses the concepts End Systems (ESs), Intermediate Systems (ISs), and Designated Routers (DRs) in the same way as has been described for OSI (see Section 8.3).

8.9.2   Logical Phase IV Networks over SMDS

Logical Phase IV Subnetworks (L4Ss) can be formed by prudent use of the SMDS Group Address feature. This assumes again that the Phase IV stations are configured to listen only to these Group Addresses for the propagation of routing information and neighbor discovery. In the simplest scenario, all ESs are configured to listen to an SMDS Group Address 4ES_GA, and all routers are configured to listen to 4IS_GA. There is a 2-level routing hierarchy, similar to that described for OSI. Thus, Level 1 and Level 2 routers may be configured to listen to 4L1IS_GA and 4L2IS_GA, respectively.

As with OSI, DEC Phase IV nodes may also be configured to listen to a mixture of SMDS Group and Individual Addresses, and to dynamically learned addresses. Unless these nodes listen only to a fixed set of addresses, other means are necessary to maintain an L4S. As for OSI (Section 8.3.2), these means are as follows:

- SMDS Address Screens

- The use of passwords in neighbor-greeting messages

8.9.3   Address Resolution and Neighbor Discovery

On 802 LANs, DEC Phase IV obtains the binding of the addresses on the internetworking layer and the physical network layer by overwriting the 6-byte MAC address with a 4-byte specified constant plus the DEC Phase IV 2-byte internetworking address. Thus, an algorithmic relationship is created between the two address layers. The 8-byte SMDS address does not lend itself to this method. Instead, a dynamic address resolution procedure is used [SIG003]. Since this protocol was first designed for use over SMDS, the key properties are described here. The packet formats and their use are illustrated in Section 8.9.5. For full details on DEC Phase IV routing, consult [DEC1], [DEC2], and [SIG003].

8.9.3.1 Neighbor Greeting

The neighbor-greeting procedure is very similar to the one described for OSI (see Section 8.3.3). Again, the concept of Designated Router (DR) is used to minimize neighbor-greeting traffic. Routers may also be statically configured with ES address bindings to avoid periodic Hello messages. Alternatively, a dynamic procedure can be used:

- ESs initially broadcast SMDS ES Hello messages to a set of preconfigured routers. This broadcast on SMDS may be directed to any set of preconfigured SMDS addresses. A simple method is to preconfigure all ESs with a single SMDS Group Address, 4IS_GA. The minimum requirement for an ES is that it should know only one (1) router, unless an IS is preconfigured to know this ES.

- Non-DR ISs that receive the SMDS ES Hello respond with an SMDS Hello Redirect providing the DR's address information. Upon receipt of this redirect, the ES will send an SMDS ES Hello to the specified SMDS Individual Address.

- The result of the two previous steps is that ESs will eventually only talk to the DR, and the DR will know about all ESs. From its configuration and from received SMDS ES Hellos, the DR establishes a minimal list, ES-SMDS-BROADCAST-ADDRESSES, of all SMDS Group or Individual Addresses that ESs listen to, in order to broadcast SMDS DR-ES Hellos. The list consists of the following:

  — The DR's configured ES addresses

  — The configured SMDS addresses in other ISs, reported in SMDS IS Hellos (Option 6 in the PDU format)

  — The SMDS Source Addresses from ESs reporting to the DR with SMDS ES Hellos

  — The SMDS Group Addresses that these ESs listen to and that are reported in the SMDS IS Hellos

A weeding procedure must be used to remove redundant addresses in the list by excluding the SMDS Individual Addresses of nodes that also listen to listed SMDS Group Addresses. In the simple example where all participating ESs are configured to listen to a single Group Address, 4ES_GA, the DR would end up using only 4ES_GA. The DR-ES relationship is maintained by periodic DR-ES Hellos by the DR to this list. ESs that receive an SMDS DR-ES Hello will now send SMDS ES Hellos only to the DR.

- The DR propagates the list of learned ES address bindings to all other routers it knows in SMDS DR-IS Hello messages.

The DR must keep a list of routers to which it sends SMDS DR-IS Hellos. This list consists of ISs that it has been configured with, and of other ISs that it has learned of through incoming SMDS IS Hello messages. The DR must keep this list, IS-SMDS-BROADCAST-ADDRESSES, up-to-date by (a) keeping track of the routers joining the fray (SMDS IS Hello message), and (b) keeping track of routers that have gone down or lost connectivity (a *Listen Timer = 3 * Hello Timer*). The DR calculates this list from the following:

- Its configured IS addresses

- The configured SMDS addresses in other ISs, reported in SMDS IS Hellos

- The SMDS Source Addresses from ISs reporting to the DR with SMDS IS Hellos

- The SMDS Group Addresses that these ISs listen to, and reported in the SMDS IS Hellos

A weeding procedure is necessary to avoid duplicates by excluding the SMDS Individual Addresses of ISs that also listen to listed SMDS Group Addresses. In the simple example where all routers are configured with the same SMDS Group Address, 4IS_GA, as reach information, the IS-SMDS-BROADCAST-ADDRESSES would end up to be precisely 4IS_GA.

The DR will also deduce an *IS adjacencies* list of the individual {PHASE IV ADDRESS, SMDS INDIVIDUAL ADDRESS} bindings from the SMDS IS Hellos, and an *ES adjacencies* list of address bindings from the SMDS ES Hellos. These lists indicate the nodes that are currently up.

All three lists, together with the list of preconfigured ES SMDS addresses (if not reported in the other lists), are broadcast in SMDS DR-IS Hellos to the routers identified by the IS-SMDS-BROADCAST-ADDRESSES. See Options 1–4 of the SMDS DR-IS Hello packet format. IS-SMDS-BROADCAST-ADDRESSES is used by all routers for broadcasting their routing information (see Section 8.9.4). The address bindings are used for the transmission of data packets.

An interesting refinement to this protocol is the consideration for the length of the SMDS DR-IS Hello message. This packet may become quite large in a sizable network, and even larger than the maximum L3_PDU size. Furthermore, devices can signal in Hello messages what the maximum message size is that they are prepared to handle. To resolve this problem, the DR calculates the allowed maximum SMDS DR-IS Hello size and sends sorted fragments of the address lists. Each fragment will indicate a range of addresses, which will overwrite previously received information for that range. For this to work, the Listen Timer needs to be reset after receipt of each fragment until the set is complete.

As pointed out in [SIG003], this sorted fragmentation technique is not necessary for SMDS IS Hellos. This optimization is achieved by a timer in the DR for remembering manually configured ESs and ISs reported in SMDS IS Hellos (Options 5 and 6 in the packet format). By setting that timer to a high value (10 minutes), the DR allows that either fragments will be sent (not necessarily sorted), or that the node whose Listen Timer runs out will report in via a Hello message. Note that the IS Hellos are more likely to be small anyway, because no addresses need to be reported in IS Hellos that are advertised in SMDS DR-IS Hellos.

8.9.3.2   DR Election

The DR election process is not very democratic, since it strictly adheres to the principle of "the most qualified wins." The procedure is the same as has been described for OSI. A router boots up with the belief that it is the DR, and persists in this belief until it hears from a more qualified router. It emits periodic SMDS DR-IS Hello messages to a preconfigured list of other routers at its level. This list is allowed to be only partially complete. The frequency is set by a local Hello Timer. This chatter of claims is resolved as follows:

1. A router stops sending SMDS DR-IS Hellos when it receives one from another more qualified router (with a higher priority or a higher HOST ID in case of a priority tie; see the packet format), and/or

2. Non-DRs will return SMDS Hello Redirects if they are aware of a more qualified router.

This will cause the first router to doubt its belief that it is the DR and to start sending SMDS IS Hellos directly to what it has calculated from the previous responses to be the real DR. Of course, this might still not be the most qualified router, in which case another Hello Redirect will be returned. Eventually, when our router receives an SMDS DR-IS Hello from the more qualified router, it knows a better-qualified router is actually active. It ceases to see itself as the DR and stops sending SMDS DR-IS Hellos. This procedure will converge quickly to a stable situation where there is general agreement on the identity of the DR. Each router will keep a check on the connectivity with a DR by setting a timer (*Listen Timer = 3 * Hello Timer*) on the receipt of SMDS DR-

IS Hellos, so that if the DR crashes, another run for the DR title will start, and eventually another router will assume the DR role.

8.9.4   DECnet Phase IV Routing over SMDS

DECnet Phase IV uses a two-level routing hierarchy, similar to that described for OSI (see Section 8.3.4), with Level 2 routers routing on {AREA} and Level 1 routers routing on {HOST}. The routing protocol is a distance-vector protocol and is comparable to (but not the same as) RIP.

Routers exchange their routing information by broadcasting periodically on the Level 1 and Level 2 IS-SMDS-BROADCAST-ADDRESSES lists received in the SMDS DR-IS Hellos. The L1 and L2 routing messages carrying the distance vectors are the normal routing messages used elsewhere in Phase IV [DEC2]. Applying split-horizon update (a technique to avoid sending information about a particular route back over the same interface it was received from, see [Perlman]), routers connected to SMDS only report routing information about routes over other than their SMDS interfaces. Unlike RIP, no time-out mechanism is used to outdate routing entries. Instead, routing updates are made on the basis of the list of address bindings advertised in the SMDS DR-IS Hellos. The absence of a router in the SMDS DR-IS Hello is interpreted to mean that the router has gone down.

Phase IV routing allows for two routing metrics, one usually based on inverse bandwidth, and one counting hops, as in RIP. Routers may be configured with a single cost for traversing SMDS. An interesting alternative is specified in [SIG003] that allows for configuration of a cost-per-range of SMDS addresses. This makes use of the hierarchical structure of the typical SMDS address, and associates the cost with an SMDS address prefix, an arbitrary number of most significant digits of SMDS addresses, in the same way as has been described for OSI, and allows for route optimization and potential cost savings.

8.9.5   PDU Formats

The PDU formats are shown in Figures 8.55–8.58 and Table 8.19.

Length in bytes	Field	Value
1	Packet Type	13_H
2	Source Phase IV Address	
2	Max Data Link Layer Blocksize	9180 (= 9188 – 8) assuming sufficient buffer space
2	Hello Timer	In seconds
8	SMDS multicast	The SMDS Group Address that this station listens to Set to 0 if none
8	Password	

Figure 8.55 DEC Phase IV SMDS ES Hello PDU Format

Length in bytes	Field		Value
1	Packet Type		15_H (L1 DR-IS Hello) 17_H (L2 DR-IS Hello) 33_H (DR-ES Hello) 19_H (L1 IS Hello) $1B_H$ (L2 IS Hello)
1	Priority		Priority for becoming DR
2	Source Phase IV Address		
2	Max Data Link Layer Blocksize		9180 (= 9188 – 8) assuming sufficient buffer space
2	Hello Timer		In seconds
1	Reserved (6 bits)	Router Type (2 bits)	Router Type = 01_B (IS L1) Router Type = 10_B (IS L2)
8	SMDS multicast		Only present in L1 IS Hellos and L2 IS Hellos The SMDS Group Address that this station listens to Set to 0 if none
8	Password		
Variable	Options		See Figure 8.57

Figure 8.56 DEC Phase IV SMDS DR-ES Hello, SMDS DR-IS Hello, and SMDS IS Hello PDU format

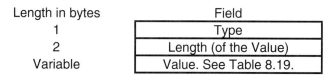

Figure 8.57 Use of the OPTIONS field

Message	Option type	Length in bytes	Field	Value
L1 and L2 DR-IS Hello	1_H	2	Lowest Phase IV address	IS adjacencies – Range of Phase IV addresses
		2	Highest Phase IV address	covered in this packet (allows for processing of
		$n \times 2$	Phase IV addresses	partial router lists) plus the list of routers that recently sent IS Hellos to the DR.
L1 DR-IS Hello	2_H	2	Lowest Phase IV address	ES adjacencies – Range of Phase IV addresses
		2	Highest Phase IV address	covered in this packet plus the list of ESs that recently sent IS Hellos to the DR.
		$n \times (2 + 8)$	Phase IV address / SMDS address bindings	
L1 DR-IS Hello	3_H	2	Lowest SMDS address	Other, configured, ES SMDS addresses –
		2	Highest SMDS address	Range of SMDS addresses covered in this packet plus the list of
		$n \times 8$	SMDS addresses	addresses configured into the DR and not listed in Option 2.
L1 and L2 DR-IS Hello	4_H	2	Lowest SMDS address	Reach information of routers on that level
		2	Highest SMDS address	advertised to other routers to send their routing
		$n \times 8$	SMDS addresses	information on, and used by the DR to transmit DR-IS Hellos.

(continued)

(Table 8.19 continued)

Message	Option type	Length in bytes	Field	Value
L1 and L2 IS Hello	5_H	$n \times 8$	SMDS addresses	Configured IS addresses – Neighbor-router reach information (SMDS Individual and/or Group Addresses).
L1 and L2 IS Hello	6_H	$n \times 8$	SMDS addresses	Configured ES addresses – Neighbor-router reach information (SMDS Individual and/or Group Addresses). Addresses reported in Option 2 or 3 are excluded.

Table 8.19   Use of the Option types for DEC Phase IV SMDS DR-ES Hello, SMDS DR-IS Hello, and SMDS IS Hello

Length in bytes	Function	Value	
1	Packet Type	31_H	
1	Redirect Type	1	Data Redirect
		2	Hello Redirect to ES
		3	Hello Redirect to L1 IS
		4	Hello Redirect to L2 IS
2	Phase IV Destination address	Ignored in Hello redirects (set to 0)	
8	SMDS address	The address to send to	
8	Password	Ignored in Data Redirects (set to 0)	

Figure 8.58 DEC Phase IV SMDS Hello Redirect format

8.9.6   Carrying DEC Phase IV Datagrams over SMDS

DEC Phase IV-over-SMDS employs the LLC1/SNAP encapsulation method, using the identification codes allocated to DEC. The resulting format is shown in Figure 8.59.

8.9.7   DECnet Phase IV Node Configuration for SMDS

A detailed configuration list is specified in [SIG003] for DEC Phase IV nodes attached to SMDS. We present this list in Tables 8.20 and 8.21. In addition, each

DEC Phase IV system will maintain a database with information that it learns based on interactions with other systems. The configuration and database information are presented in Tables 8.22 – 8.24.

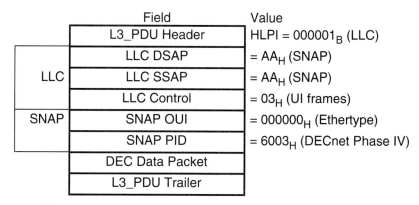

	Field	Value
	L3_PDU Header	HLPI = 000001_B (LLC)
LLC	LLC DSAP	= AA_H (SNAP)
	LLC SSAP	= AA_H (SNAP)
	LLC Control	= 03_H (UI frames)
SNAP	SNAP OUI	= 000000_H (Ethertype)
	SNAP PID	= 6003_H (DECnet Phase IV)
	DEC Data Packet	
	L3_PDU Trailer	

Figure 8.59 Encapsulation of DEC Phase IV Datagrams in L3_PDUs

Item	ES configuration information
1	Configured set of IS SMDS Group and/or Individual Addresses.
2	ES Hello Timer. The time (in seconds) between transmission of SMDS ES Hellos. Set to infinity ($FFFF_H$) in ESs whose address bindings have been configured in all routers.
3	Idle Timer. A timer (in seconds) started when no traffic needs to be forwarded to the DR. When expired, ES Hellos to the DR are discontinued. Only used if Hello Timer = $FFFF_H$
4	Destination Cache Holding Timer. The maximum time (in seconds) a cache entry should be kept that has not been refreshed by a Redirect or traffic from that Phase IV/SMDS address.

Table 8.20 Configuration information for DECnet Phase IV ESs attached to SMDS

Item	IS configuration information	IS Type
1	Link type: the link over SMDS can be configured as "Level 2 only" (L2 ISs), or "Not Level 2 only" (L1 and L2 for L2 ISs, L1 for L1 ISs).	L1 and L2
2	Configured ES addresses. If all routers are configured with a particular ES, that ES may set its Hello Timer to $FFFF_H$. For each ES: - Phase IV address - SMDS address	L1 only

(*continued*)

(Table 8.21, continued)

Item	IS configuration information	IS Type
3	Link costs. Each entry contains - SMDS address prefix length specified in the number of bits - SMDS address prefix (padded with trailing 0's to 8 bytes) - Cost from this node to this prefix	L1 and L2
4	SMDS Group Address L1IS_GA that this node receives packets on. Set to 0 if none.	L1 only
5	SMDS Group Address L2IS_GA that this node receives packets on. Set to 0 if none.	L2 only
6	Priority for becoming Level 1 DR.	L1 only
7	Priority for becoming Level 2 DR.	L2 only
8	Configured set of SMDS Group and/or Individual Addresses for reaching ESs.	L1 and L2
9	Configured set of SMDS Group and/or Individual Addresses for reaching Level 1 ISs.	L1 only
10	Configured set of SMDS Group and/or Individual Addresses for reaching Level 2 ISs.	L2 only
11	L1 Distance Vector Maximum Time Interval. The maximum time (in seconds) between transmissions of a distance to a particular IS.	L1 only
12	L2 Distance Vector Maximum Time Interval. The maximum time (in seconds) between transmissions of a distance to a particular IS.	L2 only
13	L1 Distance Vector Minimum Time Interval. The minimum time (in seconds) between transmissions of a distance to a particular IS.	L1 only
14	L2 Distance Vector Minimum Time Interval. The minimum time (in seconds) between transmissions of a distance to a particular IS.	L2 only
15	Level 1 IS-IS Hello Timer. The time (in seconds) between transmission of SMDS IS Hellos or SMDS DR-IS Hellos.	L1 only
16	Level 2 IS-IS Hello Timer. The time (in seconds) between transmission of SMDS IS Hellos or SMDS DR-IS Hellos.	L2 only
17	IS-ES Hello Timer. The time (in seconds) between transmission of SMDS DR-ES Hellos (only used if system is DR).	L1 and L2
18	Redirect cache Holding Timer. The maximum time (in seconds) a cache entry should be kept that has not been refreshed by a Redirect or traffic from that Phase IV/SMDS address.	L1 and L2

(continued)

(Tabel 8.21, continued)

Item	IS configuration information	IS Type
19	Time (in minutes) for remembering a manually configured ES or IS SMDS address reported in an SMDS IS Hello in Option types 5 or 6 (only used when the system is DR). The default is 10 minutes.	

Table 8.21 Configuration information for DECnet Phase IV ISs attached to SMDS

Item	ES database information
1	DR Information: - SMDS address - Listen Timer (3 × Hello Timer, and reported in the DR's SMDS DR-ES Hello) - Time since this cache entry was verified by receipt of DR-ES Hello. - Only if Hello Timer is $FFFF_H$: • Time since traffic sent to DR • DR's Hello Timer • Time since ES-Hello sent to DR
2	Destination cache - Set of Phase IV/SMDS address bindings - Time since the address binding was verified by an incoming message (a data packet from that address, or a Redirect with that binding specified)

Table 8.22 Database information kept by DECnet Phase IV ESs attached to SMDS

Item	IS (non-DR) database information (kept separately for L1 and L2)
1	DR Information: - Information from the SMDS DR-IS Hellos - SMDS address - Listen Timer (3 × Hello Timer, and reported in the DR's SMDS DR-ES Hello) - Time since cache entry was verified by receipt of DR-ES Hello
2	Adjacency information for each SMDS neighbor, based on received DR-IS Hellos: - Phase IV address - SMDS address - Distance vector received - Cost calculated from the configured {SMDS address prefix, cost} information
3	Redirect database (to shortcut redundant hops): - Phase IV address - SMDS address - Time since cache entry was last verified by an incoming message or Redirect

Table 8.23 Database information kept by DECnet Phase IV Non-DR ISs attached to SMDS

Item	IS database information (kept separately for L1 and L2)
1	Dynamically discovered ES neighbors. For each ES: - Phase IV address - SMDS address - Listen Timer (3 × Hello Timer, and reported in the DR's SMDS DR-ES Hello) - Time since Hello received
2	Dynamically discovered IS neighbors. For each IS: - Phase IV address - SMDS address - Listen Timer (3 × Hello Timer, and reported in the DR's SMDS DR-ES Hello) - Time since Hello received - SMDS Group Address that this IS listens to - Cost of the link to this neighbor IS - Distance vector received from this neighbor
3	Configured SMDS addresses for ISs, as discovered through Option 5 in received SMDS IS Hellos. Each entry contains: - SMDS address - Most recent time that address was reported in any received SMDS IS-Hello

(continued)

(Table 8.24, continued)

Item	IS database information (kept separately for L1 and L2)
4	Configured SMDS addresses for ESs, as discovered through Option 6 in received SMDS IS Hellos. Each entry contains: - SMDS address - Most recent time that address was reported in any received SMDS IS-Hello
5	L1-IS-SMDS-BROADCAST-ADDRESSES (kept by L1 DR only) L2-IS-SMDS-BROADCAST-ADDRESSES (kept by L2 DR only) The minimal set of addresses that will reach all ISs of the appropriate level. This includes all manually configured SMDS addresses, as configured into the DR or received by the DR in SMDS IS Hellos, that will reach all routers. All reported and configured multicast addresses are included, and any unicast SMDS addresses for routers that are not known to be included in any of the multicast groups are included.
6	ES-SMDS-BROADCAST-ADDRESSES (kept by L1 DR only) The minimal set of addresses that will reach all ESs of the appropriate level

Table 8.24 Database information kept by DECnet Phase IV DRs attached to SMDS

As explained in Section 8.3.2, an L4S can be maintained by a variety of methods, including proper use of passwords in the neighbor-greeting messages. Table 8.25 shows the configuration requirements, which are the same as for OSI. Passwords are 8 bytes long. For example, a simple configuration could be to use a single password within an L4S for all systems.

The default of the transmit passwords is the value 0. If receive passwords are not used, their presence in received messages must be ignored.

8.10   DECnet Phase V over SMDS

DECnet Phase V is described in [DEC3] and follows closely the internetworking architecture of OSI. Thus SMDS is used in DEC Phase V, as described in Section 8.3.

Device	Configured passwords	Transmit/ Receive	Applicability
ES	1	Transmit	SMDS ES Hello
	1 or more	Receive	SMDS DR-ES Hello SMDS Hello Redirect
Level 1 IS	1	Transmit	SMDS DR-ES Hello SMDS Hello Redirect (to ES)
	1	Transmit	SMDS L1 IS Hello SMDS Hello Redirect (to IS)
	1 or more	Receive	SMDS ES Hello
	1 or more	Receive	SMDS L1 IS Hello SMDS Hello Redirect (to IS)
Level 2 IS*	1	Transmit	SMDS DR-ES Hello SMDS Hello Redirect (to ES)
	1	Transmit	SMDS L2 IS Hello SMDS Hello Redirect
	1 or more	Receive	SMDS ES Hello
	1 or more	Receive	SMDS L2 IS Hello SMDS Hello Redirect

* A Level 2 IS that also acts as Level 1 IS also requires the Level 1 configuration

Table 8.25 Password configuration

9

Bridging with SMDS

Because SMDS was explicitly designed to play the role of a physical network in an internet, the typical method of interfacing to SMDS will probably be with a router. Chapter 8 details how to use SMDS for routing many of the most popular of today's (routable) network protocols. However, not all protocols in use today are routable. Furthermore, many enterprise networks have been implemented with only bridging, and it might not be attractive to have to introduce routing just to take advantage of SMDS. Consequently, we expect that bridging will be an important use of SMDS.

This chapter describes how to use SMDS for bridging. Bridging is a technique that usually relays Media Access Control (MAC)[1] frames native to one LAN to MAC frames native to another LAN. It is distinguished from routing (discussed in Chapter 8) because it does not make use of internetworking protocols such as IP [Comer1] [Comer2], IPX [Miller] [Novell1] [Novell2] [Novell3], or OSI CLNP [Piscitello]. An authoritative overview of bridging techniques is provided in [Perlman]. This chapter discusses how bridges can be interconnected by SMDS as follows:

- The application of bridging to interconnect LANs that are widely separated geographically is referred to as *Remote MAC Bridging*. In Section 9.1, we discuss this application with SMDS.
- To identify the information exchanged between bridges, the LLC/SNAP multiplexing technique described in Section 8.1 is used

---

[1]Media Access Control is a protocol layer defined by IEEE Project 802 for providing orderly access to a shared medium. The devices attached to the shared medium are identified by their MAC Address, typically a 48-bit, globally unique value.

[802.6i]. The use of this technique for bridging with SMDS is discussed in Section 9.2.

- In order to forward MAC frames properly, bridges must be manually configured with forwarding tables, or they must exchange forwarding information with other bridges and update their tables dynamically. In Section 9.3, we describe how a widely used protocol for this purpose, the Spanning Tree Protocol, can be supported over SMDS.

CPE designers should find the chapter useful in designing SMDS equipment. SMDS customers who want to use SMDS for bridging will find this chapter useful in configuring their bridged networks when using SMDS.

9.1   Remote MAC Bridging

By its very nature, SMDS is meant to interconnect LANs that are geographically widely separated. The application of bridging in this context is referred to as *Remote MAC Bridging*. Perlman [Perlman] notes that bridges connecting geographically distant LANs are sometimes called *remote bridges* or also sometimes *half bridges*, signifying that the combination of the bridges and the wide area connection can be thought of as a single bridge. This concept is illustrated in Figures 9.1 and 9.2, where the configuration of Figure 9.2 is functionally equivalent to the configuration of Figure 9.1.

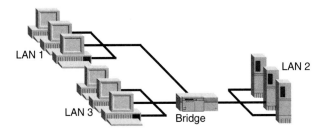

Figure 9.1 LAN bridging

There are currently no standards or industry implementation agreements for Remote MAC Bridging with SMDS. IEEE Project 802.1 is developing a standard approach to Remote Bridging, [802.1g] but this is not specific to SMDS. Consequently, in the next subsections, we propose our own approach to the use of SMDS for bridging. This approach is a straightforward application of the concepts in [802.1g].

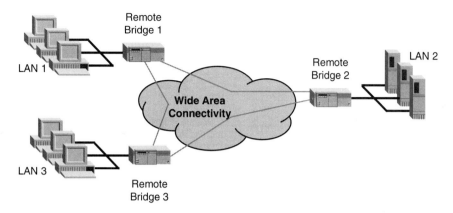

Figure 9.2 Remote MAC bridging

9.1.1   Remote Bridge Groups and Virtual Ports

When using SMDS, we recommend modeling a remote bridge as connected to two technologies: a LAN and an SNI. The protocol architecture for this model is shown in Figure 9.3, which is taken from [802.6i].[2] The protocol stack on the SNI "pant leg" reflects the encapsulation details described in Section 9.2. Communication via the LAN is modeled as occurring through the LAN Port. Communication via SMDS is modeled as occurring through the Virtual Port. Remote bridges that need to communicate among themselves via SMDS are referred to as a *Remote Bridge Group* (*RB Group* for short). The Virtual Port is the abstract vehicle for this RB Group communication. A remote bridge can be a member of more than one RB Group, in which case it is modeled as having a Virtual Port for each RB Group. When a MAC frame is received by the MAC Relay Entity from either the LAN Port or the Virtual Port, the MAC Relay Entity is responsible for deciding if the frame should be relayed by sending it to a different port.

9.1.2   Virtual LAN Configuration

To use SMDS for remote bridging, we recommend using the Virtual LAN Configuration [802.1g]. The Virtual LAN Configuration makes the Virtual Port functionally equivalent to a LAN port for the purposes of bridging. Figure 9.4

---

[2]At first glance this figure may seem to have more in common with a labyrinth than with a protocol architecture. It should be appreciated that two instances of communication are shown simultaneously, one for relaying MAC frames, and the other for applications such as the Spanning Tree Protocol described in Section 9.3. Fortunately, this method of describing a protocol architecture has not been proposed yet to describe the numerous routing protocols in routers and hosts.

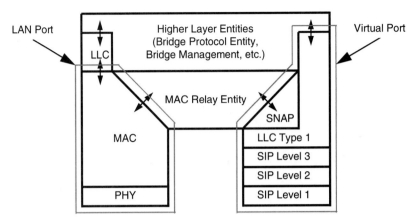

Figure 9.3 Remote bridge protocol architecture

shows an example of a Virtual LAN Configuration for an RB Group with three remote bridges. To implement this remote bridge configuration, an SMDS Group Address that identifies the SNIs for all members of the RB Group, RB_GROUP_GA, is set up. L3_PDUs addressed to RB_GROUP_GA are used to carry multicast MAC frames and occasionally (see below) unicast MAC frames. The net effect of this approach is that the remote bridges function as if they were attached to a single logical LAN.

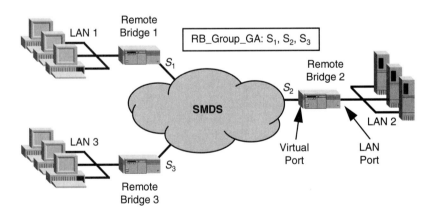

Figure 9.4 Virtual LAN configuration example

In implementing the Virtual LAN Configuration, it is desirable to minimize the use of Group Addressed L3_PDUs. One reason for this is that the performance objectives for the transport of Group Addressed L3_PDUs are less aggressive than those for Individual Addresses, and thus performance may suffer. Another reason may be economic when traffic-sensitive tariffs apply. It is reasonable to assume that such tariffs would be higher for Group Addressed transport than for Individually Addressed transport.[3]

By using multiple Group Addresses and multiple Individual Addresses, a single remote bridge can be part of multiple RB Groups. For each RB Group j, a Group Address, RB_GROUPj_GA, is obtained that identifies the SNIs for all members of the RB Group. Thus, if the remote bridge has n Virtual Ports, there are n Group Addresses: RB_GROUP1_GA, RB_GROUP2_GA, ..., RB_GROUPn_GA. In addition, n SMDS Individual Addresses (VP1_IA, VP2_IA, ..., VPn_IA), assigned to SNIs to which the remote bridge is attached, are allocated, one for each Virtual Port. Hence, up to 16 Virtual Ports can be implemented via a single SNI, as described in Section 3.4.1.5. Finally, a Virtual Port Address Table is maintained for each Virtual Port that consists of triplets: {*MAC Address*, *SMDS Individual Address*, *Age*}.

The basic idea of this implementation is to learn the individual MAC addresses that are "behind" each Virtual Port. When a MAC frame is relayed to a Virtual Port, if it has an individual destination MAC address, M_j, that is known to be behind a certain other Virtual Port in the RB Group with SMDS Individual Address, S_k, the MAC frame is encapsulated in an L3_PDU that contains S_k as the SMDS Destination Address. If M_j is not known to be associated with a specific Virtual Port, the Group Address associated with the RB Group is used as the SMDS Destination Address. In this way, the use of Group Addressing is reduced. In order to accommodate topology changes and/or end-system movement, associations between MAC Address and SMDS Individual Address are deleted if they are not used for a sufficiently long time. The following algorithms describe the implementation more precisely.

When a MAC frame is passed to Virtual Port j for relaying, the following encapsulation algorithm is used.

Step 1:   If the MAC destination address is a MAC group address, go to Step 3.

Step 2:   If the MAC destination address is contained in a triplet in the Virtual Port Address Table, encapsulate the MAC frame in an L3_PDU with SMDS Source Address = VPj_IA and SMDS Destination Address = the SMDS Individual Address from the triplet; else, go to Step 3.

---

[3]The philosophy of usage measurement for billing contained in [775] is that all L3_PDUs that are delivered by SMDS are counted. This means that a Group Addressed L3_PDU that is delivered to n destination SNIs will cause n L3_PDUs to be counted. Consequently, using Individually Addressed transport instead of Group Addressed transport in an RB Group with n remote bridges may be on the order of n times less expensive.

Step 3:   Encapsulate the MAC frame in an L3_PDU with SMDS Source
                Address = VP*j*_IA and SMDS Destination Address =
                RB_GROUP*j*_GA.

    Each time an L3_PDU is received with SMDS Destination Address =
VP*j*_IA or RB_GROUP*j*_GA, the encapsulated MAC frame is delivered to the
entity attached to Virtual Port *j*. (Note that this algorithm makes use of the fact
that the DESTINATION ADDRESS field of the delivered L3_PDU contains the
Group Address.) In addition, the Virtual Port Address Table for Virtual Port *j* is
modified according to the following algorithm.

Data: *M* = the source MAC address in the encapsulated MAC frame, *S* =
                SMDS Source Address in the L3_PDU.

Step 1:   If *M* is not contained in any triplet in the Virtual Port Address Table,
                go to Step 2; else go to Step 4.

Step 2:   If there is room in the Virtual Port Address Table for a new entry,
                add the triplet {*M*, *S*, 0} to the table, and stop; else go to Step 3.

Step 3:   Remove the triplet from the Virtual Port Address Table that has the
                largest *Age* parameter value, and go to Step 2.

Step 4:   If *M* is contained in a triplet in the Virtual Port Address Table but
                the second element of the triplet is not *S*, delete the triplet from the
                table, and go to Step 2; else go to Step 5.

Step 5:   If a triplet {*M*, *S*, *Age*} exists in the table, change the triplet to {*M*, *S*,
                0}, and stop.

    In addition to the immediately preceding algorithm, the *Age* parameter in
each triplet in the Virtual Port Address Table is incremented periodically. Any
triplet whose *Age* parameter exceeds a value, *Max_Age*, is removed from the
table. This helps to keep the Virtual Port Address Table small when there are
many end systems with low activity, and it allows end systems to be moved and
still eventually be reachable. Because the Virtual Port Address Table plays a role
similar to the Filtering Data Base[4] defined in [802.1d], we recommend setting

---

[4]The Filtering Data Base is a table constructed by a bridge that consists of associations
between MAC Addresses and a port. The bridge constructs the table by observing source MAC
addresses of MAC frames arriving at the port. Frames that arrive at the port with a destination
address in the Filtering Data Base are not forwarded because the destination end system must be on

Max_Age as discussed in Section 9.3 for the case *Topology Change* parameter equals FALSE. This approach is similar to the manipulation of the *Forwarding Database Ageing Time,* as described in Section 3.9.2 of [802.1d]. Section 9.3 revisits this parameter when the Spanning Tree Algorithm is being used.

Figure 9.5 shows an example of Virtual Port Address Tables. This example assumes that all end systems have been recently active, and thus all end-system MAC addresses are contained in the Virtual Port Address Table.

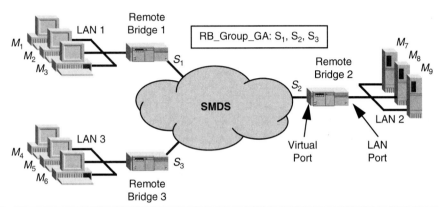

Virtual port address table at remote bridge 1			Virtual port address table at remote bridge 2			Virtual port address table at remote bridge 3		
MAC Address	SMDS Address	Age (secs)	MAC Address	SMDS Address	Age (secs)	MAC Address	SMDS Address	Age (secs)
M_4	S_3	1	M_1	S_1	0	M_8	S_2	21
M_8	S_2	8	M_4	S_3	5	M_9	S_2	13
M_9	S_2	3	M_6	S_3	20	M_1	S_1	0
M_6	S_3	10	M_2	S_1	73	M_2	S_1	23
M_5	S_3	6	M_3	S_1	124	M_3	S_1	12
M_7	S_2	15	M_5	S_3	17	M_7	S_2	53

Figure 9.5 Example of Virtual Port address tables

As shown in Chapter 8, some protocols (e.g., LLC Type 2 [802.2]) depend on MAC frames being delivered in the same sequence as the transmit sequence. For this to be the case, the Virtual LAN Configuration implementation effected by the above algorithms assumes that *all* L3_PDUs are delivered in sequence. To see this, consider an end system sending MAC frames to an end system with MAC Address M_d. Suppose that when the first such frame reaches a remote

---

the piece of a spanning tree behind the port. In the use of SMDS that we are recommending, the spanning tree is the "star" consisting of SMDS.

bridge, M_d is not in the Virtual Port Address Table. This frame will be encapsulated in a Group Addressed L3_PDU. When the next frame arrives at the remote bridge, it is possible that M_d has been entered in the Virtual Port Address Table, and thus the frame will be encapsulated in an Individually Addressed L3_PDU. To prevent the MAC frames from getting out of sequence, these two L3_PDUs must not get out of sequence even though one is Group Addressed and one is Individually Addressed. This assumption goes beyond the performance objectives in Chapter 7. However, if the service-provider network meets the requirements of [1059], then such sequentiality should be maintained.[5]

9.2   MAC Frame Encapsulation

When a bridge is attached to two different types of LAN, it can theoretically operate in either of two modes. Translation Bridging is the process where the bridge translates the format of each incoming MAC frame to the format of the outgoing MAC frame. Encapsulation Bridging means that the bridge encapsulates one MAC frame within the information field of the other MAC frame. Encapsulation bridging used with SMDS is shown in Figure 9.6. The MAC frame is being sent from the station with MAC address M_s to the station with MAC address M_d. The bridge at SNI S_s constructs the L3_PDU addressed to S_d from S_s by placing the frame within the L3_PDU INFORMATION field. The bridge at SNI S_d unwraps the original frame for delivery.

Encapsulation Bridging should be used with SMDS. The reason is that the SMDS address space is different from the MAC Address space. The ultimate destination for the MAC frame is defined by a MAC Address (M_d in Figure 9.6). Thus, this address must be either carried across SMDS or somehow reconstructed by the bridge at SNI S_d. Because of the complexity of reconstructing the MAC address, encapsulation bridging is the preferred method [802.6i].

IEEE [802.6i] defines the standard way to encapsulate MAC frames. The type of MAC frame is identified by use of the Logical Link Control Protocol (LLC) and the SubNetwork Access Protocol (SNAP) discussed in Section 8.1. Figure 9.7 shows the details of this encapsulation into the L3_PDU INFORMATION field. Note that because LLC is being used, the L3_PDU HIGHER LAYER PROTOCOL IDENTIFIER field should contain the value 1 (see Section 4.5.6). The LLC DESTINATION SERVICE ACCESS POINT (DSAP) and the LLC SOURCE SERVICE ACCESS POINT (SSAP) are set to AA_H to indicate the use of

---

[5]Bellcore [1059] calls for the routing of internal network data units based on a spanning tree that only changes when an equipment failure occurs. Such failures are vary rare, and thus L3_PDUs should stay in sequence.

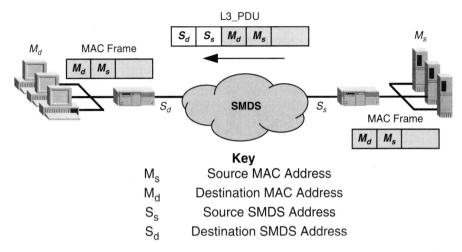

Figure 9.6 Encapsulation bridging with SMDS

SNAP. The bit order of the encapsulated MAC frame is the bit order of the native MAC protocol. This allows simple and efficient forwarding between like LANs.

LLC			SNAP		
DSAP = AA_H	SSAP = AA_H	Control = 03_H	OUI	PID	Encapsulated Bridged MAC Frame
1 byte	1 byte	1 byte	3 bytes	2 bytes	$\leq$ 9180 bytes

Key

LLC	Logical Link Control
DSAP	Destination Service Access Point
SSAP	Source Service Access Point
SNAP	SubNetwork Access Protocol
OUI	Organizationally Unique Identifier
PID	Protocol IDentification

Figure 9.7 Encapsulation in the L3_PDU INFORMATION Field

SNAP consists of two fields. The ORGANIZATIONALLY UNIQUE IDENTIFIER (OUI) is a value assigned to various organizations so that each can assign PROTOCOL IDENTIFICATION (PID) values. Table 9.1 lists the OUI/PID values that should be used. The OUI value of $0080C2_H$ is the value assigned to the IEEE 802.1 Working Group. LLC/SNAP is also used to identify network layer protocols as described in 8.1.3.

OUI	PID	Protocol
0080C2$_H$	0001$_H$	IEEE 802.3/Ethernet with FCS present
0080C2$_H$	0002$_H$	IEEE 802.4 with FCS present
0080C2$_H$	0003$_H$	IEEE 802.5 with FCS present
0080C2$_H$	0004$_H$	FDDI with FCS present
0080C2$_H$	0005$_H$	IEEE 802.6 with FCS present
0080C2$_H$	0006$_H$	IEEE 802.9 with FCS present
0080C2$_H$	0007$_H$	IEEE 802.3/Ethernet with FCS absent
0080C2$_H$	0008$_H$	IEEE 802.4 with FCS absent
0080C2$_H$	0009$_H$	IEEE 802.5 with FCS absent
0080C2$_H$	000A$_H$	FDDI with FCS absent
0080C2$_H$	000B$_H$	IEEE 802.6 with FCS absent
0080C2$_H$	000C$_H$	IEEE 802.9 with FCS absent

Table 9.1 Coding of the OUI and PID fields [802.6i]

Whenever the FRAME CHECK SEQUENCE (FCS) is present in the MAC frame,[6] we recommend that the FCS be included in the encapsulation, since this reduces processing, and the bandwidth saved by not including the FCS will be insignificant.

IEEE [802.6i] also specifies the placement of the MAC frame within the L3_PDU INFORMATION field as shown in Figures 9.8 through Figure 9.12. Padding is inserted so that the INFORMATION field of the MAC frame falls on a 4-byte boundary as a means of facilitating hardware processing. In all cases except IEEE 802.3 (Figure 9.8), this also means that the beginning of the destination MAC address falls on a 4-byte boundary.

9.3   Support of the Spanning Tree Algorithm and Protocol

Section 9.1 describes how remote bridges can be implemented to effectively transmit MAC frames via SMDS. There still remains the question of when MAC frames are to be relayed between a LAN Port and a Virtual Port. In other words, how does the MAC Relay Entity that is shown in Figure 9.3 know when to relay

---

[6]The FCS is always present for IEEE 802.3, IEEE 802.4, IEEE 802.5, and FDDI. The FCS is optional for IEEE 802.6.

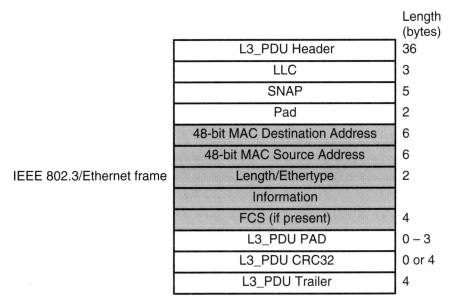

Figure 9.8 Encapsulation of IEEE 802.3/Ethernet

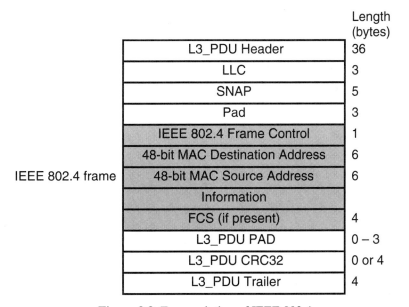

Figure 9.9 Encapsulation of IEEE 802.4

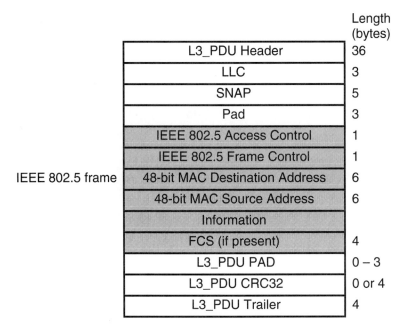

Figure 9.10 Encapsulation of IEEE 802.5

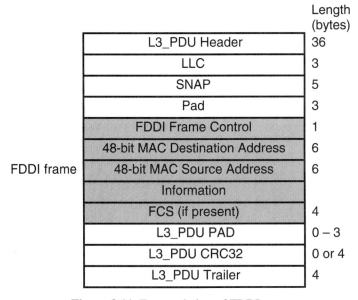

Figure 9.11 Encapsulation of FDDI

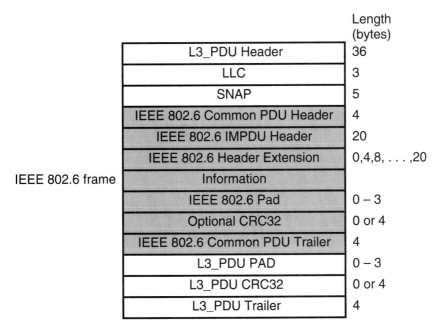

	Length (bytes)
L3_PDU Header	36
LLC	3
SNAP	5
IEEE 802.6 Common PDU Header	4
IEEE 802.6 IMPDU Header	20
IEEE 802.6 Header Extension	0,4,8, . . . ,20
Information	
IEEE 802.6 Pad	0 – 3
Optional CRC32	0 or 4
IEEE 802.6 Common PDU Trailer	4
L3_PDU PAD	0 – 3
L3_PDU CRC32	0 or 4
L3_PDU Trailer	4

IEEE 802.6 frame

Figure 9.12 Encapsulation of IEEE 802.6

MAC frames. Simple networks such as that of Figure 9.5 can be manually configured. However, for more complex networks, more sophisticated methods should be used.

Perhaps the most widely used bridging technique is the Spanning Tree Algorithm, as specified in IEEE 802.1D-1990 [802.1d] [Perlman]. IEEE [802.1g] contains the Extended Spanning Tree Protocol for extending the Spanning Tree Algorithm to the case of remote bridging. However, when the Virtual LAN Configuration is used, Section 9.1 of [802.1g] specifies that the two protocols are identical with the Virtual Ports treated equally with LAN ports. In other words, by implementing the Virtual LAN Configuration in the remote bridges when using SMDS, the remote bridges appear to the rest of the network as if they were attached to a regular LAN. Thus, the Spanning Tree Protocol can be used without modification.

The spanning tree that is constructed is a subset of the topology that is both loop free but sufficiently rich to provide a path between every pair of LANs. The key to the operation of the Spanning Tree protocol is the exchange of Bridge Protocol Data Units (BPDUs) among the bridges. This exchange allows the bridges to dynamically elect a "root" bridge, and enables other bridges to calculate the shortest and best path between themselves and the root, and to select the bridge ports that must be included in the spanning tree; that is, it prunes the topology to a spanning tree (see Figure 9.13).

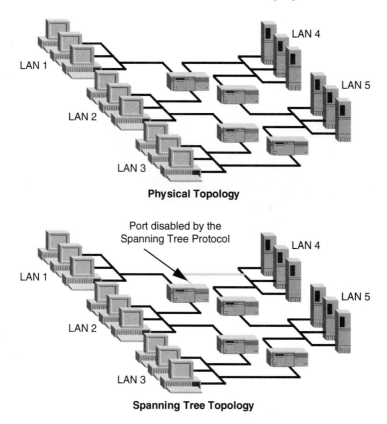

Figure 9.13   Example of Spanning Tree selection

It is beyond the scope of this book to describe the Spanning Tree Protocol in detail. Instead, we focus our attention on what needs to be done to support the protocol with SMDS (i.e., the transfer of BPDUs).

9.3.1   Encapsulation of BPDUs in L3_PDUs

When transmitted on a LAN, the destination MAC address of a BPDU is the Bridge Group Address, $(0180C2000000_H$ [802.1d]), which identifies all bridges on the LAN. When a BPDU is passed to a Virtual Port, we recommend that it be encapsulated into an L3_PDU as shown in Figure 9.14. (The LLC DSAP and SSAP value of 42_H has been allocated by IEEE P802 to identify BPDUs.) This is consistent with the algorithm specified in Section 9.1, which calls for using RB_GROUP_GA for MAC frames with group destination MAC addresses. The source MAC address is the MAC address associated with the Virtual Port. This association is necessary because the MAC address is needed to derive the Bridge Identifier for the remote bridge on the Virtual LAN configuration, which in turn is needed in computing the spanning tree.

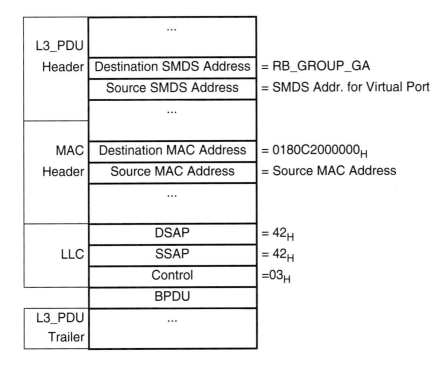

Figure 9.14 Encapsulation of BPDUs in L3_PDUs

9.3.2   Virtual Port Address Table

The Virtual Port Address Table can become invalid when the Spanning Tree Algorithm changes topology (i.e., computes a different spanning tree). As an example, consider Figure 9.15, where three remote bridges and one local bridge interconnect three LANs. In this figure, the Spanning Tree Algorithm has disabled the local bridge from forwarding frames (preventing a loop) and thus the correct Virtual Port Address Table for Remote Bridge 2 is as shown.

Figure 9.16 shows the correct Virtual Port Address Table for Remote Bridge 2 in the case where MAC frame relaying is disabled at Remote Bridge 1. In this case, all of the MAC addresses on the LAN behind Remote Bridge 1 are accessible via Remote Bridge 3.

If the Virtual Port Address Table shown in Figure 9.15 is used with the topology of Figure 9.16, then MAC frames originating behind the Remote Bridge 2 will not reach their destination. Thus, if the Spanning Tree Algorithm changes the topology, the Virtual Port Address Table that was derived during the operation of the previous topology may result in some end systems being unreachable from some other end systems. Such a condition will not persist

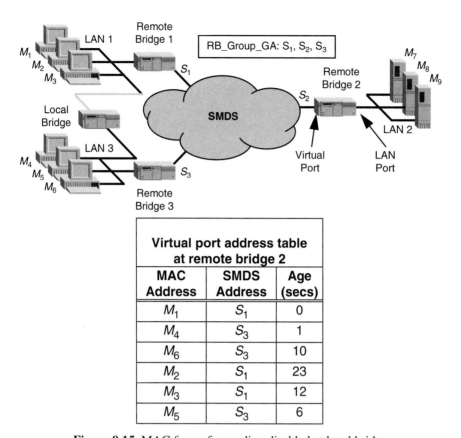

Figure 9.15 MAC frame forwarding disabled at local bridge

indefinitely because the invalid entries will not be refreshed; their *Age* will eventually exceed Max_Age and they will be deleted. This suggests setting Max_Age to a small value. However, there is a trade-off, because a small value of Max_Age will lead to a large amount of SMDS Group Addressed traffic.

To deal with this trade-off, we suggest treating the aging of the Virtual Port Address Table in much the same way as the Filtering Data Base[7] is treated in [802.1d]. Through the exchange of the BPDUs, the Bridge Protocol Entity in each remote bridge is aware that a change in topology has occurred. Procedures in [802.1d] identify this via the Topology Change parameter, which has the value TRUE when a topology change has occurred. As with the Filtering Data Base,

---

[7]When the spanning tree changes, some or all of the Filtering Data Base may not be valid. Thus, when a topology change occurs, inactive entries in the Filtering Data Base should be "aged out" quickly to remove invalid entries. The allowed inactivity time under these conditions is called the *Forward Delay* in [802.1d].

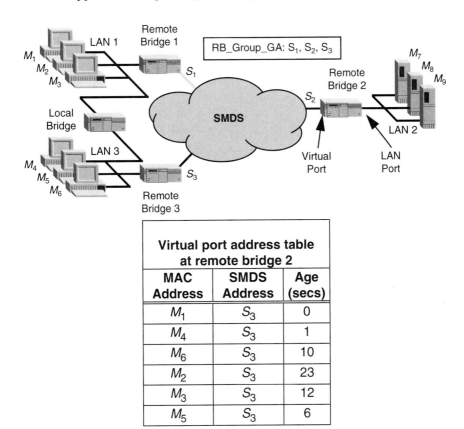

Virtual port address table at remote bridge 2		
MAC Address	SMDS Address	Age (secs)
M_1	S_3	0
M_4	S_3	1
M_6	S_3	10
M_2	S_3	23
M_3	S_3	12
M_5	S_3	6

Figure 9.16 MAC frame forwarding disabled at remote bridge 1

we recommend using the Forward Delay [802.1d] for aging out the entries in the Virtual Port Address Table when a topology change occurs. Thus, our recommendations for setting Max_Age are shown in Table 9.2.

Topology change (boolean)	Max_Age default (seconds)	Max_Age range (seconds)	Granularity (seconds)
FALSE	300	$10 - 10^6$	1
TRUE	15	4 - 30	1

Table 9.2 Recommended values for Max_Age

10

Network Management and SMDS

The configuration and monitoring features of an individual network device are key properties that enhance its usefulness in a network as a whole. This chapter describes how an SMDS environment fits into the network management of a customer network (see Chapters 8 and 9). Readers interested in SMDS troubleshooting, performance monitoring, and configuration of SMDS interfaces will find a variety of management capabilities and strategies that allow for quick trouble isolation and identification. Implementors of SMDS management capabilities in SMDS CPE or carrier networks will find detailed descriptions and background of these features.

The capabilities described in this chapter rely on the use of Simple Network Management Protocol, or SNMP [RFC1155] [RFC1157] [RFC1212] [RFC1213] [RFC1215]. The reason for this choice was the pervasive use of SNMP by potential SMDS customers in managing multivendor networks. We describe the capabilities in a such way that only minimal knowledge of SNMP is required. For readers unfamiliar with SNMP, Section 10.7 provides an overview of concepts such as Network Management Station (NMS), Management Information Base (MIB), and SNMP agent, that are necessary for the understanding of Chapters 10, 11, and 12. A more comprehensive description of SNMP can be found in [Rose].

This chapter introduces general management aspects of SMDS CPE and carrier networks. The management service provided by a carrier network is referred to as SMDS *Customer Network Management* (CNM) Service. Specifically, we describe how general SNMP system and interface management capabilities apply to SMDS CPE and SMDS CNM Service, and how this fits into the management of internets. Subsequently, Chapter 11 describes further details of the management of SMDS CPE, and Chapter 12 describes the details of the SMDS CNM Service.

10.1   Internet Management

Previous chapters showed that SMDS is usually used as a subnetwork in a customer internet. Thus, the management of SMDS must be seen in the context of the management of this internet; SMDS CPE and SMDS are *some* of the components to be managed. Figures 10.1 and 10.2 use the example network of the Bodacious Data Corp. (see Chapters 3 and 8) to illustrate this principle. Figure 10.1 shows the network of Bodacious Data being managed by three NMSs. Figure 10.2 shows an example of how the network may be represented to a network manager.

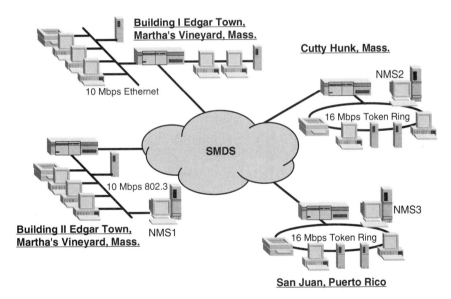

Figure 10.1 Example of Network Management Stations in a corporate internet

Network management requires a range of capabilities:

- *General system management: system identification, characterization, and status*
  An internet consists of a variety of systems, such as bridges and routers. Thus, it must be possible to distinguish system types and to identify

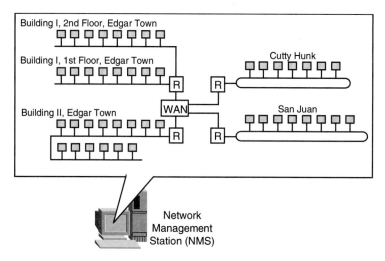

Figure 10.2 Role of LANs and WANs in network management of a corporate internet

individual systems. It must also be possible to determine the status and the physical location of each system.

- *General interface management: interface identification, characterization, and status*
  It must be possible to understand the overall network topology and to identify specific interface details within that network. For example, an NMS must be able to identify a particular interface as an Ethernet port of a particular router. It must also be possible to determine the status of the interface, that is, whether it is working.

- *Performance measurements*
  When a problem occurs, it is necessary to have access to performance measurements (traffic and error data) in network equipment to quickly isolate the nature of the problem. Performance measurements are further used to trace traffic patterns and analyze network usage.

- *Configuration management*
  Network equipment can be configured in a variety of ways. The network manager must have access to this configuration information. The network manager should also be able to make configuration changes through an NMS. This facilitates rapid reconfiguration and problem resolution, and may avoid the need to dispatch maintenance personnel.

- *Event notifications*
  Event notifications are asynchronous alerts that notify an NMS of the occurrence of events that may require attention. Link failure, link (re)establishment, system outages, and reconfigurations are examples of events that are typically sent to an NMS. At the same time it must be possible to proactively check the status of devices, since the absence of alarms may also indicate a loss of connectivity or a system-down situation.

10.2   Role of SMDS Management

The approach of resource management in an internet is applied to CPE and to SMDS. The latter is achieved by the *representation* of SMDS to a customer as a single managed resource; that is, the *service*, including the service interface, is managed by the customer. The management capabilities and information for this resource are provided as a management service, called the SMDS Customer Network Management (CNM) Service. Figure 10.3 illustrates that the NMS manages SMDS (through the CNM service) much as it manages other resources in the internet. The figure also shows that the router and CSU/DSU at customer's side of the SMDS interface are managed in combination.[1]

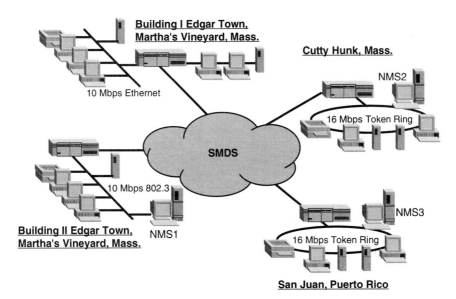

Figure 10.3 SMDS as a managed resource

---

[1]Chapter 5 discusses the roles of routers and CSU/DSUs in SMDS access. We will discuss the corresponding management aspects in Chapter 11.

10.3   Customer and Carrier Perspectives

There are two perspectives on managing SMDS: the service provider's and the customer's. Customers will be interested in management aspects of the public *service*, while the carrier will manage the *network* that provides the service.

- The *provider's interest* is to maintain the level of service promised to the customer. To achieve this, a variety of activities are necessary, including traffic and capacity management, the repair of malfunctioning equipment, performance monitoring, rerouting of traffic in cases of outages, and so on. These activities do not need to be visible to subscribers. (See the performance objectives in Chapter 7.) Customers should not be burdened by a need to understand the internal operations of the public network.

- The *customer's interest* is to maintain connectivity in the customer's private network, of which SMDS is just one part. The prime concern for the customer is whether the service interfaces are working or not. If they are working, how well is the service behaving? If they are not working, what is the nature of the problem, and is it due to malfunctioning CPE, a cut or disconnected cable, or is there a public network problem? Customers will also be interested in how the service is configured for their use, and they may want to modify this configuration.

Thus, the service provider and customer have different views of SMDS. Figure 10.4 shows this principle.

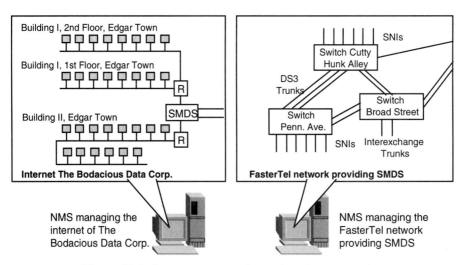

Figure 10.4 Customer perspective and carrier perspective

There are two issues that further distinguish SMDS CNM Service from the management of ordinary network equipment:

- SMDS is a public, shared, resource. For privacy and other security reasons, customers must be offered only a management view of the resources they have subscribed to (see Figure 10.5).

- A public service is not a "device down the hall." While customer equipment, such as a router, can often be quickly reached for repair or reconfiguration by operations personnel of the customer network, public network configuration or troubleshooting must often be done through telephone calls and service orders. It is desirable to avoid lengthy procedures wherever possible, and to give customers direct access to reconfiguration capabilities.

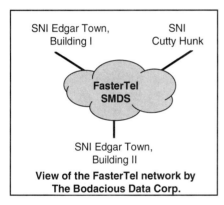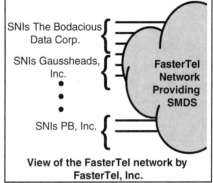

Figure 10.5 SMDS is a public, shared, managed resource — Virtual Private Networking

10.4   Interconnected Carrier Networks

The public service may be provided through a number of interconnected carriers, as discussed in Chapter 3. Each carrier may offer its own CNM Service, representing its portion of the public service (see Figures 10.6 and 10.7). In the example, the CNM service provided by an IEC would necessarily be different from that of the LECs, given their different roles. This service is called *Interexchange CNM Service*, or ICNM Service [Sher].

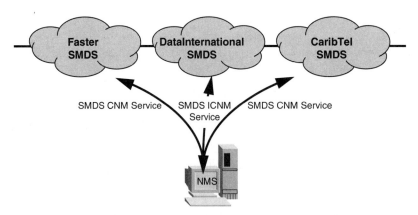

Figure 10.6 Interconnected carriers and CNM Service

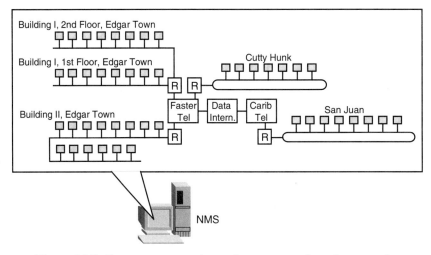

Figure 10.7 Customer perspective on interconnected carrier networks

10.5   Overview of SMDS CNM and SMDS CPE Management

This section takes a closer look at the management capabilities described in Section 10.1, and provides an overview of how these capabilities apply to the SMDS CPE and SMDS CNM Service. It also associates these capabilities with SNMP MIBs,[2] and guides the reader to the detailed descriptions of these capabilities in Section 10.8 (generic system and interface management), Chapter 11 (management of SMDS CPE), and Chapter 12 (SMDS CNM Service).

---

[2]SNMP concepts such as the MIB are explained in Section 10.7.

- *General system management: system identification, characterization, and status*
  This management capability is needed for both SMDS CNM Service and for SMDS CPE. Taking the example of Figure 10.7, retrieval of this information enables the NMS to recognize a managed resource as a router or as SMDS. Section 10.8.1 describes this capability for both SMDS CPE and SMDS CNM Service. The required MIB module for this purpose is called MIB II [RFC1213].

- *General interface management: interface identification, characterization, and status*
  Retrieval of this information enables the NMS to recognize an interface as an SMDS interface. It also applies to both SMDS CPE and to SMDS CNM Service. MIB II [RFC1213] provides this capability, as explained in Section 10.8.2.

- *Performance measurements*
  The network manager may be primarily interested in the traffic and error counts at the internet level. For SMDS, this translates into transmitted, received, and errored $L3\_PDUs$. Similar measurements can be made for supporting protocols at lower levels. By retrieving these measurements for a particular interface from both SMDS CPE and through the SMDS CNM Service, the status of the interface can be monitored, and problems can be identified and isolated. Performance measurements for SMDS CPE are described in Section 11.1. Their counterparts provided through SMDS CNM Service are similar. The differences are described in Chapter 12. The required MIB modules for this purpose are the SIP MIB [RFC1304], DS1/E1 MIB [RFC1406] and DS3/E3 MIB [RFC1407].

- *Configuration management*
  For SMDS CPE, a network manager may be interested in how applications make use of an SMDS interface (e.g., the bindings of internet level addresses and SMDS addresses; see [RFC1213]). Chapters 8 and 9 describe more examples. The management of these aspects is application-specific, and is beyond the scope of this book. SMDS CNM Service provides access to subscription parameters. Retrieval and manipulation of these parameters through SMDS CNM Service enable network managers to configure their particular use of SMDS. These capabilities are described in Chapter 12, and are contained in the Subscription MIB [Cox].

- *Alarms*
  There are two categories of alarms:

1. Generic system and interface alarms that apply to all managed resources. These alarms are a part of the SNMP specification [RFC1157], and are described in Section 10.9 for both SMDS CPE and SMDS CNM Service.

2. SMDS-specific alarms. These alarms apply to SMDS subscription management only and are provided through SMDS CNM Service (see Chapter 12 and the Subscription MIB [Cox]).

Table 10.1 summarizes the main capabilities of the relevant MIB modules, and Figure 10.8 shows how the MIB modules apply to the management of SMDS and SMDS CPE. This overview focuses on SNIs that use SIP as the access protocol to SMDS. Management aspects of DXI, SIP Relay, and ATM-based access to SMDS is in the process of being defined at the time of publication of this book.

Network Management capabilities related to SMDS	Access level	SMDS applicability		Applicable MIB module
		SMDS CPE NM	SMDS CNM Service	
1. General system management	Read-only	Section 10.8.1	Section 10.8.1	MIB II
2. General interface management	Read-only	Section 10.8.2	Section 10.8.2	MIB II
3. Performance management specific to an SMDS interface	Read-only	Section 11.1	Section 12.5	SIP MIB DS1/E1 MIB DS3/E3 MIB
4. SMDS-specific configuration management	Read-only Read-write	Not applicable	Section 12.6	Subscription MIB
5. Alarms - Generic system and interface alarms - Subscription-related alarms	—	Section 10.9 Not applicable	Section 10.9 Section 12.7	Core SNMP alarms Subscription MIB

Table 10.1 Summary of SMDS network management capabilities

We describe the full set of features that allows optimal use of SMDS. However, these capabilities are not necessarily always available. CPE MIBs must be instrumented to be manageable. Not every service-provider will initially have a CNM Service available. Furthermore, not all capabilities may immediately be supported in SMDS CPE or in SMDS CNM Service. For example, read-only capabilities are likely to be implemented first.

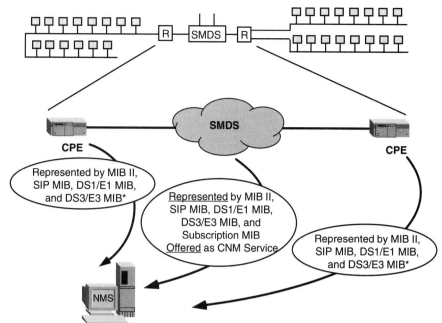

* CPE may use other MIB modules for the management of other interfaces and resources (e.g., Ethernets, FDDI, etc.).

Figure 10.8 Representation of SMDS and SMDS CPE by MIB modules

10.6   Strategies for SMDS Troubleshooting

In the rest of this chapter and Chapters 11 and 12, we provide extensive descriptions of the tools available for managing SMDS. Before launching into this detail, we pause to provide an overview of how these tools can be combined for troubleshooting.

The perspective of a user or application of SMDS may be as simple as whether the submitted L3_PDUs arrive properly. On the other hand, SMDS features, such as Address Screening, enforce the desired user configuration and cause discard of L3_PDUs that do not conform to the configured environment. This situation may point to configuration errors.

Figure 10.9 and Table 10.2 summarize conditions for L3_PDU loss and the means to verify these situations through the use of SMDS CNM Service and the management of SMDS CPE, and point to sections where these issues are addressed. The remainder of this section discusses general guidelines for troubleshooting and trouble-isolation cases.

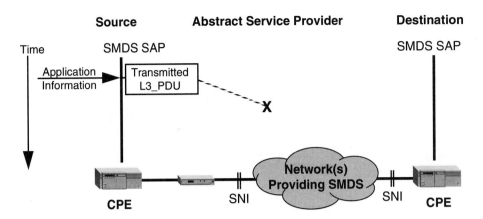

Figure 10.9 L3_PDU loss

L3_PDU Events	Reasons for L3_PDU discard, loss, nondelivery, or misdelivery	Verfication through CPE management and/or SMDS CNM Service
1. Transmission by the source station of the L3_PDU	• Cable disconnected • If a CSU/DSU is used, any errors between the source station and CSU/DSU, and any errors by the CSU/DSU • Any errors on the ingress SNI (e.g., link down, transmission / protocol errors) *	Section 10.8.1 (CPE): • Status source station Section 10.8.2 (CPE and CNM): • Status SNI Section 11.1 and 12.5 (CPE and CNM): •Problem type if the SNI is down • Is the source transmitting PDUs • Compare CPE and CNM traffic measurements to determine CSU/DSU problems • Is SMDS receiving the PDUs unerrored • Error types
2. Enforcement of the subscribed Access Class of the ingress SNI	• Access Class exceeded	Section 12.6.2 (CNM): • Measurements for this problem
3. Enforcement of the subscribed MCDUsIn of the ingress SNI	• MCDUs In exceeded	Section 12.6.2 (CNM): • Measurements for this problem

(continued)

(Table 10.2, continued)

L3_PDU Events	Reasons for L3_PDU discard, loss, nondelivery, or misdelivery	Verfication through CPE management and/or SMDS CNM Service
4. Source Address Validation	• Source Address invalid	Section 12.6.2 (CNM): • Measurements for this problem
5. Address Screening of the Destination Address against the Individual or Group Address Screen identified by the individual Source Address	• Source Address not authorized to communicate with the Destination Address	Section 12.6.2 (CNM): • Measurements for this problem Section 12.6.3 (CNM): • Address Screen contents
6. Determine whether End-user blocking is in effect.	• End-user blocking is in effect	Section 12.6.5 (CNM): • Measurements for this problem
7. Determine and route to the appropriate carrier (if needed) Replicate Group Addressed L3_PDUs. Route to network egress	• Unknown Destination Address	Section 12.5 (CNM): • Measurements for this problem
	• Group Address improperly configured	Section 12.6.4 (CNM): • Group Address contents
	• Improper Carrier Selection / Embodied SAC usage	Section 12.6.5 (CNM): • Measurements for this problem
	• Carrier unreachable	Section 10.8.2 (CNM): • Interface status between carriers
	• Any network inaccuracies *	Section 12.5 (CNM): • Compare measurements of unerrored packets accepted by SMDS with the sum of the delivered and dropped packets. Discrepancies may be caused by any of the interconnected carriers.
8. Individual Address screening of the Source Address against the Individual Address screen identified by the Destination Address	• Destination Address not authorized to communicate with the Source Address	Section 12.6.3 (CNM): • Measurements for this problem • Address Screen contents
9. Enforcement of the subscribed MCDUs Out of the egress SNI	• Buffer overflow (SMDS will attempt to buffer as much as possible)	• Measurements for this particular problem are not avalailable. Item 7 shows verification of general network inaccuracies

(continued)

(Table 10.2, continued)

L3_PDU Events	Reasons for L3_PDU discard, loss, nondelivery, or misdelivery	Verfication through CPE management and/or SMDS CNM Service
10. Transmission of the L3_PDU to the destination CPE	• Cable disconnected • Any errors on the egress SNI (e.g., link down, transmission / protocol errors) *	Section 10.8.2 (CPE and CNM): • Status SNI Section 11.1 and 12.5 (CPE and CNM): • Problem type if the SNI is down • CPE is receiving the PDUs unerrored • Error types
11. L3_PDU arrives at the CPE from the egress SNI.	• Any improper or errored delivery of the L3_PDU* • If a CSU/DSU is used, any errors by the CSU/DSU, and any errors between the CSU/DSU and the destination station	Section 10.8.1 (CPE): • Destination station running? Section 11.1 and 12.5 (CPE and CNM): • Compare CPE and CNM traffic measurements to determine CSU/DSU problems.

* See SMDS Availability and Accuracy objectives, Chapter 7.

Table 10.2 Trouble isolation and identification

Trouble isolation is not always straightforward; it depends on the configuration of a particular internet and the role that SMDS plays in that internet. In the following subsections, we discuss a number of common problems.

Trouble shooting for SMDS applications such as those described in Chapters 8 and 9 generally relates to the management of internets. For example, routing parameters such as the ones discussed in Chapter 8 may have been misconfigured. In this section, we assume that observed problems have been isolated to the SMDS environment. For example, in a TCP/IP environment, ICMP based tools such as *ping* and *traceroute* [Comer1] help to determine general connectivity at the IP level.

10.6.1 Connectivity Verification

We use the configuration of the Bodacious Data Corp., shown in Figure 10.1. As an example, we assume that a problem has been observed between Building I and Building II. The cause of the problem is suspected to be in the SMDS environment.

NMS1 should check first whether the Building II router is reachable and subsequently whether the Building I router responds, using tools such as *ping**.[3] A lack of response from the Building II router means that either that router has a problem or that a problem exists between the two routers. Unlike the situation in this example, multiple paths between NMS1 and the remote router may sometimes exist. In that case, the status of the remote router can be verified, but no conclusions can yet be drawn about the SMDS path between them.

Additional connectivity checks by NMS1 may help to isolate the problem. For example, if NMS1 can reach the Cutty Hunk router, but not the Building I router, it follows that the Building II SNI is operational. The problem may be caused by the Building I SNI, the Building II subscription configuration, or a service-provider problem.

Symptoms of a lack of connectivity through SMDS include:

- Tests such as *ping** to one or more SMDS CPE fail.

- If an SNI is disconnected, down (Sections 10.8.2 and 11.1), or in loopback mode, both the CPE and the CNM Service should send an alarm (see Section 10.9). The error counts supplied by the physical level (Section 11.1 and 12.5) should increase. It is also possible that the physical transmission facilities perform poorly, but not poorly enough to bring the interface down. In this case, no alarms are generated.

- Loss of connectivity on an intercarrier interface causes an alarm.

- A broken implementation of SIP will cause error counters discussed in Section 11.1 to increase, or may stop transmission of SIP PDUs altogether.

10.6.2 Alarms

Section 10.9 describes traps that indicate whether systems (CPE, SMDS) and SNIs are up or down. For example, if an alarm has been received from the Building II router indicating that the SNI has gone down, further diagnosis of the nature of the problem can be done using the specific performance and configuration information provided by the SMDS CPE. Chapter 11 details this information. If the SMDS CNM Agent (Chapter 12) can still be reached,[4] the

---

[3]We will use *ping** to mean *ping* or equivalent feature in internets using protocols other than TCP/IP.

[4]Chapter 12 describes how to use the SNI as the path to access the SMDS CNM Service. Hence, SNI problems also affect the ability to access the SMDS CNM Service. To circumvent this, a path dedicated to CNM may be used (e.g., a dial-up or leased line).

measurements performed by the CPE can be compared with the measurements provided through SMDS CNM Service, in order to isolate the problem.

10.6.3 Absence of Alarms

The absence of alarms does not necessarily signify the absence of problems. The absence of alarms may just mean that alarm notifications do not reach the NMS, or that a device is incapable of sending an alarm. Alternatively, it may mean that communication has not broken down entirely, but that performance is severely degraded, or that only occasional problems occur due to configuration errors (e.g., misconfiguration of an address screen).

For this reason, an NMS should periodically poll the managed systems and interfaces (Section 10.8) in order to verify their status.

10.6.4 SNI Performance Measurements

Both the CPE and SMDS can monitor the SMDS access protocols, and detect correct and incorrect protocol behavior. This information is provided to NMSs through the SIP, DS1/E1, and DS3/E3 MIBs. By using the information provided by the CPE in combination with that provided through SMDS CNM Service, it is usually possible to identify faulty protocol behavior and to determine whether the fault is on customer premises or in SMDS. Consider the following situations.

- A broken SIP implementation will cause a mismatch between the number of transmitted packets and the number of received unerrored packets at the remote end of the SNI. The SIP MIB provides this information for both SIP Level 3 and SIP Level 2, and supports measurements of different error types. For example, a high count of received protocol errors by the service provider may suggest a faulty CPE SIP implementation.

- Noisy physical facilities can be traced through information in the DS1/E1 and DS3/E3 MIBs. By checking both the SMDS CPE and SMDS CNM (if reachable), the nature of the problem can be analyzed. Physical disconnection will cause both ends to generate an alarm and make the appropriate diagnostic available through the MIB.

The comparison of CPE and CNM performance information naturally requires that the relative age of the information be interpreted correctly. This age is called *data currentness* in [1062R]. It must be assumed that, typically, the information provided by CPE is younger than that provided through SMDS CNM Service. The reason is that the CNM Agent must usually collect this information from remote switching systems. Figure 10.10 shows this effect.

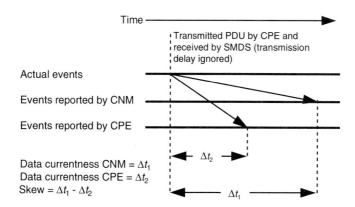

Figure 10.10 Example of different CPE and SMDS CNM Service data currentness

Chapter 12 discusses data currentness objectives for SMDS CNM Service. It is likely that in initial service offerings this effect will vary by service provider. In order to enable correct interpretation of CNM information, we recommend that service providers specify the data currentness values of their CNM service offering.

10.6.5 Misconfiguration

This section lists some misconfiguration cases, typically attributable to human error. The effect tends to be that, while the physical connections are working, logical connections may fail.

- SMDS CPE is configured with the wrong SMDS Source Address. The effect is an increase in the Source Address violations counter in SMDS CNM Service (Section 12.6.2). SMDS will discard all traffic from this CPE. Another effect is that *ping** (through SMDS) will fail.

- The SMDS CPE is configured to communicate with a wrong Group Address. For example, if the Group Address is intended to identify LIS_GA (see Section 8.2), the effect will be that the SMDS CPE will be incapable of address resolution and neighbor discovery and IP packets cannot be forwarded over SMDS. If Address Screens are used, this problem will reveal itself through an increase in the count of Address Screen violations. Otherwise, if the incorrect address happens to be unallocated within SMDS, the count of unknown destination addresses will increase. Furthermore, *ping** (through SMDS) will fail.

- Misconfigured Group Address membership has an effect similar to the previous case. Note however that this situation will not cause an increase in Address Screen violations. The contents of Group Addresses can be checked through SMDS CNM Service, as described in Section 12.6.4.

- Misconfigured Address Screens may cause L3_PDUs to be discarded unintentionally, which can be traced through the counter for Address Screen violations (Section 12.6.2). Furthermore, *ping** will fail to destinations that inadvertently are blocked. The contents of Address Screens can be checked through SMDS CNM Service, as described in Section 12.6.3.

- A high count of Access Class violations (Section 12.6.2) suggests that a higher Access Class needs to be subscribed to. Section 3.4.6 discusses Access Class selection.

Chapter 12 describes all SMDS CNM Service features to monitor and configure SMDS subscription parameters.

10.6.6 CSU/DSU Problems

Chapter 11 describes how SMDS CSU/DSUs and routers are often managed as a single device. A drawback is that problems between these two devices cannot then be directly traced through SNMP management. Steps to isolate these problems include the following:

- Compare the counters for transmitted L3_PDUs in CPE (router) and received L3_PDUs in SMDS.

- If the SNI is working (check physical layer information), and if the SMDS CNM information shows that no L3_PDUs are arriving, a CSU/DSU problem will cause the counter of received correct L2_PDUs to remain unchanged or to increase only slowly; that is, L2_PDUs are received in error by SMDS or are not received at all. (This method applies to SIP interfaces, and not to other types of access to SMDS.) This can be verified by checking counters for transmitted and received L2_PDUs at the CPE (CSU/DSU).

- Similarly, problems at the physical level (for DS1, E1, E3, and DS3) can be isolated by inspecting the performance information for that level. This check applies for all types of access to SMDS.

10.6.7 Service-Provider Problems

The accuracy and availability objectives (see Chapter 7) for SMDS can be statistically verified by periodically retrieving the appropriate counters and status information through SMDS CNM Service, and by maintaining statistics on an NMS. A customer may also request the service-provider to test the physical access facilities (e.g., through a loopback; see Chapter 12).

Connectivity between carriers may be lost, and Interexchange Carriers cannot be reached. This can be verified through interface status information (see Section 10.8.2). It is more likely that traffic is being lost due to incorrect use of Carrier Selection features, or due to End-user Blocking. Counters for this purpose are described in Chapter 12.

10.6.8 Incomplete SNMP Support by SMDS CPE

SMDS CPE that supports SNMP is likely to support at least MIB II, providing an NMS system and interface management capabilities. In conjunction with SMDS CNM Service, this situation still allows SMDS customers to perform a number of trouble isolation functions. However, some of the detailed trouble diagnoses described above are not possible. Similarly, when SMDS CPE does not support SNMP, only SMDS CNM Service can be used to trace problems. For example, this allows the NMS to determine that the provider is not receiving SMDS traffic from CPE, but it is not always possible to isolate the problem as a CPE or a provider problem.

10.6.9 Absence of SMDS CNM Service

Assuming that management information from SMDS CPE is available, this scenario allows verification of whether the CPE is working correctly. It does not allow for some of the detailed trouble diagnoses described above. On-line verification of the SMDS subscription configuration is not possible. Manual communications with the service provider are necessary to verify subscription parameters, such as the exact contents of an Address Screen or a Group Address.

10.7   An Introduction to SNMP

This section explains some basic SNMP concepts that are used in Chapters 10, 11 and 12. Readers familiar with SNMP can skip this section. Readers interested in more details about SNMP are referred to the literature, for example, [RFC1155], [RFC1157], [RFC1212], [RFC1213], [RFC1215], and [Rose]. Some key concepts in these chapters follow:

- NMSs manage network resources. The resources that are of particular interest in this book are SMDS CPE, and SMDS as provided by a public network.

- A managed resource is represented to an NMS through a MIB. In other words, a MIB is a virtual information store. A MIB consists of a collection of managed objects, the "things" to be managed.

- NMSs can access the MIB through a function called the *SNMP agent*. The protocol is SNMP.

10.7.1 Management Information Base

The MIB is chosen as a convenient representation of the managed device, in order to make it manageable in a larger context (i.e., a managed network). Conceptually, there exists a single global MIB, consisting of multiple modules, each with a set of objects designed for a specific purpose. For example, some modules important for SMDS concern the management of SIP interfaces and of DS1/E1 and DS3/E3 facilities. Colloquially, these MIB modules are simply referred to as *MIBs*. Agents will implement only those modules that are needed to support the management of the device that is represented. Thus, for an NMS, it is important to find out which modules are being supported by a managed resource.

Managed objects may correspond to parameters that are stored on the same device as the SNMP agent, or that are conveyed by remote devices to the agent, with the agent acting as proxy for the remote device. The managed objects may be identical to the actual parameters managing the device, or this may be calculated from one or more of these parameters.

An easy way to think of objects and how they are used is by considering management instructions as sets of verbs and nouns, where the nouns are formed by naming one or more managed objects, and the verbs correspond to the protocol operators (*get*, *set*, etc.).

Each managed object is defined in the following terms:

- The object semantics define the purpose of the object and its intended use.

- The object syntax defines the data type applicable to the object (e.g., an INTEGER with a certain range of permitted values).

- The particular object identification or object name distinguishes an object uniquely from other objects.

- The level of access for the object. Objects discussed in this book use the access levels read-only or read-write. The level of access determines the protocol operations that are allowed on the object.

10.7.2 Object Syntax and Encoding

The SNMP object syntax is based on the OSI defined Abstract Syntax Notation One, or ASN.1 [ISO8824] [ISO8824.1] [Steedman]. For simplicity, SNMP is designed to support only a subset of OSI's supported set. This syntax, the abstract syntax, is specified in the Structure of Management Information (SMI) [RFC1155].

With ASN.1 we can define objects in terms of their object type and object value. ASN.1 convention prescribes that types are denoted as words starting with an uppercase letter, while values start with a lower-case letter. An authoritative discussion of the full ASN.1 can be found in [Steedman]. For SMDS, the following SMI types are important:

- *INTEGER* — an integer. For human convenience, mnemonics may be used to denote enumerated INTEGER values. For example, the object `dsx3LineType` can assume the values 1 and 7 for DS3 and E3 facilities respectively. This can also be denoted as dsx3ClearChannel(1) or e3Framed(7). See Chapter 11.

- *OCTET STRING* — a string of zero or more bytes, encoded with any binary pattern. One possible use is ASCII text, for example, in some objects described in Section 10.8.1 for general system and interface management.

- *OBJECT IDENTIFIER* — used for unique identification of managed objects; see Section 10.8.

- *Counter* — a 32-bit, nonnegative integer that cannot decrease (and will wrap around when it reaches its maximum value of $2^{32} - 1 = 4294967295$). This is used extensively for SMDS performance management. See, for example, Chapter 11.

- *Gauge* — a 32-bit, nonnegative integer that may increase or decrease. This type is used for SMDS performance management of physical transmission facilities. See Chapter 11.

- *TimeTicks* — a 32-bit, nonnegative integer that counts time in hundredths of a second. See Section 10.7.7.

- *NULL* — the data type with a value of zero length.

ASN.1 also defines the rules that are needed to encode the information for transmission, the transfer syntax [ISO8825]. These rules are known as the ASN.1 Basic Encoding Rules (BER). SNMP follows these rules. It is beyond the scope of this book to detail this technique. Interested readers are referred to [Steedman] and [Rose].

10.7.3 Object Identification

Each object is uniquely identifiable. The data type used for this purpose is called *object identifier* or *OID*. An OID is a string of nonnegative integers. By convention, these identifiers are pictorially represented as branches in a tree.[5] An SNMP textual format for denoting a particular object identifier is to separate the integers with dots. For example, 1.3.6.1.2 and 1.3.6.1.2.1 are OIDs that name objects in the tree in Figure 10.11. This branch of the OID tree shows a portion of the Interfaces group of objects defined in MIB II (see Section 10.8).

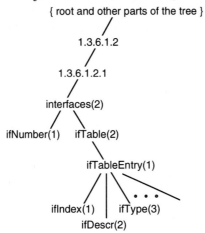

Figure 10.11 Example of a portion of the OID tree

Since a long string of integers is not convenient for human use, mnemonics called *object descriptors* are allowed. A particular object descriptor is synonymous with a particular OID. Of course, a particular object descriptor can only be used for one OID. Thus, in the example of Figure 10.11, 1.3.6.1.2.1.2 is assigned the object descriptor `interfaces`. Observe that `ifTable.1` and `ifTableEntry` are both synonyms for the object identifier 1.3.6.1.2.1.2.2.1. In this book, we will generally use object descriptors wherever possible, since the actual values of the OIDs are hardly needed for the understanding of the management of SMDS.

Each object is a scalar. Conceptual tables are formed by a clever organization of the OID tree. One typical use of a table is the characterization of a number of interfaces through a set of properties. The properties form the columns of the table, and each interface instance forms a row. SNMP MIBs make extensive use of the tabular organization of management information.

---

[5]A unique feature of this tree is that it is always pictured and discussed upside down, that is, with the *root* on top. For practical reasons, illustrations only show the portion of the tree that is of interest.

Figure 10.11 shows a portion of MIB II's `ifTable` (see Section 10.8.2). The objects `ifIndex`, `ifDescr`, and `ifType` form three columns in the table. Rows are formed by rules for allocation of OIDs under these three objects [RFC1212]. This design is tailored for efficient retrieval of these rows, and allows conceptual tables to be indexed. This is needed to scope out a particular entry or set of entries from a table. In summary, the rules for identification of object instances are as follows:

- Instances of leaf objects are identified by the concatenation of the OID of the parent object and a suffix.

- For objects that are not a part of a column in a table, the suffix is 0. For example, the object name of the (only) instance of `ifNumber` in Figure 10.11 is `ifNumber.0`.

- For objects that are a part of a column in a table, the suffix is the index of the table. The index is usually formed by the use of the value of one or more columns in the table. For example, the object `ifIndex` is the only index column of `ifTable`. For SMDS-related tables discussed in this book, the following rules are important:

  - If the index column is an integer, the suffix is the value of the integer. In the example in Figure 10.11, if `ifIndex` has the integer values 1, 2, and 3, then the first three object instances of the second row are identified by

    { ifIndex.2, ifDescr.2, ifType.2 }

  - If the index column is an octet string with fixed length, the suffix is a string of integers, where each integer corresponds to the value of a byte in the octet string.[6]

Using the same rules, a suffix can be based on a number of index columns. The suffix is formed by using the rules for the individual index columns and concatenating the result in the order as specified by the MIB. Indexing by more than one column is sometimes necessary to achieve unique identification of the row. In the discussion of SMDS objects pertinent for the management of SMDS, several examples will be shown using this technique. The details and background

---

[6]Thus, in the example of Figure 10.11, if `ifIndex` had been an octet string of 16 bits with the respective values $FFFC_H$, $FFFD_H$, and $FFFE_H$, then the three rows in the table would have been identified as follows:

{ ifIndex.255.252, ifDescr.255.252, ifType.255.252 }
{ ifIndex.255.253, ifDescr.255.253, ifType.255.253 }
{ ifIndex.255.254, ifDescr.255.254, ifType.255.254 }

of the full set of rules are described in the SNMP standards, [RFC1155], [RFC1157], [RFC1212], and in [Rose].

10.7.4 Authentication and Access Control

SNMP supports a very basic mechanism to validate that a message is from the claimed source. To each SNMP PDU, a field is tagged called *community*. The *Community String*, an OCTET STRING, serves as a password.[7] For example, the value public is a very common Community String.

When considering the issue of SNMP access to management information of a public service, it can be understood that a mechanism is needed to make certain portions of a MIB accessible only to specific customers. For example, customers should only have access to that portion of the MIB concerning their own use of the service. Similarly, it should be possible to grant read-only and read-write privileges to different users. This is achieved by pairing the community name with the objects that the community is entitled access to, and by linking this with the access mode (read-only or read-write) granted to that community. This technique has been applied to the implementation of SMDS CNM Service to achieve virtual private networking.

10.7.5 Access Protocol — SNMP

The management capabilities described in Chapters 10 through 12 make use of SNMP as the access protocol to the MIB. This section describes the protocol, provides some examples of its use, and specifies supporting protocol stacks for accessing CPE and CNM MIBs.

10.7.5.1   SNMP Capabilities and Messages

The protocol for MIB access consists of five different messages. Each message consists of a header and message data. The header specifies the version (always set to version 1) and the community name (see Section 10.7.4). The message data contain the actual SNMP PDU. The five PDUs allow for the following capabilities:

- *Read capability.*
  The SNMP PDUs for this purpose are the get-request and get-next-request PDUs issued by an NMS to an SNMP agent. Issuance of one of these PDUs will invoke a response in the form of the get-response PDU. The get-request PDU is used to obtain the value of a particular object instance. The get-next-request PDU is used to obtain the value of

---

[7]It is generally recognized that this mechanism is weak, since the password is sent with each PDU, and in the "clear." A more secure mechanism is provided in SNMP Version 2.

the object instance identified by the next available higher OID than the one identified in the PDU. It can be intuitively understood that this capability allows for simple retrieval of tables or portions thereof, by using one table row in a get-response in a subsequent get-next-request to obtain the next row. For the details of the difference between these two operators, we refer to the literature [RFC1157] [Rose]. No detailed understanding of this difference is required for reading this book.

- *Write capability.*

  The SNMP PDU for this purpose is the set-request PDU, which also invokes a get-response PDU.

- *Notification or alarm capability.*

  The SNMP PDU in this case is the trap PDU.

The get-request, get-next-request, set-request, and the get-response all have the same structure. The simplified format is shown in Figure 10.12. The encoding follows the ASN.1 Basic Encoding Rules. It is beyond the scope of this book to detail these rules. Illustrative examples can be found in [Steedman] and [Rose].

	Field
SNMP message	version
header	community
SNMP message	PDU type
data field	request-id
(contains an	error-status
SNMP PDU)	error-index
	variable-bindings

Figure 10.12 Simplified format of the SNMP get-request, get-next-request, set-request, and get-response

A request identifies one or more managed objects for which the current value is desired or to be set. The get-response identifies the same list of objects, accompanied by the returned values. A PDU TYPE distinguishes the different PDU types. A REQUEST-ID correlates requests with responses. Any error resulting from the request is conveyed in the ERROR-STATUS and ERROR-INDEX fields. The latter contains the place of the variable in the VARIABLE-BINDINGS list that caused the error. For example, if the second variable in a requested list causes an error, the ERROR-INDEX is set to 2. The ERROR-INDEX is set to 0 if there are no errors. Since the ERROR-INDEX and ERROR-STATUS are only meaningful in a GET-RESPONSE PDU, they are set to 0 in other PDUs.

The ERROR-STATUS diagnoses the error. The values of the ERROR-STATUS are noError(0), tooBig(1) when the get-response would exceed supported SNMP message size, noSuchName(2) when the requested object is unknown by the agent (the object is not supported or the requested instance is not present), or when access by the requester is not allowed, badValue(3) when the syntax or value of a set-request does not match the definition of the object, or genErr(5) for any other errors. The VARIABLE-BINDINGS is a list of objects with their values that the PDU operates on.

The SNMP trap-PDU has a different structure. The simplified format is shown in Figure 10.13.

	Field
SNMP message	version
header	community
	PDU type
SNMP message	enterprise
data field	agent-addr
(contains an	generic trap
SNMP PDU)	specific-trap
	time-stamp
	variable-bindings

Figure 10.13 Simplified format of the SNMP trap

The fields of the trap PDU follow:

- The ENTERPRISE field contains the value of the object sysObjectID (see Section 10.7.1), identifying the agent.

- The AGENT-ADDR is the network address of the agent (for SMDS CNM IP addresses are used).

- The GENERIC-TRAP identifies a number of standard events.

     - coldStart(0), and warmStart(1)

     - linkDown(2), and linkUp(3)

     - authenticationFailure(4)

     - egpNeighborLoss(5)

     - enterpriseSpecific(6)

The coldStart(0) and warmStart(1) alarms are not specific to SMDS; they indicate that the SNMP agent is (re)initializing itself. With the coldStart(0), potentially a new management view of the device is being built up (e.g., a new port has been added). With the warmStart(1), the management view is not being refreshed. The authenticationFailure(4) indicates that the SNMP agent has received a message that was not correctly authenticated. The linkDown(2) and linkUp(3) traps signify whether the link is available for communication. Events that cause these traps are specific to the type of device that is used (e.g., SMDS). The trap egpNeighborLoss(5) is specific to the use of IP. The last trap, enterpriseSpecific(6) identifies that an event has occurred that is further identified by the specific-trap field (see next item).

- The SPECIFIC-TRAP identifies the event for enterprise specific cases. For SMDS CNM Service, some enterprise specific traps have been defined (see Chapter 12).

- The TIME-STAMP field contains the value of sysUpTime of the agent (see Section 10.8.1).

- The VARIABLE-BINDINGS consist of a list of objects and their values that are relevant to the event.

10.7.5.2   Notational Conventions and Examples

This section shows examples of the use of SNMP with objects shown in Figure 10.11. These examples also show the notational conventions that are used in this book for SNMP operations.

The value of the only instance of ifNumber is obtained by

> get (ifNumber.0)

or, with the get-next

> getnext (ifNumber)

Both will invoke the desired result via a get-response PDU, for example,

> get-response (ifNumber.0 = 6)

Let us look at the retrieval of the first three objects of an entry in ifTable:

> get (ifIndex.1, ifDescr.1, ifType.1)

Consider now how the get-next is used to dump the first three columns of the whole table.

> getnext (ifIndex, ifDescr, ifType)

The result will be object names and values in the first row.

> get-response (ifIndex.1 = 1, ifDescr.1 = "SMDS interface Building I",
>   ifType.1 = 31)

The result is used for retrieval of the second row.

getnext (ifIndex.1, ifDescr.1, ifType.1)

For a table dump, this process continues until the end of the table is reached, which is detected when an object name appears in the get-response PDU that does not belong to the table.

SMDS CNM Service also allows read-write operations. The use of set-request PDUs for these operations is discussed in Section 12.4.2.

10.7.5.3   SNMP Protocol Support for SMDS

The protocol stack that is needed to support SNMP is shown in Figure 10.14, which uses the example configuration illustrated in Figure 10.1. SNMP is typically operated over the User Datagram Protocol, or UDP [RFC768] (see Figure 10.15) and IP [RFC791]. In turn, IP runs over physical networks, as explained in Section 8.2.1. The physical network that is used to access SMDS CNM Service is either SMDS, or a leased line, or a dial-up line. The latter two approaches allow continuous access to CNM information when the SMDS SNI is down. Chapter 12 provides details on SMDS CNM Service access.

The UDP SOURCE PORT and DESTINATION PORTS identify the respective applications that require communication between the hosts identified by the IP addresses. The ports assigned to SNMP are 162_D for SNMP trap messages, and 161_D for all other SNMP messages [RFC1340].

The UDP DATA field contains the SNMP message. SNMP [RFC1157] requires that messages with a length of 484 bytes or less must always be accepted by an SNMP agent. This guarantees that no segmentation will be performed on the packet.

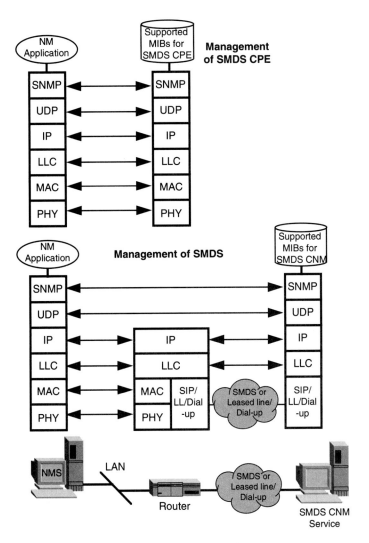

Figure 10.14 Examples of MIB access with SNMP

Length in bytes	Function
2	Source Port
2	Destination Port
2	Length in bytes
2	Checksum
Variable	Data

Figure 10.15 UDP packet format

10.7.6 Case Diagrams

We use Case Diagrams[8] as an aid in the understanding of the mutual relationship of the performance counters (see Figure 10.16).

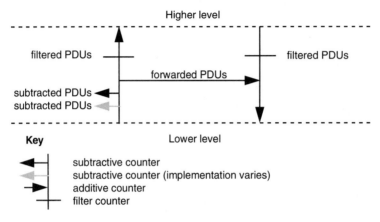

Figure 10.16 Example of a Case Diagram

A filter counter in the Case Diagram represents the number of PDUs received from or sent to another protocol level. Subtractive counters are used for PDUs that are not sent to another protocol level (e.g., discarded or forwarded to a peer entity). Additive counters refer to PDUs that are added to those received from another source.

We have added one convention. The shaded arrows represent counters that are known to have implementation problems.

10.7.7 Performance Measurements — Counters and TimeTicks

For SMDS, most performance measurements use the Counter data type. A reading of counter values is only valuable if it can be related to elapsed time. The object that measures elapsed time since (re)start is called `sysUpTime` (see Section 10.8.1). Thus, a performance measurement can be made by dividing a counter increment by the corresponding increment of `sysUpTime`.[9] Recall that a Counter is 32 bits long, and will eventually wrap to a value of zero. Thus, a

---

[8]Named after the eminent Professor Jeffrey Case (Dr. SNMP), these diagrams are used to convey pictorially simple protocol-counter relationships, and not any complex semantics or processing order. See [Case] and [Rose] for a discussion of these diagrams.

[9]Note that the definition of the Counter data type does not require counters to be reset at (re)start, although many implementations do so. In that case, the value of a counter represents the number of counted events since (re)start.

measurement requires periodic polling to be significant, and should typically be accompanied by `sysUpTime` to allow calculation of time averages.

To illustrate this, we use a Counter discussed in Chapter 11, `sipL3ReceivedIndividualDAs`, that measures received unicast L3_PDUs. Suppose two subsequent samples of `sipL3Received-IndividualDAs` and `sysUpTime` produce the following:

sipL3ReceivedIndividualDAs	sysUpTime
14294967294	14
4002	6014

Assuming that no reset has taken place during the polling period, the number of L3_PDUs received over the polling period is calculated as follows.

$$[4002 - 4294967294] \bmod 2^{32} = 4004 \text{ L3\_PDUs}$$

The values of sysUpTime are used to calculate the elapsed time over the polling period.

$$0.01 \times [6014 - 14] \bmod 2^{32} = 60 \text{ seconds}$$

Division of these two numbers produces a per-second average of 60.73 received individually addressed L3_PDUs.

The polling frequency must be greater than the roll-over frequency of the counter in order to be significant. For example, on a DS3-based SIP interface, and assuming an application with SIP_L3 PDUs of an average length of 125μsec, the `sipL3ReceivedIndividualDAs` counter would have a maximum roll-over frequency of $125 \times 10^{-6} \times 2^{32}$ seconds (in the order of 6 days).

10.8 Management of SMDS Using SNMP MIB II

The umbrella MIB module for SNMP-based management is called *MIB II* [RFC1213]. The objects in this MIB module provide an NMS with information about the general status and nature of managed devices in an internet and of their interfaces. For example, an NMS will use this MIB module to find out how many interfaces a managed device has, the interface type (Ethernet, SIP, Token Ring, etc.), and whether these interfaces are "up" or "down." This simple information helps an NMS to build up a general topology of a managed network and to identify general connectivity problems. MIB II also provides an NMS with information on any additional MIB modules that must be used to manage a particular device or interface. For example, a Token Ring MIB module provides management capabilities beyond MIB II that are specific to Token Ring interfaces. For SMDS, we will describe the use of the DS1/E1 MIB, the DS3/E3 MIB, the SIP MIB, and the SMDS Subscription MIB in Chapters 11 and 12. In this section we describe how MIB II is applied to the management of SMDS CPE and to SMDS CNM Service.

The general management approach using MIB II is shown in Figure 10.17. MIB II is organized into groups of parameters. The MIB II System group applies to basic system management, and the Interfaces group is designed for basic interface management. Both groups are applied to the management of SMDS devices, regardless of the applications that use SMDS (see Chapters 8 and 9). The Systems group characterizes the managed systems. Interfaces are characterized by a generic set of attributes, organized in a table, `ifTable`. For SMDS there is one `ifTable` entry per SNI.[10] The object `ifIndex` that is shown in the figure is used to identify an entry in this table, and will be discussed in Section 10.8.2.1. Media-specific attributes further characterize interfaces. These attributes are specified in separate MIB modules (see Chapters 11 and 12). Section 10.8.1 discusses the use of the System group. Section 10.8.2 discusses the use of the Interfaces group. Subsequently, Section 10.8.3. describes which additional MIB modules must be used to manage SMDS devices and interfaces.

Figure 10.17 illustrates that SMDS is represented to SMDS CNM Service users as a single SNMP-managed resource. This approach facilitates the objectives discussed below:

- Unnecessary details of the internal operations of the carrier's network are hidden from the customer.

- The service, as a single SNMP-managed resource, fits into an internet of other SNMP-managed resources. The interface index object `ifIndex` is a key object to achieve this integration.

- A subscriber will see only those details of the service that concern her subscription (and not those of other subscribers).

With this approach, system and interface management procedures can be the same for SMDS CPE and for SMDS CNM. Also, the same basic alarms can be used.

---

[10]Refinements to the use of the Interfaces group have been specified in [RFC1573]. This specification allows multiple entries in `ifTable` (one for each protocol layer). At the time of publication of this book, the use of this approach was not yet formalized for SMDS, or supported in SMDS CPE or SMDS CNM Service. However, we expect full support of [RFC1573] in the future.

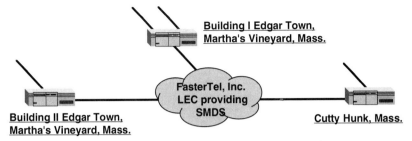

Physical view from the perspective of the Bodacious Data Corp.

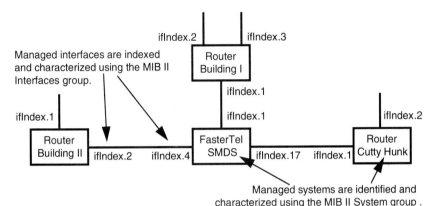

SNMP NM view from the perspective of the Bodacious Data Corp.

Figure 10.17 MIB II management of SMDS CPE and networks providing SMDS

10.8.1 System Management for SMDS CPE and SMDS CNM Service

Table 10.3 shows the use of the System group. The System group is used to identify and characterize a managed device in a managed internet.

Most of the parameter settings will not be surprising. The setting for the object `sysContact` for SMDS CNM Service may only provide limited value. The reason is that the System group in SMDS CNM Service represents an SNMP agent, which may act as a proxy for switching systems supporting a large geographical area. This means that service personnel may not be centrally located. Thus, a complementary approach is to provide a contact on a per-interface basis. The SMDS Subscription MIB does this (see `smdsContact`, Chapter 12). Service providers that offer a single point of contact to their customers should set the value of `sysContact` to the value of `smdsContact`.

MIB II's System group of objects	Semantics for SMDS CPE	Semantics in SMDS CNM Service
sysDescription	A textual description of the device type.	"<Service provider name> SMDS CNM SNMP agent"
sysObjectID	An OID that uniquely identifies the SMDS CPE.	An OID that uniquely identifies the SMDS CNM SNMP agent.
sysUpTime	The elapsed time since the SMDS CPE (re)started, measured in hundredths of a second	The elapsed time since the SMDS CNM Agent (re)started measured, in hundredths of a second
sysContact	The contact information for maintenance of this device	"See your SMDS Contact"
sysName	The name of this device	The name of the SMDS CNM SNMP agent
sysLocation	The physical location of this device	The physical location of the SMDS CNM SNMP agent
sysServices	A bitmap representing the functions this type of equipment supports. The value for SMDS CPE depends on the type of device. The values and meanings important for SMDS follow. 2 bridge 3 router 64 host	SMDS is represented by the value 2, signifying that it fulfills a role below the internetwork level.

Table 10.3 System management

10.8.2 Interface Management for SMDS CPE and SMDS CNM Service

The MIB II Interfaces group consists of a table, ifTable, and an additional single object, ifNumber. Table 10.4 shows how ifTable applies to SMDS. Many objects are self-explanatory. We will only discuss the peculiarities. Readers interested in additional details of the background of these parameters are referred to [RFC1213] and [Rose].

MIB II's ifTable objects	Semantics for SMDS CPE		Semantics in SMDS CNM Service	
ifIndex	(Table index) The interface index		(Table index) The interface index	
ifDescr	Textual description of the interface		For SIP ports: "<Service provider name> SIP port" For intercarrier connectivity: "<Service provider name> port"	
ifType	The type of interface. The value follows:		The type of interface. The values follow:	
	31	SIP	1	Other (here implying intercarrier connectivity)
			31	SIP
ifMtu	The maximum L3_PDU size (9232 bytes)		The maximum L3_PDU size (9232 bytes) (for intercarrier connectivity this object must be not-accessible)	
ifSpeed	The line speed of the managed interface in bps. For example, the values for SIP are as follows:		The line speed of the managed interface in bps. For example, the values for SIP are as follows:	
	1544000	SIP/DS1	1544000	SIP/DS1
	2048000	SIP/E1	2048000	SIP/E1
	34368000	SIP/E3	34368000	SIP/E3
	44736000	SIP/DS3	44736000	SIP/DS3
			For intercarrier connectivity, this object may be set to the aggregated speed of the intercarrier trunks.	
ifPhysAddress	The SMDS address of the interface		An octet string of zero length	

(continued)

(Table 10.4, continued)

MIB II's ifTable objects	Semantics for SMDS CPE		Semantics in SMDS CNM Service	
ifAdminStatus	The desired status of the interface. The values are as follows:		The desired status of the interface. The values are as follows:	
	1	up — L3_PDUs can be transmitted and received.	1	up — L3_PDUs can be transmitted and received.
	2	down — L3_PDUs cannot be transmitted and received.	2	down — L3_PDUs cannot be transmitted and received.
	3	testing	3	testing
ifOperStatus	The actual status of the interface (see ifAdminStatus)		The actual status of the interface (see ifAdminStatus)	
ifLastChange	The timestamp (the value of sysUptime) of the most recent change in status of the interface		The timestamp (the value of sysUptime) of the most recent change in status of the interface	
ifSpecific	The OID of the root of the SIP MIB. The value is 1.3.6.1.2.1.10.31.		The OID of the root of the SMDS Subscription MIB . The value is 1.3.6.1.4.1.148.1. The value is 0.0 for intercarrier connectivity.	

Table 10.4 Interface management of SIP ports — `ifTable`

Readers familiar with MIB II will notice that `ifTable` actually contains more objects than shown. Currently, these parameters do not apply to SMDS.[11] Other (IP-specific) information is covered in MIB II. It is beyond the scope of this book to describe the management of SMDS applications.

10.8.2.1   Interface Index

The integer `ifIndex` numbers the interfaces of a managed device and is used as an index to `ifTable`. Each SNI is represented by one `ifTable` entry. In our earlier example, the Building I router has two interfaces, numbered 1 and

---

[11]It is possible to use more parameters in `ifTable`. However, as will be explained in Chapter 11, SIP performance parameters are represented in the SIP MIB [RFC1304]. Objects that are not used must be represented with an access level of not-accessible [Rose] causing an error code of noSuchName in response to a get-request. Since the publication of RFC1304, the IETF has published refinements of the Interfaces group [RFC1573]. In the future, SMDS interfaces are expected to support the full Interfaces group, as defined in [RFC1573]. RFC1304 is expected to be aligned with RFC1573.

2 (`ifIndex.1 = 1`, `ifIndex.2 = 2`), and the interfaces visible through SMDS CNM Service are numbered 1, 4, and 17.

An interesting consideration is the treatment of connectivity with other carriers in this table. SMDS customers will not necessarily be interested in the details of carrier network interconnection. After all, it is part of the service that SMDS customers do not need to worry about these details; it is the carriers' job to provide smooth and uninterrupted service, independent of the implementation of their mutual intercarrier arrangements. The SMDS customer's interest is whether performance objectives are met. While details of intercarrier connectivity may be irrelevant to customers, the connectivity itself is relevant.

Figure 10.18 shows that the network of FasterTel and DataInternational are connected through a number of physical trunks. The trunks carry traffic from multiple SNIs. Typically, customers will not be interested in the individual trunks of the local network that is providing SMDS to other carriers. Of interest is whether the combination of trunks provides connectivity. Thus, a single `ifIndex` instance is allocated to each combined set of trunks (regardless of their location) that connects the local carrier with a remote carrier.

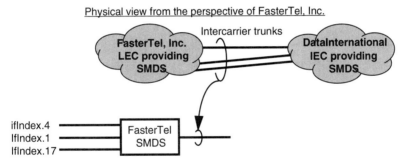

Figure 10.18 Representation of intercarrier connectivity and the use of `ifIndex`

Only a portion of the rest of `ifTable` is appropriate for this (logical) interface (see Table 10.4). Objects such as `ifSpeed` are not applied to this (logical) interface. Recall that the MIB view provided by CNM is intended to be virtually private. Thus, a parameter such as `ifSpeed` would be meaningless to a particular customer, since the connectivity is shared with other customer traffic.

This model changes if intercarrier connectivity is provided via trunks that are dedicated to a particular customer. This scenario results in the management view shown in Figure 10.19. In this case, knowledge about individual trunks and information such as `ifSpeed` and traffic statistics will be valuable to this customer.

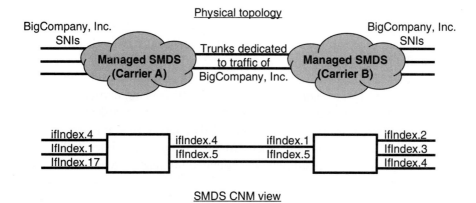

Figure 10.19 Intercarrier connectivity and customer-dedicated trunks

10.8.2.2 Number of Interfaces

In addition to `ifTable`, the Interfaces group also contains an object showing the total number of interfaces of the managed device. This parameter is `ifNumber`.

A special situation exists for the implementation of this object in an SMDS CNM Agent. Normally, `ifNumber` would be expected to show the total number of interfaces supported by SMDS. But recall that a CNM user should only get access information concerning her own use of the service. Thus, correct implementation of `ifNumber` in this case should only show the number of interfaces that are within the MIB view of this subscriber.

10.8.2.3 Interface Type

The interface type, `ifType`, enumerates different interfaces. The value 31 has been assigned to SIP. While originally intended for SIP only, we recommend that this value also be used for other SMDS access protocols, for example, DXI-based access to SMDS (see Chapter 5). The SIP MIB is expected to be updated in this regard.

Since no `ifType` value has been assigned to SMDS intercarrier connectivity, the value must be set to other(1).

10.8.2.4 Interface Physical Address

An interesting case is a configuration where multiple SMDS addresses are in use at an interface. In this case `ifPhysAddress` represents the primary address. Extensions to the Interfaces group have been published that represent the additional addresses (Individual Addresses and Group Addresses) through a separate table [RFC1573].

The network side of SMDS interfaces does not have a physical address. Hence, the object `ifPhysAddress` should not be used for SMDS CNM Service.

10.8.2.5   Interface Status

The status of the interface is represented by the objects `ifOperStatus` and `ifAdminStatus`. The former represents the actual status of the interface, while the latter shows the desired interface status. The interface status is undergoing change when these objects do not have the same value. For example, when the SMDS CNM Service shows `ifOperStatus` as down, and `ifAdminStatus` as up, it may be an indication that the service provider is trying to solve a problem. The testing status applies to loopback procedures (see Chapter 12).

10.8.2.6   Examples

The Building I router of the Bodacious Data Corp. may show the following system information (recall that the index 0 is used for nontabular objects):

sysDescr.0	"IP WAN router"
sysObjectID.0	1.3.6.1.4.1.148.525.1
sysUpTime.0	372111 (1 hour, 2 minutes, 1.11 seconds)
sysContact.0	"Mark Niederberger, (516) 758 5254"
sysName.0	"WAN router 1"
sysLocation.0	"Edgar Town Building I, Rm 1A427"
sysServices.0	4 (router)

For the same router, `ifNumber` and `ifTable` for the SMDS interface may show the following values. The table index, the integer `ifIndex`, has the value of 1 for this interface; `ifNumber` is not part of a table, and is instantiated by the suffix of 0.

ifNumber.0	2
ifIndex.1	1
ifDescr.1	"SMDS port"
ifType.1	31
ifMtu.1	9188
ifSpeed.1	1544000
ifPhysAddress.1	C15165552642FFFF
ifAdminStatus.1	1
ifOperStatus.1	1
ifLastChange.1	60480004
ifSpecific.1	1.3.6.1.2.1.10.31

This information shows that the router has two managed interfaces, and that interface 1 uses a DS1-based SMDS access interface with physical address C15165552642FFFF$_H$. The interface state is up for more than a week.

The preciseness of the object-oriented structure of the managed information lends itself well to applications that present the information in a user-friendly manner. A graphical example is shown in Figure 10.20.

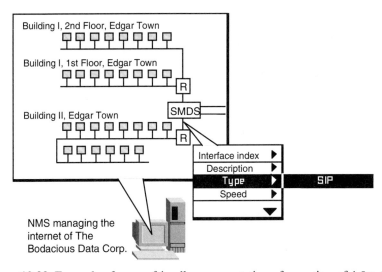

Figure 10.20 Example of a user-friendly representation of a portion of `ifTable`

10.8.3 Other MIB Modules for SMDS

The standard method for NMSs to determine which MIB modules are needed for the management of a particular interface makes use of a MIB II parameter in the Interfaces group, `ifSpecific`. This object can point to the root of a MIB module that is needed to manage the interface. Unfortunately, this simple method fell short for SMDS. A SIP interface is not monolithic; it can use a variety of physical media, such as DS1, DS3, E1, E3, for which separate MIB modules have been designed independently of SIP [RFC1406] [RFC1407]. For SMDS CNM Service, still another MIB module, the SMDS Subscription MIB, is needed for the management of service-related parameters. Thus, multiple MIB modules are needed to fully describe an SMDS interface. The solution that is used in this case relies on inspection by NMSs of other MIB II objects in the `ifTable`, `ifType` and `ifSpeed`,[12] as follows:

---

[12]This solution is rather unsatisfactory. The IETF has published [RFC1573], which provides a better approach for these cases. The SIP MIB is expected to be aligned with RFC1573.

- The method of inspecting `ifType` relies on a particular allocation convention in the `transmission` branch of the MIB II OID tree. By convention, subbranches, identified by the OID {transmission.x} are chosen so that the value of x corresponds to the value of `ifType` for that interface type. The root of the SIP MIB module corresponds with `ifType` $= 31$, that is, {transmission.31}.

- `ifSpecific` for SMDS CPE points to the root of the SIP MIB. For SMDS CNM Service, `ifSpecific` points to the root of the SMDS Subscription MIB.

- The appropriate MIB for the physical media is selected by inspection of `ifSpeed`, as shown in Table 10.5. This assumes that an NMS knows the OID of the root of the appropriate physical media MIBs. Note that the DS1/E1 MIB module covers both DS1 and E1 lines.[13] Similarly, the DS3/E3 MIB module applies to DS3 and E3 interfaces.

ifSpeed in bps	Transmission media	MIB module	OID of the root of the MIB module
1544000	DS1	DS1/E1	{ transmission.18 }
2048000	E1	DS1/E1	{ transmission.18 }
34368000	E3	DS3/E3	{ transmission.30 }
44736000	DS3	DS3/E3	{ transmission.30 }

Table 10.5 Relation of `ifSpeed` with MIB modules

10.9   Alarms (SNMP Traps)

The generic SNMP traps apply to the management of SMDS CPE and to SMDS CNM Service. The relevant traps in this context are the following (see Section 10.7.5 for a description):

- coldStart(0), and warmStart(1),

- linkDown(2), and linkUp(3),

- authenticationFailure(4).

---

[13]MIB II specifies separate values of `ifType` for DS1 and E1 transmission media, i.e, the values ds1(18) and cept(19). This assumed at the time that a separate MIB would be defined for E1 facilities. However, the management of DS1 and E1 facilities has since been defined as a single MIB module. Thus, `ifType` for E1 must be set to 18, and the value 19 must not be used.

The *linkDown*(2) trap signifies an event at the interface concerned that precludes any further successful communication through that interface. When the interface leaves the down state again, a linkUp(3) trap is sent. By convention, the first parameter in the variable list must be the interface identifier, *ifIndex*. The *linkDown*(2) and *linkUp*(3) traps can be caused by a range of events, for example, a failure in the transmission line. See Chapter 11 for details.

For SMDS CNM Service, a number of enterprise-specific traps are also defined to notify certain subscription changes. Their use is discussed in Chapter 12.

11

Management of SMDS Customer Premises Equipment

This chapter describes SNMP capabilities for SMDS CPE that provide performance and status details to a network manager beyond the generic system and interface management capabilities described in Chapter 10 (see Table 11.1).

The applicable MIB modules, [RFC1304], [RFC1406], and [RFC1407] contain objects to measure performance and to allow troubleshooting. In Section 11.1, we discuss these objects by protocol level and provide examples of their use. Section 11.2 reviews CSU/DSU implications for network management and describes the DXI Local Management Interface (LMI) for configurations where the DXI is used.

This chapter complements Chapters 10 and 12, and it should be useful to readers interested in troubleshooting, performance monitoring, and configuration of SMDS CPE. Designers of SMDS CPE or carrier networks will find detailed descriptions and background of network management features for SMDS CPE.

11.1 Performance Management of a SIP Interface

The performance of a SIP interface can be monitored by implementation of the SIP MIB module [RFC1304] and the MIB module for the applicable physical

SMDS-specific interface management capabilities	Access level	Remarks	Applicable MIB module
1. SIP Level 3 performance management	Read-only	Applies to all types of SMDS access.	SIP MIB
2. SIP Level 2 performance management	Read-only	Applies to SIP access only. Management of interfaces based on DXI, SIP Relay, and ATM is expected in the future.	SIP MIB
3. SIP PLCP performance management	Read-only	Applies to interfaces based on DS1, E1, E3, and DS3.	SIP MIB
3. SIP Level 1 performance management	Read-only	Applies to interfaces based on DS1, E1, E3, and DS3.	DS1/E1 MIB DS3/E3 MIB
4. SIP Level 1 configuration and line status	Read-only	Applies to interfaces based on DS1, E1, E3, and DS3.	DS1/E1 MIB DS3/E3 MIB

Table 11.1 SMDS NM capabilities for SMDS CPE

transmission media, the DS1/E1 MIB [RFC1406], or the DS3/E3 MIB [RFC1407]. These modules represent parameters such as counts of correct or errored PDUs at all the SIP levels, and the line configuration and status information at the physical level. The parameters can be used to measure the traffic volume on the SIP interface, as well as to pinpoint the erroneous protocol behavior discussed in Chapter 4.[1]

When provided by CPE, these measurements represent the interface behavior from the CPE's perspective. Trouble-isolation can be improved by comparing these measurements with their peers collected by the public service and represented through SMDS CNM Service (see Chapter 12).

The SIP MIB module represents management information in a number of groups:

- The SIP Level 3 group: A number of counters describing SIP Level 3 protocol behavior. This group is augmented by the SIP Error Log, which provides additional diagnostic information about syntactical errors in received SIP_L3 PDUs.
- The SIP Level 2 group: A number of counters describing the protocol behavior at SIP Level 2.

---

[1]For access based on DXI, SIP Relay, or ATM, only performance management of SIP Level 3 may be initially available. Management of the other layers is expected in the future.

- The SIP PLCP group: Information about the PLCP Level for DS1/E1- and DS3/E3-based interfaces.

These three groups are discussed in the next subsections. Two additional groups are defined in the SIP MIB. The SMDS Applications group is defined to provide information about SIP applications such as those defined in Chapter 8. The SIP MIB only defines information for IP-over-SMDS, but leaves room for future extensions. The SMDS Carrier Selection group is a placeholder in this MIB for possible future information relevant for Carrier Selection. More experimentation is necessary to determine the exact information useful for this group.

Subsequently, we describe the MIB modules for the DS1, E1, E3, and DS3 physical transmission media.

11.1.1 SIP Level 3 Performance Management

SIP Level 3 performance is managed through the use of two tables: the `sipL3Table` and the `sipL3PDUErrorTable`. The `sipL3Table` tracks performance by counting correct and errored L3_PDUs. The `sipL3PDUErrorTable` complements the error counters with detailed diagnostics.

11.1.1.1 The sipL3Table

The purpose of the `sipL3Table` of the SIP MIB is to track the SIP Level 3 protocol behavior on a particular SIP port. The table is indexed by the interface index `ifIndex` and is shown in Table 11.2.

With the exception of `sipL3VersionSupport` (an integer), all of these variables are counters.

The Case Diagram in Figure 11.1 describes the mutual relationship of the `sipL3Table` counters.

Implementation experience has shown that, in practice, it is not always possible to count the `sipL3UnrecognizedGAs` and `sipL3-UnrecognizedIndividualDAs`. This problem occurs in bus implementations where each station only copies "its own" PDUs from the bus; misaddressed PDUs will simply disappear without being counted. Thus, CPE may not be able to support these objects and should in that case return the error code "noSuchName" on requests for their value. Note that these counters relate to the stringent SMDS service objectives of 5×10^{-8} on misdelivered L3_PDUs (see Section 7.4.3).

sipL3Table objects	Semantics
sipL3Index	(Table index) Interface index (= ifIndex)
sipL3ReceivedIndividualDAs	The number of received individually addressed L3_PDUs
sipL3ReceivedGAs	The number of received group addressed L3_PDUs
sipL3UnrecognizedIndividualDAs	The number of L3_PDUs with an unrecognized individual destination address
sipL3UnrecognizedGAs	The number of L3_PDUs with an unrecognized group address
sipL3SentIndividualDAs	The number of transmitted individually addressed L3_PDUs
sipL3SentGAs	The number of transmitted Group Addressed L3_PDUs
sipL3Errors	The number of received L3_PDUs with syntax errors
sipL3InvalidSMDSAddressTypes	The number of received L3_PDUs with improper address types
sipL3VersionSupport	Set to 1 for SIP, as described in Chapter 4

Table 11.2 Measurements of SIP Level 3 syntactical errors — `sipL3Table`

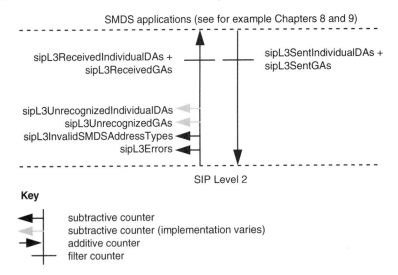

Figure 11.1 Case Diagram for SIP Level 3 counters

The sipL3Errors counter represents L3_PDUs with syntactical errors. A high `sipL3Errors` count may lead maintenance personnel to simply exchange the SIP Level 3 hardware. However, in some cases error diagnosis may be desirable, through the use of the SIP Level 3 error log, the `sipL3PDUErrorTable`. The remaining error counters in Table 11.2 represent semantic errors. An errored L3_PDU causes only one error counter to increase.

11.1.1.2   The sipL3PDUErrorTable

The `sipL3PDUErrorTable` (Table 11.3) contains the latest occurrence of syntactical errors counted in `sipL3Errors`. It records the observed Destination Address and Source Address of the discarded SIP_L3 PDU, together with an error code and a time stamp (the value of `sysUpTime` at the time of the error).

The time stamp is slightly ambiguous. Recall that `sysUpTime` is represented by a 32-bit continuous counter, which eventually rolls over. Thus, a time stamp may refer to a very old event! This is still considered acceptable in this case, however, since the error log is expected to be used in conjunction with the error counter. Only a suspicious increase in `sipL3Errors` should prompt a manager to inspect the error log. The NMS should then hunt for recent time stamps only, as the likely cause for the error-counter increase. Erroneous syntactical protocol behavior tends to be repetitive and caused by implementation problems. Thus, additional PDUs with the same error are likely to be observed. The small risk of associating an old table entry with a recent problem was considered acceptable, given the straightforward and simple implementation. The `sipL3PDUErrorTable`, which is indexed by the combination of the interface index and the error type, is shown in Table 11.3.[2]

---

[2]Note that both Error 5 and Error 8 cannot actually be detected by a SIP L3 protocol entity. The case of Error 5 (HE exceeding 12 bytes) cannot be detected, since (a) the SIP L3_PDU HE is set to 12 bytes, (see error code Error 4), and (b) the subsequent INFORMATION field is unlabeled. Thus, any excess portion of the HE is interpreted as part of the INFORMATION field. For the same reasons, an HE PAD with excessive length cannot be detected. The other two potential problems listed under error Error 8 are already covered by errors Error 6 and Error 7. Errors Error 5 and Error 8 are actually products of initial overengineering of SMDS operations. They are redundant in the SIP MIB module, but not harmful since the protocol entity would simply never set these values.

sipL3PDUErrorTable objects	Semantics	
sipL3PDUErrorIndex	(Table index)	
	Interface index (= ifIndex)	
sipL3PDUErrorType	Value	(Table index)
		Error type (see Section 4.5)
	1	Destination Address syntax error
	2	Source Address syntax error
	3	Buffer Allocation Size value error: < 32, or > 9220 (CRC32 not present), or > 9224 (CRC32 present), or $\neq 4n$(with n a positive integer)*
	4	Header Extension Length field $\neq$ 3.
	5	Header Extension exceeds 12 bytes.
	6	Invalid Header Extension Version Element: Header Extension must start with a Version Element (Length = 3, Type = 0, Value = 1). A Version Element may not appear elsewhere in the Header Extension.
	7	Invalid Header Extension Carrier Selection Element: Carrier Selection Element is used but does not follow the Version Element, or has a syntax error: Length $\neq$ (4 or 6 or 8), or Type $\neq$ 1, or Value is not a four-BCD-digit code, or The identified CIC code is invalid.
	8	Header Extension PAD Error: Header Extension PAD Length > 9 bytes, or Header Extension PAD does not start with a zero byte, or Header Extension PAD does not follow all other Header Extension Elements.
	9	Beginning-End Tags in the L3_PDU do not match.

(continued)

(Table 11.3, continued)

sipL3PDUErrorTable objects	Semantics	
sipL3PDUErrorType	Value	(Table index) Error type (see Section 4.5)
	10	Buffer Allocation Size field $\neq$ Length field.
	11	Length field $\neq$ p − 8 (where p is the number of bytes in the L3_PDU).
	12	Message Receive Interval Timeout Error — no matching BOM/EOM found within MRI (not used when the MRI timer is not implemented).
sipL3PDUErrorSA	The Source Address of the discarded L3_PDU	
sipL3PDUErrorDA	The Destination Address of the discarded L3_PDU	
sipL3PDUErrorTimeStamp	The value of sysUpTime at the time the L3_PDU was discarded.	

* Interestingly, while the L3_PDU INFORMATION field plus the padding should have a length of a multiple of 4 bytes, this check on the BASIZE is not actually required by IEEE [802.6]. As a result, the Bellcore specification for SMDS operations [774] lists this check only as optional, and not all implementations may support this check.

Table 11.3 Diagnostics of SIP Level 3 syntactical errors - `sipL3PDUErrorTable`

Table 11.4 shows an example of a log that may be retrieved for a given SNI.

SNI	Error type	Source Address	Destination Address	Time stamp	sysUpTime at retrieval
1	7	C15165552642FFFF	C18095555254FFFF	3984958678	54567
1	3	C15165552642FFFF	C15165552107FFFF	4294967294	57575

Table 11.4 Example of the use of the `sipL3PDUErrorTable`

Figure   11.2   shows   the   use   of   the   `sipL3Table`   and   the `sipL3PDUErrorTable` and the example of Table 11.4 with an imaginary user-friendly representation on an NMS.

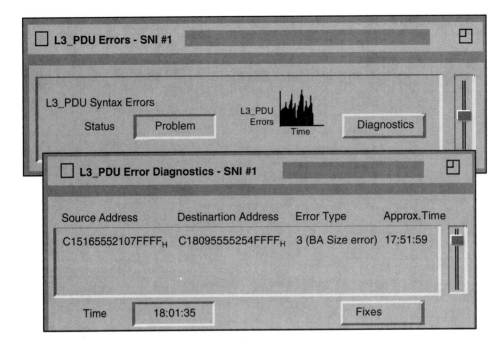

Figure 11.2 Example of user-friendly representation of the information in the `sipL3Table` and the `sipL3PDUErrorTable`

11.1.2 SIP Level 2 Performance Management — sipL2Table

The purpose of the `sipL2Table` of the SIP MIB is similar to that of the `sipL3Table`: to track erroneous protocol behavior on a particular SIP port. The `sipL2Table` consists solely of continuous counters of different L2_PDU syntax error types, and is indexed by the interface index `ifIndex`, as shown in Table 11.5.

The error situations listed in Table 11.5 are discussed in more detail in Section 4.6. Figure 11.3 illustrates the relationship between the variables in the `sipL2Table`.

The `sipL2ReceivedCounts` includes L2_PDUs that may subsequently be discarded. This occurs at the receipt of L2_PDUs with BOMs for which an active receive process is already started, and at the receipt of L2_PDUs with COMs/EOMs with an invalid Sequence Number. These events, counted in the `sipL2MidCurrentlyActiveErrors` and the `sipL2Sequence-NumberErrors` respectively, cause previously accumulated (correct) segments to be discarded (see Section 4.8.2). Thus, in order to interpret

sipL2Table objects	Semantics
sipL2Index	(Table index). Interface index (= ifIndex)
sipL2ReceivedCounts	The number of received unerrored L2_PDUs
sipL2SentCounts	The number of transmitted L2_PDUs
sipL2HcsOrCRCErrors	The number of received L2_PDUs with an Header Check Sequence* error or a CRC error
sipL2PayloadLengthErrors	The number of received L2_PDUs with: SSM payload < 28 bytes, or SSM payload > 44 bytes, or BOM/COM payload ≠ 44 bytes, or EOM payload < 4 bytes, or EOM payload > 44 bytes
sipL2SequenceNumberErrors	The number of received L2_PDUs with an unexpected Sequence Number
sipL2MidCurrentlyActiveErrors	The number of received L2_PDUs with BOMs for which an active receive process is already started
sipL2BomOrSSMsMIDErrors	The number of received L2_PDUs with: SSM with MID ≠ 0, or BOM with MID = 0
sipL2EomsMIDErrors	The number of received L2_PDUs with: EOM without matching BOM, or EOM with MID = 0

*See Section 4.6 and Appendix A. For SMDS, the NETWORK CONTROL INFORMATION must always be set to FFFFF022$_H$. HEADER CHECK SEQUENCE refers to the last byte of the NETWORK CONTROL INFORMATION. If the HEADER CHECK SEQUENCE calculation indicates that the transmission was correct, but that the NETWORK CONTROL INFORMATION ≠ FFFFF022$_H$, (i.e., non-SMDS traffic), then the sipL2-HcsOrCRCErrors must not be incremented. Note that HCS calculation is performed by SMDS but is not required for CPE.

Table 11.5 Measurements of SIP Level 2 errors — sipL2Table

sipL2ReceivedCounts correctly, we recommend that sipL2-MidCurrentlyActiveErrors and sipL2SequenceNumberErrors be inspected as well.

Invalid MIDs are only counted for BOMs, EOMs, and SSMs. Counting these errors for COMs was felt to be redundant, since this error condition would also show up in the count of EOMs with invalid MIDs.

As recommended in Chapter 4, implementations may not check on PAYLOAD LENGTH errors. If this check is not implemented, the SNMP error code noSuchName should be returned on receipt of a get-request for sipL2-PayloadLengthErrors.

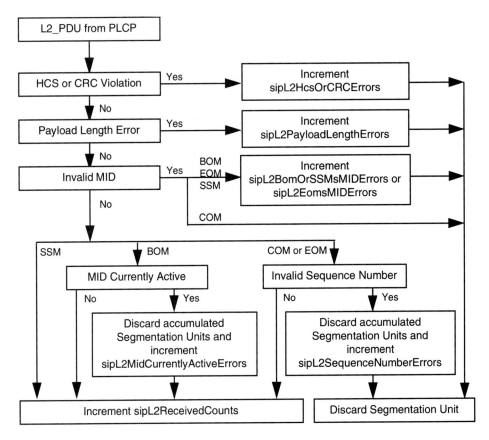

Figure 11.3 Use of SIP Level 2 counters

11.1.3 SIP PLCP Performance Management

The PLCPs for the various physical levels are described in Section 4.7. The management of this level is relatively simple, because of its strong correlation with the status and condition of the physical level. The behavior of the PLCP Level is represented to an NMS by a portion of the SIP MIB through the `sipDS1PLCPTable` and the `sipDS3PLCPTable`. These tables apply to both DS1/DS3 and to E1/E3 facilities, as shown in Table 11.6, and represent the error events and failure conditions described in Section 4.7. Both tables are again indexed by the interface index `ifIndex`.

sipDS1PLCPTable objects (Apply to E1 and DS1)	sipDS3PLCPTable objects (Apply to E3 and DS3)	Semantics	
sipDS1PLCPIndex	sipDS3PLCPIndex	(Table index) Interface index (= ifIndex)	
sipDS1PLCPSEFSs	sipDS3PLCPSEFSs	The number of seconds in which Severely Errored Framing events are declared: Both framing bytes are errored (first 2 bytes in a PLCP row), or 2 consecutive row numbers (3rd byte in a PLCP row) are invalid or nonsequential (see Section 4.7). Not counted during Unavailable Time.	
sipDS1PLCP-AlarmState	sipDS3PLCP-AlarmState	Value	The alarm condition of the PLCP (see Section 4.7):
		1	No alarm
		2	Far-end alarm (incoming Yellow Signal)
		3	A Loss-Of-Frame (LOF) failure condition Both framing bytes are errored (first 2 bytes in a PLCP row), or 2 consecutive row numbers (3rd byte in a PLCP row) are invalid or nonsequential, and this condition persists for $\Delta t = 2.5 \pm 0.5$ sec.
sipDS1PLCPUASs	sipDS3PLCPUASs	The number of Unavailable Seconds. UAS's start when a failure condition is declared and end when the condition is removed.	

Table 11.6 Performance management of the SIP PLCP Level — `sipDS1PLCPTable` and `sipDS3PLCPTable`

11.1.4 SIP Level 1 Management — The DS1/E1 and DS3/E3 MIB Modules

The management of the transmission facilities for SMDS does not differ from the management of DS1, E1, DS3, or E3 leased lines. The description of the maintenance signaling for DS1 and DS3 facilities is based on [773]. The E1 and E3 descriptions are based on [ESIG002]. For a full explanation of the appropriate MIBs and the semantics of the MIB variables, the reader is referred to the MIB module specifications, [RFC1406] and [RFC1407], and the applicable line-type specifications.

The two MIB modules have been developed simultaneously and are very similar. We will discuss them in parallel. Both MIB modules consist of the following:

- A mandatory near-end group of parameters to monitor the local side of the interface (see Figure 11.4). This group must be implemented for DS1, E1, E3, and DS3 facilities, and concerns the following:

    - A set of parameters that describes the local configuration. Examples are the line type, the line status, and so on. The corresponding MIB tables are the `dsx1ConfigTable` and the `dsx3ConfigTable`.[3]

    - A set of performance parameters that allows monitoring of the transmission facility and keeps a history of its behavior over a 24-hour time period. This concerns a number of tables: the `dsx1CurrentTable`, the `dsx1IntervalTable`, and the `dsx1TotalTable`, and their peers in the DS3/E3 MIB.

- An optional far-end group of parameters, which shows the perspective of the far-end state, conveyed to the local end via special signaling. For DS1, this signaling is part of the F-bits mentioned in Section 4.7.1. Since far-end information for DS3 can only be maintained if the C-bit application is supported (see Section 4.7.2), we will only discuss the DS1 far-end information in detail (Section 11.1.7). The far-end portion of the MIBs is very similar to the near-end information, and consists of the `dsx1FarEndCurrentTable`, the `dsx1FarEndInterval-Table`, and the `dsx1FarEndTotalTable`.

    The means by which the performance measurements are conveyed between the two ends of the transmission line is often called *layer*

---

[3]All object descriptors in the DS1/E1 MIB start with the prefix `dsx1`. The DS3/E3 MIB uses the prefix `dsx3`. This is a bit misleading since E1 and E3 facilities are fully covered in these specifications. However, the MIBs have evolved over time. The predecessors of these MIBs did not cover E1 and E3 facilities, and used the prefixes `ds1` and `ds3`. For a number of reasons, these MIBs were completely revised, and new object descriptors had to be used (the simple generic change from `ds` into `dsx`). Full coverage of E1 and E3 was then added, but the object descriptors remained to avoid the need to change implementations.

management, since it is an inherent part of the protocol used in that layer. Figure 11.4 shows this principle.

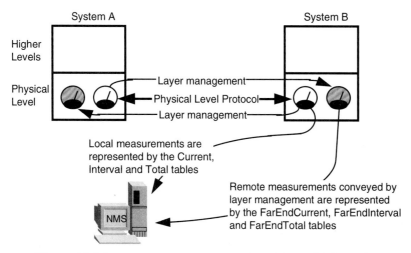

Figure 11.4 Layer management, near-end, and far-end information

- For systems that divide the DS1, E1, DS3, or E3 path into channels of separate information streams (e.g., fractional DS1, fractional DS3), a network manager will also be interested in having access to the list of active channels. The MIBs accommodate this capability. Since such facilities are not widely supported for SMDS, these tables, the dsx1FracTable and dsx3FracTable are not described here.[4]

11.1.5 Physical Level Near-End Configuration and Status Information

The parameters for near-end configuration of DS1, E1, DS3 or E3 lines are used for SMDS as defined in Tables 11.7 and 11.8. They are represented by the MIB tables dsx1ConfigTable and dsx3ConfigTable.

---

[4]We expect fractional T1 access to be more widely supported in the future (see Chapter 5), in which case these MIB capabilities can be used.

dsx1ConfigTable objects	Semantics for DS1 and E1 lines for SMDS		
dsx1LineIndex	(Table index) Another Interface index (see Section 11.1.5.1)		
dsx1IfIndex	Interface index (= ifIndex).		
dsx1TimeElapsed	The number of seconds that have elapsed in the current near-end measuring interval		
dsx1ValidIntervals	The number of available complete interval gauges since (re)start (up to 96; see Section 11.1.6)		
dsx1LineType	The line type (see Section 11.1.5.3). The values for SMDS are:		
	1	other	E1 only
	2	dsx1ESF[773]	DS1 only
	5	dsx1E1-CRC[G.704]	E1 only
dsx1LineCoding	The line coding (see Chapter 4). The values for SMDS are:		
	2	dsx1B8ZS	DS1 only
	3	dsx1HDB3	E1 only
	4	dsx1ZBTSI	DS1 only
dsx1SendCode	Used for loopbacks. SMDS does not support CPE-initiated loopbacks. The value for SMDS CPE is:		
	1	dsx1SendNoCode	
dsx1CircuitIdentifier	The transmission vendor's circuit identifier		
dsx1LoopbackConfig	The loopback configuration. SMDS supports service-provider-initiated loopbacks for DS1 (see Section 11.1.5.3). The values for SMDS are:		
	1	dsx1NoLoop	No loopback active
	3	dsx1LineLoop	Line loopback active (DS1 only)
dsx1LineStatus	The values represent a bit map that can report multiple conditions simultaneously (see Section 11.5.1.2). For SMDS facilities, the values for DS1 and E1 are:		
	1	dsx1NoAlarm	
	2	dsx1RcvFarEndLOF	Receiving Yellow / Remote alarm
	4	dsx1XmitFarEndLOF	Transmitting Yellow / Remote alarm
	8	dsx1RcvAIS	Receiving AIS failure condition
	16	dsx1XmitAIS	Transmitting AIS failure condition
	32	dsx1LossOfFrame	LOF failure condition
	64	dsx1LossOfSignal	LOS failure condition

(continued)

(Table 11.7, continued)

dsx1ConfigTable objects	Semantics for DS1 and E1 lines for SMDS		
dsx1LineStatus	The values represent a bit map that can report multiple conditions simultaneously (see Section 11.5.1.2). For SMDS facilities, the values for DS1 and E1 are:		
	128	dsx1LoopbackState	The near end is looped; the far end is performing a loopback procedure (DS1 only).
dsx1SignalMode	Indicates whether special signaling capabilities are used. The value for SMDS is:		
	1	none	
dsx1Transmit-ClockSource	The transmit clock source. The value for SMDS CPE is:		
	1	loopTiming	The loop is the transmit clock source.
	2	localTiming	The loop clock is lost.
dsx1Fdl	A bitmap describing the use of the Facilities Data Link (the D-bits of a DS1 frame; see Section 4.7.1.1)		
	2	dsx1Ansi-T1-403	Value used for DS1
	8	dsx1Fdl-none	Value used for E1

Table 11.7 Configuration   and   status   of   DS1/E1   transmission   facilities   —   `dsx1ConfigTable`

dsx3ConfigTable objects	Semantics for DS3 and E3 lines for SMDS		
dsx3LineIndex	(Table index) Another Interface index (see Section 11.1.5.1)		
dsx3IfIndex	Interface index (= ifIndex)		
dsx3TimeElapsed	The number of seconds that have elapsed in the current near-end measuring interval		
dsx3ValidIntervals	The number of available complete interval gauges since (re)start (up to 96; see Section 11.1.6)		
dsx3LineType	The line type (see Section 11.1.5.3). The values for SMDS are:		
	5	dsx3ClearChannel	DS3 only[T1.107] [773]
	7	e3Framed	E3 only[G.751]

(continued)

(Table 11.8, continued)

dsx3ConfigTable objects	Semantics for DS3 and E3 lines for SMDS		
dsx3LineCoding	The line coding (see Chapter 4). The values for SMDS are:		
	2	dsx3B3ZS	DS3 only
	3	e3HDB3	E3 only
dsx3SendCode	Used for loopbacks. SMDS does not support CPE initiated loopbacks. The value for SMDS is:		
	1	dsx3SendNoCode	
dsx3CircuitIdentifier	The transmission vendor's circuit identifier		
dsx3LoopbackConfig	The loopback configuration. SMDS does not support loopbacks for DS3 and E3. The value for SMDS is:		
	1	dsx3NoLoop	No loopback active
dsx3LineStatus	The values represent a bit map that can report multiple conditions simultaneously (see Section 11.5.1.2). For SMDS facilities, the values for DS3 and E3 are:		
	1	dsx3NoAlarm	
	2	dsx3RcvRAIFailure	Receiving Yellow / Remote alarm
	4	dsx3XmitRAIAlarm	Transmitting Yellow / Remote alarm
	8	dsx3RcvAIS	Receiving AIS failure condition
	16	dsx3XmitAIS	Transmitting AIS failure condition
	32	dsx3LOF	LOF failure condition
	64	dsx3LOS	LOS failure condition
dsx3Transmit-ClockSource	The transmit clock source. The value for SMDS CPE is:		
	2	localTiming	The clock source is local.

Table 11.8 Configuration and status of DS3/E3 transmission facilities — dsx3ConfigTable

11.1.5.1 Identifying interfaces

The indexing of the dsx1ConfigTable and the dsx3ConfigTable is somewhat special. At first glance, the design of these MIB modules could rely on the use of ifIndex, just as in other MIB modules. However, Tables 11.7 and 11.8 show two index parameters, dsx1/dsx3LineIndex, and dsx1/ds3IfIndex (=ifIndex). In fact, the MIB module specifies that only the dsx1/dsx3LineIndex must be used for indexing the table, while `dsx1/dsx3IfIndex` is just provided as an informational parameter in each row of the table. The need for two parameters is caused by certain configurations where the CSU/DSU functions are separate from a router or host, but where the router or host proxies for the management of the CSU/DSU. See also Chapter 5 and Section 11.2. To understand this design, we use the example shown in the DS1/E1 MIB (see Figure 11.5).

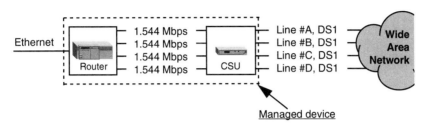

Figure 11.5 Example of a router proxying for a CSU

Figure 11.5 shows a router (not running SMDS) connected to DS1 lines via a CSU. The router provides management information for both itself and the CSU. It retrieves the management information from the CSU through some suitable method.

From an SNMP perspective, the router/CSU combination can be considered as one device (see the dotted line), with one Ethernet interface and four DS1 interfaces, each with its own `ifIndex` value. This implies that the router/CSU interfaces would be invisible from a management perspective. In order to make the router/CSU interfaces visible to NMSs, a new index was introduced, the `dsx1LineIndex`, which is used solely as the index for the configuration and performance measurement tables to identify the DS1 lines. The idea is to allocate two `dsx1LineIndex` values for each `dsx1IfIndex` value: one for the interface on the router side of the CSU, and another one for the public-network side of the CSU. Thus, the configuration and performance measurement tables must have two entries for each DS1 interface (router side and network side), which are identified by the use of `dsx1LineIndex`. The `ifIndex` value is also supplied in each entry to allow linkage with other tables, such as the interfaces table in MIB II. The value of `ifIndex` is the same for the network side and the router side of the CSU. The number allocation rules for `dsx1IfIndex` and `dsx1LineIndex` are as follows.

Case 1a: A router proxies for a CSU/DSU, with DS1 terminated at the CSU/DSU.

An example of this case is when a HSSI interface is used between the CSU/DSU and the router. In this case the `dsx1/dsx3LineIndex` must be identical to the value of `dsx1/dsx3IfIndex`.

SMDS CPE that uses SIP (Chapter 4) falls into this category. The complexity of Case 1b (see below) can be avoided. Table 11.9 shows possible index-value allocations for the configuration of Figure 11.5, with HSSI being used between the CSU/DSU and the router, and the router proxying for the CSU/DSU. Figure 11.6 shows an example for SMDS.

Interface	ifIndex = dsx1IfIndex = dsx1LineIndex
Ethernet	1
Line A, router side	Not directly managed by SNMP
Line A, network side	2
Line B, router side	Not directly managed by SNMP
Line B, network side	3
Line C, router side	Not directly managed by SNMP
Line C, network side	4
Line D, router side	Not directly managed by SNMP
Line D, network side	5

Table 11.9 Example where `dsx1LineIndex = ifIndex`

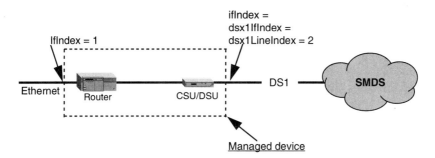

Figure 11.6 Example of Case 1a for SMDS

Case 1b: A router proxies for a CSU/DSU with DS1 on both router and network sides.

The `ifIndex` (and thus `dsx1IfIndex`) will be numbered as usual; that is, all the external interfaces of the managed device are numbered. The `dsx1LineIndex` will be numbered starting with a number greater than the highest value of `ifIndex` on the managed device, and choosing odd numbers for the interfaces on the network side and even numbers for the interfaces on the router side. Table 11.10 shows an example. Figure 11.7 shows an example for SMDS.

Interface	ifIndex = dsx1IfIndex	dsx1LineIndex
Ethernet	1 (not applicable to dsx1IfIndex)	Not applicable
Line #A, router side	2	6
Line #A, network side	2	7
Line #B, router side	3	8
Line #B, network side	3	9
Line #C, router side	4	10
Line #C, network side	4	11
Line #D, router side	5	12
Line #D, network side	5	13

Table 11.10 Example where `dsx1LineIndex` ≠ `ifIndex`

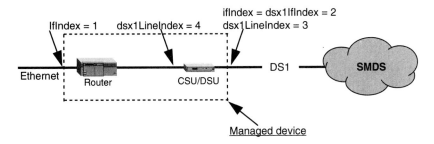

Figure 11.7 Example of Case 1b for SMDS

The MIB for DS3 and E3 interfaces follows the same structure and uses the objects `dsx3IfIndex` and `dsx3LineIndex`.

This case is only applicable to SMDS CPE if SMDS is accessed through the DXI-based protocol discussed in Chapter 5.

Case 2:   The CSU/DSU has its own SNMP agent and is managed directly.

The router-CSU/DSU interface will be allocated its own `ifIndex` value and will be visible to an NMS. Figure 11.8 shows an example for SMDS. We expect that this case will eventually become the most common case for SMDS access methods that use an external CSU/DSU.

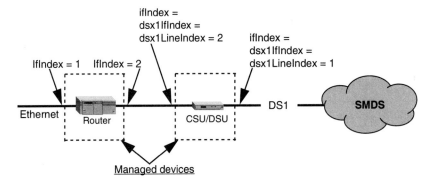

Figure 11.8 Example of Case 2 for SMDS

11.1.5.2　Line Status and Failure Conditions

The failure state of the transmission line can be read from the parameters `dsx1/dsx3LineStatus` in Tables 11.7 and 11.8. Table 11.11 provides a summary of the four error defects that may lead to failure conditions, and that are relevant for SMDS transmission facilities. The description relies mostly on definitions from [773] and [ESIG002].

When a DS1/DS3 Loss-Of-Signal (LOS) defect, an Out-Of-Frame (OOF) defect, or an Alarm Indication Signal (AIS) defect persists for a period of Δt_1, a failure condition is declared, that is, a LOS failure condition, a Loss-Of-Frame (LOF) failure condition, or an AIS failure condition respectively. In case of a LOF or AIS failure condition, a Yellow Alarm signal is transmitted to alert the far end to the problem. The failure condition is removed when the error defect has been absent for a period of at least Δt_2.

This mechanism also applies to E1 and E3 facilities, except that the E1/E3 alarm signal, the Remote Alarm Signal (RAI), is sent immediately upon detection of an error defect at the near end. The E1/E3 far end declares its failure condition when detecting RAI for a period of at least Δt_1 and removes the condition when RAI is absent for a period of at least Δt_2.[5] Removal of the LOS failure condition requires also an average pulse density of 12.5% (DS1, E1, E3) or 33% (DS3). Table 11.12 shows the values of Δt_1 and Δt_2.

As you may conclude from the above description, the error events and alarm conditions have a rather complicated relationship, and may in some cases occur simultaneously. Figures 11.9 and 11.10, based on more detailed explanations in [773] and [ESIG002], provide simplified relationships among the basic alarm conditions.

---

[5]There is no technical reason for this difference. The DS1/DS3 case follows common practice in DS1/DS3 deployments. E1/E3 follow ISDN standards.

Error defect at the incoming signal	Semantics
LOS defect	DS1 and DS3: Detection of 175±75 contiguous pulse positions with no pulses of either positive or negative polarity E1 and E3: Absence of signal transitions for at least 255 pulse positions, or the incoming signal amplitude is 20dB or more below nominal level [G.703] for a period of 1 ms, and cannot be read by the receiver.
OOF defect	DS1: ≥ 2 framing errors within 3 msec, or 2 out of 5 consecutive framing bits are in error. E1: ≥ 3 consecutive frame-alignment errors DS3: ≥ 3 errors out of 16 consecutive framing bits E3: ≥ 4 consecutive frame-alignment errors
AIS defect	DS1: Detection of an incoming signal without framing, but an all-ones pattern for 99.9% of the time for a period $\geq T$, with $3ms \leq T \leq 75ms$ DS3: A special pattern ("stuck stuffing") in the M-frame for a period $\geq T$, with $0.2ms \leq T \leq 100ms$ E1: Upon detection of 512 bits (250µs) with less than 3 zeros, or an all-ones pattern for at least 0.5 ms, or less than 2 zeros in each of two consecutive double frames E3: Detection of an incoming signal without framing, but an all-ones pattern.
Far End Yellow Alarm / Remote Alarm Indication Signal defect	DS1: Receipt of a 1111111100000000_B pattern in the 4-Kbps data link channel in the frame overhead (F-bits) DS3: Special bits (X-bits) = 0 in the M-frame E1: The A-bit has been set to 1. E3: The RAI-bit has been set to 1.

Table 11.11 DS1/E1/DS3/E3 error defects leading to failure conditions

Interface type	Range of Δt_1	Range of Δt_2
SMDS DS1/DS3	2.5 ± 0.5 seconds	15 ± 5 seconds
SMDS E1/E3	0.5 to 3 seconds	1 to 20 seconds

Table 11.12 Ranges of Δt_1 and Δt_2

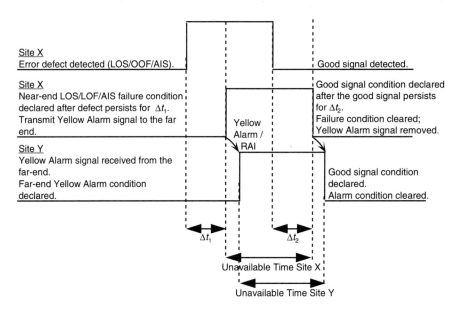

Figure 11.9 Relationships of some DS1/DS3 alarm conditions

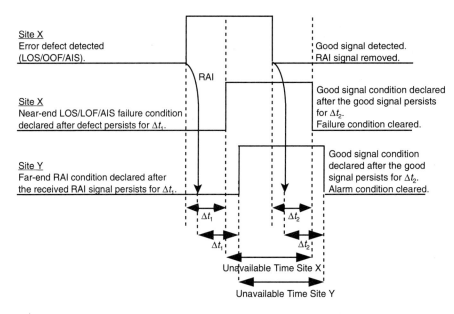

Figure 11.10 Relationships of some E1/E3 alarm conditions

When an interface becomes unavailable, a linkDown trap should be generated to the appropriate NMS, and `ifOperStatus` (see Chapter 10) for that interface should be set to down(2). When the interface becomes available again, a linkUp trap should be sent to the NMS. These alarms are discussed in Chapter 10.

From the two previous figures, the interface failure conditions can now be related to the values of the parameters `dsx1LineStatus` and `dsx3LineStatus` shown in Tables 11.7 and 11.8. Table 11.13 shows how the values of these objects relate to the condition of `ifOperStatus`.

Interface failure condition	Value of dsx1LineStatus and dsx3LineStatus	Value of the interface status ifOperStatus
No failure condition	dsx1NoAlarm(1) dsx3NoAlarm(1)	up(1)
LOS failure condition	dsx1LossOfSignal(64) dsx3LOS(64)	down(2)
LOF failure condition	dsx1LossOfFrame(32) dsx3LOF(32)	down(2)
AIS failure condition	dsx1RcvAIS(8) dsx3RcvAIS(8)	down(2)
Receiving Yellow/Remote Alarm failure condition	dsx1RcvFarEndLOF(2) dsx3RcvRAIFailure(2)	down(2)
Transmitting Yellow/Remote Alarm failure condition	dsx1XmtFarEndLOF(4) dsx3XmtRAIFailure(4)	down(2)

Table 11.13 Failure conditions — `dsx1/dsx3LineStatus` and `ifOperStatus`

11.1.5.3   The Transmission Line Type

The physical interface is characterized by the parameter `dsx1/dsx3LineType`. As discussed in Chapter 4, DS1 facilities use the ESF format, E1 uses G.704 framing with CRC, E3 uses G.751 framing, and DS3 uses the clear channel format as in [773]. Tables 11.7 and 11.8 show the values applicable to the physical facilities for SMDS.

Some configurations in Europe are special in this regard, and are represented with the `dsx1LineType` = other(1). This applies to the scenario where the service provider uses a certain type of Network Termination unit (called *NT1*) in the access line, as shown in Figure 11.11. An NT1 is located on customer premises and represents the demarcation point between the service provider and the CPE. It performs a number of maintenance functions and may also convert between a standard signal (E1) and a proprietary signal. The special case only applies to NT1s that process the G.704 signal.[6]

---

[6]Definitions of NT1s differ in the literature. The device that is meant here in some configurations only processes the electrical transmission signal. This is also referred to as *Line*

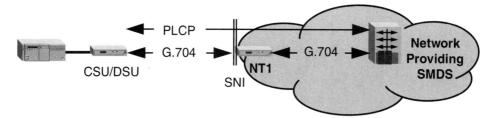

Figure 11.11 E1 Configuration with an NT1 that processes the G.704 signal

What makes this scenario interesting is that NT1s act on the G.704-CRC signal by recalculating the CRC, regardless of whether the received frame was in error. A number of other actions are taken as well. The consequence is that CPE may receive G.704 frames with a correct CRC but with an incorrect information field! Higher protocol levels, for example the PLCP BIP-8, must be used to detect this problem. This situation is not specific to SMDS. The background must be sought in ISDN standards [ETSI233]. A consequence is that the CPE performance measurements on CRC-related errors are not fully reliable in this configuration. Since the DS1/E1 MIB did not foresee this scenario, the only way to flag this access configuration is by setting the `dsx1LineType` to other(1) [ESIG003]. Thus, in order to configure CPE correctly, it is necessary for the service provider to specify the type of NT1 that is used. This information may be obtained through SMDS CNM service (Chapter 12) by inspecting the `dsx1LineType` set by the provider for this SNI.

11.1.5.4 Loopbacks

Loopbacks are used to test the physical transmission lines. The near end requests the far end to loop its received signal back as the transmitted signal. By transmitting certain test patterns over the line, the near end can compare the transmitted and received signals and assess the condition of the line.

For SMDS access through DS1 or E1 (using the NT1), service-provider-initiated loopbacks are supported. Details of the loopback service are discussed in Chapter 12. SMDS does not support loopbacks initiated by CPE. We summarize here the resulting parameter setting at the CPE.

DS1 and E1 loopbacks are service-intrusive; normal traffic is not possible during the test. Typically, this test happens when the interface is already down (reflected by `ifOperStatus`). Otherwise, the loopback initialization will cause the interface to go down, and cause a *linkDown trap* by both CPE and the SMDS CNM Service. Activation of loopback procedures places the interface at the CPE in a testing state; that is, the `ifOperStatus` value should change to testing(3).

Termination, or *LT.* In other configurations, as described here, it also processes the G.704 framing pattern.

For DS1, a loopback procedure between the switching system and the CPE can be invoked, which causes the CPE to loop the incoming signal. This is not supported for E1 facilities. For DS1 and E1, the service provider can activate loopback procedures between the switching system and SNI. The DS1 loopback effects at the CPE that can be read by an NMS follow:

- The dsx1LoopbackState(128) bit in the `dsx1LineStatus` parameter is set, indicating that the near end is looped.

- The value of the `dsx1LoopbackConfig` parameter changes from dsx1NoLoop(1) to dsx1LineLoop(3). This signifies that the CPE is looping the received signal directly back for retransmission. Payload loopbacks, which typically loop through a reframing function, are not supported for SMDS.

11.1.5.5   Other Configuration Information

The remainder of the configuration tables is relatively straightforward. The `dsx1/dsx3TransmitClockSource` shows that DS1 and E1 CPE facilities are looptimed. E3 and DS3 use a local source for the transmit clock.

The `dsx1/dsx3TimeElapsed` and `dsx1/dsx3ValidIntervals` are used for performance measurements that are discussed in the next sections.

11.1.6 Physical Level Near-End Performance information

The purpose of the performance measurement capability is to allow precise diagnosis of the behavior of the physical transmission facilities. For example, if the line is in a certain fault condition indicated by the line status, maintenance personnel can use an NMS to identify the nature of the problem. In nonfault conditions, the quality of the line can be measured. These diagnostics are common to this type of transmission equipment and are not specific to SMDS. However, for SMDS not all capabilities offered by the MIB modules are necessary. In our explanation, we will go through a number of steps (see Figure 11.12):

- A description of the type of gauges that are used (15-minute-interval gauges)

- A definition of particular error events that influence the gauges

- A description of the gauges themselves, and how the error events relate to each of them

- A discussion of how the gauges behave under the LOS, LOF, and AIS error defects that lead to failure conditions described in Table 11.11.

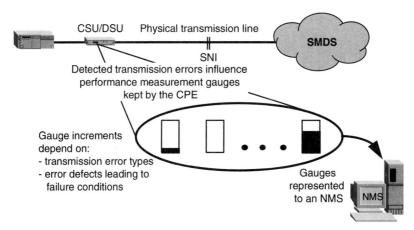

Figure 11.12 Physical transmission performance measurements and MIB representation

11.1.6.1   15-Minute-Interval Gauges

The performance counters for the physical transmission facilities are not represented as continuous counters, as used in MIB II and the SIP MIB. The behavior of the transmission facility is represented as a set of gauges that measure events over 15-minute intervals. The reason for this representation is that transmission equipment traditionally stores performance information as 15-minute counters. Thus, the corresponding objects have the syntax *Gauge* (see Chapter 10), because their value will increase during a measurement interval and be reset to zero when a new interval starts.

The MIB modules support a 24-hour history of 96 measurement intervals plus the current ongoing interval. This means that the measurements represent a sliding window on the most recent 24-hour period plus the current interval, as depicted in Figure 11.13. This technique is used for all counts in the DS1/E1 and DS3/E3 MIBs.[7] The 15-minute intervals may align with the quarter hours on a regular wall clock, but this is not required by the MIB definition.

The progression and the size of the window, relative to the gauges, are determined by the two parameters in the `dsx1/dsx3ConfigTable`, `dsx1/dsx3TimeElapsed`, and `dsx1/dsx3ValidIntervals` (see Tables 11.7 and 11.8). The parameter `dsx1/dsx3TimeElapsed` represents the number of seconds that have elapsed since the start of the current measurement interval. After `dsx1/dsx3TimeElapsed` = 899, the current

---

[7]The reason for this different way of counting as compared with most other MIBs is mostly cultural. The 15-minute-gauge approach has its roots in telecommunications equipment, where historically a 15-minute snapshot represented a sufficient level of granularity for voice applications. SNMP was initially designed for data communications equipment, where the possibility of short bursts of data necessitates performance measurements of a finer level of granularity in order to be meaningful. The burden of this difference will fall on NMSs, which must represent both formats.

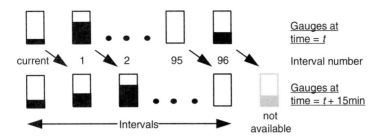

Figure 11.13 DS1/E1 and DS3/E3 MIB use of 15-minute event
gauges

measurement interval is completed; it is renumbered as history-interval number 1, and a new, current interval is started. The `dsx1/dsx3ValidIntervals` parameters indicate how many intervals besides the current interval are available for inspection. There are some situations where this may be less than 96, that is, after a restart of the system, or when a piece of equipment has implemented less than 96 interval registers.

The performance counters for both the near-end group and the far-end group are represented to an NMS by three tables. The near-end group has the `dsx1/dsx3CurrentTable`, the `dsx1/dsx3IntervalTable`, and the `dsx1/dsx3TotalTable`. The Current tables keep the information on the currently ongoing 15-minute interval. The Interval tables keep the history of up to 96 completed intervals. A restart causes the agent to flush all old information and start building up new interval history again, so that fewer than 96 intervals will be available during the first 24 hours after restart. The Total tables represent the sum of the respective gauges accumulated over the last 24 hours preceding the current interval (i.e., the sum of the values in the Interval table).[8]

11.1.6.2   Error Events

The MIB modules describe the performance measurement gauges based on the occurrence of certain error events. We summarize the error types defined in the DS1/E1 and DS3/E3 MIB modules [RFC1406] [RFC1407]. For details, the reader is referred to those specifications and the applicable specifications of the physical transmission facilities.

Error events relevant to SMDS DS1, DS3, E1, and E3 facilities follow:

- *Bipolar Violation (BPV) error event.*

---

[8]It can be argued that the Total tables represent redundant information, since they can be calculated from the Interval tables. However, since current CSU/DSU devices commonly store both the Interval information as well as the Total information, the Total tables were included in the MIBs.

A repetition of the same pulse polarity occurs (without being part of the zero substitution code), or *n* or more consecutive zeros and/or incorrect polarity occur. For B3ZS-coded signals (DS3), *n* equals 3. For HDB3-coded signals (E3), *n* equals 4.

- *Excessive Zeros (EXZ) error event.*
  The occurrence of *n* or more consecutive zeros. For B8ZS-coded signals (DS1), *n* equals 7. For B3ZS code signals (DS3), *n* is 3, and for HDB3 coded signals (E1, E3), *n* equals 4.

- *Line Code Violation (LCV) error event.*
  The occurrence of either a BPV or an EXZ.

- *P-bit Coding Violation (PCV) error event.*
  This event applies to DS3 facilities only. The P-bit is a parity function in the DS3 frame overhead. For details see [773].

- *Path Coding Violation (also abbreviated as PCV) error event.*
  This event applies to DS1 and E1 facilities only, and refers to a CRC error in the ESF or E1-CRC frames.

11.1.6.3 Performance Measurement Tables

Tables 11.14 and 11.15 show the Current, Interval, and Total tables for the near-end performance measurements and apply them to SMDS CPE. The critical gauge that measures time during which the interface is unavailable (Unavailable Seconds, or UASs) corresponds to the Unavailable Time shown in Figures 11.9 and 11.10.

dsx1CurrentTable, dsx1IntervalTable, dsx1TotalTable objects	Semantics for DS1 and E1 lines for SMDS
dsx1TotalIndex	(Table index) Interface index (=dsx1LineIndex)
dsx1IntervalNumber	(Table index) Index for the interval number (see Figure 11.13) Not present for the Current and Total tables
dsx1CurrentESs dsx1IntervalESs dsx1TotalESs	The number of Errored Seconds for this interval An ES is a second with one or more PCVs, or one or more OOFs, or an incoming AIS.

(continued)

(Table 11.14, continued)

dsx1CurrentTable, dsx1IntervalTable, dsx1TotalTable objects	Semantics for DS1 and E1 lines for SMDS
dsx1CurrentSESs dsx1IntervalSESs dsx1TotalSESs	The number of Severely Errored Seconds for this interval For DS1 lines, a SES is a second with 15 or more PCVs, or one or more OOFs, or an incoming AIS.* For E1-CRC lines, a SES is a second with 20 or more PCVs, or one or more OOFs.
dsx1CurrentSEFSs dsx1IntervalSEFSs dsx1TotalSEFSs	The number of Severely Errored Framing Seconds for this interval A SEFS is a second with one or more OOFs, or an incoming AIS.
dsx1CurrentUASs dsx1IntervalUASs dsx1TotalUASs	The number of Unavailable Seconds for this interval
dsx1CurrentCSSs dsx1IntervalCSSs dsx1TotalCSSs	The number of Controlled Slip Seconds for this interval Not applicable to SMDS facilities.**
dsx1CurrentPCVs dsx1IntervalPCVs dsx1TotalPCVs	The number of Path Coding Violations for this interval
dsx1CurrentLESs dsx1IntervalLESs dsx1TotalLESs	The number of Line Errored Seconds for this interval A LES is a second with one or more LCVs, or one or more LOS events.
dsx1CurrentBESs dsx1IntervalBESs dsx1TotalBESs	The number of Bursty Errored Seconds for this interval. Not required for SMDS facilities. If supported, a BES should measure seconds with more PCVs than in ESs, but less than SESs, and without OOF or AIS events.**
dsx1CurrentDMs dsx1IntervalDMs dsx1TotalDMs	The number of Degraded Minutes for this interval. A DM is a minute (not counting SESs) during which the interface is available, but with an error rate between10^{-6} and 10^{-3} errored bps. Not required for SMDS facilities.**

(continued)

(Table 11.14, continued)

dsx1CurrentTable, dsx1IntervalTable, dsx1TotalTable objects	Semantics for DS1 and E1 lines for SMDS
dsx1CurrentLCVs dsx1IntervalLCVs dsx1TotalLCVs	The number of Line Code Violations for this interval

*The SMDS requirement for SESs is a bit stricter than what is typical (≥15 PCVs instead of ≥ 320 PCVs for DS1 facilities, and ≥20 PCVs instead of ≥832 PCVs for E1 facilities). The background is that the SMDS requirement results in an improved bit-error rate.

**In response to a get-request for unsupported objects the SNMP error code noSuchName must be returned.

Table 11.14 Performance measurement gauges in the `dsx1CurrentTable`, the `dsx1IntervalTable`, and the `dsx1TotalTable`

dsx3CurrentTable, dsx3IntervalTable, dsx3TotalTable objects	Semantics for DS3 and E3 lines for SMDS
dsx3TotalIndex	(Table index) Interface index (=dsx3LineIndex)
dsx3IntervalNumber	(Table index) Index for the interval number (see Figure 11.13) Not present for the Current and Total tables
dsx3CurrentESs dsx3IntervalESs dsx3TotalESs	The number of P-bit Errored Seconds for this interval A PES is a second with one or more PCVs, or one or more OOFs, or an incoming AIS. Not applicable to E3 SMDS facilities.*
dsx3CurrentSESs dsx3IntervalSESs dsx3TotalSESs	The number of P-bit Severely Errored Seconds for this interval A PSES is a second with 44 or more PCVs (corresponding to an error rate of ≥10⁻bps), or one or more OOFs, or an incoming AIS. Not applicable to E3 SMDS facilities.*
dsx3CurrentSEFSs dsx3IntervalSEFSs dsx3TotalSEFSs	The number of Severely Errored Framing Seconds for this interval A SEFS is a second with one or more OOFs, or an incoming AIS.
dsx3CurrentUASs dsx3IntervalUASs dsx3TotalUASs	The number of Unavailable Seconds for this interval

(continued)

(Table 11.15, continued)

dsx3CurrentTable, dsx3IntervalTable, dsx3TotalTable objects	Semantics for DS3 and E3 lines for SMDS
dsx3CurrentLCVs dsx3IntervalLCVs dsx3TotalLCVs	The number of Line Code Violations for this interval
dsx3CurrentPCVs dsx3IntervalPCVs dsx3TotalPCVs	The number of DS3 P-bit Coding Violations for this interval Not applicable to E3 SMDS facilities.*
dsx3CurrentLESs dsx3IntervalLESs dsx3TotalLESs	The number of Line Errored Seconds for this interval A LES is a second with one or more LCVs, or one or more LOS events.
dsx3CurrentCCVs dsx3IntervalCCVs dsx3TotalCCVs	The number of C-bit Coding Violations for this interval Not required for DS3 SMDS facilities. Not applicable to E3 facilities.*
dsx3CurrentCESs dsx3IntervalCESs dsx3TotalCESs	The number of C-bit Errored Seconds for this interval Not required for DS3 SMDS facilities. Not applicable to E3 facilities.*
dsx3CurrentCSESs dsx3IntervalCSESs dsx3TotalCSESs	The number of C-bit Severely Errored Seconds for this interval Not required for DS3 SMDS facilities. Not applicable to E3 facilities.*

* In response to a get-request for unsupported objects the SNMP error code noSuchName must be returned.

Table 11.15 Performance measurement gauges in the `dsx3CurrentTable`, the `dsx3IntervalTable`, and the `dsx3TotalTable`

Note that the UASs and SESs gauges may show misleading values if the unavailable time happens at an interval boundary. As stated in the MIB module descriptions, this effect is unavoidable when using discreet (15-minute) gauges.

11.1.6.4   Performance Measurements and Failure Conditions

Table 11.16 summarizes the conditions that cause the counters in Tables 11.14 and 11.15 to increment and relates this to the defects leading to failure discussed in Section 11.1.6.2.

11.1.6.5   Examples

The Current and Total tables are indexed by the interface index. The Interval table is indexed by the interface index and the interval number. For example, the SEFS gauge for the Bodacious Data Corp.'s SNI at Edgar Town

Gauge type	Normal counter increments	Counter increments at defects leading to failure			Failure condition causing UnAvailable Time (UAT)
		LOS defect	OOF defect	AIS defect	
ES (DS1, E1) PES (DS3)	At ≥ 1 PCV/sec		✓	✓	
SES (DS1, E1) PSES (DS3)	At ≥ n PCV/sec DS1: n = 15 E1: n = 20 DS3: n = 44		✓	✓	
SEFS	At ≥ 1 OOF or AIS/sec		✓	✓	
UAS	Each sec of UAT				✓ (Partial seconds are rounded up)
LCV	Each LCV		✓	✓	
PCVs (DS1, E1, DS3)	Each PCV			DS3 only	
LES	At ≥ 1 LCV/sec	✓	✓	✓	

Table 11.16 Summary of conditions to increment performance measurement gauges

Building II (ifIndex.4) and Interval 2 (a half hour before the current interval) is obtained by the following:

    get(dsx3IntervalSEFSs.4.2)

Now consider a situation where this interface experiences a link down, signaled through an SNMP linkDown trap (discussed in Chapter 10). One simple strategy to find the nature of the problem may be to inspect the line status.

    get(dsx3LineStatus.4)

The response may be

    get-response(dsx3LineStatus.4 = 36)

Thus, the line status bits dsx3XmitRAIAlarm(4) and dsx3LOF(32) are set, indicating that the transmission equipment is transmitting a Yellow Alarm due to a LOF failure condition.

Subsequently, we may want to find out how long the facility has been unavailable:

get(dsx3CurrentUASs.4, dsx3TimeElapsed.4)

The response may be

dsx3CurrentUASs.4 = 603, dsx3TimeElapsed.4 = 603

The line has been unavailable for the whole current interval (over 10 minutes). Inspection of the previous intervals may reveal additional unavailable time for this interface. Inspection of the specific gauges can determine the nature of the problem. Recall also that *trap* PDUs may carry additional clues about the nature of the problem, by including appropriate variable bindings in the message.

11.1.7 Physical Level Far-End Performance Information

The far-end portion of the MIBs consists of the dsx1/dsx3FarEndCurrentTable, the dsx1/dsx3FarEndIntervalTable, and the dsx1/dsx3FarEndTotalTable. We will discuss how this capability can be utilized for DS1 facilities. Far-end information for DS1 facilities is conveyed by the 4-Kbps data channel in the ESF frame overhead discussed in Section 4.7. For E1 and E3, facilities, no far-end performance messages are defined between CPE and the service provider [ESIG002]. Thus, the far-end performance tables cannot be used by E1 and E3 CPE.[9] Similar capabilities for SMDS DS3 facilities are only possible for DS3 equipment using the C-bit Parity application. As pointed out in Section 4.7, this application may not be widely supported for SMDS. MIB representation of DS3 far end is therefore not described here. Interested readers are referred to [T1.107a] and [RFC1407].

From a network management perspective, there is a choice in obtaining the DS1 performance statistics measured at the service provider's side of the interface:

- An NMS can inspect the far-end information collected at the CPE, or

- An NMS can use the Customer Network Management Service, where available, to access the measurements directly (represented by the near-end tables; see Figure 11.4).

---

[9]For E1, performance report messages are defined using the Sa5-and Sa6-bits between NT1 and the switching system. These messages have only local significance to the service provider, and are not provided to the CPE.

We recommend that in cases where the network statistical measurements are available both from layer management and from CNM Service, at least the latter should be used, if the performance of the CNM Service is acceptable (for example, the data supplied from CNM must be recent enough to allow comparison with the CPE's local statistics in the near-end tables). The rationale follows:

a. The near-end parameter set is more complete than the far-end parameter set, and is directly comparable with the CPE's measurements.

b. If both the CPE and the public service just supply their near-end information to an NMS, the NMS applications that use this information may be simplified. Near-end performance observed by the CPE can be directly compared with the peer near-end information provided by SMDS CNM Service; no exception routine needs to be implemented to compare near-end and far-end information.

c. This avoids the need for CPE to process and compile the far end information.

11.1.7.1   Physical Level Far-End Performance Information For DS1 Facilities

The 4-Kbps data channel defined in the framing overhead of the DS1 ESF signal is used to carry *Performance Report Messages*, or PRMs. The idea is to send a PRM every second to the other end to report the local state of affairs. In fact, a PRM contains 4 seconds' worth of information, but is sent every second. The PRM overhead consists of an HDLC Unnumbered Information frame, similar to that discussed in Section 5.2 for the SMDS DXI. In this case, the frame is based on [Q.921], also called *LAPD*. The frame is shown in Figure 11.14. For our purpose, the only difference from the frame description in Section 5.2 is that a 2-byte ADDRESS field is required. The COMMAND/RESPONSE bit is set to 1 by the public network and to 0 by the CPE. Furthermore a special address value is used. The resulting header is $001110C0000000001000000011_B$. The FRAME CHECK SEQUENCE (FCS) is as described in Section 5.2. The time between PRMs is filled with FLAGS. The bit order of transmission is the same as explained in Section 5.2.

The INFORMATION field of the frame is always 4 words of 2 bytes each. Each word reports the status of the interface as measured at the far end. With the earlier definitions of error events and conditions, the mapping of these 2-byte words to the MIB far-end table is straightforward. The gauges in the dsx1FarEndCurrentTable can be directly maintained by this information and can be represented to an NMS. The appropriate mapping is shown in Table

11.17. The tables that keep the interval history (dsx1FarEnd-IntervalTable) and the 24-hour totals (dsx1FarEndTotalTable) can subsequently be calculated and maintained.

Byte	8	7	6	5	4	3	2	1	Bit
1	0	1	1	1	1	1	1	0	Flag
2	0	0	1	1	1	0	C/R	0	Address byte 1
3	0	0	0	0	0	0	0	1	Address byte 2
4	0	0	0	0	0	0	1	1	Control
5	G3	LV	G4	U1	U2	G5	SL	G6	Report for time t
6	FE	SE	LB	G1	R	G2	Nm	NI	Report for time t
7	G3	LV	G4	U1	U2	G5	SL	G6	Report for time t–1
8	FE	SE	LB	G1	R	G2	Nm	NI	Report for time t–1
9	G3	LV	G4	U1	U2	G5	SL	G6	Report for time t–2
10	FE	SE	LB	G1	R	G2	Nm	NI	Report for time t–2
11	G3	LV	G4	U1	U2	G5	SL	G6	Report for time t–3
12	FE	SE	LB	G1	R	G2	Nm	NI	Report for time t–3
13									Frame Check
14									Sequence

Figure 11.14 DS1 Performance Report Message (PRM)

One-second report	Semantics	Corresponding dsx1FarEndCurrentTable information
G1 = 1	CRC error event = 1	dsx1FarEndCurrentESs dsx1FarEndCurrentPCVs
G2 = 1	1 < CRC error event ≤ 5	dsx1FarEndCurrentESs dsx1FarEndCurrentPCVs
G3 = 1	5 < CRC error event ≤ 10	dsx1FarEndCurrentESs dsx1FarEndCurrentPCVs
G4 = 1	10 < CRC error event ≤ 100	dsx1FarEndCurrentSESs dsx1FarEndCurrentPCVs
G5 = 1	100 < CRC error event ≤ 319	dsx1FarEndCurrentSESs dsx1FarEndCurrentPCVs
G6 = 1	CRC error event ≤ 320	dsx1FarEndCurrentSESs dsx1FarEndCurrentPCVs
SE = 1	Severely Errored Framing event ≥ 1	dsx1FarEndCurrentSESFs
FE	Frame synchronization Error – set to 0 for SMDS	
LV = 1	≥1 Line Code Violations	dsx1FarEndCurrentLESs
SL	Slip Event detector – set to 0 for SMDS	

(continued)

(Table 11.17, continued)

One-second report	Semantics	Corresponding dsx1FarEndCurrentTable information
LB	Payload loopback – set to 0 for SMDS	
R = 0	Reserved	
U1, U2 = 0	Currently not used	
NmNI	One-second report modulo 4 counter	

Table 11.17 Relationship between the DS1 PRM and the far-end portion of the DS1 MIB

Two exceptions to this pattern can be expected:

- The Yellow Alarm condition is reported by the signal 1111111110000000000_B ($FF00_H$).

- The signal that is used for loopback activation is 1111111101110000_B ($FF70_H$; loopback at the CPE) or 1111111101001000_B ($FF48_H$; loopback at the SNI). The deactivation signal is 1111111100100100_B ($FF24_H$).

The same events are counted for near-end and far-end measurements. Thus, the MIB tables for the far-end information, including their indexing, follow the tables for the local measurements (`dsx1CurrentTable`, the `dsx1IntervalTable`, and the `dsx1TotalTable`) shown in Table 11.17 (LCVs are not used in the far end tables). Of course the names of the parameters differ. Whereas the object descriptors of the near-end gauges start with the prefix `dsx1`, for the far-end gauges the prefix `dsx1FarEnd` is used.

11.2 Management of CSU/DSUs

Chapter 5 discussed common SMDS CPE configurations of a separate CSU/DSU for SMDS access through SIP. The management technique described above can also be applied to this configuration. The analogy is shown in Figure 11.15.

The right-hand scenario depicted in Figure 11.15 has been implemented by several router and CSU/DSU vendors. The router collects management information from the CSU/DSU and subsequently represents it to an NMS. However, for this to work, a protocol is needed to convey management information between router and CSU/DSU. This protocol has been specified by the SIG [SIG002], and is called *DXI Local Management Interface* (LMI). While the LMI uses some of the concepts of SNMP, it is actually not the same. For

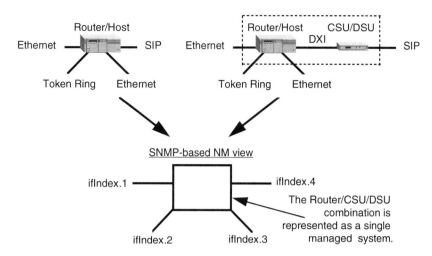

Figure 11.15 Analogy of router and router/CSU/DSU management

example, the LMI packets are carried directly in DXI frames (see Chapter 5) and do not rely on the presence of UDP/IP. This means that the router must process the LMI; it cannot just route IP packets to an NMS, as would be the case with the traditional SNMP. A simplified encoding scheme is used as compared with SNMP. This is possible because the set of managed information is always known. This allows shortcuts in the generic ASN.1 encoding rules, where a parameter is encoded by specifying its type, length, and value.[10]

Chapter 5 shows that with SMDS access through SIP, the DSU processes SIP Levels 1 and 2. Thus, the LMI must provide management information to the router for SIP Level 1 and 2. The LMI does just that. It supports the DS1/E1 MIB, the DS3/E3 MIB, and the PLCP and SIP Level 2 object groups in the SIP MIB. Figure 11.16 summarizes the role of the LMI.

11.2.1 LMI Protocol

The protocol used to retrieve the management information from the CSU/DSU follows SNMP rather closely. The protocol omits the authentication function in SNMP, that is, the use of a community string. The reason is that authentication of outside management requests is performed at the host/router. Since the LMI is running directly over the DXI, instead of over an internetwork protocol such as IP, access to the LMI can only be obtained via the host/router.

---

[10]Some have questioned whether this simplification is worthwhile; it requires a router to support two different management protocols. A more radical simplification could be to implement a periodic "dump" by the DSU to the router of the relevant MIB information in a single large packet.

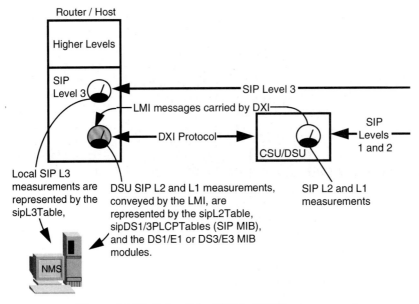

Figure 11.16 Role of the LMI in SNMP management

The LMI PDU set follows the SNMP set of PDUs. However, the LMI PDU encoding does not follow SNMP formats. Table 11.18 shows that the router or host acts in the manager role, issuing LMI GetRequest, GetNextRequest, or SetRequest PDUs. The CSU/DSU acts in the agent role; it responds with GetResponse PDUs on requests, and may issue Trap PDUs.

LMI PDU type	Transmitted by
GetRequest	Router / Host
GetNextRequest	Router / Host
GetResponse	CSU/DSU
SetRequest	Router / Host
Trap	CSU/DSU

Table 11.18 PDUs supported by LMI

As in SNMP, there are two PDU structures: the structure for the LMI Trap PDU, and the structure for the other PDUs. These PDUs are illustrated in Figures 11.17 and 11.18.

As in SNMP, the value for the LMI PDU_TYPE field identifies the PDU that is carried.

The REQUEST_ID, the ERROR_STATUS , and the ERROR_INDEX all fulfill the same function as their SNMP peers.

The OBJECT_COUNT indicates the number of objects that are listed in the

Length in bytes	Field	Value
1	PDU_type	GetRequest(0) GetNextRequest(1) GetResponse(2) SetRequest(3)
1	Request_ID	A modulo 256 counter
1	Error_status	noError(0) tooBig(1) noSuchName(2) badValue(3) genError(5)
1	Error_index	
1	Object_count	
Variable	Object-bindings	Up to 128 object-bindings. See Figure 11.19 and Table 11.19.

Figure 11.17 LMI GetRequest, LMI GetNextRequest, LMI SetRequest, and LMI GetResponse PDUs

Length in bytes	Field	Value
1	PDU_type	Trap(4)
1	Trap_index	coldStart(0) warmStart(1) linkDown(2) linkUp(3) enterpriseSpecific(6)
1	Object_count	
Variable	Object-bindings	Up to 128 object-bindings. See Figure 11.19 and Table 11.19.

Figure 11.18 LMI Trap PDU

PDU. The LMI limits the object count to a maximum of 128. This is in practice not a limitation, since typical SNMP PDUs carry just up to about 20 objects due to the payload size of the supporting protocol.

The TRAP_INDEX identifies the type of trap. The values follow SNMP. The trap authenticationFailure(5) is not supported, since it is assumed that the host/router and CSU/DSU are owned by the same party, and the host/router does not need to identify itself to the CSU/DSU.

The LMI protocol supports objects defined in SNMP MIBs, but applies a simplified encoding scheme. Bytes are transmitted starting with their least significant bit first. The encoding of variable bindings follows the structure shown in Figure 11.19. The LMI encoding rules for the object values are summarized in Table 11.19.

Length in bytes	Field
1	Object_ID Length
n	Object_ID
1	Object_value Length
m	Object_value

Figure 11.19 Object encoding structure for the LMI

Object syntax	Encoding rule
Integer	2's complement
Counter	Binary encoding — 1 to 4 bytes
Gauge	Binary encoding — 1 to 4 bytes
Octet string	Each octet is ASCII-encoded.
Object identifier	Each subidentifier is encoded in 1 or more bytes, so that the most significant bit of each byte indicates whether more bytes will follow. The least significant byte starts with a 0; all others start with a 1. For example the OID 1.129.2 is encoded in 4 bytes with the values 1, 129, 1, 2 respectively.
NULL	Object value absent — object length is 0

Table 11.19 Object syntax and encoding rules supported by the LMI

Note that the NULL (see Chapter 10) syntax must be used in LMI GetRequest and GetNextRequest PDUs to signify the absence of object values.

11.2.2 LMI Managed Information

The LMI protocol supports the objects defined in the SIP MIB[RFC1304], and the DS1/E1 and DS3/E3 MIBs [RFC1406] [RFC1407] that are applicable to SIP Levels 1 and 2.[11]

One object that is absent from the LMI is dsx1/dsx3IfIndex. Recall from Table 11.10 that ifIndex and dsx1/dsx3LineIndex in this scenario assume the same value for SMDS access through SIP. Thus, the LMI does not need to support both.

---

[11]At press time, the LMI was still aligned with a deprecated version of the DS1 and DS3 MIBs (RFC1232, and RFC1233), instead of with their successors. It is expected that the LMI will be aligned with these later versions. Since the update is very straightforward, we present here our interpretation of what this update should look like.

11.2.3 Using the LMI

The LMI by itself is a straightforward specification, but it assumes that the connected host or router proxies for the DSU when responding to NMS requests regarding the SIP Levels 1 and 2. This is sometimes explained as a direct relaying of SNMP requests by the host or router to the DSU. However, the router will have to perform at least the following tasks:

- Encoding conversion between SNMP and LMI PDUs.

- Incoming SNMP requests may concern both parameters local to the router or host and parameters resident on the DSU. Thus, the LMI must be used for the DSU portion, and the local and DSU results must then be combined to construct a single SNMP response.

- The router/host and DSU will need a common understanding of ifIndex and `dsx1/dsx3LineIndex` values. This may imply a translation between values locally used in the DSU, and values used by the router/host. Note also that the fact that the LMI does not support `ifIndex` must not cause the router/host to return a noSuchName error code. Instead the same value as for `dsx1/dsx3LineIndex` must be returned.

Furthermore, it is possible that the router may perform its own polling strategy towards the DSU, independent of the requests coming in from NMSs.

12

SMDS Customer Network Management Service

This chapter describes SNMP capabilities available through SMDS CNM Service that provide a network manager performance and status details beyond the generic system and interface management capabilities described in Chapter 10. SMDS subscription configuration capabilities (see Table 12.1) are also described. We also describe how access to the SMDS CNM Service must be configured, along with the accuracy and availability parameters that can be expected from the CNM Service.

This chapter complements Chapters 10 and 11 and explains SMDS CNM Service as defined in [1062], [1062R], and [ESIG003]. These specifications are very similar, the only major difference being that [1062] and [1062R] define the management of DS1 and DS3 facilities, while [ESIG003] specifies the management of E1 and E3 equipment. SMDS CNM Service is expected to be introduced in phases, in a way that not all capabilities may be immediately available. The first phase recommended for the RBOCs is defined in [1062R], while [1062] and [ESIG003] describe a larger set of capabilities. Potential users should find out from their service provider the exact capabilities that are supported.

This chapter should be useful to readers interested in troubleshooting, performance monitoring, and configuration of SMDS. It contains detailed descriptions and background of the SMDS CNM Service features that should also be useful to designers and implementors of SMDS CNM Service capabilities.

SMDS CNM Service capabilities	Access level	Remarks	Applicable MIB module
1. SIP performance and configuration management	Read-only	Similar to that described for SMDS CPE in Chapter 11. Differences are described in this chapter.	SIP MIB DS1/E1 MIB DS3/E3 MIB
2. SIP Level 1 loopback invocation and testing procedures	Read-only* (DS1) Read-write (E1)	Applies to DS1 and E1 based access.	DS1/E1 MIB
3. SMDS subscription management		Applies to all types of SMDS access.	Subscription MIB
- Subscriber addresses	Read-only*		
- Subscription parameters per SNI:			
• SNI location	Read-only		
• SMDS Provider contact information	Read-only		
• Access Class	Read-only*		
• MCDUs In and MCDUs Out	Read-write		
- Service violation information per SNI, i.e., lost L3_PDUs due to:	Read-only		
• Source Address Validation			
• Access Class enforcement			
• Address Screen violations			
• MCDU enforcement			
- Address Screens	Read-write		
- Group Addresses	Read-write		
- Carrier Pre-selection	Read-write		
- Information on connectivity to other carriers	Read-only		

(*continued*)

(Table 12.1, continued)

SMDS CNM Service capabilities	Access level	Remarks	Applicable MIB module
4. SMDS-specific alarms	-	Applies to all types of SMDS access.	Subscription MIB

* The read-only capability for these parameters may seem restrictive; read-write capabilities could be of significant value to customers in these cases. However, in the engineering process, not only service to customers had to be considered, but also ease of implementation, impact on the provisioning process, and potential impact on billing aspects. Some of these read-only capabilities may be reconsidered in the future.

Table 12.1 Summary of SMDS CNM Service capabilities beyond general system and interface management

For customers of public communications services, the traditional way to manage their use of the service is by telephone calls with the service provider. This method may initially also be used for SMDS. The advantages include personal contact, professional advice tailored to a particular customer situation, and the possibility of rapid troubleshooting in cases where the customer perceives misbehavior of the service. Nevertheless, there will be cases where customers will be better helped by the use of a mechanized interface that allows direct management of the service. Advantages of such an interface include precision, independence of office hours of the service provider, the possibility to program certain routine actions into scripts, and the integration of the management of the public service into the overall management of the customer's private network. The SNMP capabilities described in this chapter are designed to fulfill this role. In practice, a combination of both telephone calls and SMDS CNM Service will provide valuable management service to SMDS customers.

Since the publication of [1062] in February 1992, [1062R] and [ESIG003] were published in March 1993, which, based on experience with [1062], modified some of the SMDS CNM Service capabilities. For example, [1062R] refers to the latest version of the MIBs for the physical transmission facilities. Also, [1062R] has a narrower scope compared with [1062] and [ESIG003]; that is, it focuses on capabilities that are expected to be offered in initial service offerings by the RBOCs. The differences follow:

- MCDUs In and MCDUs Out parameters are read-only in [1062R],

- Carrier Selection or related information is not covered in [1062R],

- The SIP Level 3 diagnostic information described in Section 11.1.1.2 is not supported in [1062R].

All of these capabilities may be provided at a later stage. In this chapter, we intend to cover the broadest set of information, as allowed by the MIBs listed in Table 12.1. Actual service offerings may be different for each service provider.

12.1   The Role of SMDS CNM Service

Chapter 10 explains the customer view of SMDS and how the service is modeled as a single managed resource. Figure 12.1 summarizes this model and shows the key role of the MIB II object `ifIndex` (see Section 10.8). The subscription aspect of SMDS makes this resource different from on-premise resources, such as routers, bridges, and multiplexers. It is therefore important for SMDS users to have access to their SMDS configuration information, and that any subscription changes, such as Address Screen and Group Address modifications, can be made as conveniently as possible, so as to emulate closely the management of on-premise equipment. System and interface management of SMDS and SMDS CPE are very similar, but while SMDS CPE provides a management view as measured by the CPE, SMDS CNM Service shows the service provider's measurements. Comparison of these measurements assists in fault isolation (see Chapter 10).

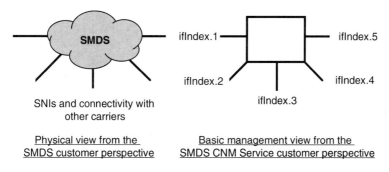

Figure 12.1 Basic service view provided by SMDS CNM Service

In Section 12.2, we explain the rules for access to the SMDS CNM Service, and the configuration requirements by a customer. The capabilities of the SMDS CNM Service and the associated MIB modules have been summarized in Table 12.1. We will discuss each of these components in detail in Sections 12.5 through 12.7. This explanation is preceded by a review of the performance and quality-of-service objectives that are pertinent to the SMDS CNM Service (Section 12.3). An explanation of some common conventions used in SMDS CNM Service is given in Section 12.4.

12.2   Access to SMDS CNM Service

The SMDS CNM Service can be viewed as provided by a server that resides in the service-provider network. For access through SNMP, this server corresponds to the SNMP agent function described in Section 10.7, which also explains that SNMP is supported by UDP [RFC768] and IP [RFC791]. Access to the SNMP agent may be provided through two different types of access paths [1062] [1062R] [ESIG003]. Service providers are expected to provide at least the first option. Figure 12.2 shows the two approaches:

- *An access path that uses SMDS.*
  In this approach, a customer utilizes one or more subscribed SNIs to obtain access to the SMDS CNM Service. The advantage in this approach is that no special communication facilities are needed for the use of the SMDS CNM Service. The disadvantage is that when the SNI is down, access to the SMDS CNM Service is cut off. This violates a key rule in network management: Network management is needed most when the network is in trouble. Access through an SNI follows the rules for running IP over SMDS, as described in Section 8.2.

- *An access path that uses a dedicated leased line or dial-up line.*
  The advantage of this approach is that the SMDS CNM Service is also accessible when the subscribed SNI is down. The disadvantage is that a special line must be used for this purpose. Access through a leased line or a dial-up line requires support of the Point-to-Point Protocol (PPP) [RFC1331].

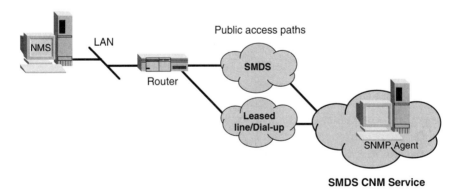

Figure 12.2 Access to an SMDS CNM server

A number of issues are relevant for correct configuration of access to the SMDS CNM Service:

- For proper CPE configuration of IP-level access to the service, it is necessary to consider the IP-level routing and associated IP address allocation by the service provider. Figure 12.3 shows the relevant aspects of the service-provider configuration in this regard and shows an example of a CPE configuration with the NMS attached to a LAN in the customer network.

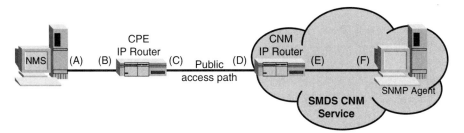

Figure 12.3 IP-level routing and address allocation for SMDS CNM Service access

Access to the SMDS CNM Service, SNMP agent is provided through a router of the service provider. To support IP routing, the router and SNMP agent must share the same NETID in their respective addresses (see Section 8.2.1). In fact, the service provider's router, the SNMP agent, and the CPE IP router share a Class B or Class C address space. This includes the addresses (C) through (F) shown in Figure 12.3. The implications of this configuration are the following:

1. The IP addresses (C) through (F) shown in Figure 12.3 are allocated by the service provider. The addresses (A) and (B) are independent of access to the SMDS CNM Service; they are allocated by the customer within her network.

2. The IP routers in Figure 12.3 that access the SMDS CNM Service, IP router through SMDS actually form a LIS, as explained in Section 8.2.2. As stipulated in the rules for supporting IP over SMDS, all members of a LIS have the same NETID. The implication is that the customer should not use this IP address for communication via SMDS with other IP stations in her network. For that purpose, the CPE router will have to support multiple IP addresses on a single interface (i.e., the SIP port).

- The SNMP agent supports such capabilities as IP *ping*, an ICMP [RFC792] echo procedure to determine availability of a remote IP station. For security reasons, the service provider's SNMP agent and IP router will not support ARP (see Section 8.2). Customers must maintain static ARP and routing tables for access to the SMDS CNM Service.

- Section 10.7 explains that typical SNMP implementations must support an SNMP message size of up to 484 bytes. However, implementations supporting larger SNMP messages do exist. For this reason, [1062], [1062R], and [ESIG003] state the objective that larger packet sizes should be supported to access the SMDS CNM Service.

- Community Strings are used for authentication and access control by the SNMP agent. They can be used to restrict MIB access privileges (read-only or read-write) and to restrict access to specific portions of the MIB. These Community Strings are at least 20 bytes in length, and they form one method of protecting the server from trial-and-error security threats. For the same reason, access is barred for a certain amount of time if excessive authentication failures are detected. The Community Strings are administered by the SMDS CNM Service provider.

- Associated with each Community String, a customer must specify to the service provider the IP address of each NMS that will be used to access SMDS CNM Service. This information is needed to determine where event notifications must be directed. It is also used as an additional level of security. Thus, when a customer wants to use a different or additional NMS for SMDS CNM Service access, its IP address must first be registered with the service provider.

12.3 Performance and Quality-of-Service Objectives

Chapter 7 discusses how certain performance objectives apply to data transfer and service availability in SMDS. This section describes similar objectives for the SMDS CNM Service. This allows effective use of the service by customers and allows vendors of NMSs to design efficient service applications. We explained before that the network management of SMDS, from the perspective of a customer, may be just one part of the management of a larger customer network. Thus, the performance of the SMDS CNM Service should be comparable with the management performance of other portions of that network (e.g., bridges and routers). Moreover, since most of the physical facilities to access SMDS are not on customer premises, and thus not under direct control, good performance of the SMDS CNM Service is a prime requirement.

We will describe the performance and quality-of-service objectives in terms similar to those used in Chapter 7. Different terminology, where necessary, will be explained here. As in Chapter 7, the figures that define the objectives are based on Bellcore specifications [1062] [1062R] to be used by the RBOCs, and apply to RBOC LEC intra-LATA networks. ESIG has recommended the same figures for European service offerings [ESIG003].

Figure 12.4 shows the extent of the service objectives of SMDS CNM Service. These objectives apply to the availability of the SNMP agent and its ability to deduce information from the service-provider network. The availability of management information to customers also depends on the public access path, but this is excluded from the service objectives. For example, [1062], [1062R], and [ESIG003] allow for SMDS CNM Service access paths via SMDS, and via dial-up or leased lines. In the former case, a link-down event on an SNI that is also used for access to the SNMP agent will make it impossible to use the SMDS CNM Service, regardless whether the service is up or down.

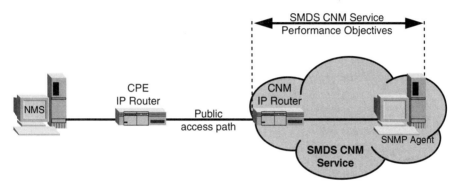

Figure 12.4 Framework for SMDS CNM Service performance and quality-of-service objectives

12.3.1 Availability Objectives

The SMDS CNM Service is planned to be up continuously, matching the scheduled service time of SMDS.

The **SMDS CNM Service Scheduled Service Time Objective** is 24 hours a day, 7 days a week.

Network management is needed most when the network is in trouble. Thus, it can be understood that the objective for the mean time between service outages must be a bit longer than for SMDS; it has been set to 2.25 service outages per year.

The **SMDS CNM Service Mean Time Between Service Outages Objective** is no less than 3893 hours.

Similar to the mean time between service outages, the objective for the mean time to restore is also a bit more strict than that of SMDS.

The **SMDS CNM Service Mean Time to Restore Objective** is no more than 3 hours.

With the previous parameters, the availability of the SMDS CNM Service can be estimated as 3893/(3893 + 3) = .999229979.

The **SMDS CNM Service Availability Objective** is 99.92%.

In other words, the service unavailability should not exceed 6.75 hours per year. Table 12.2 summarizes the SMDS CNM Service availability objectives.

Availability parameter	Objective
Scheduled Service Time	24 hours a day, 7 days a week
Mean Time Between Service Outages	No less than 3893 hours
Mean Time to Restore	No more than 3 hours
Availability	99.92%

Table 12.2 Summary of SMDS CNM Service availability objectives

12.3.2 Delay Objectives

A number of accuracy and delay parameters are important for the customer of SMDS CNM Service. They have an impact on the polling strategy and the interpretation of performance information at a customer NMS (see Section 10.6.4).

An NMS needs to make assumptions about the average response time that can be expected when requests are issued. The response time is influenced by the number of objects that are carried in a request. Data may have to be retrieved from different parts of a network to grant a request. Response times do not include the transmission time between the SNMP agent and the NMS.

The **SMDS CNM Service Response Time Objective** is 5 seconds for 95% of all SNMP requests containing one object. For objects that concern the `serviceDisagreementTable` (see Section 12.6.2.2), the response-time objective is 10 seconds for 95% of all requests.

A special response-time objective is defined for the responsiveness of the CNM Service to SNMP requests for changes in a customer profile. SMDS CNM

Service allows an NMS to request certain changes in subscription parameters, for example, in an Address Screening list. While some changes are easy to accommodate in SMDS, others may require more effort and cause delays between the SNMP set-request/get-response PDUs (request for a service change and confirmation of the receipt of the request), and the time that is required to perform "behind-the-scenes" processing by the service provider before the service change becomes effective. At the time the change becomes effective, an SNMP trap PDU specific for SMDS is usually sent to the NMS. Alternatively, an NMS may rely on a polling strategy to confirm the change. (The procedure for service modifications is described in Section 12.4.2). The subscription change delay is the time between receipt of a valid SNMP set-request PDU and transmission of an SNMP trap PDU to the NMS.

> The **SMDS CNM Service Subscription Change Delay Objective** is no more than 1 hour after receipt of the SNMP set-request PDU requesting the change.

Management information supplied to an NMS is necessarily not exactly current or real-time. Thus, it is important for NMSs and their users to know the average age of the supplied information. The data currentness is defined as the maximum elapsed time since an object value was known to be current.

> The **SMDS CNM Service Data Currentness Objective** for information provided through SMDS CNM Service (see Section 10.6.4) is 30 seconds.[1]

An SMDS CNM Service, SNMP agent that offers SMDS CNM Service will often be implemented as a proxy agent that acts on behalf of multiple devices in the physical network. It can be understood that in practice either the SMDS CNM Service response time or SMDS CNM Service data currentness, or both, are usually not as good as can be expected from SMDS CPE that is managed directly. However, in order to facilitate useful information to customers, the objective for these parameter values is set as low as possible.

Table 12.3 summarizes the SMDS CNM Service delay objectives.

---

[1]Interestingly, [1062R] is ambiguous on this point. It states an *objective* of 180 seconds, but at the same time expresses the expectation that the future *requirement* will be 30 seconds. The background is that the SMDS CNM Service designers specified 30 seconds (the original proposal was 5 seconds) in [1062]. This was based on expected customer needs (e.g., the requirement to have comparable performance between CPE NM and SMDS CNM Service, in order to make the performance information comparable). However, an initial supplier implementation could not do better than 900 seconds, which is fairly useless for performance measurements on high-speed lines. The issue was settled through a paper compromise by the current wording in [1062R].

Delay parameter	Objective
Response Time	≤ 10 seconds (serviceDisagreementTable only) ≤ 5 seconds (all other objects)
Subscription Change Delay	≤ 1 hour
Data Currentness	≤ 30 seconds

Table 12.3 Summary of SMDS CNM Service delay objectives

12.4   Conventions

In this section we describe two conventions in the use of SNMP with SMDS CNM Service. These conventions concern the representation of SMDS addresses in the SMDS Subscription MIB and the use of set-request PDUs to support modifications in subscription parameters such as Address Screens.

12.4.1 Representation of SMDS Addresses

SMDS addresses are in most cases represented in MIB modules with the same syntax as they have in L3_PDUs. The syntax available in SNMP is OCTET STRING. The string is supposed to be represented on an NMS screen by 16 BCD characters. Unfortunately, during implementation of the SMDS Subscription MIB, this syntax was felt to be user-unfriendly, especially since SMDS addresses are used as indices for some MIB tables. Recall from Section 10.7 that object identification in MIB tables that are indexed by a fixed-length OCTET STRING is of the following form:

objectDescriptor.x.y.z

In this example, `objectDescriptor` corresponds to a column in the table, and `x.y.z` is the index, derived from an index object with the syntax OBJECT STRING, and the decimal values of the bytes of the string (x, y, and z). Thus, if an SMDS address with syntax OBJECT STRING and value $C19087585254FFFF_H$ were used as a table index, an object instance in the table entry would be identified by:

objectDescriptor.193.144.135.88.82.84.255.255

While this representation could be hidden behind a more user-friendly Graphical User Interface (GUI) on an NMS, such GUIs are not necessarily always available to customers. For this purpose, a different method has been defined for indexing MIB tables with SMDS addresses. Table indices consisting of SMDS addresses have been defined in the applicable MIB module (the SMDS Subscription MIB), as a set of three[2] separate INTEGERS, consisting of

<Country Code><Destination Code><Subscriber Number>

The ADDRESS TYPE and the trailing ones in the 64-bit SMDS address are not part of this structure. This solution sufficed for most cases, since, as we will see later, the ADDRESS TYPE is usually not needed for table indexing. For example, when we use the previous example as a table index, the result would be

objectDescriptor.1.908.7585254

One remaining issue is the length allocation of the <Destination Code> and <Subscriber Number> portions of the address. This choice can be made per interface and has been left up to each SMDS CNM Service provider, since countries use different national numbering plans. It can be understood that none of the address portions should be allocated as starting with a zero. Thus, a Dutch carrier could use an SMDS address C31201234567FFFF$_H$ in Amsterdam as the following index:

objectDescriptor.31.201.234567

A managed object, smdsAddressCodes, has been defined in the SMDS Subscription MIB to convey these lengths to customers' NMSs (see Section 12.6.2.1). It can be argued that this structure is more human-friendly at the SNMP level. By the same token, it can be argued that this complexity is hard to program in a management GUI that intends to hide details such as object rules from its users, in particular since smdsAddressCodes is an OBJECT STRING. In practice, a human user may have to know how each particular SMDS address is partitioned for this purpose.

To ease this complexity, we recommend that the default length of the <Destination Code> should *always* be three digits in the partitioning of SMDS addresses for SNMP table indices, unless this causes the <Subscriber Number> to start with a zero for a particular address. In that case the <Destination Code> must have the next shorter length that does not cause the <Subscriber Number> to start with a zero. Thus, with this rule, the SMDS address C31201034567FFFF$_H$, when used as an index, is used as follows:

objectDescriptor.31.20.1034567

---

[2]Multiple integers are used, since SNMP integers are encoded in 4 bytes, providing only 9 digits, while an SMDS address is potentially 15 digits long.

12.4.2 Support of the SNMP Set-Request PDU

The SNMP set-request PDU is used to create or delete object instances (for example, entries in an SMDS Address Screening table), and to modify values of existing object instances. The SNMP set-request PDU conveys desired values of object instances. If the request is appropriate, the receiving SNMP agent generates a get-response PDU confirming the new values. An inappropriate request (such as trying to modify an object with an incorrect syntax or an out-of-bound value) will invoke a get-response with the SNMP error code badValue(3). The NMS uses the REQUEST-ID in the PDU (see Section 10.7) to correlate outstanding requests with incoming responses. A service-provider network may be large, and may rely on distributed management of its operations. Furthermore, some operations require human intervention. The implication is that it may take quite long to grant a request to change certain subscription parameters. The performance objectives in Section 12.3 specify up to 1 hour.

It is undesirable to leave an NMS that long in uncertainty on the fate of a set-request PDU. One obvious conclusion at the NMS could be that the set-request PDU was lost! Some NMSs timeout after 5 seconds and resend the request if no responses are received. Thus, a special procedure was designed to overcome this problem. The procedure uses the paradigm of the MIB II objects ifOperStatus and ifAdminStatus (see Section 10.8).

Modifiable SMDS Subscription parameters are represented by two objects, one showing the actual status of the parameter, and the other showing that a change request for that parameter is pending. The object descriptors of these objects have by convention the suffixes Status and StatusChange respectively.[3] Table 12.4 shows their semantics, and Figure 12.5 illustrates the accompanying procedure. Figure 12.5 shows also that a trap PDU (enterprise-specific) is sent to the NMS when a change has been granted or denied.[4]

An interesting situation occurs when entire table rows must be created or deleted. Examples include addition or deletion of addresses in SMDS Address Screens and Group Addresses in the SMDS Subscription MIB. The procedure in Table 12.4 and Figure 12.5 is applied, using a special trick. These cases concern situations where the table columns of interest are also index columns that

---

[3]In some cases the word Status has been left out of the object descriptor. There is no technical significance to this slight inconsistency.

[4]It can be argued that this trap is redundant, since delivery of the trap PDU is not guaranteed due to the nature of the protocol stack supporting SNMP (UDP/IP). Thus, an NMS should still maintain some polling strategy to check the status of outstanding change requests. Appropriate use of trapping and polling in general is the subject of continuous debate. The capability provided here allows for both trap-oriented and polling-oriented strategies at NMSs. We recommend that NMSs maintain some polling strategy to cover cases where traps are lost or not sent appropriately.

Object	Object semantics	Access
somenameStatus	This object indicates the actual value of the entry.	Read-only
somenameStatusChange	This object indicates the desired value of the entry. If the instances of these two objects differ, a request represented by the instance value of somenameStatusChange is pending. The request may be granted or denied. If the two object instances have the same value, no change requests are pending.	Read-write

Table 12.4 Objects used for the Write capability for SMDS CNM Service

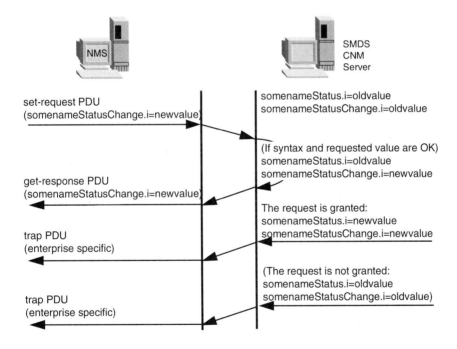

Figure 12.5 Write capability for SMDS CNM Service

determine table entries. Two other columns are used for the Status/StatusChange paradigm. Usually, the INTEGER columns Status and Status/StatusChange determine for each row, whether the table entry is valid(1) or invalid(2), or whether a change is pending, according to the procedure described before. Thus, the addition of an entry in these tables is requested by set(somenameStatusChange.someindex=valid(1))

This request, if granted, will cause the network to add a table entry and fill the index columns appropriately, using the value someindex. Similarly, removal of an entry is requested by setting the StatusChange parameter to invalid(2). If granted, this may cause the row to be removed immediately, or the Status parameter may also assume the value invalid(2).

12.5   Performance Management of a SIP Interface

Performance management for the SNIs represented by SMDS CNM Service is largely identical with that on the CPE side of the interface. In this section, we only discuss the differences.

12.5.1 SIP Level 3 Performance Statistics

The Case Diagram for SIP Level 3 counters on the two sides of the SNI differ (compare Figures 11.1 and 12.6). The reason for this difference is that the CPE side of the interface performs only monitoring of correct protocol behavior at the SIP port. On the other hand, the network side of the interface must also enforce the service aspects defined by SMDS. Thus, service violations will influence the Case Diagram. These service violations are represented by objects defined in the Subscription MIB, which will be discussed in the next sections.

The set of error counters in the Case Diagram also illustrates the order of precedence in error processing. All error counters except parts 3 and 4 of the sipL3Errors (Section 11.1.1.1) apply to L3_PDU header checks (BOM or SSM Segment Types; see Section 4.6.3). Thus, the sipL3Invalid-AddressTypes check is performed first, and the carrierBlocking-L3PDUs check is performed last. The sipL3Errors counter is incremented due to events shown in Table 12.5. This table also correlates the order of processing of SIP L3_PDU syntax errors with the error types represented by sipL3PDUErrorType (Section 11.1.1.2).

As explained in Section 11.1.1.1, it is not always possible in practice to count the sipL3UnrecognizedGAs and sipL3Unrecognized-IndividualDAs. This is unfortunate, since counting of these events by the public service (and providing the counters via SMDS CNM Service) can help to isolate certain types of configuration errors by SMDS customers. An example is the use of an errored Destination Address in a CPE routing table.[5] If these

---

[5]One possibility to address this problem would be a number-authentication service provided by the SMDS service-provider, where the service provider would verify a list of SMDS addresses to confirm their existence.

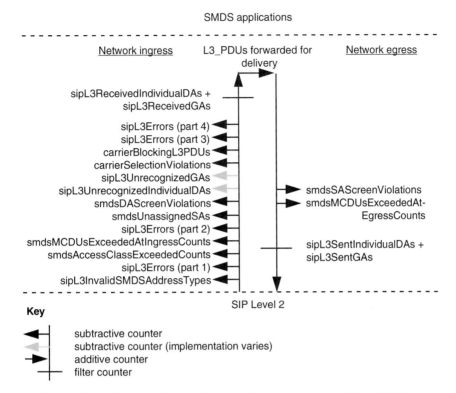

Figure 12.6 SIP Level 3 Case Diagram for a network providing SMDS

sipL3Errors part	Type of error events	sipL3PDUErrorType (Section 11.1.1.2)	Applicable Segment Types (Section 4.6.3)
1	Source or Destination Address syntax error, invalid Buffer Allocation Size field value	1, 2	BOM, SSM
2	Header Extension syntax errors	4, 5, 6, 7, 8	BOM, SSM
3	Beginning-End Tags mismatch, incorrect Length, Buffer Allocation Size / Length mismatch	9, 10, 11	EOM, SSM
4	Message Receive Interval timeout	12	-

Table 12.5 `sipL3Errors` order of precedence

counters are not supported, the SNMP error code noSuchName will be returned on requests for these counters.

12.5.2 SIP Level 2 and PLCP Performance Statistics

Performance management at SIP Level 2 and the PLCP level is identical with that for CPE.

12.5.3 SIP Level 1 Performance Statistics

Performance management of the physical transmission facilities is almost the same as for CPE. The differences follow:

- The parameters Bursty Errored Seconds (BESs) and Degraded Minutes (DMs) are not supported [773].

- For DS1, a local source is used for the transmit clock.

- The far-end measurements, even if conveyed to SMDS, are not represented in SMDS CNM Service. The assumption is that NMSs at the customer premises can most often extract them directly from the CPE.

- The network providing SMDS can activate and deactivate loopback tests for DS1 and E1 lines (see Chapter 11).

12.5.4 DS1 and E1 Loopback Service

Loopbacks are used to test transmission lines. The near end requests the far end to loop its received signal back as the transmitted signal. By transmitting certain test patterns over the line, the near end can compare the transmitted and received signals and assess the condition of the line by checking the line status and running performance measurements, as discussed in Section 11.1.5.

There are two kinds of loopback. A line loopback causes the far end to loop the received signal back directly for retransmission. In contrast, a payload loopback is typically looped through a reframing function. Payload loopbacks are not supported for SMDS.

SMDS does not support CPE-initiated loopbacks.[6] Loopbacks initiated at the service provider's side of the interface are supported for E1 and DS1 facilities only. These loopbacks *disrupt* normal SMDS service; during a loopback test, SMDS PDUs cannot be transmitted or received.

---

[6]This reflects a long-held carrier tradition of hesitancy towards the concept of a sophisticated customer environment.

For SMDS, the purpose of loopback tests is to verify physical connectivity between the SMDS serving switching system and CPE. If connectivity is lost, it must be determined whether the problem is a service-provider problem, or at the customer premises. Recall that the SNI is the demarcation between CPE and the service provider. In the DS1 case, the SNI is formed by a DS1 interface connector, also called *Smart Jack*. For E1s, the SNI is the NT1.[7]

The physical access path extends beyond the SNI (see for example Section 4.7). By performing loopback procedures on the service provider's portion, a problem with the service-provider transmission facilities can be confirmed and assessed. If no problem is found, a problem at the customer premises is implied. This type of loopback is supported for DS1 and E1 facilities. By also performing loopback procedures between the SMDS serving switching system and the CPE, a problem at the customer premises can also be confirmed and assessed. This type of loopback is supported for DS1 facilities only [773] [ESIG002]. Figure 12.7 shows the general principle.

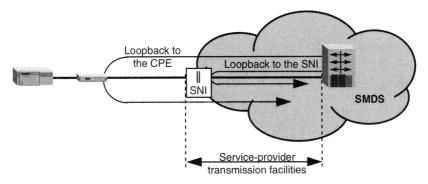

Figure 12.7 Two types of loopback

SMDS DS3 and E3 facilities do not support loopback [773] [ESIG002]. One reason is that transmission systems providing SMDS via these access facilities are expected to have intelligence that allows maintenance procedures that do not interrupt service and that can be used to test the performance of the line. In addition, the distance between CPE and service provider is expected to be relatively short: about 450 feet for DS3. Also, no standard method exists for DS3 and E3 loopbacks.

The CPE and SNI loopback procedures and possible DS1/E1 MIB parameter settings are shown in Figures 12.8 and 12.9.

---

[7]Definitions of NT1s differ in the literature. The device that is meant here in some configurations only processes the electrical transmission signal. This is also referred to as *Line Termination*, or LT. In other configurations, as described in Section 11.1.5.3, it also processes the G.704 framing pattern.

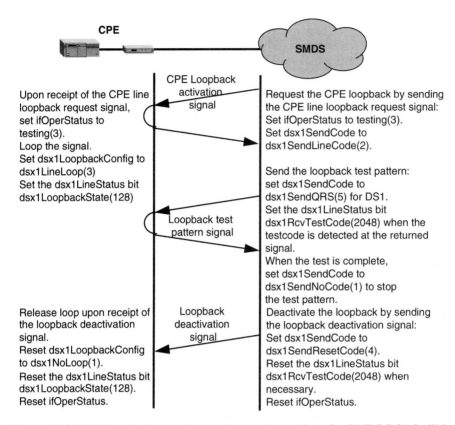

Figure 12.8 CPE loopback procedure and parameter settings for SMDS DS1 facilities

Note that customers who access SMDS CNM Service via an SNI and not via a dialup or leased line can only observe the loopback behavior of that SNI at the CPE, since loopback is a service-intrusive test and causes the SNI to go down.

For DS1, a customer can only ask for loopback tests via a telephone call with service personnel. (See the managed object `smdsContact` in Section 12.6.2.) The loopback signals generated by the service provider are Performance Report Messages (PRMs; see Chapter 11) with the following bit patterns:

1111111101110000_R ($FF70_H$)   DS1 loopback at the CPE
1111111101001000_R ($FF48_H$)   DS1 Smart Jack loopback activation
1111111100100100_R ($FF24_H$)   DS1 loopback deactivation

The test pattern is the *Quasi Random Signal*, as defined in [T1.403] and [54] and is carried in the DS1 payload. The activation signal is repeated at least ten times and may be transmitted continuously during the loopback test to maintain the loopback state and avoid the ESF data link idle pattern. The

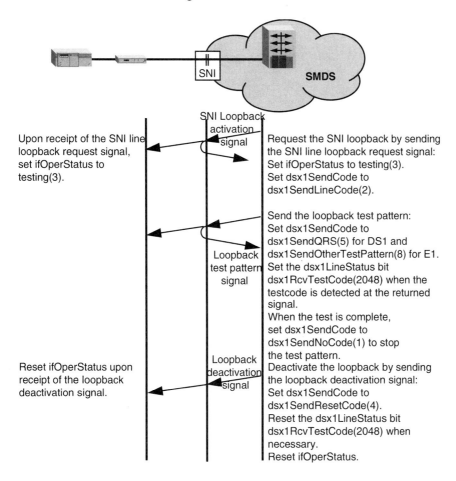

Upon receipt of the SNI line loopback request signal, set ifOperStatus to testing(3).

SNI Loopback activation signal

Request the SNI loopback by sending the SNI line loopback request signal:
Set ifOperStatus to testing(3).
Set dsx1SendCode to dsx1SendLineCode(2).

Send the loopback test pattern:
Set dsx1SendCode to dsx1SendQRS(5) for DS1 and dsx1SendOtherTestPattern(8) for E1.
Set the dsx1LineStatus bit dsx1RcvTestCode(2048) when the testcode is detected at the returned signal.
When the test is complete, set dsx1SendCode to dsx1SendNoCode(1) to stop the test pattern.

Loopback test pattern signal

Reset ifOperStatus upon receipt of the loopback deactivation signal.

Loopback deactivation signal

Deactivate the loopback by sending the loopback deactivation signal:
Set dsx1SendCode to dsx1SendResetCode(4).
Reset the dsx1LineStatus bit dsx1RcvTestCode(2048) when necessary.
Reset ifOperStatus.

Figure 12.9 SNI Loopback procedure and parameter settings for SMDS DS1 and E1 facilities

loopback may also be deactivated by recurrence of two consecutive regular PRMs. The loopbacks to the Smart Jack will not cause the CPE to go in a loopback state, but will cause the interface to go down. The behavior on the service provider's side of the interface is as shown in Figure 12.8.

For E1, the loopback is activated and deactivated by manipulation of the Sa5 and Sa6 bits in the E1-framing overhead (see Section 4.7 and Table 12.6) [ETSI233]. No loopback to the CPE is defined [ESIG002]. The loopback is activated at detection of eight consecutive loopback activation commands. It is released at eight consecutive deactivation commands, or at any other eight consecutive signals other than the loopback activation command.

Function	Relevant E1-CRC-4 submultiframe bits sent by the service provider		
	All A-bits	All Sa5-bits	Sa6-bit pattern
Loopback activation:			
Loopback 1 (a portion of the service-provider's transmission facilities)	1	0	1111
Loopback 2 (the service-provider's transmission facilities from SS to SNI)	1	0	1010*
Loopback deactivation	Don't Care	0	0000

*These two codes invoke loopbacks over different portions of the transmission facilities of the service provider with the purpose of further isolating any problems in the circuit [ETSI233]. This difference does not impact the SMDS customer.

Table 12.6 E1 Loopback activation and deactivation on the service provider transmission facilities

For E1, a service provider generated loopback can also be requested via SNMP [ESIG003], directly from an NMS by SNMP *set* commands, but only if access to the SMDS CNM Service does not depend on the circuit that needs to be tested:

set(dsx1SendCode=dsx1SendLineCode)   (Request activation[8])
set(dsx1SendCode=dsx1SendOtherTestPattern) (Request test signal)
set(dsx1SendCode=dsx1SendResetCode)   (Request deactivation)

In summary, Tables 12.7 and 12.8 show the SMDS CNM Service object settings that relate to the use of the loopback service. The CPE side is summarized in Figures 12.8 and 12.9, and in Chapter 11.

12.6 Subscription Management

The MIB module that is defined for SMDS subscription management is referred to as the *Subscription MIB* [Cox]. This MIB module is defined as enterprise-specific, which means that it is not subject to standardization by the IETF.

The Subscription MIB is reproduced in Appendix B. While this module was written to be self-explanatory, the module as a whole turned out to be quite

---

[8]The dsx1SendCode does not distinguish between the different loopbacks shown in Table 12.6. Service providers should specify which loopback is invoked. We recommend that the loopback 2, which extends from SS to the NT1, be invoked in this procedure, since it provides the most information to customers.

dsx1ConfigTable objects	Semantics for DS1 and E1 lines for SMDS	
dsx1SendCode	Used for loopbacks. The values are:	
	1	dsx1SendNoCode
	2	dsx1SendLineCode (start line loopback)
	4	dsx1SendResetCode (stop loopback)
	5	dsx1SendQRS (the test pattern used for SMDS DS1 facilities - Quasi Random Signal)
	8	dsx1OtherTestPattern (the test pattern used for SMDS E1 facilities)
dsx1LoopbackConfig	The loopback state. The value is:	
	1	dsx1NoLoop (only the CPE side is looped)
dsx1LineStatus	The line-status bit map is as described in Section 11.1.5. One additional state applies:	
	2048	dsx1RcvTestCode (The transmitted loopback test pattern is received back.)

Table 12.7   Use of the `dsx1ConfigTable` objects in SMDS CNM Service for loopbacks

dsx3ConfigTable objects	Semantics for DS3 and E3 lines for SMDS	
dsx3SendCode	Used for loopbacks. The value is:	
	1	dsx3SendNoCode
dsx3LoopbackConfig	The loopback state. The value is:	
	1	dsx3NoLoop

Table 12.8   Use of the `dsx3ConfigTable` objects for loopbacks

large and inherently complex. These sections are meant as additional guidance to the reader. Also, further refinements are still expected to be made by Bellcore, so both SMDS CNM Service Agent implementors, as well as implementors of applications that use this MIB module, should also consult the latest version of this module. (See Appendix D on how to obtain electronic or paper copies.)

The Subscription MIB contains a number of submodules. We will discuss each of these components in more detail in the subsequent sections. Table 12.9 summarizes these components.

12.6.1 SMDS Subscriber Addresses

For SMDS subscription management by SNMP, it is necessary to correlate subscribed SMDS addresses of particular SNIs with the interface index

SMDS subscription management capabilities	Remarks	Applicable portion of the Subscription MIB
1. Subscriber addresses	Correlates SMDS Individual Addresses with SNIs.	subscriberAddressesTable See Section 12.6.1.
2. Subscription information per SNI:	Provided information: • SNI location • SMDS Provider contact information • Access Class • MCDUs In and MCDUs Out	smdsSubscrTable See Section 12.6.2.
3. Lost L3_PDUs due to service violations: • Source Address Validation • Access Class enforcement • Address Screen violations • MCDU enforcement	Maintains counters and a log for subscription violations for each SNI.	smdsSubscrTable serviceDisagreementTable See Section 12.6.2.
4. Address Screens	Relates Address Screens with SNIs and provides access to the contents of the screens.	Address Screening group See Section 12.6.3.
5. Group Addresses	Provides access to the contents of Group Addresses.	groupAddressing group See Section 12.6.4.
6. Carrier Pre-selection and information on connectivity to other carriers	Service information for each SNI pertinent to traffic when IECs are used	xaSmds group See Section 12.6.5.
7. SMDS-specific alarms	Issued when changes have been made to a subscription profile.	Enterprise-specific traps; see Section 12.7.

Table 12.9 Summary of SMDS subscription management capabilities

(ifIndex) of the managed resource. As we have seen in other MIB modules, ifIndex is a key to many MIB tables. However, the value of ifIndex is locally assigned (within an SNMP agent) and may, technically, even change over time. On the other hand, an SMDS address is a fixed, subscribed parameter.

Thus, the two values must be correlated, which is the purpose of the subscriberAddressesTable, shown in Table 12.10.

subscriberAddressesTable objects	Semantics
subCountryCodeIndex subDestinationCodeIndex subSubscriberNumberIndex	(Table index) Three portions of an SMDS address used for indexing of this table (see Section 12.4.1)
subscriberAddressesOnSNI	The complete SMDS address*
subscriberAddressesIndex	SNI index (= ifIndex)

    * Note that this object is, strictly speaking, redundant, since the information is already contained in the first three objects. The inconvenience of the difference in syntax between the triplet and the full address, an ongoing debate ("Who is in Grant's tomb?") in the IETF on a related issue, and the insistence of some implementors resulted in this extra object. The same redundancy occurs in other SMDS Subscription MIB tables indexed by SMDS addresses.

Table 12.10 Matching subscribed SMDS addresses with ifIndex values — subscriberAddressesTable

The SMDS Subscription MIB correlates the local (network) value of ifIndex with SMDS addresses that are subscribed to for that interface but that have significance at the remote (customer) end. The service-provider side of the interface has no addressing information that is of significance for a customer.

The table produces for a given SMDS address the matching ifIndex value, and thus is indexed by an SMDS address. For example, for the Bodacious Data Corp., the ifIndex values for their SNIs subscribed to with FasterTel (see Figures 10.1 and 10.17) are obtained as follows:

get-next (subCountryCodeIndex, subDestinationCodeIndex,
          subSubscriberNumberIndex, subscriberAddressesIndex)

returns a get-response PDU with

subCountryCodeIndex.1.516.5552107 = 1
subDestinationCodeIndex.1.516.5552107 = 516
subSubscriberNumberIndex.1.516.5552107 = 5552107
subscriberAddressesIndex.1.516.5552107 = 4

Subsequent get-next commands would return

subCountryCodeIndex.1.516.5552286 = 1
subDestinationCodeIndex.1.516.5552286 = 516
subSubscriberNumberIndex.1.516.5552286 = 5552286
subscriberAddressesIndex.1.516.5552286 = 17
subCountryCodeIndex.1.516.5552642 = 1
subDestinationCodeIndex.1.516.5552642 = 516
subSubscriberNumberIndex.1.516.5552642 = 5552642
subscriberAddressesIndex.1.516.5552642 = 1

Further get-next commands do not provide information on these objects. This shows that this subscriber has three SNIs, where a single SMDS address is assigned to each SNI. Thus, the `ifIndex` values are 4, 17, and 1. Of course, a particular entry can also be looked up directly by

get (subscriberAddressesIndex.1.516.5552642)

It is also possible to look up a particular SMDS address for a given SNI or `ifIndex` value. The current table is not optimized for that operation, since it is anticipated that the customer network manager usually knows the subscribed address and only needs information as described above. So this lookup uses a "table walk" until the SMDS address matching a particular `ifIndex` value is found (or until the table is completely walked through). This procedure represents some overhead, but was felt to be more efficient than the introduction of an additional table, indexed by `ifIndex`. The reason is that the average length of a particular subscriber MIB view for this table is small, and the need for this operation is relatively infrequent.

12.6.2 Management of General Subscription Parameters

The SMDS CNM Service provides access to the basic subscription parameters for a given SNI. In addition, it also provides measurements of traffic discarded due to service violations. The portions of the SMDS Subscription MIB that are used for this purpose are the SMDS Subscription Parameters and Violations group and the Service Disagreements group.

12.6.2.1 SMDS Subscription Parameters and Violations

The purpose of the SMDS Subscription Parameters and Violations group is to provide access to the basic subscription parameters for a given SNI. Specifically, it allows read-only access to the subscribed Access Class and the subscribed MCDUs In and MCDUs Out. These subscription parameters are organized in a table called the `smdsSubscrTable`.

The objects representing the MCDUs In and MCDUs Out subscription (`smdsMCDUsIn` and `smdsMCDUsOut`) are actually defined as read-write, which allows subscribers to dynamically change these subscription parameters.

Traffic that is discarded because of service violations is measured as a set of continuous counters that are part of the `smdsSubscrTable`. The table also provides the information on how to use SMDS addresses for table indexing. The table is summarized in Table 12.11.

smdsSubscrTable objects	Semantics		
smdsSubscrIndex	(Table index) SNI index (= ifIndex)		
smdsContact	Contact information of the SMDS service provider		
smdsSNILocation	The location of the local switching system for this SNI		
smdsAccessClass	The subscribed access class[a]:		
	1	noClass	DS1, E1, lower-speed access
	2	class4	SIR=4Mbps (DS3, E3)
	3	class10	SIR=10Mbps (DS3, E3)
	4	class16	SIR=16Mbps (DS3, E3)
	5	class25	SIR=25Mbps (DS3, E3)
	6	class34	SIR=34Mbps (DS3)
smdsMCDUsIn smdsMCDUsInChange	The subscribed MCDUsIn.[b] Values can be:		
	1	mcdusIn1	
	2	mcdusIn16	
smdsMCDUsOut smdsMCDUsOutChange	The subscribed MCDUsOut.[b] Values can be:		
	1	mcdusOut1	
	2	mcdusOut16	
smdsUnassignedSAs	Discarded L3_PDUs due to Source Address Validation		
smdsAccessClass-ExceededCounts	Discarded L3_PDUs due to Access Class enforcement		
smdsSAScreenViolations	Discarded L3_PDUs due to Source Address Screening		
smdsDAScreenViolations	Discarded L3_PDUs due to Destination Address Screening		
smdsMCDUsExceeded-AtIngressCounts	Discarded L3_PDUs due exceeding the MCDUs In.		
smdsMCDUsExceeded-AtEgressCounts	Discarded L3_PDUs due exceeding the MCDUs Out[c]		

(continued)

(Table 12.11, continued)

smdsSubscrTable objects	Semantics
smdsAddressCodes	Textual information telling how the SMDS address is partitioned for table indexing.

^a The descriptors of the values of this object do not correspond with the convention in Section 3.4.6 (Class 1, Class 2, etc.). Theoretically, this may be slightly misleading, since, in the future, new access classes could be defined with the same SIR but different burstiness.

^b The write capability, if supported, uses the procedure in Section 12.4.2.

^c Interestingly, a correct implementation of the service should cause this counter to remain at 0 at all times(!). The reason for having this managed object may be a result of overengineering of SMDS operations and the SMDS CNM Service.

Table 12.11 Management of General Subscription Parameters and Violations — smdsSubscrTable

The parameters smdsContact and smdsSNILocation identify for each SNI who to call in case of questions or trouble, and from where the SNI is served. Note that the similar MIB II [RFC1213] parameters sysContact and sysLocation must be used when the service provider designates a single point of contact for subscribers for all SNIs. The parameter smdsContact provides more detailed information when the SMDS CNM Service represents a geographically large area with maintenance personnel spread over different locations. Similarly, while sysLocation represents the location of the SNMP agent, smdsSNILocation provides the more detailed SNI serving location for multiswitch networks.

The next six parameters are continuous counters of violations of subscription parameters and count discarded L3_PDUs. (See the Case Diagram in Figure 12.5.)

The remaining object in this group, smdsAddressCodes, provides the information needed to correctly partition the SMDS address for table indexing, as discussed in Section 12.4.1.

The table is indexed by the equivalent of ifIndex.

As an example, consider again the Bodacious Data Corp. with its three FasterTel SNIs shown in Figure 10.1. A read-out of the subscription parameters would be as follows (the ifIndex values for the SNIs are 1, 4, and 17, respectively, as deduced via the subscriberAddressesTable):

```
get-next (smdsSubscrIndex, smdsContact, smdsLocation,
        smdsAccessClass, smdsMCDUsIn, smdsMCDUsInChange,
        smdsMCDUsOut, smdsMCDUsOutChange)
```

which returns a get-response with:

```
smdsSubscrIndex.1 = 1
smdsContact.1 = "J.P. Kassie (516) 123-4567"
```

```
smdsLocation.1 = "Pennsylvania Ave. 1600, Martha's Vineyard"
smdsAccessClass.1 = 5
smdsMCDUsIn.1 = 1
smdsMCDUsInChange.1 = 1
smdsMCDUsOut.1 = 1
smdsMCDUsOutChange.1 = 1
```

The next two get-next commands would produce the remaining instances of these parameters for this subscriber:

```
smdsSubscrIndex.4 = 4
smdsContact.4 = "J.P. Kassie (516) 123-4567"
smdsLocation.4 = "Pennsylvania Ave. 1600, Edgar Town, Martha's
       Vineyard"
smdsAccessClass.4 = 1
smdsMCDUsIn.4 = 1
smdsMCDUsInChange.4 = 1
smdsMCDUsOut.4 = 1
smdsMCDUsOutChange.4 = 1
smdsSubscrIndex.17 = 17
smdsContact.17 = "Tabitha Luilak (516) 234-5678"
smdsLocation.17 = "Cutty Hunk Alley, Cutty Hunk"
smdsAccessClass.17 = 1
smdsMCDUsIn.17 = 1
smdsMCDUsInChange.17 = 1
smdsMCDUsOut.17 = 1
smdsMCDUsOutChange.17 = 1
```

Any further get-next on this table would not produce useful information, since this subscriber has only three SNIs (and SNIs of other subscribers are excluded from her view). The two Change objects show, for example,

```
smdsMCDUsIn.17 = smdsMCDUsInChange.17
smdsMCDUsOut.17 = smdsMCDUsOutChange.17
```

This means that no change request is being processed for these subscription parameters.

Periodic polling of the counters will uncover any irregular behavior of the CPE with regard to these subscription parameters and as perceived by SMDS. For example, regular inspection of smdsAccessClassExceededCounts aids in the understanding of the access class that is needed for this interface.

While this seems a bit cumbersome at first glance, the precision of this procedure lends itself to hiding it behind a user-friendly interface. A hypothetical example is shown in Figures 12.10 and 12.11. Note that the Subscriber Addresses column in Figures 12.10 also requires the use of the subscriber-AddressesTable.

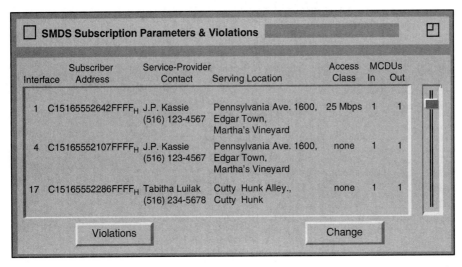

Figure 12.10 Example of user-friendly representation of the subscription information in the smdsSubscrTable

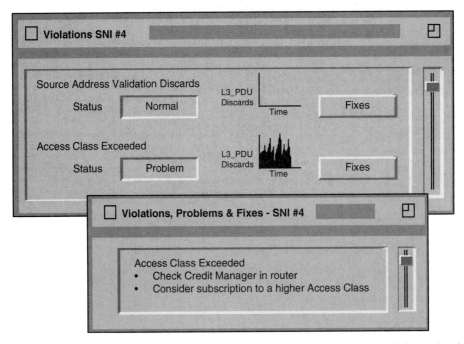

Figure 12.11 Example of user-friendly representation of service violation information in the smdsSubscrTable

12.6.2.2   Service Disagreements

The purpose of the *Service Disagreements* group is to relate three types of service violations with the Source and Destination Address pair of the most recent L3_PDU that caused these types of errors. It is considered sufficient to provide only the most recent case of these errors, since it is likely that the error is caused by configuration errors or malfunctioning equipment and is therefore repetitive. The service violations are: (1) Address Screen violations caused by the Source Address, (2) Address Screen violations caused by the Destination Address, and (3) Source Address invalidation. This function is represented to the SMDS CNM Service user by a single table and may help to pinpoint configuration errors or malfunctioning CPE.

The table, the serviceDisagreementTable, is maintained by SNI, and is indexed by SNI and the type of service violation (see Table 12.12).

serviceDisagreementTable objects	Semantics	
sniSDIndex	(Table index) SNI index (= ifIndex)	
serviceDisagreementType	(Table index) The type of service violation. The possible values are:	
	1	SA Screen violation
	2	DA Screen Violation
	3	Invalid SA for this SNI
serviceDisagreementSA	The Source Address of the most recent L3_PDU causing the error	
serviceDisagreementDA	The Destination Address of the most recent L3_PDU causing the error	
serviceDisagreementTimeStamp	The time stamp of the most recent occurrence of this type of violation	

Table 12.12 Service error diagnostics log — serviceDisagreementTable

The time stamp is expressed using the earlier described syntax TimeTicks (hundredths of a second; see Section 10.7.7) and is the value of sysUpTime, the number of TimeTicks since startup of the agent providing SMDS CNM Service, at the time of the error. Thus, when no restart has taken place, the time elapsed since startup-time for events in this table is

$$100 \times \left[\text{serviceDisagreementTimeStamp.x.y} - \text{sysUpTime.0}\right] \bmod 2^{32} \text{ seconds}$$

For example, a dump of this table for SNI #4 might produce a single entry:

```
sniSDIndex.4.3 = 4
serviceDisagreementType.4.3 = 3
serviceDisagreementSA.4.3 = C15165552108FFFF
serviceDisagreementDA.4.3 = E19987477472FFFF
serviceDisagreementTimeStamp.4.3 = 198765432
```

Retrieval of `sysUpTime` may produce the following:

```
sysUpTime.0 = 198786432
```

Thus, the event is 3.5 minutes old. The value of 3 for the error type indicates that the Source Address ($C15165552108FFFF_H$) has been used on SNI #4, which has not been allocated to that SNI. This may suggest that the CPE has been configured incorrectly. Continued polling will reveal repetitive error behavior.

The time stamp has the same slight ambiguity as the one discussed for `sipL3PDUErrorTable` in Section 11.1.1.2, but, for the same reasons, this ambiguity is acceptable here also. Note that the table must be flushed by the service provider at a restart of the SNMP agent.

This table is likely to be used as a more detailed diagnostic tool after erroneous behavior shows up via the earlier described `smdsSubscrTable` (see Section 12.6.2.1). Building on the example shown in that section, the `serviceDisagreementTable` can now be used as shown in Figure 12.12. Note that the `subscriberAddressesTable` is used to retrieve the addresses that belong to SNI #4.

12.6.3 Address Screen Management

The purpose of the Address Screening group is to provide SMDS customers with the ability to review the Address Screens for each of their SNIs and to make changes in these screens. The Address Screening group of objects is perhaps the most complex in the Subscription MIB. This complexity is necessary because

- Multiple screens (up to 4) are allowed for each SNI, and

- Each screen for an SNI must be correlated with SMDS addresses assigned to that SNI.

Fortunately, the Address Screening group has been designed so that the complexity is greatly reduced for the common case where a single Address Screen is used for an SNI. At the end of this section we will provide a simple example of the configuration of an Address Screen for this case.

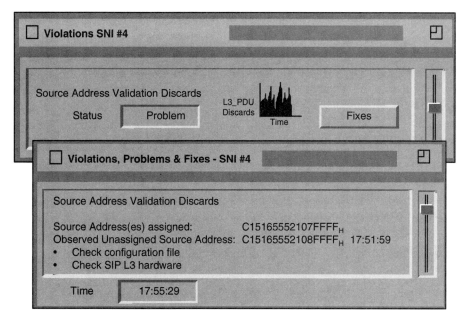

Figure 12.12 Example of user-friendly representation of the information in the `smdsSubscrTable`, `subscriberAddressesTable`, and the `serviceDisagreementTable`

12.6.3.1   Overview

For this overview we use the examples described in Section 3.4.3. Details for the example of a single pair of Address Screens per SNI are shown in Figure 12.13. The example of the multiple Address Screen pairs per SNI is detailed in Figure 12.15. The overviews of the MIB objects to manage these cases are shown in Figures 12.14 and 12.16 respectively. In summary, these objects provide the following functions:

- **Screen type, screen status, and screen index**

  The `addressScreeningMasterTable` shows for each SNI the `screenType`, and `screenStatus`/`screenStatusChange` parameters, which determine whether a screen is active and whether it is an inclusionary screen (allowed addresses) or exclusionary screen (disallowed addresses). To accommodate the multiple screen-pair case, a `screenIndex` is used. The use of this table is discussed in Section 12.6.3.2.

- **Associating SNI addresses with Address Screens**

  When multiple screen pairs per SNI are used, addresses on an SNI (addresses A and E in Figure 12.15) must be linked with the appropriate screens. This linking function is provided through the `associatedAddressesIndScreenTable` and the `associated-AddressesGrpScreenTable`. The contents of these tables can be modified and do not need to be used for the scenario with a single screen-pair per SNI. Section 12.6.3.3 describes these tables.

- **The contents of the Address Screens**
  The contents of the Address Screens are represented by the `individualAddressScreenTable`, and the `groupAddress-ScreenTable`. These tables list the addresses in L3_PDUs that need to be screened and allow modifications to the list. Section 12.6.3.4 explains these tables.

- **Screen utilization and default screens**
  Since Address Screens are subject to size limitations, the SMDS CNM Service provides information such as the number of addresses that are actually listed in a particular screen at a given time. It is also convenient to designate default screens, for example, to simplify the representation of a single Address Screen pair per SNI. These features are represented by the `numberAndDefaultScreeningTable`, which is discussed in Section 12.6.3.5.

In Section 12.6.3.6 we make recommendations for the use of these objects and provide some examples.

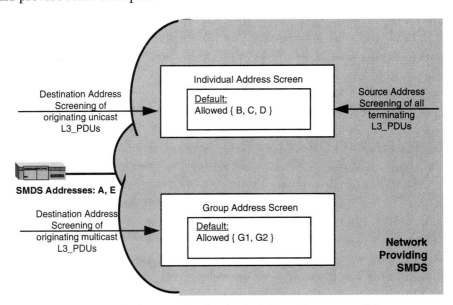

Figure 12.13 Example of a single Address Screen per SNI

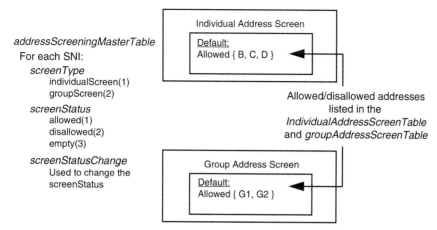

Figure 12.14 Example of the use of the Address Screening group for a single Address Screen per SNI

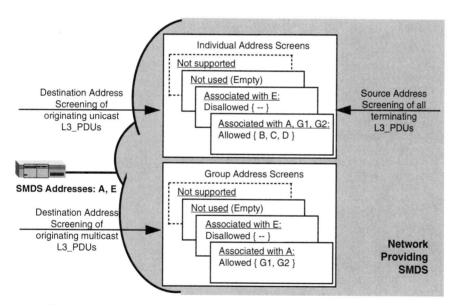

Figure 12.15 Example of the use of multiple Address Screens per SNI

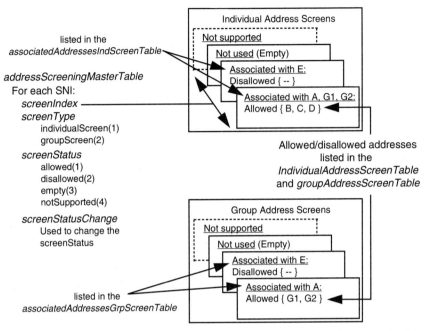

Figure 12.16 Example of the use of the Address Screening group with multiple Address Screens per SNI

12.6.3.2   Address Screen Allocation and Activation

The `addressScreeningMasterTable` (Table 12.13) serves to label and type Address Screens for each SNI, correlates them with SNIs, and provides both the screen status and the capability to change the status.

The `addressScreeningMasterTable` provides the screen status for each screen, by SNI, and by screen type. Thus, the table must be indexed by the following object triplet:

{ sniScreenIndex, screenIndex, screenType }

The SNI index is `sniScreenIndex` and equals `ifIndex`. A screen index is represented by the object `screenIndex`. This parameter is necessary to distinguish multiple Address Screens for an SNI. The table is designed so that for a given SNI, four entries for each screen type are always present. For each screen type, the index ranges between 1 and 4. The screen type `screenType` determines whether the screen consists of SMDS Group Addresses or SMDS Individual Addresses.

The screen status (`screenStatus`) of each Address Screen shows whether the screen contains allowed or disallowed addresses, is empty, or is not

addressScreeningMasterTable objects	Semantics	
sniScreenIndex	(Table index) The SNI index (=ifIndex)	
screenIndex	(Table index) Numbering of the screens from 1 to 4	
screenType	(Table index) Indicates an IA screen or a GA screen	
	1	Individual Address Screen
	2	Group Address Screen
screenStatus screenStatusChange	A screen status* can be:	
	1	allowed (an active inclusionary screen)
	2	disallowed (an active exclusionary screen)
	3	empty (an inactive screen)
	4	notSupported (the service provider supports less than 4 screens)

* The procedure in Section 12.4.2 is used for modifications.

Table 12.13 Address Screen allocation and activation — `addressScreening-MasterTable`

supported by the service provider. The number of Individual or Group Address Screens for a given SNI and type that is supported by the service provider of SMDS equals the number of entries that have a `screenStatus` value other than notSupported. An active subscribed screen has a `screenStatus` value of allowed or disallowed, indicating an inclusionary or exclusionary Address Screen. The value empty means that Address Screening is not activated for addresses associated with this screen. The procedure to modify the screen status follows that of Section 12.4.2.

Thus, the status of {SNI #17, screen #1, Group Address Screen type} is obtained by

get (screenStatus.17.1.2)

which may produce a response of

screenStatus.17.1.2 = empty(3)

To change this screen to an exclusionary screen with disallowed addresses requires

set (screenStatusChange.17.1.2 = disallowed(2))

Polling of `screenStatus.17.1.2` and `screenStatusChange.17.1.2` will verify whether and when the change has been accepted by SMDS (see also Section 12.4.2 on the use of the set command).

The implementation of the value empty(3) in the SMDS CNM Service Agent provides the SMDS CNM Service user with a nice shortcut to flush a whole screen at once. Setting the `screenStatusChange` column to empty(3) will cause the Agent to remove the contents of the whole screen. A set-request of the `statusChange` column to notSupported(4), or from notSupported(4) to another value will not be granted by the Agent. The SNMP error code badValue will be returned on these requests.

12.6.3.3 Linking SNI Addresses and Address Screens

Two tables serve to link the addresses associated with an SNI (including Group Addresses) to the respective screens that are used for traffic from and to these addresses. This is necessary to accommodate support of configurations with multiple Address Screen pairs per SNI. It must be possible for the SMDS CNM Service user to make changes in these tables, for example, to add a new Group Address that identifies one of the stations on the SNI. The two tables are the `associatedAddressesIndScreenTable` and the `associated-AddressesGrpScreenTable`. These tables do not need to be used for configurations with a single Address Screen pair per SNI.

Both tables work in the same manner. The table index consists of the concatenation of the values of the SNI index (equaling `ifIndex`), the screen index (equaling `screenIndex` in the Master Table), and an SMDS address (represented by the partitioned-address technique explained in Section 12.4.1).

An Individual Address Screen is used for both Source and Destination Address Screening. Thus, Individual Addresses as well as Group Addresses that identify an SNI may have to be linked with the Individual Address Screens of that SNI. This link is represented by the `associatedAddresses-IndScreenTable`. Since a Group Address Screen is only used for Destination Address Screening, the other table, the `associatedAddresses-GrpScreenTable`, links Group Address Screens only with Individual Addresses that identify the SNI. No address type index is needed in this table.

The `Status/StatusChange` parameters allow SMDS CNM Service users to add and remove entries in the tables. The descriptors of the objects are shown in Table 12.14.

For example, the Group Address E19987477472FFFF$_H$ that includes the Bodacious Data Corp.'s Cutty Hunk router (see Figure 10.1) is linked with Individual Address Screen #1 of that SNI (`ifIndex` = 17) with:

```
set (associatedAddressIndStatusChange.17.1.2.1.998.7477472 =
     valid(1))
```

associatedAddresses-IndScreenTable objects	associatedAddresses-GrpScreenTable objects	Semantics	
associatedSNIIndIndex	associatedSNIGrpIndex	(Table index) SNI index (=ifIndex)	
associatedScreenIndIndex	associatedScreenGrpIndex	(Table index) Screen index (=screenIndex)	
associatedAddressTypeIndex	(Not needed in this table)	(Table index) Address type:	
		1	individual
		2	group
assocIndCountryCodeIndex assocIndDestination-CodeIndex assocIndSubscriber-NumberIndex	assocGrpCountryCodeIndex assocGrpDestination-CodeIndex assocGrpSubscriber-NumberIndex	(Table index). Three SMDS address portions[a]	
associatedAddressInd	associatedAddressGrp	The complete SMDS address	
associatedAddressIndStatus associatedAddressInd-StatusChange	associatedAddressGrpStatus associatedAddressGrp-StatusChange	The status can be:[b]	
		1	valid
		2	invalid

[a] Used for table indexing; see Section 12.4.1.
[b] The procedure in Section 12.4.2 is used for modifications.

Table 12.14 The associatedAddressesScreenTables

As described in Section 12.4.2, this action will cause the SMDS CNM agent to create a new table row with the following column values:

{ 17, 1, 2, 1, 998, 7477472, E19987477472FFFF, 2, 1 }

If the request is granted by SMDS, the status column will change its value to 1. If the request is rejected, the status-change column will change its value to 2. Rows with both the status and the status-change columns set to invalid may be removed by the Agent.

The appropriate trap is sent out on these events. Through a polling strategy, the NMS can check when and whether the request has been granted (see Section 12.4.2).

12.6.3.4 Address Screen Contents

The purpose of the `individualAddressScreenTable` and the `groupAddressScreenTable` is to provide access to the contents of the respective screens for review and possible modification. The contents of a screen consist of the addresses that the screen allows or disallows. The two tables work in the same manner and are structurally the same as the previously described `associatedAddressesIndScreenTable` and `associated-AddressesGrpScreenTable`, except that the SMDS Addresses in these tables now represent the screen itself (see Table 12.15).

individualAddress-ScreenTable objects	groupAddress-ScreenTable objects	Semantics	
iAScreenSNIIndex	gAScreenSNIIndex	(Table index) SNI index (=ifIndex)	
iAScreenIndex	gAScreenIndex	(Table index) Screen index (=screenIndex)	
iACountryCodeIndex iADestinationCodeIndex iASubscriberNumberIndex	gACountryCodeIndex gADestinationCodeIndex gASubscriberNumberIndex	(Table index) Three SMDS address portions[a]	
iAScreeningAddress	gAScreeningAddress	The complete SMDS address	
iAScreeningAddressStatus iAScreeningAddress-StatusChange	gAScreeningAddressStatus gAScreeningAddress-StatusChange	The status can be:[b]	
		1	valid
		2	invalid

[a] Used for table indexing; see Section 12.4.1.
[b] The procedure in Section 12.4.2 is used for modifications.

Table 12.15 Address Screen contents — `individualAddressScreenTable` and `groupAddressScreenTable`

For example, a dump of the Individual Address Screen #1 of the SNI for the Bodacious Data Corp.'s Cutty Hunk location (`ifIndex = 17`) could be initiated with:

```
getnext (iAScreenSNIIndex.17.1, iAScreenIndex.17.1,
        iACountryCodeIndex.17.1, iADestinationCodeIndex.17.1,
        iASubscriberNumberIndex.17.1, iAScreeningAddress.17.1,
        iAScreeningAddressStatus.17.1,
        iAScreeningAddressStatusChange.17.1 )
```

Together with subsequent get-next PDUs, the following Address Screen table may be retrieved:

17	1	1	516	5552107	C15165552107FFFF	1	1
17	1	1	516	5552642	C15165552642FFFF	1	1
17	1	1	809	5555254	C18095555254FFFF	1	1

Observe that, as expected, this table shows that only one Individual Address Screen is configured for SNI #17. The inspected Individual Address Screen consists of the three addresses of the SNIs at the other Bodacious Data branch offices, as configured in Figure 10.1. The status objects show that all three addresses are valid and that no change is pending. Further checks in previously described tables would reveal the station address(es) that use this screen, and whether this screen is inclusionary or exclusionary.

Removal of the last address in the list requires

```
set (iAScreeningAddressStatusChange.17.1.1.809.5555254 =
    invalid(2))
```

12.6.3.5   Default Screens and Screen Utilization

One purpose of the `numberAndDefaultScreeningTable` is to keep track of the combined number of addresses that are listed in all (maximum 8) screens of a given SNI. This is useful, since (as explained in Chapter 3), there is a maximum to this number. After this maximum is reached, attempts to add additional addresses to any of the screens will not be granted. As we have seen in the previous section, in that case a request to add an entry to the table representing the screen contents will not cause the STATUS column in that entry to turn to valid, and the requested entry will be removed again.

The second purpose of this table is to deal with situations where an address associated with an SNI is not linked with any Address Screen of that SNI (i.e., is not included in the `associatedAddressesIndScreenTable` or the `associatedAddressesGrpScreenTable`). In such a situation, incoming and outgoing traffic will be screened against the appropriate *default* Address Screen. The `numberAndDefaultScreeningTable` lists the indices of the default screens.

The three situations that require a default screen index are as follows:

Case 1:   This case concerns the default screen for Individually Addressed L3_PDUs that cannot be correlated with an Individual Address Screen (both Source and Destination Address Screening).

Case 2:   This case concerns the default screen for Group Addressed L3_PDUs that cannot be correlated with an Individual Address Screen for Source Address Screening.

Case 3:   This case concerns the default screen for Group Addressed L3_PDUs that cannot be correlated with a Group Address Screen for Destination Address Screening.

A handy use of the defaults includes the common case of a single Address Screen pair per SNI. Since this case concerns only one Individual Address Screen and one Group Address Screen, we can use the default tables and avoid the need to fill out the tables that explicitly bind the SNI address(es) with the screen index (`associatedAddressesIndScreenTable` and `associated-AddressesGrpScreenTable`). For example, when an Individual Address is included in an additional Group Address and the Address Screens need to be updated to include the new Group Address, the use of a default screen avoids the need to update the `associatedAddressesIndScreenTable`.

Table 12.16 shows the resulting organization of the `number-AndDefaultScreeningTable`. The table is indexed by the SNI index.

numberAndDefault-ScreeningTable objects	Semantics
sniNumberIndex	(Table index) SNI index (=ifIndex)
deflAScreenForIAs deflAScreenForIAsChange	Case 1. Values range from 1 to 4. The procedure in Section 12.4.2 is used for modifications.
deflAScreenForGAs deflAScreenForGAsChange	Case 2. Values range from 1 to 4. The procedure in Section 12.4.2 is used for modifications.
defGAScreenForIAs defGAScreenForIAsChange	Case 3. Values range from 1 to 4. The procedure in Section 12.4.2 is used for modifications.
numberValidEntries	Total number of current and valid entries in the Address Screens

Table 12.16 `numberAndDefaultScreeningTable`

The modification of a default value follows the technique that uses a `Status/StatusChange` paradigm, as discussed for the support of set commands in Section 12.4.2. The values of these two parameters equal the screen index of the Address Screen that is determined to be the default.

As an example, in the single-address case for SNI 17, the defaults can be set as follows:

```
set (deflAScreenForIAsChange.17 = 1,
     deflAScreenForGAsChange.17 = 1,
     defGAScreenForIAsChange.17 = 1)
```

This configuration means that all traffic to and from SNI #17 is screened against screen number 1.

The `numberValidEntries` is an aggregate of all valid entries in the combined Address Screens. Chapter 3 defines the maximum for this value (i.e., 128). Comparison of the value of `numberValidEntries` for a given SNI with the maximum supported by the configuration (and the service provider) will determine whether additional addresses can be added to the screens.

12.6.3.6   Recommended Use

The configuration of a single Address Screen pair per SNI allows a simple way to use the Address Screening group in the SMDS Subscription MIB. We recommend the following use:

- The `addressScreeningMasterTable` should be configured with the `screenIndex` set to 1.

- The `associatedAddressesIndScreenTable` and the `associatedAddressesGrpScreenTable` should not be used.

- The defaults in the `numberAndDefaultScreeningTable` should be set to 1.

To illustrate the manipulation of the Address Screens, we will conclude the explanation of Address Screen capabilities with a set of practical examples.

Installing an Address Screen:

Default: Set the defaults. This step can be skipped in the case where the service provider supports just one screen per screen type for an SNI:

```
set (defIAScreenForIAsChange.17 = 1,
     defIAScreenForGAsChange.17 = 1,
     defGAScreenForIAsChange.17 = 1)
```

Activate: For both the individual Address Screen and the Group Address Screen, set the screen status to allowed to configure an inclusionary screen, or to disallowed to create an exclusionary screen:

```
set (screenStatusChange.17.1.1 = allowed(1),
     screenStatusChange.17.1.2 = allowed(1))
```

Adding and deleting addresses in an existing Address Screen:

Add: Fill the individual Address Screen and the Group Address Screen:

```
set (iAScreeningAddressStatusChange.17.1.1.516.5552107 = valid(1),
     iAScreeningAddressStatusChange.17.1.1.809.5555254 = valid(1),
     iAScreeningAddressStatusChange.17.1.1.516.5552642 = valid(1),
     gAScreeningAddressStatusChange.17.1.1.199.7477472 = valid(1))
```

Delete: Set the `StatusChange` parameter for the address to be deleted to invalid(2).

Checking the number of addresses in the Address Screens:

Check size: The combined size of the screens is obtained by the following:

> get (numberValidEntries.17)

This returns, for our example,

> get-response (numberValidEntries.17 = 4)

Flushing installed Address Screens:

Flush: Set the screen status to empty(3) for the individual Address Screen or the Group Address Screen that must be flushed:

> set (screenStatusChange.17.1.1 = empty(3),
>   screenStatusChange.17.1.2 = empty(3))

Figure 12.17 shows a hypothetical user-friendly representation of the management of Address Screens.

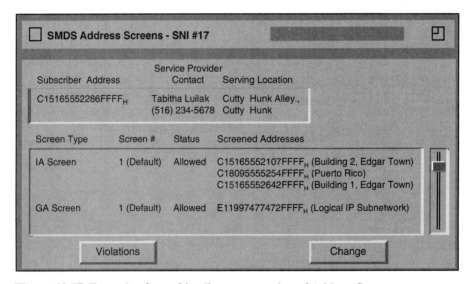

Figure 12.17 Example of user-friendly representation of Address Screen management

12.6.4 Group Address Management

The purpose of the Group Addressing Information group is to enable an SMDS CNM Service user to review and modify his use of Group Addresses for his SNIs. Two capabilities are available:

1. The list of the Individual Addresses that are members of a particular Group Address can be reviewed and modified. This function is represented by the `groupAddressTable`.

2. The list of the Group Addresses that a particular Individual Address is a member of can be reviewed and modified. This function is represented to the SMDS CNM Service user by the `memberGroup-AddressTable`.

The `memberGroupAddressTable` is a representation of the same information that is used to represent the `groupAddressTable`, but the principal information elements (the Group Address and the Individual Address) are correlated in opposite ways. Technically, a single table can do the same job. If, for example, just the `groupAddressTable` is used, the other function (to find all Group Address memberships of a particular Individual Address) can be performed by traversing the whole table. However, since these tables are potentially lengthy, even for a single SMDS customer, the two-table approach offers a more efficient service.

A number of rules that relate to access control and orderly Group Address management are imposed on the access to this information. Unlike other information offered in the SMDS CNM Service, the Group Address lists do not represent a resource tied to a particular SNI. A Group Address list may even span a combination of service providers! Thus, the SMDS CNM Service has some rules on access to Group Address list information:

Rule 1. Group Addresses themselves cannot be added or deleted from the tables. The reason for this requirement is that allocation and withdrawal of addresses may involve more than an electronic command (for example, number allocation). Thus, for now, a Group Address can only be requested or deleted by telephone or service order.

Rule 2. Only Group Address information can be accessed for which the SMDS service provider acts as Group Address Agent (see Section 3.4.2). The opposite would require that SMDS service providers dynamically exchange Group Address information, which is an unrealistic expectation at this time. It does mean that multiple SNMP agents may have to be accessed to obtain all Group Addressing information for a given SMDS customer, assuming that all of these SMDS service providers offer SMDS CNM Service. A simple approach is to register all your Group Addresses with the same service provider.

Rule 3.   Only members of a given Group Address and its Sponsor (see Chapter 3) are permitted to retrieve the entries in the tables of the Group Addressing Information group that concern that Group Address.

Rule 4.   Only the Sponsor of a given Group Address is permitted to modify the entries in the tables of the Group Address Information group that concern the membership of that Group Address.

Rules 2, 3, and 4 are implemented by the pairing of appropriate MIB Views with the authorized communities (see Section 10.7.4).

Both tables are straightforward and shown in Tables 12.17 and 12.18. Both tables are indexed by a pair of matching Group and Individual Addresses. Modifications to these tables rely again on the `Status/StatusChange` paradigm described in Section 12.4.2.

groupAddressTable objects	Semantics	
groupCountryCodeGAIndex groupDestinationCodeGAIndex groupSubscriberNumberGAIndex	(Table index) Three portions[a] of an SMDS Group Address	
groupCountryCodeIndex groupDestinationCodeIndex groupSubscriberNumberIndex	(Table index) Three portions[a] of an SMDS Individual Address that is a member of the Group Address	
groupMemberStatus groupMemberStatusChange	The status can be:[b]	
	1	valid
	2	invalid

[a] Used for table indexing; see Section 12.4.1.
[b] The procedure in Section 12.4.2 is used for modifications.

Table 12.17 Group Address members — `groupAddressTable`

Since these tables seem to allow sponsors of Group Addresses to freely modify their use of Group Addressing, a reminder is in order that there are limits to (1) the number of members that can belong to a Group Address, (2) the number of Group Addresses a particular Individual Address can belong to, and (3) the number of Group Addresses that identify any of the addresses on a particular SNI. These limits are described in Chapter 3. Since it is a bit cumbersome for SMDS CNM Service users to keep track of these limits, access to three additional tables is offered as a convenience to show whether any of the three limits have been reached. These tables are the `numberMemberAddressesTable`, the `numberGAForAddressTable`, and the `numberGAsForSNITable` respectively; they are shown as Tables 12.19 – 12.21.

memberGroupAddressTable objects	Semantics	
memberCountryCodeIndex memberDestinationCodeIndex memberSubscriberNumberIndex	(Table index) Three portions[a] of an SMDS Individual Address	
memberCountryCodeGAIndex memberDestinationCodeGAIndex memberSubscriberNumberGAIndex	(Table index) Three portions[a] of an SMDS Group Address that the Individual Address is a member of	
associatedGroupAddressStatus associatedGroupAddressStatusChange	The status can be:[b]	
	1	valid
	2	invalid

[a] Used for table indexing; see Section 12.4.1.
[b] The procedure in Section 12.4.2 is used for modifications.

Table 12.18 Group Address membership — `memberGroupAddressTable`

numberMemberAddressesTable objects	Semantics
numberCountryCodeIndex numberDestinationCodeIndex numberSubscriberNumberIndex	(Table index) Three portions[a] of an SMDS Group Address
numberIndAddresses	The actual number of Individual Addresses that are members of the Group Address

[a] Used for table indexing; see Section 12.4.1.

Table 12.19 Group Address membership size — `numberMemberAddressesTable`

numberGAsForAddressTable objects	Semantics
numberGAsCountryCodeIndex numberGAsDestinationCodeIndex numberGAsSubscriberNumberIndex	(Table index) Three portions[a] of an SMDS Individual Address
numberGroupAddresses	The actual number of Group Addresses that the Individual Address is a member of

[a] Used for table indexing; see Section 12.4.1.

Table 12.20 Number of Group Addresses that an Individual Address is a member of — `numberGAsForAddressTable`

numberGAsForSNITable objects	**Semantics**
numberGAsSNIIndex	(Table index)
	SNI index (= ifIndex)
numberGAs	The actual number of Group Addresses
	in use for the stations on this SNI

Table 12.21 Number of Group Addresses identifying an SNI — `numberGAsForSNI-Table`

Since the five tables in the Group Address group all operate on the same set of information, a modification in either the `memberGroupAddressTable` or the `groupAddressTable` will cause changes in the other tables as well. A subtle issue is the complete removal of all members of a particular Group Address. This causes removal of all entries related to this Group Address in all tables except the `numberMemberAddressesTable`, which would show the Group Address with zero members. This indicates that the Group Address still exists and is at the disposal of that customer. It corresponds to Rule 1 mentioned earlier, which states that Group Addresses cannot be removed from the tables via SMDS CNM Service. Similarly, a Group Address cannot be added to the tables via SMDS CNM Service.

A simple rule is that after obtaining a Group Address, the Group Address can only be populated after it appears in the `numberMember-AddressesTable`.

Requests that would overpopulate a Group Address or otherwise exceed the aforementioned limits are not granted by the service provider. This can be detected by the SMDS CNM Service user by inspection of the relevant `status/statusChange` parameters.

As an example, consider a newly obtained Group Address, $E19987477472FFFF_H$. Thus:

numberIndAddresses.1.998.7477472 = 0

The Group Address is now populated with the Individual Addresses $C15165552642FFFF_H$, $C15165552107FFFF_H$, and $C15165552286FFFF_H$ by setting the `groupMemberStatusChange` parameters to valid(1).

set (groupMemberStatusChange.1.998.7477472.1.516.5552642 = 1,
     groupMemberStatusChange.1.998.7477472.1.516.5552286 = 1,
     groupMemberStatusChange.1.998.7477472.1.516.5552107 = 1)

A value of valid(1) of the respective `groupMemberStatus` parameters will show that the requests have been activated, at which point,

numberIndAddresses.1.998.7477472 = 3

Figure 12.18 shows a hypothetical user-friendly representation of Group Address management.

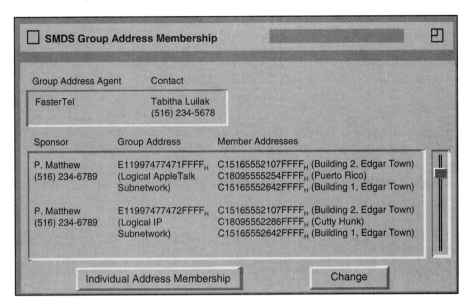

Figure 12.18 Example of user-friendly representation of Group Address management

12.6.5 Management of Access to Other Carriers

The subscription parameters for access to other carriers are particularly important in North America. Management features of these parameters are represented to the SMDS CNM Service user by means of the Interexchange Carrier Access group of objects in the Subscription MIB. This group implements three functions:

- The Carrier Pre-selection subscription parameter (see Chapter 3) and a counter of the number of L3_PDUs that were discarded because of improper use of the explicit Carrier Selection field in L3_PDUs. The Carrier Pre-selection can be modified via SMDS CNM Service. These functions are represented by the `xaSmdsSubscrTable`.

- On behalf of a connected carrier, a LEC may block traffic from a certain customer to the connected carrier. This rare event may occur, for example, in cases of nonpayment by the customer to that carrier. SMDS CNM Service provides a list of carriers to which traffic has been blocked. The `carrierBlockingTable` represents this function.

- A support function identifies carriers that the local service provider of SMDS gives access to, which are represented by the `carrierIndexTable`.

12.6.5.1 Carrier Pre-selection Management

The `xaSmdsSubscrTable` correlates the SNI index (`ifIndex`) and the Carrier Pre-selection that is in effect for that interface. The technique for making changes to the Carrier Pre-selection information follows the `Status/Status-Change` paradigm described before. Note that the service provider will not grant requests for preselection of a carrier that is not connected to the local SMDS service provider or requests that specify a CIC code[9] that is nonexistent. The `carrierSelectionViolations` counter measures any improper use of the CARRIER SELECTION field in L3_PDUs, as described in Chapters 3 and 4. The `xaSmdsSubscrTable` is shown as Table 12.22.

xaSmdsSubcrTable objects	**Semantics**
xaSmdsSubscrIndex	(Table index) SNI index (= ifIndex)
carrierPreselection carrierPreselectionChange	An integer representing the CIC code of the preselected carrier*
carrierSelectionViolations	The number of discarded L3_PDUs due to Carrier Selection errors

* The procedure in Section 12.4.2 is used for modifications.

Table 12.22 Carrier Pre-selection and Carrier Selection — `xaSmdsSubscrTable`

As an example, the Carrier Pre-selection for Bodacious Data Corp.'s SNI at Cutty Hunk (`ifIndex=17`) is obtained by

get (carrierPreselection.17, carrierSelectionChange.17)

The response indicates the use of the DataInternational carrier with CIC code 199:

get-response (carrierPreselection.17=199,
   carrierSelectionChange.17=199)

This also indicates that no change to the Carrier Pre-selection is pending.

12.6.5.2 Blocking by Other Carriers

Carriers that have requested blocking of traffic from an SNI (End-user blocking; see Chapter 3) are listed in the (read-only) `carrier-BlockingTable`. Only IECs can request blocking. The table is indexed by the

---

[9]According to [1060], Carrier Pre-selection applies to IECs only. IECs are identified by a CIC code. NECA codes do not apply to this case. See also Chapter 3.

SNI index and the CIC code[10] of carriers that requested blocking. The table also shows the status of the blocking and provides a counter of the number of L3_PDUs that were discarded due to blocking. When blocking is turned off, this counter value is still available[11]. When blocking is turned on, the counter is reset to zero. Only carriers that have requested blocking are listed. The table is shown in Table 12.23.

carrierBlockingTable objects	Semantics	
carrierBlockingIndex	(Table index) SNI index (= ifIndex)	
carrierBlockingCodeIndex	An integer representing the primary CIC code of the carrier requesting blocking	
carrierBlockingStatus	The actual status of the blocking:*	
	1	on
	2	off
carrierBlockingL3PDUs	The number of PDUs that have been discarded due to blocking of this carrier	

* The object descriptor is slightly misleading. Despite the suffix `Status` (see Section 12.4.2), this object is read-only; the value is not meant to be changed by SMDS CNM Service customers.

Table 12.23 Carriers blocking an SNI — `carrierBlockingTable`

For example, a dump of this table for the Bodacious Data Corp. may produce

```
1      288    1      0
1      882    1      0
```

This example shows that the carriers with CIC code 288 and 882 have requested that traffic from SNI with index 1 to those carriers be blocked. It also shows that no PDUs have been discarded. Since the example shows a table dump, it also shows that for other SNIs of this customer, no End-user blocking has been requested.

---

[10]According to [1060], End-user blocking can be requested by IECs only. IECs are identified by a CIC code. NECA codes do not apply to this case. See also Chapter 3.

[11]The semantics of the `carrierBlockingStatus` may be slightly confusing, in that it does not specify whether the value off(2) means that blocking is impending, or whether blocking is over. The correct interpretation is that blocking is over. Note also that an entry with the value off(2) may be removed again. This occurs if that particular carrier has again requested blocking, or possibly if the SNMP Agent providing the SMDS CNM Service is restarted. Removal of this entry should not be considered significant, since the entry is not time-stamped, and is therefore of limited historic value.

12.6.5.3   Identification of Connected Carriers

It is convenient for SMDS CNM Service users to have an overview of the accessible carriers. This could be achieved by a dump of the SMDS CNM Service instance of the MIB II interface table (ifTable), in particular the columns ifIndex, ifDescr, and ifType. (see Section 10.8). The intercarrier entries in this table have an ifType value of other(1), and the ifDescr value gives a textual clue to which carrier is connected via that interface. The carrierIndexTable provides a slightly more precise method and also enables an NMS to find the ifIndex value for a given carrier. Recall that carriers may be identified by a CIC code or a NECA code (see Chapter 3). Thus, the table implementing this function is indexed by the carrier identification and the carrier type (CIC or NECA), as shown in Table 12.24.

carrierIndexTable objects	Semantics	
carrierIndexCode	(Table index) An integer representing the CIC or NECA code of the carrier of interest	
carrierCodeType	(Table index) The type of connected carrier:	
	1	CIC code
	2	NECA
carrierIndex	Interface index (= ifIndex)	

Table 12.24 Connected carrier identification — carrierIndexTable

As an example, the interface index for the connectivity with the carrier identified by CIC code 199 (DataInternational in the Bodacious Data example of Section 10.8.2.1) is obtained by

get (carrierIndex.199.1)

which returns

get-response (carrierIndex.199.1= 387)

Another way of using this table is to list all carriers that are accessible. This is done by a table dump using the get-next PDU, starting by:

get-next (carrierIndex)

which returns

get-response (carrierIndex.199.1= 387)

Subsequent get-next commands will yield the rest of the table:

```
get-next (carrierIndex.199.1)
      get-response (carrierIndex.288.1= 758)
get-next (carrierIndex.288.1)
      get-response (carrierIndex.882.1= 121)
```

Thus, the provider of SMDS CNM Service is connected to carriers with CIC codes 199, 288, and 882 through interfaces with ifIndex values of 387, 758, and 121, respectively.

12.6.5.4 Example

Figure 12.19 shows an example of a hypothetical user-friendly representation of Carrier-access management. For the SNI shown, the preselected carrier is DataInternational. Carriers 288 and 822 have requested blocking to this SNI. The SNI shows also some discarded traffic due to incorrect use of the CARRIER SELECTION field, which may suggest misconfiguration at the CPE.

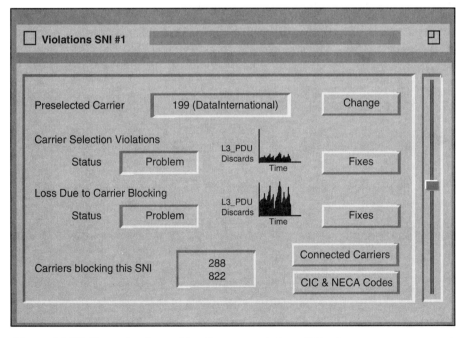

Figure 12.19 Example of user-friendly representation of Carrier-access management

12.7 Alarms

SMDS CNM Service supports the standard SNMP alarms (see Section 10.9), except the authenticationFailure. This trap is not supported because of security concerns. In addition, a number of alarms have been defined to alert the SMDS CNM Service user to certain changes in a subscription profile. Table 12.25 summarizes these alarms.

Trap sent	Event
smdsSubscrEntryChange	A change for this SNI has occurred in: smdsContact smdsSNILocation smdsAccessClass smdsMCDUsIn smdsMCDUsOut
smdsAddressesEntryChange	A change in the subscriberAddressesTable of this SNI has occurred.
individualAddressScreenEntryChange	A change in an Individual Address Screen configuration of this SNI has occurred.
groupAddressScreenEntryChange	A change in a Group Address Screen configuration of this SNI has occurred.
groupAddressChange	A change in a Group Address concerning this SNI has occurred.
xaSmdsSubscrChange	A request for a change in the carrierPreselection for this SNI has occurred.
carrierBlockingEntryChange	An entry in the carrierBlockingTable has been added or deleted, or a change in the carrierBlockingStatus has occurred.

Table 12.25 Alarms for SMDS subscription changes

13

Asynchronous Transfer Mode Access to SMDS

In recent years, Asynchronous Transfer Mode (ATM) has become the subject of intense interest across all segments of the communications industry. Examples of this interest include the following:

- The ATM Forum, an industry consortium that is dedicated to the proliferation of ATM, has grown from four members in October 1991 to over 500 members in 1994.

- Time-Warner, the large cable television provider, has purchased ATM switching equipment to use for providing new services to cable subscribers.

- Telephone companies are aggressively announcing new ATM-based services and/or trials.

- Data networking vendors are falling all over each other to announce their ATM plans for their future products.[1]

With all of this interest, it is not surprising that confusion surrounding ATM has developed. Much of the confusion stems from the fact that the term *ATM* is attached to many different concepts including:

---

[1]At the August 1993 Interop trade show, we suspected that someone with an ATM stencil and a spray paint can had engaged in a form of high tech graffiti the evening before the opening of the show.

415

- A high-speed multiplexing and switching technology with the potential to carry many different types of traffic

- The underlying technology for the Broadband Integrated Services Digital Network (BISDN)

- A unifying network architecture to provide seamless networking across all network environments[2]

- The technology basis for supporting existing and new public carrier services

As a grand unifying architecture, one might conclude that ATM will replace everything and that all new investment and spending on network equipment should be postponed until the arrival of ATM, the networking nirvana.

A much more realistic view of ATM is that it is a technology that will be used by public carriers as both a vehicle for new services and as a means to improve both the cost and performance of existing services, for example, SMDS.[3] This support of SMDS by ATM is the topic of this chapter. The chapter begins with some background information on ATM as a technology. Then the use of ATM to provide access to SMDS via a multiple-service interface is described, and the use of ATM within the carrier network to implement SMDS is discussed. Finally, the impact on service features is explored.

CPE designers should find the chapter useful in designing SMDS equipment that will attach to ATM interfaces. SMDS customers should be interested in the chapter as an example of the use of ATM that should clarify the relationship between this new technology and network services such as SMDS.

13.1 Brief Tutorial on ATM and BISDN

In the early 1980s, the telephone industry infrastructure (switches and transmission systems) was rapidly converting to digital technology. The primary motivation was reduced cost and improved performance for Plain Old Telephone Service (POTS). It was realized that once the telephone network was extensively converted to digital technology, new digital services could be offered to

---

[2]A common hyperbole is that ATM will provide seamless LAN/WAN interworking. Given the speeds defined for ATM and the implications for the cost of wide-area bandwidth for ATM, we doubt that many network implementors will want to treat the boundary between the LAN and the WAN as seamless. Generally, we believe that pitches about seamless networking should be viewed as curve balls where the seams have been used to enhance the curvature.

[3]It is also (perhaps more) realistic to view ATM as a technology that can be used in private networks such as LANs. However, this use of ATM is beyond the scope of this book.

customers. This concept, called the *Integrated Services Digital Network* (ISDN), has been the subject of intense standardization efforts since 1980.

The basic idea of ISDN is illustrated in Figure 13.1. The interface to the customer uses digital transmission and is divided into channels by means of Time Division Multiplexing (TDM). The channels can be circuit-switched at various rates (e.g., 64 Kbps and 384 Kbps, as in Figure 13.1), in order to support various types of traffic. The channels can also be used to carry packet-switched traffic.

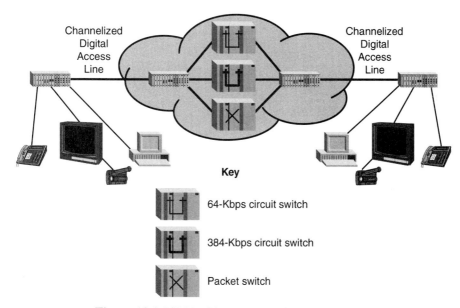

Figure 13.1 ISDN with separate switch technologies

Separate switches are shown in Figure 13.1 because the technology of the early 1980s dictated the use of different switching hardware for each different circuit rate for circuit switching as well as different hardware for packet switching. This is of concern because it means that to support a new service (e.g., 768-Kbps circuit switched connections in Figure 13.1), a new network of dedicated switches must be installed. Thus, implementing a new service is both time-consuming and expensive. Consequently, researchers began to look for a new switching approach that avoids the proliferation of separate switches implied in Figure 13.1.

The approach that became the focus of interest was fast packet switching. The concept is that all traffic types are converted to packets of a form that can be switched by dedicated hardware at very high rates. For digital circuit switching, continuous bit streams are collected into the packets at the entrance to the fast packet network. At the exit of the fast packet network, the payloads of the packets are unwrapped and converted back to the original continuous bit stream.

In the mid 1980s, the emergence of fiber optic transmission and the expected need for higher bandwidth connectivity for applications such as high-definition video resulted in the extension of the ISDN concept to Broadband ISDN (BISDN). BISDN standards adopted the fast packet switching concept with fixed-size[4] (53 bytes)[5] packets that are called *cells*. In addition, instead of a channelized interface, BISDN standards define a cell-based customer interface that is called the *User Network Interface* (UNI). These two concepts are the essence of Asynchronous Transfer Mode (ATM) and are illustrated in Figure 13.2. For a more detailed discussion of the motivation and details for ATM concepts, see [dePrycker].

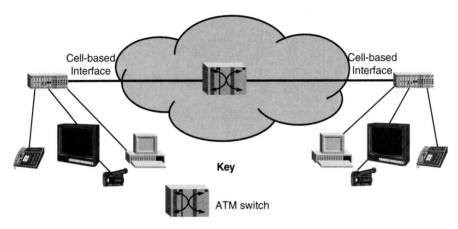

Figure 13.2 BISDN with ATM switching

Like Frame Relay, ATM switches use virtual connections. While Frame Relay transports HDLC frames, the fundamental protocol element of ATM is the cell. The format of the cell at the UNI is shown in Figure 13.3. The payload is 48 bytes, and the header is 5 bytes. ATM is inherently connection-oriented, and virtual connections called *Virtual Channel Connections* (VCC) are used. The VCCs are identified at the UNI by the combined VIRTUAL PATH IDENTIFIER and VIRTUAL CHANNEL IDENTIFIER fields (VPI/VCI).[6] The details of the

---

[4]The decision to use fixed-length cells was a subject of intense debate within CCITT in the mid-1980s. Variable length cells are claimed to be more efficient in the use of bandwidth, while fixed-length cells are claimed to lead to less complex switches. As might be expected in a telephone-oriented context, switching was given high consideration, and the fixed-length approach won out.

[5]The length of 53 bytes is the result of a standards compromise in CCITT. It is hard to imagine a rational technical analysis leading to a length that is a prime number.

[6]Strictly speaking, ATM has two kinds of virtual connection: Virtual Channel Connections and Virtual Path Connections. Virtual Path Connections can be thought of as a set of virtual channels that are switched in a single bundle. For our purposes, we can ignore the distinction and simply refer to VCCs.

syntax and semantics of fields in the cell header are beyond the scope of this discussion. Details can be found in [UNI3].

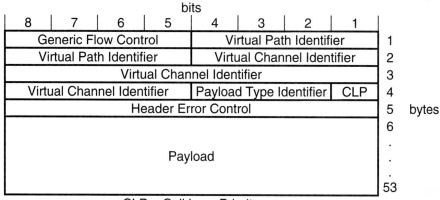

CLP = Cell Loss Priority

Figure 13.3 ATM cell format at the UNI

Devices attached to the UNI can make use of VCCs to communicate with multiple other devices, as shown in Figure 13.4. When a device is sending cells into the ATM network, the value of the VPI/VCI in the cell header identifies the destination UNI. Similarly, when a device receives a cell, the value of the VPI/VCI in the cell header identifies the source UNI.[7] VCCs can be established administratively (e.g., via a paper service order), in which case the VCC is called a *permanent virtual connection* (PVC). VCCs can also be established dynamically by interaction between the devices attached to UNIs and the ATM network, using a signaling protocol [UNI3]. Such a connection is called a *Switched Virtual Connection* (SVC).

The ability to exchange cells using ATM VCCs is not of much use unless the content of the cells can be interpreted. The protocols that provide this capability are called *ATM Adaptation Layer* (AAL) *Protocols.* To adapt ATM to the needs of different types of traffic or service, different AAL protocols are defined. Figure 13.5 shows the protocol architecture for ATM, including the role of AAL. Details of the ATM layer and the ever-increasing assortment of physical layers (PHY) can be found in [UNI3], [G.703], [G.707], [G.708], [G.709], [G.804], and [G.832]. Figure 13.5 shows that the AAL layer is transparent to the ATM network and is composed of three sublayers. Since we are primarily interested in packet data traffic, we describe the role of each AAL sublayer in that context.

---

[7]The value of the VPI/VCI will, in general, change as the cell progresses through the ATM network. These translations are always the same for a given virtual connection and are transparent to the devices attached to the UNI.

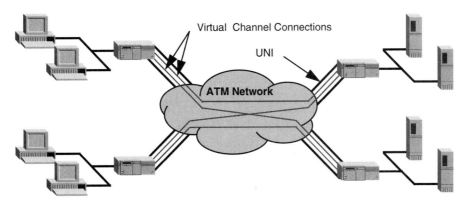

Figure 13.4 ATM Virtual Channel Connections

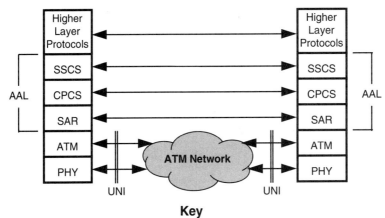

Key

AAL	ATM Adaptation Layer
SSCS	Service-Specific Convergence Sublayer
CPCS	Common Part Convergence Sublayer
SAR	Segmentation and Reassembly Sublayer
ATM	Asynchronous Transfer Mode Layer
PHY	Physical Layer

Figure 13.5 ATM protocol architecture

On transmission, the Segmentation and Reassembly (SAR) sublayer is responsible for breaking up large, variable-length packets into pieces that can be carried in ATM cells. On reception, the SAR sublayer reverses the process by reassembling the pieces of the packet from incoming cells into the original variable-length packet.

The Common Part Convergence Sublayer (CPCS) is responsible for detecting errors that may have occurred in the segmentation and reassembly process. For example, the SAR sublayer may not detect lost cells, which would mean that the product of the reassembly process would be missing some data.

The CPCS can detect this by using a length field. The CPCS only detects errors. Higher layer protocols are expected to recover (if necessary) from such errors.

The Service Specific Convergence Sublayer (SSCS) is dependent on the traffic type that is being carried. For example, it could provide for reliable data transfer by implementing procedures for recovering from the errors detected at the lower layers.

One of the services currently being standardized for BISDN is called *Broadband Connectionless Data Service*.[8] The current working definition of this service was motivated by SMDS. The ITU-T [I.364] describes the current BISDN view of how Connectionless Broadband Data Service can be accessed via the ATM UNI. The service and access protocols are very similar to SMDS and the access to SMDS described in the next subsection. Indeed, SMDS accessed via the ATM UNI is considered to be a proper subset of the final BISDN standards for Connectionless Broadband Data Service.

13.2   Access to SMDS via the ATM UNI

The material for this section is primarily drawn from [SIG008], which in turn references [BICI], which deals with carrying SMDS traffic across an ATM-based interface between two carrier networks. The SIG [SIG008] draws on this material and molds it to apply to the case of CPE service access via the ATM UNI.

The basic idea of access to SMDS via the ATM UNI is illustrated in Figure 13.6. In this figure, each small pipe represents a VCC that is carrying a different service. In the case of Figure 13.6, example services other than SMDS are selected to emphasize that ATM is promised to be useful for multimedia. Instead of SMDS being accessed via a physical link dedicated to SMDS, a dedicated VCC is used. Also note that multiple offerings of SMDS from different service providers (GoliathNet and DaveNet in Figure 13.6) can be simultaneously accessed via the UNI.

In addition to providing a multiservices interface, ATM technology can also be used by a service provider in implementing SMDS. The use of ATM for access to SMDS is described in the next subsection, and then the use of ATM for implementing SMDS within the service-provider network is discussed in Section 13.2.2.

---

[8]Many times this service will be called Connectionless Broadband Data Service (CBDS) which is the name given to similar standardization work in ETSI.

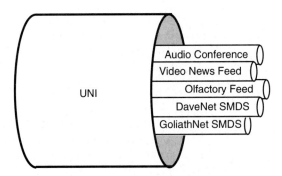

Figure 13.6 SMDS Access via virtual connections over the ATM UNI

13.2.1 Access Protocol

The access protocol for SMDS over ATM is derived from the relationship between SIP and the ATM protocols, which is shown in Figure 13.7. The SIP Connectionless Service Layer (SIP_CLS) is one of the higher layer protocols shown in Figure 13.5, which implies that there is a null SSCS layer; i.e., it is not used. AAL3/4 [I.363][9] is one of the standard protocols for carrying large, variable-length packets with ATM.[10]

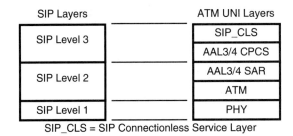

Figure 13.7 Comparison of SIP and ATM layers [SIG008]

The relationships of Figure 13.7 apply when AAL3/4 is used for the transfer of variable-length packets over ATM. In fact, the leading 4 bytes and the trailing 4 bytes of the L3_PDU are identical in format to the AAL3/4 CPCS, as illustrated in Figure 13.8. However, the names of the fields in the AAL3/4 CPCS

---

[9]The number of AAL proposals was large enough that the AALs had to be numbered. Over time, AAL weeding took place, and it was discovered that AAL3 and AAL4 should be merged, keeping the name AAL3/4 as an artifact.

[10]As can be seen in the subsequent discussion in this chapter, AAL3/4 is similar, but not identical, to the segmentation and reassembly protocol of [802.6].

are not the same as the corresponding fields in the L3_PDU. The coding and interpretation of these fields are identical.[11]

	L3_PDU		SIP_CLS and AAL3/4 CPCS		
	Rsvd	AAL3/4	CPI	1 byte
	BEtag	CPCS	Btag	1 byte
	BAsize		BAsize	2 bytes
	DA		DA	8 bytes
	SA		SA	8 bytes
	HLPI		HLPI	6 bits
	PL		PL	2 bits
SMDS	QOS	SIP	QOS	4 bits
Feature-	CIB	Connectionless	CIB	1 bit
Related	HEL	Service	HEL	3 bits
Fields	Brdg	Layer	Brdg	2 bytes
	HE		HE	12 bytes
	Info		Info	≤ 9188 bytes
	PAD		PAD	0 - 3 bytes
	CRC32		CRC32	0 or 4 bytes
	Rsvd	AAL3/4	Algn	1 byte
	BEtag	CPCS	Etag	1 byte
	Length		Length	2 bytes

L3_PDU   **SIP_CLS and AAL3/4 CPCS**

Key

Rsvd	Reserved	QOS	Quality of Service
BEtag	Beginning-End Tag	CIB	CRC32 Indicator Bit
BAsize	Buffer Allocation Size	HEL	Header Extension Length
DA	Destination Address	Brdg	Bridging
SA	Source Address	HE	Header Extension
HLPI	Higher Layer Protocol Identifier	Info	Information
PL	PAD Length	CRC32	32-bit Cyclic Redundancy Check
CPI	Common Part Indication	Btag	Beginning Tag
Algn	Alignment	Etag	End Tag

Figure 13.8 L3_PDU, SIP_CLS, and AAL3/4 CPCS formats

An important observation from the above discussion is that when accessing SMDS via an ATM UNI, the SMDS feature-related fields of the L3_PDU, as shown in Figure 13.8, are used unchanged, as they are with all SMDS access protocols (see Chapters 4, 5, and 6). Because the L3_PDU and associated procedures are identical to the combination of the SIP Connectionless Service

---

[11][BICI] specifies that the values of the BEGINNING TAG field and END TAG field be computed by a separate counter for each MULTIPLEXING IDENTIFICATION field. This would require multiple counters. The SIG [SIG008] requires the use of only one counter, as implied by [I.364], which is identical to the computation for the BEGINNING-END TAG fields (see Chapter 4).

Layer and the AAL3/4 CPCS layer, the protocol layering for ATM UNI access to SMDS is that shown in Figure 13.9.

SIP Level 3
AAL3/4 SAR
ATM
PHY

Figure 13.9 Protocol layering for SMDS access via the ATM UNI

Figure 13.10 shows the format of the AAL3/4 SAR layer PDU. This format is identical to the last 48 bytes of the L2_PDU (see Section 4.6), with the correspondences between the fields as shown in Table 13.1.

ST	SN	MID	User Information	Fill	LI	CRC
2 bits	4 bits	10 bits	44 bytes		6 bits	10 bits

Key
ST   Segment Type
SN   Sequence Number
MID   Multiplexing Identification
LI   Length Indication
CRC   Cyclic Redundancy Check

Figure 13.10 AAL3/4 SAR layer PDU format

L2_PDU field names	AAL3/4 SAR PDU field names
Segment Type	Segment Type
Sequence Number	Sequence Number
Message Identifier	Multiplexing Identification
Segmentation Unit	User Information and Fill
Payload Length	Length Indication
Payload CRC	Cyclic Redundancy Check

Table 13.1 Correspondence between AAL3/4 SAR and L2_PDU fields

The coding and interpretation of the SEGMENT TYPE, SEQUENCE NUMBER, and CYCLIC REDUNDANCY CHECK fields are identical to those for the corresponding fields in the L2_PDU. The USER INFORMATION field is populated exactly as the data portion of the SEGMENTATION UNIT field, and the FILL field is sized to make the combined User Information and Fill be 44 bytes long. The LENGTH INDICATION field is set to the length of the USER INFORMATION field.

The semantics of the MULTIPLEXING IDENTIFICATION field are similar to the semantics of the MESSAGE IDENTIFIER field, in that the MULTIPLEXING IDENTIFICATION field in all SAR PDUs associated with a particular CPCS PDU must have the same value. However, the values used in the MULTIPLEXING IDENTIFICATION field differ from those used in the MESSAGE IDENTIFIER field. According to [I.363], the MULTIPLEXING IDENTIFICATION field is set to 0 when CPCS PDUs are not interleaved on the VCC (i.e., only one CPCS PDU is transmitted at a time). When CPCS PDUs are interleaved, the associated MULTIPLEXING IDENTIFICATION fields are to have nonzero values. Furthermore, [SIG008] specifies that on a particular VCC, either 1 or 16 multiple concurrent L3_PDUs be supported. Therefore, the allowed values of the MULTIPLEXING IDENTIFICATION field are as shown in Table 13.2.[12] When 16 multiple concurrent L3_PDUs are in force, each side of the ATM UNI is to use only 16 unique values in the MULTIPLEXING IDENTIFICATION field.[13]

Number of multiple concurrent L3_PDUs	Values of the Multiplexing Identification field
1	0
16	1 - 1023

Table 13.2 Appropriate values for the MULTIPLEXING IDENTIFICATION field

From the CPE point of view, reassembly is more complex when accessing SMDS via the ATM UNI than when accessing SMDS via SIP.[14] Consider the situation where an EOM is lost, for example, due to ATM switch cell-buffer overflow. If the corresponding value of the MULTIPLEXING IDENTIFICATION field is not reused, the partially reassembled L3_PDU and corresponding context will continue to exist, thus consuming resources (e.g., high-speed memory). To deal with this problem, a timer is called for in [BICI]. The use of this timer constrains the length of time that a reassembly context can exist. The operation of this timer is described in the context of the state machine of Figure 13.11.[15]

---

[12]There appears to be no validation by the receiver on this use of the MULTIPLEXING IDENTIFICATION field. Thus, it appears that L3_PDU transfer would be successful if a nonzero MULTIPLEXING IDENTIFICATION field is used, but only one L3_PDU is transferred at a time (no interleaving). Perhaps this would be grounds for a nighttime visit by the Protocol Police.

[13]This is a similar requirement to that imposed on the SS in the case of SIP. See Chapter 4.

[14]This additional CPE complexity arises from the different philosophies of [772] and [BICI], which is the basis of [SIG008]. CPE simplification is a key objective of [772] (see Chapter 4). This is in stark contrast to [BICI], where the goal is the interconnection of large, complex ATM switches and/or multiplexers.

[15]As with SIP, the fact that the SS will use at most 16 unique values of the MULTIPLEXING IDENTIFICATION field (as specified in [SIG008]) means that such a timer is not necessary. Nevertheless, [BICI] calls for the use of a reassembly timer, and [SIG008] calls for compliance with [BICI]. Consequently, this CPE complexity cannot be avoided without becoming non-compliant.

Another source of increased CPE complexity is the requirement that additional error checking is mandated in [BICI]. This is all described by the state machine shown in Figure 13.11, where the conditions that cause a state transition are listed above the arrow representing the transition. The actions taken in association with each state transition are listed below the corresponding arrow. If MCDUs Out is 1, then a single state machine must be implemented in the CPE. If MCDUs Out is 16, then 16 state machines must be maintained, one state machine for each possible value of the MULTIPLEXING IDENTIFICATION field. Comparing the state machine of Figure 13.11, which is taken from [BICI], with the similar state machine in Section 4.8.2 reveals the complexity increase required of the CPE when accessing SMDS via ATM.

Each state transition is discussed below:

- **(IA1)** This is the normal initiation of a reassembly for the particular value of the MULTIPLEXING IDENTIFICATION field. In addition to storing the fragment of the L3_PDU, the expected value of the next SEQUENCE NUMBER field (RxSN) is calculated, and a reassembly timer is started.

- **(II1)** This represents an error condition where an error is detected in the LENGTH INDICATION field. The reassembly is not initiated.

- **(II2)** This represents an error condition where the BOM was lost or errored. The COMs and EOM are discarded.

- **(II3)** For an L3_PDU that consists of a single segment, no reassembly context needs to be established.

- **(AA1)** This represents an error condition where the EOM was lost or errored. The partially reassembled L3_PDU is discarded, and a new reassembly context is established by storing the new fragment, computing the expected value of the next SEQUENCE NUMBER field, and restarting the reassembly timer.

- **(AA2)** This is the normal reception of a COM. The new fragment is stored, and the expected value of the next SEQUENCE NUMBER field is computed.

- **(AI1)** This represents an error condition where the EOM was lost or errored, and the new BOM is errored by having an incorrect LENGTH INDICATION field. The partially reassembled L3_PDU is discarded, and the reassembly context is destroyed.

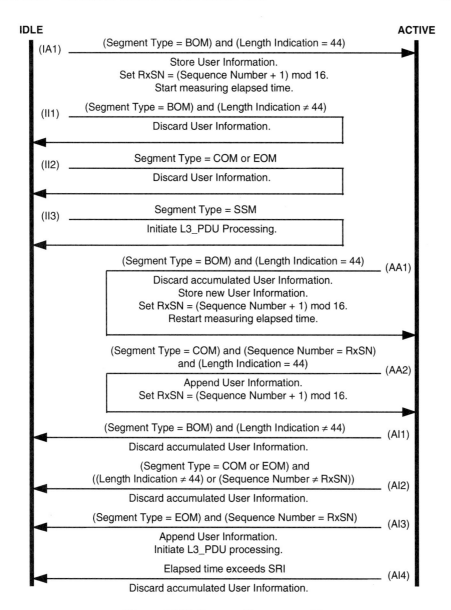

Figure 13.11 Reassembly state machine

- **(AI2)** This represents an error condition where the COM or EOM contains an errored LENGTH INDICATION field and/or an errored SEQUENCE NUMBER field. The partially reassembled L3_PDU is discarded, and the reassembly context is destroyed.

- **(AI3)** This is the normal completion of the reassembly process. The L3_PDU is ready for further processing, and the reassembly context is destroyed.

- **(AI4)** This represents an error condition where the EOM was lost or excessively delayed, which is detected when the timer exceeds the SAR Receive Interval (SRI). (Choosing a value for the SRI is discussed below.) The partially reassembled L3_PDU is discarded, and the reassembly context is destroyed.

The ATM Forum [BICI] states that the value of the SRI is a subject for further study. This is understandable, since setting the SRI appears to be quite challenging. A lower bound can be derived by examining the minimum time that will be required to transmit one L3_PDU across the UNI. From Figure 13.6, it can be seen that the full bandwidth of the physical link may not be available for SMDS. In general, the bandwidth that can be used on a virtual connection carrying SMDS will be limited. The techniques for such limiting, referred to as *Traffic Management*, are described in [UNI3]. It is beyond the scope of this discussion to describe the details of this arcane subject. Suffice it to say that it is likely that a Peak Cell Rate (PCR) in cells per second will be specified. Since the maximum-size L3_PDU requires 210 cells, SRI should satisfy the following:

$$SRI \geq \frac{210}{PCR} \text{ seconds}$$

However selecting a specific value for SRI is more difficult. Regardless of the value of PCR, the actual bandwidth available on the UNI will depend on the bandwidth consumed by the other services and their priority relative to SMDS. Thus, the time to transmit the L3_PDU will depend on the actual bandwidth available to the virtual connection, which depends on both the configuration of the UNI and the level of traffic of the other services at the time the L3_PDU is transmitted. One approach to this problem is to configure the UNI and the service priorities in such a way that a Minimum Cell Rate (MCR) is guaranteed for SMDS. Then SRI can be set as

$$SRI = \frac{210}{MCR} \text{ seconds}$$

The situation becomes more complex if pipelining is used (see Chapter 4) in the service-provider network. In this case, the MCR of the originating UNI may control the time to receive the L3_PDU. If MCR_o is the MCR of the originating UNI, and MCR_d is the MCR of the destination UNI, then ideally,

$$SRI = \frac{210}{\min(MCR_o, MCR_d)} \text{ seconds}$$

Unfortunately, it is probably impossible to compute this value, since MCR_o will in general be different for L3_PDUs from different source SNIs and is likely to be unknown at the destination CPE in any event. Thus we recommend that

$$SRI = \frac{210}{MCR} + \delta \text{ seconds}$$

where δ is a fudge factor to account for the MCR of the originating UNI and other uncertainties, such as delay variations in the service-provider network(s). Note that δ should not be chosen too large, since that implies increased cost in the CPE for increased reassembly resources. We think that an effective value for SRI can only be derived from implementation experience.[16]

13.2.2 Service-Provider Network Implementation

In addition to supporting service access for SMDS, ATM technology can be used within the service provider network. One view of such an implementation, which we call the *Server-Forwarding* approach, is shown in Figure 13.12, which is taken from [I.364]. In this approach, a server is used to provide all service functions "above" ATM. In particular, the Connectionless Service Functions, (CLSF) implemented in CLSF servers, forward L3_PDUs among themselves as well as to and from CPE. Thus, as shown in Figure 13.12, all L3_PDUs exchanged between SMDS and a CPE are carried via a VCC between the CPE and a CLSF server. The CLSF servers use other VCCs to exchange the content of L3_PDUs.[17] This results in all customer data flowing through one or more CLSF servers, as illustrated in Figure 13.12.

A disadvantage of the server-forwarding approach is that the customer data must flow through some ATM switches twice. This is avoided in an alternative approach that we call *Server-Assisted Forwarding,* which is illustrated in Figure 13.13. In this arrangement, the VCC carrying SMDS across the UNI is terminated in the ATM switch. The information required to forward an L3_PDU is cached in the ATM switch. This information is obtained from the CLSF server and includes service-feature information (e.g., Access Classes) and the identity

---

[16]The challenge of choosing SRI is not specific to SMDS. It applies to the transfer of any large, variable-length packets over a multiple-services ATM UNI.

[17]L3_PDUs cannot provide all of the functions required for an internal network protocol. Thus, CLSF servers exchange much information in addition to the content of L3_PDUs.

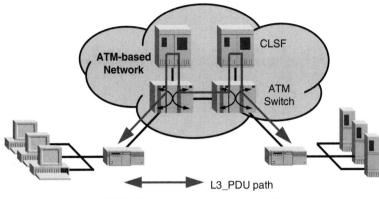

Figure 13.12 Server-forwarding for SMDS

of the destination ATM switch(es).[18] With this information, an ATM switch can set up a virtual connection to the destination ATM switch(es) and use this connection to forward L3_PDUs. This connection can be cleared during long periods of inactivity. Thus, the delay caused by traversing the same ATM switch twice is avoided, and the number of virtual connections that are maintained through each ATM switch is decreased. The cost of obtaining these advantages is that the ATM switch requires functionality beyond that of a simple ATM layer device.

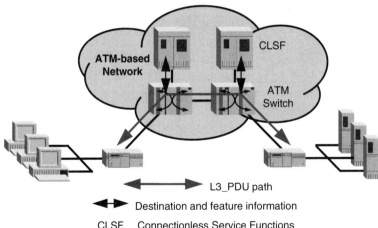

Figure 13.13 Server-assisted forwarding for SMDS

---

[18]Multiple-destination switches can be involved when a multipoint connection is used to support SMDS Group Addressing.

13.3   Service Aspects

With two exceptions, all of the service features of SMDS are available when accessing the service via the ATM UNI. The exceptions are multi-CPE configurations and Access Classes. The nature of the modifications to these features are discussed in the next two subsections.

Performance and quality of service may also be affected by the use of the ATM UNI. These are discussed in the third subsection.

13.3.1 Multi-CPE

The ATM UNI in [UNI3] is defined as a point-to-point interface. Thus the multi-CPE configuration in which distributed CPE (see Section 3.2) share the bandwidth of the service interface is not supported. On the other hand, multiple CPE can easily share the ATM UNI through the multiplexing of VCCs supporting SMDS. Figure 13.14 illustrates an example. In this figure, a CSU/DSU multiplexes two SMDS DXI interfaces onto a single ATM UNI by using two VCCs, one associated with each SMDS DXI. In this arrangement, the two routers are attached to two logically separate SMDS interfaces and thus can only communicate via SMDS. There is no local traffic in the sense of local traffic on an Access DQDB when a Multi-CPE configuration is used with SIP.

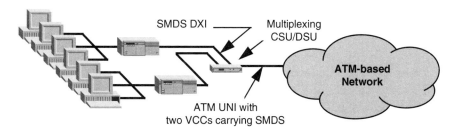

Figure 13.14 Multiple routers sharing an ATM UNI for access to SMDS

13.3.2 Access Classes

As described in Chapter 3, Access Classes are defined for DS3 and E3 based access to SMDS. These Access Classes may be available when accessing SMDS via an ATM UNI, provided that the proper PCR on the VCC supporting SMDS is configured as shown in Table 13.3. (Recall from Chapter 4 that DS3 and E3 PLCP frames have a duration of 125 µsec, and carry 12 and 9 cells respectively.) When the PCR is less than that shown in Table 13.3, some or all of the Access Classes will not be available.

Access Classes	Peak Cell Rate (cells/second)
DS3 SNI Access Classes	96,000
E3 SNI Access Classes	72,000

Table 13.3 Peak cell rates for Access Classes [SIG008]

When higher-rate links are used for service access (e.g., 155 Mbps), or different PCR values are used, additional Access Classes are likely to be defined and offered. For these Access Classes, the Credit Manager Algorithm (see Section 4.9) is slightly modified. Instead of executing the algorithm each time an ATM cell is received, the algorithm is executed periodically at the PCR. This results in the following expression for Sustained Information Rate:

$$\text{SIR} = \left[8 \frac{\text{bits}}{\text{byte}} \right] \times \left[\frac{\text{PCR cells}}{\text{second}} \right] \times \left[\frac{N_{\text{inc}} \text{ bytes}}{I_{\text{inc}} \text{ cells}} \right] \text{Mbps}$$

As an example, if PCR = 40,000 cells per second, $N_{\text{inc}} = 13$, and $I_{\text{inc}} = 1$, (these values of N_{inc} and I_{inc} correspond to Access Class 2 for a DS3-based SNI), then SIR = 4.16 Mbps. In the case of a DS3-based SNI, these values of N_{inc} and I_{inc} yield SIR = 9.98 Mbps. The expression for the Maximum Burst Size remains:

$$\text{Maximum Burst Size} = \left[\frac{C_{\text{max}}}{44 - \frac{N_{\text{inc}}}{I_{\text{inc}}}} \right] \times 44 = \left[\frac{I_{\text{inc}} \times C_{\text{max}}}{44 \times I_{\text{inc}} - N_{\text{inc}}} \right] \times 44 \text{ bytes}$$

However, the definition of a burst must change. In the case of SMDS access via the ATM UNI, it is the number of L3_PDU INFORMATION field bytes that can be transmitted in ATM cells at the PCR. Thus, if we use the parameter values from the previous example and assume $C_{\text{max}} = 9188$, the Maximum Burst Size = 13041 bytes, just as it does for Access Class 2. However, the time to transmit this burst is approximately 7.4 ms (= 297 cells/40,000 cells per second), compared to approximately 3.1 ms for Access Class 2 on a DS3-based SNI.

There may be situations in which Table 13.3 does not apply. As mentioned in the discussion of choosing the SRI, bandwidth on a VCC may be limited by the use of Traffic Management by the service provider. In particular, the number of cells that can be sent at the PCR may limited in number, and cells that violate this constraint are subject to higher levels of discard than those that comply.[19] The result can be that traffic that abides by an Access Class experiences

---

[19]The marking of cells for discard that violate the traffic management constraint is commonly called traffic policing. The Protocol Police appears to be a growth organization in the Information Age.

intermittent, high levels of L3_PDU loss. Our advice is to be sure your carrier is exercising Traffic Management that is consistent with the Access Class.

13.3.3 Performance Objectives

The performance objectives described in Chapter 7 should generally apply to the case of SMDS access via ATM UNIs served by a single LEC network. However, the PCR affects the delay that will be experienced by L3_PDUs. The SIG [SIG008] implies that the delay objectives for SMDS access via ATM should be calculated as described in Chapter 7 by substituting the cell rate for the access path bit rate. Table 13.4 shows the result for delay of Individually Addressed L3_PDUs for transfers between ATM UNIs. Table 13.5 shows the result for Group Addressed L3_PDUs for transfers between ATM UNIs. The numbers in Table 13.4 and Table 13.5 assume that all L3_PDU transfers across the ATM UNI occur at the PCR for the VCC supporting SMDS. A more extensive compilation of delay objectives is contained in Chapter 7.

Peak Cell Rates (cells/second)		95th percentile of delay (ms)
UNI A	UNI B	
96,000	96,000	20
96,000	3,333	80
3,333	3,333	140

Table 13.4 95th percentile bounds on delay for Individually Addressed L3_PDUs

Peak Cell Rates (cells/second)		95th percentile of delay (ms)
UNI A	UNI B	
96,000	96,000	100
96,000	3,333	160
3,333	3,333	220

Table 13.5 95th percentile bounds on delay for Group Addressed L3_PDUs

Appendix A

Overview of Distributed Queue Dual Bus

This appendix provides background material on the Distributed Queue Dual Bus (DQDB). It is intended as an aid to understanding the SMDS Interface Protocol (SIP). For a complete technical description of DQDB, [802.6] should be consulted.

A.1   DQDB Functional Architecture

Figure A.1 shows a highly simplified diagram of the functional architecture of a DQDB station. The functions depicted in gray are not included in [802.6] but were the subject of ongoing standardization when [802.6] was completed. The MAC Service to Logical Link Control is that defined in [802.2] and is the connectionless data capability provided by all IEEE 802 LANs and FDDI. This is the capability used for accessing SMDS. The connectionless protocol service is supported by means of a large, variable-length PDU called the *Initial MAC Protocol Data Unit* (IMPDU). The MAC Convergence Function is responsible for segmenting and reassembling the IMPDU to and from small PDUs for transmission on the DQDB. The Queued Arbitrated Functions carry out the basic DQDB algorithm to effect orderly use of the transmission bandwidth on the buses by the small PDUs.

The Isochronous Services are services that receive and deliver SDUs in a periodic function. For example, a 64-Kbps circuit could be implemented as the reception and delivery of a byte every 125 μsec. Access to the bandwidth on the

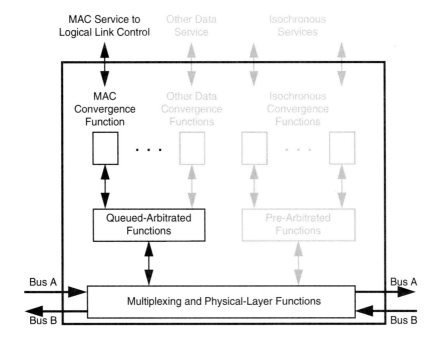

Figure A.1 Simplified DQDB station functional architecture

buses is provided by the Pre-Arbitrated Functions. Although the specification for Pre-Arbitrated media access was not complete when [802.6] was published, the Standard was carefully developed so that stations with only Queued Arbitrated capability would operate on a DQDB with stations having the Pre-Arbitrated capability.

Since SIP exploits the MAC Service to Logical Link Control, we focus our discussion on that aspect of DQDB in this appendix.

The next four sections of this appendix describe DQDB, covering physical topology, media access control, segmentation and reassembly, and allocation of MIDs. Section A.6 discusses DQDB performance issues and the implications for SMDS. Section A.7 shows the correlation between SIP and IEEE Std. 802.6-1990.

A.2   Physical Topology

DQDB makes use of contra-flowing dual busses configured as either an Open Bus Topology, as shown in Figure A.2, or as a Looped Bus Topology, as shown in Figure A.3. Each bus is composed of a series of equal-speed transmission links (e.g., DS1 or DS3). At the head of each bus is a special function called *Head-of-Bus*. Head-of-Bus A generates empty slots on Bus A and terminates Bus

B. Head-of-Bus B generates empty slots on Bus B and terminates Bus A. The delimitation of the slots is effected by the use of the Physical Layer Convergence Procedure (PLCP), as described in Section 4.7. Since SIP is based on the Open Bus Topology, we limit the discussion to this case.

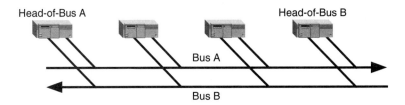

Figure A.2 Open Bus Topology

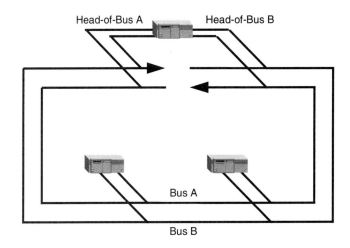

Figure A.3 Looped Bus Topology

When a failure is detected, the Head-of-Bus function can be assumed by any station. Figure A.4 illustrates this with the Open Bus Topology. In this case, the network becomes segmented, but stations within each segment can continue to communicate among themselves. The SMDS Switching System (SS) plays the role of Head-of-Bus A. Thus, Figure A.4 represents the case of a multi-CPE configuration (see Section 3.2) with a failure on the access path between the SS and the customer premises. In such a situation, local communications among the CPE could continue.

The two busses and the Heads-of-Bus are not identical in function. They play different roles in reconfiguration in the face of failures and in the MID Page Allocation. MID Page Allocation is described later in this appendix.

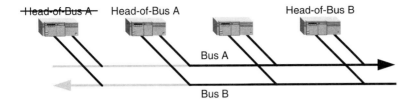

Figure A.4 Failure in the Open Bus Topology

A.3   Media Access Control

Media access is based on the slots that roughly correspond to the L2_PDU (see Section A.7). The key is the ability of a station to both read and overwrite bits. This concept is illustrated by Figure A.5. A station can be viewed as attached to a bus with a byte-wide shift register that can first be read and then possibly overwritten before being forwarded to the next station on the bus.[1] Thus, if a station does not overwrite a bit, it repeats that bit on to the downstream station.

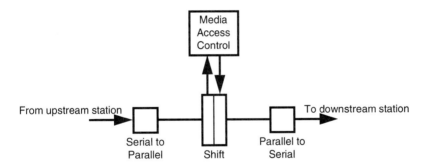

Figure A.5 Conceptual attachment to a bus

Access to the media is done on a slot-by-slot basis. The format of the slot is presented in Figure A.6. The ACCESS CONTROL field contains the bits that are used to arbitrate access to each bus. It is shown in Figure A.7.

Access Control	Segment
1 byte	52 bytes

Figure A.6 DQDB slot format

---

[1]This discussion is meant for ease of exposition and should not be considered to imply a particular design. Indeed, many of the details of IEEE Std. 802.6-1990 were based on an assumption of 32-bit computations.

Busy	SL_TYPE	PSR	Reserved	REQ_2	REQ_1	REQ_0
1 bit	1 bit	1 bit	2 bits	1 bit	1 bit	1 bit

Figure A.7 Access Control Field format

If the BUSY bit = 0, the slot is available for write access by a station, and if the BUSY bit = 1, then the slot SEGMENT field has already been written by a station and must not be written by any other station. The SL_TYPE bit is used to indicate if a slot is a Pre-Arbitrated slot[2] or a Queued Arbitrated slot.[3] Since we are only concerned with the data aspects of DQDB, we can assume that this bit is always set to 0. The PSR bit is set to 1 under certain conditions (see Section 5.1.2.2.2 in [802.6]) when a slot is received by a station. It is included to allow the use of an eraser node that could set the BUSY bit from 1 back to 0, thus allowing slot reuse.[4] The RESERVED bits are set to 0. The last three bits, REQ_2, REQ_1, and REQ_0, are used by a station to request empty slots on the opposite bus with three levels of priority.

The BUSY, REQ_2, REQ_1, and REQ_0 bits are used for accessing Queued Arbitrated slots on a given bus. To see how this works, consider the case where all stations are sending at the lowest priority; that is, the REQ_2 and REQ_1 bits are always set to 0. In this case, each station maintains two nonnegative counters, a Countdown Counter and a Request Counter, for controlling access to each bus: a total of four counters. Figures A.8 and A.9 illustrate the operation of these counters for Bus A.

When a station has no data to send on Bus A, it maintains the Request Counter as illustrated in Figure A.8. Each time a slot on Bus B has the REQ_0 bit set to 1, the counter is incremented by 1. Each time a slot on Bus A has the BUSY bit set to 0, the counter is decremented by 1 but not below 0. Thus, while the station has no data to send, the value in the Request Counter can be viewed as an approximation of the number of stations downstream on Bus A that have requested free slots on Bus A by setting a REQ_0 bit to 1 on Bus B and that have not yet seen a free slot. Notice that since Bus A and Bus B are of equal speed, the rate at which REQ_0 bits are set on Bus B cannot exceed the rate at which free slots are generated by the Head-of-Bus A.

---

[2]During the development of IEEE Std. 802.6-1990, there was a substantial effort to maintain alignment with the emerging Broadband ISDN standards. BISDN principles declare that time-division multiplexing shall not be used. Therefore, rather than calling slots *isochronous*, which would imply strict timing, the term *Pre-Arbitrated* was invented.

[3]*Queued Arbitrated* is the fancy term for data (the opposite of isochronous).

[4]A slot that has been received by a station that is the only destination will have its PSR bit set. In theory, a special function, called an *eraser node*, can overwrite the header in such slots, thus allowing the slot to be reused further along the bus. The eraser node is the subject of future standardization by IEEE Project 802.6.

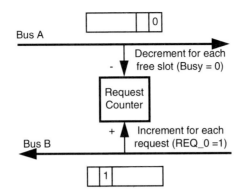

Figure A.8 Station not trying to send on Bus A

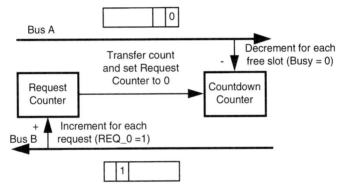

Figure A.9 Station trying to send on Bus A

When a station transitions from the state of having no data to send to having data (a slot) to send, the value of the Countdown Counter is set to the current value of the Request Counter, and the Request Counter is reset to 0, as indicated in Figure A.9. At the same time, the station "queues a request bit" on Bus B. This means that the station establishes a process that exists until it sees a REQ_0 bit = 0 on Bus B, which it sets to 1. The term *queues* is used because it is possible for several such processes to be established before the next REQ_O bit = 0 is observed. These processes can be thought of as a queue of request bits. This means that a request bit is set to 1 on Bus B for every slot transmitted on Bus A.

While the station has a slot to send, it maintains the counters as shown in Figure A.9. The Request Counter is incremented for every REQ_0 bit = 1 on Bus B, and the Countdown Counter is decremented for every free slot observed on Bus A. During this process, the value of the Countdown Counter approximates the number of downstream stations on Bus A that requested a slot *before* this station that have not yet received a free slot to satisfy their requests. The Request Counter approximates the number of downstream stations on Bus A that requested a slot *after* this station that have not yet received a free slot to satisfy their requests.

When the Countdown Counter reaches 0, the station seizes (writes data into) the next free slot available on Bus A. If it then has another slot to send, it sets the values of the Counters as above and repeats the countdown process. Thus, if stations downstream on Bus A have slots to send, this station cannot seize all slots but will honor their requests for free slots.

If the requests for free slots could be recognized instantly by all upstream stations, the resulting system would operate as a perfect First-In-First-Out queue with respect to slots. This is illustrated in Figures A.10.A through A.10.H.

Figure A.10.A shows the initial conditions. None of the stations have slots to send, and thus their Countdown Counters are undefined. All Request Counters are assumed to be 0.

Figure A.10.A Initial conditions

The next event is that Station 2 gets a slot to send on Bus A. Figure A.10.B shows the counters after this event. Station 1 observed the request bit set by Station 2, and thus its Request Counter has a value of 1.

Figure A.10.B Station 2 gets a slot to send

Next Station 3 gets a slot to send, which means that both Stations 1 and 2 increment their Request Counters as shown in Figure A.10.C.

Next Station 1 gets a slot to send. The only impact is that Station 1 sets its Countdown Counter to 2 and clears its Request Counter. The result is shown in Figure A.10.D.

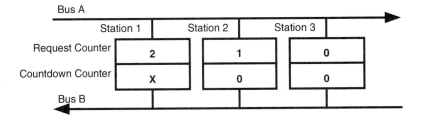

Figure A.10.C Station 3 gets a slot to send

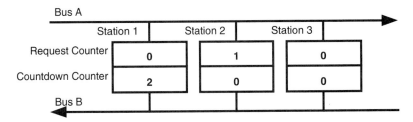

Figure A.10.D Station 1 gets a slot to send

Now a free slot arrives on Bus A. Station 1 lets it pass and decrements its Countdown Counter. Station 2 has its Countdown Counter = 0, so it uses the free slot. The result is shown in Figure A.10.E.

Bus A

	Station 1	Station 2	Station 3
Request Counter	0	1	0
Countdown Counter	1	X	0

Bus B

Figure A.10.E Free slot appears and is seized by Station 2

After sending the slot, Station 2 immediately gets another slot to send, thus causing its Countdown Counter to take on the value 1 and causing the Request Counter in Station 1 to be incremented as shown in Figure A.10.F.

The next free slot is passed by Stations 1 and 2 because their Countdown Counters are not 0. Thus, Station 3 seizes this slot, resulting in the counter values in Figure A.10.G.

Finally, another free slot arrives, which is seized by Station 1 since its Countdown Counter is 0. The resulting counters, shown in Figure A.10.H, indicate that the next free slot will be seized by Station 2. Thus, the arrival order of slots to the system (2, 3, 1, 2) is the order in which they are sent on Bus A.

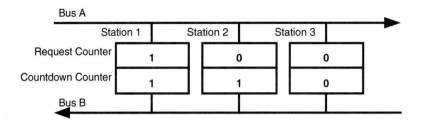

Figure A.10.F Station 2 gets another slot to send

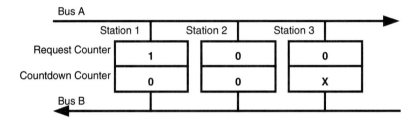

Figure A.10.G Next free slot is seized by Station 3

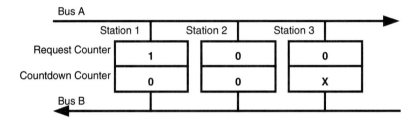

Figure A.10.H Next free slot is seized by Station 1

Of course, the assumption used in Figures A.10.A–H that the requests are immediately communicated to upstream stations is not valid. It is easy to formulate examples where the propagation time of the request bits leads to non-FIFO behavior. In fact, the performance characteristics of DQDB have become a topic of high interest. We will consider this phenomenon in Section A.6.

Finally, the REQ_1 and REQ_2 bits are used to implement two higher levels of priority for slot access. It is straightforward to generalize the DQDB algorithm by defining a Request Counter and a Count Down Counter for each of the three levels of DQDB Priority. Thus, if a station has used the REQ_2 bit to request a free slot and the request bit has propagated to the end of Bus B, it will

receive a free slot before all stations that have requested a free slot using the
REQ_0 bit or the REQ_1 bit.

With the above explanation in mind, we can now consider how the ACCESS
CONTROL field is handled in SMDS. Since SMDS is a data service, it does not use
Pre-Arbitrated slots; hence, the SS always sets the SL_TYPE bit to 0 (see Figure
A.21). In order to allow the use of Pre-Arbitrated slots for local communications
in a multi-CPE configuration, the SS ignores this bit on reception. Since the SS
never receives slots on Bus A, it always sets the PSR bit to 0. In the event that
the eraser node is standardized, the SS ignores this bit on reception so that an
eraser node could be incorporated in the multi-CPE configuration case. To
comply with [802.6], the SS sets the RESERVED bits to 0 and ignores them on
reception, so they could be used for local communications in the multi-CPE
configuration case if they become standardized in the future. Since the SS never
transmits on Bus B, it never needs to request free slots for that bus; hence, the SS
always sets REQ_0 bit = REQ_1 bit = REQ_2 bit = 0. Of course, to allow
local communications in the multi-CPE configuration case, the SS processes
these bits as described in Chapter 4.

A.4   Segmentation and Reassembly

The DQDB algorithm provides a means for several stations to transmit slots onto
the shared dual bus in an orderly way. What remains to be described is the
method by which the appropriate stations receive from the dual bus. In principle,
a number of different techniques can coexist to effect an integrated services
network. To understand how these techniques are differentiated, we need to look
at the format of the SEGMENT field, as shown in Figure A.11. (Recall that the
SEGMENT is a field of the slot; see Figure A.6.)

Virtual Channel Identifier	Payload Type	Segment Priority	Header Check Sequence	Segment Payload
20 bits	2 bits	2 bits	8 bits	48 bytes

Figure A.11 SEGMENT field format

When the VIRTUAL CHANNEL IDENTIFIER field contains the value 1111
11111111 11111111_B = $FFFFF_H$, the SEGMENT field is identified as carrying
connectionless data, and the SEGMENT PAYLOAD field contains what is called a
Derived MAC Protocol Data Unit (DMPDU), whose format is shown in Figure
A.12. The only valid value for both the PAYLOAD TYPE field and the SEGMENT
PRIORITY field is 00_B. (All other values are reserved.) Thus, since for
connectionless data these three fields always equal $FFFFF0_H$, the HEADER CHECK

SEQUENCE field is also constant, and can be calculated to be 00100010_B.[5] Thus, the SEGMENT HEADER equals the constant $FFFFF022_H$.

Segment Type	Sequence Number	Message Identifier	Segmentation Unit	Payload Length	Payload CRC
2 bits	4 bits	10 bits	44 bytes	6 bits	10 bits

Figure A.12 DMPDU format

The SEGMENTATION UNIT field contains a piece of the large, variable-length IMPDU, which is very similar to the L3_PDU. The format of the IMPDU and how it compares to the L3_PDU are presented in the last section of this appendix. For the purposes of this discussion, the important aspect of the format of the IMPDU is that a complete 64-bit destination address field is contained within the first 44 bytes.

To send an IMPDU, the transmitting station chooses a currently unused MESSAGE IDENTIFIER (MID) and segments the IMPDU into 44-byte units that form the SEGMENTATION UNIT field. The first DMPDU has the SEGMENT TYPE field = Beginning of Message (BOM), the last has SEGMENT TYPE = End of Message (EOM), and the intervening have SEGMENT TYPE field = Continuation of Message (COM). (SEGMENT TYPE field = Single Segment Message (SSM) is also theoretically possible.)

Potential receiving stations observe the passing slots. SEGMENT fields of busy slots are further processed if the VIRTUAL CHANNEL IDENTIFIER field = $FFFFF_H$. If the SEGMENT TYPE field = BOM, the destination address of the IMPDU is examined to see if it identifies this station. If it does, then the station establishes a reassembly process that is identified by the value of the MID. If the SEGMENT TYPE field = COM or EOM, the MID is compared against those that identify ongoing reassembly processes. If there is a match, the SEGMENTATION UNIT field is appended to the IMPDU being reassembled. (If the SEGMENT TYPE field = SSM, only a receive decision based on the destination address is made; no reassembly process needs to be started.)

Notice that a station can simultaneously be receiving IMPDUs from multiple sources on the dual bus. The method by which the SEGMENTATION UNIT fields are appended to the correct IMPDU is the MID. This means that the MIDs being used to transmit IMPDUs on a given bus must be unique to each transmitting station. The technique used to guarantee this is described in the next section.

---

[5]As noted before, the SIP protocol stack provides ample opportunity to test one's CRC skills. This value can be verified by using Appendix C and the generator polynomial of degree 8, $G(x) = x^8 + x^2 + x + 1$.

A.5   MID Page Allocation

Since accurate reassembly requires each station that is transmitting on a bus to be using a unique MID, there is a technique for distributing MIDs, called *MID Page Allocation*. In describing the MID Page Allocation, we first describe the algorithm and then describe the details of the protocols that implement the algorithm. The algorithm starts with messages generated by the Head-of-Bus A. Each message indicates a particular MID value,[6] and thus the Head-of-Bus A cycles through the MID values. As a message passes by a station, if that station believes that it "owns" the MID value indicated in the message and it wants to keep it, the station "marks" the message. If the message was already marked, the station removes the MID value from its ownership list, since there is a conflict with another station upstream on Bus A. This process is called the *keep phase* of the algorithm. If a message reaches the Head-of-Bus-B unmarked, then the MID value indicated by the message is available to be claimed for use by any station.

The Head-of-Bus B relays the messages unchanged onto Bus B which is the beginning of the *claim phase* of the algorithm. A station wishing to claim a new MID value observes the messages and when it sees one that is unmarked, it marks it and adds the indicated MID value to its ownership list. Figure A.13 shows an overview of the algorithm.

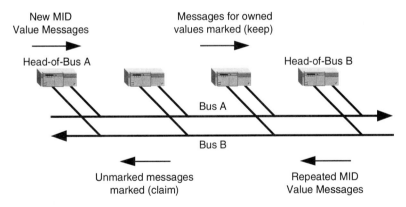

Figure A.13 Overview of the MID Page Allocation algorithm

---

[6]One might conclude from the name of this protocol that it allocates MID values in groups (pages). However, this is not the case. The values are allocated one at a time. At one time in the development of IEEE Std. 802.6-1990, the MESSAGE IDENTIFIER field was proposed to be 14 bits, and MID values were allocated in pages of 4. In an attempt to maintain alignment with the emerging BISDN standards, four bits were taken away from the MESSAGE IDENTIFIER field when the draft document was nearly complete, and it was deemed easier to leave the name of the protocol unchanged and simply define a page to equal 1.

It should be evident that when a station successfully claims an MID value, it will be the only station owning the value. But how can two stations try to keep an MID value? The answer is that this can happen if a dual bus has been segmented due to a failure and then repaired. Such conflicts will be short-lived; they will be resolved as soon as the Head-of-Bus A has cycled through all possible MID values. For example, using the DS3 PLCP, an MID-value message is generated every 125 µsec. Thus all values will be resolved in no more than $2^{10} \times 125$ µsec = 128 ms.[7]

In [802.6], the messages used for the MID Page Allocation are carried in the MID PAGE ALLOCATION FIELD (MPAF), which is shown in Figure A.14. This field is a part of the Type 1 SIP Level 1 Control Information (see Section 4.7.5).

Page Reservation	Page Counter Modulus	Page Counter Control
2 bits	2 bits	2 bits

Figure A.14 MID PAGE ALLOCATION FIELD format

Clearly the MPAF cannot explicitly specify the 10 bits of the MID. Instead, the value of the MID is specified implicitly by the use of two counters (one for each bus) that are maintained by each station. When an MPAF is received, the value of the Page Counter is the MID value whose status is indicated by the PAGE RESERVATION field. Table A.1 shows the interpretation of this field. When a station wants to either keep or claim an MID value, it sets the PAGE RESERVATION field to 11_B.

Page Reservation Field value	Bus A interpretation	Bus B interpretation
00_B	Not Reserved	Not Reserved
01_B	Not Reserved	Reserved
10_B	Not Reserved	Reserved
11_B	Reserved	Reserved

Table A.1 Page Reservation field interpretation

After the PAGE RESERVATION field is processed, the PAGE COUNTER CONTROL (PCC) field and the PAGE COUNTER MODULUS (PCM) field are processed to control the Page Counter. The PCM is used to check the value of the Page Counter. It is the MID value modulo 4 or, equivalently, the two least

---

[7]Actually, the limit is 127.875 ms, since MID = 0 is reserved for SSMs and thus is never indicated in the messages generated by the Head-of-Bus A.

significant bits of the binary representation of the MID value. The PCC indicates whether the counter should be incremented or reset according to Table A.2.

PCC value	Interpretation
00_B	Increment
01_B	Reset
10_B	Increment
11_B	Increment

Table A.2 PCC interpretation

Figure A.15 is a simplified[8] state machine representation of how the PCM and PCC are used to control the Page Counter. Being in the Active state implies that the Page Counter is synchronized, while being in the Idle state implies a loss of synchronization. Consequently, a station can only mark messages (by setting PAGE RESERVATION field = 11_B) when the Page Counter is in the Active state. The actions taken in association with each state transition are listed below the corresponding arrow. Each state transition is discussed below:

- **(AA1)** This is the normal Page Counter increment operation.

- **(AA2)** This is the normal Page Counter reset. It normally occurs when the Page Counter = 1023. The Page Counter is set back to 1 because MID = 0 is reserved for use by SSMs.

- **(AI1)** A failure of the PCM to match the value of the Page Counter modulo 4 indicates a loss of synchronization, and the Idle state is entered.

- **(II1)** This is the operation while in the Idle state waiting for the reset.

- **(IA1)** Reception of PCC = Reset implies that the Page Counter should be 1 and synchronization is restored.

A.6   DQDB Performance

In the last few years, a seemingly uncountable number of papers and conference presentations have appeared analyzing the performance of DQDB and proposing modifications to the basic algorithm. In particular, many of the authors have addressed what they call the "fairness" of DQDB. We do not attempt a thorough

---

[8][802.6] specifies a slightly more complicated procedure in order to prevent counter overflow. The details are not important to our overview.

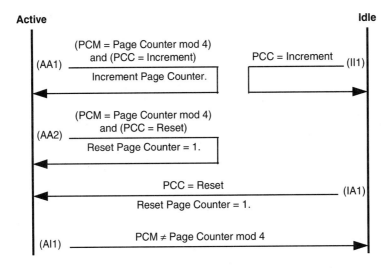

Figure A.15 Simplified Page Counter state machine

review of the literature here. However, we cannot resist having our say about the DQDB "fairness" and the implications for SMDS.

We begin with an example of the type of analysis that has been used to raise the issue of fairness. Figure A.16 shows two stations, X and Y, that are separated by 3 slot times (approximately 7.5 Km if the stations are separated by a .8 speed-of-light propagation medium, and DS3 transmission is used). Assume that X has been continuously transmitting slots on Bus A and, at time $T = 0$, Station Y wants to start transmitting on Bus A. Further assume that only X and Y are active on the DQDB, which means that X is always receiving empty slots on Bus A. Figure A.16 shows the situation at $T = 0$ with Y having just set a request bit on Bus B.

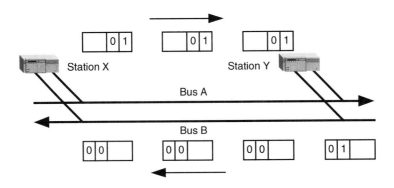

Figure A.16 Two stations separated by 3 slot times, $T = 0$

Because of the busy slots en route on Bus A, Y will not see an empty slot in the time interval $T = 0$ to $T = 6$ slot times. The situation at $T = 3$ slot times is illustrated in Figure A.17. Here we see that the request from Y has just reached X. This means that the next slot leaving X will be empty, as shown in Figure A.18.

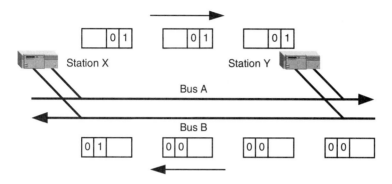

Figure A.17 Situation at time $T = 3$ slot times

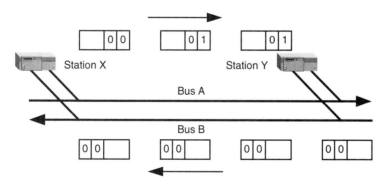

Figure A.18 Situation at time $T = 4$ slot times

Figure A.18 shows that Y will not begin sending its slot until time $T = 6$ slot times, at which point Y will again set a request bit, and the process will repeat itself. As a result, X obtains 5/6 of the Bus A bandwidth, while Y obtains 1/6.

A conclusion that is commonly drawn from the above type of example is that DQDB is unfair. Both stations are always trying to use Bus A and, if the metric of fairness is that each gets an equal share of the bandwidth, then the conclusion follows.

However, the practical implications of such an analysis are questionable. When data networks are fully loaded, they are *dead*. Full utilization means that queues are growing without bound, which in turn means that higher layer protocols (e.g., transport layer protocols), are experiencing broken connections. Worrying about bandwidth share under such conditions is the equivalent of optimizing the placement of deck chairs on the Titanic.

The question of practical importance is "Does DQDB exhibit unfairness under heavy load?" To answer this question requires a different metric of fairness since, for DQDB, when the offered load on the network is less than 100%, all stations are obtaining all the bandwidth they request. We believe that a reasonable measure of fairness under heavy loading is the variation in delay in sending IMPDUs relative to position on the bus. For example, if d_j is the average delay for sending IMPDUs for station j and there are n stations, then a measure of fairness, F, can be defined as follows:

$$F = \frac{\max\{d_j \mid j = 1, \ldots, n\}}{\min\{d_j \mid j = 1, \ldots, n\}}$$

$F = 1$ represents perfect fairness, and the larger the value of F, the more unfair the performance.

Unfortunately, analytical techniques for determining F under realistic traffic-arrival models have not been discovered. As a result, only simulation studies have been performed. In fact, during the final stages of development of IEEE Std. 802.6-1990, Sayeed Ghani (technical editor of the document) and Ray Schnitzler (then a Bellcore representative) performed extensive simulation studies. The results indicated that stations located near the Head-of-Bus experienced modestly lower IMPDU delay than those near the end of the bus when loads were over 95%. These differences were nowhere close to what is suggested by the fully loaded analytical examples.

Another interesting result from these studies involves Bandwidth Balancing. Bandwidth Balancing is a technique included in [802.6] to prevent bandwidth-sharing anomalies under 100% loading such as that described above. When Bandwidth Balancing is invoked, each station increments its Request Counter for every transmission of N Queued Arbitrated slots. N is called the *Bandwidth Balancing Modulus*, and [802.6] calls out a default value of 8. The simulation results suggested that the increase in IMPDU delay due to the lost bandwidth resulting from Bandwidth Balancing totally masked any improvement in IMPDU delay variation based on bus location. This is why Bandwidth Balancing is not required for the SS in [772].

If we accept the fact that there is some modest IMPDU delay advantage depending on location on the bus, then the question becomes "What does this mean for SMDS?" First of all, it means nothing for the single-CPE Access. For the multi-CPE configuration, we need to examine the physical layout of the DQDB. Figure A.19 shows this layout, with the longest part of the DQDB being between the SS and CPE.

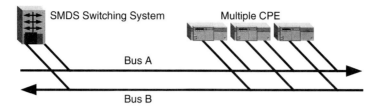

Figure A.19 Physical layout of Access DQDB with SMDS

The distance between the SS and the CPE could be as long as tens of kilometers, while the CPE stations will typically be located relatively close to each other within the customer's building or campus. Since the SS never transmits on Bus B, its delay disadvantage relative to the CPE is irrelevant. The CPE, being relatively clustered, will have approximately equal delay performance in transmitting SMDS traffic to the SS. On Bus A, SMDS traffic is only transmitted by the SS, and thus the delay variation is irrelevant.[9]

Thus we conclude that the so-called unfairness of DQDB is probably of modest practical importance in MANs and, in any event, is not relevant to SMDS.

A.7   Correlation Between SIP and IEEE Std. 802.6-1990

As an aid in understanding the relationship between SIP and IEEE Std. 802.6-1990, we compare the SIP PDUs (see Chapter 4) with the corresponding PDUs specified in [802.6]. Figure A.20 shows the relationship between the fields of the L3_PDU and the IMPDU.

Figure A.21 shows the relationship of the fields of the L2_PDU to the fields of the slot, the SEGMENT field, and the DMPDU.

Figure A.22 shows the relationship of the fields of the SIP Level 1 Control Information to the fields of the DQDB Layer Management Information.

---

[9]Arriving SMDS traffic will have a delay advantage over local traffic on Bus A, but this local traffic is not part of SMDS.

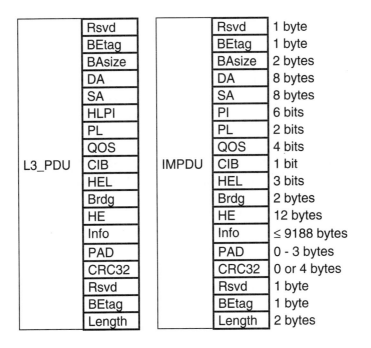

Key

Rsvd	Reserved		QOS	Quality of Service
BEtag	Beginning-End Tag		CIB	CRC32 Indicator Bit
BAsize	Buffer Allocation Size		HEL	Header Extension Length
DA	Destination Address		Brdg	Bridging
SA	Source Address		HE	Header Extension
HLPI	Higher Layer Protocol Identifier		Info	Information
PL	PAD Length		CRC32	32-bit Cyclic Redundancy Check
PI	Protocol Identification			

Figure A.20 Fields in the L3_PDU and the IMPDU

L2_PDU CPE→SS		L2_PDU SS→CPE				
	Busy		Busy		Busy	1 bit
	X		0_B	Slot	Slot Type	1 bit
	X		0_B	Header	PSR	1 bit
	XX		00_B		Rsvd	2 bits
	Req		00_B		Req	3 bits
	$FFFFF_H$		$FFFFF_H$		VCI	20 bits
	00_B		00_B	Segment	Pay Type	2 bits
	00_B		00_B	Header	Seg Pri	2 bits
	00100010_B		00100010_B		HCS	8 bits
	Seg Type		Seg Type		Seg Type	2 bits
	Seq Num		Seq Num		Seq Num	4 bits
	MID		MID	DMPDU	MID	10 bits
	Seg Unit		Seg Unit		Seg Unit	44 bytes
	Pay Len		Pay Len		Pay Len	6 bits
	Pay CRC		Pay CRC		Pay CRC	10 bits

Key

X	Bit not processed by the SS	Slot Type	SL_TYPE
Req	REQ_2, REQ_1, REQ_0	PSR	Previous Segment Received
Seg Type	Segment Type	Rsvd	Reserved
Seq Num	Sequence Number	VCI	Virtual Channel Identifier
MID	Message Identifier	Pay Type	Payload Type
Seg Unit	Segmentation Unit	Seg Pri	Segment Priority
Pay Len	Payload Length	HCS	Header Check Sequence
Pay CRC	Payload CRC		

Figure A.21 Fields in the L2_PDU, slot, Segment, and DMPDU

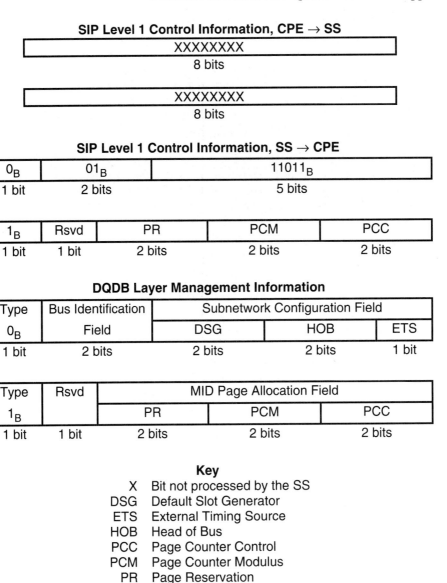

Figure A.22 Fields in SIP Level 1 Control Information and DQDB Layer Management Information

Appendix B

The SMDS Subscription
MIB Version 2.1

B.1   Introduction

This appendix contains the formal definition of the SMDS Subscription MIB, as described in Chapter 12 and published in [Cox]. This is version 2.1 of this MIB module. Implementors are encouraged to check the public enterprise-specific MIB archive for any more recent versions of this MIB module. The public enterprise-specific MIB archive is maintained on venera.isi.edu (see Appendix D).

B.2   Definition of the SMDS Subscription MIB version 2.1

```
SMDS-Subscription-MIB DEFINITIONS ::= BEGIN

IMPORTS
    enterprises, Counter, TimeTicks
      FROM RFC1155-SMI
    DisplayString, ifIndex
      FROM RFC1213-MIB
    OBJECT-TYPE
      FROM RFC-1212
    TRAP-TYPE
```

```
                    FROM RFC-1215;
```

-- This MIB module uses the extended OBJECT-TYPE macro as defined in
-- RFC1212 and the TRAP-TYPE macro as defined in RFC1215.

-- This is the MIB module for the SMDS Subscription related objects.

```
bellcore          OBJECT IDENTIFIER ::= { enterprises 148 }
requirements      OBJECT IDENTIFIER ::= { bellcore 1 }
taTsv001062       OBJECT IDENTIFIER ::= { requirements 1 }
smdsSubscr        OBJECT IDENTIFIER ::= { taTsv001062 2 }
```

-- This is version 2.1 of this MIB module and obsoletes version 1.0
-- and version 2.0.

-- All representations of SMDS addresses in this MIB module use, as a
-- textual convention (i.e., this convention does not affect their
-- encoding), the data type:

```
SMDSAddress ::= OCTET STRING (SIZE (8))
```
-- the 60-bit SMDS address, preceded by 4 bits with the following
-- values:
-- "1100" when representing an individual address
-- "1110" when representing a group address

-- This MIB is divided into six MIB modules: SMDS Subscription
-- Parameters and Violations Group, SMDS Address Table Group, Address
-- Screening Group, Group Addressing Information Group, Service
-- Disagreements Group, and Exchange Access Component of Inter-exchange
-- SMDS Group.

-- The SMDS Subscription Parameter and Violations Group contains the
-- SNI's service related information (e.g., Access Class and Maximum
-- Concurrent Data Units In and Out) along with counts of SIP L3_PDUs
-- that were discarded because of a service violation (e.g., exceeded
-- the subscribed to access class).

-- The SMDS Address Table Group contains the mapping between SMDS
-- Addresses and the ifIndex for an SNI. An SNI may have up to 16
-- addresses assigned to it.

-- The Address Screening Group is a collection of six tables. These six
-- tables are used to identify up to 4 Individual Address Screens and up
-- to 4 Group Address Screens. Two tables are used to identify all the
-- screens (i.e., there may be up to 8 screens) and the default screens
-- for each SNI. New screens can be created and deleted by using these
-- tables. The default screens may be changed also. The Associated
-- Addresses Group is used to associate the addresses assigned to the
-- SNI to a particular individual address screen and a particular group
-- address screen. This information is read/writable. The Screened
-- Addresses Group identifies the addresses to be screened (i.e.,
-- whether you want to receive SIP L3_PDUs from or send them to a

-- particular address) within the Individual Address Screens (up to 4)
-- and the Group Address Screens (up to 4). This information is
-- read/writable.

-- The Group Addressing Information Group is a collection of 5 tables.
-- The Group Address Group identifies the group address and the
-- individual addresses that are identified by the group address, and
-- this group also provides the number of individual addresses that are
-- associated with the group address. New individual addresses can be
-- identified by the group address by adding it to this table, and
-- addresses can also be deleted from this table. Only the owner of the
-- group address has read/write access on this information. Members of
-- the group address have only read access. New group addresses can not
-- be created by using this table, new group addresses can only be
-- assigned by the service provider. The Member Group Address Group
-- identifies the individual address and all of the group addresses with
-- which it is associated. Using this table, the group addresses can
-- only be disassociated from the individual addresses; meaning that the
-- group member may only delete the row and not create a new row in this
-- table. This capability is under study. Allowing the group member to
-- disassociate their individual address from This group also provides
-- the number of group addresses an individual address belongs and the
-- number of group addresses that are assigned to each SNI.

-- The Service Disagreement Group provides the latest occurrences of SIP
-- L3_PDUs that were discarded because of particular service violations.
-- This information is provided in a log format.

-- The Exchange Access Component of Inter-exchange SMDS Group is divided
-- into three groups; the Exchange Access SMDS Subscription Parameters
-- and Violations Group, the Carrier Blocking Group, and the Carrier
-- Index Group. The Exchange Access SMDS Subscription Parameters and
-- Violations Group provides subscription parameter information (e.g.,
-- the Carrier selected to provide Exchange Access SMDS for this SNI)
-- and counts of violations. The Carrier Blocking Group provides
-- information on the carriers that are blocking an SNI and the number
-- of packets that were discarded per carrier. The Carrier Index Group
-- associates the carrier's interface(s) to the SMDS network as one
-- interface and assigns an ifIndex to it.

-- The SMDS Subscription Parameters and Violations Group
-- Implementation of this group is mandatory if providing SMDS CNM.
-- Although some of the objects in this group are read-write, the write-
-- capability is not supported by the agent. However, in the future, the
-- management station when authorized may change the values for
-- smdsMCDUsIn and smdsMCDUsOut. Assuming that the objects are in the
-- customer's MIB View and the Access Control Table allows read-write
-- access, in the mean time, the agent will return badValue for any
-- Secure SNMP SET-Request on a read-write object. The agent will
-- return noSuchName for community-string based SET-Request on a read-
-- write object.

```
smdsSubscrTable  OBJECT-TYPE
   SYNTAX  SEQUENCE OF SmdsSubscrEntry
   ACCESS  not-accessible
   STATUS  mandatory
   DESCRIPTION
      "This  table  contains  Subscriber-Network  Interface
      (SNI) parameters and state variables, one entry per
      SIP port."
   ::= { smdsSubscr 1 }

smdsSubscrEntry  OBJECT-TYPE
   SYNTAX  SmdsSubscrEntry
   ACCESS  not-accessible
   STATUS  mandatory
   DESCRIPTION
      "This  list  contains  Subscriber-Network  Interface
      (SNI) parameters and state variables."
   INDEX   { smdsSubscrIndex }
   ::= { smdsSubscrTable 1 }

SmdsSubscrEntry  ::= SEQUENCE {
   smdsSubscrIndex
      INTEGER,
   smdsContact
      DisplayString,
   smdsSNILocation
      DisplayString,
   smdsAccessClass
      INTEGER,
   smdsMCDUsIn
      INTEGER,
   smdsMCDUsInChange
      INTEGER,
   smdsMCDUsOut
      INTEGER,
   smdsMCDUsOutChange
      INTEGER,
   smdsUnassignedSAs
      Counter,
   smdsAccessClassExceededCounts
      Counter,
   smdsSAScreenViolations
      Counter,
   smdsDAScreenViolations
      Counter,
   smdsMCDUsExceededAtIngressCounts
      Counter,
   smdsMCDUsExceededAtEgressCounts
      Counter,
   smdsAddressCodes
      DisplayString
```

```
}


smdsSubscrIndex  OBJECT-TYPE
   SYNTAX   INTEGER (1..65535)
   ACCESS   read-only
   STATUS   mandatory
   DESCRIPTION
       "The value of this object identifies the SIP port
       interface for which this entry contains management
       information.   The value of this object for a
       particular interface has the same value as the
       ifIndex object, defined in RFC1213, for the same
       interface."
   ::= { smdsSubscrEntry 1 }

smdsContact OBJECT-TYPE
   SYNTAX   DisplayString (SIZE(0..255))
   ACCESS   read-only
   STATUS   mandatory
   DESCRIPTION
       "The textual identification of the contactperson(s)
       or organization(s) for thesubscriber of this managed
       SNI, together withinformation on how to contact this
       person   ororganization   (e.g.,   BCC   information
       telephone number, or email address)."
   ::= { smdsSubscrEntry 2 }

smdsSNILocation OBJECT-TYPE
   SYNTAX   DisplayString (SIZE(0..255))
   ACCESS   read-only
   STATUS   mandatory
   DESCRIPTION
       "The physical location of the termination point for
       this  SNI  on  the  Switching  System  (e.g.,  CO
       Location)."
   ::= { smdsSubscrEntry 3 }

smdsAccessClass OBJECT-TYPE
   SYNTAX INTEGER {
noClass (1),
class4  (2),
class10 (3),
class16 (4),
class25 (5),
class34 (6)
   }
   ACCESS   read-only
   STATUS   mandatory
   DESCRIPTION
```

```
    "The currently subscribed-to access class for this
    SNI.  For a DS3-based access path, the value for
    this information indicates access class and the
    Sustained Information Rate in Mbps {4, 10, 16, 25,
    34}.  There is no Access Class enforcement for DS1-
    based access paths and hence no related information
    (i.e., noClass)."
::= { smdsSubscrEntry 4 }

smdsMCDUsIn OBJECT-TYPE
    SYNTAX INTEGER {
        mcdusIn1 (1),
        mcdusIn16 (2)
    }
    ACCESS  read-only
    STATUS  mandatory
    DESCRIPTION
        "The maximum number of SMDS data units that may be
        transferred concurrently over the SNI to the SMDS
        SS. Values can be 1 or 16."
    ::= { smdsSubscrEntry 5 }

smdsMCDUsInChange OBJECT-TYPE
    SYNTAX INTEGER {
        mcdusIn1 (1),
        mcdusIn16 (2)
    }
    ACCESS  read-write
    STATUS  mandatory
    DESCRIPTION
        "This object is used to change the value of
        smdsMCDUsIn.  When the values of this object and
        smdsMCDUsIn are equal, then no change is being
        processed by the agent.  If they are not equal, then
        the agent is processing a requested change.  The
        agent may refuse the change to be made and thus
        return the value for smdsMCDUsInChange to its
        previous value which is equal to the smdsMCDUsIn
        value.  If the agent accepts the change, the
        smdsMCDUsIn value will be set equal to the
        smdsMCDUsInChange value.  The maximum number of SMDS
        data units that may be transferred concurrently over
        the SNI to the SMDS SS. Values can be 1 or 16."
    ::= { smdsSubscrEntry 6 }

smdsMCDUsOut OBJECT-TYPE
    SYNTAX INTEGER {
        mcdusOut1 (1),
        mcdusOut16 (2)
    }
    ACCESS  read-only
```

```
    STATUS   mandatory
    DESCRIPTION
        "The maximum number of SMDS data units that may be
        transferred concurrently over the SNI from the SMDS
        SS. Values can be 1 or 16."
    ::= { smdsSubscrEntry 7 }

smdsMCDUsOutChange OBJECT-TYPE
    SYNTAX INTEGER {
        mcdusOut1 (1),
        mcdusOut16 (2)
    }
    ACCESS   read-write
    STATUS   mandatory
    DESCRIPTION
        "This object is used to change the value of
        smdsMCDUsOut. When the values of this object and
        smdsMCDUsOut are equal, then no change is being
        processed by the agent. If they are not equal, then
        the agent is processing a requested change. The
        agent may refuse the change to be made and thus
        return the value for smdsMCDUsOutChange to its
        previous value which is equal to the smdsMCDUsOut
        value. If the agent accepts the change, the
        smdsMCDUsOut value will be set equal to the
        smdsMCDUsOutChange value. The maximum number of SMDS
        data units that may be transferred concurrently over
        the SNI from the SMDS SS. Values can be 1 or 16."
    ::= { smdsSubscrEntry 8 }

smdsUnassignedSAs OBJECT-TYPE
    SYNTAX   Counter
    ACCESS   read-only
    STATUS   mandatory
    DESCRIPTION
        "The number of SIP L3_PDUs that have been discarded
        by the SMDS SS because the source addresses were not
        assigned to the SNI."
    ::= { smdsSubscrEntry 9 }

smdsAccessClassExceededCounts OBJECT-TYPE
    SYNTAX   Counter
    ACCESS   read-only
    STATUS   mandatory
    DESCRIPTION
        "A count of the number of L3_PDUs that were
        discarded because the access class for this SNI has
        been exceeded."
    ::= { smdsSubscrEntry 10 }

smdsSAScreenViolations OBJECT-TYPE
```

```
   SYNTAX   Counter
   ACCESS   read-only
   STATUS   mandatory
   DESCRIPTION
       "The  number  of  SIP  L3_PDUs   that  violated  the
       address screen based on source address screening for
       an SNI."
 ::= { smdsSubscrEntry 11 }

smdsDAScreenViolations OBJECT-TYPE
   SYNTAX   Counter
   ACCESS   read-only
   STATUS   mandatory
   DESCRIPTION
       "The  number  of  SIP  L3_PDUs   that  violated  the
       address   screen   based   on   destination   address
       screening for an SNI."
 ::= { smdsSubscrEntry 12 }

smdsMCDUsExceededAtIngressCounts OBJECT-TYPE
   SYNTAX   Counter
   ACCESS   read-only
   STATUS   mandatory
   DESCRIPTION
       "The number of L3_PDUs that were discarded because
       the  MCDU  was  exceeded  in  the  CPE  to  SMDS  SS
       direction."
 ::= { smdsSubscrEntry 13 }

smdsMCDUsExceededAtEgressCounts OBJECT-TYPE
   SYNTAX   Counter
   ACCESS   read-only
   STATUS   mandatory
   DESCRIPTION
       "The number of L3_PDUs that were discarded because
       the  MCDU  was  exceeded  in  the  SMDS  SS  to  CPE
       direction."
 ::= { smdsSubscrEntry 14 }

smdsAddressCodes OBJECT-TYPE
   SYNTAX   DisplayString (SIZE(0..255))
   ACCESS   read-only
   STATUS   mandatory
   DESCRIPTION
       "This object provides hints on how an SMDS Addressis
       divided into three fields.  These three fields are
       used as indices into tables that need to be indexed
       by an SMDS address.  These three fieldsprovide for a
       user-friendly/readable format in order to do SETs
       and GETs.  The  three  fields  are  country  code,
       destination code, and subscriber number.  Each field
```

MUST only contain 1 to 9 digits and must NOT start
with a zero. All SMDS addresses will have a country
code. Most SMDS addresses will have a destination
code (e.g., in the US this number is the area code).
The subscriber number is the rest of the SMDS
address, which is less than or equal to the
remaining 9 digits. For those SMDS addresses that
do not have a destination code or whose subscriber
number is more than 9 digits long, the destination
code and the subscriber number must be divided in a
logical way. Also, if a field starts with zero(s),
then these zero(s) must be the trailing zero(s) of
the previous field. It is up to the service
provider to determine this logic. This object
describes the way that the SMDS addresses are
divided for this SNI (ifIndex). For example, in the
US, this object will contain the following text:
'Country code = 1. Destination code = area code
(e.g., 908). Subscriber number = the remaining 7
digits (e.g., 7582107). The OID looks like
objectName.1.908.7582107 and the SMDSAddress =
C19087582107FFFF in Hex'."
   ::= { smdsSubscrEntry 15 }

-- The SMDS Address Table Group
-- Implementation of this group is mandatory if providing SMDS CNM.

```
subscriberAddressesTable  OBJECT-TYPE
   SYNTAX   SEQUENCE OF SubscriberAddressesEntry
   ACCESS   not-accessible
   STATUS   mandatory
   DESCRIPTION
      "This table contains the SMDS addresses assigned to
      each SNI (up to 16 addresses per SNI)."
 ::= { smdsSubscr 2 }

subscriberAddressesEntry  OBJECT-TYPE
   SYNTAX   SubscriberAddressesEntry
   ACCESS   not-accessible
   STATUS   mandatory
   DESCRIPTION
      "A valid SMDS individual address for this SNI and an
      SNI index."
   INDEX    { subCountryCodeIndex, subDestinationCodeIndex,
      subSubscriberNumberIndex }
 ::= { subscriberAddressesTable 1 }

SubscriberAddressesEntry  ::= SEQUENCE {
   subCountryCodeIndex
     INTEGER,
   subDestinationCodeIndex
     INTEGER,
```

```
subSubscriberNumberIndex
  INTEGER,
subscriberAddressesOnSNI
  SMDSAddress,
subscriberAddressesIndex
  INTEGER
}

subCountryCodeIndex OBJECT-TYPE
  SYNTAX  INTEGER (1..4294967295)
  ACCESS  read-only
  STATUS  mandatory
  DESCRIPTION
    "The country code portion of the SMDS Address. For
    example, the country code of North America is (1),
    the UK is (44), and Germany is (49)."
  ::= { subscriberAddressesEntry 1 }

subDestinationCodeIndex OBJECT-TYPE
  SYNTAX  INTEGER (1..4294967295)
  ACCESS  read-only
  STATUS  mandatory
  DESCRIPTION
    "The destination code portion of the SMDS Address.
    For example, in North American it is the Area Code.
    For many European countries, it is the city code
    portion of the address.  For SMDS addresses that do
    not distinguish such a code, this field is the next
    set  of  numbers  that  make  logical  sense.  See
    smdsAddressCodes object."
  ::= { subscriberAddressesEntry 2 }

subSubscriberNumberIndex OBJECT-TYPE
  SYNTAX  INTEGER (1..4294967295)
  ACCESS  read-only
  STATUS  mandatory
  DESCRIPTION
    "The  remaining  digits  of  the  SMDS  address.  This
    field will always be less than or equal to 9 digits
    long.  In North America, this field contains the
    rest of the SMDS address (e.g., the last 7 digits
    following  the  area  code).  See smdsAddressCodes
    object."
  ::= { subscriberAddressesEntry 3 }

subscriberAddressesOnSNI OBJECT-TYPE
  SYNTAX  SMDSAddress
  ACCESS  read-only
  STATUS  mandatory
  DESCRIPTION
    "An SMDS address that belongs to this SNI."
```

```
    ::= { subscriberAddressesEntry 4 }

subscriberAddressesIndex  OBJECT-TYPE
    SYNTAX   INTEGER (1..65535)
    ACCESS   read-only
    STATUS   mandatory
    DESCRIPTION
        "The value of this object identifies the SIP port
        interface for which this entry contains management
        information.   The value   of   this   object   for   a
        particular interface has the same value as the
        ifIndex object, defined in RFC1213, for the same
        interface."
    ::= { subscriberAddressesEntry 5 }



-- The Address Screening Group
-- Implementation of this group is mandatory if providing SMDS CNM.

addressScreening OBJECT IDENTIFIER ::= { smdsSubscr 3 }

-- The Address Screening Master Group

addressScreeningMasterTable OBJECT-TYPE
    SYNTAX   SEQUENCE OF AddressScreeningMasterEntry
    ACCESS   not-accessible
    STATUS   mandatory
    DESCRIPTION
        "This is the table for the address screens. There
        can be up to s individual address screens and up to
        s group address screens per SNI (sniScreenIndex).
        The initial value for s (screenIndex) is equal to 4.
        In the future a higher value of s may be supported.
        The screens are distinguished by their screenType
        (i.e., individual or group) and by the screenIndex
        (i.e., a value between 1 and s).

        This list identifies the s screens associated with
        an SNI accompanied by an indication (screenStatus)
        of   whether   the   screening   comprises   'allowed
        addresses' or 'disallowed addresses' (i.e., whether
        the   screen   is   applied   as   an   inclusionary   or
        exclusionary restriction), or whether the screen is
        not used (i.e., screening is turned off and all SIP
        L3_PDUs are allowed; this is identified by an empty
        list) or multiple individual and group address
        screens are not supported by the network supporting
        SMDS.

        Different addresses on an SNI may be associated with
        different address screens (one individual and one
```

group address screen per associated SNI individual address, and one individual address screen per associated SNI group address). This information is included in the associatedAddressesIndScreenTable and associatedAddressesGrpScreenTable. The associatedAddressesIndScreenTable includes all the addresses (associatedAddressInd) assigned to an SNI (i.e., both individual and group addresses) that are associated with a particular Individual Address Screen (associatedScreenIndIndex). The associatedAddressesGrpScreenTable includes all the addresses (associatedAddressGrp) assigned to an SNI (i.e., only individual addresses) that are associated with a particular Group Address Screen (associatedScreenGrpIndex).

For every SNI, there are: 1) defIAScreenForIAs; the default Individual Address Screen used for destination address screening at the network ingress and source address screening at the network egress of individually addressed L3_PDUs when the associated SNI address is an Individual Address. 2) defGAScreenForIAs; the default Group Address Screen used for destination address screening at the network ingress of group addressed L3_PDUs. The associated SNI address will always be an Individual Address (i.e., it is the Source Address). 3) defIAScreenForGAs; the default Individual Address Screen used for source address screening at the network egress of individually addressed L3_PDUs when the associated SNI address is a Group Address (i.e., it is the Destination Address).

The individual address screen (all the iAScreeningAddresses for the s iAScreenIndices in the individualAddressScreenTable) and the group address screen (all the gAScreeningAddress for the s gAScreenIndices in the groupAddressScreenTable) together consist of up to n addresses. The initial value of n (numberValidEntries in the numberAndDefaultScreeningTable) is defined as 128. In the future a value of n up to 2048 may be supported.

The individual address screen (iAScreeningAddress in the individualAddressScreenTable) is used to perform Destination Address Screening for individually addressed data units (performed at the network ingress) and Source Address Screening for all data units (performed at the network egress). The group address screen (gAScreeningAddress in the

```
            groupAddressScreenTable)    is    used    to    perform
            Destination  Address  Screening  for  group  addressed
            data units."
       ::= { addressScreening 1 }

addressScreeningMasterEntry OBJECT-TYPE
    SYNTAX  AddressScreeningMasterEntry
    ACCESS  not-accessible
    STATUS  mandatory
    DESCRIPTION
        "This  list  contains  the  SNI  Index,  the  Screening
        Table  Index,  whether  the  screening  table  is  an
        Individual  Address  Screen  or  Group  Address  Screen,
        whether   the   screen   is   a   list   of   allowed   or
        disallowed  addresses,  whether  the  screen  is  empty,
        or  whether  multiple  individual  and  group  address
        screens  are  not  supported.   See  reference  TR-TSV-
        000772."
    INDEX { sniScreenIndex, screenIndex, screenType }
    ::= { addressScreeningMasterTable 1 }

AddressScreeningMasterEntry   ::= SEQUENCE {
    sniScreenIndex
        INTEGER,
    screenIndex
        INTEGER,
    screenType
        INTEGER,
    screenStatus
        INTEGER,
    screenStatusChange
        INTEGER
    }

sniScreenIndex  OBJECT-TYPE
    SYNTAX  INTEGER (1..65535)
    ACCESS  read-only
    STATUS  mandatory
    DESCRIPTION
        "The  value  of  this  object  identifies  the  SIP  Port
        interface  for  which  this  entry  contains  management
        information.   The  value  of  this  object  for  a
        particular  interface  has  the  same  value  as  the
        ifIndex,  defined  in  RFC1213,  for  the  same
        interface."
       ::= { addressScreeningMasterEntry 1 }

screenIndex  OBJECT-TYPE
    SYNTAX  INTEGER (1..4)
    ACCESS  read-only
    STATUS  mandatory
```

DESCRIPTION
"The value of this object identifies the individual
or group address screening list. There may be up to
s individual address screening lists and up to s
group address screening lists per SNI. The initial
value of s is defined to be 4. In the future more
screening lists per SNI may be allowed. For each
SNI, there must be at least one individual address
screen and one group address screen."
::= { addressScreeningMasterEntry 2 }

screenType OBJECT-TYPE
   SYNTAX INTEGER {
       individualScreen (1),
       groupScreen (2)
   }
   ACCESS read-only
   STATUS mandatory
   DESCRIPTION
       "The value of this object identifies whether the
       screening table is either an individual address
       screen or a group address screen."
   ::= { addressScreeningMasterEntry 3 }

screenStatus OBJECT-TYPE
   SYNTAX INTEGER {
       allowed (1),
       disallowed (2),
       empty (3),
       notSupported (4)
   }
   ACCESS read-only
   STATUS mandatory
   DESCRIPTION
       "The object identifies whether the screen contains
       allowed or disallowed addresses. The value of this
       object is identical for an entire address screen.
       The value of empty implies that screening is turned
       off (i.e., all L3_PDUs are allowed). The value of
       notSupported implies that this particular
       screenIndex is not available for this SNI
       (sniScreenIndex) (i.e., the SNI supports less than s
       individual address screens and less than s group
       addresses screens). An SNI must have at least one
       Individual Address Screen and one Group Address
       Screen in which all their SNI addresses are
       associated with those screens. See reference TR-
       TSV-000772 for the requirements and objectives on
       address screening."
   ::= { addressScreeningMasterEntry 4 }

```
screenStatusChange OBJECT-TYPE
    SYNTAX   INTEGER {
        allowed (1),
        disallowed (2),
        empty (3),
        notSupported (4)
    }
    ACCESS   read-write
    STATUS   mandatory
    DESCRIPTION
        "This object is used to change the screenStatus. If
        this object is different from the screenStatus, then
        the screenStatus is undergoing change.  When these
        objects  are  the  same,  then  the  screenStatus  is
        stable.  The agent may refuse the change to be made
        and thus return the value for screenStatusChange to
        its  previous  value  which  is  equal  to  the
        screenStatus  value.   If  the  agent  accepts  the
        change, the screenStatus value will be set equal to
        the screenStatusChange value.  An NMS may SET the
        screenStatus to empty to clean out all the addresses
        in  an  individualAddressScreenTable  or  a
        groupAddressScreenTable.   The  addresses  in  the
        associatedAddressesIndScreenTable                and
        associatedAddressesGrpScreenTable  would  need  to  be
        moved  to  another  screening  list  (otherwise,
        screening would be turned off for these addresses
        and all packets will be allowed through for these
        associated SNI addresses).  An NMS may not SET the
        STATUS  of  screenStatusChange  if  the  value  of
        screenStatus is equal to notSupported and the value
        of screenStatusChange is equal to notSupported.  If
        an  NMS  tries  to  SET  the  STATUS  of
        screenStatusChange  to  notSupported  or  to  move  it
        from the notSupported state, then the agent will
        return badValue.  An SNI must have at least one
        Individual Address Screen  and  one  Group  Address
        Screen, in which case all their SNI addresses are
        associated with that screen.  See reference TR-TSV-
        000772  for  the  requirements  and  objectives  on
        address screening."
    ::= { addressScreeningMasterEntry 5 }

-- The number of addresses in the screening table group along with
-- information about the default screens. Implementation of this group
-- is mandatory if providing SMDS CNM.

numberAndDefaultScreeningTable  OBJECT-TYPE
    SYNTAX   SEQUENCE OF NumberAndDefaultScreeningEntry
    ACCESS   not-accessible
    STATUS   mandatory
    DESCRIPTION
```

"This list identifies the total number of addresses
that are in all of the screens for the particular
SNI. This list also identifies the default screens.
For every SNI, there are: 1) defIAScreenForIAs; the
default Individual Address Screen used for
destination address screening at the network ingress
and source address screening at the network egress
of individually addressed L3_PDUs when the
associated SNI address is an Individual Address. 2)
defGAScreenForIAs; the default Group Address Screen
used for destination address screening at the
network ingress of group addressed L3_PDUs. The
associated SNI address will always be an Individual
Address (i.e., it is the Source Address). 3)
defIAScreenForGAs; the default Individual Address
Screen used for source address screening at the
network egress of individually addressed L3_PDUs
when the associated SNI address is a Group Address
(i.e., it is the Destination Address)."
```
   ::= { addressScreening 2 }

numberAndDefaultScreeningEntry  OBJECT-TYPE
   SYNTAX  NumberAndDefaultScreeningEntry
   ACCESS  not-accessible
   STATUS  mandatory
   DESCRIPTION
      "An SNI index along with the number of addresses in
      all of the screening lists and the default screens
      for this SNI."
   INDEX { sniNumberIndex }
   ::= { numberAndDefaultScreeningTable 1 }

NumberAndDefaultScreeningEntry    ::= SEQUENCE {
   sniNumberIndex
      INTEGER,
   defIAScreenForIAs
      INTEGER,
   defIAScreenForIAsChange
      INTEGER,
   defIAScreenForGAs
      INTEGER,
   defIAScreenForGAsChange
      INTEGER,
   defGAScreenForIAs
      INTEGER,
   defGAScreenForIAsChange
      INTEGER,
   numberValidEntries
      INTEGER
   }
```

```
sniNumberIndex   OBJECT-TYPE
   SYNTAX   INTEGER (1..65535)
   ACCESS   read-only
   STATUS   mandatory
   DESCRIPTION
       "The value of this object identifies the SIP Port
       interface for which this entry contains management
       information.   The value of this object for a
       particular interface has the same value as the
       ifIndex, defined in RFC1213, for the same
       interface."
   ::= { numberAndDefaultScreeningEntry 1 }

defIAScreenForIAs   OBJECT-TYPE
   SYNTAX   INTEGER (1..4)
   ACCESS   read-only
   STATUS   mandatory
   DESCRIPTION
       "The value of this object identifies the default
       Individual Address Screen for all Individual
       Addresses associated with this SNI.   This value is
       to guard against an assigned SNI Address not being
       represented in one of the
       associatedAddressesIndScreenTable."
   ::= { numberAndDefaultScreeningEntry 2 }

defIAScreenForIAsChange   OBJECT-TYPE
   SYNTAX   INTEGER (1..4)
   ACCESS   read-write
   STATUS   mandatory
   DESCRIPTION
       "This object is used to change the
       defIAScreenForIAs.   When the value of this object
       and defIAScreenForIAs are equal, then no change is
       being processed by the agent.   If they are not
       equal, then the agent is processing the requested
       change.   The agent may refuse the change to be made
       and thus return the value for
       defIAScreenForIAsChange to its previous value which
       is equal to the defIAScreenForIAs value.   If the
       agent accepts the change, the defIAScreenForIAs
       value will be set equal to the
       defIAScreenForIAsChange value."
   ::= { numberAndDefaultScreeningEntry 3 }

defIAScreenForGAs   OBJECT-TYPE
   SYNTAX   INTEGER (1..4)
   ACCESS   read-only
   STATUS   mandatory
   DESCRIPTION
```

"The value of this object identifies the default
Individual Address Screen for all Group Addresses
associated with this SNI. This value is to guard
against an assigned SNI Address not being
represented in one of the
associatedAddressesIndScreenTable."
    ::= { numberAndDefaultScreeningEntry 4 }

defIAScreenForGAsChange OBJECT-TYPE
    SYNTAX INTEGER (1..4)
    ACCESS read-write
    STATUS mandatory
    DESCRIPTION
        "This object is used to change the
        defIAScreenForGAs. When the value for this object
        and defIAScreenForGAs are equal, then no change is
        being processed by the agent. If they are not
        equal, then the agent is processing the requested
        change. The agent may refuse the change to be made
        and thus return the value for
        defIAScreenForGAsChange to its previous value which
        is equal to the defIAScreenForGAs value. If the
        agent accepts the change, the defIAScreenForGAs
        value will be set equal to the
        defIAScreenForGAsChange value."
    ::= { numberAndDefaultScreeningEntry 5 }

defGAScreenForIAs OBJECT-TYPE
    SYNTAX INTEGER (1..4)
    ACCESS read-only
    STATUS mandatory
    DESCRIPTION
        "The value of this object identifies the default
        Group Address Screen for all Individual Addresses
        associated with this SNI. This value is to guard
        against an assigned SNI Address not being
        represented in one of the
        associatedAddressesGrpScreenTable."
    ::= { numberAndDefaultScreeningEntry 6 }

defGAScreenForIAsChange OBJECT-TYPE
    SYNTAX INTEGER (1..4)
    ACCESS read-write
    STATUS mandatory
    DESCRIPTION
        "This object is used to change the
        defGAScreenForIAs. When the value of this object
        and defGAScreenForIAs are equal, then no change is
        being processed by the agent. If they are not
        equal, then the agent is processing the requested
        change. The agent may refuse the change to be made

and   thus   return   the   value   for
defGAScreenForIAsChange to its previous value which
is equal to the defGAScreenForIAs value.   If the
agent accepts the change, the defGAScreenForIAs
value   will   be   set   equal   to   the
defGAScreenForIAsChange value."
  ::= { numberAndDefaultScreeningEntry 7 }

numberValidEntries OBJECT-TYPE
   SYNTAX   INTEGER (0..128)
   ACCESS   read-only
   STATUS   mandatory
   DESCRIPTION
      "This value identifies the total number of screened
      addresses in all (up to s+s = 8) address screens.
      The individual address screens (up to s) and the
      group address screens (up to s) together consist of
      up to n addresses.   The value of s is initially
      equal to 4.   The initial value of n is defined as
      128.   In the future a value of n up to 2048 may be
      supported."
  ::= { numberAndDefaultScreeningEntry 8 }

-- The Associated Addresses Group
-- Implementation of this group is mandatory if providing SMDS CNM.

-- The Associated Addresses within an Individual Address Screen Group

associatedAddressesIndScreenTable OBJECT-TYPE
   SYNTAX   SEQUENCE OF AssociatedAddressesIndScreenEntry
   ACCESS   not-accessible
   STATUS   mandatory
   DESCRIPTION
      "This list identifies the associated SNI addresses
      per individual address screen.   Different addresses
      on an SNI may be associated with different
      individual address screens (one individual address
      screen per associated address on an SNI)."
  ::= { addressScreening 3 }

 associatedAddressesIndScreenEntry OBJECT-TYPE
   SYNTAX   AssociatedAddressesIndScreenEntry
   ACCESS   not-accessible
   STATUS   mandatory
   DESCRIPTION
      "An   SNI   index,   a   screening   list   index,   the
      associated addresses for the SNI for the individual
      address screen, and whether the associated address
      for the screen is valid or invalid."
   INDEX   { associatedSNIIndIndex,
      associatedScreenIndIndex, assocAddressTypeIndex,

```
        assocIndCountryCodeIndex,
        assocIndDestinationCodeIndex,
        assocIndSubscriberNumberIndex }
  ::= { associatedAddressesIndScreenTable 1 }

AssociatedAddressesIndScreenEntry     ::= SEQUENCE {
  associatedSNIIndIndex
    INTEGER,
  associatedScreenIndIndex
    INTEGER,
  assocAddressTypeIndex
    INTEGER,
  assocIndCountryCodeIndex
    INTEGER,
  assocIndDestinationCodeIndex
    INTEGER,
  assocIndSubscriberNumberIndex
    INTEGER,
  associatedAddressInd
    SMDSAddress,
  associatedAddressIndStatus
    INTEGER,
  associatedAddressIndStatusChange
    INTEGER
  }

associatedSNIIndIndex OBJECT-TYPE
  SYNTAX   INTEGER (1..65535)
  ACCESS   read-only
  STATUS   mandatory
  DESCRIPTION
      "The value of this object identifies the SIP Port
      interface for which this entry contains management
      information.   The   value   of   this   object   for   a
      particular  interface  has  the  same  value  as  the
      ifIndex,  defined  in  RFC1213,  for  the  same
      interface."
  ::= { associatedAddressesIndScreenEntry 1 }

associatedScreenIndIndex   OBJECT-TYPE
  SYNTAX   INTEGER (1..4)
  ACCESS   read-only
  STATUS   mandatory
  DESCRIPTION
      "The value of this object identifies the individual
      address  screening  list.   There  are  at  least  one
      individual  address  screen  and  at  most  s  individual
      address screens per SNI. The initial value of s is
      defined to be 4.   In the future more screening lists
      per SNI may be allowed.   The values of this object
```

```
        correspond  to  the  values  of  screenIndex  in  the
        addressScreeningMasterTable."
    ::= {  associatedAddressesIndScreenEntry 2 }


assocAddressTypeIndex   OBJECT-TYPE
    SYNTAX  INTEGER  {
        individual(1),
        group(2)
    }
    ACCESS  read-only
    STATUS  mandatory
    DESCRIPTION
        "The  value  of  this  object  identifies  the  type  of
        address that is identified by the three address sub-
        object       identifiers       assocIndCountryCodeIndex,
        assocIndDestinationCodeIndex,
        assocIndSubscriberNumberIndex.  The  address  type  can
        either  be  an  individual  or  group  address.   See  the
        object associatedAddressInd."
    ::= {  associatedAddressesIndScreenEntry 3 }


assocIndCountryCodeIndex OBJECT-TYPE
    SYNTAX  INTEGER (1..4294967295)
    ACCESS  read-only
    STATUS  mandatory
    DESCRIPTION
        "The  country  code  portion  of  the  SMDS  Address.  For
        example,  the  country  code  of  North  America  is  (1),
        the UK is (44), and Germany is (49)."
    ::= { associatedAddressesIndScreenEntry 4 }


assocIndDestinationCodeIndex OBJECT-TYPE
    SYNTAX  INTEGER (1..4294967295)
    ACCESS  read-only
    STATUS  mandatory
    DESCRIPTION
        "The  destination  code  portion  of  the  SMDS  Address.
        For  example,  in  North  American  it  is  the  Area  Code.
        For  many  European  countries,  it  is  the  city  code
        portion  of  the  address.   For  SMDS  addresses  that  do
        not  distinguish  such  a  code,  this  field  is  the  next
        set   of   numbers   that   make   logical   sense.   See
        smdsAddressCodes object."
    ::= { associatedAddressesIndScreenEntry 5 }


assocIndSubscriberNumberIndex OBJECT-TYPE
    SYNTAX  INTEGER (1..4294967295)
    ACCESS  read-only
    STATUS  mandatory
    DESCRIPTION
```

"The remaining digits of the SMDS address. This
field will always be less than or equal to 9 digits
long.   In North America, this field contains the
rest of the SMDS address (e.g., the last 7 digits
following the area code).   See smdsAddressCodes
object."
    ::= { associatedAddressesIndScreenEntry 6 }

associatedAddressInd OBJECT-TYPE
    SYNTAX   SMDSAddress
    ACCESS   read-only
    STATUS   mandatory
    DESCRIPTION
        "The value of this object identifies one of the SMDS
        addresses   for   the   SNI   identified   by   the
        associatedSNIIndIndex   that   belongs   to   this
        individual   address   screen
        (associatedScreenIndIndex). This list will contain
        both individual and group addresses, because this
        list is used for both Destination Address Screening
        and   Source   Address   Screening;   the   destination
        address in the L3_PDU that is undergoing Source
        Address   Screening   may   be   either   a   group   or
        individual address that is assigned to that SNI.
        One screen will have a maximum of 64 associated
        addresses;   up   to   a   maximum   of   16   individual
        addresses identifying an SNI and up to a maximum of
        48 group addresses identifying an SNI."
    ::= { associatedAddressesIndScreenEntry 7 }

associatedAddressIndStatus OBJECT-TYPE
    SYNTAX   INTEGER {
        valid (1),
        invalid (2)
    }
    ACCESS   read-only
    STATUS   mandatory
    DESCRIPTION
        "The   object   identifies   whether   the   associated
        address is valid or invalid."
    ::= { associatedAddressesIndScreenEntry 8 }

associatedAddressIndStatusChange OBJECT-TYPE
    SYNTAX   INTEGER {
        valid (1),
        invalid (2)
    }
    ACCESS   read-write
    STATUS   mandatory
    DESCRIPTION

"This object is used to change the associatedAddressIndStatus. When the value of this object and associatedAddressIndStatus are equal, then no change is being processed by the agent. If they are not equal, then the agent is processing the requested change. The agent may refuse the change to be made and thus return the value for associatedAddressIndStatusChange to its previous value which is equal to the associatedAddressIndStatus value. If the agent accepts the change, the associatedAddressIndStatus value will be set equal to the associatedAddressIndStatusChange value. This object is used to add/delete associated SNI addresses -- associatedAddressInd (either individual or group addresses) to this table."
```
    ::= { associatedAddressesIndScreenEntry 9 }
```

-- The Associated Addresses within a Group Address Screen Group

```
associatedAddressesGrpScreenTable  OBJECT-TYPE
    SYNTAX   SEQUENCE OF AssociatedAddressesGrpScreenEntry
    ACCESS   not-accessible
    STATUS   mandatory
    DESCRIPTION
        "This list identifies the associated SNI addresses
        per group address screen.  Different addresses on an
        SNI may be associated with different group address
        screens (one group address screen per associated
        address on an SNI)."
    ::= { addressScreening 4 }

associatedAddressesGrpScreenEntry  OBJECT-TYPE
    SYNTAX   AssociatedAddressesGrpScreenEntry
    ACCESS   not-accessible
    STATUS   mandatory
    DESCRIPTION
        "An SNI index, a screening list index, the
        associated addresses for the SNI for the group
        address screen, and whether the associated address
        for the screen is valid or invalid."
    INDEX    { associatedSNIGrpIndex,
        associatedScreenGrpIndex, assocGrpCountryCodeIndex,
        assocGrpDestinationCodeIndex,
        assocGrpSubscriberNumberIndex }
    ::= { associatedAddressesGrpScreenTable 1 }

    AssociatedAddressesGrpScreenEntry    ::= SEQUENCE {
    associatedSNIGrpIndex
        INTEGER,
    associatedScreenGrpIndex
        INTEGER,
```

```
    assocGrpCountryCodeIndex
      INTEGER,
    assocGrpDestinationCodeIndex
      INTEGER,
    assocGrpSubscriberNumberIndex
      INTEGER,
    associatedAddressGrp
      SMDSAddress,
    associatedAddressGrpStatus
      INTEGER,
    associatedAddressGrpStatusChange
      INTEGER
    }

associatedSNIGrpIndex OBJECT-TYPE
    SYNTAX   INTEGER (1..65535)
    ACCESS   read-only
    STATUS   mandatory
    DESCRIPTION
        "The value of this object identifies the SIP Port
        interface for which this entry contains management
        information.   The  value  of  this  object  for  a
        particular  interface  has  the  same  value  as  the
        ifIndex,  defined  in  RFC1213,  for  the  same
        interface."
  ::= { associatedAddressesGrpScreenEntry 1 }

 associatedScreenGrpIndex   OBJECT-TYPE
    SYNTAX   INTEGER (1..4)
    ACCESS   read-only
    STATUS   mandatory
    DESCRIPTION
        "The value of this object identifies the group
        address  screening  list.    There  are  at  least  one
        group  address  screen  and  at  most  s  group  address
        screens per SNI. The initial value of s is defined
        to be 4.  In the future more screening lists per SNI
        may  be  allowed.    The  values  of  this  object
        correspond  to  the  values  of  screenIndex  in  the
        addressScreeningMasterTable."
  ::= { associatedAddressesGrpScreenEntry 2 }

assocGrpCountryCodeIndex OBJECT-TYPE
    SYNTAX   INTEGER (1..4294967295)
    ACCESS   read-only
    STATUS   mandatory
    DESCRIPTION
        "The country code portion of the SMDS Address. For
        example, the country code of North America is (1),
        the UK is (44), and Germany is (49)."
  ::= { associatedAddressesGrpScreenEntry 3 }
```

```
assocGrpDestinationCodeIndex OBJECT-TYPE
    SYNTAX   INTEGER (1..4294967295)
    ACCESS   read-only
    STATUS   mandatory
    DESCRIPTION
        "The destination code portion of the SMDS Address.
        For example, in North American it is the Area Code.
        For many European countries, it is the city code
        portion of the address.  For SMDS addresses that do
        not distinguish such a code, this field is the next
        set  of  numbers  that  make  logical  sense.  See
        smdsAddressCodes object."
    ::= { associatedAddressesGrpScreenEntry 4 }

assocGrpSubscriberNumberIndex OBJECT-TYPE
    SYNTAX   INTEGER (1..4294967295)
    ACCESS   read-only
    STATUS   mandatory
    DESCRIPTION
        "The remaining digits of the SMDS address.  This
        field will always be less than or equal to 9 digits
        long.  In North America, this field contains the
        rest of the SMDS address (e.g., the last 7 digits
        following  the  area  code).  See smdsAddressCodes
        object."
    ::= { associatedAddressesGrpScreenEntry 5 }

associatedAddressGrp OBJECT-TYPE
    SYNTAX   SMDSAddress
    ACCESS   read-only
    STATUS   mandatory
    DESCRIPTION
        "The value of this object identifies one of the SMDS
        addresses   for   the   SNI   identified   by   the
        associatedSNIGrpIndex  that  belongs  to  this  group
        address   screen   (associatedScreenGrpIndex).   This
        list will contain only individual addresses, because
        this  list  is  used  for  only  Destination  Address
        Screening; The Source Address in the L3_PDU that is
        undergoing Destination Address Screening is always
        an  individual  address.   One  screen  will  have  a
        maximum of 16 associated addresses; up to a maximum
        of 16 individual addresses identifying an SNI."
    ::= { associatedAddressesGrpScreenEntry 6 }

associatedAddressGrpStatus OBJECT-TYPE
    SYNTAX   INTEGER {
        valid (1),
        invalid (2)
    }
    ACCESS   read-only
```

```
STATUS   mandatory
DESCRIPTION
    "The  object  identifies  whether  the  associated
    address is valid or invalid."
::= { associatedAddressesGrpScreenEntry 7 }

associatedAddressGrpStatusChange OBJECT-TYPE
    SYNTAX   INTEGER {
        valid (1),
        invalid (2)
    }
    ACCESS   read-write
    STATUS   mandatory
    DESCRIPTION
        "This       object      is       used       to       change
        associatedAddressGrpStatus.  When the value of this
        object   and   associatedAddressGrpStatus   are   equal,
        then no change is being processed by the agent.  If
        they are not equal, then the agent is processing the
        requested change.  The agent may refuse the change
        to   be   made   and   thus   return   the   value   for
        associatedAddressGrpStatusChange   to   its   previous
        value       which      is       equal       to       the
        associatedAddressGrpStatus   value.   If   the   agent
        accepts  the  change,  the  associatedAddressGrpStatus
        value     will     be     set     equal     to     the
        associatedAddressGrpStatusChange value.  The object
        identifies whether the associated address is valid
        or   invalid.   This   object   is   used   to   add/delete
        associated  SNI  addresses  --  associatedAddressGrp
        (only individual addresses) to this table."
    ::= { associatedAddressesGrpScreenEntry 8 }


-- The Screened Addresses Group
-- Implementation of this group is mandatory if providing SMDS CNM.

-- The Individual Address Screen Group

individualAddressScreenTable  OBJECT-TYPE
    SYNTAX   SEQUENCE OF IndividualAddressScreenEntry
    ACCESS   not-accessible
    STATUS   mandatory
    DESCRIPTION
        "This list identifies the individual addresses that
        will  be  screened  per  individual  address  screen
        table.  The are up to s (s is equal to 4) individual
        address screens per SNI and at least one individual
        address  screen  per  SNI.  The  Individual  Address
        Screens  and  the  Group  Address  Screens  together
        consist of up to n addresses. The initial value of n
        is defined as 128. In the future a value of n up to
```

2048 may be supported. The Individual Address Screen
is used to perform Destination Address Screening for
individually addressed data units and Source Address
Screening for all data units.   The Group Address
Screen is used to perform Destination Address
Screening for group addressed data units."
```
::= { addressScreening 5 }

individualAddressScreenEntry  OBJECT-TYPE
    SYNTAX   IndividualAddressScreenEntry
    ACCESS   not-accessible
    STATUS   mandatory
    DESCRIPTION
        "An SNI      INDEX, a screening list    INDEX, the
        individual   addresses   to   be   screened   for   the
        individual address screen, and whether the screened
        address is valid or invalid."
    INDEX   { iAScreenSNIIndex, iAScreenIndex,
        iACountryCodeIndex, iADestinationCodeIndex,
        iASubscriberNumberIndex }
  ::= { individualAddressScreenTable 1 }

IndividualAddressScreenEntry   ::= SEQUENCE {
    iAScreenSNIIndex
      INTEGER,
    iAScreenIndex
      INTEGER,
    iACountryCodeIndex
      INTEGER,
    iADestinationCodeIndex
      INTEGER,
    iASubscriberNumberIndex
      INTEGER,
    iAScreeningAddress
      SMDSAddress,
    iAScreeningAddressStatus
      INTEGER,
    iAScreeningAddressStatusChange
      INTEGER
    }

iAScreenSNIIndex OBJECT-TYPE
    SYNTAX   INTEGER (1..65535)
    ACCESS   read-only
    STATUS   mandatory
    DESCRIPTION
        "The value of this object identifies the SIP Port
        interface for which this entry contains management
        information.   The value of this object for a
        particular interface has the same value as the
```

```
        ifIndex,   defined   in   RFC1213,   for   the   same
        interface."
 ::= { individualAddressScreenEntry 1 }
```

iAScreenIndex OBJECT-TYPE
    SYNTAX   INTEGER (1..4)
    ACCESS   read-only
    STATUS   mandatory
    DESCRIPTION
        "The value of this object identifies the individual
        address screening list.   There are at least one
        individual address screen and at most s individual
        address screens per SNI. The initial value of s is
        defined to be 4.   In the future more screening lists
        per SNI may be allowed.   The values of this object
        correspond to the values of screenIndex in the
        addressScreeningMasterTable."
     ::= { individualAddressScreenEntry 2 }

iACountryCodeIndex OBJECT-TYPE
    SYNTAX   INTEGER (1..4294967295)
    ACCESS   read-only
    STATUS   mandatory
    DESCRIPTION
        "The country code portion of the SMDS Address. For
        example, the country code of North America is (1),
        the UK is (44), and Germany is (49)."
     ::= { individualAddressScreenEntry 3 }

iADestinationCodeIndex OBJECT-TYPE
    SYNTAX   INTEGER (1..4294967295)
    ACCESS   read-only
    STATUS   mandatory
    DESCRIPTION
        "The destination code portion of the SMDS Address.
        For example, in North American it is the Area Code.
        For many European countries, it is the city code
        portion of the address. For SMDS addresses that do
        not distinguish such a code, this field is the next
        set of numbers that make logical sense. See
        smdsAddressCodes object."
     ::= { individualAddressScreenEntry 4 }

iASubscriberNumberIndex OBJECT-TYPE
    SYNTAX   INTEGER (1..4294967295)
    ACCESS   read-only
    STATUS   mandatory
    DESCRIPTION
        "The remaining digits of the SMDS address.   This
        field will always be less than or equal to 9 digits
        long.   In North America, this field contains the

> rest of the SMDS address (e.g., the last 7 digits following the area code). See smdsAddressCodes object."
  ::= { individualAddressScreenEntry 5 }

iAScreeningAddress OBJECT-TYPE
    SYNTAX   SMDSAddress
    ACCESS   read-only
    STATUS   mandatory
    DESCRIPTION
> "The value of this object identifies one of the individual addresses to be screened for source and destination address screening for the SNI identified by the iAScreenSNIIndex and for the particular individual address screen (iAScreenIndex)."
  ::= { individualAddressScreenEntry 6 }

iAScreeningAddressStatus OBJECT-TYPE
    SYNTAX   INTEGER {
        valid (1),
        invalid (2)
    }
    ACCESS   read-only
    STATUS   mandatory
    DESCRIPTION
> "The object identifies whether the screened address is valid or invalid."
  ::= { individualAddressScreenEntry 7 }

iAScreeningAddressStatusChange OBJECT-TYPE
    SYNTAX   INTEGER {
        valid (1),
        invalid (2)
    }
    ACCESS   read-write
    STATUS   mandatory
    DESCRIPTION
> "This object is used to change the iAScreeningAddressStatus. When the value of this object and iAScreeningAddressStatus are equal, then no change is being processed by the agent. If they are not equal, then the agent is processing the requested change. The agent may refuse the change to be made and thus return the value for iAScreeningAddressStatusChange to its previous value which is equal to the iAScreeningAddressStatus value. If the agent accepts the change, the iAScreeningAddressStatus value will be set equal to the iAScreeningAddressStatusChange value. This object is used to add/delete individual addresses in

```
            the Individual Address Screens -- iAScreeningAddress
            to this table."
   ::= { individualAddressScreenEntry 8 }
```

-- The Group Address Screen Group

```
groupAddressScreenTable  OBJECT-TYPE
    SYNTAX   SEQUENCE OF GroupAddressScreenEntry
    ACCESS   not-accessible
    STATUS   mandatory
    DESCRIPTION
            "This list identifies the group addresses that will
            be screened per group address screen table. The are
            up to s (s is equal to 4) group address screens per
            SNI and at least one group address screen per SNI.
            The Individual Address Screen and the Group Address
            Screen together consist of up to n addresses.  The
            initial value of n is defined as 128. In the future
            a value of n up to 2048 may be supported.  The
            Individual  Address  Screen  is  used  to  perform
            Destination  Address  Screening  for  individually
            addressed data units and Source Address Screening
            for all data units.  The Group Address Screen is
            used to perform Destination Address Screening for
            group addressed data units."
    ::= { addressScreening 6 }

groupAddressScreenEntry  OBJECT-TYPE
    SYNTAX   GroupAddressScreenEntry
    ACCESS   not-accessible
    STATUS   mandatory
    DESCRIPTION
            "An SNI index, a screening list index, the group
            addresses to be screened for the group address
            screen, and whether the screened address is valid or
            invalid."
    INDEX   { gAScreenSNIIndex, gAScreenIndex,
            gACountryCodeGAIndex, gADestinationCodeGAIndex,
            gASubscriberNumberGAIndex }
    ::= { groupAddressScreenTable 1 }

GroupAddressScreenEntry     ::= SEQUENCE {
    gAScreenSNIIndex
        INTEGER,
    gAScreenIndex
        INTEGER,
    gACountryCodeGAIndex
        INTEGER,
    gADestinationCodeGAIndex
        INTEGER,
    gASubscriberNumberGAIndex
```

```
      INTEGER,
   gAScreeningAddress
      SMDSAddress,
   gAScreeningAddressStatus
      INTEGER,
   gAScreeningAddressStatusChange
      INTEGER
   }

gAScreenSNIIndex OBJECT-TYPE
   SYNTAX   INTEGER (1..65535)
   ACCESS   read-only
   STATUS   mandatory
   DESCRIPTION
      "The value of this object identifies the SIP Port
      interface for which this entry contains management
      information.   The value of this object for a
      particular interface has the same value as the
      ifIndex, defined in RFC1213, for the same
      interface."
   ::= { groupAddressScreenEntry 1 }

gAScreenIndex  OBJECT-TYPE
   SYNTAX   INTEGER (1..4)
   ACCESS   read-only
   STATUS   mandatory
   DESCRIPTION
      "The value of this object identifies the group
      address screening list.  There are at least one
      group address screen and at most s group address
      screens per SNI. The initial value of s is defined
      to be 4.  In the future more screening lists per SNI
      may be allowed.  The values of this object
      correspond to the values of screenIndex in the
      addressScreeningMasterTable."
   ::= {  groupAddressScreenEntry 2 }

gACountryCodeGAIndex OBJECT-TYPE
   SYNTAX   INTEGER (1..4294967295)
   ACCESS   read-only
   STATUS   mandatory
   DESCRIPTION
      "The country code portion of the SMDS Group Address.
      For example, the country code of North America is
      (1), the UK is (44), and Germany is (49)."
   ::= { groupAddressScreenEntry 3 }

gADestinationCodeGAIndex OBJECT-TYPE
   SYNTAX   INTEGER (1..4294967295)
   ACCESS   read-only
   STATUS   mandatory
```

DESCRIPTION
    "The destination code portion of the SMDS Group
    Address. For example, in North American it is the
    Area Code. For many European countries, it is the
    city code portion of the address. For SMDS
    addresses that do not distinguish such a code, this
    field is the next set of numbers that make logical
    sense. See smdsAddressCodes object."
::= { groupAddressScreenEntry 4 }

gASubscriberNumberGAIndex OBJECT-TYPE
    SYNTAX   INTEGER (1..4294967295)
    ACCESS   read-only
    STATUS   mandatory
    DESCRIPTION
        "The remaining digits of the SMDS Group Address.
        This field will always be less than or equal to 9
        digits long. In North America, this field contains
        the rest of the SMDS address (e.g., the last 7
        digits following the area code). See
        smdsAddressCodes object."
    ::= { groupAddressScreenEntry 5 }

gAScreeningAddress OBJECT-TYPE
    SYNTAX   SMDSAddress
    ACCESS   read-only
    STATUS   mandatory
    DESCRIPTION
        "The value of this object identifies one of the
        group addresses to be screened for destination
        address screening for the SNI identified by the
        gAScreenSNIIndex and for the particular group
        address screen (gAScreenIndex)."
    ::= { groupAddressScreenEntry 6 }

gAScreeningAddressStatus OBJECT-TYPE
    SYNTAX   INTEGER {
        valid (1),
        invalid (2)
    }
    ACCESS   read-only
    STATUS   mandatory
    DESCRIPTION
        "The object identifies whether the screened address
        is valid or invalid."
    ::= { groupAddressScreenEntry 7 }

gAScreeningAddressStatusChange OBJECT-TYPE
    SYNTAX   INTEGER {
        valid (1),
        invalid (2)

```
            }
         ACCESS    read-write
         STATUS    mandatory
         DESCRIPTION
              "This     object     is     used     to     change     the
              gAScreeningAddressStatus.   When  this  object  and
              gAScreeningAddressStatus  are  equal,  then  no  change
              is  being  processed  by  the  agent.   If  they  are  not
              equal,  then  the  agent  is  processing  the  requested
              change.   The  agent  may  refuse  the  change  to  be  made
              and       thus       return       the       value       for
              gAScreeningAddressStatusChange  to  its  previous  value
              which  is  equal  to  the  gAScreeningAddressStatus
              value.    If   the   agent   accepts   the   change,   the
              gAScreeningAddressStatus  value  will  be  set  equal  to
              the   gAScreeningAddressStatusChange   value.    This
              object  is  used  to  add/delete  group  addresses  in  the
              Group  Address  Screens  --  gAScreeningAddress  to  this
              table."
         ::= { groupAddressScreenEntry 8 }


     -- The Group Addressing Information Group
     -- Implementation of this group is mandatory if providing SMDS CNM.
     -- The Group Addressing Information is divided into two groups.  The
     -- Group Address Group provides all the individual addresses that are
     -- members of a particular group address.  The Member Group Address
     -- Group provides all the group addresses that a particular individual
     -- address is a member.

     groupAddressing OBJECT IDENTIFIER   ::= { smdsSubscr 4 }


     -- The Group Address Group
     -- Implementation of this group is mandatory if providing SMDS CNM.

     groupAddressTable  OBJECT-TYPE
         SYNTAX   SEQUENCE OF GroupAddressEntry
         ACCESS   not-accessible
         STATUS   mandatory
         DESCRIPTION
              "A  table  of  all  group  addresses  in  the  network  and
              the  associated  individual  addresses  identified  by
              each  group  address.   A  group  address  identifies  up
              to  m  individual  addresses.   An  SMDS  SS  supports  up
              to  n  group  addresses.   An  group  address  can  be
              identified  by  up  to  p  individual  addresses.   A
              particular  SNI  is  identified  by  up  to  48  group
              addresses.   The  initial  values  of  m,  n,  and  p  are
              defined  as  128,  1024,  and  32,  respectively.   In  the
              future  values  of  m  and  n  of  2048  and  8192,
              respectively,  may  be  supported.
```

```
        Changes in this table cause corresponding changes in
        the                          memberGroupAddressTable,
     numberMemberAddressesTable,
     numberGAsForAddressTable, and numberGAsForSNITable."
  ::= { groupAddressing 1 }

groupAddressEntry  OBJECT-TYPE
   SYNTAX  GroupAddressEntry
   ACCESS  not-accessible
   STATUS  mandatory
   DESCRIPTION
      "A Group Address and an address in that group and
      whether that association is valid or invalid."
   INDEX   { groupCountryCodeGAIndex,
      groupDestinationCodeGAIndex,
      groupSubscriberNumberGAIndex, groupCountryCodeIndex,
      groupDestinationCodeIndex,
      groupSubscriberNumberIndex }
  ::= { groupAddressTable 1 }

GroupAddressEntry     ::= SEQUENCE {
   groupCountryCodeGAIndex
      INTEGER,
   groupDestinationCodeGAIndex
      INTEGER,
   groupSubscriberNumberGAIndex
      INTEGER,
   groupCountryCodeIndex
      INTEGER,
   groupDestinationCodeIndex
      INTEGER,
   groupSubscriberNumberIndex
      INTEGER,
   groupAddress
      SMDSAddress,
   groupMember
      SMDSAddress,
   groupMemberStatus
      INTEGER,
   groupMemberStatusChange
      INTEGER
   }

groupCountryCodeGAIndex OBJECT-TYPE
   SYNTAX  INTEGER (1..4294967295)
   ACCESS  read-only
   STATUS  mandatory
   DESCRIPTION
      "The country code portion of the SMDS Group Address.
      For example, the country code of North America is
      (1), the UK is (44), and Germany is (49)."
```

```
    ::= { groupAddressEntry 1 }

groupDestinationCodeGAIndex OBJECT-TYPE
    SYNTAX   INTEGER (1..4294967295)
    ACCESS   read-only
    STATUS   mandatory
    DESCRIPTION
        "The destination code portion of the SMDS Group
        Address.  For example, in North American it is the
        Area Code.  For many European countries, it is the
        city code portion of the address.  For SMDS
        addresses that do not distinguish such a code, this
        field is the next set of numbers that make logical
        sense.  See smdsAddressCodes object."
    ::= { groupAddressEntry 2 }

groupSubscriberNumberGAIndex OBJECT-TYPE
    SYNTAX   INTEGER (1..4294967295)
    ACCESS   read-only
    STATUS   mandatory
    DESCRIPTION
        "The remaining digits of the SMDS Group Address.
        This field will always be less than or equal to 9
        digits long.  In North America, this field contains
        the rest of the SMDS address (e.g., the last 7
        digits following the area code).  See
        smdsAddressCodes object."
    ::= { groupAddressEntry 3 }

groupCountryCodeIndex OBJECT-TYPE
    SYNTAX   INTEGER (1..4294967295)
    ACCESS   read-only
    STATUS   mandatory
    DESCRIPTION
        "The country code portion of the SMDS Address. For
        example, the country code of North America is (1),
        the UK is (44), and Germany is (49)."
    ::= { groupAddressEntry 4 }

groupDestinationCodeIndex OBJECT-TYPE
    SYNTAX   INTEGER (1..4294967295)
    ACCESS   read-only
    STATUS   mandatory
    DESCRIPTION
        "The destination code portion of the SMDS Address.
        For example, in North American it is the Area Code.
        For many European countries, it is the city code
        portion of the address.  For SMDS addresses that do
        not distinguish such a code, this field is the next
        set of numbers that make logical sense.  See
        smdsAddressCodes object."
```

```
    ::= { groupAddressEntry 5 }

groupSubscriberNumberIndex OBJECT-TYPE
    SYNTAX   INTEGER (1..4294967295)
    ACCESS   read-only
    STATUS   mandatory
    DESCRIPTION
        "The remaining digits of the SMDS Address.  This
        field will always be less than or equal to 9 digits
        long.  In North America, this field contains the
        rest of the SMDS address (e.g., the last 7 digits
        following the area code).  See smdsAddressCodes
        object."
    ::= { groupAddressEntry 6 }

groupAddress OBJECT-TYPE
    SYNTAX   SMDSAddress
    ACCESS   read-only
    STATUS   mandatory
    DESCRIPTION
        "A Group Address."
    ::= { groupAddressEntry 7 }

groupMember OBJECT-TYPE
    SYNTAX   SMDSAddress
    ACCESS   read-only
    STATUS   mandatory
    DESCRIPTION
        "An individual SMDS address that belongs to this
        Group Address."
    ::= { groupAddressEntry 8 }

 groupMemberStatus OBJECT-TYPE
    SYNTAX   INTEGER  {
        valid (1),
        invalid (2)
    }
    ACCESS   read-only
    STATUS   mandatory
    DESCRIPTION
        "The object identifies whether the groupMember is
        valid or invalid.  See reference TA-TSV-001062."
    ::= { groupAddressEntry 9 }

groupMemberStatusChange OBJECT-TYPE
    SYNTAX   INTEGER  {
        valid (1),
        invalid (2)
    }
    ACCESS   read-write
    STATUS   mandatory
```

DESCRIPTION
>   "This object is used to change the
>   groupMemberStatus. When the value of this object
>   and groupMemberStatus are equal, then no change is
>   being processed by the agent. If they are not
>   equal, then the agent is processing the requested
>   change. The agent may refuse the change to be made
>   and thus return the value for
>   groupMemberStatusChange to its previous value which
>   is equal to the groupMemberStatus value. If the
>   agent accepts the change, the groupMemberStatus
>   value will be set equal to the
>   groupMemberStatusChange value. This object is used
>   to add/delete a group member to a group address.
>   Changes can only be made by a Group Address Sponsor
>   (the subscriber who requested the group address from
>   the service provider). See reference TA-TSV-001062.
>   Changes in this table affect other tables in this
>   group and the Member Group Address Group."
> ::= { groupAddressEntry 10 }

numberMemberAddressesTable   OBJECT-TYPE
    SYNTAX   SEQUENCE OF NumberMemberAddressesEntry
    ACCESS   not-accessible
    STATUS   mandatory
    DESCRIPTION
>   "This table contains the number of individual
>   addresses that are associated with a group address.
>   Initially, there may be up to 128 individual
>   addresses that are identified by the group address."
> ::= { groupAddressing 2 }

numberMemberAddressesEntry   OBJECT-TYPE
    SYNTAX   NumberMemberAddressesEntry
    ACCESS   not-accessible
    STATUS   mandatory
    DESCRIPTION
>   "A group address and the number of individual
>   addresses that are identified by it."
    INDEX { numberCountryCodeGAIndex,
        numberDestinationCodeGAIndex,
        numberSubscriberNumberGAIndex }
> ::= { numberMemberAddressesTable 1 }

NumberMemberAddressesEntry   ::= SEQUENCE {
    numberCountryCodeGAIndex
        INTEGER,
    numberDestinationCodeGAIndex
        INTEGER,
    numberSubscriberNumberGAIndex
        INTEGER,

```
    numberGroupAddress
      SMDSAddress,
    numberIndAddresses
      INTEGER
    }

numberCountryCodeGAIndex OBJECT-TYPE
    SYNTAX   INTEGER (1..4294967295)
    ACCESS   read-only
    STATUS   mandatory
    DESCRIPTION
        "The country code portion of the SMDS Group Address.
         For example, the country code of North America is
         (1), the UK is (44), and Germany is (49)."
    ::= { numberMemberAddressesEntry 1 }

numberDestinationCodeGAIndex OBJECT-TYPE
    SYNTAX   INTEGER (1..4294967295)
    ACCESS   read-only
    STATUS   mandatory
    DESCRIPTION
        "The destination code portion of the SMDS Group
         Address. For example, in North American it is the
         Area Code. For many European countries, it is the
         city code portion of the address. For SMDS
         addresses that do not distinguish such a code, this
         field is the next set of numbers that make logical
         sense. See smdsAddressCodes object."
    ::= { numberMemberAddressesEntry 2 }

numberSubscriberNumberGAIndex OBJECT-TYPE
    SYNTAX   INTEGER (1..4294967295)
    ACCESS   read-only
    STATUS   mandatory
    DESCRIPTION
        "The remaining digits of the SMDS Group Address.
         This field will always be less than or equal to 9
         digits long. In North America, this field contains
         the rest of the SMDS address (e.g., the last 7
         digits following the area code). See
         smdsAddressCodes object."
    ::= { numberMemberAddressesEntry 3 }

numberGroupAddress OBJECT-TYPE
    SYNTAX   SMDSAddress
    ACCESS   read-only
    STATUS   mandatory
    DESCRIPTION
        "A Group Address."
    ::= { numberMemberAddressesEntry 4 }
```

```
numberIndAddresses OBJECT-TYPE
    SYNTAX   INTEGER (0..128)
    ACCESS   read-only
    STATUS   mandatory
    DESCRIPTION
        "This value identifies the total number of
        individual addresses that are associated with a
        group address.  Initially, there may be up to 128
        individual addresses that are associated with a
        group address.  A group address may have no
        members."
    ::= { numberMemberAddressesEntry 5 }


-- The Member Group Address Group
-- Implementation of this group is mandatory if providing SMDS CNM.

memberGroupAddressTable  OBJECT-TYPE
    SYNTAX   SEQUENCE OF MemberGroupAddressEntry
    ACCESS   not-accessible
    STATUS   mandatory
    DESCRIPTION
        "A table of all individual addresses that are
        members of group addresses and the group address(es)
        they belong to.  A group address identifies up to m
        individual addresses.  An SMDS SS supports up to n
        group addresses.  An individual address can be
        identified by up to p group addresses.  A particular
        SNI is identified by up to 48 group addresses.  The
        initial values of m, n, and p are defined as 128,
        1024, and 32, respectively.  In the future values
        of m and n of 2048 and 8192, respectively, may be
        supported.

        Changes in this table cause corresponding changes in
        the groupAddressTable, numberMemberAddressesTable,
        numberGAsForAddressTable, and numberGAsForSNITable."
    ::= { groupAddressing 3 }

memberGroupAddressEntry  OBJECT-TYPE
    SYNTAX   MemberGroupAddressEntry
    ACCESS   not-accessible
    STATUS   mandatory
    DESCRIPTION
        "An address and a Group Address in which it is a
        member and whether that association is valid or
        invalid."
    INDEX   { memberCountryCodeIndex,
        memberDestinationCodeIndex,
        memberSubscriberNumberIndex,
        memberCountryCodeGAIndex,
```

```
        memberDestinationCodeGAIndex,
        memberSubscriberNumberGAIndex }
   ::= { memberGroupAddressTable 1 }


MemberGroupAddressEntry      ::= SEQUENCE {
   memberCountryCodeIndex
      INTEGER,
   memberDestinationCodeIndex
      INTEGER,
   memberSubscriberNumberIndex
   INTEGER,
   memberCountryCodeGAIndex
      INTEGER,
   memberDestinationCodeGAIndex
      INTEGER,
   memberSubscriberNumberGAIndex
      INTEGER,
   memberAddress
      SMDSAddress,
   associatedGroupAddress
      SMDSAddress,
   associatedGroupAddressStatus
      INTEGER,
   associatedGroupAddressStatusChange
      INTEGER
   }


memberCountryCodeIndex OBJECT-TYPE
   SYNTAX  INTEGER (1..4294967295)
   ACCESS  read-only
   STATUS  mandatory
   DESCRIPTION
      "The country code portion of the SMDS Address. For
      example, the country code of North America is (1),
      the UK is (44), and Germany is (49)."
   ::= { memberGroupAddressEntry 1 }


memberDestinationCodeIndex OBJECT-TYPE
   SYNTAX  INTEGER (1..4294967295)
   ACCESS  read-only
   STATUS  mandatory
   DESCRIPTION
      "The destination code portion of the SMDS Address.
      For example, in North American it is the Area Code.
      For many European countries, it is the city code
      portion of the address.  For SMDS addresses that do
      not distinguish such a code, this field is the next
      set  of  numbers  that  make  logical  sense.  See
      smdsAddressCodes object."
   ::= { memberGroupAddressEntry 2 }
```

```
memberSubscriberNumberIndex OBJECT-TYPE
    SYNTAX   INTEGER (1..4294967295)
    ACCESS   read-only
    STATUS   mandatory
    DESCRIPTION
        "The remaining digits of the SMDS Address.  This
        field will always be less than or equal to 9 digits
        long.  In North America, this field contains the
        rest of the SMDS address (e.g., the last 7 digits
        following the area code).  See smdsAddressCodes
        object."
    ::= { memberGroupAddressEntry 3 }

memberCountryCodeGAIndex OBJECT-TYPE
    SYNTAX   INTEGER (1..4294967295)
    ACCESS   read-only
    STATUS   mandatory
    DESCRIPTION
        "The country code portion of the SMDS Group Address.
        For example, the country code of North America is
        (1), the UK is (44), and Germany is (49)."
    ::= { memberGroupAddressEntry 4 }

memberDestinationCodeGAIndex OBJECT-TYPE
    SYNTAX   INTEGER (1..4294967295)
    ACCESS   read-only
    STATUS   mandatory
    DESCRIPTION
        "The destination code portion of the SMDS Group
        Address.  For example, in North American it is the
        Area Code.  For many European countries, it is the
        city code portion of the address.  For SMDS
        addresses that do not distinguish such a code, this
        field is the next set of numbers that make logical
        sense.  See smdsAddressCodes object."
    ::= { memberGroupAddressEntry 5 }

memberSubscriberNumberGAIndex OBJECT-TYPE
    SYNTAX   INTEGER (1..4294967295)
    ACCESS   read-only
    STATUS   mandatory
    DESCRIPTION
        "The remaining digits of the SMDS Group Address.
        This field will always be less than or equal to 9
        digits long.  In North America, this field contains
        the rest of the SMDS address (e.g., the last 7
        digits following the area code).  See
        smdsAddressCodes object."
    ::= { memberGroupAddressEntry 6 }

memberAddress OBJECT-TYPE
```

```
   SYNTAX   SMDSAddress
   ACCESS   read-only
   STATUS   mandatory
   DESCRIPTION
        "An individual SMDS address."
 ::= { memberGroupAddressEntry 7 }

associatedGroupAddress OBJECT-TYPE
   SYNTAX   SMDSAddress
   ACCESS   read-only
   STATUS   mandatory
   DESCRIPTION
        "A Group Address of which the individual address is
        a member."
 ::= { memberGroupAddressEntry 8 }

associatedGroupAddressStatus OBJECT-TYPE
   SYNTAX   INTEGER   {
        valid (1),
        invalid (2)
   }
   ACCESS   read-only
   STATUS   mandatory
   DESCRIPTION
        "The       object       identifies       whether       the
        associatedGroupAddress is valid or invalid.    See
        reference TA-TSV-001062."
  ::= { memberGroupAddressEntry 9 }

 associatedGroupAddressStatusChange OBJECT-TYPE
   SYNTAX   INTEGER   {
        valid (1),
        invalid (2)
   }
   ACCESS   read-write
   STATUS   mandatory
   DESCRIPTION
        "This    object    is    used    to    change    the
        associatedGroupAddressStatus.   When  the  value  of
        this  object  and  associatedGroupAddressStatus  are
        equal,  then  no  change  is  being  processed  by  the
        agent.  If  they  are  not  equal,  then  the  agent  is
        processing  the  requested  change.   The  agent  may
        refuse  the  change  to  be  made  and  thus  return  the
        value  for  associatedGroupAddressStatusChange  to  its
        previous   value   which   is   equal   to   the
        associatedGroupAddressStatus  value.    If  the  agent
        accepts  the  change,  the  associatedGroupAddressStatus
        value    will    be    set    equal    to    the
        associatedGroupAddressStatusChange   value.    This
        object  is  used  to  only  remove  the  Individual  Address
```

```
          (memberAddress) from being associated with a Group
          Address (associatedGroupAddress). Changes may only
          be made by the Group Member. This capability is
          under study. See reference TA-TSV-001062."
     ::= { memberGroupAddressEntry 10 }

numberGAsForAddressTable  OBJECT-TYPE
     SYNTAX   SEQUENCE OF NumberGAsForAddressEntry
     ACCESS   not-accessible
     STATUS   mandatory
     DESCRIPTION
          "This table contains the number of group addresses
          that are associated with this individual address.
          Initially, there may be up to 32 group addresses
          that are associated by the individual address."
     ::= { groupAddressing 4 }

numberGAsForAddressEntry  OBJECT-TYPE
     SYNTAX   NumberGAsForAddressEntry
     ACCESS   not-accessible
     STATUS   mandatory
     DESCRIPTION
          "An individual address and the number of group
          addresses that are associated with it."
     INDEX { numberGAsCountryCodeIndex,
          numberGAsDestinationCodeIndex,
          numberGAsSubscriberNumberIndex }
     ::= { numberGAsForAddressTable 1 }

NumberGAsForAddressEntry  ::= SEQUENCE {
   numberGAsCountryCodeIndex
       INTEGER,
   numberGAsDestinationCodeIndex
       INTEGER,
   numberGAsSubscriberNumberIndex
       INTEGER,
   individualAddress
       SMDSAddress,
   numberGroupAddresses
       INTEGER
   }

numberGAsCountryCodeIndex OBJECT-TYPE
     SYNTAX   INTEGER (1..4294967295)
     ACCESS   read-only
     STATUS   mandatory
     DESCRIPTION
          "The country code portion of the SMDS Address. For
          example, the country code of North America is (1),
          the UK is (44), and Germany is (49)."
     ::= { numberGAsForAddressEntry 1 }
```

```
numberGAsDestinationCodeIndex OBJECT-TYPE
    SYNTAX   INTEGER (1..4294967295)
    ACCESS   read-only
    STATUS   mandatory
    DESCRIPTION
        "The destination code portion of the SMDS Address.
        For example, in North American it is the Area Code.
        For many European countries, it is the city code
        portion of the address.  For SMDS addresses that do
        not distinguish such a code, this field is the next
        set  of  numbers  that  make  logical  sense.  See
        smdsAddressCodes object."
    ::= { numberGAsForAddressEntry 2 }


numberGAsSubscriberNumberIndex OBJECT-TYPE
    SYNTAX   INTEGER (1..4294967295)
    ACCESS   read-only
    STATUS   mandatory
    DESCRIPTION
        "The  remaining  digits  of  the  SMDS  Address.  This
        field will always be less than or equal to 9 digits
        long.   In  North  America,  this  field  contains  the
        rest  of  the  SMDS  address  (e.g.,  the  last  7  digits
        following  the  area  code).   See  smdsAddressCodes
        object."
    ::= { numberGAsForAddressEntry 3 }


individualAddress OBJECT-TYPE
    SYNTAX   SMDSAddress
    ACCESS   read-only
    STATUS   mandatory
    DESCRIPTION
        "An  individual  SMDS  Address  that  has  at  least  one
        group address associated with it."
    ::= { numberGAsForAddressEntry 4 }


numberGroupAddresses OBJECT-TYPE
    SYNTAX   INTEGER (1..32)
    ACCESS   read-only
    STATUS   mandatory
    DESCRIPTION
        "This  value  identifies  the  total  number  of  group
        addresses  that  are  associated  with  an  individual
        address.   Initially,  there  may  be  up  to  32  group
        addresses  that  are  associated  with  an  individual
        address.   This  table  only  contains  the  individual
        addresses  that  are  associated  with  at  least  one
        group address."
    ::= { numberGAsForAddressEntry 5 }


numberGAsForSNITable  OBJECT-TYPE
```

```
     SYNTAX  SEQUENCE OF NumberGAsForSNIEntry
     ACCESS  not-accessible
     STATUS  mandatory
     DESCRIPTION
         "This table contains the number of group addresses
         that are associated with an SNI. Initially, there
         may be up to 48 group addresses that identify the
         SNI."
     ::= { groupAddressing 5 }

numberGAsForSNIEntry  OBJECT-TYPE
     SYNTAX  NumberGAsForSNIEntry
     ACCESS  not-accessible
     STATUS  mandatory
     DESCRIPTION
         "An SNI    INDEX along with the number of group
         addresses that are identify it."
     INDEX { numberGAsSNIIndex }
     ::= { numberGAsForSNITable 1 }

NumberGAsForSNIEntry   ::= SEQUENCE {
     numberGAsSNIIndex
         INTEGER,
     numberGAs
         INTEGER
     }

numberGAsSNIIndex OBJECT-TYPE
     SYNTAX  INTEGER (1..65535)
     ACCESS  read-only
     STATUS  mandatory
     DESCRIPTION
         "The value of this object identifies the SIP port
         interface for which this entry contains management
         information.  The  value  of  this  object  for  a
         particular interface has the same value as the
         ifIndex object, defined in RFC1213, for the same
         interface."
     ::= { numberGAsForSNIEntry 1 }

numberGAs OBJECT-TYPE
     SYNTAX  INTEGER (0..48)
     ACCESS  read-only
     STATUS  mandatory
     DESCRIPTION
         "This value identifies the total number of group
         addresses that identify an SNI. Initially, there
         may be up to 48 group addresses that identify an
         SNI."
     ::= { numberGAsForSNIEntry 2 }
```

-- The Service Disagreements Group

-- Implementation of this group is mandatory if providing SMDS CNM.

```
serviceDisagreementTable  OBJECT-TYPE
    SYNTAX   SEQUENCE OF ServiceDisagreementEntry
    ACCESS   not-accessible
    STATUS   mandatory
    DESCRIPTION
        "A table that contains the latest occurrence of a:
        - Source Address Screening Violation,
        - Destination Address Screening Violation, and
        - Unrecognized Source Address for SNI.
        Each  entry  is        INDEXed  by  SNI  and  service
        disagreement type, and accompanied by a time-stamp.
        When  the  serviceDisagreementTimeStamp  is  equal  to
        zero, the ServiceDisagreementEntry does not contain
        any valid information."
  ::= { smdsSubscr 5 }

serviceDisagreementEntry  OBJECT-TYPE
    SYNTAX   ServiceDisagreementEntry
    ACCESS   not-accessible
    STATUS   mandatory
    DESCRIPTION
        "An entry in the service disagreement table."
    INDEX   { sniSDIndex, serviceDisagreementType }
  ::= { serviceDisagreementTable 1 }

ServiceDisagreementEntry   ::= SEQUENCE {
    sniSDIndex
      INTEGER,
    serviceDisagreementType
      INTEGER,
    serviceDisagreementSA
      SMDSAddress,
    serviceDisagreementDA
      SMDSAddress,
    serviceDisagreementTimeStamp
      TimeTicks
    }

sniSDIndex OBJECT-TYPE
    SYNTAX   INTEGER (1..65535)
    ACCESS   read-only
    STATUS   mandatory
    DESCRIPTION
        "The value of this object identifies the SIP port
        interface for which this entry contains management
        information.   The  value  of  this  object  for  a
        particular  interface  has  the  same  value  as  the
        ifIndex object, defined in RFC1213, for the same
        interface."
  ::= { serviceDisagreementEntry 1 }
```

```
serviceDisagreementType OBJECT-TYPE
   SYNTAX   INTEGER {
       sourceAddressScreenViolation (1),
       destinationAddressScreenViolation (2),
       invalidSourceAddressForSNI (3)
   }
   ACCESS   read-only
   STATUS   mandatory
   DESCRIPTION
       "The type of service disagreement."
 ::= { serviceDisagreementEntry 2 }

serviceDisagreementSA OBJECT-TYPE
   SYNTAX   SMDSAddress
   ACCESS   read-only
   STATUS   mandatory
   DESCRIPTION
       "A rejected SMDS source address."
 ::= { serviceDisagreementEntry 3 }

serviceDisagreementDA OBJECT-TYPE
   SYNTAX   SMDSAddress
   ACCESS   read-only
   STATUS   mandatory
   DESCRIPTION
       "A rejected SMDS destination address."
 ::= { serviceDisagreementEntry 4 }

serviceDisagreementTimeStamp OBJECT-TYPE
   SYNTAX   TimeTicks
   ACCESS   read-only
   STATUS   mandatory
   DESCRIPTION
       "The timestamp for the service disagreement.  The
       timestamp contains the value of sysUpTime at the
       latest   occurrence  of  this  type  of  service
       disagreement.  See textual    DESCRIPTION under
       serviceDisagreementTable for boundary conditions."
 ::= { serviceDisagreementEntry 5 }


-- The information to support the exchange access component of inter-
-- exchange SMDS. See reference TR-TSV-001060 for requirements.
-- Implementation of this group is mandatory if providing SMDS CNM and
-- Exchange   Access SMDS.

xaSmds    OBJECT IDENTIFIER    ::= { smdsSubscr 6 }

-- The Exchange Access SMDS Subscription Parameters and Violations Group
-- Implementation of this group is mandatory if providing SMDS CNM and
-- Exchange Access SMDS.
```

-- Although some of the objects in this group are read-write, the write-
-- capability is not supported by the agent. However, in the future, the
-- management station, when authorized, may change the value for
-- carrierPreselection. Assuming that the objects are in the customer's
-- MIB View and the   Access Control Table allows read-write   Access,
-- in the mean time, the agent will return badValue for any Secure SNMP
-- SET-Request on a read-write object. The agent will return noSuchName
-- for community-string based SET-Request on a read-write object.

```
xaSmdsSubscrTable  OBJECT-TYPE
    SYNTAX   SEQUENCE OF XaSmdsSubscrEntry
    ACCESS   not-accessible
    STATUS   mandatory
    DESCRIPTION
        "This  table  contains  Subscriber-Network  Interface
        (SNI) parameters and state variables, one entry per
        SIP port, that is applicable for providing interLATA
        SMDS to the end customer."
  ::= { xaSmds 1 }

xaSmdsSubscrEntry  OBJECT-TYPE
    SYNTAX   XaSmdsSubscrEntry
    ACCESS   not-accessible
    STATUS   mandatory
    DESCRIPTION
        "This  list  contains  Subscriber-Network  Interface
        (SNI)  parameters  for  interLATA  SMDS  and  state
        variables."
    INDEX    { xaSmdsSubscrIndex }
  ::= { xaSmdsSubscrTable 1 }

XaSmdsSubscrEntry    ::= SEQUENCE {
    xaSmdsSubscrIndex
      INTEGER,
    carrierPreselection
      INTEGER,
    carrierPreselectionChange
      INTEGER,
    carrierSelectionViolations
      Counter
    }

xaSmdsSubscrIndex  OBJECT-TYPE
    SYNTAX   INTEGER (1..65535)
    ACCESS   read-only
    STATUS   mandatory
    DESCRIPTION
        "The value of this object identifies the SIP port
        interface for which this entry contains management
        information.   The value  of  this  object  for  a
        particular  interface  has  the  same  value  as  the
```

```
        ifIndex object, defined in RFC1213, for the same
        interface."
  ::= { xaSmdsSubscrEntry 1 }

 carrierPreselection OBJECT-TYPE
    SYNTAX   INTEGER (1..9999)
    ACCESS   read-only
    STATUS   mandatory
    DESCRIPTION
        "The preselected carrier used to send inter-
        exchange SMDS L3_PDUs.  If a carrier is not
        preselected than this SMDS carrier code is all
        zeros.  This object is equal to the CIC code for the
        carrier."
  ::= { xaSmdsSubscrEntry 2 }

 carrierPreselectionChange OBJECT-TYPE
    SYNTAX   INTEGER (1..9999)
    ACCESS   read-write
    STATUS   mandatory
    DESCRIPTION
        "This object is used to change the
        carrierPreselection.  When the value of this object
        and carrierPreselection are equal, then no change is
        being processed by the agent.  If they are not
        equal, then the agent is processing the requested
        change.  The agent may refuse the change to be made
        and thus return the value for
        carrierPreselectionChange to its previous value
        which is equal to the carrierPreselection value. If
        the agent accepts the change, the
        carrierPreselection value will be set equal to the
        carrierPreselectionChange value."
  ::= { xaSmdsSubscrEntry 3 }

 carrierSelectionViolations OBJECT-TYPE
    SYNTAX   Counter
    ACCESS   read-only
    STATUS   mandatory
    DESCRIPTION
        "The number of SIP L3_PDUs that were discarded
        because an explicit carrier (CIC code) was selected
        in the Carrier Selection field of the Header
        Extension of an SIP L3_PDU and the Destination
        Address was structured as an embodied Service
        ACCESS Code (SAC) plus the number of SIP L3_PDUs
        that were discarded because of an unauthorized
        carrier (CIC) was selected plus the number of SIP
        L3_PDUs that were discarded because they contained
        an explicit Carrier Selection element (CIC code)
        that the SMDS SS did not recognize.  The CIC may be
```

a valid code for SMDS. However, this SMDS SS that is
serving this SNI is not connected to that carrier or
does not recognize the code specified.   In some
jurisdictions not all carriers are authorized to
provide exchange service.   Hence, if the carrier
selection field contains a carrier's CIC code (i.e.,
an explicit carrier selection has been made) and
that carrier is not authorized to provide service
between destination and source addresses within the
exchange service area, then the SIP L3_PDU will be
discarded.   See TR-TSV- 001060."
    ::= { xaSmdsSubscrEntry 4 }

-- The Carrier Blocking Group
-- Implementation of this group is mandatory if providing SMDS CNM and
-- Exchange Access SMDS.

carrierBlockingTable OBJECT-TYPE
    SYNTAX   SEQUENCE OF CarrierBlockingEntry
    ACCESS   not-accessible
    STATUS   mandatory
    DESCRIPTION
      "This table contains a list of carriers that are
      blocking   the   end-customer's   Subscriber-Network
      Interface (SNI), whether the blocking is turned on
      or off, and contains the number of SIP L3_PDUs that
      were discarded because the carrier blocked packets
      from this SNI.   Initially, if no carriers are
      blocking an SNI, then this table contains no
      information."
    ::= { xaSmds 2 }

carrierBlockingEntry OBJECT-TYPE
    SYNTAX   CarrierBlockingEntry
    ACCESS   not-accessible
    STATUS   mandatory
    DESCRIPTION
      "This list contains the Subscriber-Network Interface
      (SNI)   INDEX, the carriers that are blocking
      packets from that SNI, and the number of SIP L3_PDUs
      that were blocked per SMDS CIC code per SNI."
    INDEX   { carrierBlockingIndex, carrierBlockingCodeIndex
        }
    ::= { carrierBlockingTable 1 }

CarrierBlockingEntry   ::= SEQUENCE {
    carrierBlockingIndex
      INTEGER,
    carrierBlockingCodeIndex
      INTEGER,
    carrierBlockingStatus

```
    INTEGER,
  carrierBlockingL3PDUs
    Counter
  }

carrierBlockingIndex  OBJECT-TYPE
   SYNTAX   INTEGER (1..65535)
   ACCESS   read-only
   STATUS   mandatory
   DESCRIPTION
       "The value of this object identifies the SIP port
       interface for which this entry contains management
       information.   The value of this object for a
       particular interface has the same value as the
       ifIndex object, defined in RFC1213, for the same
       interface."
   ::= { carrierBlockingEntry 1 }

carrierBlockingCodeIndex  OBJECT-TYPE
   SYNTAX   INTEGER (1..9999)
   ACCESS   read-only
   STATUS   mandatory
   DESCRIPTION
       "The value of this object identifies the carrier
       code (CIC) in decimal form. There may be up to 16
       carriers that are blocking a particular SNI.  Only
       interexchange carriers may block an SNI."
   ::= { carrierBlockingEntry 2 }

carrierBlockingStatus OBJECT-TYPE
   SYNTAX   INTEGER  {
       on  (1),
       off (2)
   }
   ACCESS   read-only
   STATUS   mandatory
   DESCRIPTION
       "Whether the carrier is presently blocking this SNI
       (on) or whether blocking is turned off.  When the
       carrierBlockingStatus is changed from on to off, the
       carrierBlockingL3PDUs     for     this     particular
       carrierBlockingCodeIndex remain pegged at the value
       when turned off.  When the carrierBlockingStatus is
       turned  on,  the  carrierBlockingL3PDUs  for  this
       carrierBlockingCodeIndex is reset to zero."
   ::= { carrierBlockingEntry 3 }

carrierBlockingL3PDUs OBJECT-TYPE
   SYNTAX   Counter
   ACCESS   read-only
   STATUS   mandatory
```

```
    DESCRIPTION
        "The number of SIP L3_PDUs that were discarded,
        because the carrier blocked packets from that SNI.
        This count may be zero. When the
        carrierBlockingStatus is changed from off to on, the
        carrierBlockingL3PDUs counter is reset to zero."
    ::= { carrierBlockingEntry 4 }


-- The Carrier Index Group
-- Implementation of this group is mandatory if providing SMDS CNM and
-- Exchange Access SMDS.

carrierIndexTable  OBJECT-TYPE
    SYNTAX   SEQUENCE OF CarrierIndexEntry
    ACCESS   not-accessible
    STATUS   mandatory
    DESCRIPTION
        "The value of this object identifies the
        interface(s) between the local service provider and
        the particular other carriers for which this entry
        contains management information. The value of this
        object for a particular interface has the same value
        as the ifIndex object, defined in RFC1213, for the
        same interface."
    ::= { xaSmds 3 }

carrierIndexEntry  OBJECT-TYPE
    SYNTAX   CarrierIndexEntry
    ACCESS   not-accessible
    STATUS   mandatory
    DESCRIPTION
        "This list contains the carrier code of the carriers
        and the respective ifIndex. Only the interfaces
        table from MIB II (RFC1213) is applicable for this
        ifIndex and only the following items: ifDescr,
        ifType, ifOperStatus, and ifLastChange."
    INDEX    { carrierIndexCode, carrierCodeType }
    ::= { carrierIndexTable 1 }

CarrierIndexEntry    ::= SEQUENCE {
    carrierIndexCode
      INTEGER,
    carrierCodeType
      INTEGER,
    carrierIndex
      INTEGER
    }


carrierIndexCode  OBJECT-TYPE
    SYNTAX   INTEGER (1..9999)
    ACCESS   read-only
```

```
STATUS   mandatory
DESCRIPTION
      "The  carrier's  code  (CIC  or  NECA  code)  which  is
      connected to the serving network supporting SMDS."
::= { carrierIndexEntry 1 }

carrierCodeType  OBJECT-TYPE
   SYNTAX   INTEGER  {
        cic (1),
        necacc (2)
   }
   ACCESS   read-only
   STATUS   mandatory
   DESCRIPTION
        "Whether  the  carrier's  code  which  is  connected  to
        the serving network supporting SMDS is a CIC or NECA
        CC."
   ::= { carrierIndexEntry 2 }


carrierIndex  OBJECT-TYPE
   SYNTAX   INTEGER (1..65535)
   ACCESS   read-only
   STATUS   mandatory
   DESCRIPTION
        "The carrier's ifIndex from RFC1213. For SMDS CNM,
        this      INDEX  models  all  the  interfaces  (ICIs)
        between  an  LEC  and  an  ILEC  or  IEC  as  the  same
        interface."
   ::= { carrierIndexEntry 3 }
```

-- Enterprise-specific traps for use with the SNMP-based SMDS Customer
-- Network Management Service. Implementation of these traps are
-- mandatory if providing SMDS CNM.

-- This is the SMDS CNM Subscription MIB trap module.

-- Trap definitions that follow are specified compliant with the SMI
-- RFC1155, as amended by the extensions specified for concise MIB
-- specifications RFC1212 and using the conventions for defining event
-- notifications RFC1215.

```
smdsSubscrEntryChange TRAP-TYPE
   ENTERPRISE   bellcore
   VARIABLES    { ifIndex }
   DESCRIPTION
        "An  smdsSubscrEntryChange  trap  signifies  that  for
        this SNI one or more of the following subscription
        parameters have been changed:
        smdsContact(1)
        smdsSNILocation(2)
        smdsAccessClass(3)
```

```
        smdsMCDUsIn(4)
        smdsMCDUsOut(5)."
  ::= 1

smdsAddressesEntryChange TRAP-TYPE
  ENTERPRISE  bellcore
  VARIABLES   { ifIndex }
  DESCRIPTION
      "An smdsAddressesEntryChange trap signifies that for
      this SNI the list of associated SMDS addresses has
      been changed."
  ::= 2

individualAddressScreenEntryChange TRAP-TYPE
  ENTERPRISE  bellcore
  VARIABLES   { ifIndex }
  DESCRIPTION
      "An      individualAddressScreenEntryChange      trap
      signifies that for this SNI a change has been made
      to the individual address screening tables."
  ::= 3

groupAddressScreenEntryChange TRAP-TYPE
  ENTERPRISE  bellcore
  VARIABLES   { ifIndex }
  DESCRIPTION
      "An  groupAddressScreenEntryChange  trap  signifies
      that for this SNI a change has been made to the
      group address screening tables."
  ::= 4

groupAddressChange TRAP-TYPE
  ENTERPRISE  bellcore
  VARIABLES   { groupAddress }
  DESCRIPTION
      "A groupAddressChange trap signifies that for the
      list of SMDS addresses for this group address has
      been changed, or that this group address has been
      added or deleted."
  ::= 5

excessiveAuthenticationFailure TRAP-TYPE
  ENTERPRISE  bellcore
  VARIABLES   { ifIndex }
  DESCRIPTION
      "An  excessiveAuthenticationFailure  trap  signifies
      that n consecutive authentication failures have been
      received for management requests for this SNI. The
      value of n is 100."
  ::= 6
```

```
xaSmdsSubscrEntryChange TRAP-TYPE
   ENTERPRISE  bellcore
   VARIABLES   { ifIndex }
   DESCRIPTION
       "An xaSmdsSubscrEntryChange trap signifies that for
       this SNI the carrierPreselection has been changed."
   ::= 7

carrierBlockingEntryChange TRAP-TYPE
   ENTERPRISE  bellcore
   VARIABLES   { ifIndex }
   DESCRIPTION
       "A carrierBlockingEntryChange trap signifies that
       for this SNI a new carrierBlockingCode has been
       turned on (added to the list) or one has been turned
       off."
   ::= 8

  END
```

-- Acknowledgments

-- This document was produced by the Bellcore SMDS CNM TEAM:

-- Jim Alfieri, Ted Brunner, Tracy Cox, Thom Farese, Steven Jaffe,
-- Deirdre Kostick, Dave Piscitello, and Kaj Tesink.

-- In addition, the comments of the following individuals are also
-- acknowledged: Jeff Case and Ron Reuss.

Appendix C

Cyclic Redundancy Checks

Several protocols described in this book utilize one or more Cyclic Redundancy Checks, or CRCs. This appendix provides a brief overview on how these checks work. The information discussed is based on [McNamara], which provides a much more in-depth treatment of this technology, as well as additional references to relevant literature. A comparative analysis of some CRC codes is described in [Witzke].

CRCs are used to achieve error detection in bit transmissions with a high degree of effectiveness. They can also be used for error correction, but we restrict our discussion to error detection, which is their predeominant use in SMDS. In descriptions of CRCs, a bit string is conventionally considered to be the coefficient vector of a polynomial. The presence of a term corresponds to a binary 1, and the absence to a binary 0. The value of the mth least significant bit represents the coefficient of the x^{m-1} term. A polynomial with a length of j bits is said to be of degree $(j-1)$. For example, the polynomial $x^4 + x + 1$ is of degree 4, and corresponds to 10011_B. Similarly, $x^3(x^4 + x + 1)$ corresponds to the polynomial $x^7 + x^4 + x^3$, and the bit string 10011000_B. Note that the multiplication represents a logical shift operation of 3 bits.

The objective of a CRC is, with a minimum of hardware, to calculate from a binary message, represented as the polynomial $M(x)$ with a length of k bits, a code that is to a high degree unique for that message. This code, represented as the polynomial $C(x)$, is the calculated CRC value. In HDLC [ISO3309] it is called the *Frame Check Sequence* or FCS. The code is calculated by the use of a generator polynomial $G(x)$, a bit string with a length and value that are specific to the type of CRC that is used. For example, the generator polynomial for a common CRC of degree 4 is $x^4 + x + 1$. This polynomial is chosen so that the

510

generated CRC has a high error-detection probability. For example, the term x^0 is included to allow detection of single-bit errors. See [McNamara] and [Witzke] for properties of $G(x)$. In the basic CRC algorithm, used for CRCs such as described in Sections 4.6.2 (CRC-8), 4.6.8 (CRC-10), 4.7.1 (CRC-6), and 4.7.3 (CRC-4), the idea is to produce a codeword $F(x)$, such that $F(x)$ is the concatenation of $M(x)$ and $C(x)$, and that $F(x)$ is evenly divisible by $G(x)$. In other words:

1. $F(x) = x^{n-k}[M(x)] + C(x)$, where n is the length in bits of $F(x)$, and

2. The remainder of the division of $F(x)$ by $G(x)$ is zero.

Step 1 is produced in the transmitter by dividing $x^{n-k}[M(x)]$ by $G(x)$. The remainder of this division is $C(x)$, and it is added to $x^{n-k}[M(x)]$ to produce $F(x)$. The division is binary without carries or borrows (modulo 2 division).

Step 2 is verified at the receiver by dividing $F(x)$ by the generator polynomial $G(x)$.

To understand the power of this method, as compared with, for example, the parity-bit method, we point to a simple typical implementation, which is identical for transmitter and receiver, and shown in Figure C.1. The example shows the case for the generator polynomial of degree 10, $G(x) = x^{10} + x^9 + x^5 + x^4 + x + 1$ (see Section 4.6.8). The figure shows a 10-bit shift register combined with logical XOR gates. The most significant bit of the register corresponds to the term with the coefficient of 1, and is on the left. The placement of the XOR gates corresponds to the generator polynomial $G(x)$. The message to be checked ($M(x)$ at the transmitter, or $F(x)$ at the receiver) is the input. The data are shifted in starting with the most significant bit of the polynomial. (See also the example shown below.)

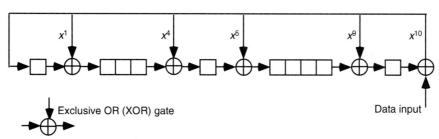

Figure C.1 A typical implementation of the CRC mechanism

In the transmitter, the register is initialized at all zeroes, and after processing $M(x)$, the contents of the register is $C(x)$. The highest polynomial term of $C(x)$ is transmitted first. The receiving register is also initialized with all zeroes. Processing of $F(x)$ must produce all zeroes again, since if the message has been transmitted without errors, upon receipt of the $C(x)$ portion of $F(x)$, the register must contain the same value as $C(x)$. Shifting the $C(x)$ portion of $F(x)$ bit-wise into the Data input of the register results in an XOR of $C(x)$ with its equivalent and produces all zeroes.

Note that the HDLC CRCs, discussed in Chapter 5, deviate slightly, in that the initial contents of the register used to calculate the $C(x)$ is all ones, and the transmitted remainder is the ones-complement of the calculated remainder (compare with Section 5.2.2.5). The consequence is that the receiver will end with a nonzero result. In the absence of transmission errors, the result at the receiver for the HDLC CRC-16 must be 0001110100001111_B, and for the HDLC CRC-32, it must be $11000111000001001101101011111011_B$.

As observed by McNamara, the key to the effectiveness of this arrangement is that the effect of any bit is reflected in the various bits of the shift register for a considerable time after that bit is transmitted. It can be intuitively understood that increasing the length of $G(x)$ will enhance the probability of detecting error bursts.

We conclude with a brief example using the CRC-10 for the 13-bit message $M(x)$.

$M(x) = 1100011001011_B$ or $x^{12} + x^{11} + x^7 + x^6 + x^3 + x^1 + 1$, and
$G(x) = 11000110011_B$ or $x^{10} + x^9 + x^5 + x^4 + x + 1$

Since $n-k = 10$ in this case, we get

$x^{n-k}[M(x)] = x^{10}(x^{12} + x^{11} + x^7 + x^6 + x^3 + x^1 + 1)$, or
$11000110010110000000000_B$

Division by $G(x)$ (binary, no carries, no borrows) corresponds to a series of XOR and shift operations (see Figure C.1), and produces $C(x) = 1011111111_B$:

$$\frac{x^{(n-k)}M(x)}{G(x)} = 11000110011 \overline{)\begin{array}{l} 00000000001000000000101 \\ 11000110010110000000000 \\ \underline{11000110011} \\ 11100000000 \\ \underline{11000110011} \\ 10011001100 \\ \underline{11000110011} \\ 1011111111 \end{array}}$$

Thus, $F(x) = 11000110010111011111111_B$. At the receiver, the received $F(x)$ is divided by $G(x)$. A remainder of 0 indicates correct transmission:

$$\frac{F(x)}{G(x)} = 11000110011 \overline{)\begin{array}{l} 0000000000 1000000000101 \\ 11000110010111011111111 \\ \underline{11000110011} \\ 11110111111 \\ \underline{11000110011} \\ 11000110011 \\ \underline{11000110011} \\ 00000000000 \end{array}}$$

Appendix D

More Information and SMDS Interest Groups

Details for how to obtain documents and information relevant to SMDS are presented in this appendix.

D.1   Bellcore

A summary of the latest service- and product-related technical information made available to the industry by Bellcore is published in a monthly magazine, the Bellcore Digest. To order the Bellcore Digest, Technical References, Technical Advisories, Framework Advisories, and Special Reports, contact

Bellcore Customer Service
8 Corporate Place
Piscataway, NJ 08854-4156

(800) 521-CORE (within the USA and Canada)
(908) 699-5800 (all foreign calls)
(Mastercard, VISA, American Express)

The SMDS Subscription MIB (Appendix B) is electronically available only by anonymous FTP from venera.isi.edu/mib.

D.2   Internet Requests For Comments and Internet-Drafts

Internet RFCs are available by (electronic) anonymous FTP. This requires access to the Internet. Login with the user name "anonymous" and password "guest." After logging in, type

```
cd rfc
get <title>.
```

RFCs directories are located at the following primary repositories: DS.INTERNIC.NET, NIS.NSF.NET, NISC.JVNC.NET, FTP.ISI.EDU, WUARCHIVE.WUSTL.EDU, SRC.DOC.IC.AC.UK, FTP.CONCERT.NET, and FPT.SESQUI.NET.

For more information on retrieving RFCs, send an electronic mail message to RFC-INFO@ISI.EDU with a single line that says "HELP:HELP."

D.3   SMDS Interest Group (SIG)

To obtain SIG information, information on how to join the SIG, or SIG documentation, contact

SMDS Interest Group Inc.
303 Vintage Park Drive
Foster City, CA 94404-1138

(415) 578-6979

(415) 525-0182
(415) 688-4314 (Fax-on-demand;
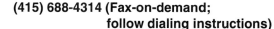
              follow dialing instructions)

sig@interop.com

SIG specifications are available by anonymous FTP (see Section D.2). The host address is ftp.acc.com. The directory is /pub/smds.

D.4   European SMDS Interest Group (ESIG)

Information from the ESIG can be obtained at

European SMDS Interest Group
John Roberts (Chair)
Merlin House
Station Road
Chepstow
Gwent, UK NP6 5PB

+44 (0) 291 620425

+44 (0) 291 627119

D.5   Pacific Rim Frame Relay/ATM/SMDS Interest Group (PR FASIG)

Information from the PR FASIG can be obtained at

Pacific Rim Frame Relay/ATM/SMDS Interest Group
Maria B. P. Chou (Chair)
AT&T Taiwan Inc.
12th Floor Overseas Trust Building
249, Sec. 1, Tun Hwa South Road
Taipei,106, Taiwan, R.O.C.

+886-2-775-6398

+886-2-775-6356

mbc@attitw.attmail.com

D.6   IEEE

The IEEE Computer Society can be contacted at the following address:

IEEE Computer Society
10662 Los Vaqueros Circle
Los Alamitos, CA 90720

(800) 272-6657

(714) 821-4641

cs.books@compmail.com

Standards and other books may be obtained at

IEEE Service Center
445 Hoes Lane
P.O. Box 1331
Piscataway, NJ 08855

(800) 678-4323

(908) 981-9667

D.7   ITU (CCITT)

Before 1993, the ITU consisted of five permanent organizations, including the International Radio Consultative Committee (CCIR) and the International Telegraph and Telephone Consultative Committee (CCITT). In early 1993, the ITU was reorganized, and the standards-making activities of the CCITT and CCIR have been consolidated into the Telecommunication Standardization Sector (ITU-T). CCITT Recommendations will continue to be available, but references to CCITT should be replaced by ITU-T. To obtain specifications or other information, contact

International Telecommunication Union
Information Services Department
Place de Nations
1211 Geneva 20
Switzerland

+41 22 730 5554

+41 22 730 5337

 internet: helpdesk@itu.ch
X.400:   S=helpdesk; A=arcom; P=itu; C=ch

In the United States ITU recommendations are available from

 U.S. Department of Commerce
National Technical Information Service
5285 Port Royal Road
Springfield, VA 22161

 (703) 487-4650

 (703) 321-8547

and from

 United Nations Bookstore
Room 32B
United Nations Plaza
New York, NY 10017

The ITU also provides electronic access to much of their documentation, using an electronic document distribution service called *ITUDOC*. For instructions, send a message with HELP in the message body to

 Internet: itudoc@itu.ch
X.400:   S=teledoc, P=itu, A=arcom, C=ch

The ITUDOC is also accessible by anonymous Telnet. (Login as anonymous guest.) FTP and Kermit services are available. Telnet to one of the following addresses:

 ties.itu.ch (156.106.4.75) or
chi.itu.ch (156.106.4.16)

Some ITU information resources are available in multiple formats and/or languages (e.g., English, French, and Spanish).

D.8 ANSI and ISO

ANSI is the American National Standards Institute. The ISO is the International Standardization Organization. In the United States, ANSI and ISO specifications are available from

American National Standards Institute
11 W. 42nd Street
New York, NY 10036

(212) 642-4900

D.9 Some Electronic Discussion Groups on SMDS

Many engineering questions relevant for SMDS are discussed by electronic mail. Table D.1 lists some of these discussion groups.

To join these lists, send email to X-request@Y, where X is the login and Y the host name of the discussion group in Table D.1. For example, mail to atommib-request@thumper.bellcore.com will reach the administrator of the atommib discussion list. Use a subject line of "Subscribe."

Subject	Email (Internet) address
SMDS discussions	smdstc@thumper.bellcore.com
SNMP, SNMP II, MIB II, SIP MIB	snmp@psi.com
DS1/E1 MIB, DS3/E3 MIB	trunk-mib@saffron.acc.com
ATM MIB, SONET MIB	atommib@thumper.bellcore.com

Table D.1 Electronic discussion groups relevant to SMDS

D.10 ATM Forum

The ATM Forum can be contacted at the following address:

ATM Forum
303 Vintage Park Drive
Foster City, CA 94404

(415) 578-6860

(415) 525-0182

 info@atmforum.com

D.11 Reaching the Authors

The authors' email addresses are

 Bob_Klessig@3mail.3com.com

 kaj@cc.bellcore.com

Icon Glossary

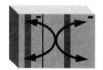

ATM Switch

Bridge/Router

Carrier Network or Service

Circuit Switch

Connectionless Service Function Server

Customer Access Node

Digital Cross Connect

End System

End System

End System

Frame Relay Switch

Multiplexer

**SMDS/Frame Relay
Interworking Unit**

Packet Switch

SMDS Switching System

Telephone Set

Video Camera

Video Monitor

Acronym List

A

AAL	ATM Adaptation Layer
AARP	AppleTalk Address Resolution Protocol
AE bit	Address Extension bit
AFI	Authority and Format Identifier
AIS	Alarm Indication Signal
AMT	Address Mapping Table
ANSI	American National Standards Institute
ARP	Address Resolution Protocol
ASN.1	Abstract Syntax Notation One
ATM	Asynchronous Transfer Mode

B

B3ZS	Bipolar with 3-Zero Substitution
B8ZS	Bipolar with 8-Zero Substitution
BAsize	Buffer Allocation Size
BCD	Binary Coded Decimal
BECN	Backward Explicit Congestion Notification

Bellcore	Bell Communications Research
BER	Basic Encoding Rules
BES	Bursty Errored Second
BETag	Beginning-End Tag
BGP	Border Gateway Protocol
BIP-8	Bit Interleaved Parity-8
BISDN	Broadband Integrated Services Digital Network
BOM	Beginning of Message
BPDU	Bridge Protocol Data Unit
BPV	Bipolar Violation

C

C/R bit	Command/Response bit
CAN	Customer Access Node
CATV	Community Antenna Television
CBDS	Connectionless Broadband Data Service
CCIR	International Radio Consultative Committee
CCITT	International Telegraph and Telephone Consultative Committee
CIB	CRC32 Indicator Bit
CIC	Carrier Identification Code

CIR	Committed Information Rate	DSX	Digital cross-connect
CLNP	Connectionless Layer Network Protocol	DXI	Data Exchange Interface
CLP	Cell Loss Priority	**E**	
CLSF	Connectionless Service Functions	E1	European transmission level 1
CNM	Customer Network Management	E3	European transmission level 3
COM	Continuation of Message	EGP	Exterior Gateway Protocol
CPCS	Common Part Convergence Sublayer	EIA	Electronics Industry Association
CPE	Customer Premises Equipment	ELAP	EtherTalk Link Access Protocol
CRC	Cyclic Redundancy Check	EOM	End of Message
CRCn	n-bit Cyclic Redundancy Check	ES	End System
CRS	Cell Relay Service	ES	Errored Second
CSMA/CD	Carrier Sense Multiple Access with Collision Detection	ESF	Extended Superframe
		ESIG	European SMDS Interest Group
CSNP	Complete Sequence Number PDU	ETSI	European Telecommunications Standards Institute
CSU	Channel Service Unit	EXZ	Excessive Zeros
D		**F**	
DA	Destination Address		
DARPA	Defense Advanced Research Program Agency	FCS	Frame Check Sequence
DDP	Datagram Delivery Protocol	FDDI	Fiber Distributed Data Interface
DLCI	Data Link Connection Identifier	FEBE	Far-End Block Error
DM	Degraded Minute	FECN	Forward Explicit Congestion Notification
DMPDU	Derived MAC Protocol Data Unit	FRP	Fragmentation and Reassembly Protocol
DOS	Disk Operating System	FRPVC	Frame Relay Permanent Virtual Circuit Service
DQDB	Distributed Queue Dual Bus		
DR	Designated Router	FRSVC	Frame Relay Switched Virtual Circuit Service
DS0	Digital Signal 0		
DS1	Digital Signal 1	FTP	File Transfer Protocol
DS3	Digital Signal 3		
DSAP	Destination Service Access Point	**G**	
DSP	Domain Specific Part	GCRA	Generic Cell Rate Algorithm
DSU	Data Service Unit	GUI	Graphical User Interface

H

HDB3	High Density Bipolar order 3
HDLC	High-level Data Link Control
HE	Header Extension
HEL	Header Extension Length
HLPI	Higher Layer Protocol Identifier
HSSI	High Speed Serial Interface

I

IANA	Internet Assigned Numbers Authority
ICIP	Inter-Carrier Interface Protocol
ICNM	Interexchange CNM
IDI	Initial Domain Identifier
IDP	Internetwork Datagram Protocol
IDRP	Inter-Domain Routing Protocol
IEC	Interexchange Carrier
IEC	International Electrotechnical Commission
IEEE	Institute of Electrical and Electronic Engineers
IETF	Internet Engineering Task Force
IMPDU	Initial MAC Protocol Data Unit
IP	Internet Protocol
IPX	Internetwork Packet Exchange
IS	Intermediate System
ISDN	Integrated Services Digital Network
ISO	International Standardization Organization
ISSIP	Inter-Switching System Interface Protocol
ITU	International Telecommunications Union

L

L1_PDU	Level 1 Protocol Data Unit
L2_PDU	Level 2 Protocol Data Unit
L3_PDU	Level 3 Protocol Data Unit
L3S	Logical 3+ Subnetwork, Logical 3+Open Subnetwork
L4S	Logical DECnet Phase IV Subnetwork
LAN	Local Area Network
LAPB	Link Access Procedure - Balanced
LAPD	Link Access Procedure for the D-channel
LAPF	Link Access Procedure Frame-mode
LATA	Local Access and Transport Area
LCV	Line Code Violation
LEC	Local Exchange Carrier
LES	Line Errored Second
LI	Length Indication
LIS	Logical IP Subnetwork
LLC	Logical Link Control
LMI	Local Management Interface
LOF	Loss-Of-Frame
LOS	Loss-Of-Signal
LSA	Logical SMDSTalk AppleTalk network
LSP	Link State PDU
LVS	Logical VINES Subnetwork
LXS	Logical XNS Subnetwork

M

MAC	Media Access Control
MAN	Metropolitan Area Network
MCDUs	Maximum Concurrent Data Units
MCR	Minimum Cell Rate
MIB	Management Information Base
MID	Message Identifier

MID	Multiplexing Identification	PLCP	Physical Layer Convergence Procedure
MPAF	MID Page Allocation Field		
MRI	Message Receive Interval	PMD	Physical Medium Dependent
		POTS	Plain Old Telephone Service
N		PR FASIG	Pacific Rim Frame Relay/ATM/SMDS Interest Group
NANP	North American Numbering Plan		
		PRM	Performance Report Message
NBP	Name Binding Protocol	PSES	P-bit Severely Errored Second
NCP	NetWare Core Protocol		
ND	Names Directory	PSNP	Partial Sequence Number PDU
NLPID	Network Layer Protocol Identifier		
		PSR bit	Previous Segment Received bit
NLSP	NetWare Link State Protocol		
NMS	Network Management Station	PUP	PARC Universal Packet
		PVC	Permanent Virtual Channel
NPA	Numbering Plan Area	PVC	Permanent Virtual Connection
NSAP	Network Service Access Point		
NT1	Network Termination unit 1	**Q**	
		QOS	Quality of Service
O			
OID	Object Identifier	**R**	
OOF	Out-Of-Frame		
OSI	Open Systems Interconnection	RAI	Remote Alarm Indication
		RARP	Reverse Address Resolution Protocol
OSPF	Open Shortest Path First		
OUI	Organizationally Unique Identifier	RB Group	Remote Bridge Group
		RBOC	Regional Bell Operating Company
P		RIP	Routing Information Protocol
		RTMP	Routing Table Maintenance Protocol
PARC	Palo Alto Research Center		
PCC	Page Counter Control	RTP	Routing Update Protocol
PCM	Page Counter Modulus		
PCR	Peak Cell Rate	**S**	
PCV	P-bit Coding Violation		
PDU	Protocol Data Unit	SA	Source Address
PEP	Packet Exchange Protocol	SAC	Service Access Code
PES	P-bit Errored Second	SAP	Service Access Point
PHY	Physical layer	SAP	Service Advertising Protocol
PID	Protocol Identification	SAR	Segmentation And Reassembly
Ping	Packet Internet Groper		
PL	PAD Length	SDLC	Synchronous Data Link Control

SEATF	SMDS Early Availability Task Force	TLAP	TokenTalk Link Access Protocol
SEFS	Severely Errored Framing Second	TPC	The Phone Company
SEL	Selector	**U**	
SES	Severely Errored Second		
SIG	SMDS Interest Group	UAS	Unavailable Second
SIP	SMDS Interface Protocol	UAT	Unavailable Time
SIR	Sustained Information Rate	UDP	User Datagram Protocol
SMDS	Switched Multi-megabit Data Service	UI frame	Unnumbered Information frame
SMI	Structure of Management Information	UNI	User Network Interface
SN	Sequence Number	**V**	
SNAP	SubNetwork Access Protocol		
SNI	Subscriber Network Interface	VCC	Virtual Channel Connection
SNMP	Simple Network Management Protocol	VCI	Virtual Channel Identifier
		VCI	Virtual Circuit Identifier
SONET	Synchronous Optical Network	VFRP	VINES Fragmentation and Reassembly Protocol
SPP	Sequenced Packet Protocol	VINES	Virtual Networking Systems
SPX	Sequenced Packet Exchange	VPI	Virtual Path Identifier
SRI	SAR Receive Interval	VPN	Virtual Private Network
SRI	SIP Relay Interface		
SS	SMDS Switching System	**W**	
SSAP	Source Service Access Point		
SSCS	Service Specific Convergence Sublayer	WACCO	Wire and Cable Company
		WAN	Wide Area Network
SSM	Single Segment Message		
ST	Segment Type	**X**	
STS-3c	Synchronous Transport Signal 3c	XNS	Xerox Network System
SVC	Switched Virtual Connection		
		Z	
T			
		ZBTSI	Zero Byte Time Slot Interchange
TCP	Transmission Control Protocol	ZIP	Zone Information Protocol
TDM	Time Division Multiplexing	ZIT	Zone Information Table

References

[1059]   Bellcore Technical Advisory TA-TSV-001059, *Inter-Switching System Interface Generic Requirements in Support of SMDS Service*, December 1990.

[1060]   Bellcore Technical Reference TR-TSV-001060, Issue 1, *Switched Multi-megabit Data Service Generic Requirements for Exchange Access and Intercompany Serving Arrangements*, December 1991.

[1062]   Bellcore Technical Advisory TA-TSV-001062, Issue 2, *Generic Requirements for SMDS Customer Network Management Service,* February 1992.

[1062R]   Bellcore Technical Reference TR-TSV-001062, Issue 1, *Generic Requirements for Phase 1 SMDS Customer Network Management Service*, March 1993.

[1110]   Bellcore Technical Advisory TA-NWT-001110, Issue 1, *Broadband ISDN Switching System Generic Requirements*, August 1992.

[1239]   Bellcore Technical Advisory TA-TSV-001239, Issue 1, *Generic Requirements for Low Speed SMDS Access*, June 1993.

[1240]   Bellcore Technical Advisory TA-TSV-001240, Issue 1, *Generic Requirements for Frame Relay Access to SMDS*, June 1993.

[1369]   Bellcore Technical Reference TR-TSV-001369, Issue 1, *Generic Requirements for Frame Relay PVC Exchange Service*, May 1993.

[1408]   Bellcore Technical Advisory TA-TSV-001408, Issue 1, *Generic Requirements for Exchange PVC Cell Relay Service*, August 1993.

[253]   Bellcore Technical Advisory TA-NWT-000253, Issue 6, *Synchronous Optical Network (SONET) Transport Systems: Common Generic Criteria*, September 1990.

[2775]   Bellcore Special Report SR-TSV-002275, *BOC Notes on the LEC Networks,* March 1991.

[301]   Bellcore Technical Reference TR-TSY-000301, Issue 2, *Public Packet Switched Network Generic Requirements (PPSNGR)*, December 1988.

[54]   Bellcore Technical Reference TR-NPL-000054, Issue 1, *High-Capacity Digital Service (1.544 Mbps) Interface Generic Requirements for End Users*, April 1989.

[772.1]   Bellcore Technical Advisory TA-TSY-000772, Issue 1, *Metropolitan Area Network Generic Framework System Requirements in Support of Switched Multi-megabit Data Service*, February 1988.

[772.2]   Bellcore Technical Advisory TA-TSY-000772, Issue 2, *Generic System Requirements in Support of Switched Multi-megabit Data Service*, March 1989.

[772.3]   Bellcore Technical Advisory TA-TSV-000772, Issue 3, *Generic System Requirements in Support of Switched Multi-megabit Data Service*, October 1989.

[772.3S]   Bellcore Technical Advisory TA-TSV-000772, Issue 3, Supplement 1, *Generic System Requirements in Support of Switched Multi-megabit Data Service*, January 1991.

[772]   Bellcore Technical Reference TR-TSV-000772, Issue 1, *Generic Requirements in Support of Switched Multi-megabit Data Service*, May 1991.

[773]   Bellcore Technical Reference TR-TSV-000773, Issue 1, *Local Access System Generic Requirements, Objectives, and Interfaces in Support of Switched Multi-megabit Data Service*, June 1991.

[774]   Bellcore Technical Reference TR-TSV-000774, Issue 1, *SMDS Operations Technology Network Element Generic requirements*, March 1992.

[775]   Bellcore Technical Reference TR-TSV-000775, Issue 1, *Usage Measurement Generic Requirements in Support of SMDS*, June 1991.

[802.1d]   IEEE Std 802.1D - 1990, *Media Access Control (MAC) Bridges*.

[802.1g]   IEEE P802.1G/D7, *Remote MAC Bridging, Draft D7*, December 30, 1992.

[802.2]   IEEE Std 802.2-1989/ISO International Standard 8802-2, *Information Processing Systems—Local Area Networks—Part 2: Logical Link Control*, IEEE August 1989, ISO 1989.

[802.3]   IEEE Std 802.3-1985, *Carrier Sense Multiple Access with Collision Detection (CSMA/CD)*.

[802.4]   IEEE Std 802.4-1985, *Token-Passing Bus Access Method and Physical Layer Specifications*.

[802.5]   IEEE Std 802.5-1989, *Token Ring Access Method and Physical Layer Specification*.

[802.6]   IEEE Std 802.6-1990, *Distributed Queue Dual Bus (DQDB) Subnetwork of a Metropolitan Area Network*.

[802.6i]   IEEE P802.6I/D5, *Remote LAN Bridging Using IEEE Std. 802.6—1990 MAN, Draft D5*, Document 93/01.

[802]   IEEE Std 802-1990, *Overview and Architecture*.

[802Req]   IEEE Computer Society, IEEE P802-D5.9, *Local Area Network Functional Requirements*, July 1989.

[93]   Bellcore Technical Reference TR-EOP-000093, *Telephone Area Code Directory*, September 1991.

[Apple]   Apple Computer, Inc., *AppleTalk Network System Overview*, Addison-Wesley, 1989.

[ATM1]   ATM Forum, ATM Data Exchange Interface (DXI) Specification, June 1993.

[Banyan1]   Banyan Systems Inc., *VINES Architecture Definition*, Publication 092015-001, 1988.

[Banyan2]   Banyan Systems Inc., *VINES Protocol Definition*, Publication DA254-00, 1989

[BICI]   ATM Forum, *BISDN Inter Carrier Interface (B-ICI) Specification, Version 1.0*, August 1993.

[Brown]   Brown, C. M., *"Sizing Up ESF Service Units"*, Data Communications, May 1990

[Case]   Case, J. D., and C. Partridge, *"Case Diagrams: A First Step to Diagrammed Management Information Bases"* Computer Communication Review, January, 1989.

[Comer1]   Comer, D. E., *Internetworking with TCP/IP*, Volume I, *Principles, Protocols, and Architecture*, Second Edition, Prentice Hall, 1991.

[Comer2]   Comer, D. E., and D. L. Stevens, *Internetworking with TCP/IP*, Volume II, *Design, Implementation, and Internals*, Prentice Hall, 1991.

[Cox]   Cox, T. A., and K. Tesink, *Definitions of Managed Objects for SMDS Subscription*, Version 2.1, Enterprise-specific MIB, Bellcore, August 1992.

[DEC1]   Digital Equipment Corp., *DECnet Phase IV General Description*, Publication AA-N149A-TC.

[DEC2]   Digital Equipment Corp., *DECnet Phase IV manual*, Publication AA-X435A-TK.

[DEC3]   Digital Equipment Corp., *DECnet, DIGITAL Network Architecture (Phase V)*, Publication EK-DNAPV-GD.

[dePrycker] de Prycker, M., *Asynchronous Transfer Mode: Solution for Broadband ISDN*, Ellis Horwood, 1991.

[Druce] Druce, C., private communication.

[E.163] CCITT Recommendation E.163, *International Numbering Plan for Telephone Systems*, CCITT Blue Book, 1988. (Note: E.163 is expected to be fully incorporated in E.164 after 1992, after which E.163 will not be reprinted; the reader is then referred to E.164 instead.)

[E.164] CCITT Recommendation E.164, *Numbering Plan for the ISDN Era*, CCITT Blue Book, 1988.

[EIA422A] EIA 422A, *Electrical Characteristics Of Balanced Voltage Digital Interface Circuits*, 1978.

[EIA449] EIA 449, *General Purpose 32-Position and 9-Position Interface for Data Terminating Equipment and Data Circuit-Terminating Equipment Employing Serial Binary Data Interchange*, 1977.

[EIA530A] EIA 530A, *High Speed 25-Position Interface for Data Terminating Equipment and Data Circuit-Terminating Equipment Including Alternative 26-Position Connector*, 1992.

[EIA612] EIA612, *Electrical Characteristics for an Interface at Data Signaling Rates up to 52 Mbit/s*, P-2795, Draft, TIA Subcommittee TR 30.2, August 1992

[EIA613] EIA613, *High Speed Serial Interface for Data Terminal Equipment and Data Circuit-terminating Equipment*, SP-2796, Draft, TIA Subcommittee TR 30.2, August 1992.

[ESIG001] European SMDS Interest Group, *SMDS Subscriber Network Access Facility Service and Level 2 and 3 Subscriber Network Interface Specification*, Edition 1.1, ESIG-TS-001, 22 June 1992.

[ESIG002] European SMDS Interest Group, *SMDS Subscriber Network Interface Level 1 Specification*, Edition 1.0, ESIG-TS-002, June 1993.

[ESIG003] European SMDS Interest Group, *SMDS Customer Network Management Service and Access*, ESIG-TS-003/93, March 93.

[ESIG006]   European SMDS Interest Group, *Interconnection of Public Telecommunication Operator (PTO) Networks Supporting SMDS*, Edition 1, ESIG-TS-006/93, March 1993.

[ETSI213]   ETSI 300-213, *Metropolitan Area Networks (MAN) Physical Layer Convergence Procedure for 2,048 Mbit/s.*

[ETSI214]   ETSI 300-214, *Metropolitan Area Networks (MAN) Physical Layer Convergence Procedure for 34,368 Mbit/s.*

[ETSI233]   ETSI, *Transmission and Multiplexing (TM)*; Digital section for ISDN Primary Rate access, ETS 300 233, 1993.

[FDDI]   ANSI X3.139-1987, *Fiber Distributed Data Interface (FDDI)—Token Ring media Access Control (MAC).*

[FRF-1]   Frame Relay Forum, *Implementors Agreement*, FRF-1, January 1992.

[G.702]   CCITT Recommendation G.702, *Digital Hierarchy Bit Rates*, CCITT Blue Book, Geneva 1989.

[G.703]   CCITT Recommendation G.703, *Physical/Electrical Characteristics Of Hierarchical Digital Interfaces*, CCITT Blue Book, Geneva 1989.

[G.704]   CCITT Recommendation G.704, *Synchronous Frame Structures Used At Primary And Secondary Hierarchical Levels*, CCITT Blue Book, Geneva 1989.

[G.706]   CCITT Recommendation G.706, *Frame Alignment and Cyclic Redundancy Check (CRC) Procedures Relating to Basic Frame Structures Defined in Recommendation G.704*, CCITT Blue Book, Geneva 1989.

[G.707]   CCITT Recommendation G.707, *Synchronous Digital Hierarchy Bit Rates*, Geneva 1991.

[G.708]   CCITT Recommendation G.708, *Network Node Interface for the Synchronous Digital Hierarchy*, Geneva 1992.

[G.709]   CCITT Recommendation G.709, *Synchronous Multiplexing Structure*, Geneva 1992.

[G.751]   CCITT Recommendation G.751, *Digital Multiplex Equipment Operating at the Third Order Bit Rate Of 34368 Kbit/S and the Fourth Order Bit Rate Of 139264 Kbit/S and Using Positive Justification*, CCITT Blue Book, Geneva 1989.

[G.804]   CCITT Recommendation G.804, *ATM Cell Mapping into Plesiochronous Digital Hierarchy (PDH)*, Geneva 1993.

[G.832]   CCITT Recommendation G.832, *Transport of SDH Elements on PDH Networks: Frame and Multiplexing Structures*, Geneva 1993.

[Gill]   Gill, J., Bellcore, private conversation.

[Gusella]   Gusella, R., *"A Measurement Study of Diskless Workstation Traffic on an Ethernet,"* IEEE Transactions on Communications, Vol. 38, No. 9, September 1990.

[Hemrick]   Hemrick, C. F., R. Klessig, and J. M. McRoberts, *"Switched Multi-megabit Data Service and Early Availability Via MAN Technology,"* IEEE Communications Magazine, April 1988.

[Hemrick2] Hemrick, C. F., *The OSI Network Layer Addressing Scheme, Its Implications, and Considerations for Implementation*, NTIA Report 85-186, U.S. Department of Commerce, National Telecommunications and Information Administration, 1985.

[Hindin]   Hindin, E. M., *"HSSI Sizzles"*, Data Communications, November 1991.

[I.363]   CCITT Recommendation I.363, *BISDN ATM Adaptation Layer (AAL) Specification*, June 1992.

[I.364]   CCITT Recommendation I.364, *Support of Broadband Connectionless Data Service on B-ISDN*, June 1992.

[ISO10589] International Organization for Standardization(ISO) and International Electrotechnical Committee (IEC), Information Processing Systems—Telecommunications and Information Exchange between Systems—*Intermediate system to Intermediate system Intra-Domain routeing information exchange protocol for use in conjunction with the Protocol for providing the Connectionless-mode Network Service*, International Standard ISO/IEC 10589, Draft 1992-01-15.

[ISO10747] ISO/IEC, Information Processing Systems—Telecommunications and Information Exchange between Systems, *Protocol for Exchange of Inter-domain Routeing Information among Intermediate Systems to Support Forwarding of ISO 8473 PDUs*, ISO CD 10747, ISO/IEC/JTC1/SC6N7196, March 16, 1992.

[ISO3309]   ISO, International Standardization Organization—Information Processing Systems, Data Communication, *High-Level Data Link Control Procedures—Frame Structure*, International Standard ISO 3309, 1984.

[ISO4335]   ISO, Information Processing Systems—Data. Communications, *High-level Data Link Control Elements of Procedures*, International Standard ISO 4335, 1987.

[ISO7498]   ISO, Information Processing Systems—Data Communications, *Open Systems Interconnection—Basic Reference Model*, International Standard ISO7498, 1984.

[ISO7809]   ISO, Information Processing Systems—Data Communications, *High-level Data Link Control Procedures, Consolidation of Classes of Procedures*, International Standard ISO 7809, 1991.

[ISO8073]   ISO, Information Processing Systems—Open Systems Interconnection, *Connection Oriented Transport Protocol Specification*, International Standard ISO/IEC 8073, 1988.

[ISO8348]   ISO, Information Processing Systems—Data Communications, *Network Service Definition*, International Standard ISO 8348, 1987.

[ISO8348.2] ISO, Information Processing Systems—Data Communications, *Network Service Definition, Addendum 2: Network Layer Addressing*, International Standard ISO 8348:1987/AD2:1988.

[ISO8473]   ISO, Information Processing Systems—Data Communications, *Protocol for Providing the Connectionless-mode Network Service and Provision for the Underlying Service*, International Standard 8473, 1988.

[ISO8509]   ISO, Information Processing Systems—Open Systems Interconnection, *Service Conventions*, Technical Report ISO 8509, 1987.

[ISO8648]   ISO, Information Processing Systems—Data Communications, *Internal Organization of the Network Layer*, International Standard ISO 8648, May 1987.

[ISO8824]   ISO, Information Processing Systems—Open Systems Interconnection, *Abstract Syntax Notation One (ASN.1)*, International Standard ISO 8824, 1987.

[ISO8824.1]   ISO, Information Processing Systems—Open Systems Interconnection, *Abstract Syntax Notation One (ASN.1), Addendum 1: Extensions to ASN.1*, Addendum ISO 8824/AD1.

[ISO8825]   ISO, Information Processing Systems—Open Systems Interconnection, *Specification of Basic Encoding Rules for Abstract Syntax Notation One (ASN.1)*, International Standard ISO 8825, 1987.

[ISO9542]   ISO, Information Processing Systems—Telecommunications and Information Exchange between Systems, *End system to intermediate system Routeing exchange protocol for use in conjunction with the protocol for providing the connectionless-mode network service (ISO 8473)*, International Standard ISO 9542, 1988.

[ISO9575]   ISO/IEC, Information Technology—Telecommunications and Information Exchange between Systems, *OSI Routeing framework*, International Standard ISO/IEC TR9575, 1989.

[ISO9577]   ISO/IEC, Information Technology—Telecommunications and Information Exchange between Systems, *Protocol Identification in the OSI Network Layer*, 2nd ed., International Standard ISO/IEC TR9577, 1993.

[Kessler]   Kessler, G. C., and D. A. Train, *Metropolitan Area networks*, McGraw-Hill, 1991.

[Martin]   Martin, J., and K. K. Chapman, *Local Area Networks*, Prentice Hall, 1989.

[MCI]   MCI Telecommunications Corporation, *Hyperstream[SM] Switched Multi-megabit Data Service*, brochure distributed at ICA, May 1993.

[McNamara] McNamara, J. E., *Technical Aspects of Datacommunication*, 2nd ed., Digital Press, Digital Equipment Corporation, 1982.

[Miller] Miller, Mark A., *LAN Protocol Handbook*, M&T Books, 1990.

[Neibaur] Neibaur, Dale, *"Understanding XNS: The Prototypical Internetwork Protocol,"* Data Communications, September 21, 1989.

[Novell1] Novell, *Netware System Interface Technical Overview*, Addison-Wesley, 1990.

[Novell2] Novell, *IPX Router Specification, Revision A*, Part Number 107-000029-001, June 16, 1992.

[Novell3] Novell, *Netware Link Services Protocol (NLSP) Specification*, Part Number 100-001708-001, March 31, 1993.

[Perlman] Perlman, R., *Interconnections, Bridges, Routers*, Addison-Wesley, May 1992.

[Piscitello] Piscitello, D. M., and A. L. Chapin, *Open Systems Networking: TCP/IP and OSI*, Addison-Wesley, 1993.

[Q.921] CCITT Recommendation Q.921, *ISDN User-Network Interface—Data Link Layer Specification*, CCITT Blue Book, Geneva 1989.

[RFC1006] Rose, M. T., and D. E. Cass, *ISO Transport Service on top of the TCP*, Version 3, RFC1006, InterNIC Information Services, May 1987.

[RFC1058] Hedrick, C., *Routing Information Protocol*, RFC1058, InterNIC Information Services, June 1988.

[RFC1112] Deering, S.E., *Host Extensions for IP Multicasting*, RFC1112, InterNIC Information Services, August 1989.

[RFC1155] Rose, M. T., and K. McCloghrie, *Structure and Identification of Management Information for TCP/IP–based Internets*, RFC 1155, InterNIC Information Services, March 1991.

[RFC1157]   Case, J. D., M. Fedor, M. L. Schoffstall, and C. Davin, *Simple Network Management Protocol*, RFC 1157, InterNIC Information Services, May 1990.

[RFC1171]   Perkins, D., *The Point-to-Point Protocol for the Transmission of Multi-Protocol Datagrams Over Point-to-Point Links*, RFC 1171, InterNIC Information Services, July 1990.

[RFC1209]   Piscitello, D. M., and J. Lawrence, *Transmission of IP Datagrams over the SMDS Service*, RFC 1209, InterNIC Information Services, March 1991.

[RFC1212]   Rose, M. T., and K. McCloghrie, eds., *Concise Mib Definitions*, RFC 1212, InterNIC Information Services, March 1991.

[RFC1213]   Rose, M. T., ed., *Management Information Base for Network Management of TCP/IP-based Internets*, RFC 1213, InterNIC Information Services, March 1991.

[RFC1215]   Rose, M. T., *A Convention for Defining Traps for Use with the SNMP*, RFC 1215, InterNIC Information Services, March 1991.

[RFC1237]   Colella, R., E. Gardner, and R. Callon, *Guidelines for OSI NSAP Allocation in the Internet*, RFC1237, InterNIC Information Services, July 1991.

[RFC1267]   Lougheed, K., and Y. Rekhter, *Border Gateway Protocol 3 (BGP-3)*, RFC 1267, InterNIC Information Services, October 1991.

[RFC1304]   Cox, T. A., and K. Tesink, eds., *Definitions of Managed Objects for the SIP Interface Types*, RFC 1304, InterNIC Information Services, May 1992.

[RFC1331]   Simpson W., *The Point-to-Point Protocol (PPP) for the Transmission of Multi-Protocol Datagrams over Point-to-Point Links*, RFC 1331, InterNIC Information Services, November 1991.

[RFC1340]   Reynolds, J., and J. Postel, *Assigned Numbers*, RFC 1340, InterNIC Information Services, July 1992.

[RFC1406]   Baker, F., and J. Watt, *Definitions of Managed Objects for the DS1 Interface Type*, RFC 1406, InterNIC Information Services, January 1993.

[RFC1407]   Cox, T. A., and K. Tesink, eds., *Definitions of Managed Objects for the DS3 Interface Type*, RFC 1407, InterNIC Information Services, January 1993.

[RFC1433]   Garrett, J., J. Hagan, and J. Wong, *Directed ARP*, RFC 1433, InterNIC Information Services, March 1993.

[RFC1483]   Heinanen, J., *Multiprotocol Encapsulation over ATM Adaptation Layer 5*, RFC 1483, InterNIC Information Services, July 1993.

[RFC1490]   Bradley, T., C. Brown, and A. Malis, *Multiprotocol Interconnect over Frame Relay*, RFC 1490, InterNIC Information Services, July 1993.

[RFC1573]   McCloghrie, K., and F. Kastenholz, *Evolution of the Interfaces Group of MIB-II*, RFC 1573, InterNIC Information Services, January 1994.

[RFC1583]   Moy, J., *OSPF Version 2*, RFC 1583, InterNIC Information Services, March 1994.

[RFC768]   Postel, J., *User Datagram Protocol*, RFC768, InterNIC Information Services, August 1980.

[RFC791]   Postel, J., *Internet Protocol*, RFC768, InterNIC Information Services, September 1981.

[RFC792]   Postel, J., *Internet Control Message Protocol*, RFC792, InterNIC Information Services, September 1981.

[RFC793]   Postel, J., *Transmission Control Protocol*, RFC793, InterNIC Information Services, September 1981.

[RFC826]   Plummer, D., *Ethernet Address Resolution Protocol: or Converting Network Protocol Addresses to 48 bit Ethernet Address for Transmission on Ethernet Hardware*, RFC 826, November 1982.

[RFC891]   Mills, D.L., *DCN Local-Network Protocols*, RFC891, InterNIC Information Services, December 1983.

[RFC896]   Nagle, J., *Congestion Control in TCP/IP Internetworks*, InterNIC Information Services, January 6, 1984.

[RFC904]   Mills, D.L., *Exterior Gateway Protocol Formal Specification*, InterNIC Information Services, 1984.

[Rose]   Rose, M., *The Simple Book—An Introduction to Management of TCP/IP-Based Internets*, Prentice Hall, 1991.

[Rose2]   Rose, M., *The Open Book—A Practical Perspective on OSI*, Prentice Hall, 1990

[RuxLiles]   Rux, P. T., and C. V. Liles, "*ESF, Rx for Healthy T1 Nets*", Data Communications, May 1990.

[Sher]   Sher, P., and K. Tesink, "*Potential Network Management Services and Capabilities Associated With SMDS*", Third IFIP/IEEE International Symposium on Integrated Network Management, San Francisco, April 18–23, 1993.

[Sidhu]   Sidhu, G, S., Richard F. Andrews, and A. B. Oppenheimer, *Inside AppleTalk*, 2nd ed., Addison-Wesley, 1990.

[SIG.cbit]   Tsou, W. W., *DS3 C-Bit Parity Application*, SMDS Interest Group Contribution, January 28, 1992.

[SIG001]   SMDS Interest Group, *SMDS Data Exchange Protocol, Revision 3.2*, SIG-TS-001/1991, October 22, 1991.

[SIG002]   SMDS Interest Group, *SMDS DXI Local Management Interface Revision 2.0*, SIG-TS-002/1991, May 19, 1992.

[SIG003]   SMDS Interest Group, *Implementation of Phase IV DECnet over SMDS*, SIG-TS-003/1992, Revision 1.1, May 3, 1994.

[SIG004]   SMDS Interest Group, *Specification for Implementation of Connectionless OSI over SMDS*, SIG-TS-004/1992, Revision 1.1, May 3, 1994.

[SIG005]   SMDS Interest Group, *Frame Based Interface Protocol for SMDS Networks, Data Exchange Interface / Subscriber Network Interface Revision 1.0*, SIG-TS-005/1993, February 2, 1993.

[SIG006]   SMDS Interest Group, *Frame Based Interface Protocol for Network Supporting SMDS—SIP Relay Interface*, Revision 1.0, SIG-TS-006/1993, February 1993.

[SIG008]   SMDS Interest Group, *Protocol Interface Specification for Implementation of SMDS over an ATM-based Public UNI*, Revision 1.0, SIG-TWG-008/1994, May 3, 1994.

[SIG019]   Oppenheimer, A. B., *SMDSTalk: Apple Talk over SMDS*, SMDS Interest Group Informational Specification, SIG-TWG-019/1992, August 17, 1992.

[SIG042]   Israel, J. E., *Transmission of Novell IPX Datagrams over the SMDS service*, Version 1.0 - SMDS Interest Group Informational Specification, SIG TWG-1993/042 July, 1993.

[Steedman]   Steedman, D., *Abstract Syntax Notation One (ASN.1): The Tutorial and Reference*, Technology Appraisals Ltd., Great Britain, 1990.

[T1.107]   ANSI T1.107-1988, American National Standard for Telecommunications, *Digital Hierarchy—Format Specifications.*

[T1.107a]   ANSI T1.107a-1990, American National Standard for Telecommunications, *Digital Hierarchy—Supplement To Formats Specifications (DS3 Format Applications).*

[T1.403]   ANSI T1.403.1989, American National Standard for Telecommunications, *Carrier-to-Customer Installation—DS1 Metallic Interface.*

[T1.617]   ANSI T1.617-1991, American National Standard for Telecommunications, *DSSI—Signaling Specification for Frame Relay Bearer Service.*

[UNI3]   ATM Forum, *ATM User-Network Interface Specification, Version 3.0*, September 10, 1993.

[V.35]   CCITT Recommendation V.35, *Data Transmission at 48 kilobits per Second Using 60-108 KHz Group Band Circuits*, CCITT Red Book, Malaga-Torremolinos 1984.

[Vissers]   Vissers, C.A., *Interface—Definition, Design, and Description of the Relation of Digital System Parts*, Ph.D. Thesis, Twente University, The Netherlands, 1977.

[Witzke]   Witzke, K. A., and C. Leung, "*A Comparison of Some Error Detecting CRC Code Standards*", IEEE Transactions on Communications, Vol. COM-33, No. 9, September 1985.

[X.137]   CCITT, Recommendation X.137, *Availability Performance Values for Public Data Networks When Providing International Packet-Switched Service*, CCITT Blue Book, Melbourne, 1988.

[X.140]   CCITT, Recommendation X.140, *General Quality of Service Parameters for Communication via Public Data Networks*, CCITT Blue Book, Melbourne, 1988.

[X.21]   CCITT Recommendation X.21, *Interface between Data Terminal Equipment (DTE) and Data Circuit-terminating Equipment (DCE) for Synchronous Operation on Public Data Networks*, CCITT Blue Book, Geneva, 1989.

[X.25]   CCITT Recommendation X.25, *Interface between Data Terminal Equipment (DTE) and Data Circuit-terminating Equipment (DCE) for Terminals Operating in the Packet Mode and Connected to Public Data Networks by Dedicated Circuit*, CCITT Blue Book, Geneva, 1989.

[X.27, V.11]   CCITT Recommendation V.11/X.27, *Electrical Characteristics for Balanced Double-current Interchange Circuits for General Use with Integrated Circuit Equipment in the Field of Data Communications*, CCITT Blue Book, Geneva, 1989.

[X3.216]   ANSI, Structure and Semantics of the Domain Specific Part (DSP) of the OSI Network Service Access Point (NSAP) Address, ANSI Draft Standard X3.216, X3S3.3/91-151R.

[Xerox]   Xerox Systems Integration Standard, *Internet Transport Protocols*, XSIS 028112, Xerox Corp., Stamford, Connecticut, December 1981.

Index